YOUNG POLAND

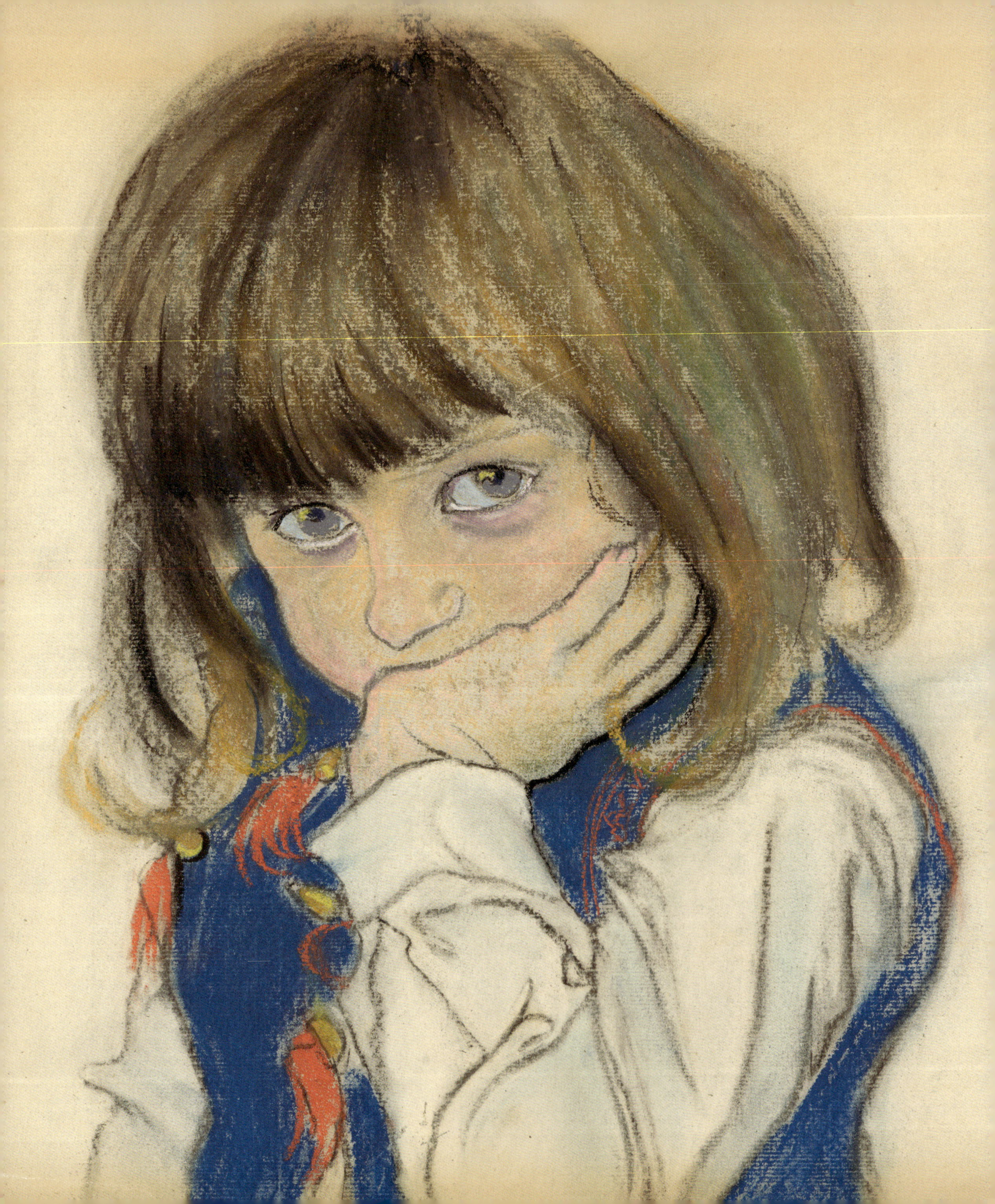

YOUNG POLAND

• THE POLISH ARTS AND CRAFTS MOVEMENT •
1890–1918

Edited by
Julia Griffin and Andrzej Szczerski

LUND HUMPHRIES

First published in 2020 by Lund Humphries
Reprinted in 2021

Lund Humphries
Office 3, Book House
261A City Road
London EC1V 1JX
UK
www.lundhumphries.com

Young Poland: The Polish Arts and Crafts Movement, 1890–1918

ISBN: 978-1-84822-453-7

A Cataloguing-in-Publication record for this book is available from the British Library

Copy-edited by Abigail Grater
Art direction and design by Adrian Hunt
Young Poland co-art direction by Anna Myczkowska-Szczerska
Set in Trieste and Monotype Italian Old Style
Printed in Belgium

Endpapers and typographic ornaments based on 'Caterpillars', 'Squirrels', and 'Crickets' paper cuttings by Karol Kłosowski (*c.*1908-1925, coloured papers, images from a Private Collection. By Descent from the Artist; see fig.8.6 on p.121 for the original complete designs).
Endpapers: designed by Anna Myczkowska-Szczerska
Composite illustrations and map on p.10 by Marta Podolska

FRONTISPIECE:
Stanisław Wyspiański
Portrait of Józio Feldman, 1905
Pastel on paper, 38 × 38 cm
National Museum in Kraków
MNK III-r.a-2505

P.7:
Karol Kłosowski
'Cockerels' paper cutting, *c.*1908-1925
Coloured papers, 22 cm in diameter
Private Collection. By Descent from the Artist

FRONT COVER:
Stanisław Wyspiański
'Pansies' repeating pattern mural decoration, 1897
Franciscan Church, Kraków

BACK COVER:
Karol Kłosowski, *At Bobbin Lacemaking (Legend)*, undated,
Chalk on paper, 63 × 75 cm
Private Collection. By Descent from the Artist

LUND HUMPHRIES
WILLIAM MORRIS GALLERY
MNK MUZEUM NARODOWE W KRAKOWIE
POLISH CULTURAL INSTITUTE LONDON
Ministry of Culture and National Heritage of the Republic of Poland.

Co-financed by the Minister of Culture and National Heritage of Poland within the framework of the 'Inspiring Culture' Programme.

Contents

Young Poland Partnership Acknowledgements

Published ahead of a major exhibition on the subject at the William Morris Gallery in autumn 2021, this book could not have come to life without the collaborative spirit central to Young Poland and the Arts and Crafts Movement. It is the result of an international partnership between the William Morris Gallery, London Borough of Waltham Forest (WMG), the National Museum in Kraków (NMK) and the Polish Cultural Institute in London (PCI), generously funded by the 'Inspiring Culture' grant from the Ministry of Culture and National Heritage of the Republic of Poland, as well as support from the WMG, NMK and PCI. Special thanks to the heads of the partner institutions for enabling the project to become a reality: Andrzej Szczerski, Director of the National Museum in Kraków; Louise Fitton, Head of Museum, Gallery & Archives – London Borough of Waltham Forest; and Marta de Zuniga, Director of the Polish Cultural Institute. We are grateful to Marta de Zuniga for providing the initial funding commitment and vital help with fundraising.

Editors' Acknowledgements

We would like to extend special thanks to the book's godmothers – Rowan Bain, Senior Curator, William Morris Gallery and Lucy Clark, Commissioning Editor, Lund Humphries – for believing in the value of this publication and making it possible.

To Roisin Inglesby, Curator, William Morris Gallery for her advocacy and expertise as Young Poland Co-Curator and offering valuable comments on the manuscript of this book; Linda Parry for acting as Academic Consultant; Anna Myczkowska-Szczerska, lecturer of Visual Communication at the Jan Matejko Academy of Fine Arts in Kraków, for expert graphic design advice and help with the illustrations, not least creating the splendid group portrait of our story's cast of characters, as well as her vital encouragement with the project; Magdalena Laskowska, Curator of Works on Paper at the National Museum in Kraków, for providing specialist advice regarding Stanisław Wyspiański's life and work; colleagues at the William Morris Gallery: James Gray, Marketing and Audience Development Manager, who first came up with the idea for a Young Poland exhibition, and Mhairi Muncaster, Retail and Commercial Development Manager, for her creative ideas; National Museum in Kraków: Kamila Hyska, Young Poland Project Manager (NMK), for her tireless professionalism and friendly manner, Dominika Treit, Head of Exhibitions, Joanna Niewidok, Head of Fundraising, curatorial and conservation staff – Alicja Kilijańska, Marta Kłak-Ambrożkiewicz, Bożena Kostuch, Joanna Regina Kowalska, Urszula Kozakowska-Zaucha, Monika Paś, Łucja Skoczeń-Rąpała, Head of Paper and Leather Conservation, Magdalena Szewczyk, Registrar, Halina Marcinkowska, Senior Curator and Head of NMK Library, NMK Finance Department – Katarzyna Bednarska and Anna Olak, NMK Photographic Department – Beata Drabek, Patrycja Dzięgiel, Karol Kowalik, Tomasz Markowski, Adam Oleksy, Anna Olchawska, Joanna Pawłowska, Ewelina Słowińska, Łukasz Wojciechowski, Katarzyna Wojdyła; the Polish Cultural Institute: Konrad Zielinski, Paulina Latham, Joanna Śnieg; Lund Humphries: Lucy Myers, Sarah Thorowgood, the excellent project manager Anna Norman, and Rochelle Roberts; graphic designer Adrian Hunt; the extraordinarily expert copy-editor Abigail Grater; all contributors, institutions and individuals who have helped with this publication in a multitude of ways – kindly facilitating research, loans and/or the use of images of artworks from their collections: Anna Wende-Surmiak, Director of the Tatra Museum for generous help on all fronts, not least lending the museum's expert conservator during a photographic session in Zakopane; William Morris Gallery; National Museum in Kraków, Collegium Maius Museum, Seweryn Udziela

Ethnographic Museum in Kraków, Franciscan Church in Kraków, Museum of Kraków including Rydlówka Manor House Branch, State Municipal Archive in Kraków, Wawel Cathedral, Wojciech Weiss Museum Foundation; Jan Matejko Academy of Fine Arts in Kraków: Faculty of Industrial Design, Museum, Main Library; Society of Friends of the Fine Arts, Kraków (TPSP), S.G. Żeleński Stained Glass Workshop; Bank PKO S.A., National Museum in Warsaw, Literature Museum in Warsaw, Museum and Archive of the Academy of Fine Arts in Warsaw, Okna Sztuki Auction House, Polish Army Museum, Rempex Auction House, Mazovian Museum in Płock, National Museum in Kielce, National Museum in Poznań and the Raczyński Foundation at Rogalin Palace, owners of Dom pod Jedlami (House Under the Firs Trust) and Willa Cicha (Silent Villa), Madonna of Częstochowa Old Church in Zakopane, Maria and Jan Szczepkowski Foundation, Lithuanian National Museum of Art in Vilnius, Victoria and Albert Museum, anonymous private collections; Antoni Bartosz, Edyta Barucka, Andrzej Betlej, Urszula Bukowska, Jacek Bukowski, Barbara Bogoczek, Katarzyna Chrudzimska-Uhera, Agata Ciołek, David Crowley, Maria Dziedzic, Ewa Gaczoł, Mariusz Gad, Maria Gajek, Roksana Gawrońska, Przemysław Gembiak, Anna Grochal, Agnieszka Grunwald, Michał Hankus, Tony Howard, Lynn Hulse, Katarzyna Jakimiak, Danuta Janusz, Elżbieta Jastrzębowska, Joanna Kania, Jarosław Klejnocki, Zygmunt Kłosowski, Piotr Kopszak, Mikołaj Kornecki, Łukasz Kossowski, Anna Kozak, Carien Kremer, Łukasz Lutostański, Justyna Masłowiec, Anna Mason, Ewa Mickiewicz, Marcin Miller, Zbigniew Moździerz, Michał Murzyn, Michał Niezabitowski, Maria Ochalska, Patricia O'Connor, Małgorzata Oleszkiewicz, Piotr Ostrowski, Małgorzata Palka, Anna and Kasper Pawlikowscy, Kamilla Pijanowska, Helena Pitoń, Marta Podolska, Zuzanna Przypkowska, Karolina Puchała-Rojek, Natalia Puchalska, Agnieszka Rosales Rodríguez, Ewa Rossal, Anna Rudzińska, Jan Rydel, Barbara Schabowska, Leszek Józef Sibila, Agnieszka Skalska, Alison Smith, Pamela Smith, Małgorzata Sokołowska, Marcin Starkowski, Marek Szczepanowski, Stanisław Tabisz, Aleksandra Trybuła, Zofia Weiss, Małgorzata Wichowska, Jadwiga Wielgut-Walczak, Marta Winiarczyk, Monika Wiśniewska, Henryk Woźniakowski.

Last but not least we would like to thank our families, especially Anna and Piotr Dudkiewicz and Ted Griffin.

Andrzej Szczerski and Julia Griffin

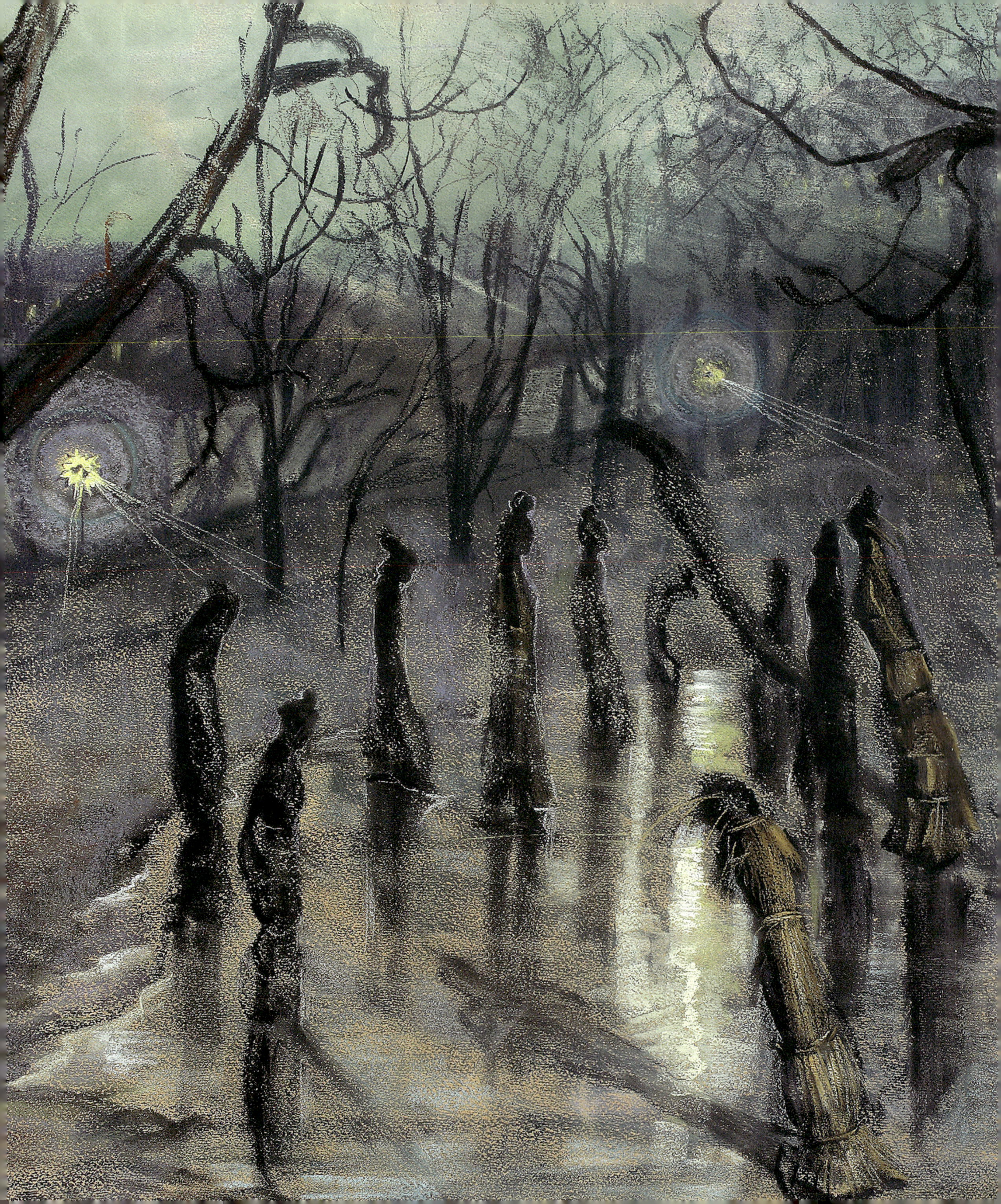

Preface: Young Poland and the Search for a National Style

Alison Smith

In the years around 1900 there developed, in the former lands of the Polish-Lithuanian Commonwealth, a dynamic arts movement that sought to fuse the fine and decorative arts in proclaiming freedom of expression and the reassertion of national identity. Called Młoda Polska, or Young Poland, it was both inward- and outward- looking, taking inspiration from nature and indigenous folk traditions, but expressing its ideals in a distinct modernist language that brought it close to other European design reform movements such as the British Arts and Crafts and Swedish Hemslöjd movements, Art Nouveau and the Vienna Secession.

In the geopolitical context of the time, however, the term Młoda Polska would have appeared something of an oxymoron in that Poland as a political entity did not exist, having disappeared from the map of Europe in 1795. This date marks the demise of the kingdom established at the end of the 16th century when Poland and Lithuania united to form the Rzeczpospolita Obojga Narodów (Polish-Lithuanian Commonwealth), becoming a major power in Europe. By the 18th century the Commonwealth had become so weakened by internal divisions that it was vulnerable to the influence of its rivals Russia, Prussia and Austria and, in 1772, an alliance between those three nations' monarchs – Catherine the Great, Frederick the Great and Joseph II – led to the first three-way partition of Poland. A second partition in 1793 ceded more territory to Russia and Prussia, culminating in the third annexation in 1795 when the Polish king Stanisław II August Poniatowski was forced to abdicate and the entire country was divided between Prussia, Russia and Austria. Poland thus ceased to exist as a state for the next 123 years.

There followed a long period of struggle to regain independence. Two abortive military uprisings in 1830–31 and 1863–4 were followed by severe reprisals that included execution, imprisonment, deportation, exile and the confiscation of property. The harshest of these punishments were enforced by the Russian and Prussian governments after 1863, added to which came a ban on the use of the Polish language and the introduction of strict censorship. With the failure of military action, culture became an alternative vehicle for communicating political aspiration both inside the partitioned nation and

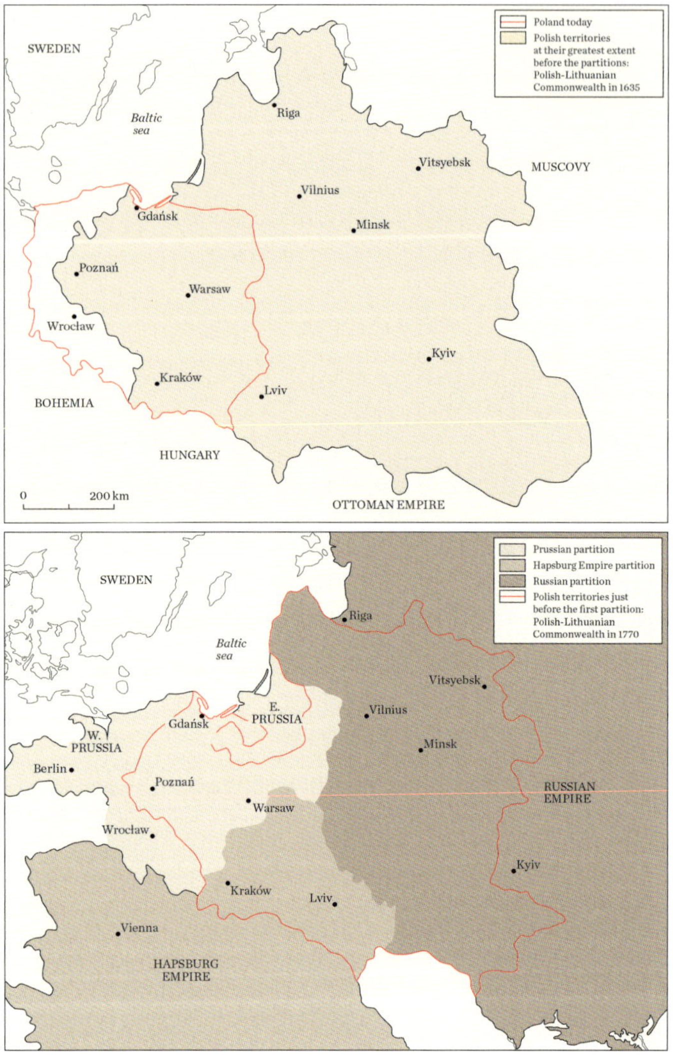

(p.8)
Detail of fig. 5.1, Stanisław Wyspiański, *Chochoły* (*Straw-Protected Bushes*), 1897–9

0.1 (LEFT)
Maps showing Polish territories before, during and after the third partition, using modern place names for clarity

0.2 (OPPOSITE)
Jan Matejko
Polonia, 1864
Oil on canvas, 158 cm × 232 cm
National Museum in Kraków, MNK XII-453

beyond, including in Britain. In 1833 Alfred Tennyson published his rousing sonnets on Poland. Fifteen years later the young members of the Pre-Raphaelite Brotherhood named the freedom fighter Tadeusz Kościuszko among the List of Immortals that helped launch their revolutionary movement.[1]

A major pioneer in the visual arts was the academic painter Jan Matejko (1838–1893) whose vast canvases depicting epic scenes from Polish history did much to fuel the idea of a once glorious nation brought low, as shown in *Polonia* (fig.0.2), Matejko's dramatic threnody concerning the January Uprising of 1863. In the picture Russian officers oversee the shackling of a female personification of Poland; the blonde woman to her side represents Lithuania. The painting remained unfinished because, fearing for his life and seeking to avoid persecution, the artist arranged for it to be hidden from view. But it lived on in the imaginings of others. Thirty years later, Matejko's former student and arguably Young Poland's foremost artist, Stanisław Wyspiański (1869–1907), reprised the motif in emotive Symbolist terms – representing Polonia, the spirit of the non-existent country, as a dying queen (fig.0.3) – the theme of trauma and martyrdom passing like a baton from one generation to another.[2]

It is no coincidence that both Matejko and Wyspiański were based in Kraków situated in the more liberal region of Galicia, which, as the century progressed, experienced a greater degree of political and economic autonomy under its Hapsburg (i.e. Austrian) rulers. By the 1890s Kraków had emerged as a vibrant cultural centre, while in the nearby mountainous Podhale area, many of the former insurrectionists who had settled there became interested in indigenous craft and building practices as a means of preserving local heritage from foreign influence and as a source for contemporary national revival.

This vernacular revival centered on the remote village of Zakopane in the Tatra mountains and it was here artists such as Stanisław Witkiewicz (1851–1915) and Karol Kłosowski (1882–1971) championed the Zakopane Style in architecture and interior decoration based on the adaptation of traditional skills of the indigenous Highlander population, such as building, carving and weaving. One has only to compare some of the everyday objects from this period – peasant costumes, carved wooden spoons and cheese moulds (see fig.0.10), for instance – with the artists' very personal reinterpretations of traditional motifs to appreciate just how reverential and creative they were in their endeavour to recreate the past in a distinct modern idiom. The Zakopane Style was both organic and

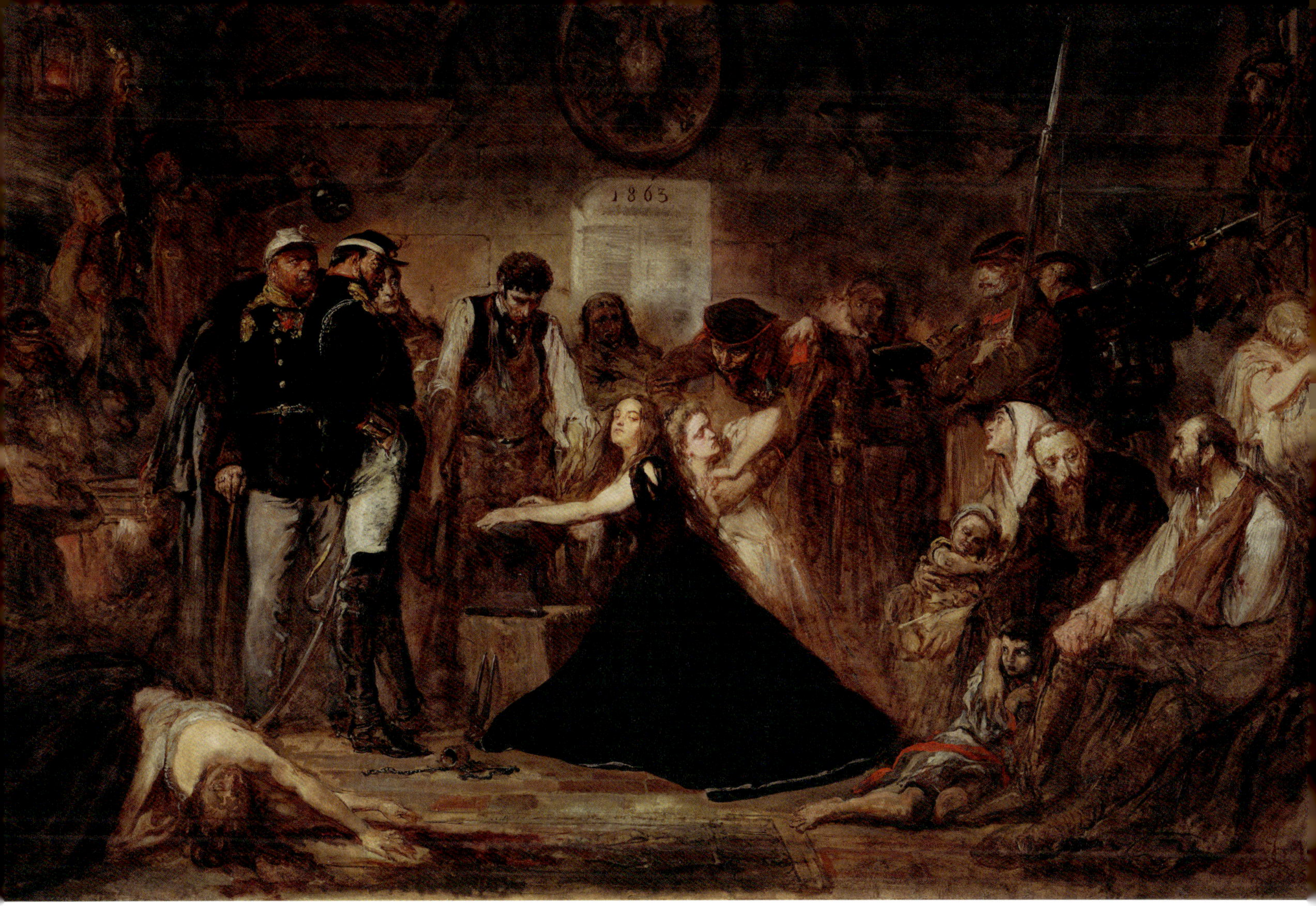

all-embracing, as seen in Witkiewicz's House Under the Firs and Kłosowski's Silent Villa, both conceived as *Gesamtkunstwerk* ('total works of art') projects but made to feel homely and familiar, as anyone who has visited the houses themselves will have experienced. This approach gave rise to the term *swojski,* meaning home-like, alluding not just to a cosy domestic environment but to an ideal of nationhood that continues to underpin a particular folksy image of Polish culture today.

Kraków, the historic seat of the Polish monarchs and the nation's original capital, symbolised for many Poles its former power and cultural heritage. Wawel Castle and Cathedral were often depicted by artists, as was the Planty Park, established in the early 19th century in place of the old medieval city walls. In Wyspiański's mysterious nocturne *Chochoły* (1897–9, see fig.5.1 and Chapter 5), the shapes of straw-wrapped shrubs in the park assume an anthropomorphic dimension, appearing like Giacometti-type figures expectantly waiting for something, each isolated in its own world. The power and poetry of the image has given rise to many interpretations, both personal and political.

Wyspiański is widely regarded as the most original artist associated with the movement, a figure only just beginning to be appreciated outside Central Europe. A polymath, like Witkiewicz, his art encapsulates the spirit of youth, vitality and sheer energy that propelled Young Poland. In this book Wyspiański is presented as a kindred spirit to the British Arts and Crafts pioneer William Morris (1834–1896), sharing similar antiquarian and ecological interests, working freely across the fine and decorative arts, and being politically motivated.

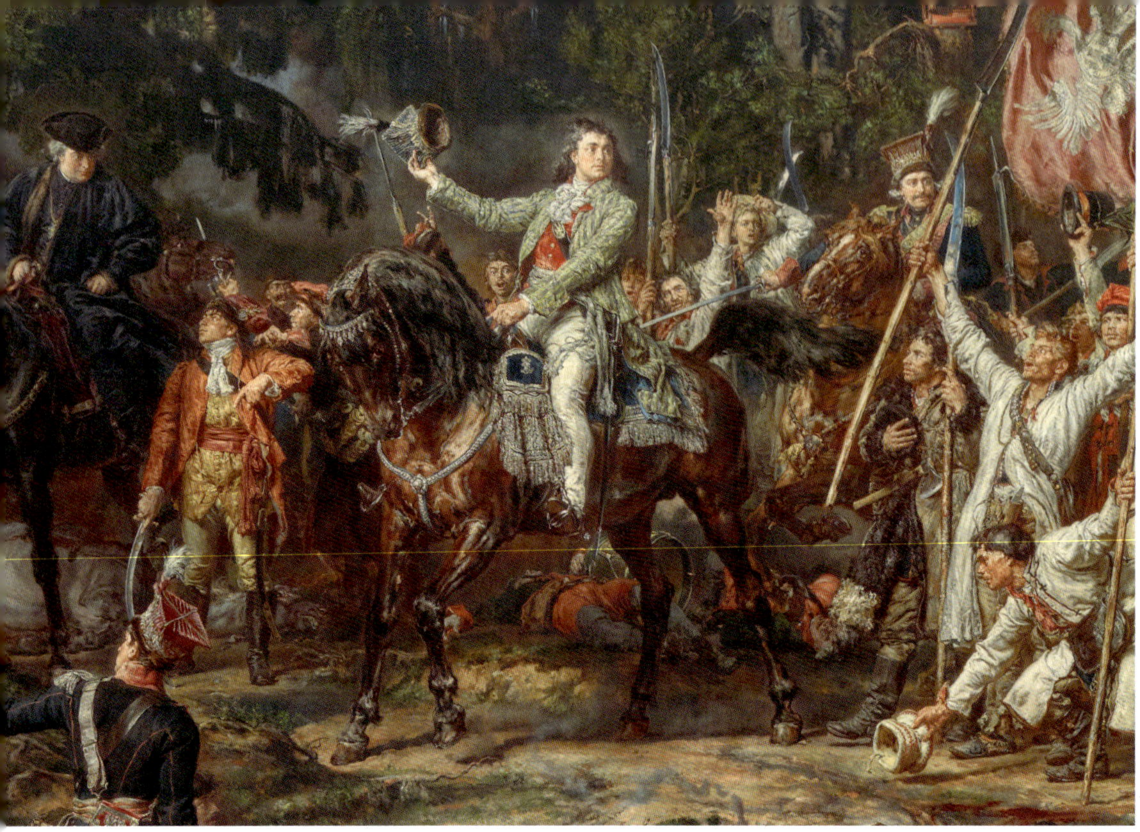

0.3 (OPPOSITE)
Stanisław Wyspiański
Polonia, 1894, replica of unrealised stained-glass design for Lviv Cathedral
Pastel, paper, canvas
299 × 175 cm
National Museum in Kraków, MNK III-r.a-10686

0.4 (LEFT)
Jan Matejko
Kościuszko at Racławice (detail), 1888
Oil on canvas, 465 × 897 cm
National Museum in Kraków
MNK II-a-151

Both artists were passionate about flowers and one of the most riveting objects illustrated in this publication is Wyspiański's small herbal containing sketches of native plants which he later adapted for wall paintings, hangings and various other decorative objects (see figs 2.4, 2.6). These drawings will put Morris enthusiasts in mind of the designer's own textile and wallpaper designs, although Wyspiański's style is more electric and nervy – cosmic rather than homely. The furniture he designed (see figs 11.3–11.6) also ranged beyond the familiar and comfortable; in fact, it takes the idea of *swojski* into another realm, according to the writer Tadeusz Żeleński (pen name 'Boy'), who remarks that Wyspiański's un-upholstered wooden furniture seemed more suited 'for spirits or people from other planets than for human beings'.[3] In other words, he took the Arts and Crafts idea of simplicity to an extreme.

The theatrical and otherworldly aspects of Wyspiański's art also characterise the work of many of his peers; it can be seen in the paintings and decorative arts of Józef Mehoffer (1869–1946), for example, or in the fairy-tale imaginings of Maria Pawlikowska-Jasnorzewska (1891–1945) (see figs 10.0–10.10). Despite its preoccupation with historicism and folk culture, Young Poland was essentially modern in that the artists were motivated as much by aesthetic considerations as they were by social and political concerns. This can be seen in their penchant for bold geometric shapes and vividly coloured patterns, and in the abstraction of natural forms that brought their creations into line with some of the most advanced contemporary movements in Europe. This was evident in the work of the first and second generation of Young Poland artists such as Witkiewicz, Wyspiański and Mehoffer, as well as their disciples from the Kraków Workshops (Warsztaty Krakowskie) association (1913–26). In this sense Young Poland was both a national and a universal phenomenon. It fuelled the struggle for freedom that led to Poland regaining independence in 1918 at the end of the First World War but endured beyond that, creating a meaningful legacy even in the darkest moments of the 20th century.

This book, the first on this subject in any language, charts the rich history of the Polish Arts and Crafts movement, placing it at the centre of the pan-European design reform phenomenon. Written by an international team of scholars, the chapters that follow in this wide-ranging and fully illustrated compilation examine the ideas that propelled the movement and introduce the artists, designers and craftspeople whose decorative schemes and objects came to define it.

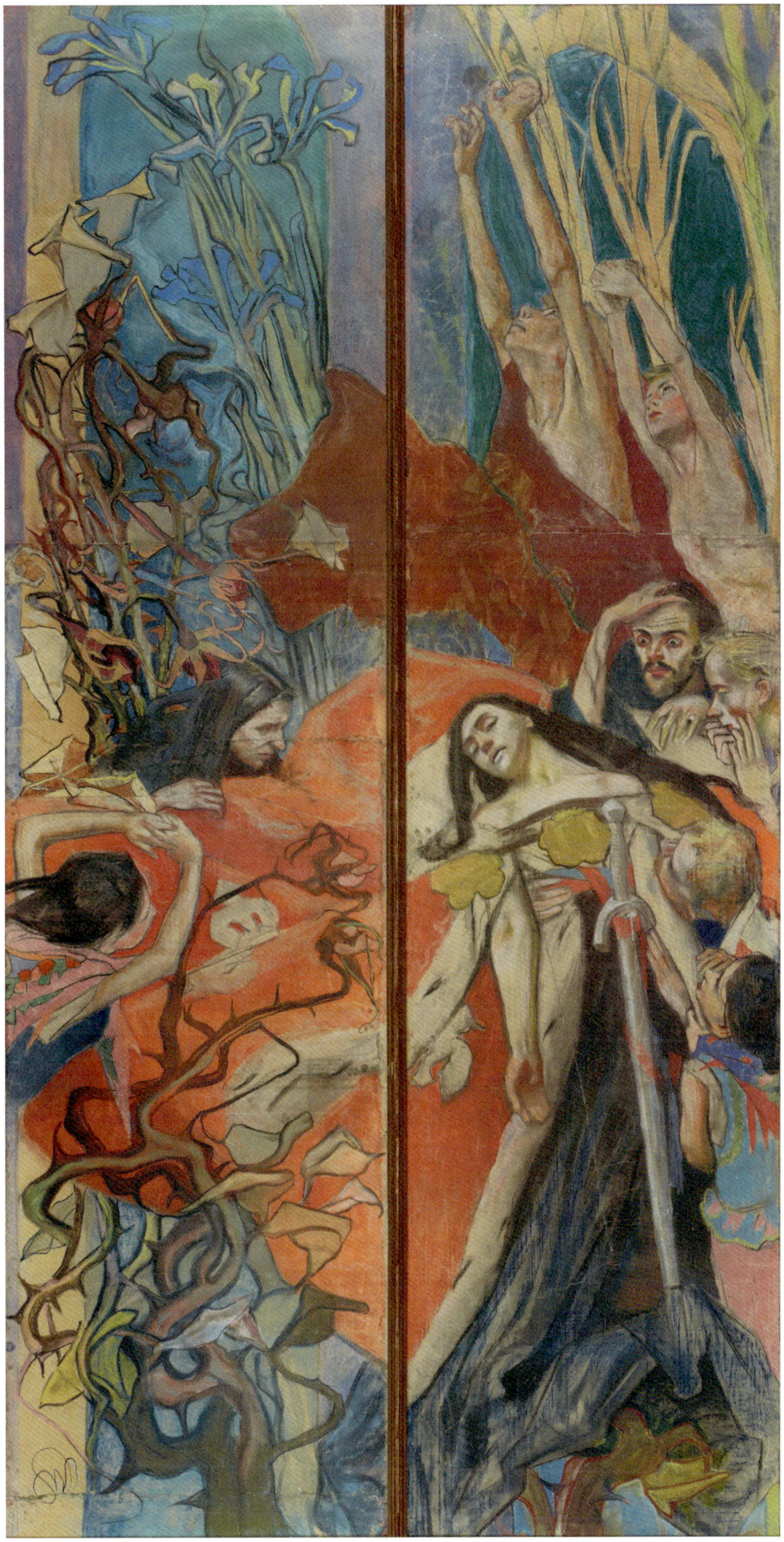

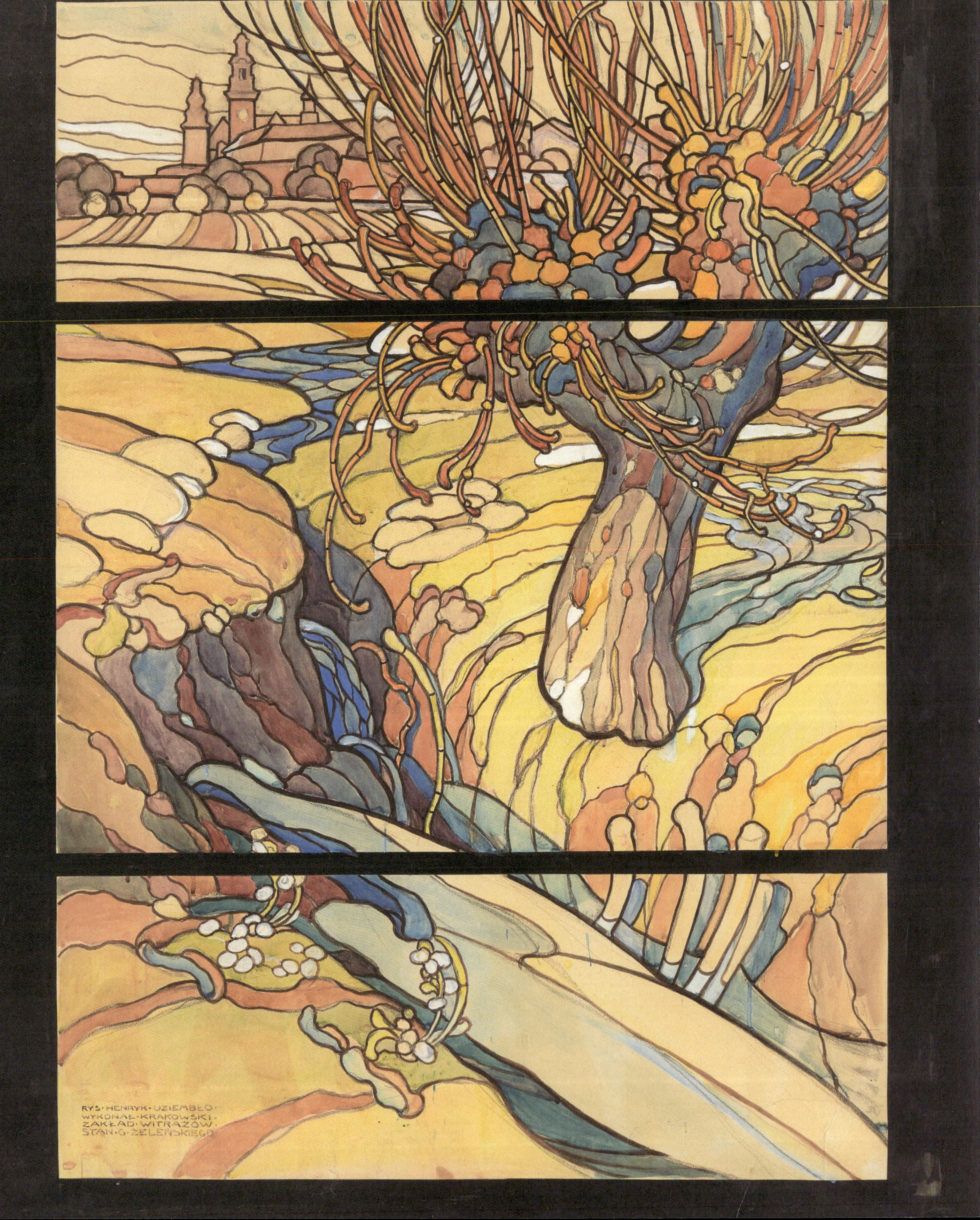
RYS·HENRYK·UZIEMBŁO·
WYKONAŁ·KRAKOWSKI·
ZAKŁAD·WITRAŻÓW·
STAN·G·ŻELEŃSKIEGO·

Editors' Introduction: Young Poland and the Arts and Crafts Movement, 1890–1918 – A New Perspective

Andrzej Szczerski and Julia Griffin

Young Poland (1890–1918) was arguably one of the most wide-ranging and original movements within Polish art and continues to enjoy unrivalled popularity today. Whilst Young Poland painting has been accorded exposure and scholarly attention abroad, mainly in the context of European Symbolism, its applied arts have not hitherto been equally and systematically presented on the international arena. This is the first monograph exclusively dedicated to a key – yet relatively little known and thus far neglected – aspect of Young Poland, namely the Polish Arts and Crafts movement.

In their pioneering study *International Arts and Crafts* (2005), Linda Parry and Karen Livingstone convincingly demonstrate that:

> Arts and Crafts was an international movement that flourished in Britain, Europe and America from the 1880s until the First World War, and in Japan from the 1920s until the Second World War . . . Developed initially in Britain, it had a widespread influence. It was originally based on an idealistic set of principles for living and working, which were taken up and adapted in many parts of the world to meet specific social and national needs, integrating heritage, local skills and resources.[1]

Although the resulting Arts and Crafts objects are often visually quite different, 'what bound them together was a unity of ideas'.[2] Our book argues that the culturally and politically motivated proliferation of applied arts and the revival of handicrafts during the Young Poland period constituted the Polish interpretation of the Arts and Crafts Movement's principles.

We also adopt a fundamental distinction between Arts and Crafts and Art Nouveau, proposed by Linda Parry.[3] Despite being frequently confused, the two movements are quite different on account of the nature of work produced, and their competing stances on the ethos of handicraft. In simplest terms, the Art Nouveau was a cosmopolitan, sensuous and pleasure-seeking style, following the doctrine of 'art for art's sake'. It favoured symbolic imagery, sumptuous materials and elaborate applied surface decoration such as veneers, frequently relying on the use of modern technical equipment

0.5 (p.14)
Henryk Uziembło
Spring stained-glass window design for the Żeleński Stained-Glass Workshop, Kraków, *c.*1908
Gouache and Indian ink on paper
176 × 130 cm
National Museum in Warsaw, MNW 183415

0.6
Józef Mehoffer
Nature and Art, 1901
Watercolour on paper laid on canvas
145 × 353 cm
National Museum in Kraków, MNK III-r.a-17376

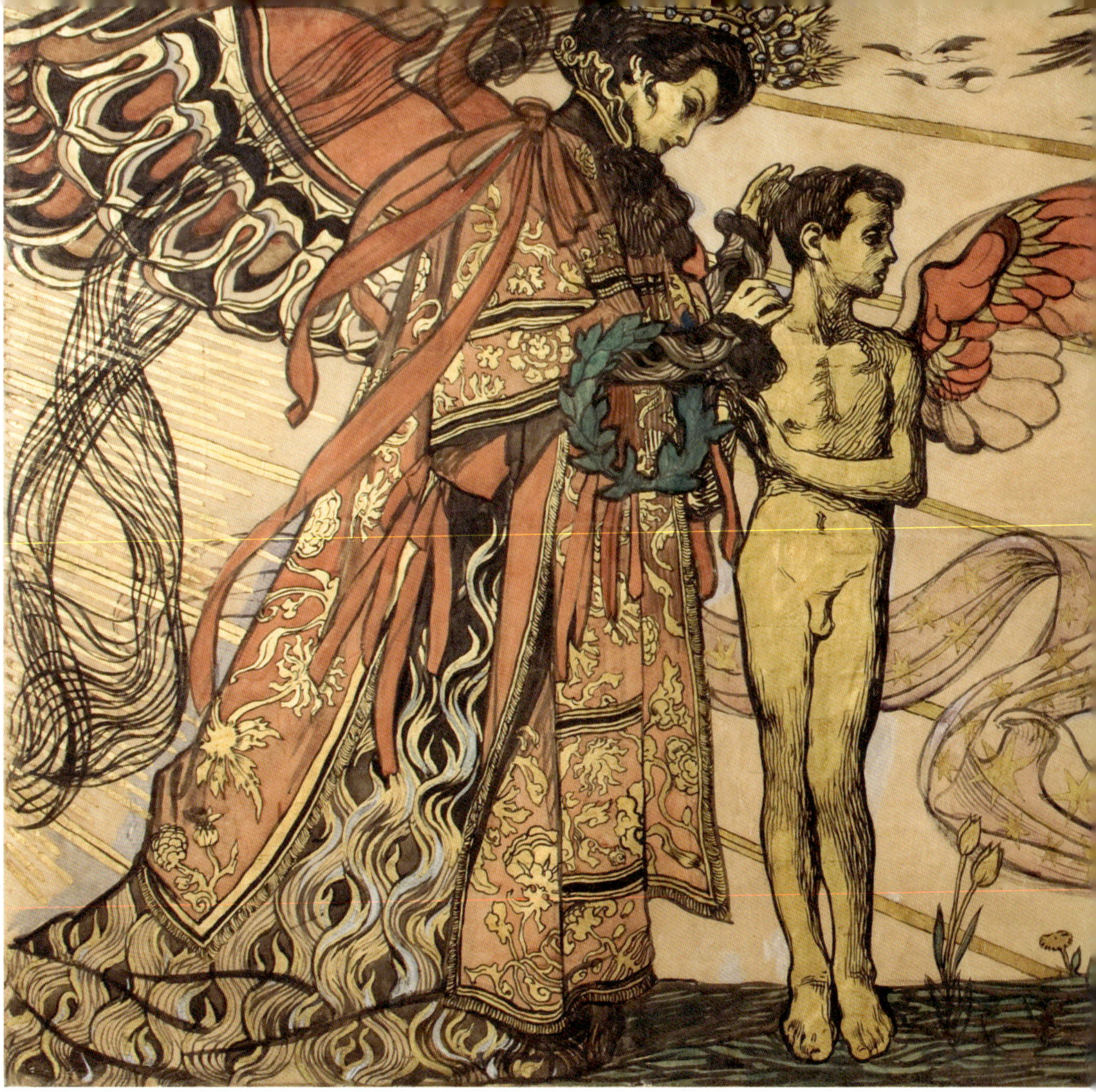

rather than handicraft skills. On the other hand, the Arts and Crafts Movement was based on an ideology revolving around moral and social values, striving to change the world. It championed simplicity and honesty of design and materials, elevated the status of craft and celebrated the process of its making.[4]

For over a century the applied arts of Young Poland have been almost exclusively considered in the context of European Art Nouveau, not allowing for a more nuanced understanding of the complexity and underlying ideology of the makers and the objects they produced. Notably, from the outset the validity of the Art Nouveau perspective had been called into question by the Young Poland makers themselves. For example, annoyed by the reception of his newly completed decorative scheme at the Medical Society (Towarzystwo Lekarskie) in Kraków, Wyspiański published the following satirical poem in 1905. In this Wyspiański uses the word 'Secesja', being the generic Polish term for any strand of European Art Nouveau, including French, Belgian and Austrian works:

> Somebody taught a parrot some words about art
> And one has to admit he soon had them by heart.
> So once he got his tongue around the word 'Secession'
> He greeted all new works with the same expression.
> Take the style of my chairs in the Medical House:
> He pronounced them 'Secession!' with a pitch-perfect flounce.

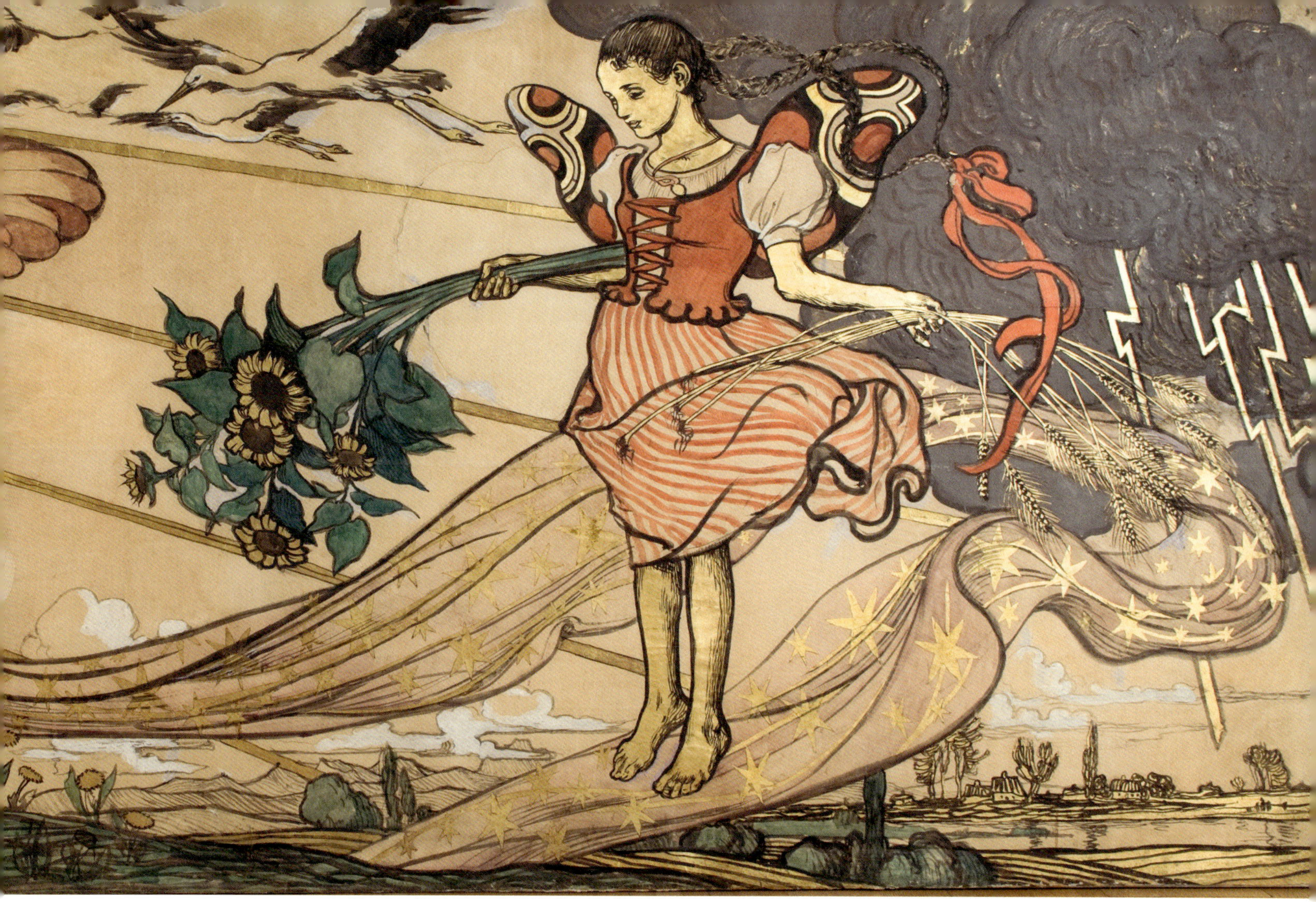

Be patient, bear with it, because before it's dead
They'll bang a new cliché in the parrot's head.
And though art's shape won't change in response to his spell,
One cliché is enough to send THOUGHT to hell![5]

Young Poland was a complex and multifaceted movement, and any attempts to frame it within strictly stylistic categories are futile. As Jan Cavanaugh demonstrates in *Out Looking In: Early Modern Polish Art, 1890–1918* (2000), one of the defining qualities (and paradoxes) of Young Poland art was that it was both culturally autonomous from the rest of Europe, and simultaneously cosmopolitan.[6] Polish artists turned inward, aspiring to devise a new visual language to cultivate their own national character. Yet they embraced progressive artistic trends in Western Europe, striving for universality of expression – and with it, international recognition for Poland as an independent cultural force. Consequently, on a stylistic level Young Poland's fine and decorative art reflected numerous strands within Western European modernism, frequently blending, of which Art Nouveau was just one.[7] Crucially, it also displayed more fundamental ideological parallels with the British Arts and Crafts Movement, and this is the subject of our book.[8]

Józef Mehoffer's powerful allegory *Nature and Art* (1901, fig.0.6) perceptibly conveys the quintessence of the new arts of Young Poland whilst also capturing an apparently incongruous duality between their underlying ethos and their superficial

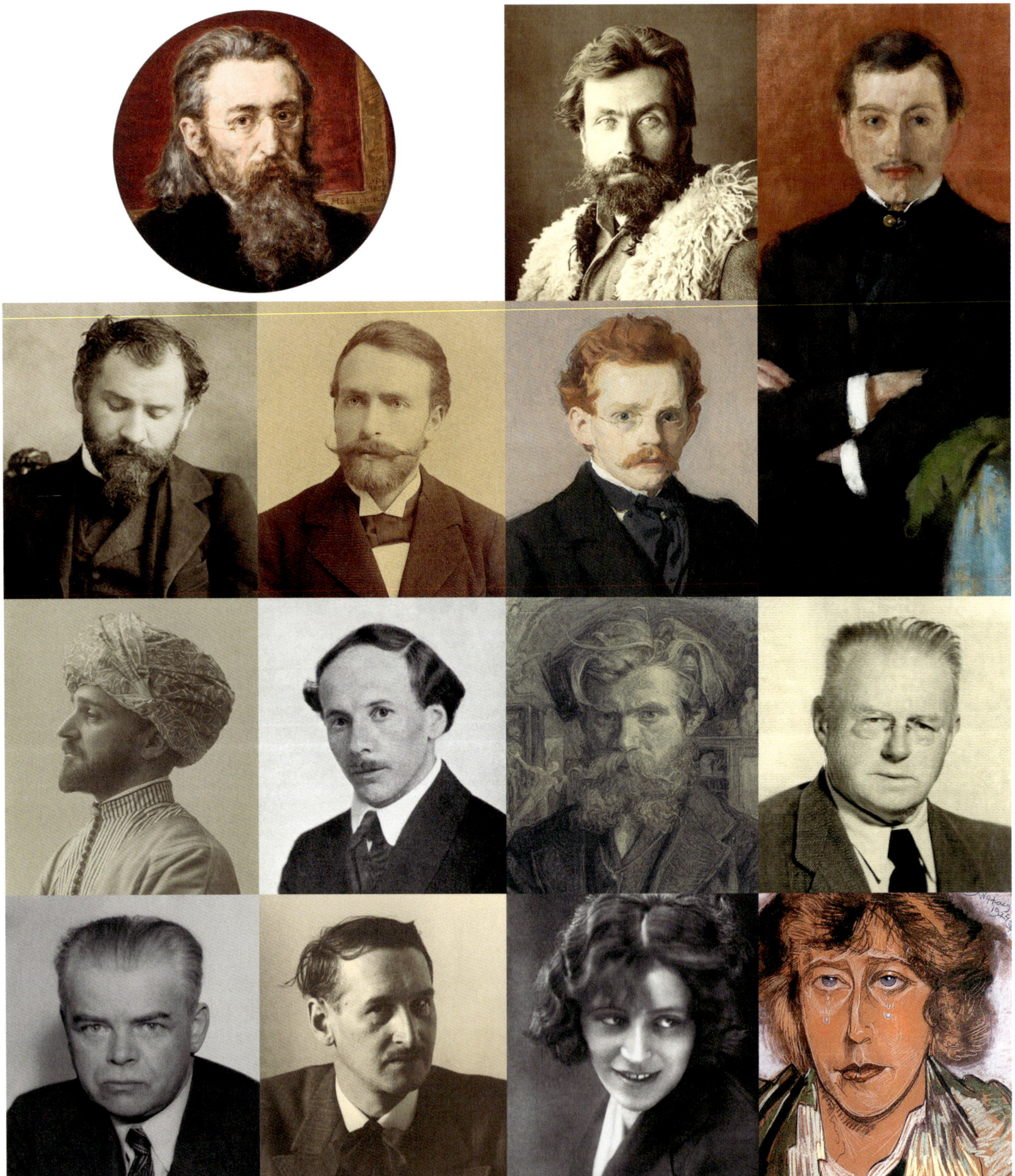

0.7
Young Poland's main protagonists:
TOP ROW – Jan Matejko, Stanisław Witkiewicz, Józef Czajkowski; SECOND ROW – Stanisław Przybyszewski, Stanisław Wyspiański, Józef Mehoffer; THIRD ROW: Jerzy Warchałowski, Bonawentura Lenart, Karol Kłosowski, Antoni Buszek; BOTTOM ROW: Wojciech Jastrzębowski, Zdzisław Gedliczka, Zofia Stryjeńska, Maria Pawlikowska-Jasnorzewska
Combination of archival photographs and painted portraits
National Museum in Kraków; Tatra Museum; National Museum in Warsaw; National Digital Archive; Archive of the Academy of Fine Arts in Warsaw; Private Collection. By Descent from the Artist; Literature Museum

stylistic variation. The personification of Art, dressed in a sumptuous gown resembling a vestment, points the Artist, represented as a nude youth, towards the only worthwhile preoccupations – celebration of nature and the ideal simple life of the country dweller. In stark contrast with the refined High Priestess of Art depicted in an overtly Art Nouveau style, the peasant girl and the archetypal Polish countryside evoke the simplicity and beauty of the new sources of the art revival, also extolled by the protagonists of the Arts and Crafts Movement. This powerful image unequivocally demonstrates that it was the Arts and Crafts ethos which lay at the core of Young Poland's yearning for political independence despite its known recourse to Art Nouveau stylistic traits.

The Arts and Crafts approach to the applied arts of Young Poland has been debated since the 1990s. David Crowley, in his pioneering book *National Style and Nation-State: Design in Poland from the Vernacular Revival to the International Style* (1992)[9] coined the term 'the Polish Arts and Crafts movement', referring specifically to the Zakopane Style, an approach continued by Cavanaugh. Andrzej Szczerski's seminal monographs *Wzorce Tożsamości* (Eng. *Models of Identity*) (2002)[10] and its expanded English-language version, *Views of Albion: The Reception of British Art and Design in Central Europe, 1890–1918* (2015),[11] presented the first systematic analysis of the wider ideological links between Poland and Britain around 1900. Szczerski substantially expanded the Arts and Crafts perspective and has also called into question the validity of the Franco-centric approach within art history, revolving around the assumed primacy of the French influence over the rest of Europe, instead acknowledging the parallel cultural exchange between Britain and Poland. This was particularly justified given that Poles perceived the Pre-Raphaelites and the British Arts and Crafts as aspirational models of national art (see Chapter 1). The Polish Arts and Crafts have also been explored in a number of informative articles by Edyta Barucka (formerly Supińska-Polit) focusing mainly on the artistic colony in the Tatras, of which 'Redefining Polishness: the revival of crafts in Galicia around 1900' (2010) offers a broad view of the topic.[12] Young Poland applied arts have previously been accorded chapters in the international surveys of the Arts and Crafts Movement conceived by Livingstone and Parry (2005),[13] and Rosalind Polly Blakesley (2006).[14]

Our book is the first opportunity to showcase a comprehensive and fully illustrated range of the best of the applied arts and handicrafts of Young Poland. The book comprises two parts presented as 17 chapters. Part 1 explores the key ideas, makers, craft societies, sites and decorative schemes, which collectively made up the landscape of the Polish Arts and Crafts movement. Part 2 includes object-based overviews of particular branches of Polish crafts featuring iconic interiors and furniture, textiles, ceramics, toys and Christmas decorations, and the book beautiful. Accompanying texts offer insights into their making as well as the ethos of craft pedagogy prevalent at the time. The book closes with a discussion of Young Poland painting used as another lens for viewing the preoccupations of the movement.

***

In 1898 literary critic Artur Górski published a series of articles in the Kraków art journal *Życie*, with a single title 'Młoda Polska' ('Young Poland').[15] All of them defined the new movement in Polish literature, based on the rediscovery of Romanticism and its intrinsic values. Górski believed that he lived in an epoch of fundamental changes that were expressed by the new art which radically departed from earlier Positivism, with its scientific approach to the world. In the new times emotions and personal feelings mattered. However, most importantly, he called for the revival of Polish national ambitions and hopes for independence, based on moral values. In contrast to the previous generation, which had to abandon its irredentist agenda in the aftermath of the failed 1863–4 January Uprising against Russia, the new one once again raised the national flag. This was Young Poland, reawakened thanks not only to political ambitions, but above all to the new art and artists who stood for its vitality and cultural force (see fig.0.7). Artur Górski, although not the first to notice that change, proved to be the most influential. His articles gave a name to the whole movement not only in literature but also in other arts. The decade of their publication is commonly understood as the beginning of the Young Poland era.

The revival, which started in the 1890s, reflected the cultural, social and political tensions in the lands of the former Polish-Lithuanian Commonwealth, proving that the status quo was unacceptable to Poles. Despite the efforts of Russia, Prussia and Austria to suppress any hopes for Poland's re-emergence on the map of Europe, national ambitions once again turned out to be invincible. The arts expressed these sentiments and were grounded in the historical realities of the epoch, which ended with Poland's declaration of independence in 1918. Even though most of the Young Poland artists remained active after that date, they needed to reflect on a contrasting set of issues, radically different from their pre-First World War preoccupations. The spirit of Young Poland gradually waned, and new generations started to view it from a historical perspective.

Although Young Poland is chiefly known for its fine arts, an Arts and Crafts revival was an essential part of it. Through the appreciation of applied arts based on vernacular and folk art models, designers were keen to find a distinctive national style which would express the uniqueness of Polish culture. The discussions about such a style began as early as the 1860s and concentrated on the revival of historic architectural styles, mainly regional versions of Gothic and Renaissance, for different reasons deemed particularly Polish. Yet at the end of the century, with the influence of the British Arts and Crafts Movement, the national style started to be defined in new terms. The distinct British achievements, known mostly through publications as well as translations of works by John Ruskin (1819–1900) and William Morris, were primarily an inspiring example of what Poles were also striving for – innovative national art and design, based on local artistic traditions. Secondly, in contrast to late 19th-century historicism and academic high art, the British Arts and Crafts Movement showed in more ways than one how forgotten vernacular applied arts or building traditions can be the inspiration for a design revival. In Poland, where handicrafts had survived in provinces unchanged by industrialisation, the British example proved that what seemed otherwise backward might in fact be beneficial as a source for the new national art. The human dimension, especially in William Morris's writings, with its emphasis on social cohesion, also had particular appeal. Polish protagonists of the Arts and Crafts promoted the idea of national unity across social divisions. Hence the appreciation of folk art as the source of a national style could be read as a political manifesto and a call for bridging gaps between peasants and upper classes in the spirit of national unity. Last but not least, as the most advanced country of global importance, Britain showed how the national art revival went hand in hand with modernity, and therefore did not mean retro-utopian escapism, but the opposite. In Poland, which struggled to become a modern nation, capable of regaining independence, the British model was therefore particularly relevant.

The roots of the Polish design revival were to be found in the activities of the Museum of Technology and Industry (Muzeum Techniczno-Przemysłowe), founded in 1868 in Kraków, then part of the relatively liberal Austro-Hungarian Empire. Based on London's South Kensington Museum (later to become the Victoria and Albert Museum), it was the private initiative of the medical doctor Adrian Baraniecki (1828–1891) and developed thanks to financial support from the city of Kraków. The Young Poland artists and designers usually functioned thanks to similar initiatives on the local and regional level, where Poles were given autonomy by the Austrian authorities. Yet they did not have substantial support from any state authorities, as these did not fully approve of their independence agenda. Artists also formed groups and associations which enabled exhibitions, publications and/or the sale of works. The most important among these was the 'Sztuka' ['Art'] Society of Polish Artists (Towarzystwo Artystów Polskich 'Sztuka'), established in Kraków in 1897, which united Young Poland artists from all three partitions. Its exhibition venue was the Palace of Art, run by the Kraków-based Society of Friends of the Fine Arts (Towarzystwo Przyjaciół Sztuk Pięknych), a non-governmental organisation where new art could be freely viewed and discussed. 'Sztuka' also promoted Polish artists abroad, thanks to an international network of artistic exchanges, but within the limits set by the Austrian state. Some of the prominent members of 'Sztuka' joined the Viennese Secession and exhibited in its pavilion designed in 1898 by Joseph Maria Olbrich (1867–1908). Young Poland artists were not only confined to their non-existent country. In the 1890s there was a large Polish community in Paris, where the exponents of Impressionism, Post-Impressionism and Symbolism lived and studied. The writer and poet Stanisław Przybyszewski (1868–1927), who lived in Berlin in the 1890s, turned Poles' attention to Scandinavia and early German Expressionism, while literary critics appreciated Symbolist poetry in Belgium and Italy, as well as Bohemia. Apart from the Arts and Crafts Movement, the Pre-Raphaelites were also an important source of inspiration. Poles not only studied abroad, but also took an active part in the artistic life of various European countries, including of those which divided their country. Given these contacts, artists were familiar with the international idiom, yet infused it with national meanings, referring to particular cultural sources, iconography or details such as ornamentation or particular symbols. The adherents of the Polish Arts and Crafts revival also established societies, although some of the main figures worked independently. Among them three most important associations and figures stood out: the Polish Applied Arts Society (Towarzystwo Polska Sztuka Stosowana) and its founding member Stanisław Wyspiański; Stanisław Witkiewicz, founder of the Zakopane Style; and the Kraków Workshops.

The Polish Applied Arts Society was established in Kraków in 1901 by ardent supporters – painters, architects and art critics – of the idea of a national style in design. Its members,

0.8
Stanisław Wyspiański
Study of eagle's head and claws,
possibly a study for the unrealised frieze of birds in flight for the Franciscan Church, Kraków, 1895
Pastel on paper
72 × 49.3 cm
National Museum in Warsaw, Rys.Pol.14712 MNW

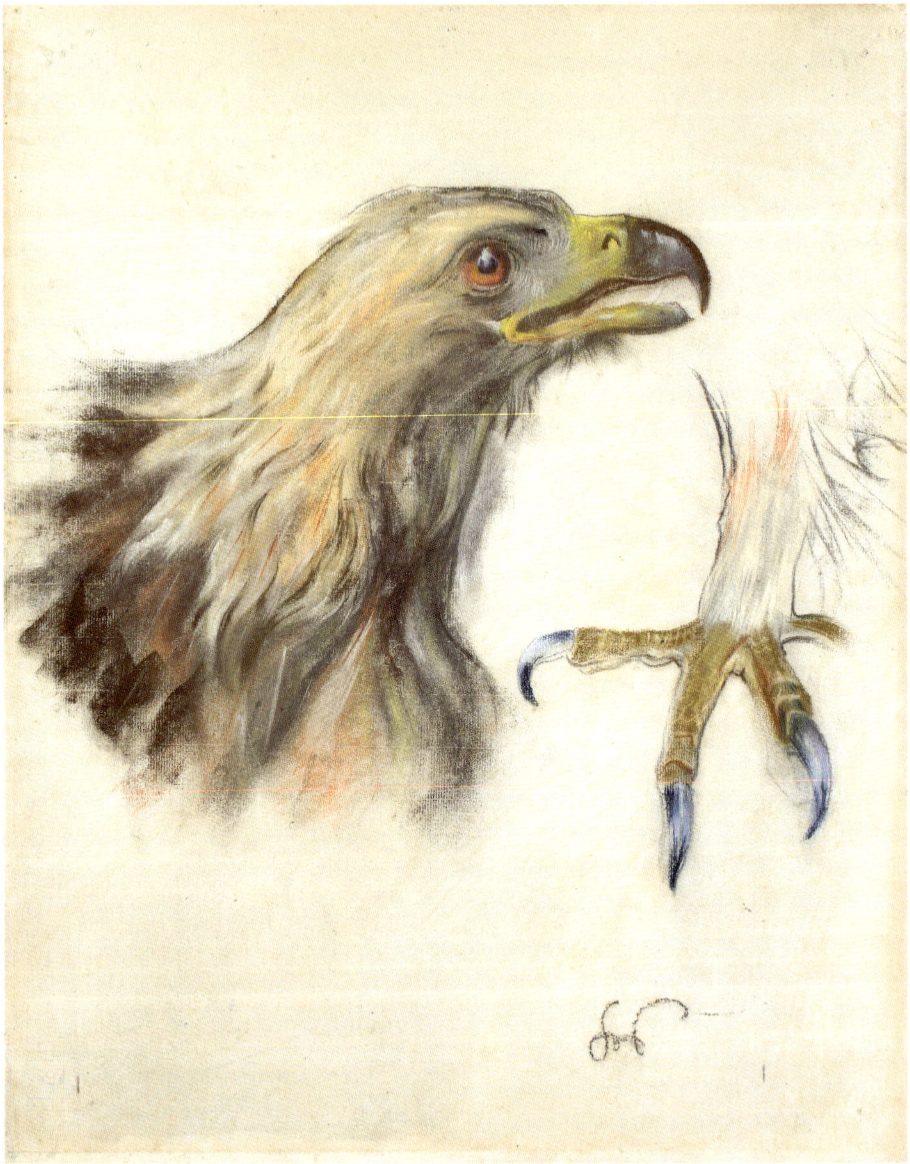

among them Jerzy Warchałowski (1874–1939), Józef Czajkowski (1872–1947) and Józef Mehoffer, considered modern design to be the perfect vehicle for expressing the distinctive Polish cultural identity. They found inspiration mostly in folk art and provincial vernacular architecture, following the pattern known particularly in Central Europe and Scandinavia. Significantly, the Society tried to find inspiration in the legacy of different religions and ethnic groups of the Polish-Lithuanian Commonwealth. It was equally interested in Catholic, Greek Catholic and Orthodox wooden churches, Jewish shtetls and synagogues, as well as folk ornaments from different regions in the Carpathian Mountains. Folk art was elevated to the status of a repository of primordial national cultural values, timeless and resistant to international influences.

Among members of the Society, Stanisław Wyspiański occupied the most prominent place. He saw the rebirth of Poland not only in political terms but also, above all, as a spiritual process that would enable Poles to achieve freedom.

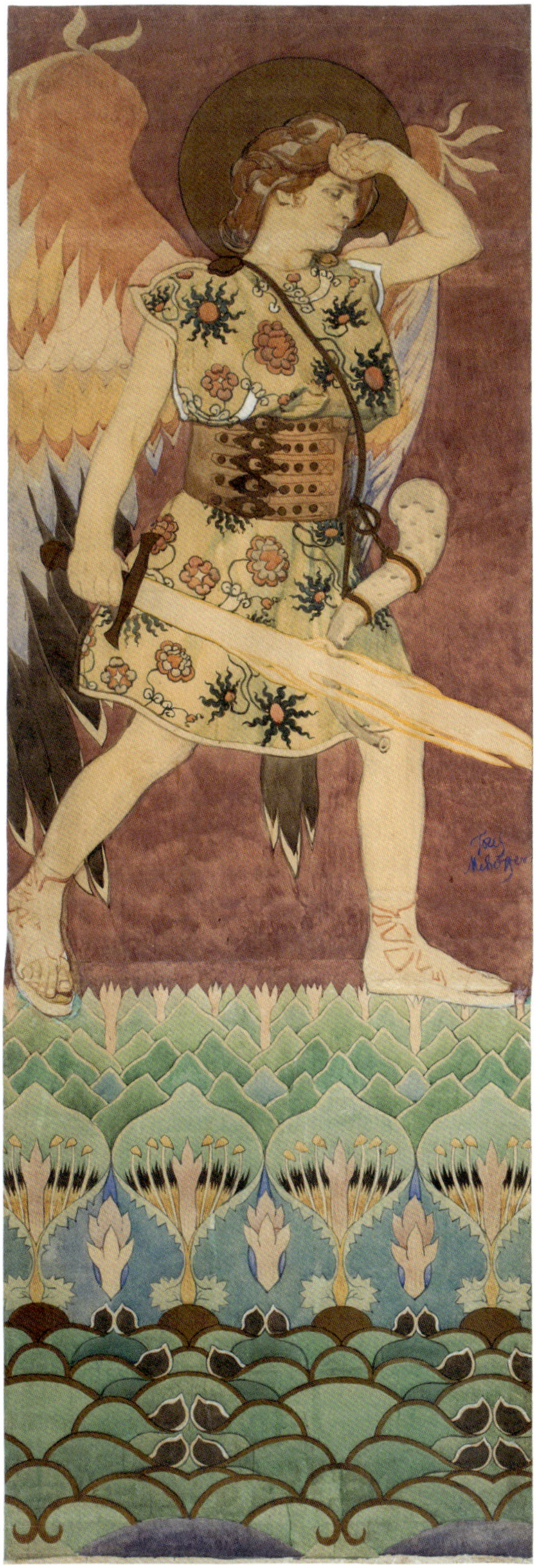

0.9
Józef Mehoffer
Saint Michael (*Angel of War*), design for a wall painting at the Wawel Treasury, 1901. Saint Michael is shown wearing a Highlander belt
Watercolour on paper laid on canvas
415.5 × 143 cm
National Museum in Poznań, MNP Gr 594

His versatile talents allowed him to work in pastel and design stained-glass windows, wall paintings, furniture, posters, engage in graphic design and also be a theatre reformer, dramatist, stage designer, local politician and teacher in the Academy of Fine Arts in Kraków. Wyspiański focused on creating powerful symbols and visionary interpretations of Polishness, which would look into the national past but also comment on the present. The artist's masterpiece, the wall paintings and stained-glass windows of the Franciscan Church in Kraków (1894–1904), show his interest in the Arts and Crafts Movement. Here Wyspiański elaborated a complex visual language based on curvilinear and expressionist Art Nouveau combined with Arts and Crafts floral motifs and ornaments. Folk art turned out to be just one of his sources of inspiration, used freely for certain ornamental motifs or in the image of the Madonna, who was given the look of a peasant woman.

Other Society members also pursued the decorative language based on the fusion of folk art and international Art Nouveau styles. Józef Mehoffer was the most successful in the application of these principles. His conference room in the Chamber of Commerce and Industry in Kraków (1906) echoed the spatial arrangement of provincial wooden churches; the wall paintings copied the decoration of peasants' wooden chests. Mehoffer mastered the ability to combine the Polish vernacular with the international Art Nouveau visual language, winning several prestigious commissions, such as those for the stained-glass windows in St Michael's Church in the Swiss city of Fribourg (1895–1936) and for the mosaic decoration of the Armenian Cathedral in Lviv (known in Polish as Lwów) (1906–13).

In contrast, Stanisław Witkiewicz, painter and art critic, initially worked alone. In the 1890s he developed a national

0.10
Stanisław Witkiewicz
Set of drawings of Kraków and the village of Zakopane, including Highlanders' huts and everyday objects, produced for *The English Illustrated Magazine*, 1888 and 1889
TOP ROW – interior and exterior of a traditional Podhale Highlander's hut; MIDDLE ROW – Highlander shepherd with sheep in the Tatras; carved spoon rack, cheese mould and drinking cup; BOTTOM ROW – entrance to the village of Zakopane with Mount Giewont in the background; Wawel from the Vistula river, Kraków
Various sizes: *c.*20 × 20 cm
National Museum in Warsaw, Rys.Pol.160113–14 MNW, 160124 MNW, Rys.Pol. 1154/3–4,6 MNW

style in architecture and design, based solely on folk art and vernacular buildings from the mountainous region of Podhale and the Tatra mountains, south of Kraków. It took its name from Zakopane, the principal village at the foothills of the mountains, which since the 1870s had been turning into a fashionable spa and a meeting point for artistic circles and middle-class Poles from all three partitions. Most importantly the Podhale region became famous for the rich folk culture of Highlanders (known as *Górale*), which Witkiewicz saw as the reservoir of Polish national culture unspoiled by cosmopolitan influences. Significantly, he believed that ornaments and building techniques preserved in the Podhale region were once used throughout the whole lands of the former Polish-Lithuanian Commonwealth, and therefore stood for its cultural affinities and common identity. He also hoped that wooden forms of Podhale architecture could be translated into stone and brick, applicable in the construction of modern cities. He designed a variety of buildings, mainly houses and chapels, but also the local Tatra Museum (Muzeum Tatrzańskie) in Zakopane. Witkiewicz soon attracted a group of professional architects and designers who followed his ideas. Thanks to them, the Zakopane Style quickly spread all over the lands of the former Polish-Lithuanian Commonwealth, though its limited impact was restricted mostly to residential manor house and interior decoration schemes.

The third main tendency in the Arts and Crafts revival was represented by the Kraków Workshops. Founded in 1913 by several former members of the Polish Applied Arts Society and representatives of the younger generation, it was led by Jerzy Warchałowski, Karol Tichy (1871–1939) and Wojciech Jastrzębowski (1884–1963). They also focused on the idea of a national style in design and architecture, but abandoned decorative, ornament-based projects of their predecessors. The new group looked for a more synthetic language of forms, based on structure and its geometric principles, in line with emerging modernism. Their activities were gaining momentum just before the outbreak of the First World War. During the war the Kraków Workshops' members worked on a limited scale and also ran design courses for war veterans.

Even though after the end of the war the art and design of Young Poland had become history, it nevertheless continued to exercise a decisive influence on Polish culture. One may argue, that subsequent generations of artists have never managed to create an equally distinctive and influential artistic movement since 1918. They have either argued for or against it, but have always had to confront its legacy. The achievements of Young Poland immediately entered the canon of Polish art. In the period of the Second Polish Republic (1918–39) the new state institutions of the art world and education gave it prominence as the source of modern culture of the country which had regained its freedom. After the Second World War, in Soviet-dominated Poland, Young Poland once again performed the role of upholding the spirit of independence. For contemporary Poles this more than hundred-year-old art still remains the most popular period in Polish art history and continues to inspire debates about national identity.

1354

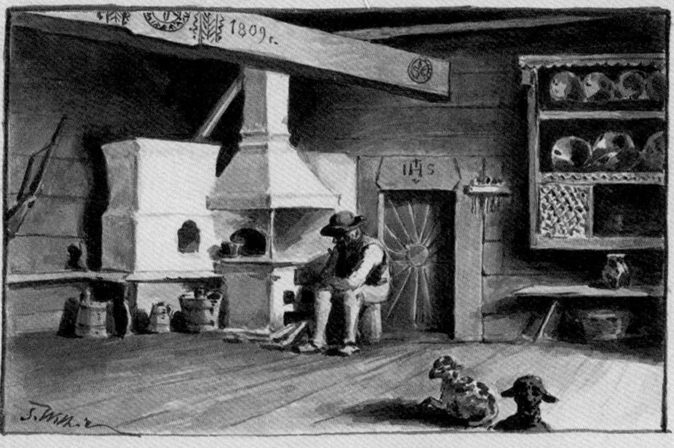

1355

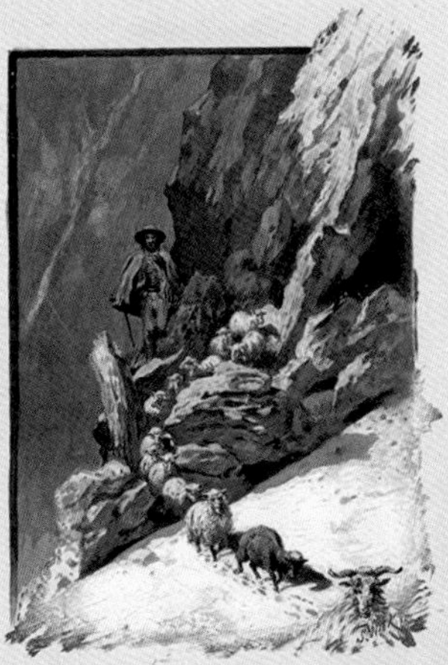

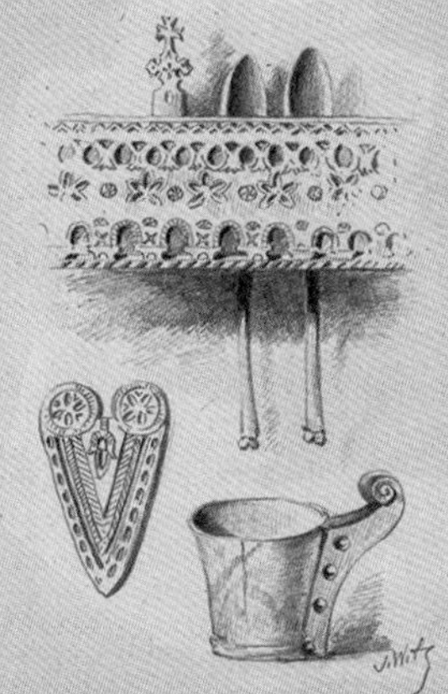

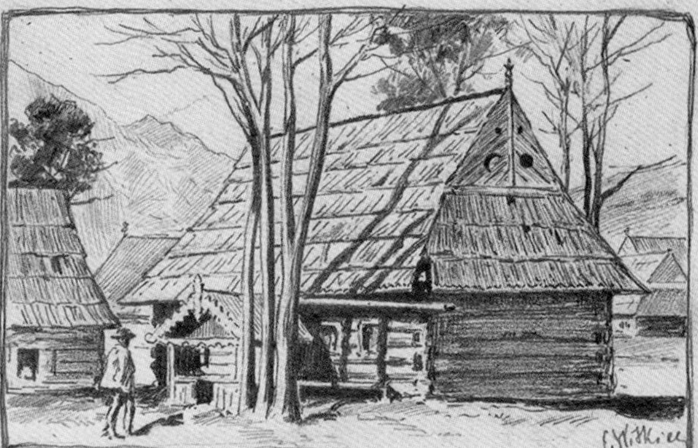

Chata góralska.

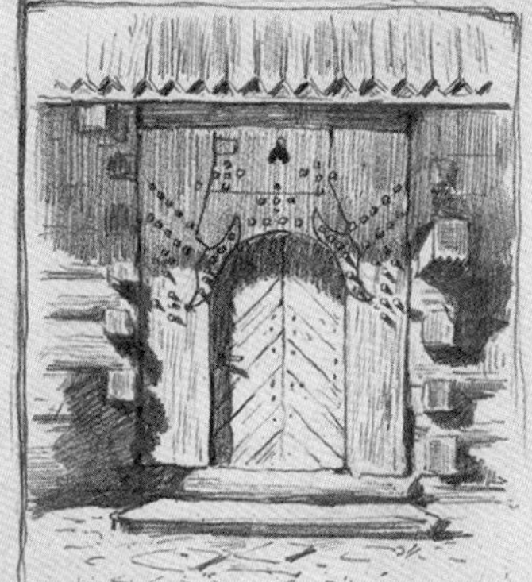

Drzwi.

1353

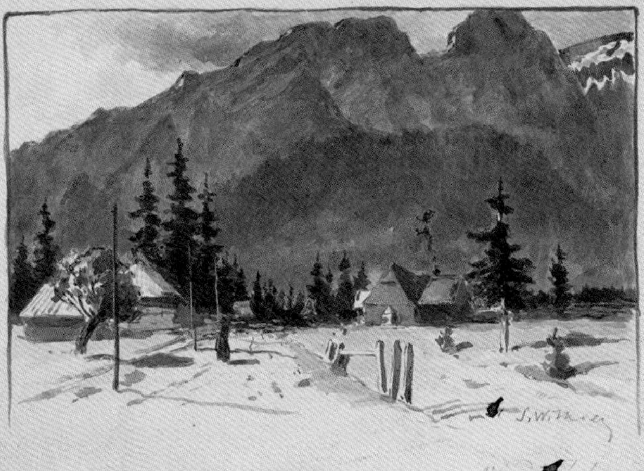

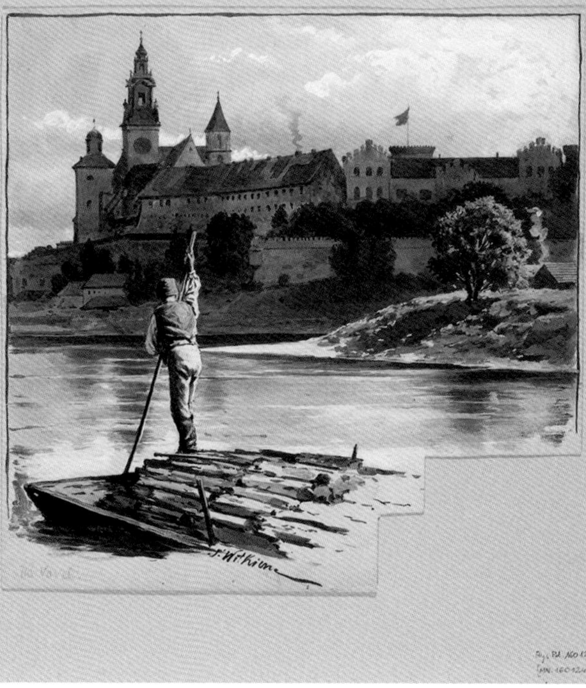

1

The Making of the Polish Arts and Crafts Movement: Key People, Places and Ideas

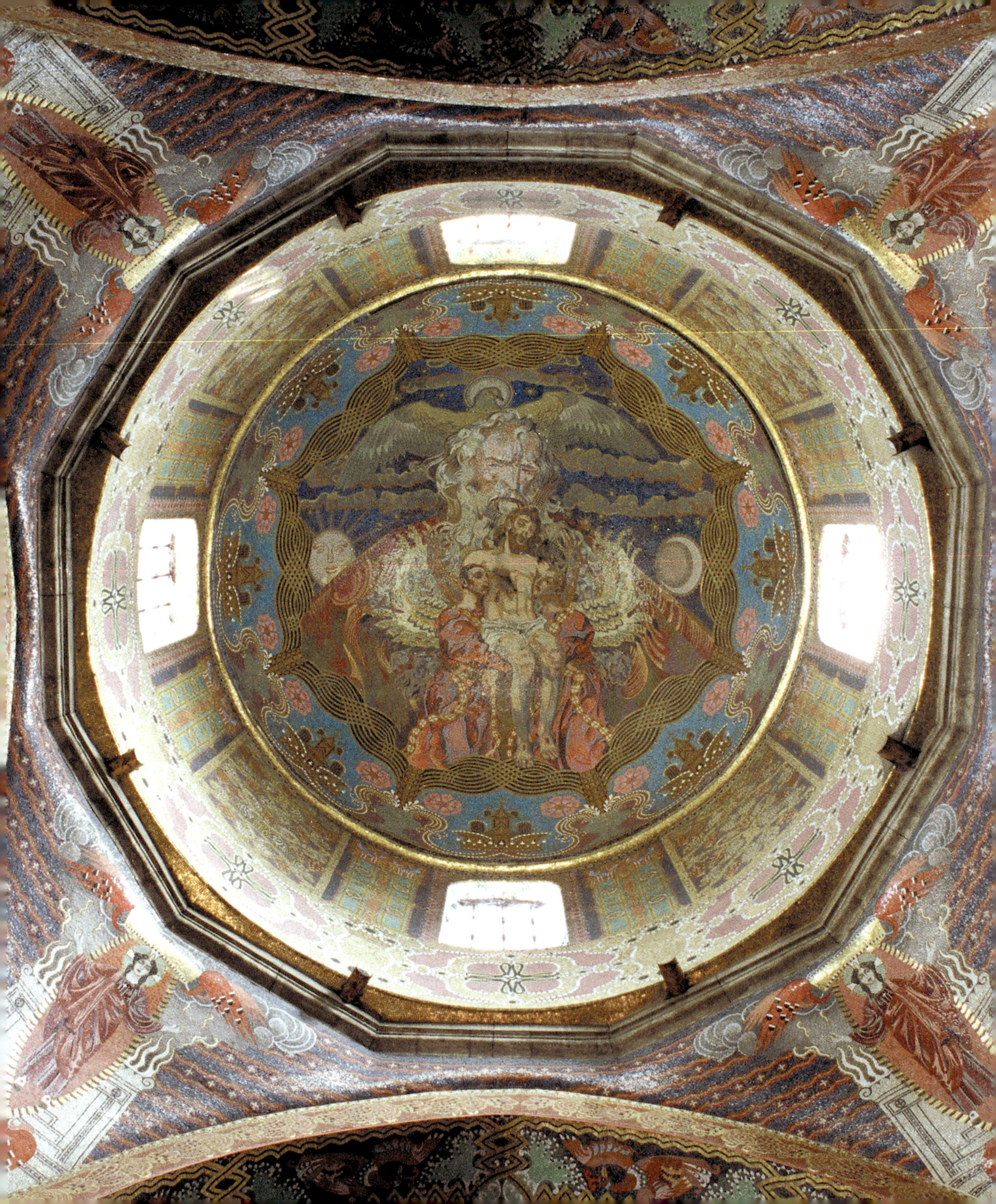

1

The Reception of the Pre-Raphaelites and the Arts and Crafts Movement in Poland

Andrzej Szczerski

In Stanisław Wyspiański's literary masterpiece, the play *The Wedding* (*Wesele*, 1901), one of the main characters, Rachela, is portrayed as if in a 'melancholic mood' which allows her to communicate with the invisible world of ghosts and phantoms.[1] In the words of the Poet her looks are typical of a painting by Edward Burne-Jones (1833–1898):

> Gladly, I'll observe you – tortured
> wandering through that dreary orchard,
> like some soul astray in love –
> half-maid, half-angel, as you rub
> against a straw-protected shrub,
> like a painting by Burne-Jones –
> while I stand watching, safe and warm.[2]

The reference to a contemporary British artist in the Polish play, although unusual, should not be surprising and Wyspiański himself must have been certain that it would be understood by his Polish audience. Even though the Pre-Raphaelites' original works were not exhibited in Poland and the direct contacts between Polish and British artists did not develop significantly, Polish cultural life in the years around 1900 was permeated by British influences. This popularity resulted from the continental fame of the Pre-Raphaelites, which had already begun in the 1870s, particularly in France, and influenced numerous Polish artists and art critics who studied and lived in Paris. Secondly, publications about British art proliferated, including those written by Polish authors such as Kazimierz Chłędowski and Feliks Jasieński (the latter under the pen name 'Manggha') who travelled to Britain and gave first-hand accounts of the local art scene. However, Polish translations of books by the Parisian critic Robert de La Sizeranne, published as *Ruskin i kult piękna* (*Ruskin and the Cult of Beauty*) in 1898 and *Malarstwo współczesne Anglii* (*Contemporary Painting in England*) in 1901, played the most important role. As a result, the Pre-Raphaelites were often

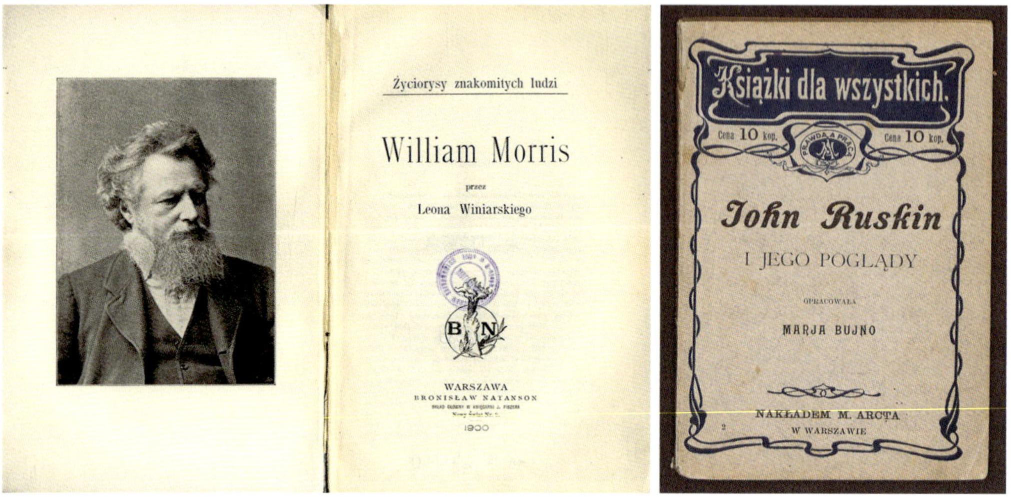

1.0 (p.28)
Józef Mehoffer
The Holy Trinity, mosaic in the cupola of the Armenian Cathedral, Lviv, 1912–13

1.1
Polish books about William Morris by Leon Winiarski (published in Warsaw in 1900 by publisher Bronisław Natason in the series 'Życiorysy Znakomitych Ludzi' ('Lives of Eminent People')), and about John Ruskin by Maria Bujno (published in Warsaw in 1901 by Michał Arct under the title *John Ruskin i jego poglądy* (*John Ruskin and His Ideas*))

associated with his generic labels such as particular types of female beauty, sensitivity, emotionalism and romanticism, or references to medieval and Early Renaissance painting.

The reception of John Ruskin's works began as early as the 1880s and was initially based exclusively on translations of writings about him, mainly those by La Sizeranne. Gradually, in the 1890s, the first Polish critical studies began to appear, while after 1900, a total of ten translations of Ruskin's works were in print, including excerpts from major publications such as *The Seven Lamps of Architecture* (1849) and ones less known in the art circles such as *The Crown of Wild Olive* (1873) or *The Ethics of the Dust* (1865). The selection of works was random and greatly hampered any attempts at independent and original assessments of Ruskin. Interestingly, apart from publicists and social activists, it was mainly architectural and literary critics who discussed him, concentrating on art theory and not on his writings about particular works of art. Ruskin was quoted by representatives of different circles: modernists emphasised his aesthetic beliefs; left-wing writers focused on references to social issues; adherents of Symbolism were chiefly interested in the spiritual and 'divinist' elements of his doctrine.

William Morris did not excite equal interest; however, his life and work were also discussed in magazines and books published around the same time as translations of Ruskin. Both were usually associated with the Pre-Raphaelites and the revolt against the dehumanising aspects of machine production, which contested the dominant Victorian taste. Though praising the noble idealism and aesthetics of Morris's social theories, his major Polish advocate Leon Winiarski nevertheless criticised his utopian concepts, such as rejecting machine production. He saw Morris mainly as an artist and aesthete, and his role 'in the contemporary world was about merging beauty with mysticism and bringing art to industry, though not for utilitarian but for purely artistic reasons'.[3]

The most widespread sources of information about Britain were numerous reproductions of British artworks, published in Polish art journals or sold as prints in bookshops such as the Altenberg Bookshop in Lviv (fig.1.2). Due to the well-developed distribution networks of art magazines, Polish readers also received additional information from foreign publications, with *The Studio* especially highly appreciated among art circles. Walter Crane (1845–1915) was the only principal protagonist of the Arts and Crafts Movement whose original works were exhibited in a Polish institution. In 1895 they were on display in the Municipal Industrial Museum (Muzeum Przemysłowe Miejskie) in Lviv, as part of a touring exhibition organised by the Royal Austrian Museum of Art and Industry (K.K. Österreichische Museum für Kunst und Industrie) in Vienna. Walter Crane himself collaborated with Polish Socialist émigré organisations in London, which from the 1890s onwards published his political posters and postcards.

The perception of the Pre-Raphaelite Brotherhood took place on a number of levels. First of all, French criticism made the movement seem like a branch of contemporary Symbolist art. It was actually the Pre-Raphaelites who were thought to be the best representatives of sophisticated aestheticism –

1.2 (LEFT)
Reproductions of Dante Gabriel Rossetti's *Dante's Dream* (1871) and Edward Burne-Jones's *Laus Veneris* (1873–8) in Adam Cybulski, *Przewodnik artystyczny* (*The Art Guide*), published by the H. Altenberg Bookshop in Lviv, 1902

1.3 (RIGHT)
A cartoon from Walter Crane's *Cartoons for the Cause* (1896), reproduced on the cover of *Kalendarz Robotniczy* (*The Workers' Calendar*), published by Polish socialist journals *Naprzód* (*Forward*) and *Nowy Robotnik* (*New Worker*), 1897

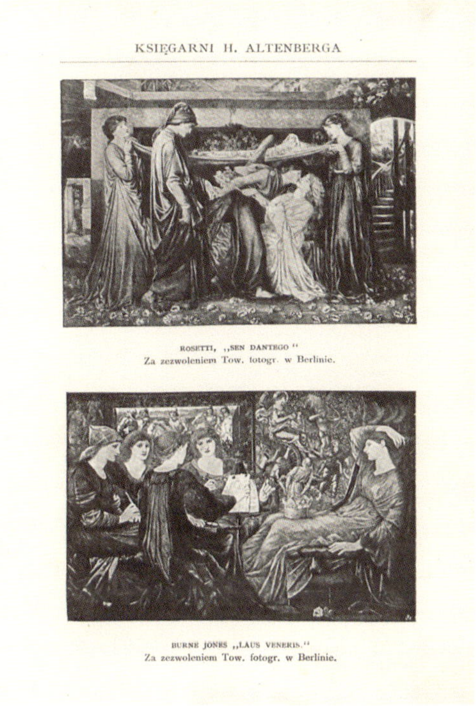
KSIĘGARNI H. ALTENBERGA

ROSETTI, „SEN DANTEGO"
Za zezwoleniem Tow. fotogr. w Berlinie.

BURNE JONES „LAUS VENERIS."
Za zezwoleniem Tow. fotogr. w Berlinie.

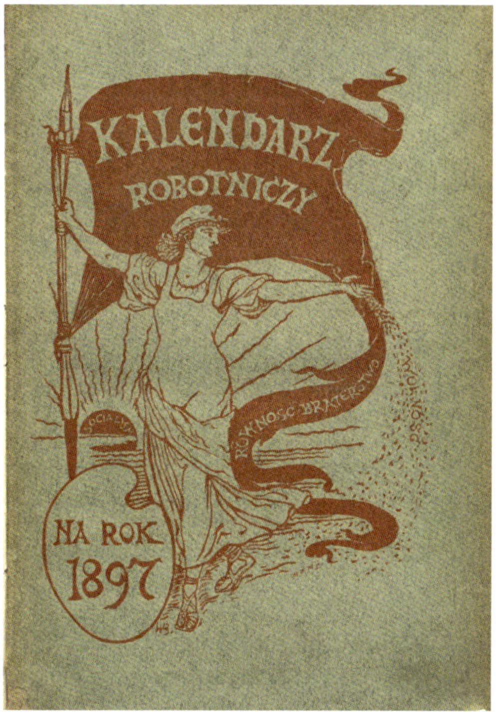

'art for art's sake' – and exoteric eulogists of mannerist beauty. Ignacy Matuszewski, a leading art critic of Young Poland, in his book *Słowacki i nowa sztuka* (*Słowacki and the New Art*, 1902) praised Ruskin and the Pre-Raphaelites for their idealism, equating it to the modernist rejection of materialism. He also valued their belief in the power of art which could bring solutions to social issues by transferring them onto aesthetic and ethical levels. Matuszewski observed the existence of a community of ideas between the Romantic poetry of Polish poet Juliusz Słowacki (1809–1849), the theories of John Ruskin, and the paintings of the Pre-Raphaelites, whom he recognised as a variation of Romanticism. He even wrote that the similarity between *The Love Song* (1868–77) by Burne-Jones and some fragments of *Król-Duch* (*The Spirit King*, 1847) by Słowacki was so great that one could actually postulate the presence of direct influences if it were not for the absurdity of such a thesis. He claimed there existed similarities between the Pre-Raphaelites and Young Poland artists such as Stanisław Wyspiański, Leon Wyczółkowski (1852–1936) and Jacek Malczewski (1854–1929), due to the appearance in their works of:

> something that was fairly non-existent in the epoch of the classical world . . . something which thoroughly permeated the mystical art of the Middle Ages (Dante) and of the early Renaissance (Fra Angelico, Botticelli), and which later almost completely disappeared, to rise up again in Romanticism and, having matured on the soil of contemporary individualism, to blossom in a flower of a repulsive stench – a flower known as mood.[4]

However, apart from such indirect connections, it would be difficult to find references to particular works of the Pre-Raphaelites among Young Poland artists. There are certain affinities to be found in paintings and graphic art by Edward Okuń (1872–1945) and lesser figures such as Stanisław Roman Lewandowski and Franciszek Siedlecki; Stanisław Wyspiański's stained-glass window titled *Apollo: Copernicus's Solar System* in the Medical Society in Kraków (1904, fig.1.4) refers to *The Wheel of Fortune* (1883) and *The Depths of the Sea* (1887) by Edward Burne-Jones. Whilst Polish artists were outward-looking and keen to emphasise their versatility and interaction with contemporary European art, especially Symbolism and

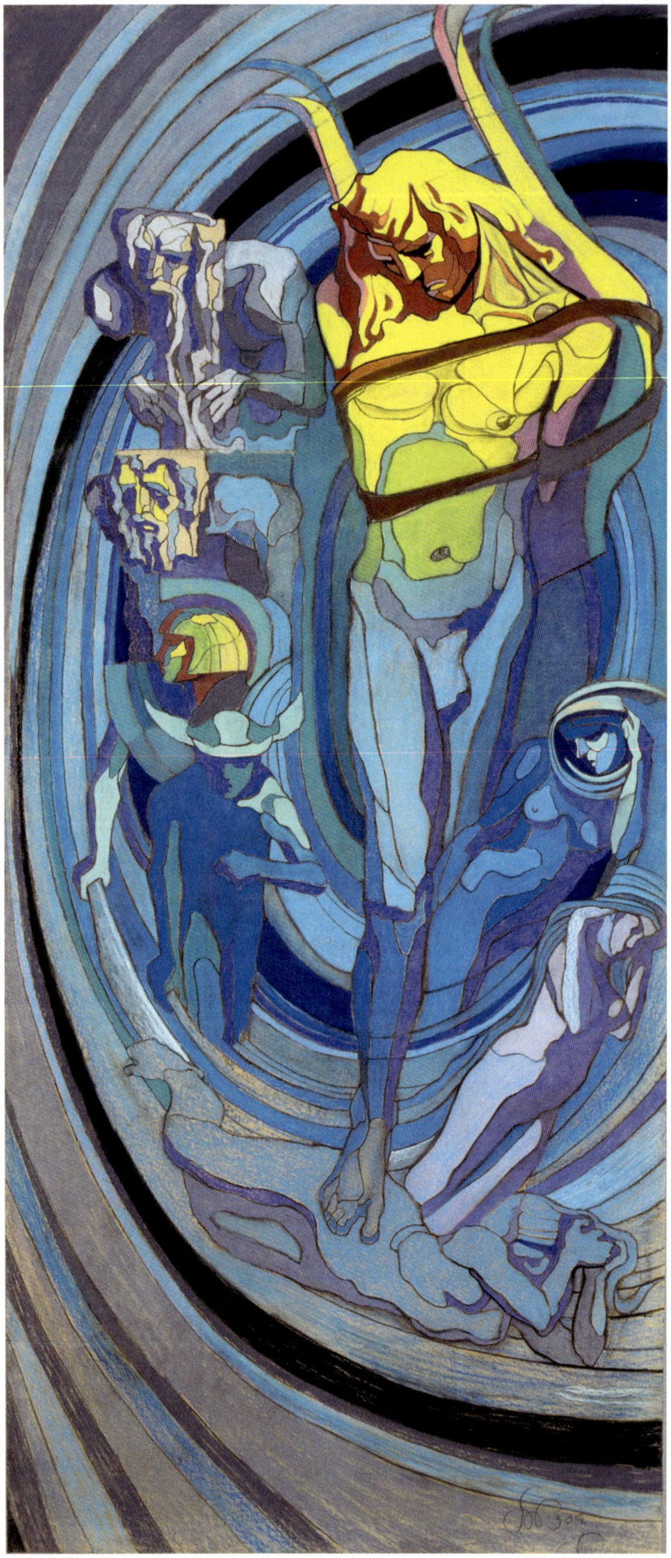

1.4
Stanisław Wyspiański
Apollo: Copernicus's Solar System (1904)
cartoon for a stained-glass window
Pastel on paper
343 × 146 cm
National Museum in Kraków,
MNK III-r.a-10898

Expressionism, they were more often interested in creating their own artistic forms. Hence they avoided any obvious connections to any other national schools, including the British.

There was yet another concurrent strand of Pre-Raphaelite reception, propagated by the circles associated with the Arts and Crafts revival. This emphasised that the paintings of Burne-Jones and of Dante Gabriel Rossetti (1828–1882), along with their furniture and stained-glass window designs, proved that applied arts had a similar value to high art, and therefore endorsed the entire programme of the Arts and Crafts Movement, with its focus on the reform of both arts and society. According to this interpretation, the Pre-Raphaelites and the Arts and Crafts Movement were seen as a unique, national school of art, different from the rest of contemporary art and especially independent from French influences. As a result, the Polish reception of British ideas showed ambitions to merge the notions of modernity and artistic reform with the hopes for national rebirth, both in the cultural and political spheres.

The latter point was already anchored in the interpretations of La Sizeranne's book *La peinture anglaise contemporaine* (*Contemporary Painting in England*). The author did not hesitate to make associations between, for example, appeals from Ford Madox Brown (1821–1893) to reject French influences, and the Pre-Raphaelite idea of creating a national school. Such opinions had important consequences in Poland, a country divided between the three empires of Russia, Germany and Austria, where art was an expression of national sentiments and hopes for regaining independence. Helena d'Abancourt in her preface to the Polish translation of La Sizeranne's book claimed that the French critic's publication offered a fuller description than usual of the whole movement which was, incidentally, then enjoying increasing popularity and which 'gave itself the name of Pre-Raphaelitism'.[5] Popular opinion up to that point had predominantly followed the stereotype that 'Pre-Raphaelitism . . . was based on a certain pre-Raphael convention, on excessive elongation of figures, on the so-called Botticellian type, etc.' La Sizeranne, however, showed that 'Pre-Raphaelitism is not keen on performing a shift towards emulating the predecessors of Raphael but on feeling their truth, seeing it as a rule for composition and for simplicity in the use of technical means'. The greatest value of La Sizeranne's book lay, according to d'Abancourt, in another place:

> What further, or rather especially engaged the translator in English Pre-Raphaelitism, arresting her with its great charm, was its distinctiveness, its 'autonomy' which La Sizeranne captured and accentuated so well. For those of us who strive to create an art all of our own, one which would be nationally different, this trait is not something we can dismiss in foreign painting. We cannot dismiss the path which others have taken towards their desired goal – they have made it there, reached it, creating art which is most individually separate – an English national art.

Thanks to La Sizeranne's book, British art could therefore be seen as an ideal standard for national art.

The national interpretation of British models became the source of renewed interest in the works of Polish romantic poet Cyprian Kamil Norwid (1821–1883) in the mid-19th century. The aim was to demonstrate the parallels between Polish and British artistic explorations, and was promoted by Zenon Przesmycki (known as 'Miriam'), editor of the prominent Young Poland journal *Chimera* in Warsaw. In volume VIII of the journal (1904) he praised Norwid's epic poem *Promethidion,* published in Paris in 1851, as an appraisal of a new national art, based on motifs found in folk art. The process of renewal was to be based on manual labour, which was understood as work-as-artistic-creativity and which would serve as a field for a general consensus across all social strata, thus creating a national and cultural community. Norwid also claimed that dividing art into high and applied art did not make any sense, believing that the element of beauty reveals itself equally powerfully in all fields of art. Therefore the main message of *Promethidion* sounded similar to the ideals of the Arts and Crafts Movement.

These similarities should not be surprising. Norwid closely followed information about British industrial reforms of that time and the Great Exhibition in London in 1851, which he refers to in *Promethidion.* Yet his work is more diverse than the writings of the British theoreticians of the design revival and more romantic in character. But for Przesmycki it was the precursor of the British ideas which now governed the world. He wrote in *Chimera* in 1904:

> The great Polish thought – as a result of the reluctance of its own people – failed to make its presence known and conquer the world. It was the others who conquered it, those who were more fortunate, the English, the Ruskins, the Morrises, the ones who developed analogous ideas, though not in a comparably comprehensive and empirical manner . . . Despite the victory of the great British reformers, they [Norwid's works] still harbour the yet undiscovered but nutritious seeds of truths which are great, fundamental and revolutionary.[6]

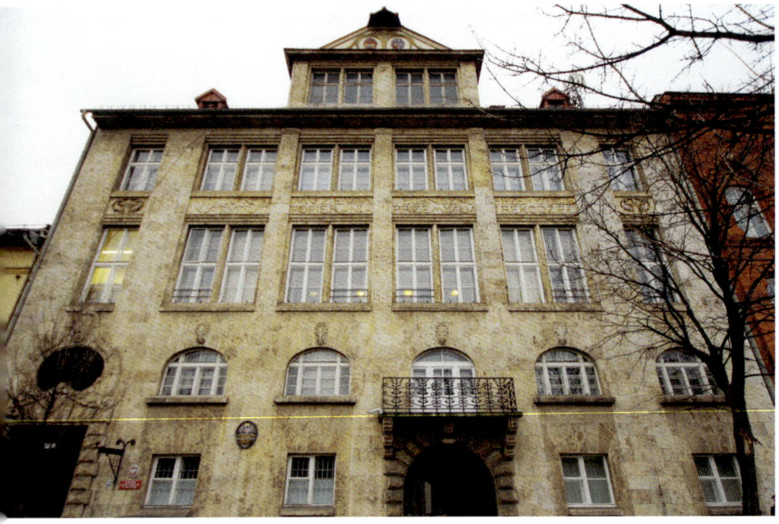

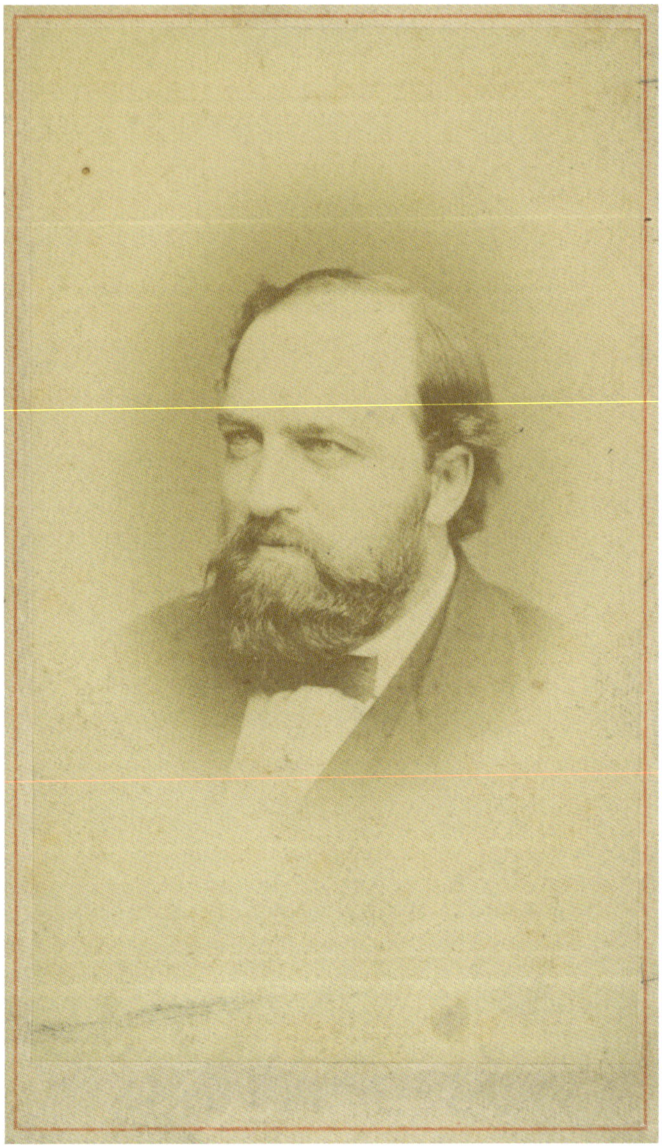

Przesmycki allowed British ideas to be seen in parallel to the forgotten Polish tradition and therefore as even more acceptable and inspiring for Polish artists.

The unique example of the reception of British design reform was the foundation of the Museum of Technology and Industry in Kraków in 1868 (fig.1.5).[7] Thanks to the relatively liberal Austrian partition of Poland where Kraków was located, and with the endorsement of city authorities dominated by Poles, Adrian Baraniecki (fig.1.6) was able to create an institution independent of the Viennese authorities. In its programme he combined the call for industrial arts reform with patriotic ideology. Baraniecki came from the region of Podolia, at that time part of Russia, and took part in a failed Polish January Uprising against the Tsar in 1863–4. At the time of post-uprising repressions, he had to flee from his estate and settled in the Austrian partition. In 1864, he travelled to Paris, London and Edinburgh, where he took care of Polish émigrés while studying contemporary arts institutions. Apparently Baraniecki remained in Britain for three years, chiefly in London, but also in Manchester and Liverpool, where he visited industrial museums. Inspired especially by the South Kensington Museum in London and the Edinburgh Museum of Science and Art, he decided to establish a similar institution in partitioned Poland. With his private resources Baraniecki began collecting raw material samples, machinery, industrial tools and samples of craftsmanship and industrial art, which he purchased in Britain and in Paris after the Exposition Universelle of 1867. Thanks to an agreement he signed with Józef Dietl, the mayor of Kraków, the new museum opened as a municipal institution in 1868, with a collection approximating 5,000 artefacts in total. Before moving to its own building in 1913, the museum operated in a wing of the Franciscan monastery in the city's historic centre. Its collection, thanks to numerous donations by Polish collectors, already numbered 30,000 objects by 1880, including specimens not only of industrial production but also of Polish folk art and

1.5
Tadeusz Stryjeński, Franciszek Mączyński and Józef Czajkowski
The Museum of Technology and Industry, Kraków, 1909–13

1.6
Photograph of Adrian Baraniecki (1828–1891), *c.*1880
State Municipal Archive in Kraków, MPA 27

ethnographic collections from Polish explorers of Siberia, Africa and Latin America.

Baraniecki was keen to follow the British model of an institution which, apart from collecting, researching and displaying artefacts, also engaged in extensive educational activities. He wanted it to serve 'professional and industrial production purposes as well as being a museum of civilisation', and to showcase all aspects of modernity to Polish audiences.[8] Moreover, Baraniecki attached great importance to the education of women: having noted the growing interest of Kraków's female residents, he swiftly transformed the irregular, occasional lectures held in the museum into Higher Learning Courses for Women; in 1870, they were rebranded as the Higher Learning Scientific College for Women. The college had five departments: natural sciences, fine arts, history and literature, commerce, and economics, with eminent lecturers such as the painter Jan Matejko, university professors and political activists. Furthermore, Baraniecki used his own money to run commercial courses for young people (1870–75), free Sunday lectures for craft workers (until 1876) as well as the Commercial Sciences College for Men (1870–77).

Educational activities notwithstanding, it is worth mentioning the carefully designed Polish ethnographic division of the museum, with its first artefacts donated by the founder of Polish ethnography Zygmunt Gloger. The division collected folk art from the majority of Poland's pre-partition regions; its political meaning was more than obvious, showing the persistence and vitality of Polish culture across the political borders of the partitioning powers. Nonetheless, one should also bear in mind the artistic dimension of folk art collections: following the Arts and Crafts Movement's interest in the vernacular, Polish folk art was seen as a source for the revival of contemporary applied art and for giving it a national character.

Baraniecki's coherent vision of the Museum's mission based on the British model turned out to be very personal and closely connected with the man himself. Notwithstanding the changes introduced by his successors, the Museum retained its prominent role in the promotion of Arts and Crafts reforms and became the seedbed of the first Polish associations of designers in the beginning of the 20th century. Although similar museums of art and industry were founded also in Warsaw and Lviv in the 1870s, they were formed on the wave of pan-European interest in industrial art rather than through British influence and did not play such an important role in the history of Polish design as the Kraków institution.

The interpretation of the Arts and Crafts Movement as a source of national art found its extraordinary expression in attempts to create a national style on the basis of folk art and architecture from the Podhale region at the foot of the Tatra mountains in southern Poland (see Chapter 6).[9] Its founder, Stanisław Witkiewicz, a painter and art critic, who settled there with his family in 1890, called it the Zakopane Style, after the principal village of the region. In his writings Witkiewicz recalls that when creating the stylistic concept he had been unaware of works by John Ruskin or William Morris; and yet he admitted that their basic ideals had much in common. In 1903, he wrote: 'knowing nothing of Ruskin or Morris, we could in real life pursue their theoretical conclusions; and we made one of their dreams come true.'[10] In the early 1890s – when the Zakopane Style concept had yet to fully mature – Witkiewicz was following vernacular-inspired architecture tendencies, mainly in Germany and Russia to which he had been exposed, especially during his studies at the St Petersburg Academy of Fine Arts (1868–71). He had not encountered Arts and Crafts Movement ideals before 1898, but he was influenced by examples of how British art and design were received in mainland Europe. Having read Ruskin's works, Witkiewicz was quick to appreciate his role in creating ideological foundations for an artistic reform of which he believed himself to be a continuator.

This is evidenced by the attempts made in Witkiewicz's circles to win Ruskin's personal support for the cause of the Zakopane Style. Most probably in 1899, Jadwiga Sienkiewicz, the daughter of Witkiewicz's personal friend Henryk Sienkiewicz (the Polish Nobel Prize winner in literature in 1905), sent a set of photographs showing Zakopane Style works to Ruskin, requesting his opinion. In the words of another friend of Witkiewicz's, the art critic and journalist Antoni Chołoniewski, 'Ruskin, who had a tendency to exaggerate when it came to his love for the primeval, declared the "Polish style" to be original, and expressed regret that his old age prevented him from making such a long journey to see these artefacts in real life – something he would have been happy to do.'[11] The correspondence with Ruskin was further confirmed by an advocate of the Zakopane Style, the painter and doctor Stanisław Eljasz-Radzikowski (1869–1935), who in his book *Styl zakopiański* (*The Zakopane Style*), published in Kraków in 1901, added that Ruskin 'entrusted [him] to thank Miss Jadwiga Sienkiewicz [for her letter]' from his sickbed, conveying through him a letter dated 26 August 1899, written at the Brantwood estate.[12] Regrettably no evidence of such correspondence with Ruskin has been found either in Poland or in Britain. Witkiewicz's fascination with Ruskin was also apparent in his theoretical papers. The Polish artist mentioned Ruskin repeatedly, and his concept of the role of art in human life and society in particular. In 1906, in the second edition of his well-known book *Na przełęczy* (*On the Mountain Pass*), he wrote, 'What Ruskin dreamed of and Morris attempted to realise happened here [in Zakopane]: the poor and the rich come closer to one another in art.'[13]

Despite its ideological connections to Ruskin and Morris's ideas, the Zakopane Style may be primarily attributed to Witkiewicz. His concept is a blend of the idea of national style, the appraisal of the social function of art, and a hope for modern art to be created, with any ties to the traditions of 19th-century historicism severed. Witkiewicz wanted to create a Polish national style unaffected by foreign influence, one recognised as a source of cultural revival in Poland. The style had to be based on original and primeval sources of Polishness which he believed had survived in the material culture of Podhale inhabitants, the Highlanders (*Górale*). The social aspect of the style was of equal importance. Witkiewicz believed that the folk-art-based concept for reviving national art would lead to national solidarity, and to the gradual evening-out of any social inequalities. Finally, despite having attached greatest importance to architecture, Witkiewicz argued against any distinction between high and low art, giving the same prominence to fine and applied arts; indeed, the Zakopane Style became most pronounced in interior decoration and applied arts, as in his masterpiece, the House Under the Firs for the Pawlikowski family in Zakopane (1897–8).

Similar concepts of the vernacular revival were also followed in Lviv, where both Polish and Ukrainian artists promoted the Hutsul culture of the eastern Carpathians as a source of a new national art.[14] It is enough to recall the fascination of painter Jan (Iwan) Trusz (1869–1941) with Hutsul folk art, or Hutsul inspirations in the paintings and applied art designs of Kazimierz Sichulski (1879–1942), not to mention the decorations by Modest Sosenko at the Institute of Music in Lviv (1914–15) or paintings by Ołeksa Nowakiwski (1872-1935). Numerous examples of the adaptation of Hutsul wooden architecture and ornamental motifs were shown at the National Exhibition in Lviv (1894), both in architecture (the Ukrainian societies' pavilion designed by Julian Zachariewicz) and interior design (furniture by Władysława Gostyńska, Teodor Prokopowicz, et al.). Artists and architects such as Julian Zachariewicz (1837–1898) and Edgar Kováts (1849–1912) even attempted to develop an 'Eastern Galician' or 'Hutsul' style to counterbalance the influence of Zakopane Style, and the issue became an important matter of debate in Lviv around the year 1900.

Interest in Hutsul art was justified in studies by Kazimierz Mokłowski, especially in his 1903 book *Sztuka ludowa w Polsce* (*Folk Art in Poland*), published in Lviv. In this work, Mokłowski focuses on folk art from the region of Lviv, as well as the Kingdom of Poland, the Grand Duchy of Poznań, Silesia, and the territories of present-day Lithuania, Belarus and Ukraine – that is, the lands of the former Polish-Lithuanian Commonwealth. While some of the analyses that Mokłowski offers seem dubious, it is worth noting his rejection of 'the kind of "Zakopane methods" suggested' and his call to adopt an 'emblem of Polish folk style'. Mokłowski identifies traces of such a style throughout the territory of the former Commonwealth, including the 'lovely' construction traditions of the Hutsuls, recognised as one of the varieties of Carpathian Highlanders' folk culture. He writes: 'Further research shows that despite the proven unity of the single woodland type, the multitude of ornamental styles displayed would make any attempt to limit the source of studies and motifs to the single narrow Nowy Targ district [Podhale] an unpardonable error; indeed, the scope of research and photography ought to be expanded to include all of Poland.'[15] The artistic values of Hutsul construction proved of interest to many architects, including the most eminent residents of Lviv, such as Tadeusz Obmiński (1874–1932) and Jan (Iwan) Lewiński (1851–1919).

As the Zakopane Style and Hutsul Style developed, a new generation of artists approached British ideas with renewed interest. Their base was the Museum of Technology and Industry in Kraków. The first association they established was the Polish Applied Arts Society, founded in 1901 by a group consisting of painters Karol Tichy, Włodzimierz Tetmajer and Stanisław Goliński, architects Józef Czajkowski and Edward Trojanowski (1873–1930), and Stanisław Wyspiański. The lawyer and critic Jerzy Warchałowski was their theoretician. He wrote that the ultimate purpose of the Society's work was to:

> replace ugliness with beauty, wherever and however expressed; . . . counterfeits – with precious materials, pretence – with simplicity; . . . the terrible and fatal boredom of the workshop climate – with a fresh breath of new effort; and, last but not least, persistence in adoring anything branded with historical style or flaunting foreign charm – with an intense listening to the pulse of one's own life, a feel for the nation's modern spirit and ideals of leading individuals.

In time, the Society was joined by prominent Kraków artists, architects, art historians and ethnographers, such as Jan Bukowski (1873–1938), Karol Frycz (1877–1963), Feliks Kopera (1871–1952), Józef Mehoffer, Karol Potkański (1861–1907), Jan Szczepkowski (1878–1964), Seweryn Udziela (1857–1937), Henryk Uziembło (1879–1949) and Ludwik Wojtyczko (1873–1949). The Society focused on propagating an applied art revival by organising exhibitions, art education initiatives and competitions, publishing, and collecting and researching Polish crafts and applied art. Nonetheless, the association's primary intent was to create an innovative artistic form, simultaneously modern and national in nature; the programme's key components consisted also of a desire to imbue all aspects of life with beauty and a social message relating to the idea of the democratisation of art. Beginning in 1902, the Society published its own periodical, *Wydawnictwo Towarzystwa Polskiej Sztuki Stosowanej: materiały* (*Publications of The Polish Applied Arts Society: Materials*) (fig.1.7), which in 1906 was renamed as simply *Sztuka Stosowana* (*Applied Art*), and which ran until 1914. Furthermore, the Society organised a number of exhibitions with a carefully designed programme (in Kraków, Lviv and Warsaw) to present folk art collections, folk-art-inspired contemporary artworks, and historic examples of Polish crafts and applied art. The *Architecture and Interiors in a Garden Setting* exhibition in Kraków in 1912 was of particular importance. It showed model solutions for 'residences suitable for all social classes' in the spirit of the Garden City Movement instigated in Britain by Ebenezer Howard (1850–1928): the suburban house, houses for workers and craftspeople and the peasant cottage. Key projects of the Society included the interior design for Kraków Town Hall (1907–11), a rebuilding of the Old Theatre in Kraków (1905–6), and Doctor Dłuski's Sanatorium in Zakopane (1910) (see Chapter 11).

The Society's work was notable primarily for its renewed attempts to blend British Arts and Crafts Movement inspirations with the search for a national style. For Kraków artists, patriotic content linked in with ideas of modernity as well as with a will to sever ties with historicism. While recognising the Society's indebtedness to British inspiration, Warchałowski wrote that Polish design was developing 'independently of any contemporary movements abroad'.[16] Józef Czajkowski dreamed of the new organisation becoming a role model for all of Poland; in a well-known fragment from his memoir, the artist described the entire country with 'thousands of studios: woodwork, kilim, carpet and tapestry weaving workshops, fabric making and dyeing works, ceramic kilns, metal and glassworks, stone and wood sculpting ateliers, leather, bookbinding, printing, stained-glass, embroidery, and toy-making workshops'.[17] The vision, in itself as idealistic as the society imagined in Morris's *News from Nowhere* (1890), does, however, bear witness to the diverse activities of members of the Society.[18] The Society drew on Morris's experience in designing the concept of model workshops where craftspeople were trained. Craftsmen were considered equal to artists as creators of works, this belief being expressed in the fact that they were credited by the Society for their products by name. Among the members of the Society Stanisław Wyspiański and Józef Mehoffer in particular shared some similarities with the British Arts and Crafts Movement, due to their medievalism, inspiration from nature, interest in various applied arts, from prints to stained-glass design, and decoration of complete interiors.

The ideas of the Polish Applied Arts Society were developed by the Kraków Workshops association formed in Kraków in 1913

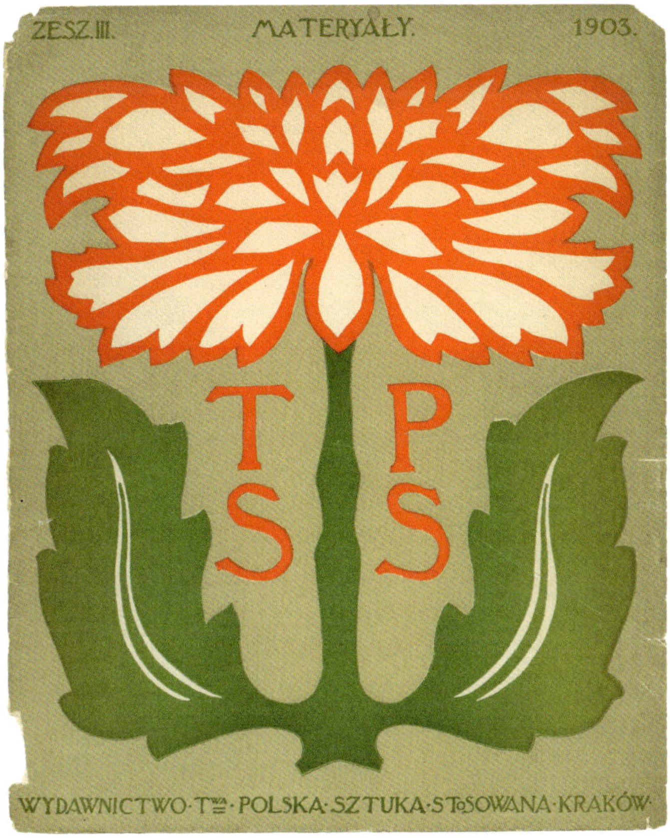

1.7
Jan Bukowski
Cover of *Wydawnictwo Towarzystwa Polska Sztuka Stosowana: materiały* (*Publications of the Polish Applied Arts Society: Materials*), no.3 (1903)

(see Chapter 9). The two formally merged in early 1914. While the Society's connections to the Museum of Technology and Industry in Kraków had been based on common ideals, indirect cooperation, and attempts to influence the facility's operational programme, the Kraków Workshops actually made the museum their headquarters. They differed from the Polish Applied Arts Society in that they belonged to a younger generation and supported a new approach to the idea of a national style and to the utilisation of folk art. Founding members of the association, which operated as a commercial cooperative of artists and craftspeople, included Karol Homolacs (1874–1962), Wojciech Jastrzębowski, Włodzimierz Konieczny (1886–1916), Kazimierz Młodzianowski (1880–1928), Kazimierz Witkiewicz (1880–1973) and Stanisław Till (1875–1945), who was director of the Museum of Technology and Industry at the time.

Instead of focusing on a need to create a national style, the Kraków Workshops' programme spoke of a centre to unite the efforts of artists, people who cared about the development of an artistic industry, and of craftsmen striving to make crafts more noble and precious.[19] While they alluded to the British Arts and Crafts Movement programme, the Workshops had more in common with artists' and craftspeople's associations formed in Europe at the time, which focused on the development of a modern and synthetic language of form of industrial art and design rather than on the handicrafts revival. Wojciech Jastrzębowski, the Workshops' main designer and theoretician, wrote of how the association was well aware that new art was not about new forms or ornamentation, but about a new way of thinking;[20] young artists accused the Polish Applied Arts Society of lacking such new vision and of eclecticism in the use of folk art motifs. To Jastrzębowski, 'perfect knowledge of craftsmanship and technique, and the understanding of properties of the material used' were all that mattered. 'The national character of our art was not discussed extensively, it was self-evident. We fought artistic paper projects not based on proper foundations or sufficient knowledge of technique or material, as well as the excessively novel – the so-called *moderna*.'[21] Kraków artists were also against ornamentation, but, as Jastrzębowski claimed, William Morris remained their master; they held true to his declaration that, of all things unnecessary, ornament is the most unnecessary.

While the outbreak of the First World War prevented the Kraków Workshops from developing further, they significantly contributed to the process by which Polish artists and designers adopted the British paradigm. The association was also instrumental in creating the first 'Morrisian' workshop in Poland, operated by Antoni Buszek (1883–1954). A painter by background, Buszek proceeded to set up a model community workshop in Kraków, employing peasant girls from nearby

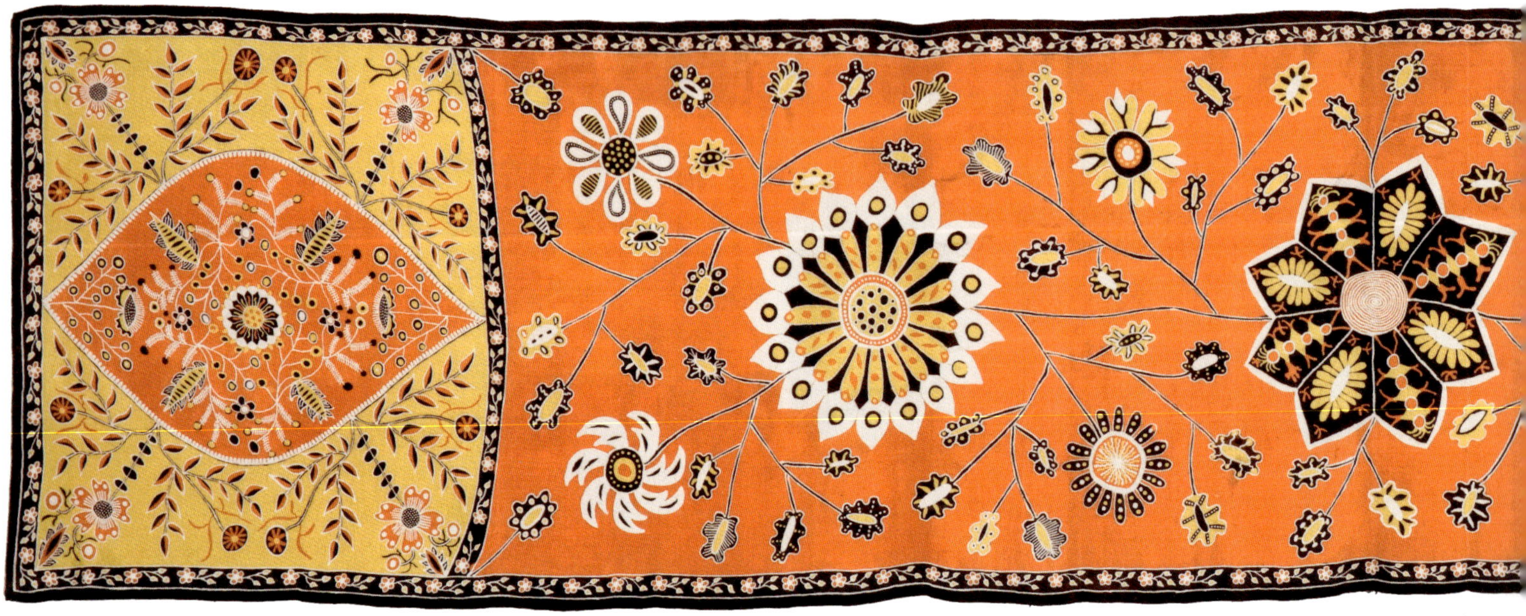

villages as designers. The process of teaching art techniques, especially batik decoration of textiles and wooden products, to an uneducated audience was to serve the purpose of unleashing their creative potential while promoting the belief that a revolutionary change in the way of approaching art was close at hand. Beauty ceased to be owned by elites only; concurrently, artists began sharing their work with members of society formerly denied access to high culture.

Kraków groups were not the only associations promoting the ideals of the Arts and Crafts Movement. Others included the Podhale Arts Society (Towarzystwo Sztuka Podhalańska) formed in Zakopane in 1909 and focusing on craft traditions in the Podhale region, and the Kilim Association (Stowarzyszenie Kilim) established in the same town in 1910 to preserve traditional weaving techniques for use in the production of modern design. Antonina Sikorska led an artistic weaving workshop in Czernichów near Kraków, and many workshops opened in the eastern Carpathians. Lviv had a number of arts and crafts associations and studios as well, such as the 'Golden Horn' Applied Art Association (Stowarzyszenie Sztuki Stosowanej 'Złoty Róg', founded 1901) and the 'Seed' Art Lovers Society (Towarzystwo Miłośników Sztuki 'Ziarno', 1902–5). The most important of them was 'Union' ('Zespól'), established in 1911, with its membership comprising the leading artists of the Lviv scene – such as painters Władysław Jarocki (1879–1965) and Fryderyk Pautsch (1877–1950), architects Wiesław Grzymalski and Marian Osiński, and with artist and designer Marian Olszewski (1881–1915) as its leader. It offered a wide range of creative work at its exhibitions: artistic advertising, locksmith plaques, stained glass, kilim designs and posters, as well as interior decoration, residential and church architecture through to home garden design. As noted by art critics, 'Union' artists strove to make their work homely and distinctly local. The creativity of the Lviv art community was also apparent in interior architecture at the Krakowski Hotel (1913–14), Feliks Wygrzywalski's decorative scheme for the 'Art' cafe (1908), Kajetan Stefanowicz's frescoes at Zofia Strzałkowska's private girls' school (1912–13), and the decoration of the Armenian Cathedral between 1912 and 1929 by Józef Mehoffer (mosaic) (fig.1.0), Karol Maszkowski (stained glass), and Henryk Rosen (wall paintings).

The reception of British art and design in Poland shows the ambition to merge the ideology of modernity with national rebirth, in both the cultural and political spheres. British works were seen by Poles as an example of a national art and they were treated – at the ideological level – as the

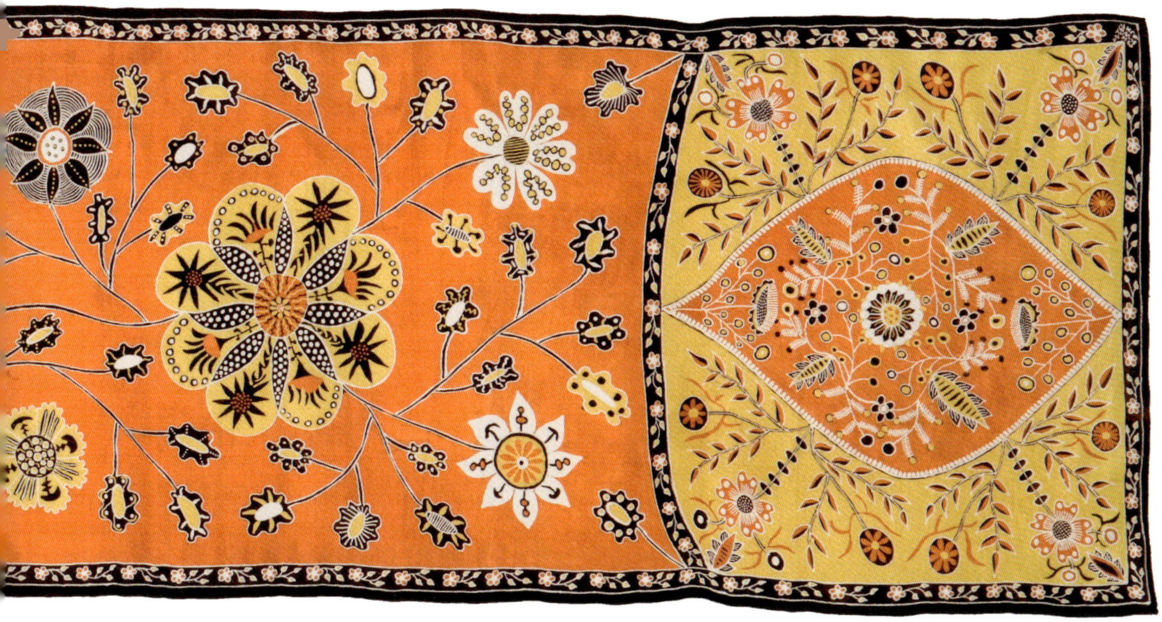

1.8
Zofia Kogut
Shawl, made in the Kraków Workshops, 1921
Batik-decorated silk
216 × 47.5 cm
National Museum in Kraków, MNK XIX-3256

inspiration to pursue the idea of a Polish 'national style'. Such a conviction was concurrent with their attempts to undertake the modernisation of art and design, which the reformers believed could serve as the beginning of the revival of national culture as a whole. The nation's cultural distinctness was eventually to lead to independence. Together with their political connotations, the writings of Ruskin and Morris served as a model for those who promoted their visions of modernity predominantly based on socialist reforms. British sources of inspiration indicated the mutual interdependence of the national and international elements in the art of Young Poland. The intensity of the cultural exchange and the access to information, mostly through various periodicals but also through studies, travels and personal contacts, made artists throughout Europe aware of the new artistic trends, not only in the artistic centre of Paris. The model based on the distinction between centre versus periphery can no longer be deemed adequate to account for and explain the pattern of artistic dissemination, as the peripheries did not have to look to the centres for sources of inspiration, but rather established direct contact between themselves, such as between Poland and Britain. In these circumstances, the national character of art in a particular country was seen as valuable, as it served to underscore its distinctiveness and original character. International dialogue and exchange were therefore possible because of the discovery of separate national identities which opposed a uniformity dictated by the centre. British art and design, perceived as distinct and unique, served as an example of such a national school which was worthy of appreciation, not least because it emphasised the value of modernity and the vernacular inspirations so crucial for Polish artists and designers. Importantly, in the years around 1900, the national idea also attracted the attention of Polish artists as it corresponded with the political revival which ultimately led to the regaining of independence after the First World War. The reception of British models therefore proved that at the turn of the 20th century the national and international dimensions overlapped, coexisted and mutually influenced each other, giving the art scene the diversity which proved to be the basis of artistic values and freedoms.

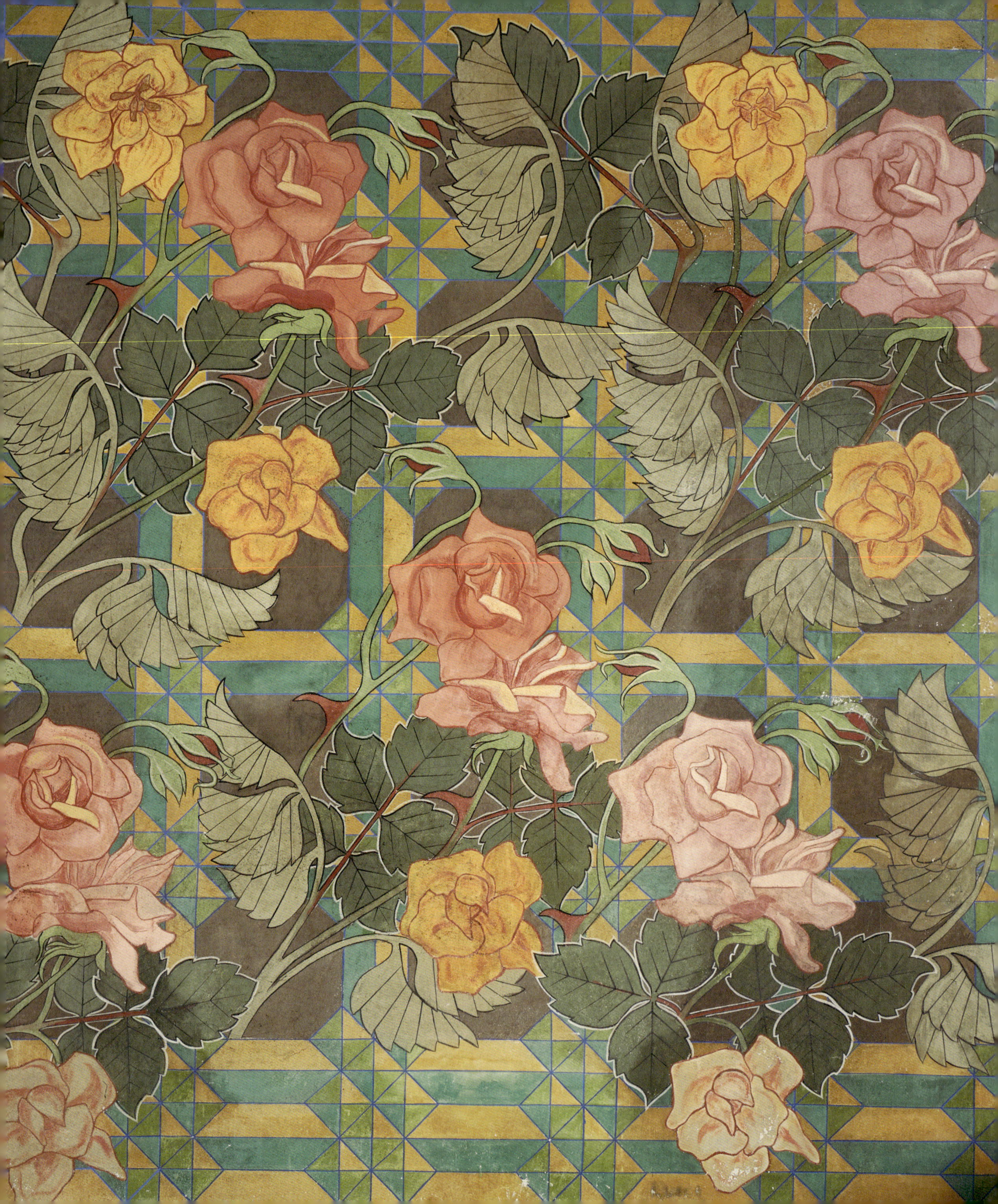

Fellow Arts and Crafts Reformers Stanisław Wyspiański and William Morris: Parallel Lives

Julia Griffin

This chapter charts the artistic achievements of Stanisław Wyspiański (1869–1907), arguably the greatest design reformer in Poland's history, with special reference to striking parallels with William Morris's life and work.[1] The two artists came from different generations and never met. However, they had a lot in common in terms of their reformist outlook, remarkable creative versatility as applied arts designers and interior decorators, shared interests and commitment to similar causes, and last but not least their character traits and work ethic. As J.W. Mackail, the author of Morris's first official biography *The Life* (1899), perceptively stated, Morris's two greatest inspirations were history and nature;[2] the same was true for Wyspiański. This chapter goes on to show that Wyspiański was William Morris's closest counterpart within the Polish Arts and Crafts movement.

When Wyspiański was born in Kraków in 1869, within the former Polish lands then under Austrian rule, the 35-year-old Morris had been building up his cutting-edge design firm, Morris, Marshall, Faulkner & Co., for almost a decade, with a number of high-profile commissions, such as the Green Dining Room at the South Kensington Museum (1866) and the decorative scheme of St James's Palace (1866–7), under his belt. Morris was also on the cusp of establishing his reputation as a foremost British poet on account of the serial publication of *The Earthly Paradise* (1868–70). Three notable milestones would mark Wyspiański's rise to prominence in the visual arts: the acclaimed completion of the first stage of the Franciscan Church decorative scheme in 1895 (see Chapter 3); his appointment as Artistic Director of the short-lived although very influential Young Poland periodical *Życie* in 1898; and being awarded the Probus Barczewski Endowment Prize, the most prestigious fine art prize in partitioned Poland at the time, by the Academy of Learning (Akademia Umiejętności) in 1901 for his King Casimir the Great stained-glass design intended for Wawel Cathedral (see fig.4.2).[3] He also became a national bard in the last year due to the staging of his play *The Wedding*. There is little space here to chart in full Wyspiański's

2.0 (p.42)
Stanisław Wyspiański
'Roses' repeating pattern
mural decoration, 1897
Franciscan Church, Kraków

2.1
Antiquarian interests shared with William Morris. CLOCKWISE FROM TOP LEFT: Wyspiański's drawings of the 16th-century vernacular Church of Sts Philip and James in the village of Sękowa, West Galicia (1889), and a French Gothic cathedral (1890); the *Madonna* of Krużlowa (*c.*1410); an antiquarian article in *Życie* weekly (6 November 1897) about the history and insensitive restoration of Kraków's Church of the Holy Cross; and William Morris's antiquarian article about 17th-century Kelmscott Manor in *The Quest* (vol.2, no.4, November 1895)
National Museum in Kraków, MNK III-r.a-4858, MNK III r.a-2676/19, MNK-I-119

early training and formative influences – the role of his master and mentor Jan Matejko, his studies at the School of Fine Arts in Kraków, involvement in the renovation and redecoration of St Mary's Basilica, and his intermittent education in Paris for almost three years, including classes at the Académie Colarossi. What is certain is that his creative journey was intrinsically linked to his unique heritage and the symbolic significance of Kraków, his home town. Following his return to Poland from Paris in 1894, Wyspiański became an influential force on the art scene, undertaking a number of innovative design projects which broke the boundaries between fine and decorative arts.

Wyspiański and Morris's lives display numerous parallels. First and foremost, they shared a tireless work ethic and restless energy, which can be credited for the enormity of their respective outputs. Both men are known to have sought rest in switching to another type of work. As recalled by Wilfrid Blunt, 'Morris sought little relaxation beyond a change of occupation – from designing to writing, or vice versa'.[4] Similarly, Wyspiański's cousin Zenon Parvi noted that the artist:

> had a fantastical, superhuman work ethic. Rest or temporary idleness were unknown to him and this surely accounts for his incredibly prolific output, especially with reference to paintings, which he created during, regrettably, such a very short life. With Wyspiański, action instantly followed any idea . . . after completing any strenuous piece of work he looked for rest in another job ... As a rest from designing the Wawel stained-glass cartoons he wrote rhapsodies and plays.[5]

Secondly, Wyspiański and Morris shared a passion and reverence for history, which fuelled many of their activities. Apart from the benefit of classical training, both reformers had great antiquarian knowledge of architecture and particularly medieval churches, as well as decorative arts, rare books and Old Masters (including a mutual love of Albrecht Dürer (1471–1528) and of Sandro Botticelli (1445–1510), for instance). An image of Botticelli's *Primavera* (*c.*1480) adorned their respective work spaces in the 1890s – Wyspiański's atelier at 14 Rue de l'Échaudé in Paris's Saint-Germain district, and Morris's study at Kelmscott House in Hammersmith, London.[6] Crucially, both Morris and Wyspiański were early advocates for the preservation of ancient buildings and heritage in general. In Morris's case, Kelmscott Manor, his 17th-century house in Oxfordshire, is considered as the embodiment of these preoccupations, which ultimately led to his foundation of the Society for the Protection of Ancient Buildings in 1877. For his part, as an art student Wyspiański went on expeditions surveying vernacular buildings organised by Professor Władysław Łuszczkiewicz (1828–1900). Some of his drawings were later published in the *Teka Grona Konserwatorów Galicji Zachodniej* (*Cahiers of the West Galicia Conservators Group*), for example the Gothic wooden Church of Sts Philip and James in Sękowa.[7] During one of these field trips he discovered the hitherto unknown 15th-century polychrome wooden carving of a Madonna from Krużlowa, subsequently acquired by the National Museum in Kraków (Muzeum Narodowe w Krakowie). In 1890 he embarked on a European tour of the 'masterpieces of architecture and church decoration', including impactful visits to many of the French Gothic cathedrals that had also enchanted Morris on his three pilgrimages in the 1850s – for example Chartres, Rouen and Amiens.[8] Wyspiański was involved with a number of ecclesiastical renovation projects

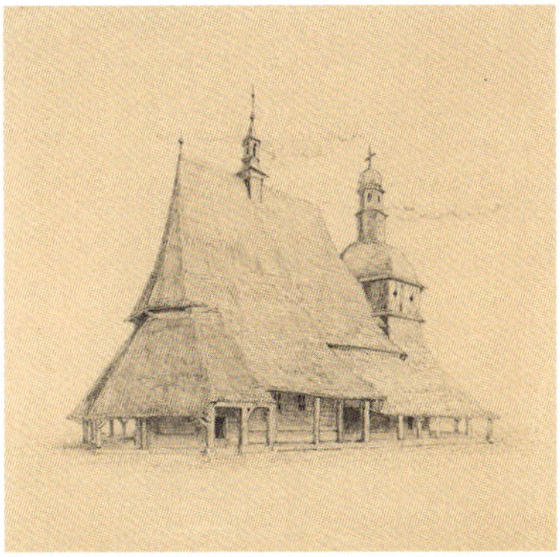

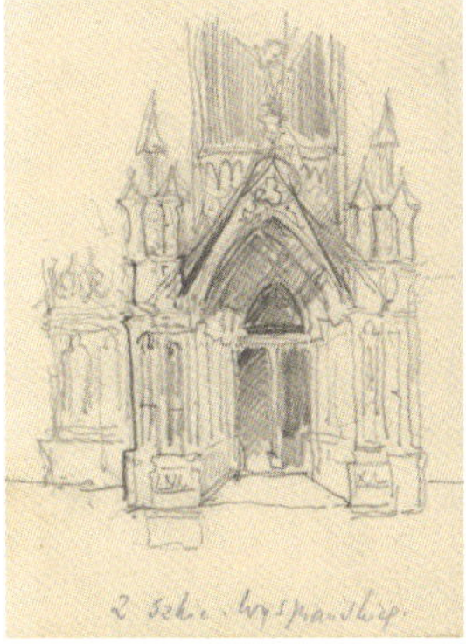

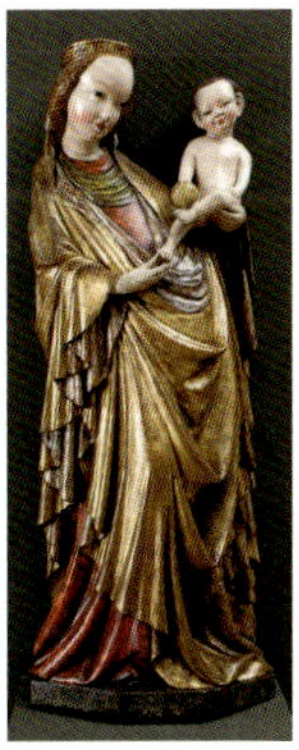

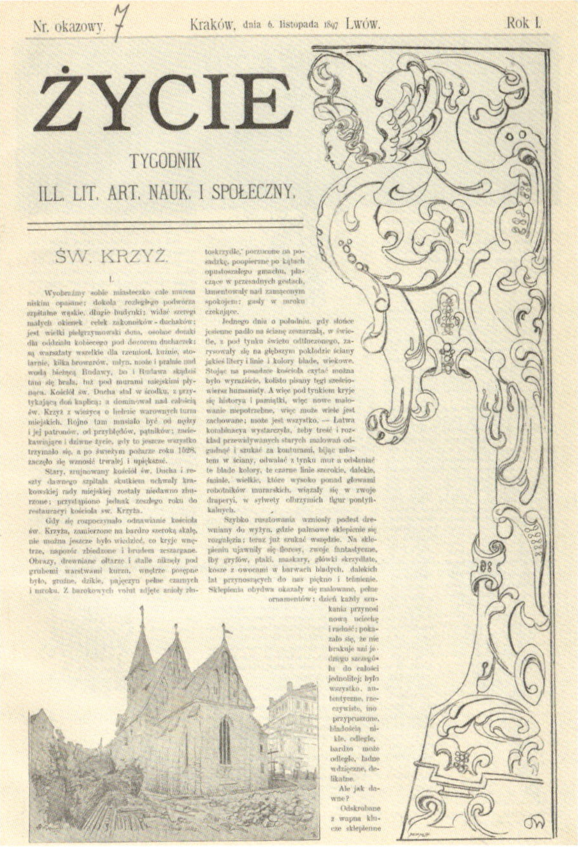

Nr. okazowy. 7 Kraków, dnia 6. listopada 1897 Lwów. Rok I.

ŻYCIE

TYGODNIK

ILL. LIT. ART. NAUK. I SPOŁECZNY.

ŚW. KRZYŻ.

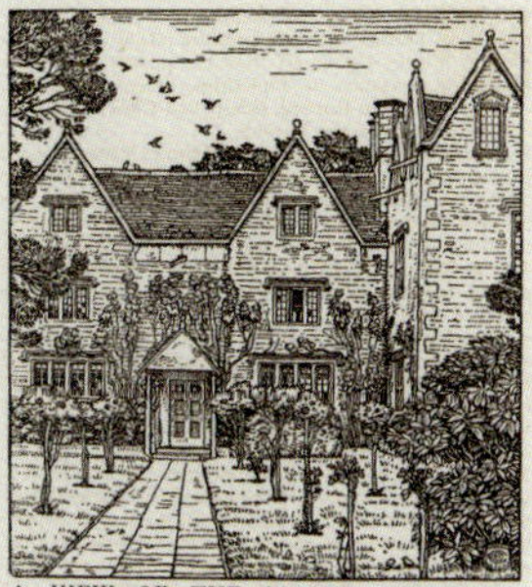

A VIEW OF THE MANOR HOUSE AT KELMSCOTT, IN OXFORDSHIRE, FROM THE GARDEN GATE.

GOSSIP ABOUT AN OLD HOUSE ON THE UPPER THAMES.

THE Village of Kelmscott lies close to the Thames on the Oxfordshire side of it, some five miles (by water) from the present end of the navigation at Inglesham, where the Colne, coming down from Fairford, Bibury and Chedworth, joins the main stream of the Thames.

Kelmscott lies on the plain of the Thames Valley, but the ground rises up from it gradually, with little interruption of the rise, till the crest of the ridge is gained which lies between Oxfordshire and Worcestershire, culminating in the Broadway Beacon some thirty miles from Kelmscott. To the N.E. of the village lies the nearly treeless piece of ground formerly Grafton Common, and beyond it is a string of pretty inland villages, or rather two strings, the westward comprising little Faringdon, Broughton Poggs and Filkins; the eastward, Langford, Broadwell, and Kencott. Of these Langford with its church partly 13th century, partly preconquest, Broadwell with its lovely 13th century tower and spire, and the curious little church of Broughton Poggs are specially interesting.

Turning south from Kelmscott one comes on the Thames, with the weir of Eaton Hastings on the foot-path from the village, but on the Berkshire side a range of heights low, but well designed, rise up from the flat meadows here, and running eastward well into a higher range on which Faringdon lies. Three miles down the river is a very pretty 15th century bridge of three arches which carries the road from Bampton to Faringdon over the Thames at Radcot. On the Eyott and the fields about here was fought a battle between the Earl of Oxford, Richard II

5

in Kraków, such as the reconstruction of medieval stained glass at the Dominican Church of the Holy Trinity (1895–6) and the documentation of newly discovered wall paintings in the Church of the Holy Cross (1896–7). He was passionate about preserving all forms of architectural heritage, complaining in a letter of 1 December 1896 to his lifelong friend Lucjan Rydel (1870–1918) about the unsympathetic and unimaginative restoration of the Lviv Cathedral: 'It is truly tragic that our great cathedrals are entrusted to the hands of people who tart them up, destroy them and spoil them'.[9] He even contemplated embarking on a PhD in the history of medieval stained glass. Wyspiański published various antiquarian articles on the history and renovation of historic buildings and decorative arts in the Young Poland periodicals *Życie* and *Rocznik Krakowski*. The latter was an academic journal set up by the Society for the Lovers of Kraków's History and Ancient Monuments (Towarzystwo Miłośników Historii i Zabytków Krakowa). Wyspiański was a co-founder of the Society and sat on the committee between 1899 and 1902. Safeguarding relics of history remained at the core of Wyspiański's public life right up to his death. As a City Councillor, one of his final initiatives was calling for the formation of the Art and Preservation Commission in 1907. Poland's history was also the predominant subject of his artistic and literary production.

Thirdly, Wyspiański and Morris were both polymaths, characterised by great versatility as writers, artists and applied arts designers, especially in terms of the wide range of crafts they both experimented with. They also shared a firm belief in the equality of fine and decorative arts, which Morris advocated in his lecture 'The Lesser Arts' (1877).[10] Morris wrote poetry and prose romances, and ran two design companies: Morris & Co. (successor to Morris, Marshall, Faulkner & Co.), which designed and made embroideries, tapestries, carpets, printed cottons, wallpapers, furniture, stained glass and tiles; and the Kelmscott Press, founded in 1891 with the

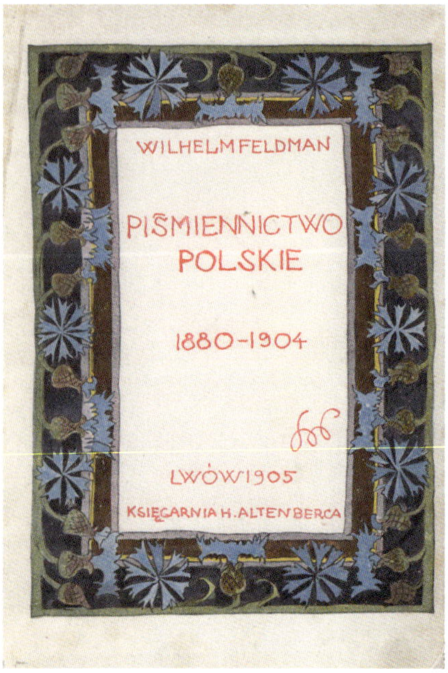
WILHELM FELDMAN
PIŚMIENNICTWO POLSKIE
1880-1904
LWÓW 1905
KSIĘGARNIA H. ALTENBERGA

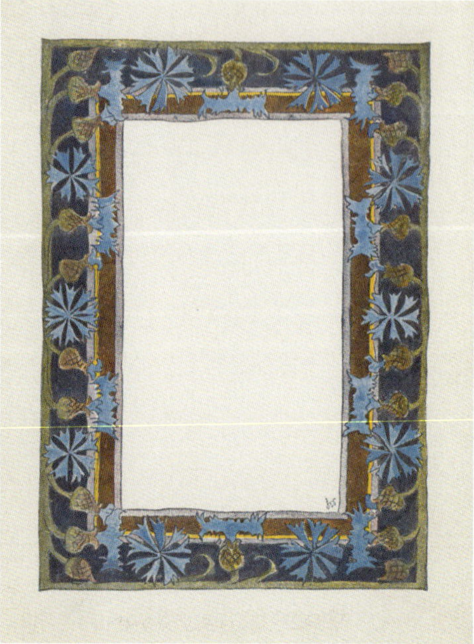

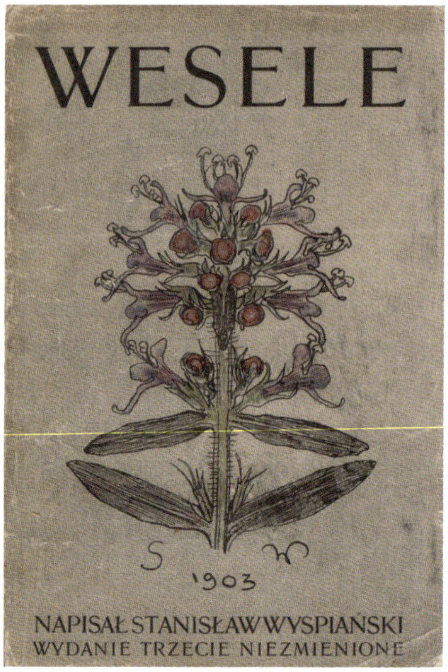
WESELE
1903
NAPISAŁ STANISŁAW WYSPIAŃSKI
WYDANIE TRZECIE NIEZMIENIONE

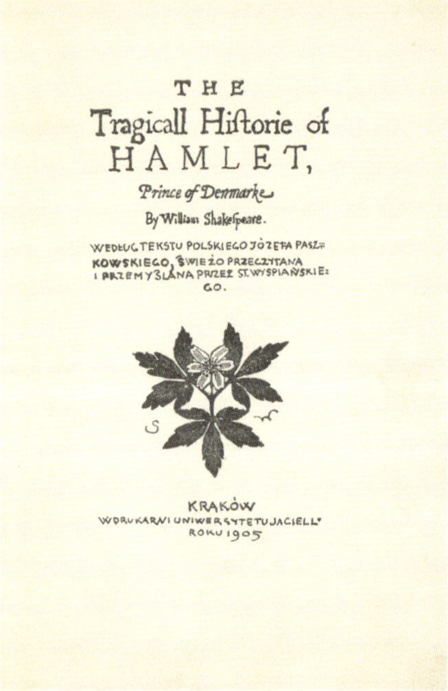
THE
Tragicall Historie of
HAMLET,
Prince of Denmarke
By William Shakespeare.
WEDŁUG TEKSTU POLSKIEGO JÓZEFA PASZ=
KOWSKIEGO, ŚWIEŻO PRZECZYTANA
I PRZEMYŚLANA PRZEZ ST. WYSPIAŃSKIE=
GO.
KRAKÓW
W DRUKARNI UNIWERSYTETU JACIELL.
ROKU 1905

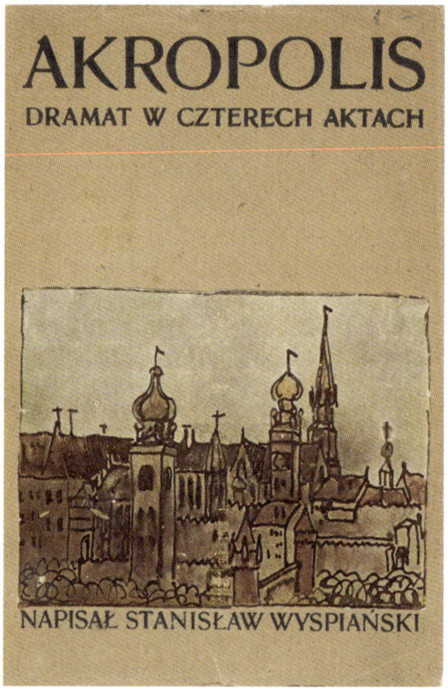
AKROPOLIS
DRAMAT W CZTERECH AKTACH
NAPISAŁ STANISŁAW WYSPIAŃSKI

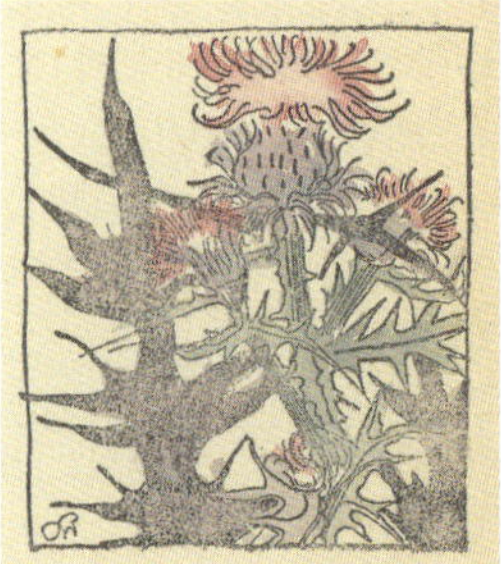

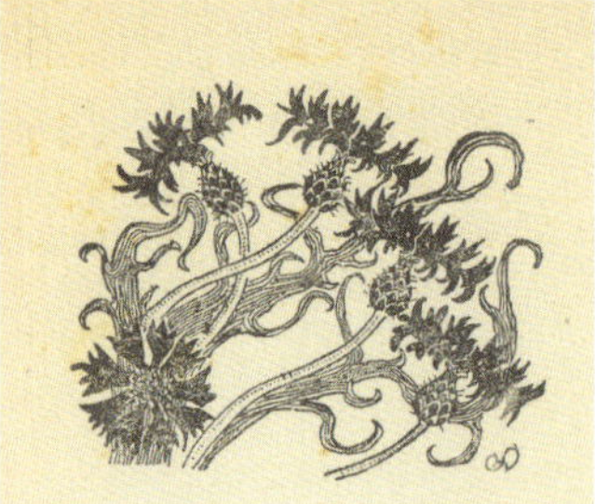

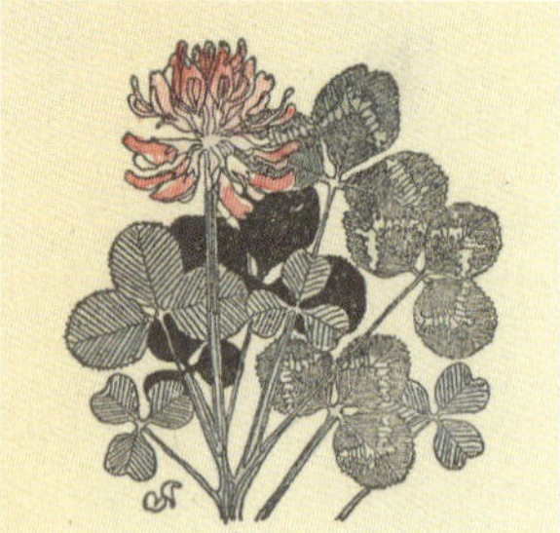

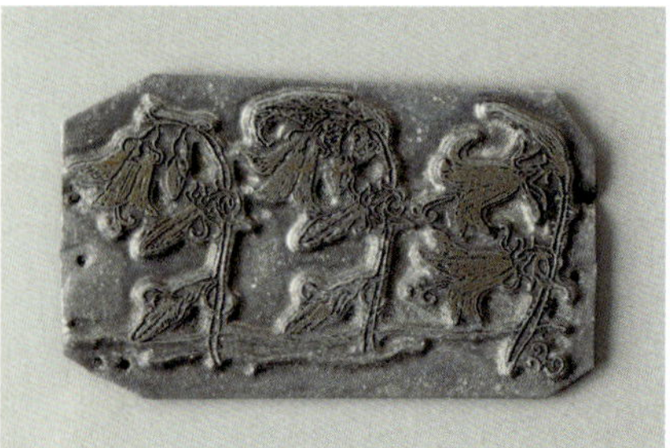

2.2
Selection of Wyspiański's book arts, including the cornflower decorative border, various book cover designs, floral typographic ornaments, nettle-leaved bellflower zinc printing plate, and (centre) the Kelmscott Press decorative border for the title page of *The Story of the Glittering Plain* (1891)
National Museum in Kraków, MNK Biblioteka - II 7086, MNK BIBLIOTEKA II 7067, Wyspiański's unfoliated scrap box, MNK III-kl.-1355, MNK III-SW-MP-4, MNK III-SW-19-20; Literature Museum, II.16271; William Morris Gallery, K134

intention of memorialising and redesigning many of Morris's favourite books. In addition to being an accomplished painter, playwright and poet, Wyspiański turned his hand to designing furniture (see Chapter 11), embroidery (see Chapter 13), kilims (fig.2.7), stained glass (see Chapters 3 and 4), book arts (fig.2.2) and entire theatrical productions (fig.2.8). Wyspiański's correspondence with the doctor and artist Stanisław Eljasz-Radzikowski suggests that he also contemplated designing wallpapers, although it is unknown if any have materialised. On 26 August 1904 Wyspiański wrote: 'Thank you so much for sending me the photographs of the wild mountain pine . . . How splendid would a room look adorned with a wallpaper pattern showing thickets of wild mountain pine. I would draw out the pattern for you straight away if only I had a live branch.'[11] Similarly, there is no evidence Wyspiański had a hand at designing commercial printed cottons, but he did create three stencil-printed linen wall friezes with repeating patterns (see figs 2.9 and 13.2).

In contrast with England, Austrian-ruled Galicia remained relatively unaffected by industrialisation in Wyspiański's lifetime. Consequently, whilst handicrafts were seen as vehicles for the preservation of the Polish national identity and way of life, the ethos of handiwork did not have the same pre-industrial and/or anti-capitalist connotations as it did for the protagonists of the British Arts and Crafts Movement.[12] Unlike Morris, Wyspiański did not carry out his own designs or have his own workshop, but rather collaborated with a number of artisans based in or near Kraków, such as those in Andrzej Sydor's cabinet-making workshop, in Antonina Sikorska's weaving workshop, the embroiderer Helena Czeremuga, as well as the Kraków Stained Glass Workshop set up by Władysław Ekielski and Antoni Tuch (later S.G. Żeleński Stained Glass Art Company) and in the Józef Gorecki Metalworks, a renowned manufactory which specialised in making artistic and ornamental objects. Nevertheless, in common with Morris, Wyspiański firmly believed that a designer's practical understanding of the working methods and materials used in particular craft techniques was a prerequisite for creating beautiful decorative arts objects. He imparted this principle to a younger colleague, Henryk Uziembło, who recalled that Wyspiański always personally supervised the making of any of his designs in the workshops, as if 'directing the hand of the craftsman-maker'.[13] Moreover, as this chapter goes on to show, Wyspiański exerted scrupulous levels of quality control in this respect, revealing an uncompromising attitude to his work.

Just as Morris is credited with reviving the book arts through the Kelmscott Press, Wyspiański is largely responsible for the typographical reform and the development of the ideal book in partitioned Polish lands. As Artistic Director of *Życie* from September 1898 until July 1899, he revolutionised the appearance of the journal in terms of its layout and choice of typefaces. He also designed and selected floral borders, ornaments and illustrations, and supervised the quality of printing undertaken at the printing house of Kraków's Jagiellonian University.[14] Wyspiański continued to pursue the book arts until the end of his life, spending his last years undertaking the graphic design and overall supervision of the printed editions of his own plays and other literary works. His one unfulfilled ambition was to create a new Polish national font. It was to be a distilled amalgam of the handwriting samples of Poland's foremost writers, artists and scholars, collated, generalised and adapted to form a typeface fit for purpose.[15]

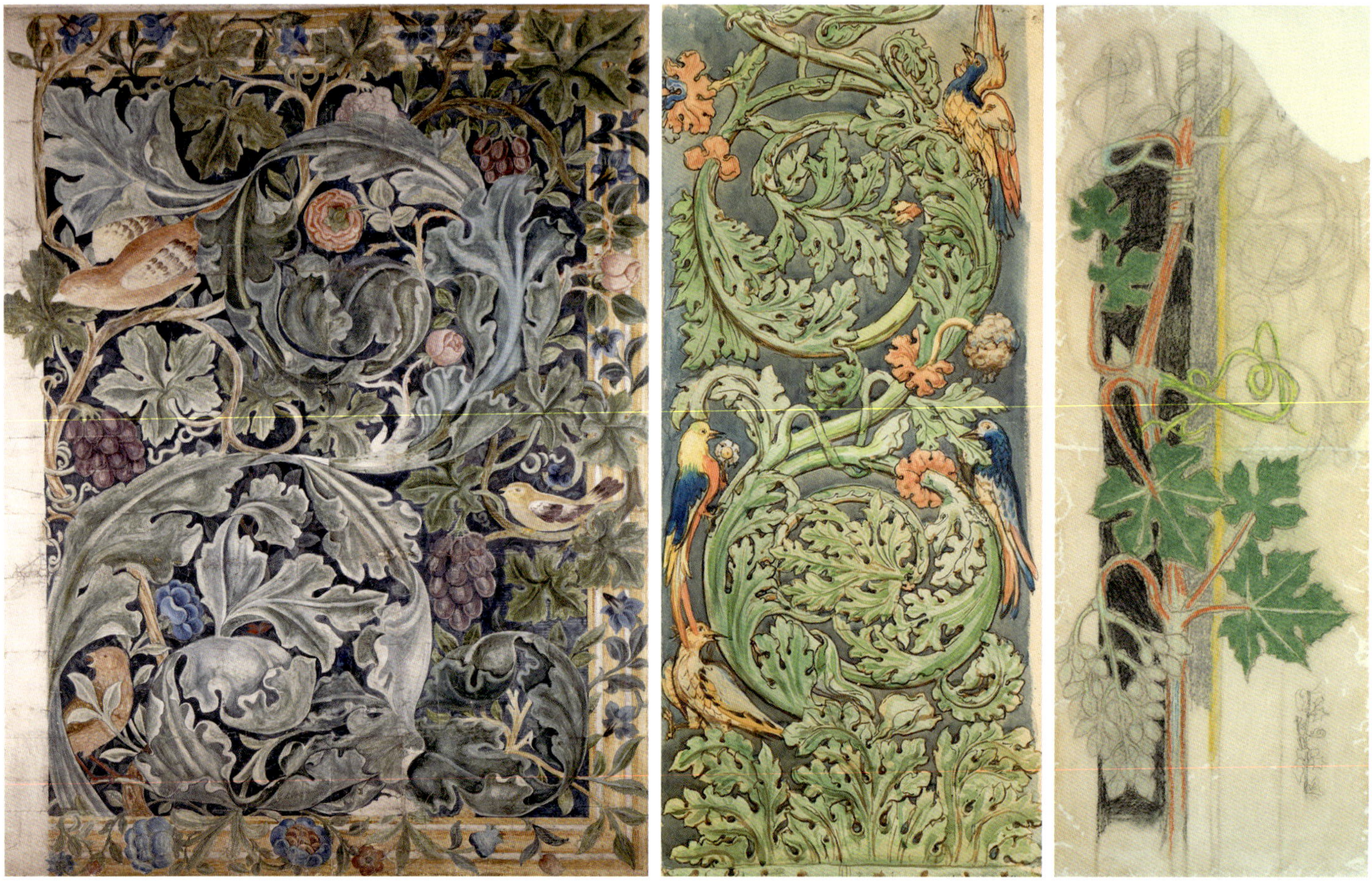

According to contemporary critics it was thanks to Wyspiański that the books acquired the status of a work of art and everyone involved in their production was given credit:

> Wyspiański's books have made a mark: their appearance on the market has marked a turning point. The spirit of beauty has entered the printers and publishing houses; they begin to succumb to it . . . The three main principles are: beautiful cover, shape of font and typesetting, and last but not least – instead of a banal illustration the overall decoration mirroring the spirit of the work . . . Wyspiański's books were equally novel, distinctive and fresh (in terms of form) as he himself. Their pictorial shape, print quality, layout, ornamentation and colour schemes were identical with the thoughts contained in the books.[16]

This was the case for one of his patriotic plays *Acropolis* (*Akropolis*, 1904), in which the action is set at Wawel Cathedral and Castle and the protagonists include the statues and characters from the tapestries, brought to life: on the cover he illustrated Wawel Hill (see Chapter 4). Likewise his critical study *Tragicall Historie of Hamlet, Prince of Denmarke by William Shakespeare (. . . According to the Polish Text by Józef Paszkowski, Freshly Read and Considered by St. Wyspiański*, 1905):[17] the cover bears the original English title whilst Wyspiański's handwritten lettering and overall layout echo the typeface and title page of the earliest editions of Shakespeare's play, mostly the second Quarto of 1604/1605 printed by James Roberts for Nicholas Ling (fig.2.2). As with Morris's Kelmscott Press, Wyspiański's book arts revolved mostly around floral decoration. For example, he adorned the cover of his play *The Wedding* (1901) with a drawing of wild thyme. Clover, thistle and nettle-leaved bellflower

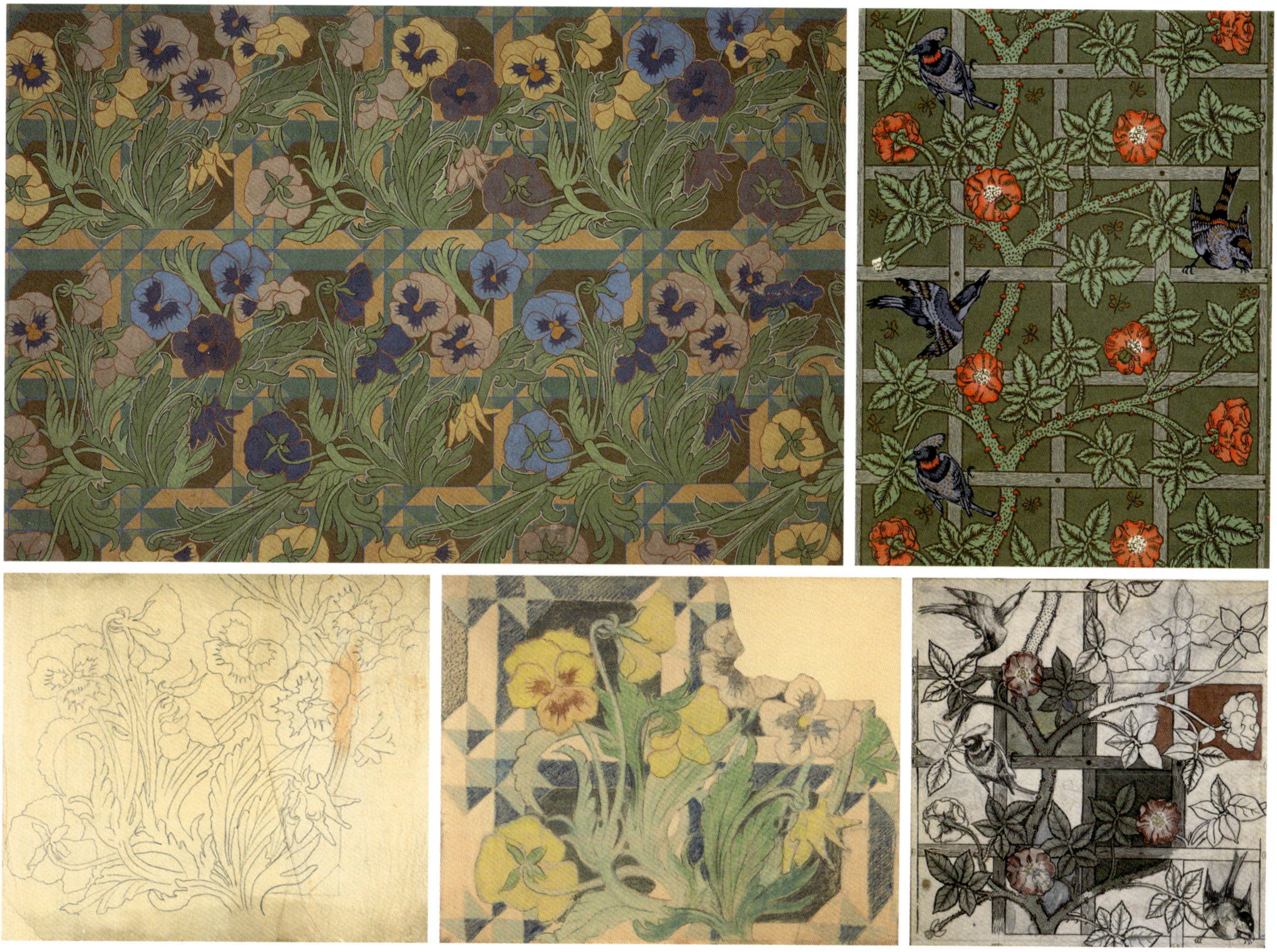

2.3 (OPPOSITE)
Ornamental leaf motifs: cartoon for *Acanthus and Vine* tapestry by Morris (1879), 'Birds and Acanthus' design for a St Mary's Basilica wall painting by Jan Matejko (1889) and 'Vines' design for a Franciscan Church wall painting by Wyspiański (1895)
Drawings on paper: pencil and watercolour; watercolour; pastel
Victoria and Albert Museum, London, E.3472-1932; National Museum in Kraków, MNK IX-61, MNK III-r.a-10737

2.4 (ABOVE)
Morris's and Wyspiański's repeating patterns – from design to realisation. CLOCKWISE FROM TOP RIGHT: Morris's 'Trellis' wallpaper and wallpaper design (1862, registered in 1864); Wyspiański's 'Pansies' design, cartoon and wall painting (1897)
Wallpaper sample; watercolour and pastel designs; cartoon; wall painting
William Morris Gallery, London, BLA472, B128; Bank PKO S.A.; National Museum in Kraków, Franciscan Church

appear in his typographic ornaments. In keeping with Arts and Crafts practices and that of Morris & Co., Wyspiański reused the same design in different media. For instance, he adapted the cornflower decorative border originally used a decade earlier around a stained-glass window in the Franciscan Church (see Chapter 3, fig.3.11), on the cover of Wilhelm Feldman's *Piśmiennictwo Polskie 1880–1904* (*Polish Literature 1880–1904*, 1905). Wyspiański preserved the loose border together with other examples of his book arts (now held at the National Museum in Kraków; fig.2.2, middle of top row).[18]

Furthermore, Morris and Wyspiański shared a passion for indigenous plants and nature as a key source of inspiration. In fact, Wyspiański was the first Polish artist to have developed a

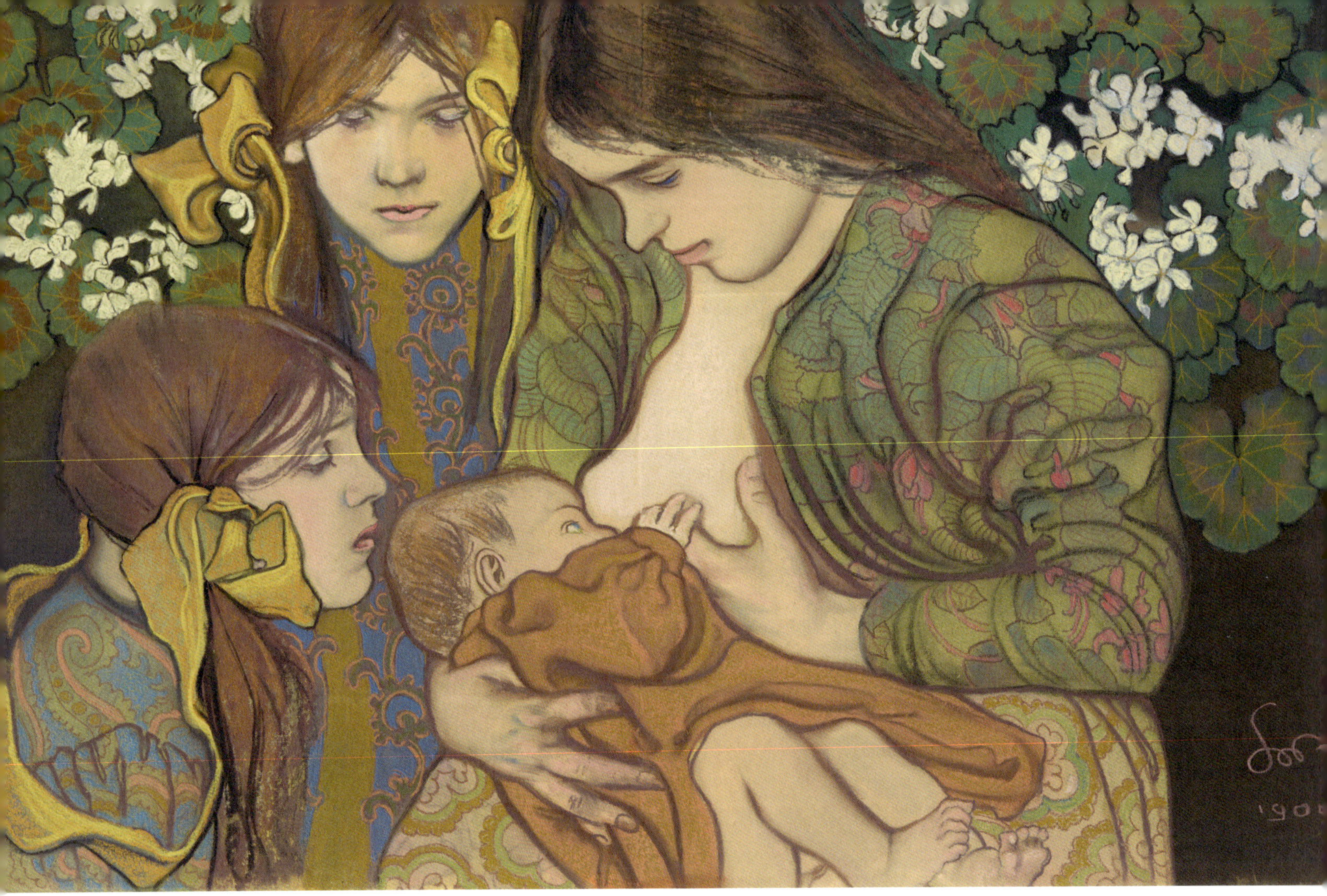

preoccupation with flowers as significant subject matter. His first notable involvement with plant ornamentation is likely to have been during the decoration of the Gothic St Mary's Basilica (1889–90) directed by Jan Matejko. Aimed at stripping the church back to its authentic medieval features and creating a sympathetic wall painting scheme, it was arguably the first project in the spirit of the Arts and Crafts Movement on Polish lands. It would provide inspiration for key Young Poland decorative schemes. Entrusted with preparing cartoons, painting Matejko's designs onto the walls and supervising the work of all the other painters, the 20-year-old Wyspiański thus received the very best training in ornamental decoration, which would inform much of his later output. Apart from angels and heraldic motifs, Matejko's design concept comprised scrolling acanthus leaves with birds. This has a strong similarity to Morris's patterns such as the *Acanthus and Vine* tapestry (1879) and shows clearly the men's shared interest in historical ornamentation based on plant leaves, which Matejko would have imparted to Wyspiański (fig.2.3). Wyspiański developed his distinctive floral style at the Franciscan Church, characterised by simplicity and modernity and a genius for repeating pattern, being a further commonality with Morris (see Chapter 3). Alongside using the decoration of the vine, as Morris frequently did, he also drew designs that included dozens of types of indigenous wayside flowers such as cornflowers, camomile, sunflowers and poppies, as well as flowers invested with Christian symbolism, such as lilies (see figs 2.0, 2.4, 3.4, 3.5, 3.11, 3.15 and 3.10). His later patterns of roses, nasturtiums and pansies set against a monumental trellis (1897) are especially evocative of Morris's wallpapers and

2.5
Stanisław Wyspiański
Maternity, 1905
Pastel on paper
58.8 × 91 cm
National Museum in Kraków,
MNK III-r.a-10898

printed cotton patters (fig.2.4).[19] Wyspiański refrained from excessive stylisation or historicising styles, striving to retain the character of each plant. On 19 February 1896 he explained to Rydel about his natural ability: 'I am so pleased that I don't need to go to any trouble – all I need is to pick up a plant, examine and consider it, and to understand how it grows, and once I have understood its distinctive style I can then take another look and easily begin to arrange it into a design.'[20]

Wyspiański's interest in plants found expression in studies from nature as well as ornamental textbooks. In 1896–7 he created a herbal of wayside flowers which became his working portfolio of design ideas (fig.2.6). Flowers and floral patterns continued to inspire his prolific painting practice, blurring boundaries with the decorative arts. The pastel drawing *Maternity* (1905) is a Symbolist portrait of Wyspiański's peasant wife, Teodora Teofila, posing in a jacket richly patterned with fuchsias and against a backdrop of geraniums, a recurrent motif in Wyspiański's design practice (fig.2.5).

Like Morris, Wyspiański also had an interest in birds. In response to the story of St Francis, he envisaged a frieze of birds in flight, but unfortunately this was surprisingly turned down by the Franciscans for the decoration of their church. Writing to Rydel, Wyspiański stated: 'Dearest Lucek, can you imagine, birds are forbidden in the Franciscan Church.'[21] It is unclear which birds Wyspiański had in mind, as no designs for this idea have been identified to date. There are surviving depictions of an eagle and a swan, which may relate to the concept. There is also a reference to a woodpecker.[22] Given the prominence accorded to birds in the British Arts and Crafts Movement, it is particularly disappointing that Wyspiański did not have a chance to realise the idea (see fig.0.8).

Another parallel between Wyspiański and Morris was their versatility as interior decorators, with their all-encompassing work extending to domestic and civic as well as ecclesiastical buildings (discussed in Chapters 3, 4 and 11). As a *Gesamtkunstwerk*, the decoration of the Kraków Medical Society's headquarters is a notable example of Wyspiański's holistic approach to interiors in terms of both intellectual concept and style. The scheme represents the unity of science and art symbolised by the natural world (motifs of snowflakes and plants), adopting Apollo, the god of the arts, healing and the sun, as the patron of doctors and also honouring the Polish astronomer Nicolaus Copernicus. The scheme combined his virtuosity at integrating diverse crafts, as well as his prowess as a colourist (see Chapter 11). Wyspiański strongly opposed the identification of his style as Art Nouveau; in fact it adopts many British traits. Andrzej Szczerski has demonstrated that the centrepiece of the scheme, the stained-glass *Apollo: Copernicus's Solar System* (see fig.1.4), displays the influence of Burne-Jones (see Chapter 1).[23] Similarly, both the distinctive motif of the chestnut leaf used on the staircase banister and on the wall frieze, as well as the bright yellow of the interior, may have been inspired by another British influence: from illustrations in Owen Jones's *Grammar of Ornament* (1856) with which Wyspiański was familiar (fig.2.6).[24] Plate XCI in the section 'Leaves and Flowers from Nature' showing 'Horse-chestnut Leaves' displays striking parallels. The Medical Society scheme also clearly demonstrates Wyspiański's uncompromising artistic vision. The tone of his letter of 18 December 1904, overleaf, addressed to Antonina Sikorska, owner of the weaving workshop, calls to mind Morris's similar perfectionism and dedication to his work through angry letters to Thomas Wardle

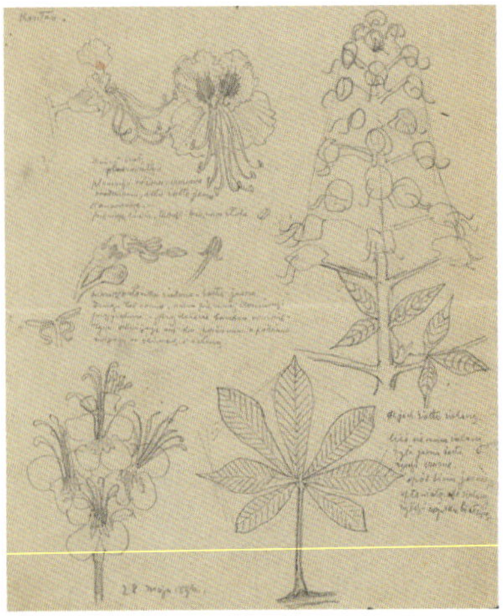

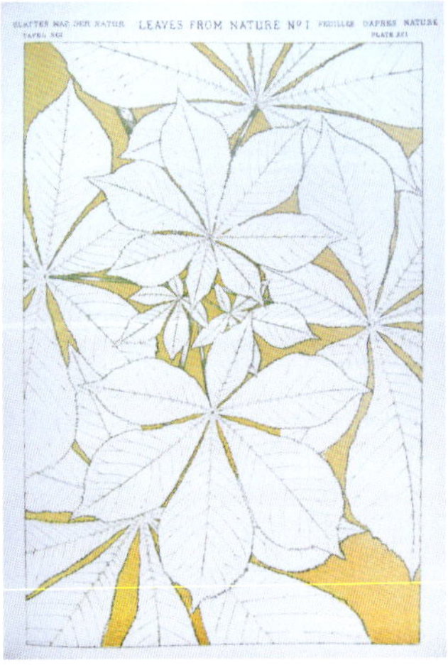

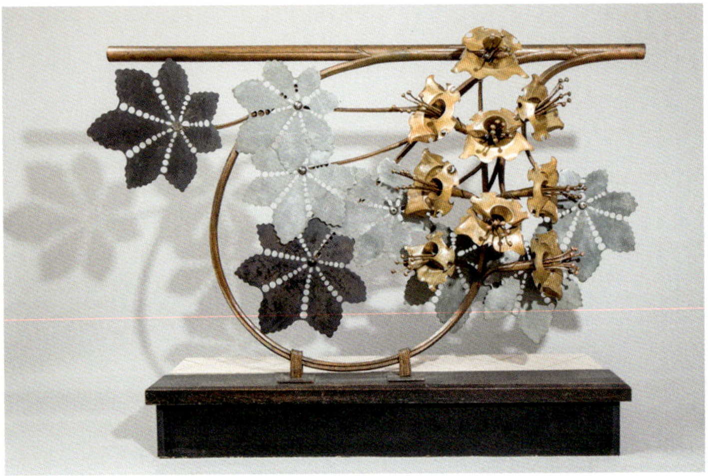

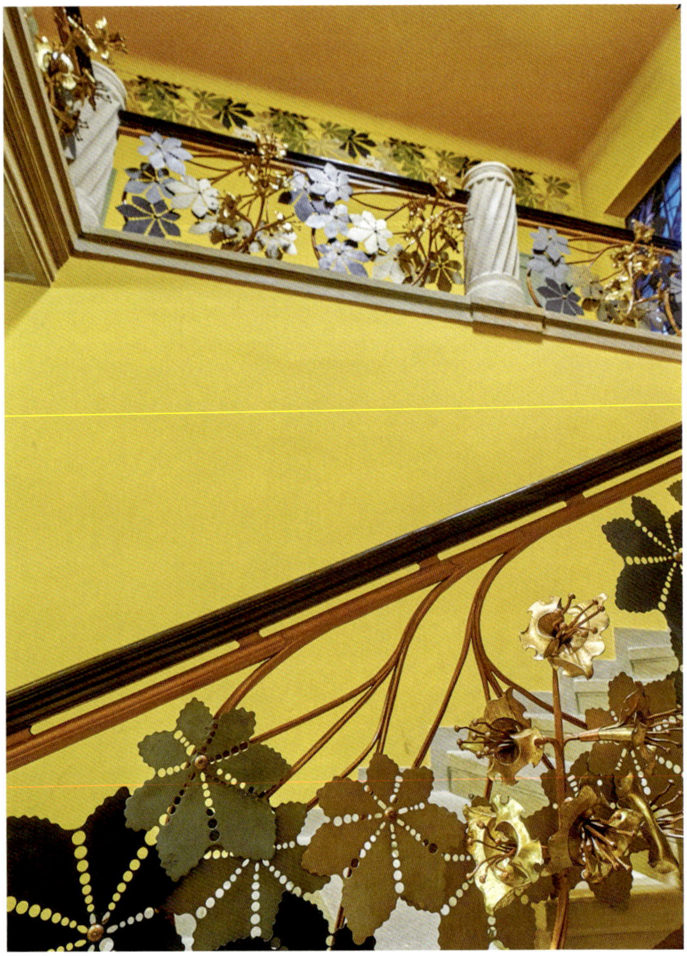

of Leek. Wardle had collaborated with Morris on the dyeing and printing of cottons. Wyspiański was making a sarcastic complaint about the inadequate workmanship of the German craftsmen, and in particular the wrong colour scheme of the kilims intended for the Medical Society's meeting hall (fig.2.7):

> The little kilim is bad. It is bad because the workman, who dyes the yarns, not asked or authorised to do so, undertook to harmonise the colours. You must also have some fool – a painter, who in overseeing the making process also aspires to keep an artist's eye in terms of harmony. This painter (I wish he would disappear) together with the workman felt sorrow in their souls at the sight of my colours and decided to make me more subtle and delicate. And because they have the Universe's greatest feel for harmony, so they have made my sharp and deep pink tone like a candy, bland as men's hair oil, like toothpaste, kalodont etc. . . .
>
> The above-mentioned Germans also made my two bright shades of yellow more subdued and pleasant and more accessible to my own soul.
>
> Furthermore, I have not asked for the gaps on the edges of the pattern to be sewed up, which has been done, but I have asked for a 50-centimetre sample to be sent to me for approval and not the finished kilim.[25]

Wyspiański exerted similar levels of artistic control with respect to other elements of the scheme at the Medical Society to ensure his vision would be carried out accurately. For example, he insisted on making a model and ordering a prototype of the chestnut banister before production began,

2.6 (OPPOSITE)
Wyspiański's design concept for the staircase at the Medical Society headquarters (1904).
CLOCKWISE FROM TOP LEFT: page from Wyspianki's herbal (1896); Owen Jones's *Grammar of Ornament* (1856); 'Chestnut Leaf' balustrade *in situ* (2020); and the design prototype (1904)
Drawing; historical plate; modern view of the decorative scheme; metalwork and wood design prototype
National Museum in Warsaw, rkps 924/19 MNW; National Museum in Kraków, MNK IV-M-2773

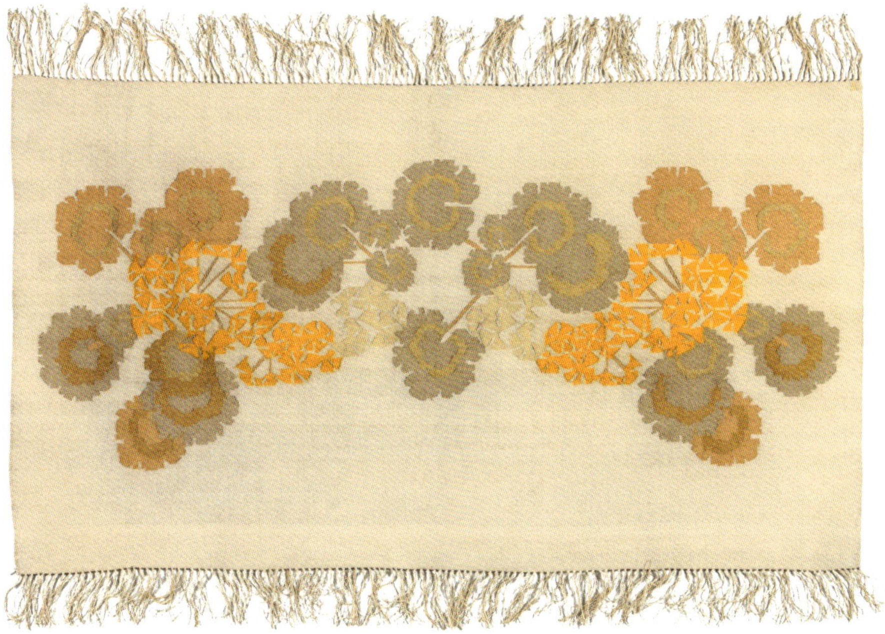

2.7 (RIGHT)
Kilim with geranium motif, related to the Medical Society headquarters scheme, designed by Stanisław Wyspiański, executed by the Antonina Sikorska workshop in Czernichów, 1904
Linen and wool
111 × 194 cm
National Museum in Kraków, MNK XIX-5096

and on having part of the *Apollo* window remade as some of the glass used was unsuitable.[26]

Native vernacular architecture and country crafts of England and Galicia were other interests shared by Morris and Wyspiański. In Morris's case these studies were arguably the inspiration behind his creation of his homes – Red House in Bexleyheath, Kent (carefully selecting materials found in local buildings), and at Kelmscott Manor in the Oxfordshire countryside (where Morris was charmed by the simplicity and beauty of this yeoman farmhouse skilfully created by country builders rather than by a professional architect). These influences also determined the underlying approach to production by all craftspeople of the Arts and Crafts Movement. Unlike in Galicia and other parts of Europe, English peasantry and their rural handicraft traditions had ceased to exist before Morris's day as a result of the effects of the Industrial Revolution. However, as Tanya Harrod points out, there were still some 'existing, if endangered, country skills' such as chair bodging.[27] It is notable that one of Morris's most popular products, the Sussex Chair, was based on a chair being produced in the village of East Hoathly in that county.[28] He also owned a set of the wheelback Windsor chairs made in the traditional manner by country craftsmen. In Galicia, there was renewed interest in the country crafts of peasants, viewed as vehicles for preserving the unique national character. Athough there was no immediate risk of these traditions disappearing due to the advent of industrialisation and/or the prospect of rural depopulation, there was concern about their vulnerability to the influence of foreign fashions. Wyspiański developed a strong and wide-ranging preoccupation with the vernacular craft tradition of the Podhale Highlanders, which had also inspired Stanisław Witkiewicz's Zakopane Style (see Chapter 6). Wyspiański knew Witkiewicz personally, and both were members of the Polish Applied Arts Society. Although Wyspiański only made one recorded visit to Zakopane, in 1902, he methodically studied the material culture of the region, by annotating his own copies of Matlakowski's ethnographic volumes – *Budownictwo ludowe na Podhalu* (*Vernacular Building in Podhale*, 1892) and *Zdobienie i sprzęt ludu polskiego na Podhalu* (*Decorations and Household Objects of Polish Folk in Podhale*, 1901).[29] He commissioned rubbings of cheese moulds, spoon racks and ornamentation found in Highlander huts, and was equally interested in the ornamentation of the badges worn by Highlander Tatra guides.[30] He based theatrical designs for his own play, *Bolesław the Bold* (*Bolesław Śmiały*, 1904), largely on the Podhale heritage, including the design of the King's crown on the Highlanders' shirt pins, and the shields of the monarch and his court on the enlarged form of Podhale heart-shaped

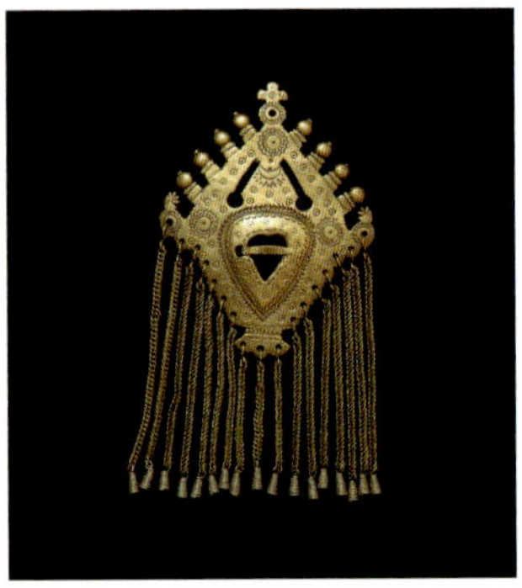

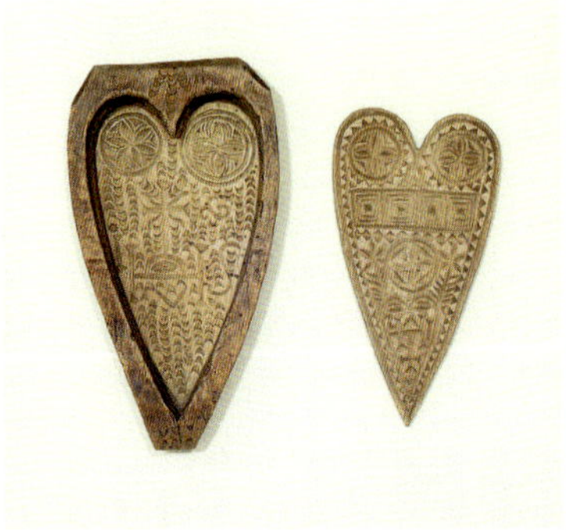

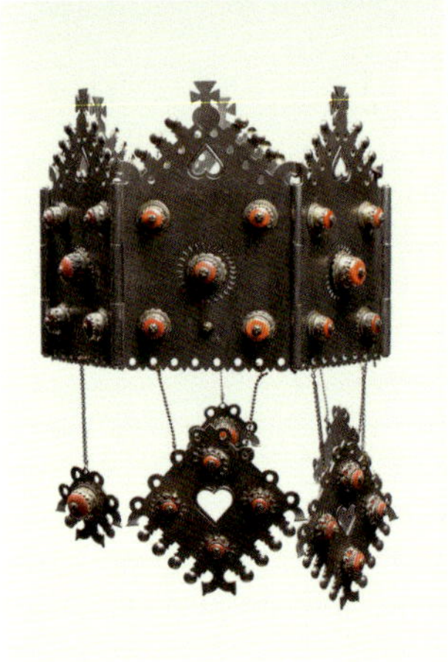

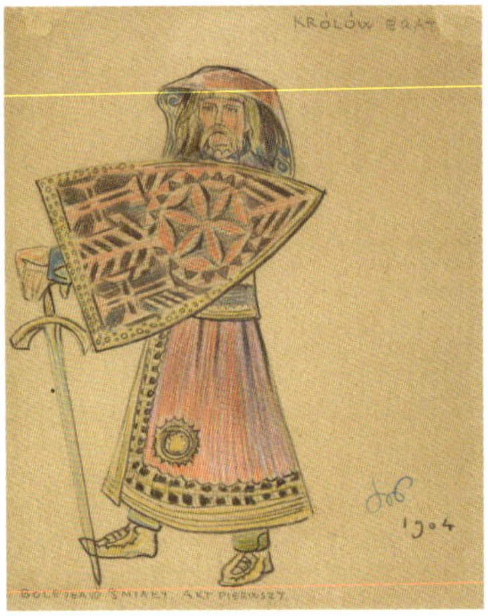

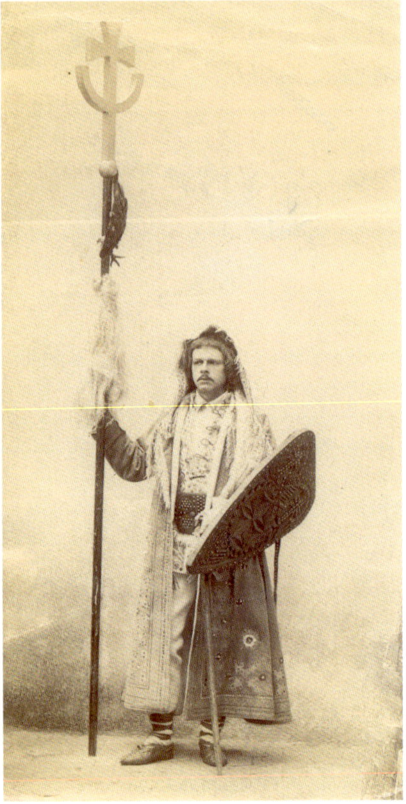

cheese moulds (fig.2.8).[31] Wyspiański's furniture and textile designs and book art also assimilate Highlander heritage, such as a wall frieze and chair designs that are based on the *kijanka*, a wooden device also known as a washing bat, used for beating wet clothes (fig.2.9). Similarly, the dining-room chair designed for Zofia and Tadeusz Żeleński's apartment features the motif of the Podhale six-petal rosette. It is notable that the chair appears to have been originally intended for the decorative scheme of 'Świetlica' (Great Hall), a gallery of works by members of the 'Sztuka' ['Art'] Society of Polish Artists, at the Society of Friends of the Fine Arts anniversary exhibition in the autumn of 1904, largely inspired by Podhale handicrafts (see Chapter 11, figs 11.6a, 11.6b, 11.3).[32] His ongoing deep engagement with Podhale ornamentation has not been previously acknowledged and is worthy of further investigation.

Both Morris and Wyspiański supported political causes: in the case of Morris, socialism; and in the case of Wyspiański, utilising his creative practice as a vehicle for helping his divided country regain independence. In addition to using his plays and artworks as a political statement,[33] he willingly agreed to lend his support to the charismatic military leader and statesman Józef Piłsudski (see fig.17.8) when, in early 1905, the latter was seeking major cultural figures to help him secure donations from the public to fund the establishment of a Polish army, with a view to an eventual uprising. Wyspiański was prepared to self-publish materials for dissemination and to donate proceeds from his artworks, and even wrote a letter of resignation from his post at the Austrian-run Academy of Fine Arts. He suggested that the printed appeal to the Polish nation to rise should take the form of his own rendition of a 9th-century religious hymn, *Veni Creator*, and offered to sponsor an edition of 100,000 lithographs of the Madonna of Częstochowa, symbolic Queen and protectress of Poland, to promote the cause. However, unlike Morris, Wyspiański was not prepared to engage directly with the media, and attempts to establish a mutually agreeable form for his involvement in Piłsudski's plan therefore stalled, the letter appearing to have remained unsent.[34]

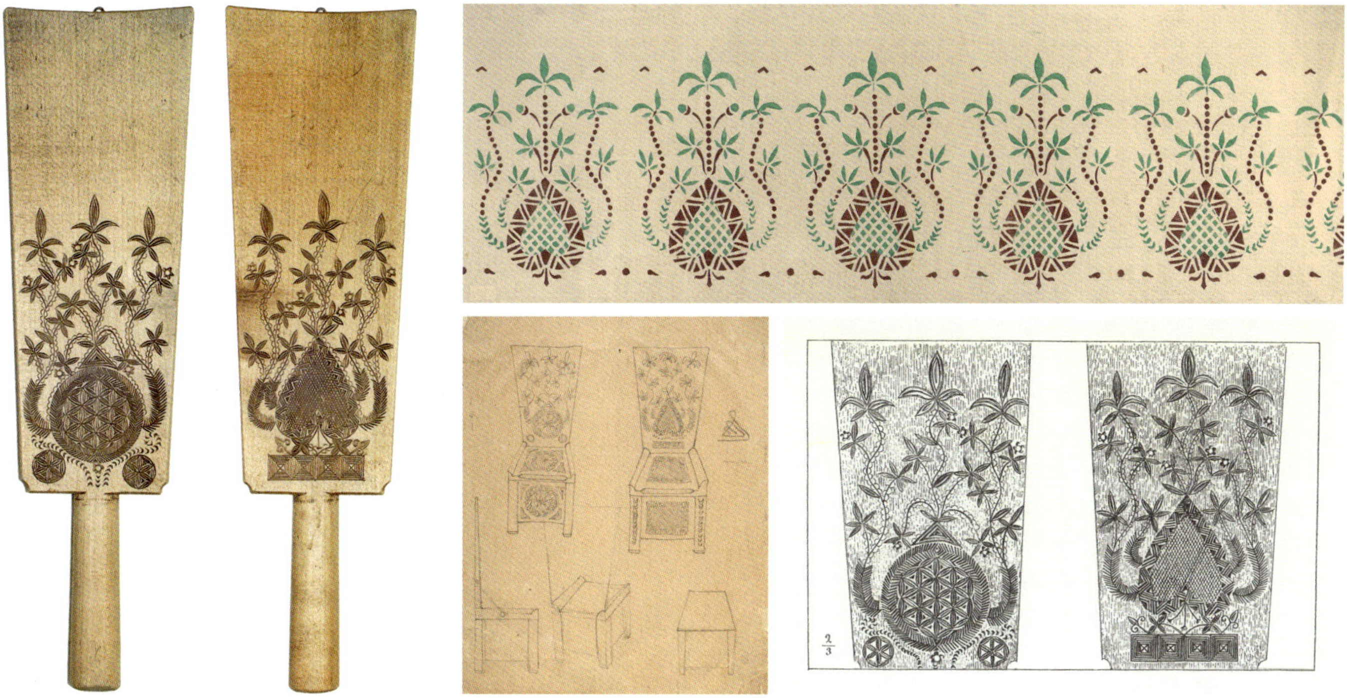

Wyspiański died prematurely at the age of 38. His experimental vision and uncompromising manner meant that his applications to carry out of a number of public arts commissions were rejected. In his very short life and despite numerous setbacks, he made a vital contribution to raising the standard and status of the Polish applied arts. He achieved this as a founding member of influential arts and crafts societies such as the 'Sztuka' Society of Polish Artists (1897) and the Polish Applied Arts Society (1901) – a counterpart of the British Arts and Crafts Exhibition Society, founded in London in 1887 in honour of Morris's creative philosophy. Wyspiański won a number of awards for his applied arts, and in so doing helped break down the entrenched division between the fine and decorative arts. He was a major influence on the development of all visual arts in Poland at what was to prove a decisive moment in the history of the nation. And it is only fair that his considerable contribution should be recognised. Reflecting on Wyspiański's aims and legacy on the 20th anniversary of his death in 1928, his friend and critic Adolf Nowaczyński remarked: 'I got the impression that . . . his intention was to play the same role in Poland as Morris did in England.'[35]

2.8 (OPPOSITE)
Wyspiański's vernacular inspirations from the material culture of the Podhale Highlanders in the stage designs for *Bolesław the Bold* (1903). CLOCKWISE FROM TOP LEFT: traditional 19th-century Zakopane Highlander shirt pin; 19th-century Zakopane Highlander cheese mould from the Dembowski ethnographic collection created between 1886-1893; historical photograph of the Sieciech character from the play; drawing of the King's Brother character with the shield based on the form of a cheese mould; first design of the King's crown featuring the motif of Highlander shirt pins
Tatra Museum, E/1072/MT, E/2477/a/b/MT; Museum of Kraków, MHK-FS 1766/VI; National Museum in Kraków, MNK III-r.a-3283; Museum of Kraków, MHK 752/VI

2.9 (ABOVE)
Wyspiański's vernacular inspirations from the material culture of the Podhale Highlanders in his furniture and textile designs.
FAR LEFT: two sides of a 19th-century Zakopane Highlander kijanka, a wooden device used to do laundry by beating the wet clothes, with the motif of scrolling leaves known as gaje, from the Zygmunt Gnatowski ethnographic collection created between 1890-1906.
BOTTOM RIGHT: drawing from Władysław Matlakowski's book *Zdobienie i sprzęt ludu polskiego na Podhalu* (*Decorations and Domestic Utensils of Polish People in Podhale*, Kraków, 1901, vol.2, pl.XL), showing Gnatowski's kijanka. The kijanka was the source for Wyspiański's stencilled wall frieze (1904–5, top) and design for two chairs (bottom left).
Tatra Museum, E/1801/MT; National Museum in Kraków, MNK XIX-9390; National Museum in Warsaw, rkps 926/1 MNW

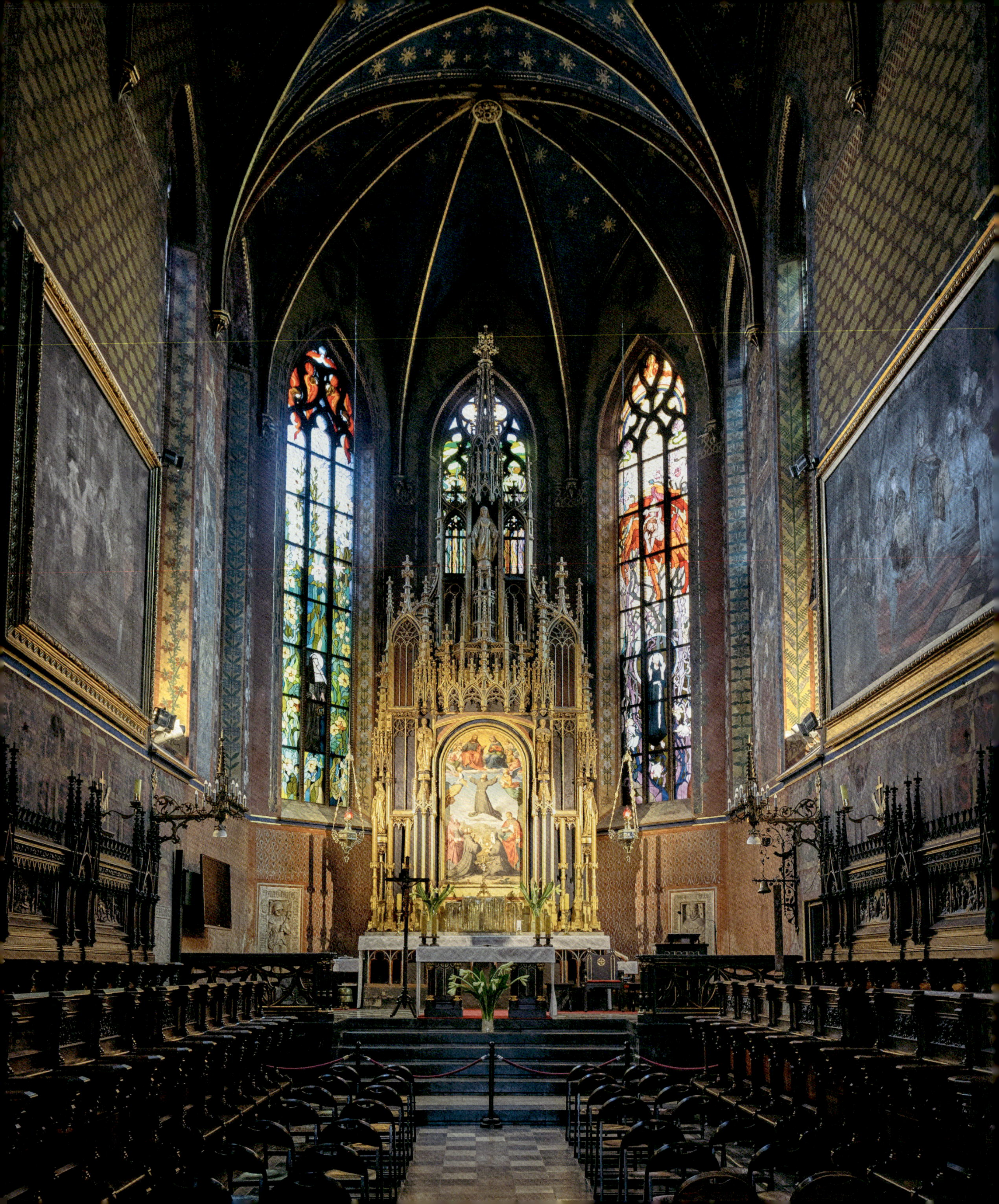

3

'Let Us Surround Ourselves With Our Own Beauty': Stanisław Wyspiański's Decorative Scheme for the Franciscan Church in Kraków

Magdalena Laskowska

'Stanisław Wyspiański was amongst those who declared war on mindless compilation, who demanded sacrifice and effort from the whole of Polish society working towards the liberation of Polish art, fulfilling the motto 'let us surround ourselves with our own beauty'.'

Marjan Dienstl, *Znaczenie Wyspiańskiego dla polskiego zdobnictwa* (*The Significance of Wyspiański for the Polish Applied Arts*), 1908[1]

The decorative scheme of the medieval Franciscan Church in Kraków, designed, supervised and in part carried out by Stanisław Wyspiański, counts amongst the most outstanding achievements of European art of the 19th and 20th centuries.[2] It is also the pinnacle of Young Poland monumental wall painting.[3] This *Gesamtkunstwerk* project was masterfully carried out by the poet-painter when he was still in his twenties. Many factors and wide-ranging influences contributed to the design concept for the decorative scheme, namely Wyspiański's great talent, his well-rounded education in Kraków, his European tour of Gothic cathedrals as well as studies in contemporary Paris, extensive reading, visiting exhibitions and historic sites, going to the theatre and the opera and contact with other artists and art critics.[4] The interior decorative scheme was carried out by a group of artisan-painters working alongside Wyspiański, which reflected the ethos of the Arts and Crafts Movement. Wyspiański's creative outlook embodied the ideal of the master-craftsman.[5]

The earliest record of Wyspiański's evolving design concept for the church survives in a letter to his friend, playwright and poet Lucjan Rydel, dated 16 November 1894. Here Wyspiański outlines his idea for two large-scale easel paintings in oils which were to adorn the church walls:

> I will mention the two main compositions for the Franciscans – their subjects are: – [one] the garden of complete happiness – so lovely, pleasant, and peaceful as can never be, and has never been on the Earth . . . [the other] the forest of despondency, struggle, difficulties, adversity, obstacles – remaining there is terrible, scary; that is as much

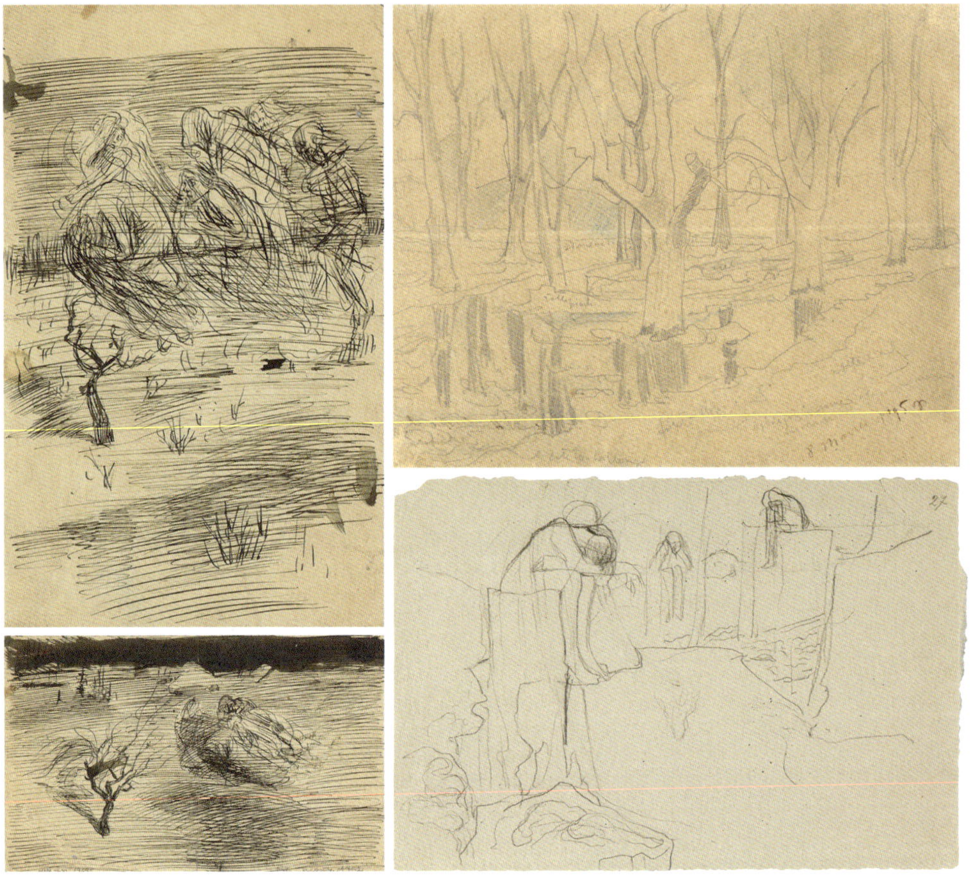

3.0 (p.56)
Chancel of the Franciscan Church looking towards the main altar with stained-glass windows of St Francis of Assisi and Blessed Salome
Franciscan Church, Kraków

3.1
Evolution of the creative concept for the unrealised 'Forest of Despondency' composition: *Symbolic Landscape with the Figure of Death* (1894–5); *Sketch with Figures seated on the rocks* (c.1894–5); *Trees* (1895)
Ink and pencil on paper; pencil on paper
20.4 × 12.6 cm; 17.5 × 25 cm; 19.0 × 23.5 cm
National Museum in Kraków, MNK III-r.a-19695; Collegium Maius Museum; private collection

> as I can say about the fundamental difference between these two paintings. I am going to carry them out, even if I don't get the commission (for it is a well-known fact that the outcome of the competition has long been decided).[6]

Surviving drawings of desolate mountainous landscapes and woods of leafless trees, as well as sketches depicting suffering entangled figures, all dating to the beginning of 1895, may have been preparatory studies for the Forest of Despondency (fig.3.1). One of them shows the figure of Death leading petrified people through a dead landscape.[7] Reminiscences about Wyspiański confirm that he was preoccupied with such images, found for instance in depictions of the 'Four Horsemen of the Apocalypse' by Albrecht Dürer and by the British Symbolist painter G.F. Watts (1817–1904). Wyspiański's cousin the poet Antoni Waśkowski recalled: 'I remember his concept for the painting for the Franciscan chancel – Death riding on a white horse, covered in a white shroud held down around the head with a wreath made up of scorpions'.[8] Crevices, marshland and wasteland would become recurrent motifs in Wyspiański's work in the following years, 1896–7, giving rise to large-scale pastel compositions: *Marshland* (*Moczar*), *Swamp* (*Topiel*), *Castles on the Ice Stars in the Water* (*Zamki na lodzie gwiazdy we wodzie*) and *Sesame's Treasures* (*Skarby Sezamu*) (fig.3.2). Wyspiański's art thus took an entirely new direction, marking the beginning of his engagement with Symbolism. He began to create fantastical pictures, with a multitude of symbolic meanings, turning to subject matter from imagination, dreams and legends. On 3 July 1897, the artist commented about this mode of expression:

> it will become my staple visual repertoire enabling me to express all my thoughts and visions. It will be Art. I am very much looking forward to this prospect. This

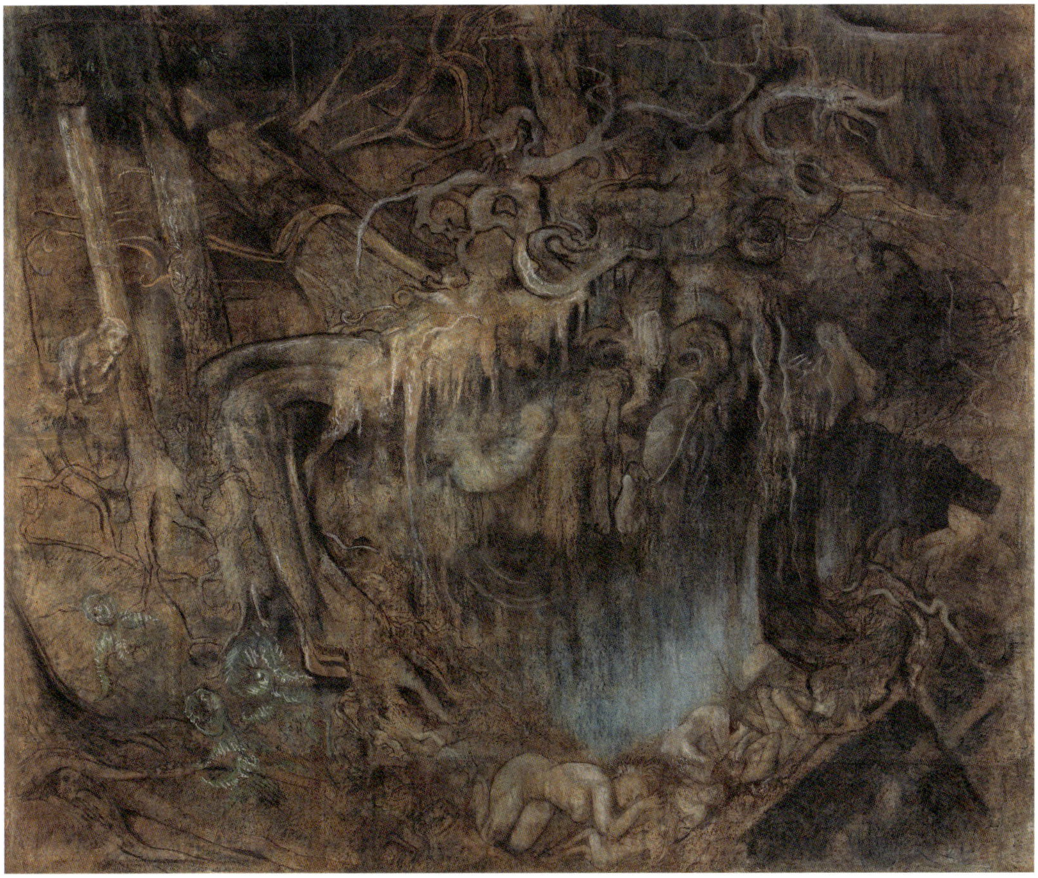

3.2
Stanisław Wyspiański
Sesame's Treasures, before 1897
Pastel on paper laid on canvas
202 × 240 cm
National Museum in Kielce,
MNKi/M/162

> visual language is distinctively and entirely my own
> whilst simultaneously homely [*swojska*] and *our own*.
> I will necessarily produce miracles and wonders.
> More like painted plays, romances, strange poems in paint.[9]

The Great Fire of Kraków in 1850 damaged the Franciscan Church and its interior. Following restoration work, the Franciscans and the city's Society of Friends of the Fine Arts organised a design competition for a painted mural scheme to decorate the chancel and transept of the Basilica. It was announced on 16 February 1894 in the Kraków newspaper *Czas*. At the time Wyspiański and his close friend Józef Mehoffer were studying art in Paris. Their protector and mentor, the architect in charge of the renovation of St Mary's Basilica, Tadeusz Stryjeński (1849–1943), notifed them about the competition. Wyspiański and Mehoffer had been employed on the renovation of St Mary's Basilica back in 1889. It appears that it was Mehoffer who first conceived a general idea for the decorative scheme, some elements of which were to give rise to Wyspiański's highly original vision for the church. On 21 February 1894 Mehoffer noted in his diary:

> Stryj[eński] sent through details of the competition, which I will enter. I already have a general idea how I will go about it. The whole scheme will be light in tone, its colours standing out against a white background, appearing to form coloured blooms, as it were, growing out of the walls – amongst them red and gold and green scrolls across the white walls … Above the pews large figurative compositions contained within irregular frames made up by the surrounding floral ornamentation of the walls. On the right – Polish saints – gloomy and skinny – overlooking from behind the flowers and candles placed at the altar – Saint Jadwiga, Queen of Poland, Blessed Salomea and

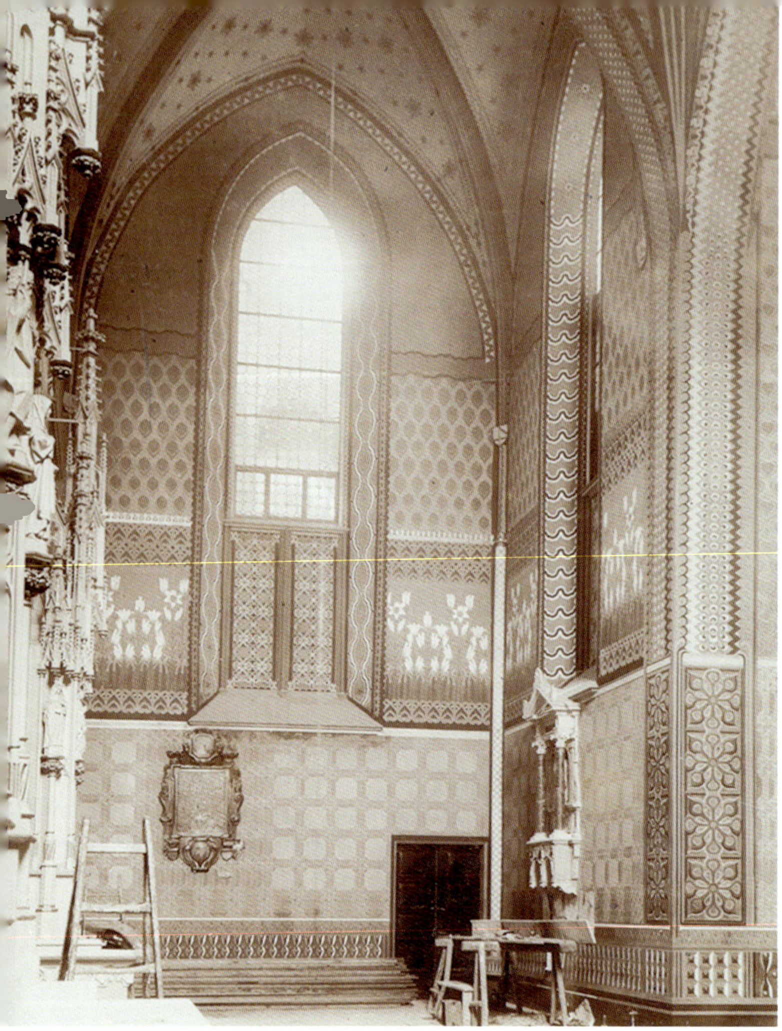
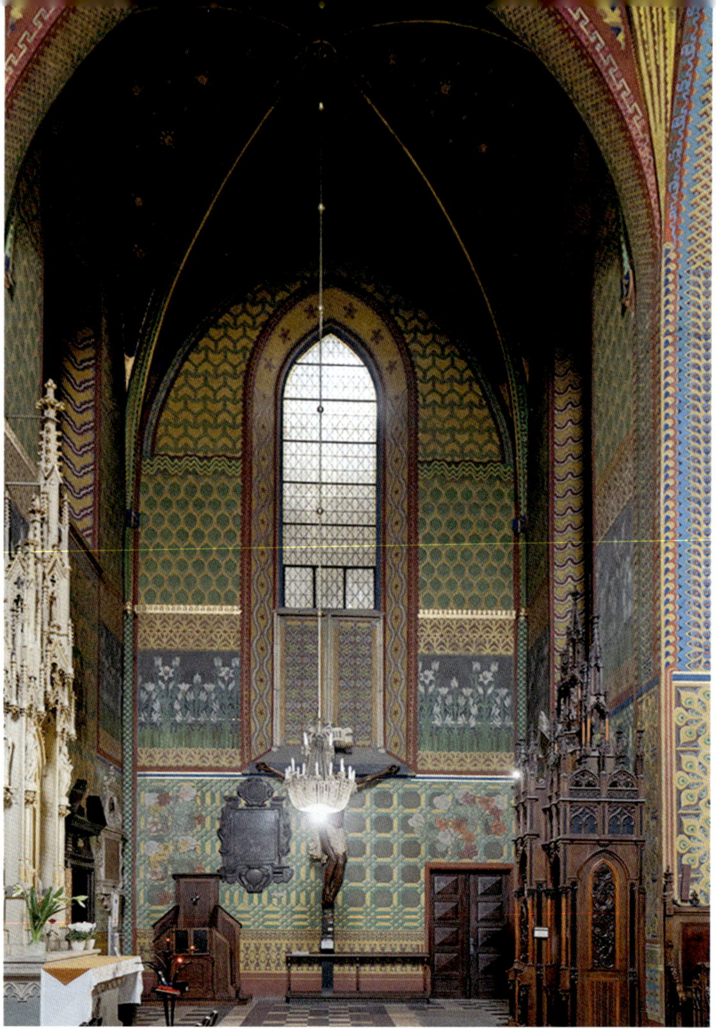

Saint Bronisława of Poland (I will utilise my old concept here once designed for St Mary's Basilica). In fact the whole chancel is to be devoted to the ghosts of this first era of Poland's history – the age of chivalry, with flourishing civilisation. On the left – a choir of knights singing Bogurodzica ['Mother of God' – the oldest Polish anthem dating to the 10th–13th centuries]. They may be singing at the Battle of Legnica [of 1241; Polish army fought under Duke Henry II the Pious against the Tatars].[10]

After initially planning to use realistic imagery to achieve the *trompe-l'œil* effect, intending 'to clothe the church in painted banners, trophies, draperies, flowers – just as if these had been attached to it in reality', Mehoffer eventually decided to follow the teaching of his master. On 9 April he declared: 'I am adopting Matejko's approach to the selection of ornamentation, i.e. I won't attempt to imitate real decoration, which may have adorned this church during some ceremonial occasion.'[11] Given that Wyspiański and Mehoffer shared a living space and studio at this time, the decoration of the church must have been the subject of their conversations, namely the necropolis of Prince Bolesław V the Chaste (1226–1279), Blessed Salomea, King Władysław I the Elbow-High (*c.*1260–1333) and his sons Stefan and Władysław. Wyspiański would subsequently draw on Mehoffer's concept to depict 'the spirit of the Polish Middle Ages', as well as his original idea to cover parts of the walls with paintings imitating heraldic banners hung in churches for great ceremonies.

On 10 May 1894 the Franciscan Church judging committee met to select the winner, but none of the entries – not even the winning design by the painters Józef Mikulski and Franciszek Górski – fulfilled the brief. The newspaper *Czas* commented on the designers' universal failure to embrace 'the chief requirement of the scheme: to be sympathetic to the historic architectural and stylistic features of the Franciscan church'.[12] Mikulski

3.3 (OPPOSITE)
Modern view of the south transept of the Franciscan Church juxtaposed with an archival photograph of 1895 by Juliusz Mien
Franciscan Church, Kraków; National Museum in Kraków, MNK XX-f-1583

3.4 (RIGHT)
Detail of the painted mural decoration in the blind window in the north transept
Franciscan Church, Kraków

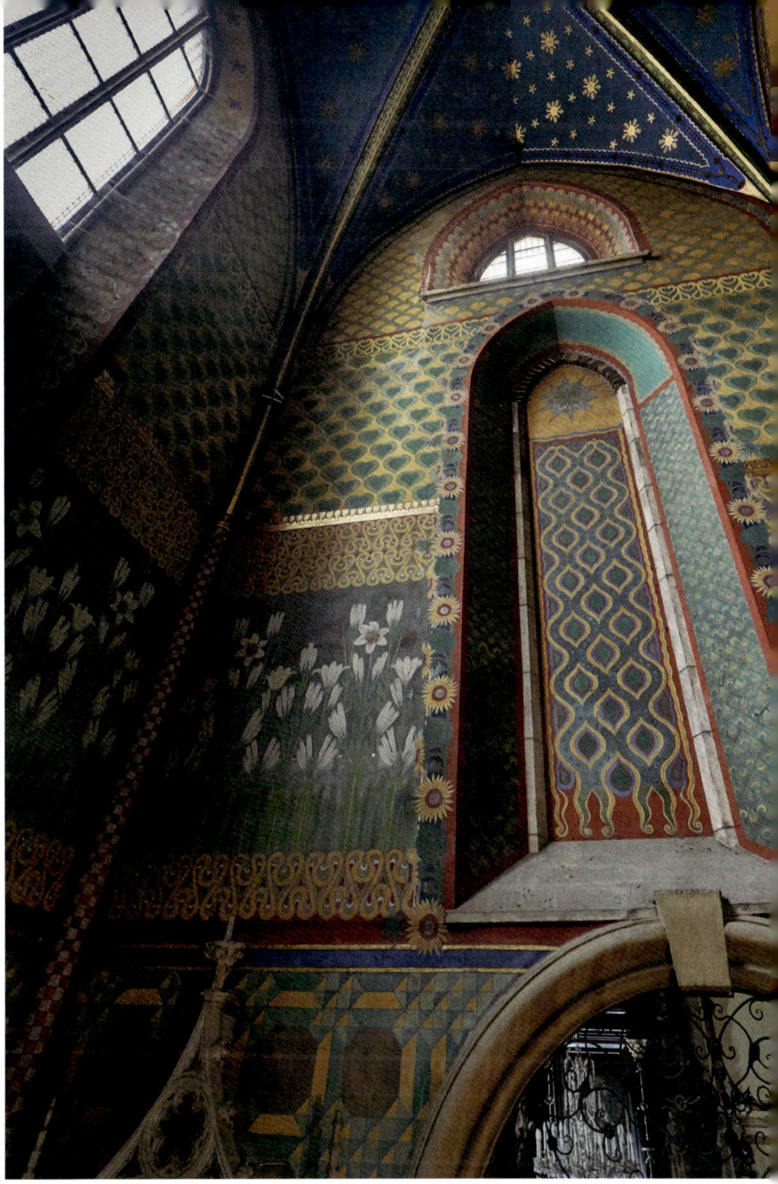

and Górski's design also came first in the new competition the following year, and the architect Władysław Ekielski (1855–1927) was to supervise the works. After commissioning a sample of the painted mural decoration, Ekielski abandoned the project, and entrusted Wyspiański with the scheme.[13]

It is unclear when exactly Wyspiański began the concept development for the wall paintings. On 15 December 1894 he wrote to Rydel about his background reading for the project: 'it is a pity that ... you did not leave me Fioretti [*The Little Flowers of Saint Francis*, 14th century], as I am on a quest for a copy. – I have now worked out all the compositions for the Franciscans – I am reading the life of Saint Francis and finding legends there'.[14] The same letter reveals that by this time Wyspiański had already spoken to the prior with a view to presenting his ideas to him, 'and if he engages with them and likes them, I would execute them on a larger scale'.[15] Mehoffer and Wyspiański's surviving notes show that their original design concept for the decorative scheme was the result of collaborative arts practice.[16] However, in the end, by 12 June 1895 the commission was entrusted solely to Wyspiański.[17]

Wyspiański's task was to cover the walls and vaulting of the chancel and transept with ornamental and figurative decoration. The work took almost six months to complete, and was recorded by Rydel in his first-hand detailed account published in the weekly *Tygodnik Illustrowany*. Rydel frequently joined Wyspiański on the scaffolding, following progress on a weekly basis, commenting that:

> Wyspiański was extremely happy about the opportunity, and threw himself into the work with passion . . . every couple of days he received the dimensions of walls or vaults which had to be filled with ornament immediately: often there was not even enough time for producing watercolour cartoons, as the medium of watercolour takes a bit of time to dry and does not allow more considerable revisions or corrections; he then turned to pastels and chalks, in order to keep up with the workmen painting in the church. Often a barely-finished sheet was almost snatched from his hands; and then the committee demanded changes and alterations, so original concepts had to be adapted.[18]

The artist drew on his wide practical knowledge of monumental wall painting acquired six years earlier whilst serving as Matejko's assistant with the decorative scheme at

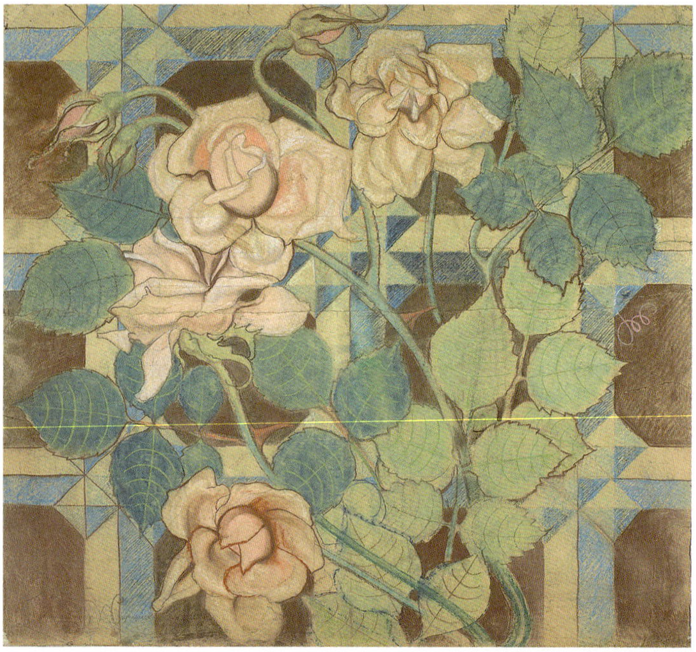
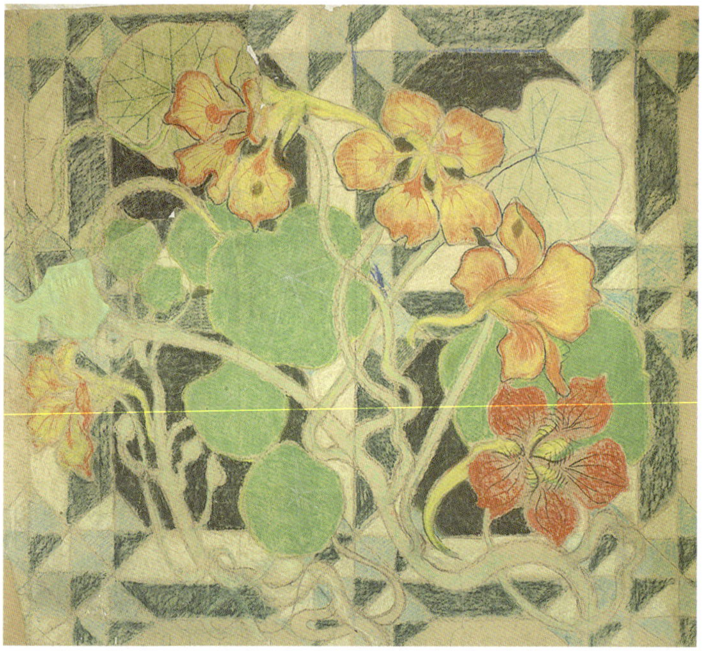
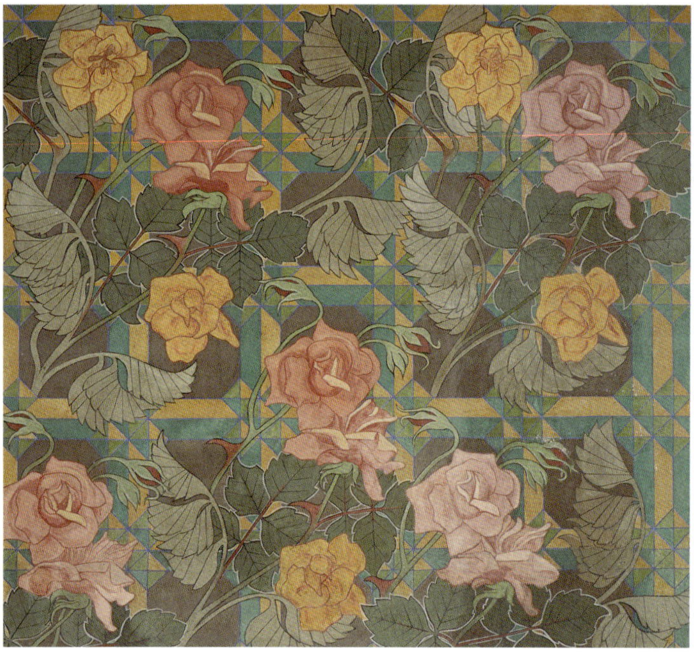
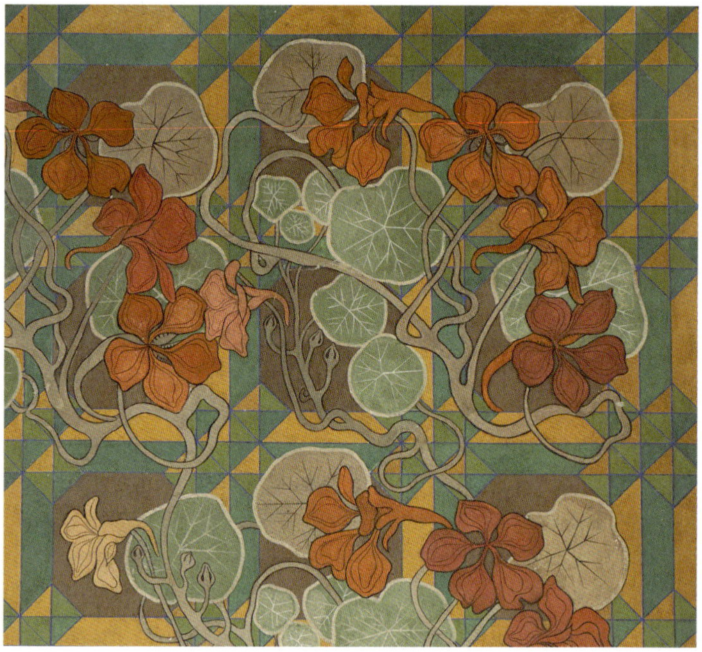

St Mary's Basilica in Kraków. He produced designs which were transferred by painters onto the wall by means of pouncing, then filled with colour and modelling. Wyspiański himself painted the figurative compositions in the chancel. He divided the walls into zones, which he filled with strips of ornament (figs 3.3, 3.4, 3.5, 3.6 and 3.7): the lowest with trellis-style latticework and the upper zone in the chancel with a design based on Jagiellonian coins and medieval heraldic Polish eagles. The Jagiellonians, responsible for creating 16th-century Wawel (see Chapter 4), were one of the most powerful dynasties in Polish history and in Renaissance Europe. Inspired by Matejko's scheme at St Mary's Basilica, Wyspiański's choice

3.5 (OPPOSITE)
Detail of rose and nasturtium floral painted mural decoration in the chancel and transepts of the Franciscan Church: original designs in pastel on paper, and finished wall paintings
Designs: 139.8 × 150.5 cm; 119 × 130 cm
National Museum in Kraków, MNK III-r.a-16970, MNK III-r.a-12560

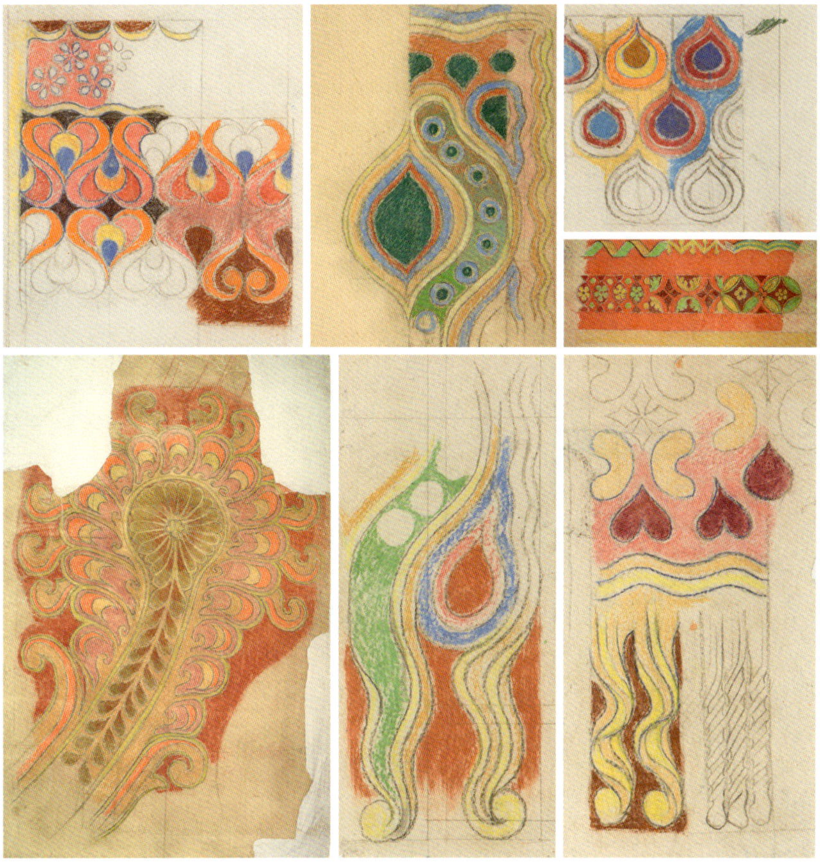

3.6 (TOP)
Various pastel designs for the ornamental painted mural decoration in the chancel and transepts of the Franciscan Church
Pastel on paper
CLOCKWISE FROM TOP LEFT: 65 × 54.2 cm; 82.2 × 58.7 cm; 73.5 × 60.5 cm; 101 × 46.5 cm; 79.5 × 38 cm; 80.5 × 35.5 cm; 140.2 × 91.5 cm
National Museum in Kraków, MNK III-r.a-4930, MNK III-r.a-4910, MNK III-r.a-4909, MNK III-r.a-12563, MNK III-r.a-4915, MNK III-r.a-4908, MNK III-r.a-10699

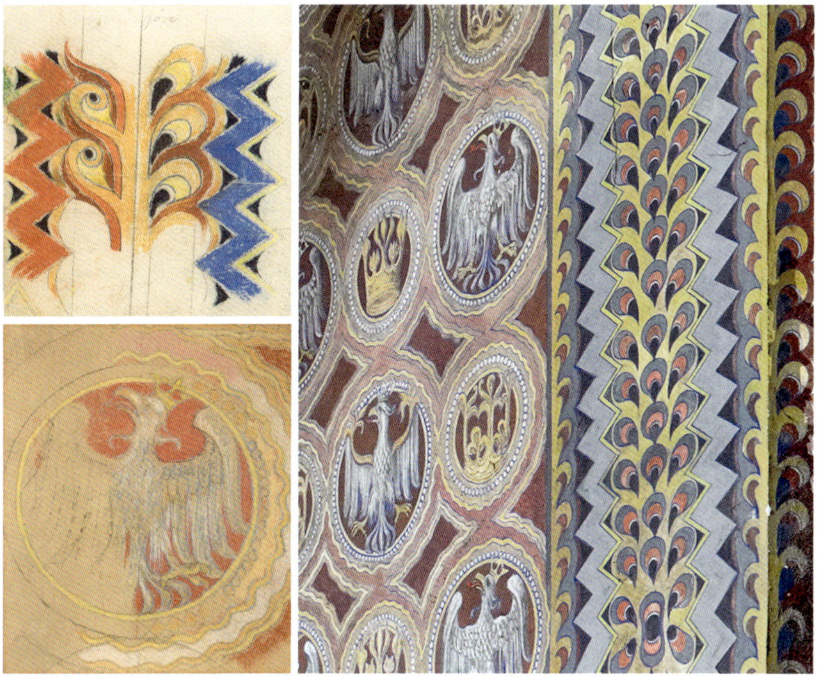

3.7 (BOTTOM)
Detail of and pastel designs on paper for the ornamental painted mural decoration in the chancel and transepts of the Franciscan Church: motifs of heraldic eagles, zigzags and peacock's eyes
Designs: 81.5 × 62.7 cm; 91.5 × 79 cm
National Museum in Kraków, MNK III-r.a-4912; Bank PKO S.A.

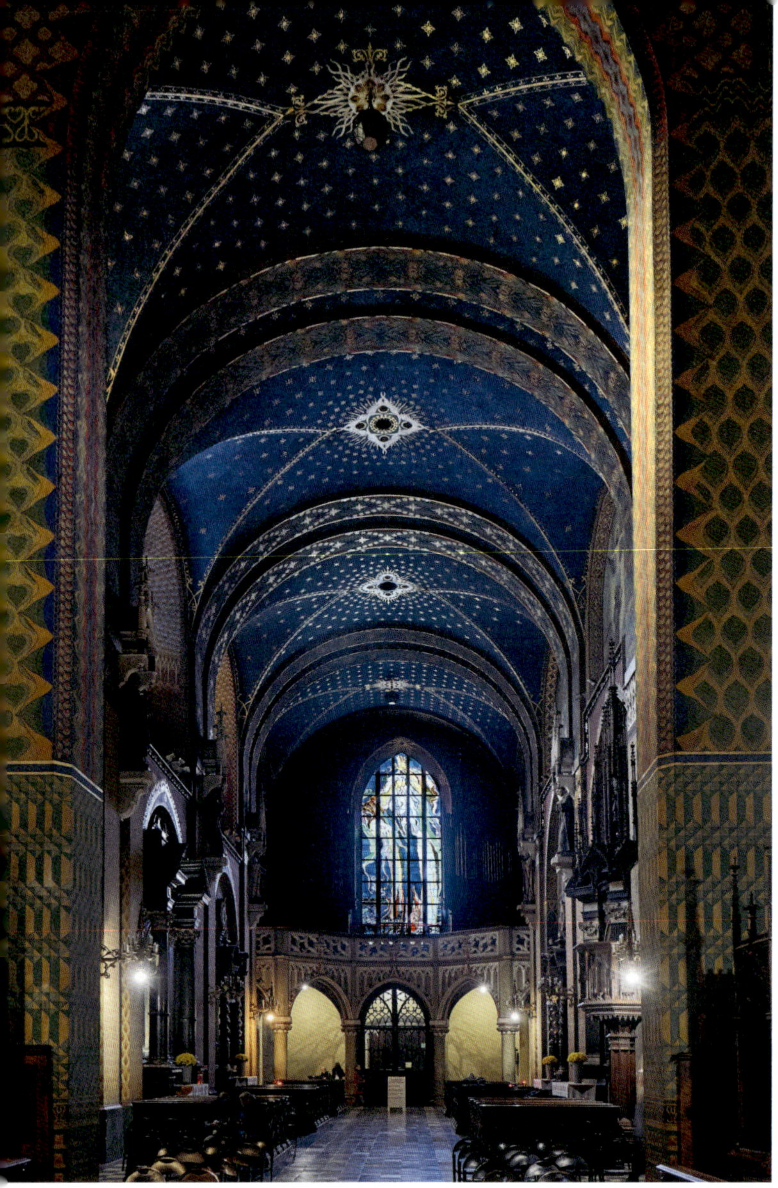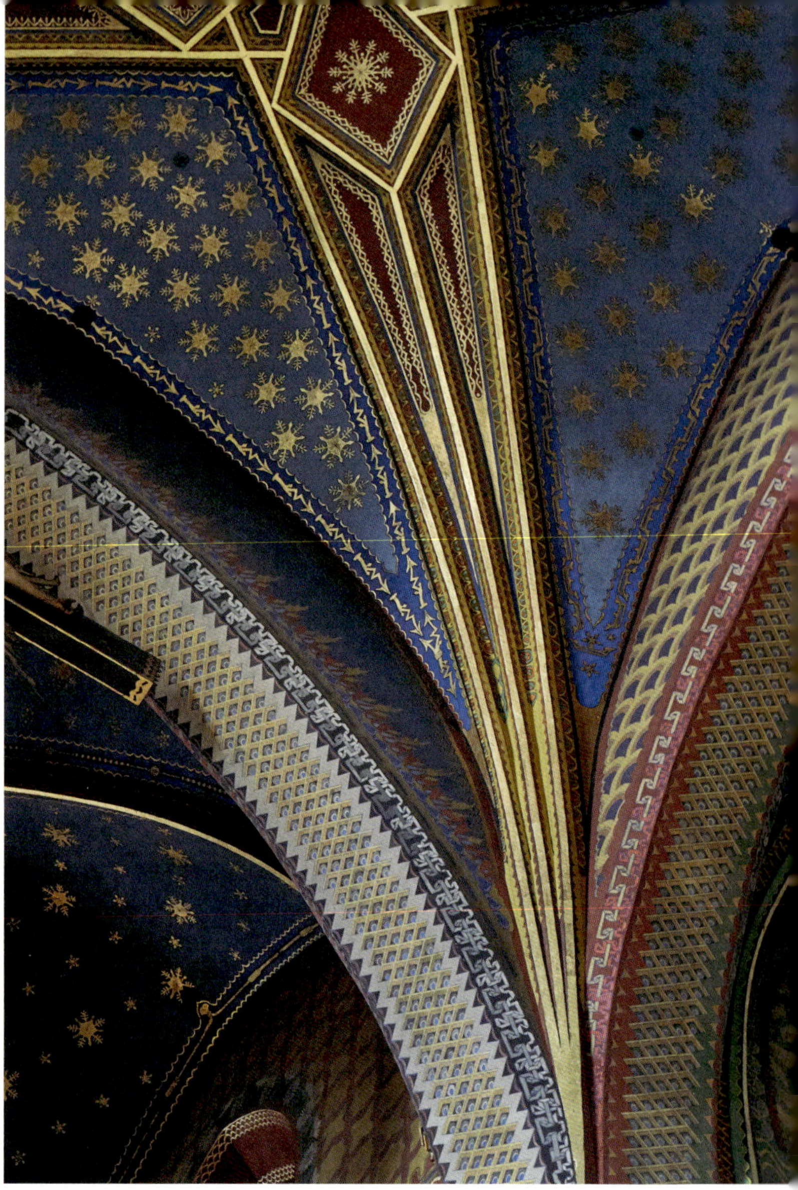

of heraldic motifs referenced the history of the Franciscan Church, including its medieval patrons and funders, as well as Poland's past greatness. The iconography was based on the numismatic antiquarian study *Dawne monety polskie dynastyi Piastów i Jagiellonów* (*Old Polish Coins of the Piast and Jagiellonian Dynasty*, 1885) by Kazimierz Stronczyński.

The upper zone in the transept comprised a border of lilies. Wyspiański had originally planned to fill this with a frieze of birds in flight, but this idea had been opposed by the Franciscans, to his astonishment (see Chapter 2).[19] The highest zone was filled with ornamentation made up of several motifs – hearts, peacocks' eyes, flames, chessboards and palmettes. 'The most beautiful and most novel idea in the entire decorative scheme,' Rydel wrote, 'is the framing of the windows with decorative borders made up of stylised wild meadow flowers, such as camomiles, sunflowers, cornflowers, poppies, corn cockles . . . Other varieties of flowers are glowing in the recesses for the windows, namely: mulleins, forget-me-nots, buttercups, violet field vetch, woodland bluebells, etc.'[20]

Wyspiański painted gold stars on the blue vaulted ceiling of the church (figs 3.8 and 3.9), drawing on the shapes of 'the limitless variety of star-like snow-crystals, which can be found magnified – in every physics textbook'.[21] Other decorative motifs included the girdle of St Francis, the rosary, as well as

3.8 (OPPOSITE, LEFT)
Nave looking towards the western stained-glass window of God the Creator
Franciscan Church, Kraków

3.9 (OPPOSITE, RIGHT)
Detail of ornamental painted mural decoration on the arched ceiling of the Franciscan Church, Kraków

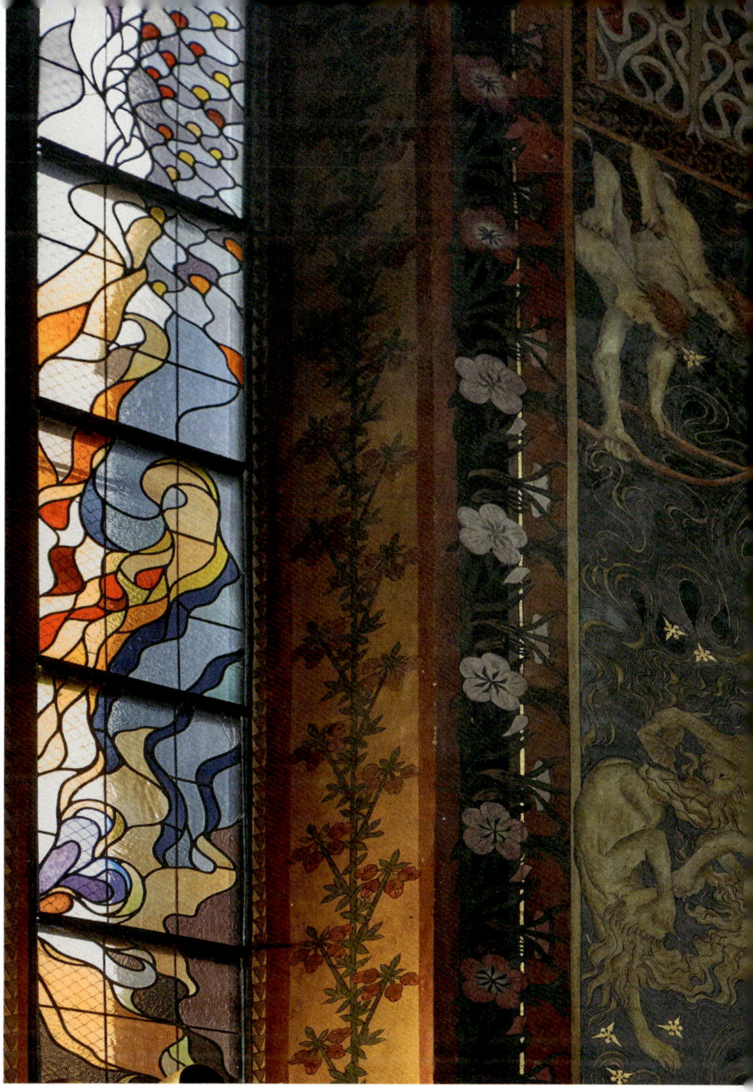

3.10 (TOP)
Stanisław Wyspiański
Detail of 'Fallen Angels' wall painting, Franciscan Church, Kraków

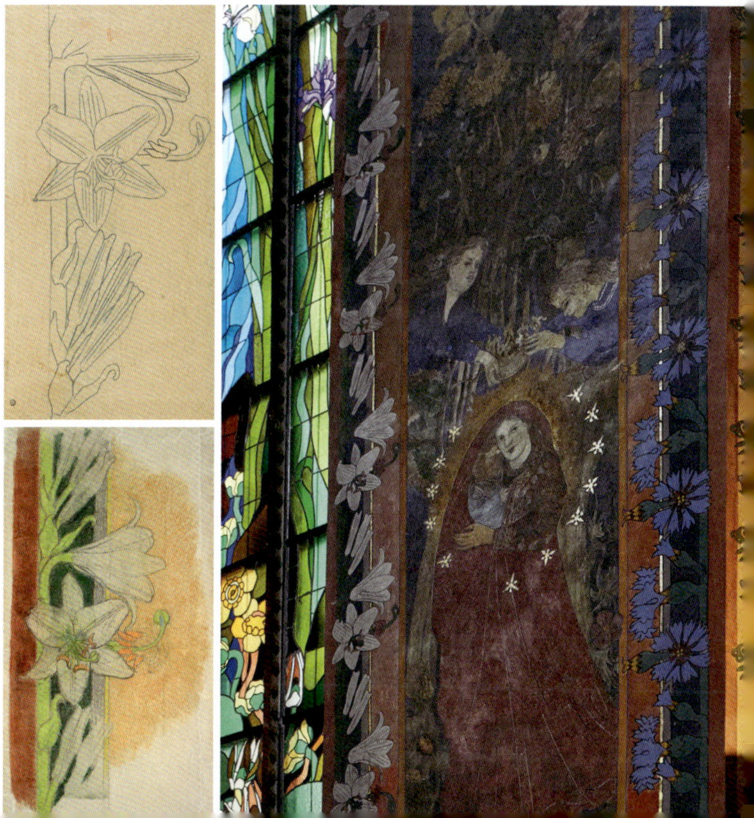

3.11 (BOTTOM)
Stanisław Wyspiański
Pastel, crayon and pencil designs of the white lily motif, and its use as the decorative border of the 'Rustic Madonna' wall painting, 1895
Designs: 92.5 × 46.5 cm; 114 × 54.5 cm
National Museum in Kraków, MNK III-r.a-4932, MNK III-r.a-10743

elements of the Friars Minor habit. He adorned the western bay of the vaulted ceiling with the undulating 'Milky Way'. In the pentagonal apse the walls above the window-openings were filled with symbols: a chalice, the Crown of Thorns, and the Host. These images were initially depicted between adoring angels, for whom altar-boys with worn-out shoes had served as models. This idea met with disapproval from the Franciscans, however, and the figures were painted over.[22]

Wyspiański designed figurative subjects for the chancel walls between the windows of the choir. On the north side he depicted Saint Michael, with the Fall of the Rebel Angels below (fig.3.10); on the south side an image of Caritas – Christian love – with Mary and the Child Jesus beneath (fig.3.11). A year after their completion Lucjan Rydel wrote:

> On one of these narrow, tall strips of wall (in between two windows each surrounded by decorative borders of lilies and cornflowers respectively) he painted the Madonna and Child against the background of an enormous mound of flowers. Two angels support the crown over the head of the Madonna. His intention was to create a rustic depiction of God's Mother in accordance with folk tradition, hence similar to the type depicted in miraculous religious paintings, featuring gilded dresses, adorned with precious stones. And since peasant-girls from villages around Kraków wear richly patterned kaftans adorned with beads and sequins for festive occasions, so Wyspiański dressed his rustic Madonna similarly, somehow evoking the iconography of a miraculous religious picture. He also depicted her in a scarlet cloak in

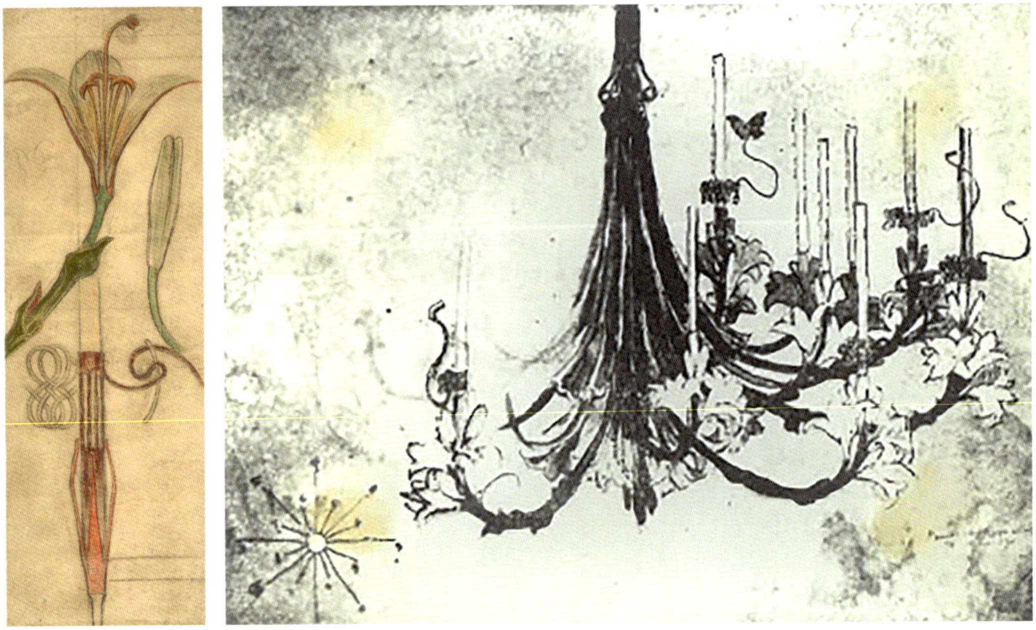

3.12
Stanisław Wyspiański
Unrealised pastel design for the lily chandelier, Franciscan Church, and photographic print from the museum card index catalogue by Gustaw Puchalski
Design: 112.5 × 38 cm
National Museum in Kraków, MNK III-r.a-10694

which she wraps both the Child and herself, in a manner not dissimilar to how peasant mothers wrap themselves in scarves in the countryside, when nursing babies ... The crown over her head held up by angels endows her with the dignity of the Queen of Heavens. Above the Madonna is another, smaller fresco, framed by a beautiful decorative border. The figures of two small girls, in a sisterly embrace, overlook from behind a splendid giant Iris flower ... This is 'Caritas', that spirit of Christian love, one of the three Cardinal Virtues, which St Paul called the greatest of virtues ... Opposite, on a narrow strip of wall (between two windows adorned with decorative borders made of strawflowers and corn cockles respectively), there is a wall painting of the Fall of the Rebel Angels. Just as we had seen the apotheosis of divine motherhood and sacred, immaculate Love, so here we have the fall of sinful creatures tarnished by guilt. Their entwined bodies tumble down, stunned by their fall, without resistance ... to their fatal destiny ... chased by youthful angels firing flaming arrows at them. One must finally mention the fourth painting, which parallels the above-mentioned 'Caritas'. This is the Archangel Michael in full armour, located above the 'Fall of the Rebel Angels', supported by a fiery sword. In stark contrast to the soft and sweet caresses of those girls, he embodies tough and severe strength.[23]

The completed scheme was presented to the committee on 30 December 1895. Its members – including the City Historic Buildings Conservator, Stanisław Tomkowicz, the architect Karol Zaremba and the painter Ludomir Benedyktowicz – requested a few alterations to the trellis-style latticework sections of the walls. Wyspiański therefore continued to work. In March 1896 he designed a candlestick in the form of a bouquet of lilies (unrealised; fig.3.12), and a year later he complemented the latticework with a striking large pattern of roses, nasturtiums and pansies (figs 2.0, 2.4, 3.5). Nature was an overarching source of inspiration to him. In a letter to Rydel dated 9–10 May 1896, Wyspiański revealed how he uses nature as sourcebook for his applied arts designs: 'I have been going to Bielany, to the banks of the Vistula river, to the meadows to get flowers which I then stylise and immediately conceive designs for lamps, candlesticks, columns, pillars, borders, friezes, walls. I want to live and breathe this entire glistening and mysterious world of nature. What miracles it holds.'[24]

He also designed a scene of the Last Judgement with Christ seated upon a rainbow among angels playing musical instruments, which he planned to locate in one of the transept arches.[25]

In a letter to Rydel from 8 September 1897, Wyspiański records the subsequent commission to design seven stained-glass windows – six in the chancel and one for the west window in the nave of the church.[26] 'The Franciscan stained-glass windows are the last of this kind of work that I'll do for nothing, since I am receiving 360 złoty in all, but since I want to do this work, and there isn't a similar opportunity available anywhere else in Europe, I am therefore pleased.'[27] Cartoons for these windows were presented at the Society of Friends of the Fine Arts in Kraków in December 1897.[28] Józef Ryszkiewicz discussed them in *Tygodnik Illustrowany*:

> According to the regulations guiding the Society's competition exhibition only paintings or sculptures within the field of pure art were eligible. Since Wyspiański's works already have the distinct features of applied art, the only solution was to exclude them from the competition, without removing them from the competition exhibition. The Society's Committee was thus happy to be able to carry out its mission as the only institution in the country having as its purpose the encouragement of visual arts in all their manifestations.[29]

Ryszkiewicz praised the great originality of the creative idea behind each stained-glass composition, and in particular the ornamental concept behind the representation of the elements – fire and water – also derived from plant forms, for example in the case of the former the petals of poppies and yellow lilies assuming the form of flames. He argued that whilst 'modern ornamentation' by other artists also frequently featured botanical forms, these were usually isolated motifs; Wyspiański on the other hand can be credited for creating his own integrated floral style.

On 29 November 1897, Guardian Father Samuel Rajss commissioned the execution of the cartoons in glass by the Innsbruck firm Tiroler Glasmalerei und Mosaik-Anstalt.[30] In September 1898 Wyspiański travelled to Innsbruck to select the colours of the glass, and on 6 December the firm sent its estimate for the windows. Wyspiański was also asked to supply the missing drawings for the east window and the tracery sections of the windows. As Ekielski wrote, the Franciscans protested about the representation of their saints in the window with the three Poor Clares, claiming they looked like dead figures.[31] The conflict became so heated that a figure of Blessed Salomea designed by Władysław Rossowski ultimately replaced the three nuns. Only in 1908 was this replaced by the figure Wyspiański had designed in 1902 (fig.3.14).[32] The windows were installed in July 1899. On 20 December 1903 Wyspiański resumed work on the window depicting God the Father (fig.3.13). The art historian Julian Pagaczewski recalled:

> When work was going to commence on the execution of the stained-glass window ... the cartoon was laid out in one of the galleries of the National Museum in the Sukiennice [the Cloth-Halls in Kraków], and a casket was brought with numbered samples of coloured glass together with the stained glass itself. Wyspiański, having come to the Museum, selected the glass, looking at it against the light and comparing its tones with the colours on the cartoon. In the event, there weren't any samples identical in tone to those in the cartoon. So Wyspiański selected one of the tones as basic, and chose the others according to the degree to which they harmonised with this. The result is that the selection of tones and their intensity in the completed window is different from those in the cartoon and, despite this, the colour scheme of the stained-glass window should be regarded as an authentic

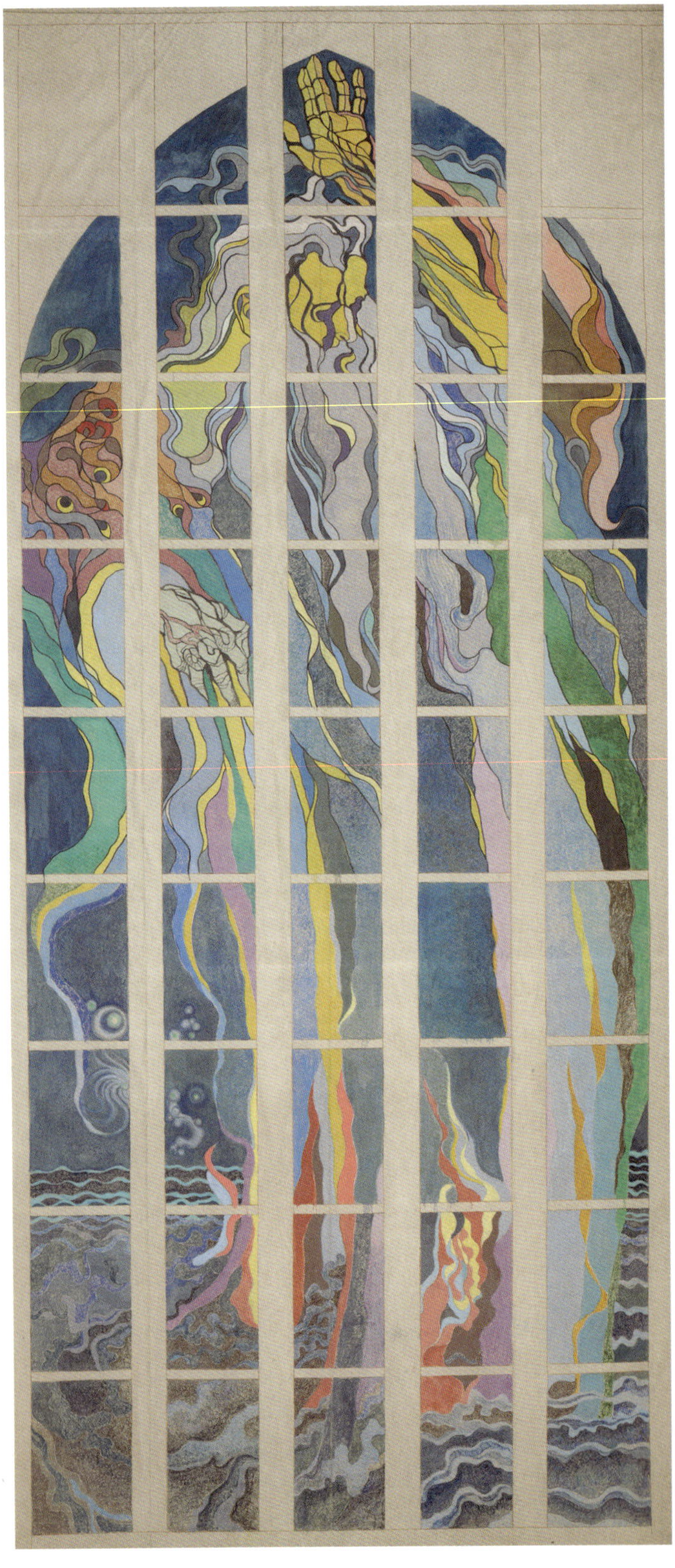

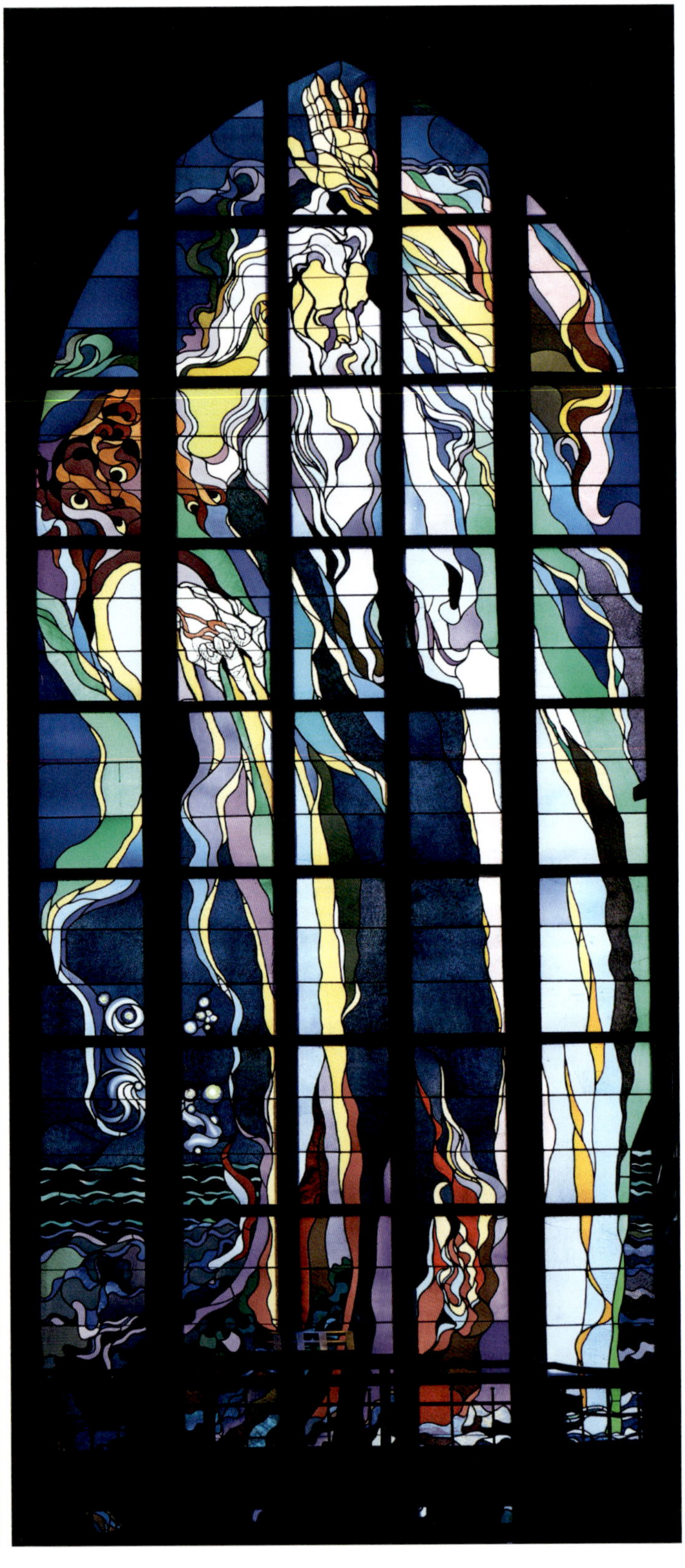

3.13
Stanisław Wyspiański
Juxtaposition of the stained-glass window 'God the Creator' in the west of the nave, Franciscan Church, with the tempera and crayon version of the design, 1904
Design: 877 × 391 cm
National Museum in Kraków, MNK II-b-514

> work by Wyspiański, since he had made the ultimate decision regarding the selection of colour shades.[33]

The installation of the window commenced on 21 October 1904.

The iconographic scheme for the Franciscan wall paintings and stained glass had taken its origin in a variety of sources. Antoni Waśkowski reported an exchange with Wyspiański:

> We both stood near the main altar, beneath his Madonna from Bronowice, and held our first conversation ever. The subjects? Renan – deism – atheism – the Middle Ages – ecclesiastical art – Gothic – wall painting decoration – Puvis de Chavannes – the frescoes in the Sorbonne – Viollet-le-Duc – Matejko – painted mural decoration of St Mary's Basilica in Kraków – and again the Franciscans – designs for wall paintings – ceiling compositions.[34]

Wyspiański's extensive reading of literary and scholarly texts undoubtedly played an enormous role. He knew the *Fioretti di San Francesco*, which was the source for individual scenes: Saint Francis receiving the stigmata and preaching to the birds (a planned but never realised painted composition for the transept). The source for the idea of covering the walls with flowers and herbs and the vaulting with stars and the Milky Way, with 'Brother Fire' and 'Sister Water', is from Francis's 'Canticle of the Sun'. Another medieval source for the motif of the flowering Paradise may have been *De diversis artibus* (*On Diverse Arts*) by Theophilus Presbyter.[35] This includes descriptions of ideal church interiors: 'dearest son, entering with confidence the House of God, you have decorated it with such loveliness, its ceilings and walls with all the variety of art, and dressing it in numerous colours have given to it the likeness of a Divine flowering Paradise, green with grass and leaf'.[36] The French architect, art historian and pioneer of heritage conservation Eugène-Emmanuel Viollet-le-Duc (1814–1879) regarded this treatise as essential reading for the understanding of the principles of wall painting, and Wyspiański in turn studied Viollet-le-Duc's encyclopaedia on Gothic architecture, the *Dictionnaire raisonné de l'architecture française du XIe au XVIe siècle* (1854–68), 'with unheard-of conscientiousness and attention'.[37] Wyspiański was also familiar with the *Poradnik dla zajmujących się utrzymaniem i restauracją kościołów i kościelnych sprzętów* (*Hand-book for Those Engaged in the Care and Restoration of Churches and Ecclesiastical Furniture*) by Władysław Łuszczkiewicz, painter and Professor at the School of Fine Arts in Kraków, published in 1887. This book appears among the reading recorded by Wyspiański in his sketchbook from 1887–8.[38] Łuszczkiewicz urged that painting should conform to the existing architecture, should be in harmony with the style in which the church is constructed.[39] As regards medieval painted mural decoration,

> The feeling of colourfulness is predominant in it; it loves patterning, it covers three sides of wall-columns with it, the ribs of vaulting, the drapery of statues; it abhors all effects of chiaroscuro painting, all imitations of convexness. Flat coloured ornamentation is characteristic of the medieval period, by virtue of which it is so appropriate to making surfaces visible; colourfulness supplements the modelling of mouldings or arcades, it strongly emphasises the springing of ribs, it covers walls with a network of silent ornament.[40]

3.14
Stanisław Wyspiański
Cartoons for the stained-glass windows 'Blessed Salomea' (before 1902) and 'St Francis of Assisi' (1897)
Pastel and charcoal on paper
184.3 × 45 cm; 183 × 44.5 cm
National Museum in Kraków, MNK III-r.a-1331; National Museum in Warsaw, 183356 MNW

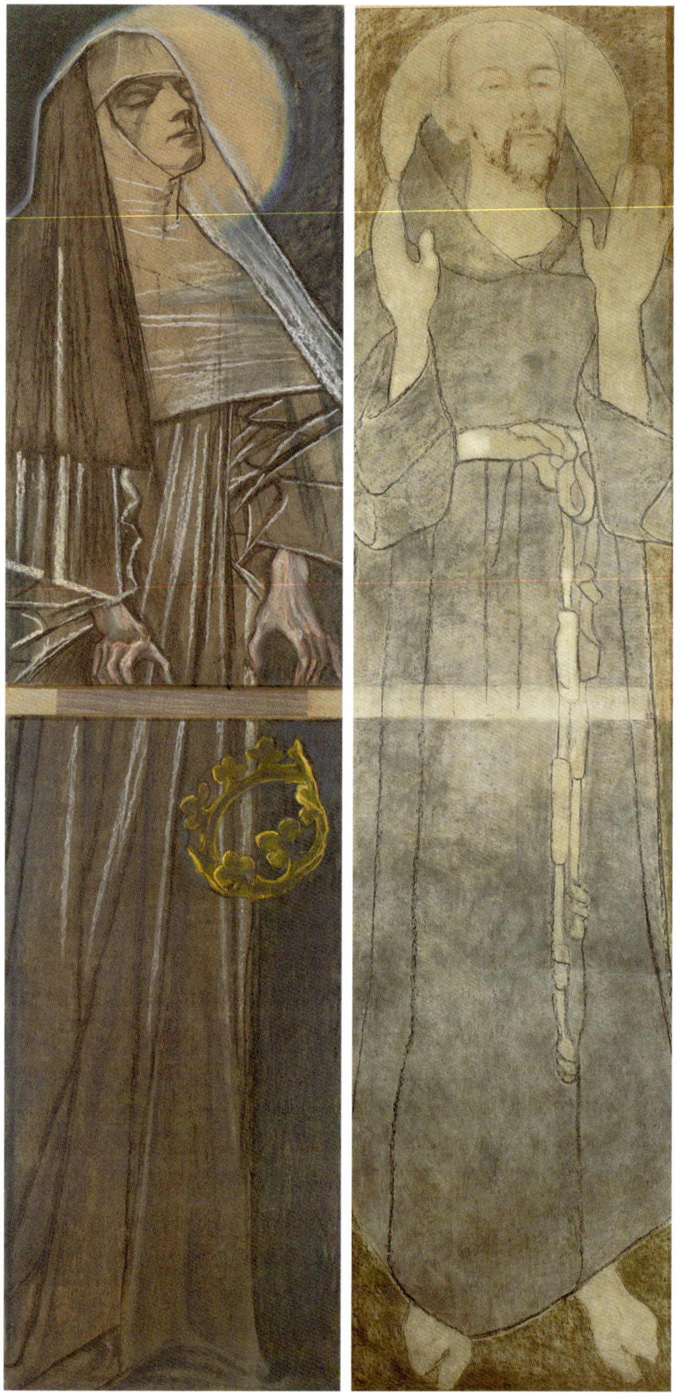

Wyspiański became familiar with the architecture and sculpture of the Middle Ages while on the scaffolding in St Mary's Basilica in Kraków, when working on the painted decoration of the chancel in 1889. He acquired much of his knowledge from his master Jan Matejko, who was credited by his contemporaries with according equal value and status to painted decoration as to architecture. The critic, art historian and painter Wacław Husarski (1883–1951) wrote about the merits of reviving the unity of the arts:

> This was ... a reflection of the breakthrough in European art at the time . . . by the mid-19th century the notion of the unity of the arts had more or less been ultimately lost; architecture, painting and sculpture were living autonomous existences, without any connection between them; decorative arts had been wholly relegated outside of the sphere of artistic creative production proper, becoming the object of soulless factory production, or else descending to the level of the then-despised craftsmanship. This had been the case with wall painting, having been wholly relegated to guild-based master-craftsmen, irrespective of whether the job involved painting a staircase or the painted mural decoration of a church. There were obviously attempts to improve this situation but for a long time these had solely taken place in England, where the disciples of the Pre-Raphaelites worked towards improvement in this direction. Only towards the end of the century did these new notions of reinstating the rightful status to the decorative arts arrive on the Continent, and of renewing this lost connection between architecture, painting and sculpture, the latter two conceived as the

decorative complements to architecture. These ideas also reached Poland, influencing the undertaking to add artistic painted mural decoration to St Mary's Basilica, which led to Matejko himself having been entrusted with this work. The choice of this medieval temple as the arena for this first act of renewal can be explained by, among other things, the fact that the Pre-Raphaelites and the adherents of their views regarded the Renaissance as the start of a decline in art, consequently returning to Gothic, which they saw as the pinnacle of the development of art in general, and of the decorative arts in particular.[41]

Wyspiański learned about medieval wall painting by visiting European Gothic cathedrals. His descriptions and sketches of these buildings appear in his correspondence with his friends and patrons. He understood the complex iconography of cathedral decoration: he saw this in metaphorical terms as 'theatrical decoration', 'as if . . . an enchanted palace' adorned with wall paintings likened to 'an opulent tapestry spread out', an act of a Shakespearean play; 'centuries were required to create such scenes'.[42]

Moreover, there was pressure exerted by contemporary art, including contemporary monumental painting. The name of Pierre Puvis de Chavannes (1824–1898) appears frequently in Wyspiański's letters from Paris. He was familiar with Puvis de Chavannes' frescoes in the Sorbonne, *The Allegory of the Sorbonne* (1889), as well as his easel-paintings, particularly *Inter artes et naturam* (*Between Art and Nature, c.*1890–95), exhibited at the Salon du Champ-de-Mars. This kind of work aroused his admiration, but also regret at the lack of of similar works at home. On 22 May 1890 he wrote to Rydel:

I was in the Panthéon ... Many frescoes inside – French art – painting here in particular provides evidence of all its strength ... everywhere you see a nation which is alive – confident in its dignity and its powers ... you leave the place stupefied – overwhelmed and oppressed that we are different and that we have nothing similar to this – that we are incapable of a life of such daring ... [43]

All of the knowledge and influences absorbed by Wyspiański were applied in practice in his extraordinary work of art at the Franciscan Church. He adapted his decorative bands and figurative paintings to existing architectural divisions, using colour to distinguish individual elements of the structure. The predominant tones – red in the chancel and green in the transept – harmonised perfectly with the existing medieval painted mural decoration in the adjacent monastic cloister. Wyspiański dismissed an approach to ornamentation alien to his own in an article devoted to the state of conservation work on the Cathedral in Lviv at this time, published in *Życie* on 9 October 1897: 'in the section of painted decorations not one single motif is beautiful, not one is composed with any thought, all is "torn" from hand-books, all would be appropriate in entrance-halls, corridors and other locations to which the viewer is indifferent'.[44] In 1896 Rydel emphasised Wyspiański's limitless imagination, which meant he would never have been satisfied just 'looking through some *L'art gothique* or *Gotische Ornament*' in order to copy an existing pattern. He drew attention to the painter's exceptional talent in schematic synthesis, 'which comprised the essence of decorative art', with a faithful representation of motifs drawn from nature.[45] Wyspiański was among those European artists

3.15
Stanisław Wyspiański
Rustic Madonna with Child, 1896
Pastel on paper laid on cardboard
484 × 97 cm
National Museum in Poznań,
MNBP Mp 1991

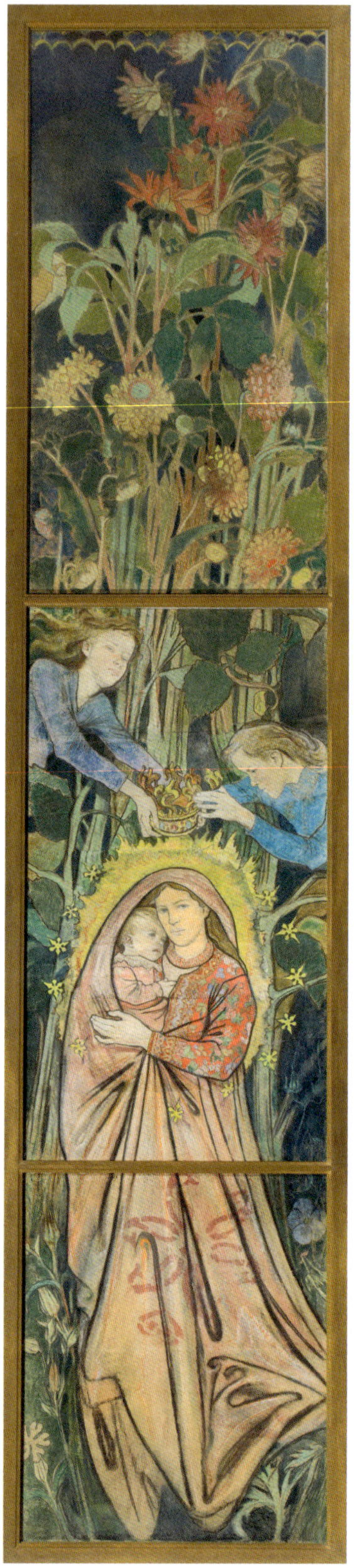

who had decided to break away from imitation in decoration; these included Eugène Grasset (1845–1917), according to whom mural decoration and stained glass ought to possess a non-naturalist and flat character, their forms marked with clear outlines, and the artist ought to turn to nature before creating new ornaments.[46] The motif of a row of flowers in Grasset's *Nativity Among Lilies*, reproduced in the December 1891 issue of *Harper's Bazaar*, appears to have been virtually copied by Wyspiański in the frieze of lilies in the transept of the Kraków church. Wyspiański was familiar with Grasset's work – the French artist was the subject of a retrospective exhibition in March 1894 in Paris, during the period of Wyspiański's studies there, and issue 122 of *La Plume*, dated 15 May 1894, was entirely devoted to him.[47] Wyspiański owned a copy of the catalogue of Grasset's exhibition, which he sent as a gift to Rydel,[48] and his contemporaries 'accused him of importing French models'.[49] Making flowers monumental almost became Wyspiański's trademark. This tendency may have had its origins in the poster art of Alphonse Mucha (1860–1939), whom Wyspiański had met in Paris. Japanese woodcuts may have been a source for his compositional device of placing ornamental floral motifs in the foreground, although he deprecated these prints in letters to his friends. Contemporary journalists and critics picked up on the seeming Far Eastern influence in Wyspiański's stylisation of plants – thus Marjan Dienstl wrote in 1908:

> He takes the entire vegetal organism from nature, with all its fibres and fluids. He creates an organic schema out of a rose, within which all its characteristics are indicated with the minuteness of a Japanese draughtsman. This schema is enlarged appropriately to decorative conditions, forming

> some sort of hugely powerful, super-natural flowers, which nevertheless do not lose their suppleness, their delicate nature and their freshness, thanks to a subtle emphasis on all their characteristics by graphic means, all their features as vegetal organisms.[50]

Six years earlier Adam Cybulski-Łada had drawn attention to the inspiration of his 'Japanese and English contemporaries' in the composition of stained-glass windows emphasising their 'medieval character alongside all their modernism'.[51] There was likewise no shortage of critical voices – thus Antoni Sygietyński mocked Wyspiański's stylisation of flowers, suggesting that they would serve excellently as 'ornaments for perfume-bottles, on powder-boxes, on perfumed soaps', but were completely inappropriate when used as decoration for church walls.[52]

A further major source of inspiration for Wyspiański was folk art, a characteristic part of early Central European modernism. Even his contemporaries suggested that 'his art arises from the lanes of the village of Bronowice'.[53] The colour scheme and ornamentation of the the Franciscan Church evoked Kraków peasants' dress, decoration of their cottages and everyday vernacular objects. Motifs of stylised peacocks' eyes, hearts, lozenges and plait-work recalled the decoration of peasant women's bodices and men's caps; the flowers used to decorate the church interior were not exotic but rather familiar indigenous wayside blooms. The 'Rustic Madonna' is depicted in an embroidered bodice adorned with red beads (fig.3.15), traditionally worn by peasant women from the region of Kraków in Wyspiański's day (see fig.17.10).

The painted and stained-glass decoration of the Franciscan Church is an exceptionally interesting example of the embodiment of the ideal of the artist-craftsman.[54] Wyspiański aestheticised his own everyday experience. He was solely responsible for the interior decoration of his successive studios and homes, choosing the wall colours, decorative schemes, furniture designs, as well as the textiles. He ensured that all constituent elements of the civic buildings he designed were executed by local craftsmen using native materials. He continued to realise this artistic philosophy when he became a professor at the Academy of Fine Arts in Kraków. During a speech at the inauguration of the academic year 1902–3, he stated: 'I do not understand why I was appointed as Professor of the Decorative Arts, since all art is decorative.'[55]

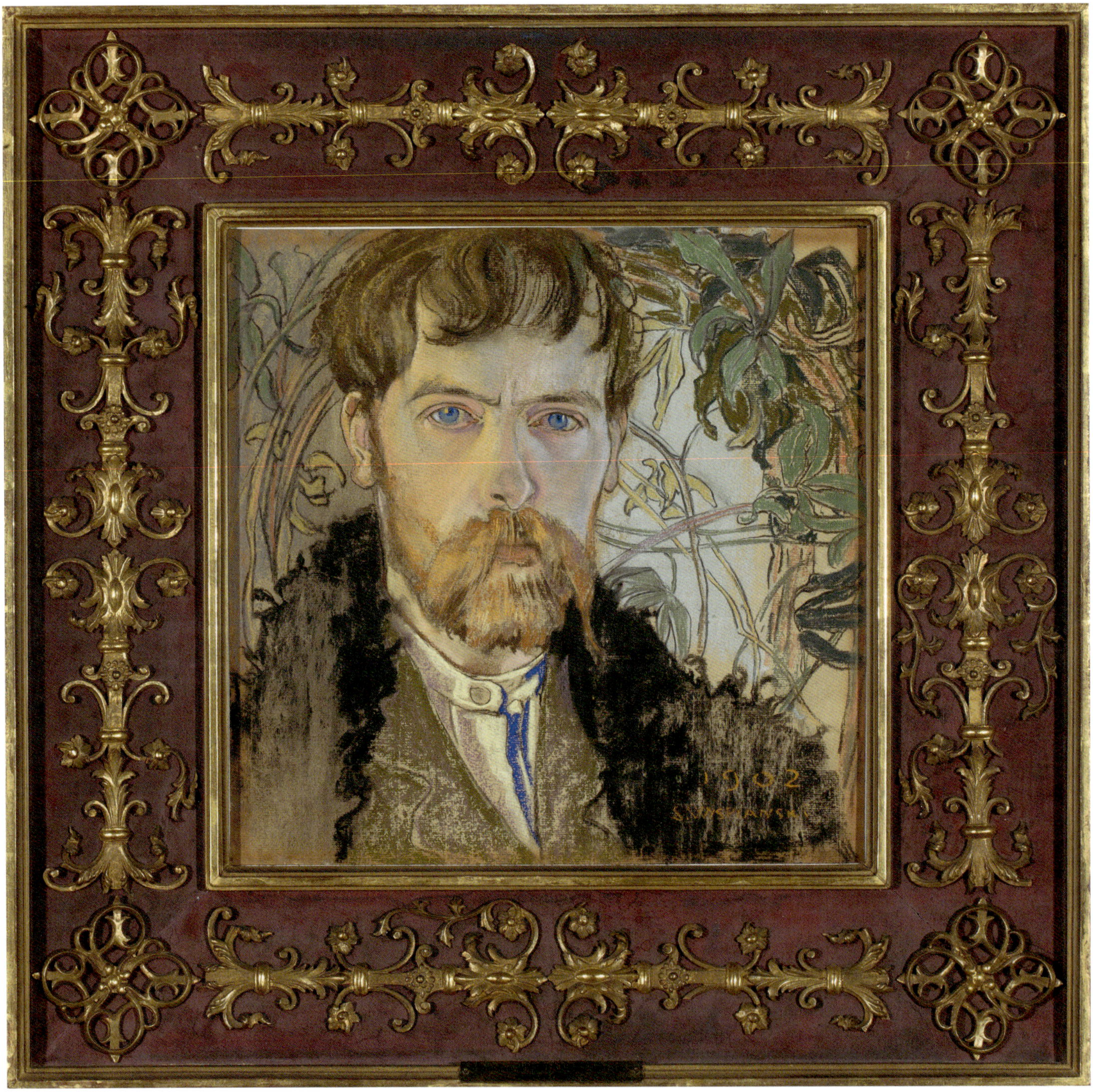

4

'Disappointed Love': Stanisław Wyspiański and Wawel

Anna Rudzińska

Late 19th-century Kraków had two facets. On the one hand it was a small, impoverished and conservative town. Historical events had deprived it of its political significance as the country's capital. Numerous decrees issued by the Austrian partitioning authorities from 1846 onwards, not least the order to surround the city with a ring of fortifications (known as Kraków Fortress), blocked any possibility of development. On the other hand Kraków enjoyed a certain measure of political independence, the free use of Polish as the language of instruction, and the tradition of the 500-year-old Jagiellonian University. Thanks to the School of Fine Arts, which, following Julian Fałat's reforms achieved the status of an Academy by 1900, Kraków became a centre of new art, propagated by professors educated in Paris and Munich. Kraków brought together artistic individualists – painters, writers, architects.[1] It was a town of numerous monuments, which were witnesses to Poland's former greatness. Kraków's magical atmosphere exuded attachment to the past. Wawel was a place of special significance (see figs 0.10 and 17.2). Wawel Hill with its Castle and Cathedral presiding over it, the latter used for the coronation and burial of Polish kings,[2] was a place inextricably connected with the country's history, a symbol of Polish national identity and patriotism.[3] Always highly regarded, the Cathedral itself was perceived as the sphere of sacrum – a national relic. Its role as the resting place not only of kings, princes, saints and clergymen but also, from the 19th century onwards, of national heroes and the most eminent poets, as had been the case at Westminster Abbey, established its status as a treasure-house of history. Monuments facilitated learning history and ensured that the existing sense of community which underlay the national spirit was not forgotten. During the partitions direct exposure to relics from the past became the source of sad reflection, melancholy, longing for what had been lost, regret and tears.

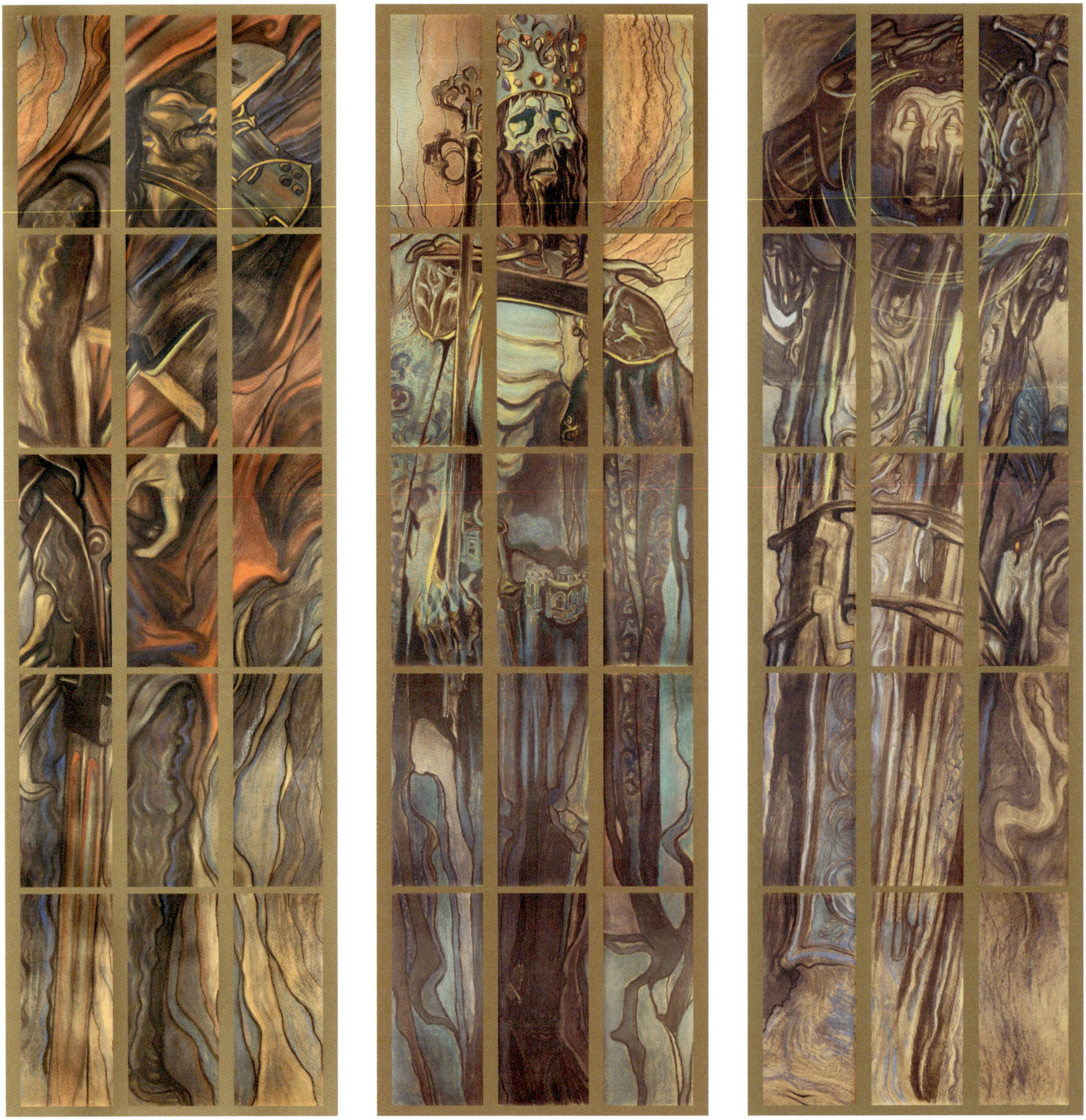

4.0 (p.74)
Stanisław Wyspiański
Self-Portrait, 1902
Pastel on lined paper laid on cardboard; frame constructed from deciduous wood strengthened with pine, with carved deciduous wood (birch?) glued to a slat painted with purple gouache, and elements finished with gilding
37.5 × 36.8 cm; external dimensions of the frame: 62 × 62 × 7 cm
National Museum in Warsaw, 128465 MNW

4.1 (OPPOSITE, LEFT)
Stanisław Wyspiański
Unrealised stained-glass design for the chancel of Wawel Cathedral, 1900:
Prince Henry the Pious
Pastel on paper
436 × 148 cm
National Museum in Kraków, MNK III-r.a-13007

4.2 (OPPOSITE, CENTRE)
Stanisław Wyspiański
Unrealised stained-glass design for the chancel of Wawel Cathedral, 1900:
King Casimir the Great
Pastel on paper
436 × 148 cm
National Museum in Kraków, MNK III-r.a-13005

4.3 (OPPOSITE, RIGHT)
Stanisław Wyspiański
Unrealised stained-glass design for the chancel of Wawel Cathedral, 1900:
Saint Stanislaus
Pastel on paper
436 × 148 cm
National Museum in Kraków, MNK III-r.a-13006

The Viennese authorities' decision to hand over Wawel Castle to Austrian troops was regarded as a particularly humiliating act. In consequence, many buildings on the hill were partially or completely demolished and/or crudely rebuilt at this time, and centuries-old furnishings pillaged. The partitioning power had turned the former seat of kings into barracks in 1796. Although the adjoining Cathedral formally remained in the hands of the Kraków Archdiocese, access was restricted. Polish society did not, however, give up its efforts to be able to care for its heritage. The Cathedral Renovation Committee was instituted in 1886. Its thorough archival and architectural research and documentation in the form of measured survey drawings formed the basis for future remedial work. The renovation of the building would commence in 1891, starting with Sigismund's Chapel. Works on the main building began in 1895. Six years later the Cathedral was made available to the congregation.

Stanisław Wyspiański was emotionally attached to Wawel Hill all his life, from childhood. Growing up, he spent much of his time in his father's sculpture workshop situated at the foothill of the Castle. As a schoolboy and art student he ardently followed the renovation of this historic building, dreaming of finding himself amongst the artists selected to decorate it. The prospect of professional involvement with Wawel arose in the second half of the 1890s. The decision rested in the hands of Sławomir Odrzywolski, the architect in charge of the renovation and a professor at the Technical Institute, and Cardinal Jan Puzyna. Odrzywolski and Wyspiański made contact in 1896, following the discovery of Gothic wall paintings at the Cathedral, when the architect gave the painter access to its interior in order to examine them. Wyspiański had already written at this time: 'I am proceeding ... with great caution, I don't want to put him off in any way, because I am anxious that the Cathedral may pass into inappropriate hands'.[4] The following years were dominated by Wyspiański's efforts to secure the commission to decorate the temple.

In 1899 Odrzywolski commissioned seven stained-glass windows from workshops in Munich and Freiburg im Breisgau, Germany. This decision met with severe protests on behalf of the Polish intelligentsia from all three partitions. The notion of entrusting the decoration of the most important national temple to foreign makers was deemed deeply unpatriotic and as such unacceptable. In keeping with his temperament, in the event Wyspiański declared that it was inadequate to just condemn and protest – it was time for him to propose his own scheme. Encouraged by the positive outcome of his efforts to win the Franciscan Church commission (see Chapter 3), Wyspiański began work on the Cathedral stained-glass designs, at his own risk and expense. He completed initial drawings that year. By 1900, when the first German window was being installed, Wyspiański was creating four full-scale pastel cartoons, together with sketches and studies of ideas for the remaining windows.[5] He was simultaneously writing rhapsodies – poems dedicated to a heroic figure or heroic deeds, and characterised by seriousness and pathos – which explained and complemented the extraordinary ideas embodied in his designs.

Wyspiański's unfinished design is known only partially. Nevertheless, surviving works make it possible to recreate the overall theme and reach conclusions regarding the artist's intentions.[6] The architectural divisions within the Gothic Cathedral's windows required each composition to be split into two parts, of unequal heights: each window had an internal horizontal division separating it into a lower section roughly measuring one third of the overall height, and a larger, upper section comprising the other two thirds. The artist made use of an idea that is characteristic in stained-glass art – the subject situated in the upper panels (here specifically in the form of individual figures) was complemented by a representation of related scenes in the lower. Wyspiański's concept was based on a departure from simple illustrations in favour of conveying one overarching idea, which all the windows would serve – the idea of a summoning to action, to unyielding combat in order to regain independence. He intended to express this by means of introducing important figures from Polish history and culture. From mythical times came Wanda, the daughter of Krakus (Krak), the legendary founder of Kraków, and Piast with his son Ziemowit, the mythical peasant founder of the dynasty named after him. Historical times were to be respectively represented by the Piast kings and princes, among them Henry II the Pious (1196/1207–1241; Duke of Silesia, Kraków and Greater Poland), King Władysław I the Elbow-High (*c.*1260–1333) and his son King Casimir the Great (1310–1370); followed by the Jagiellon dynasty, beginning with its founder Władysław II Jagiełło (*c.*1352/62–1434) together with his wife, Queen Regnant Jadwiga of Anjou (1373/4–1399), the grand-daughter of Casimir the Great's sister – marrying her ensured that the Polish Crown passed to the Lithuanian prince. The final years of this dynasty were to be represented by King Sigismund the Old (1467–1548) and his son King Sigismund II Augustus (1520–1572). Wyspiański also considered the figure of Zawisza the Black (*c.*1370–1428), the model of knightly virtues, and that of Wernyhora, the Cossack lyre-player and bard, who, according to literary accounts, prophesied both the partitions of Poland and its subsequent unification. In Wyspiański's most celebrated drama, *The Wedding* (1901), Wernyhora brings the Golden Horn, which was to sound the signal summoning all social strata to commence armed battle for the liberation of their country.

Whether historical or legendary, the heroes of the stained-glass panels situated at the top were to be depicted as spirits embodied in their human forms, immortalised by the patriotic expression of their heroic deeds. They would preside and watch over subsequent generations of their compatriots, serving as role models. In the case of Henry the Pious, his heroic action was his death in battle against the Tatars at Legnica (Liegnitz) in 1241. The prince had an opportunity to unite the country and succeed to the Polish crown, but instead his sense of duty compelled him to fight against the White Horde in defence of his country and faith. The mythical figure of Wanda was depicted at the moment of her drowning in the Vistula river, sacrificing her life to the Slavic deity Zhiva in return for her help in the defence of Kraków. Casimir the Great, the lawgiver, creator of the modern and powerful state and constructor of towns and fortifications, was represented as a wise ruler and protector of his country. The (actual) opening of his tomb in the Cathedral in 1869 had interrupted his spirit's wanderings in the other world. Wyspiański's master, Jan Matejko, who witnessed the event, recorded it in a painting (fig.4.4). In Wyspiański's poetical rhapsody 'Kazimierz Wielki' ('Casimir the Great', 1900),[7] contemporary Poles make pilgrimages to the remains of the ruler awaiting reburial, complaining of the hardships of living in a subjugated country. Saddened by the tragic condition of his people, the King resolves that he will not return to the other world. Instead he will remain – in the state

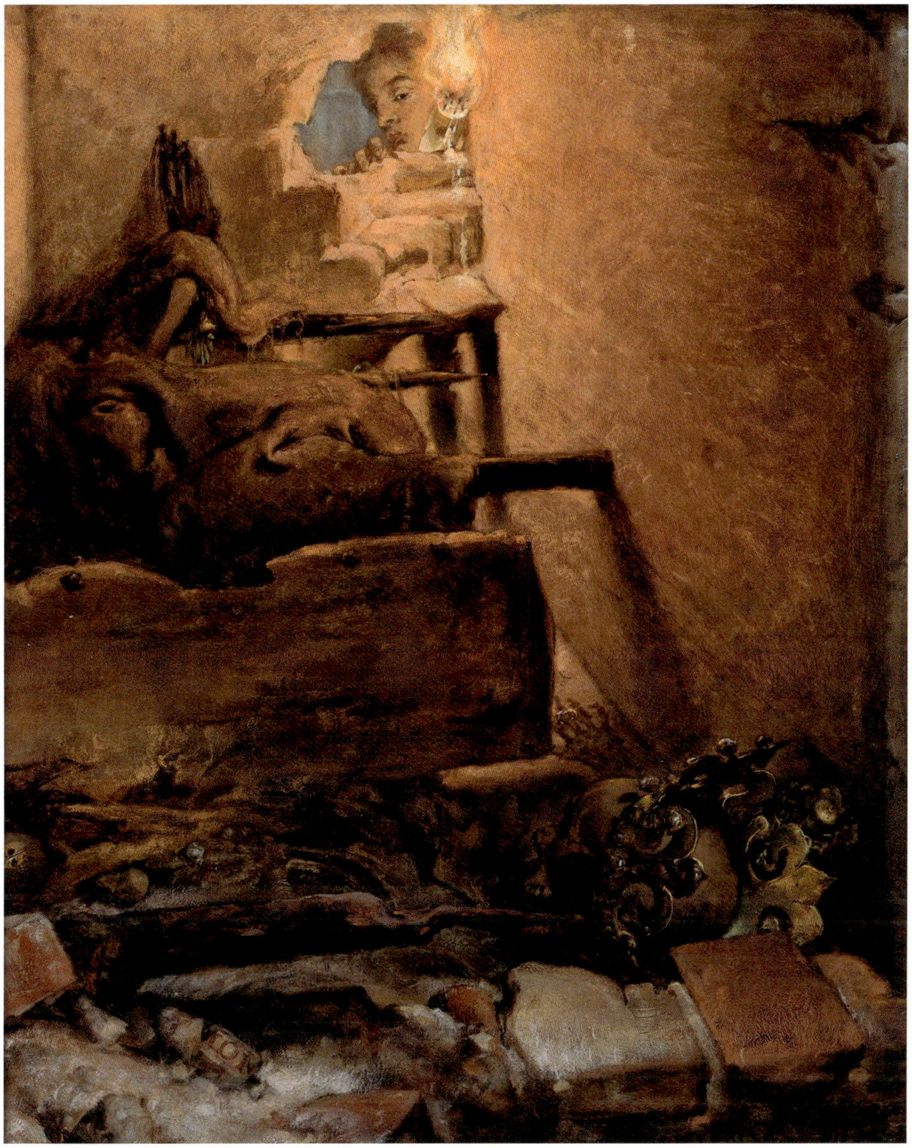

4.4
Jan Matejko
Inside the Tomb of King Casimir the Great, 1869
Oil on panel
60.5 × 47.5 cm
National Museum in Kraków, MNK IX-9

in which he was awoken – in order to watch over the destiny of his people, supporting and encouraging them to fight to regain their freedom.

Wyspiański envisaged a representation of the patron saint of the Cathedral, Bishop Stanislaus of Szczepanów (*c.*1030–1079), the first Pole to have been canonised, as the framing device to bring out the overarching idea of his scheme. In the artist's opinion, the contemporary fate of his homeland was the aftermath of events triggered by the conflict between the bishop and King Bolesław the Bold (or Bolesław II the Generous, 1039–1081). Stanislaus accused the monarch of abusing his power, denied him the Eucharist and pronounced an anathema against him, thus excommunicating him. The King accused the bishop of treason, and sentenced him to death by dismemberment. According to the myth, Stanislaus lost his life while saying Mass at the altar, executed at the hands of the King himself. The dark legend of the excessively impetuous and irascible King spread rapidly. It was soon exploited by noblemen in order to weaken royal authority, bringing about the King's exile abroad and his imminent

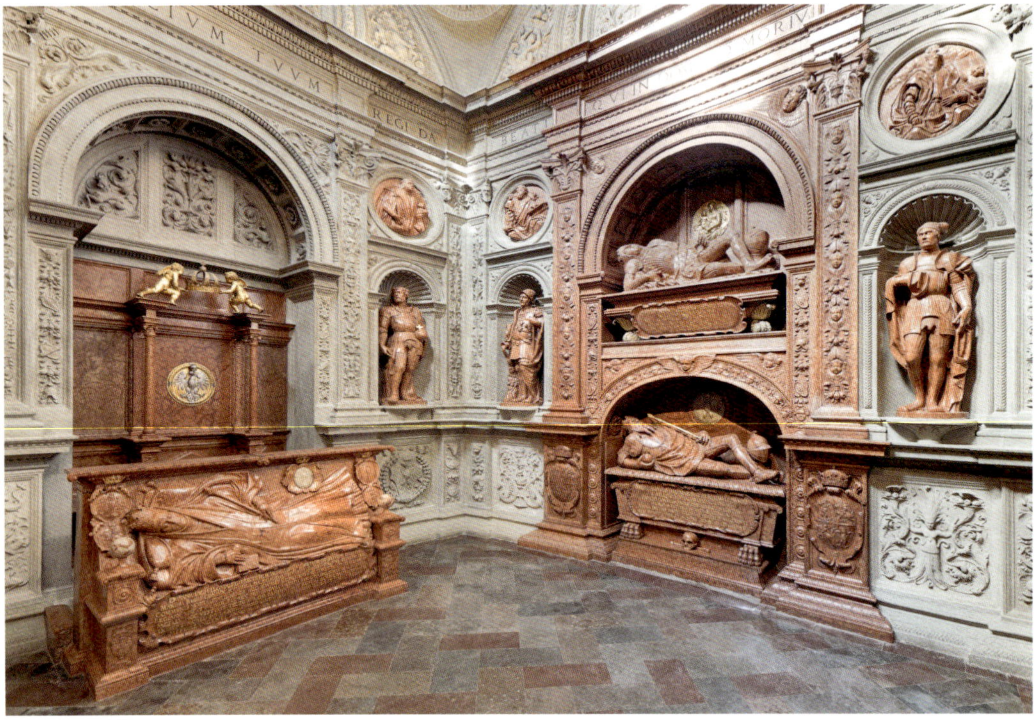

4.5 (LEFT)
Modern photograph of
Sigismund's Chapel
Wawel Cathedral on Wawel Hill

4.6 (OPPOSITE)
Leon Wyczółkowski
Saint Stanislaus's Shrine at Wawel Cathedral and *Saint Stanislaus's Reliquaries (for hand and head)*,
from *Wawel Treasury Cycle*, 1907
Pastel on paper laid on cardboard
101 cm × 150 cm; 72 cm × 58 cm
National Museum in Warsaw,
180838, 180847 MNW

death. Accounts of a miracle – the bishop's dismembered body growing back together – assiduously promoted by the Church and the nobility, were disseminated throughout Poland. Within just ten years of his death, Stanislaus's remains were buried at Wawel Cathedral. The analogous event in England, the conflict between King Henry II and the Archbishop of Canterbury Thomas à Becket leading to the latter's murder in the cathedral, only contributed to the growing cult of the Polish clergyman. Becket's canonisation in 1173 expedited the Polish episcopate's efforts to have Stanislaus canonised, which was accomplished in Assisi in 1253. The Polish saint's cult had gained momentum over the centuries. His grave had become a place of pilgrimage for Polish and neighbouring kings and peasants alike, all keen to pray at the foot of his silver sarcophagus-reliquary located in the centre of Wawel Cathedral – a site known as *Ara Patriae* (Altar of the Fatherland). Władysław the Elbow-High, credited for uniting the Polish state after two hundred years of fragmentation into independent princedoms, took the decision to hold his coronation in Kraków (in 1320), and not in the historic capital of Gniezno, based on a belief in the power of Stanislaus's saintly intercession. Coronations as well as burials of Polish kings had thenceforth taken place in Wawel Cathedral right up until the fall of the Polish-Lithuanian Commonwealth. Saint Stanislaus's shrine had become the site where rulers and triumphant military leaders paid their respects by hanging war trophies (such as from the battles of Grunwald in 1410 and Vienna in 1683), offered thanks for war victories and played for support at times of national hardship. Successive generations had viewed Saint Stanislaus as their indomitable defender against royal tyranny. The clergy exploited his cult in their own power struggle for the primacy of the church over the state. Saint Stanislaus's martyrdom was equally useful for the nobility and subsequently the gentry, in their endeavours to strengthen the status of their own social strata. Such attitudes led the country to anarchy, which in turn resulted in the fall of the Polish-Lithuanian Commonwealth in 1795. Following the loss of independence, the cult of Saint Stanislaus, whose dismembered body was miraculously reassembled, only intensified under the partitions, being perceived as a prophecy of the reunification of the country.

Rather than opposing Stanislaus himself, Wyspiański was taking a stance against the saint's cult, symbolised by

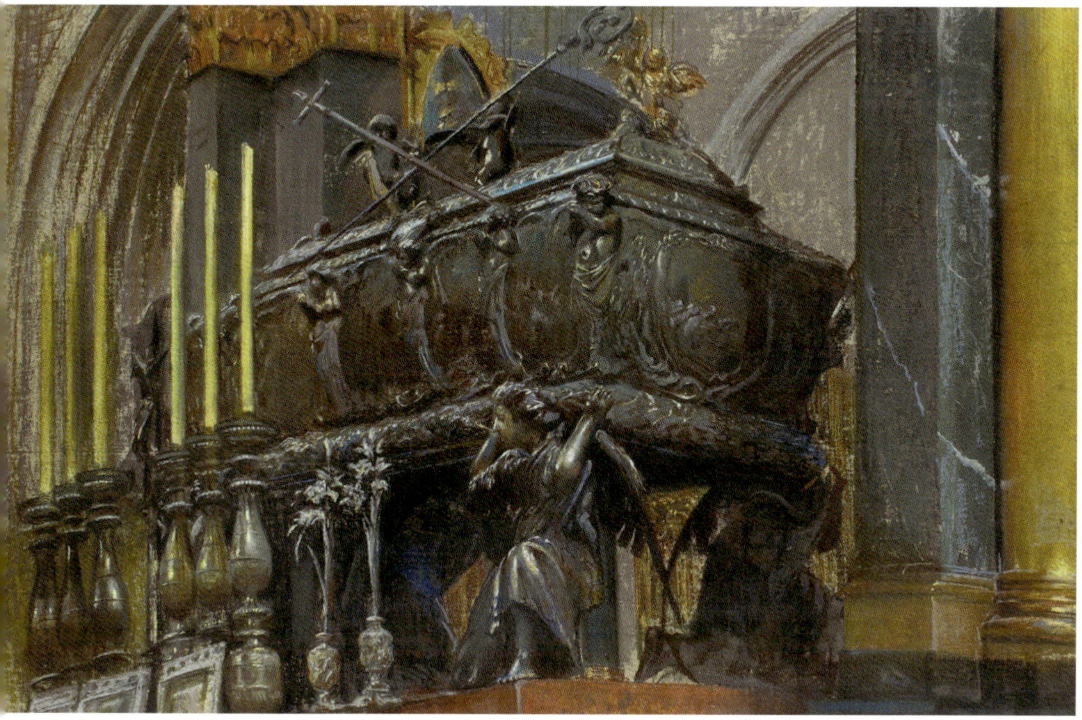

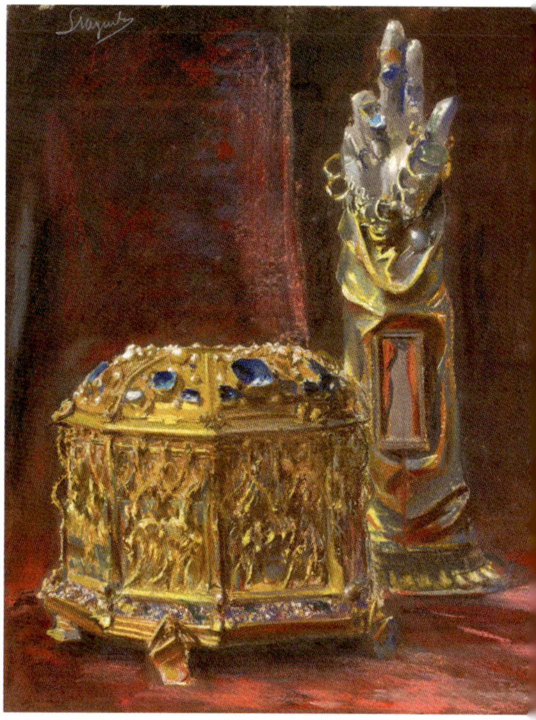

the silver coffin-reliquary (fig.4.6). The artist viewed the cult as a destructive force responsible for sending to sleep and de-energising the nation, which had fallen into a state of inertia whilst awaiting a miracle. Instead of trying to stand up to political subjugation, the nation's sole response to painful historical events had become limited to composing literary works, mainly in the genre of 19th-century messianic poetry. Wyspiański's stained-glass design (fig.4.3) depicted the phantom corpse of Saint Stanislaus, crushed by his silver coffin, frozen in eternity in the act of casting the curse (anathema) over the partitioned country. The inspirational deeds of national heroes from the remaining stained-glass windows were to help Polish society regain its nation-building instinct and agency. A strong leader capable of encouraging the nation to fight for freedom would emerge. The saint's cursing gesture, which Wyspiański modelled on the relic stored in the Cathedral's treasury, would turn into one of blessing. Only then would the curse cast upon the sovereign – the original reason for Poland's downfall – be lifted, and the trapped spirit of the saint released.

Wyspiański's designs were a reaction against the destructive and toxic cult of tombs, symbolised in his art by the historical monuments in the Cathedral, as well as by Wawel itself. Wyspiański felt that turning graves into national fetishes poisoned the souls of Poles, and took away the will to act. Living in the past anaesthetised the instinct for life and prevented progress. The present should become the nation's focus, reviewing one's own attitudes and undertaking action – leading to victorious battle to regain one's country. Apparitions of heroes presiding over their fellow countrymen from the Cathedral windows were role models intended to serve as motivators. The artist felt that society needed to be shaken very hard to awaken it from the state of lethargy, its 'slumber of servitude' (see Chapter 5). For this reason the Wawel Cathedral stained-glass designs were intended to shock with both their content and form.

Erudite and well versed on the historical iconography of the heroes he was depicting, Wyspiański made free use of them as models. His stained-glass designs feature references to Wawel Cathedral tombs and reliquaries, as well as well-known paintings and prints. Wyspiański utilised his own earlier experiences. His idea to fill each cathedral window with a monumental figure is likely to have originated from his encounter with a 16th-century painted mural scheme during the renovation of the Church of the Holy Cross in Kraków (in 1896–7). The wall paintings in question featured individual historical figures whose great size and iconic status held a fascination for the artist (and their scale was echoed in the Cathedral's stained-glass designs). Wyspiański shared his impressions of them: 'I am making copies of these giants and every day I bring them over to my place ... Paris is delicious, and one has to know it but ... here [Kraków] is seeing a Renaissance – a rebirth – and these rediscovered frescoes are to me the symbol of this Renaissance ... My room will explode ... They make up my whole world, vast, humanist.'[8]

The compositional devices employed by Wyspiański are key to the impact of the Wawel stained-glass designs. The narrow and tight framing of the figures drew attention to the message conveyed by each character. The artist achieved the impression of their incorporeality by means of blurring the contour lines of each silhouette, using lines and fields of colour far removed from the concretion of form. The figures seem to be rising upwards, a suggestion strengthened by the fact they are shown at an angle. Apart from the figure of Saint Stanislaus, whose posture is largely determined by the importance of the coffin and the cursing-cum-blessing gesture, all the other figures are also shown slightly leaning backwards, resulting in foreshortening, which strengthens the impression of being viewed from below. Their raised heads indicate the direction of movement, and Wyspiański's indeterminate treatment of their lower parts means that they do not seem to be 'anchored' to the ground. The figures in the windows were to give an impression of being lifted off the ground by the prayers of the congregation, as if emerging from the smoke of burning candles depicted in the stained-glass scenes within the lower panels directly beneath.

The artist presented his large-scale cartoons at exhibitions in Kraków, Vienna and Warsaw, where they attracted universal attention. Arousing a wide array of emotions, from objection to enthusiasm, they shocked and fascinated in equal measure. Their detractors criticised the lack of sacral references, their strange, incomprehensible content and their excessively expressive forms, while their advocates took delight in their creator's genius and rewarded him. During the period when Wyspiański was battling to be allowed to decorate the Cathedral, his artistic standing changed considerably. The play *The Wedding* had brought him unprecedented fame and the status of the fourth national bard – but the church authorities stuck by their refusal to engage Wyspiański. The aforementioned protest of the intelligentsia against introducing foreign makers' designs into the Cathedral had resulted in the cancellation of the German commissions and the removal of an existing window, but in spite of this, Wyspiański did not get the commission. His proposed interpretation of the national past proved to be too controversial, even blasphemous in the case of the Saint Stanislaus, threatening the interests of the Church, which rendered it impossible to accept.

Wyspiański's *Self-Portrait* of 1902 (fig.4.0) comprises the artist's personal commentary on his endeavours to be afforded the opportunity to decorate Wawel Cathedral. The artist painted his own likeness only rarely, and usually at important moments of his life; but only this once did he stylise his image – idealising his appearance, using a leaf motif in the background and personally designing the frame. The significance of this image as a rare and stylised self-portrait is therefore the key to understanding the thoughts of the artist. The frame attracts attention through its massiveness

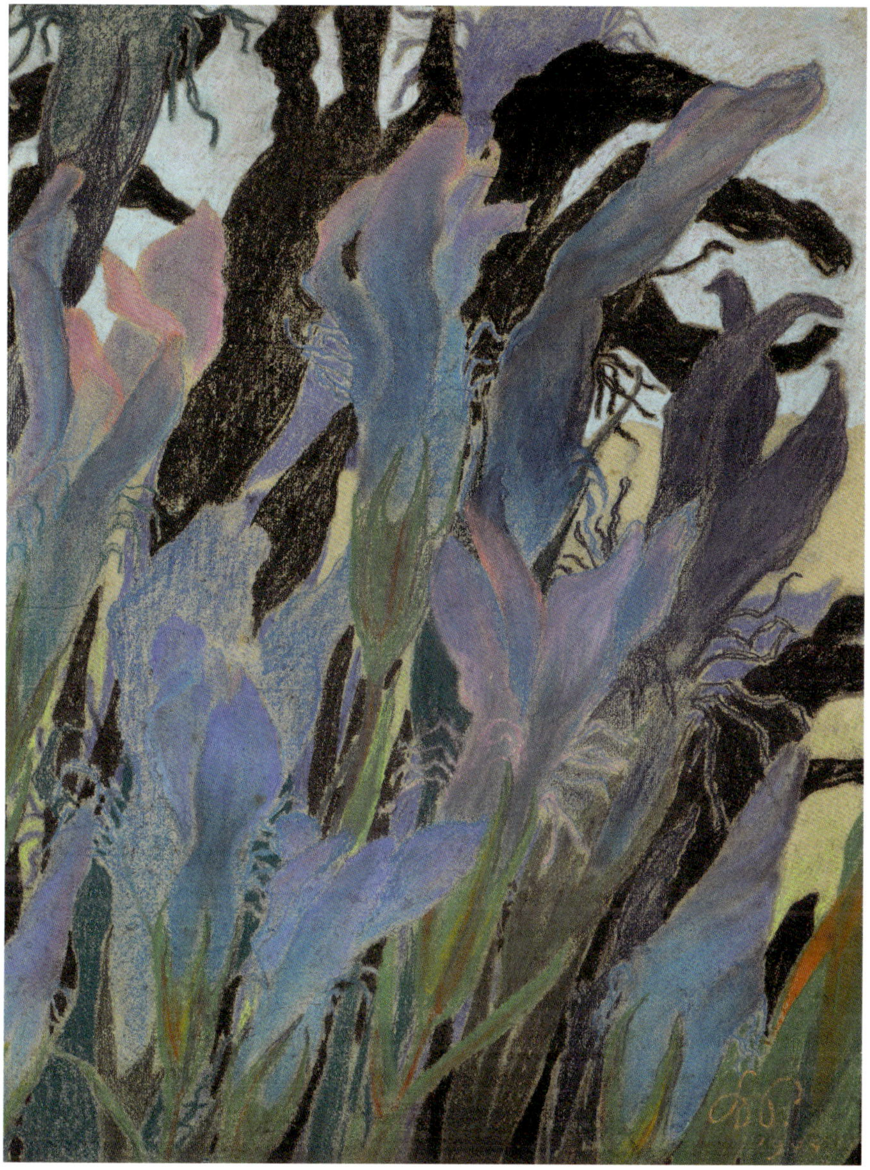

4.7
Stanisław Wyspiański
Flowers (Irises), 1904
Pastel on paper laid on cardboard
60.9 × 47 cm
National Museum in Warsaw,
Rys.Pol.7664 MNW

in comparison with the portrait itself. It is square with a frame filled with carved decoration, whose meticulous, masterly execution evokes the old handicraft traditions. Wyspiański based it on Renaissance picture frames and on the arabesque–grotesque ornamentation of the sculpted pilasters at Sigismund's Chapel (fig.4.5) – the royal chapel at Wawel Cathedral – borrowing the latter's motif of entwined floral tendrils: the mode of their arrangement, as well as the style of leaves and flowers.[9] The self-portrait therefore makes reference to the burial-place of the most powerful dynasty in Poland's history, the Jagiellons – the creators of 16th-century Wawel. Accordingly, the artist himself has to be viewed through the lens of this royal residence. By projecting his image from within a Renaissance-style frame, whose decoration directly references the Cathedral, in all probability he was going beyond indicating its thematic context: he was also presenting himself as an artist aware of his own potential, capable of bringing about the rebirth of Polish art. Details of his dress highlight his regard and

4.8
Model based on Stanisław Wyspiański and Władysław Ekielski's 'Acropolis' design for the renovation and expansion of Wawel, 1907
Model made by Jacek Czubiński and Jerzy Porębski, 1981
National Museum in Kraków, MNK IV-PN-1307

consideration for all social strata – for the peasants, expressed by his rustic sheepskin coat, and for the workmen through his shirt with a stand-up collar. Wyspiański's countenance is serious, his look direct and penetrating, and the black collar of his sheepskin coat covers his shoulders like a pall, a symbol of sorrow and mourning. Using the patterns of canes and shoots in the background as well as the distribution of light and shade falling on his face, the artist created a semblance of scenery – he stands at the threshold of an arbour covered in vines, with the drooping vine leaves evoking melancholy. His left cheek reflects the sunrays that are also showing in the pupil of his eye, while the left cheek takes on the blue of the sky visible in the background.

Ever since his youth, plants had occupied an important role in Wyspiański's life and work. Flowers grown commercially in greenhouses and meticulously arranged by professional florists held no interest for him. Instead Wyspiański took delight in plants from country gardens, meadows and fields, common herbs and weeds. He was moved by their unostentatious character, simplicity and subtle charm. It was Wyspiański's mother who instilled a love of wayside flowers in him when he was a boy, as she used to decorate his father's sculpture studio with blooms she had picked in meadows around Kraków. He would decorate his own studios in the same way throughout his adult life. He was the first Polish artist to make flowers an important theme in his art (see Chapters 2 and 3). In both his art and poetry Wyspiański treated plants as living beings. He endowed them with a soul, and ascribed emotions to them – they rejoiced or felt sadness, suffering along with humanity, just like the irises in the pastel drawing produced whilst the artist was seriously ill (fig.4.7). Here the irises' appearance is deformed by the shadows of imminent death. The ivy, which accompanies the artist in his self-portrait, is an emotional expression of his feeling of disappointment. A poem written in his youth, *Jak pomnę . . .* (*When I remember . . .*, 1888/9), evoked suffering in a similar manner, then in reference to a weeping woman:

> she stood on a step leading to the shade
> of a large arbour . . .
> held by greenery
> as if in a frame
> . . .
> that's how I saw her then – sad.
> A coiled vine bent over her, as if crying
> in sympathy with her sorrow, trying
> to wipe a tear from her eye from above
> . . .
> an odd thing – just where her tear
> dewed the page, I read: 'disappointed love'.[10]

Wyspiański was not destined to participate in the decoration of the Cathedral, but his love for Wawel faithfully endured for the rest of his life. He spoke of it in his poetry, and set the action of his successive plays on the royal hill – *Liberation* (*Wyzwolenie*, 1903), *Bolesław the Bold* (1903), *Legend II* (*Legenda II*, 1904) and *Acropolis* (1904). Acropolis was also the name given to his project aimed at the revitalisation of Wawel Hill.[11] In July 1903 the Galician State Department signed an agreement with the Austrian government regarding the departure of troops occupying the Royal Castle (the first group of soldiers left a year later and the last ones in 1911). In collaboration with the Kraków-based architect Władysław

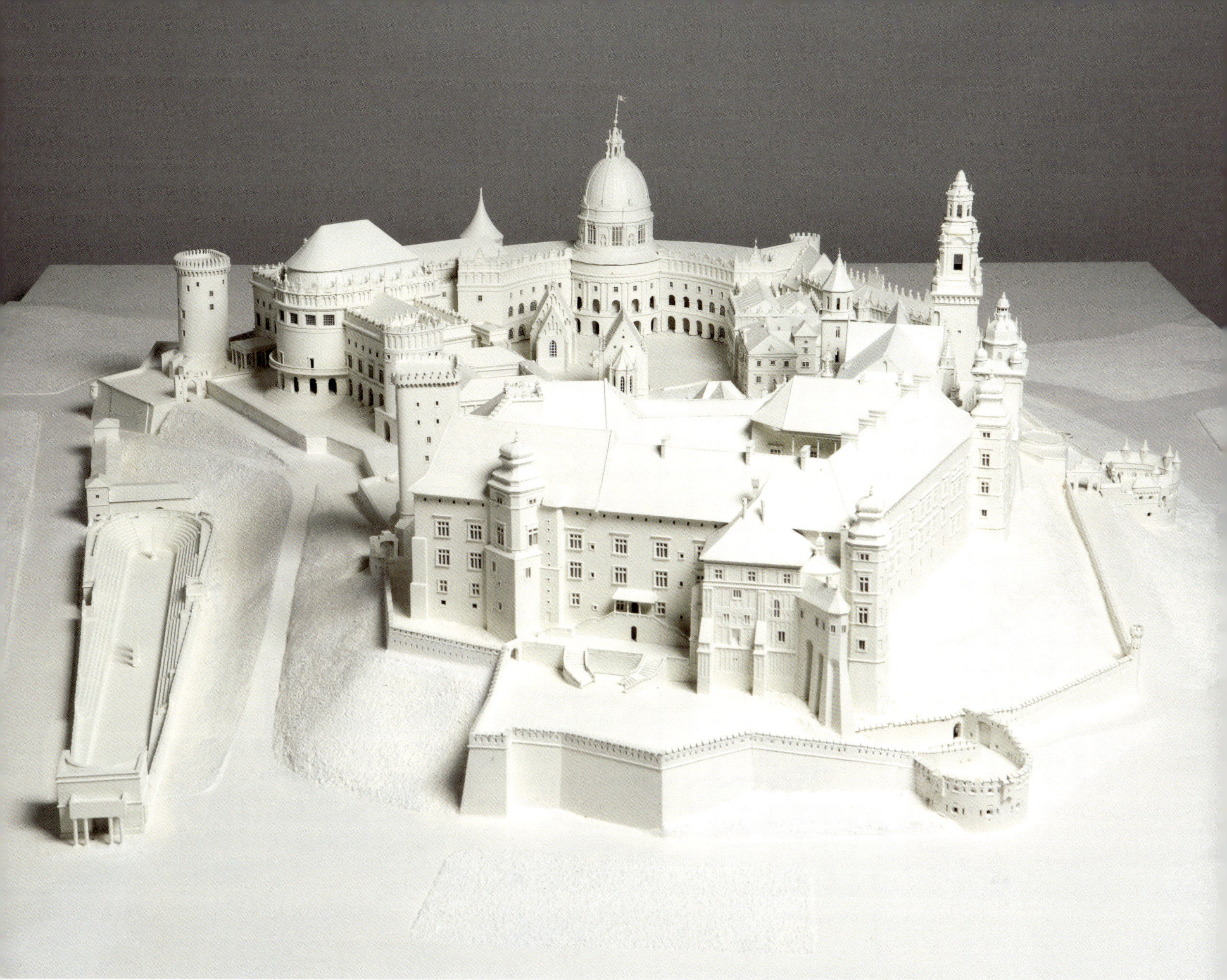

Ekielski, from autumn 1904 Wyspiański began to develop a grand scheme for converting the royal hill into the headquarters of the most important institutions envisaged for the reinstated country: including the Houses of Parliament (the Sejm and the Senate), the Academy of Learning, the National Museum, theatres and a stadium, etc. (fig.4.8).[12] The historical buildings including the Royal Castle, the Cathedral and the fortifications, were to remain intact. Wawel was to become the focal point and hub of the life of the nation, an expression of its culture in terms of state and academia. Ekielski admired Wyspiański. The architect ended his account of their collaboration, written after Wyspiański's death, with the following words: 'Perhaps someday similar buildings will stand on our MOST PRECIOUS SITE, on our POLISH ACROPOLIS, which remembers our beginnings, our Kings, our Victories, our Defeats and our Hopes, and which – God willing – will be witness to our BETTER FUTURE.'[13] Wyspiański's Acropolis project was not destined to be realised either.

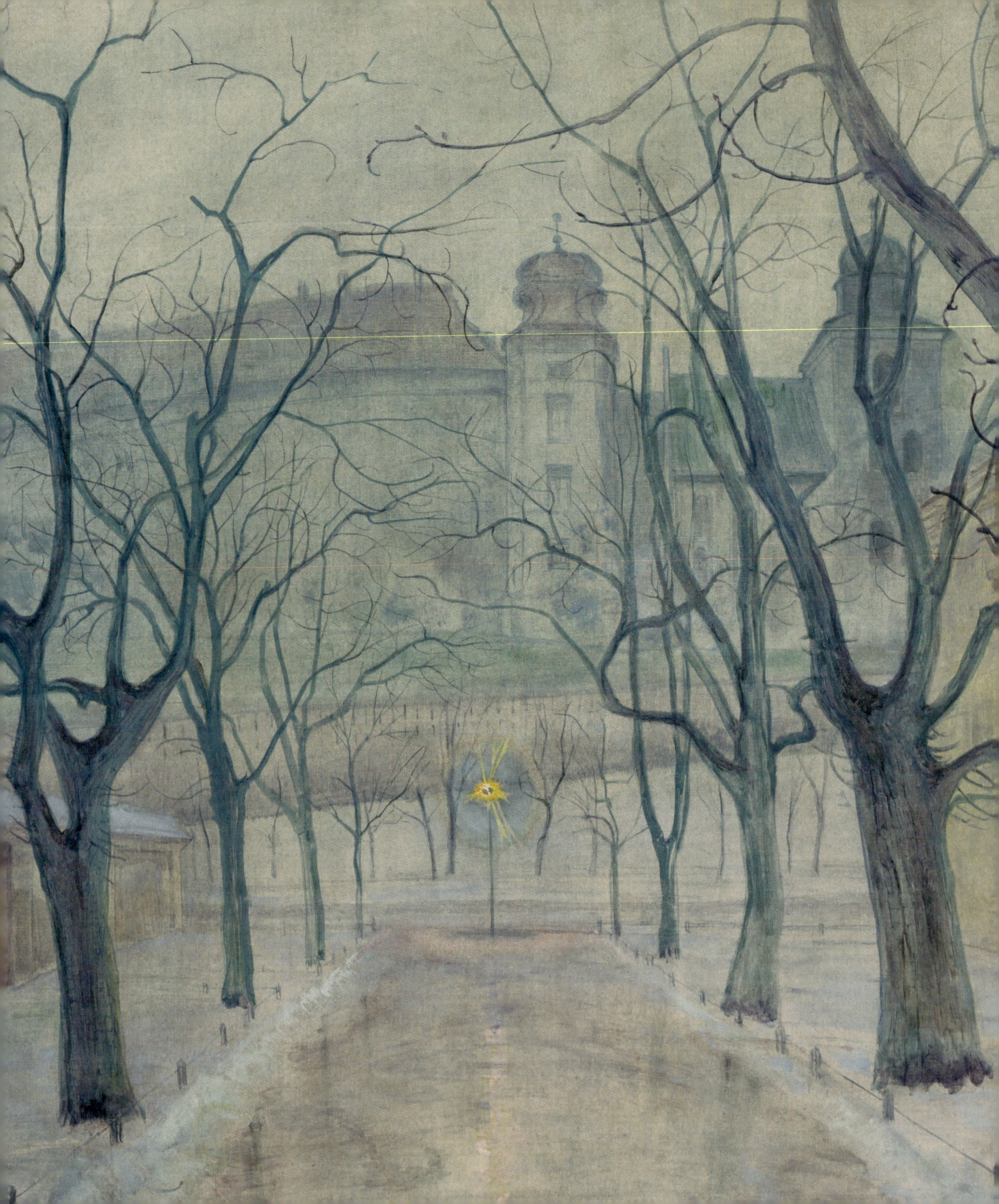

5

Wyspiański's *Chochoły*: A Meditation on the 'Straw Man' Generation

Anna Rudzińska

Directly after returning from Paris in 1894, Wyspiański produced several works featuring Wawel Castle in the background.[1] The pastel that the artist entitled *Pałuby na plantach tańczące* (*Straw Men Dancing in the Planty*, 1897–9; fig.5.1) – known today as *Chochoły* – was the first work in which Wyspiański expressed issues of the most profound importance for his generation by means of multifaceted symbols encoded in an apparently neutral landscape.[2]

The muted, minor-key tonality of this nocturne, in which greys, blacks and browns predominate, evokes a mood of disquiet and the impression of frozen time. Wyspiański's night is the time of apparitions. In this view of the Planty Park, Wawel Castle, the historic seat of Polish kings, by then occupied by Austrian troops, looms above the leafless treetops. Among the trees, on ground flooded with water, there is a circle of *chochoły* – rosebushes wrapped in straw to insulate them from the cold. The definition of the straw bundles becomes indistinct in the twilight, lit only by the faint glow of streetlamps, leaving one to wonder if the circle is made up of straw men, dummies, or of people frozen in sleep. The shadow cast by the most brightly illuminated *chochoł* dispels any doubt: it is the silhouette of a human figure.

The picture is a visual meditation on the political situation and spiritual state of Polish society at the end of the 19th century. Wyspiański synthesised his current creative inspirations, his professional and social experiences – as Artistic Director of the weekly periodical *Życie*, and as a member and insightful portraitist of the intelligentsia, whose gatherings he frequented. Since at least 1892 the messianic poem *Przedświt* (*The Moment Before Dawn*) by Zygmunt Krasiński (1812–1859) had become a source of inspiration for Wyspiański. Furthermore, since 1898 he had worked on the theme of the cyclical renewal of life, with reference to the myth of Demeter and Persephone (a subject he would soon utilise in his 1904 play *Noc listopadowa* (*November Night*)). He was also working on his decorations for Wawel Cathedral. The artist complemented his famous design for the stained-glass window showing King Casimir the Great with a verse

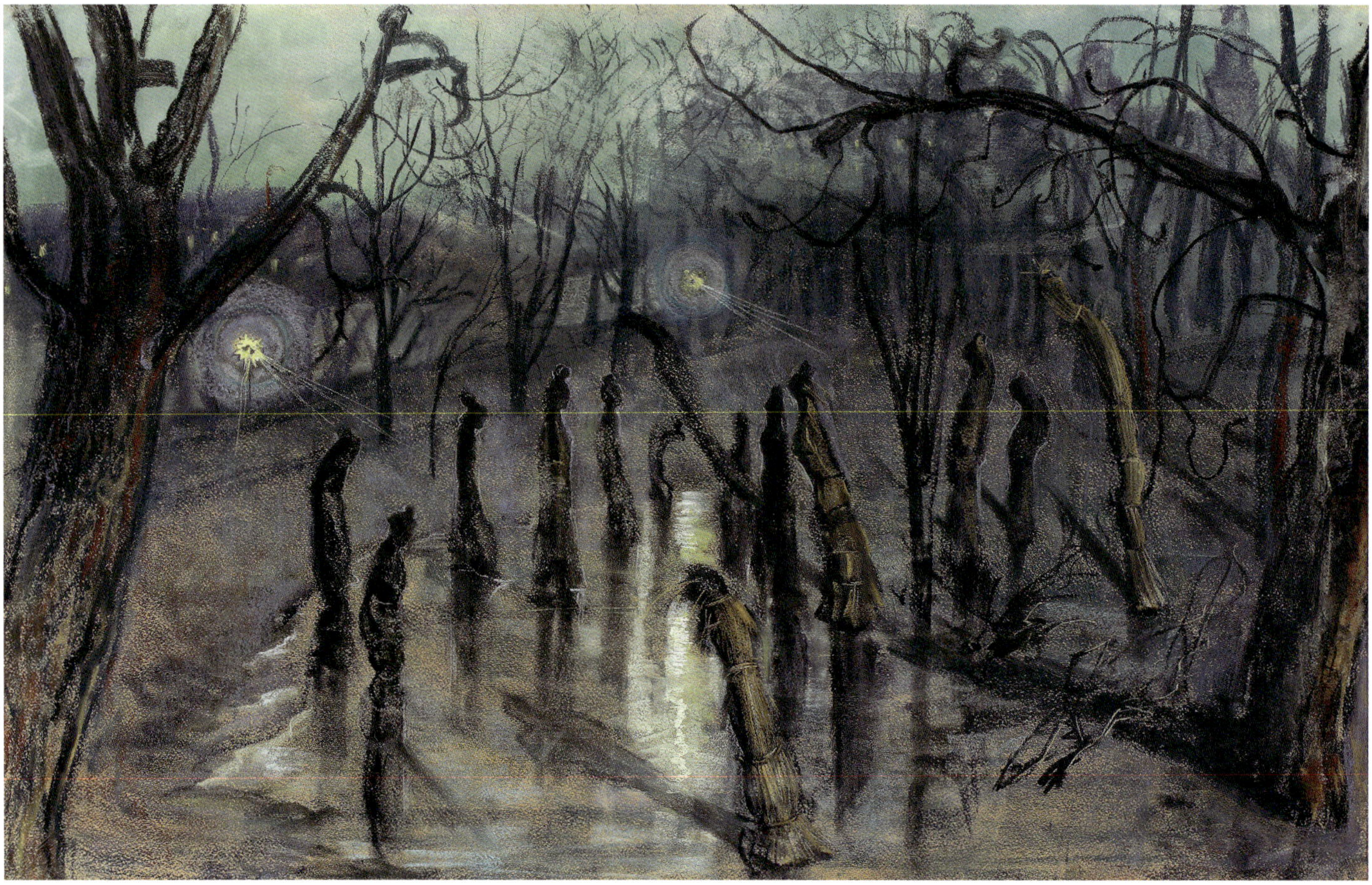

rhapsody, in which he expounded his visual concept in poetic language. The rhapsody includes verses describing the morale of contemporary Poles, also conveyed in the pastel by means of the *chochoły* motif.[3]

The turn-of-the-century generation had fallen into a state of lethargy. No wonder Wyspiański identified them with the figure of the *pałuba* (straw man) – a term used to describe dummies which imitated the shape of a live figure, and, by analogy, also meaning a person of only nominal importance, a figurehead, who merely keeps up an appearance of addressing serious issues. Left exhausted by futile attempts to regain national independence, and conscious of the irrecoverable destruction of many generations' legacy, the turn-of-the-century generation is portrayed as one of silent complainants, ashamed of their own weakness. Resigned to dozy apathy, they concern themselves solely with prosaic and insignificant matters. Such low spirits impeded the chance to regain sovereignty of an independent state, which is symbolised in the picture by Wawel Castle. The royal hill is simultaneously the metaphor for the burden placed upon the shoulders of this generation by its sense of patriotic duty, which has anchored contemporaries to the martydom of the past, preventing them from moving forward. In the pastel, the silhouette of the Castle, barely visible in the distance, is brutally slashed through by the trunk of a tree towering above a group of slumbering *pałuby-chochoły*. The *chochoł*, like a spectre casting the spell of non-agency upon whatever it conceals, kept Polish society lethargically asleep – such an interpretation was subsequently popularised in Wyspiański's play *The Wedding* (1901). On the other hand, the *chochoł* also symbolises protection of life, safeguarding what is most precious in the anticipatory lead-up to the reawakening of nature. Just as plants have a chance of surviving thanks to their protective covers, so society is also capable of rebirth.

5.0 (p.86)
Detail of fig.17.2
Stanisław Wyspiański
Morning at the Foot of Wawel Hill, 1894
Oil on canvas
100 × 201 cm
National Museum in Kraków
MNK ND-7791

5.1 (OPPOSITE)
Stanisław Wyspiański
Chochoły (Straw-Protected Bushes), 1897–9
Pastel on paper laid on board
69 × 107 cm
National Museum in Warsaw, inv.no.75564
MNW (donated by Franciszek and Józefa Krzyształowicz, 1932)

5.2 (BELOW)
Modern photograph of *Chochoł* in front of the Rydlówka Manor House
Museum of Kraków

But it needed a powerful impetus to awaken it from the slumber of disheartenment, inspiring it to realise the overarching objective of regaining freedom. Wyspiański regarded the theatre as the best medium for deep reflection, and for providing the impact capable of getting through to the most sensitive Polish sensibility.

The composition of the picture corresponds to a theatrical stage: trees placed in the wings give the illusion of a performance; the actors play their roles in the centre of the stage; and footlights indicate the chief protagonist, who is key to the understanding of the message – the *chochoł* in the foreground, with his shadow. The background for this pictorial spectacle is a contemporary, mundane view along the Planty avenue, which would become the opening scene for Wyspiański's play *Liberation* (1903), and Wawel Hill with its rich store of historical associations. Wyspiański was a total artist, responsible for every aspect of his works – their concept, form, realisation. His notion of devoting the theatre – a temple of art – to the service of the most fundamental and serious matters, opening it out to debates on the current condition of the state and the nation, dominated the 20th century, and remains vital today. Looking at this pastel, viewers may have the impression that they are witnessing the birth of Wyspiański's dramaturgy in its most mature form.

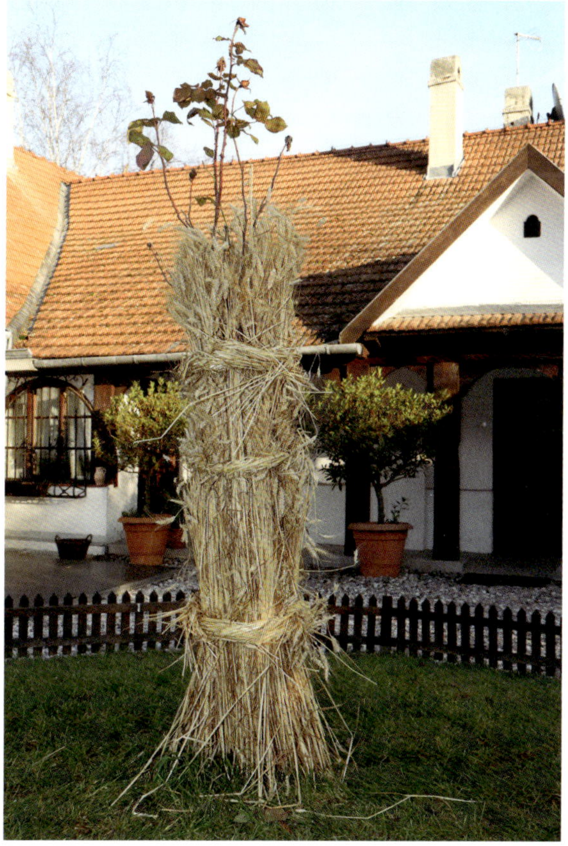

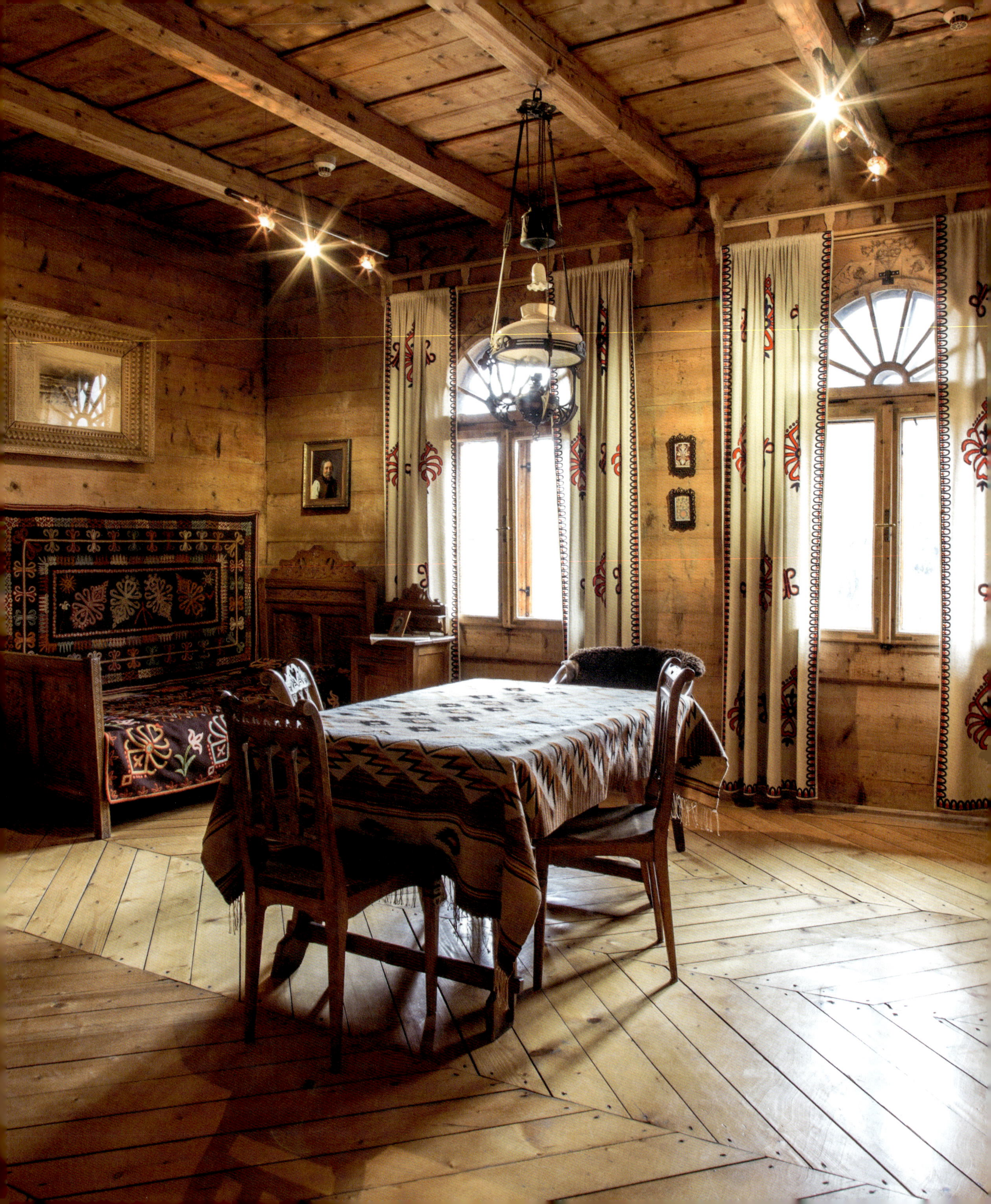

6

The Zakopane Style of Stanisław Witkiewicz

Zbigniew Moździerz in collaboration with Anna Wende-Surmiak

This chapter discusses the origin and development of the Zakopane Style in the wider context of the formative influences of its polymath founder, Stanisław Witkiewicz.[1] It also examines the making of Witkiewicz's most iconic building, the House Under the Firs, and the designer's attempts to promote the Zakopane Style abroad.

The Zakopane Style was the first Polish national style which went beyond theoretical discussions and concepts. In addition to becoming adopted in the eponymous village of Zakopane and the wider Podhale region of the Tatras, it also spread to many places across the partitioned Polish lands.

A renowned Young Poland art critic, painter, illustrator and design reformer, Witkiewicz only ever realised 13 Zakopane Style building designs – ten in Zakopane itself and three elsewhere.[2] However, his influential vision inspired a national design movement which gained a following amongst local Podhale vernacular makers as well as professional architects from many other localities. Witkiewicz had a holistic philosophy, declaring: 'a style is a certain intrinsic character of form; wherever and whenever a style has ever existed, it has always extended to everything that can be the artistic expression of a particular time and people: everything from a pin to a cannon'.[3] Accordingly, the Zakopane Style extended to residential, civic and church architecture and interior decoration as well as the applied arts, including fashion. Diverse in terms of function and location, realisations included manor houses and villas, an apartment building in Warsaw and even a narrow-gauge railway station in Syłgudyszki in Lithuania. The style spanned three decades from about 1892 to 1922. The first ever Zakopane Style building was Witkiewicz's Willa Koliba (meaning shepherd's shelter) (1892–3) whilst his last realisation, which he did not live to see, was the Tatra Museum in Zakopane (1913–22, co-designed with Franciszek Mączyński (1874–1947)).[4] Conceived at the time when Poland did not exist on the map of Europe, Zakopane Style designs served as carriers of patriotic meanings.

The idea of creating a Polish national style based on the vernacular architecture and craft traditions of the Podhale Highlanders, the indigenous population of the northern Tatras,

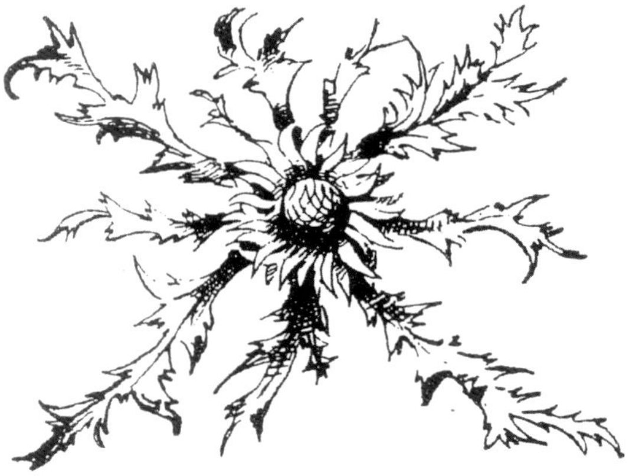

6.0 (p.90)
Zygmunt Gnatowski's room in Willa Koliba
Tatra Museum, Willa Koliba

6.1 (LEFT)
Stanisław Witkiewicz
Drawing of stemless carline thistle (*Carlina acaulis*) – a decorative motif used in Zakopane Style, 1890

6.2 (OPPOSITE)
Willa Koliba, designed by Stanisław Witkiewicz, 1891–3, with west extension wing designed by Tadeusz Prauss, 1901: view from the south-east
Tatra Museum, Willa Koliba

arose as a result of Witkiewicz's first visit to Zakopane when suffering from tuberculosis in the winter of 1886. Located at the northern foothills of the Tatras (the highest mountain range in Central Europe, part of the Carpathians), Zakopane was at that time becoming established as a health resort for the treatment of respiratory diseases thanks to the efforts of Dr Tytus Chałubiński (1820–1889).[5] Situated in Galicia (the Austrian partition), Zakopane enjoyed relative political freedom. Poles from all three partitions visited the village, usually between June and September, hence its being known informally as 'Poland's summer capital'. It was during this first visit that Witkiewicz was drawn to the Podhale vernacular wooden architecture, and specifically to the Highlander hut.

Witkiewicz's patriotic unbringing and exposure to many facets of vernacular architecture stood him in good stead to conceive the first Polish national style. Born into a landed gentry family on 21 May 1851 under the Russian partition, he lived in the family's manor house in the village of Poszawsze in Samogitia (present-day Lithuania) until the age of 12. He grew up in close proximity to country folk and the Samogitian vernacular wooden architecture with its unique ornamentation and furnishings. One distinctive element of the region was the roadside shrine in the form of a cross (*smutkalis*). This exerted such great influence on the artist that it was his last wish to have one on his grave.

Following the Poles' unsuccessful uprising against Russia in 1863–4, Witkiewicz's parents, Ignacy and Elwira, were exiled to the Tomsk province of Western Siberia, accompanied by their children, including the 13-year-old Stanisław.[6]

Witkiewicz would remain in that place of exile for five years, and it was here that he was once again exposed to highly ornamental and distinctive vernacular wooden architecture. Following his return from Siberia in 1869, Witkiewicz undertook painting studies at the Academy of Fine Arts in St Petersburg. He quite probably came under the influence of the outstanding art critic Vladimir Stasov (1824–1906), generally known among the Academy's students. Stasov was the leading proponent of the Russian vernacular revival – a Russian national style realised in wooden architecture which developed throughout the 1860s and 1870s. The two main architects associated with the Russian Style, Viktor Hartmann and Ivan Pavlovich Ropet, both trained at the Academy of Fine Arts in St Petersburg, the latter at the same time as Witkiewicz. It is likely that Witkiewicz would have attended the All-Russia Industrial Exhibition in St Petersburg in 1870, which was the first display of Russian vernacular handicraft. The exhibition pavilions in the Russian Style were designed by Hartmann.

At the beginning of the 1870s Witkiewicz visited Western Europe, including undertaking a short stint of painting studies in Munich. He was an acute observer, particularly interested in questions concerning the relationship between art and tradition, and his experience abroad served as a further catalyst for the development of his ideas, which would prove useful for his conception of the Zakopane Style. It is notable that between 1890 and 1898 Witkiewicz would specifically refer to Russian and German models, and did not mention anything about the vernacular revival in England, originated by John Ruskin and William Morris. This is because he had first-hand knowledge of the contemporary art and design scenes in Russia and Germany, whereas he remained unaware of the British Arts and Crafts Movement until 1898 (see Chapter 1). Even so, as Andrzej Szczerski convincingly argues, 'Witkiewicz's

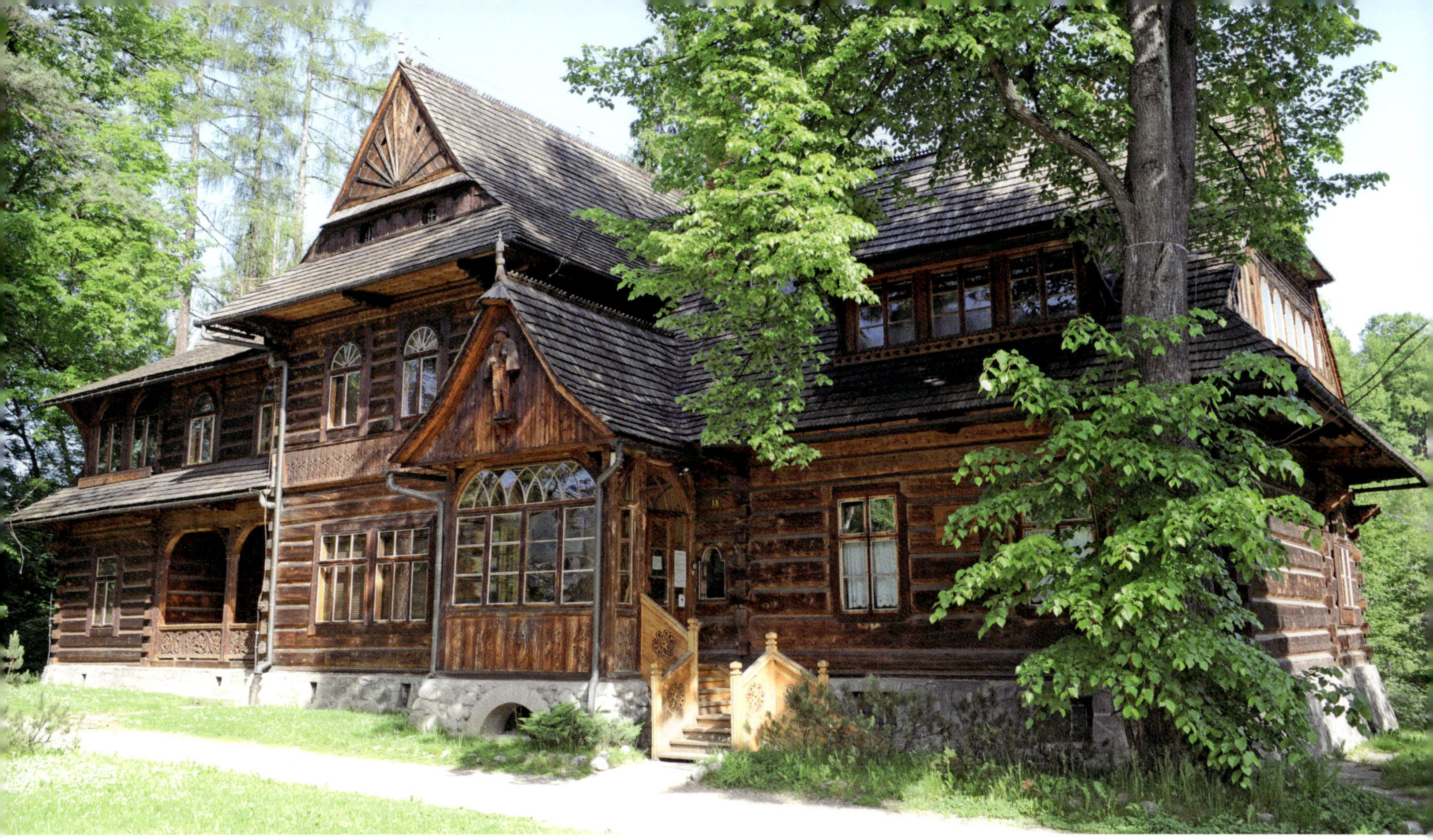

imagination was formed and shaped by examples of how British art and design were received in Germany and in Russia'.[7] In the light of this, the emergence of the Zakopane Style was a reflection of the spirit of the age.

It is worth noting that the earliest attempts to incorporate Podhale vernacular inspirations into contemporary applied arts had predated Witkiewicz's first visit to Zakopane by a year.[8] In 1885 Countess Róża Krasińska (née Potocka) (1849–1937) had commissioned the Wood Industry Vocational School (Szkoła Fachowa Przemysłu Drzewnego) in Zakopane to produce a bed, a chair and a screen decorated with traditional Podhale ornamental motifs. These were designed by Magdalena Butowt-Andrzejkowiczówna, with adjustments made by Franciszek Neužil (1845–1899), the School's first director. It was also Neužil who first used Podhale ornamentation in architecture as the designer of the 'Under the Mother of God' Villa (Willa Pod Matką Boską) in 1886. In subsequent years, following publication of several pieces of writing by Witkiewicz – the report 'Tatry w śniegu' ('The Tatras in the Snow', 1886),[9] 'Styl zakopiański' ('The Zakopane Style', 1891),[10] but most of all the influential volume of essays *Na przełęczy* (*On the Mountain Pass*, 1891)[11] – some newly erected Swiss-chalet-style villas in Zakopane began to feature decorative borrowings from Podhale architecture. The first ideological attempt to systematically embrace all elements of Podhale vernacular architecture, from form through ornamentation to the original construction methods, was the design by the Warsaw architect Józef Pius Dziekoński (1844–1927) for the wooden headquarters of the Tatra Museum in Zakopane (1892), named after Dr Chałubiński.[12] It was, however, an unsuccessful attempt at the Zakopane Style in design terms, not least because it displayed only modest references to vernacular stylistic features, mainly in the form of pegged doorframes.

It was probably professional architects' unsatisfactory attempts to utilise Podhale vernacular architecture that prompted Witkiewicz to design the first Zakopane Style building, Willa Koliba, for Zygmunt Gnatowski in 1891 (fig.6.2). Gnatowski came from a Ukrainian landed gentry

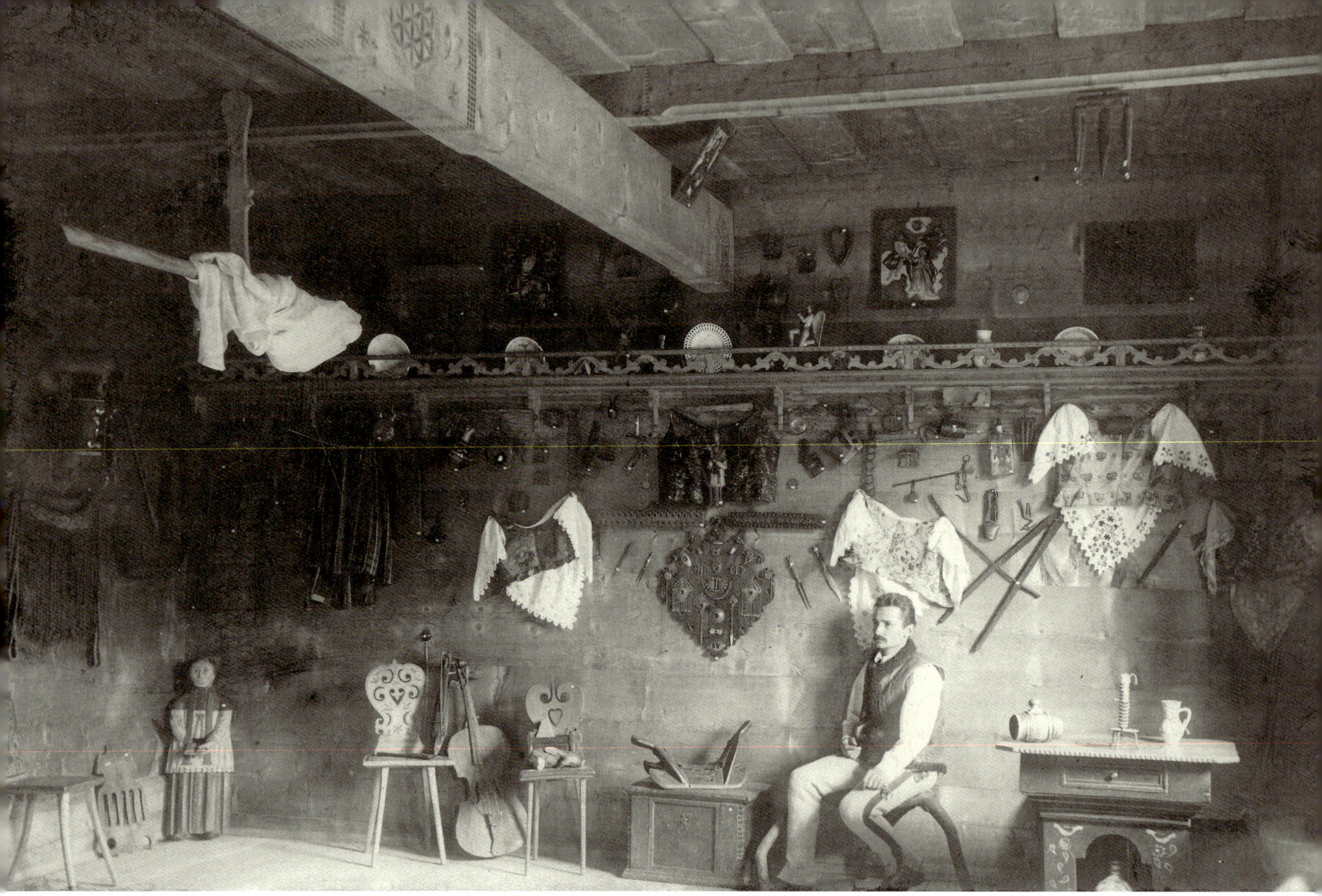

family and was a philanthropist and champion of the Zakopane Style. Willa Koliba's construction in 1892–3 was in keeping with the current of European National Romanticism, which had been present in the arts for almost half a century. Begun in late spring, the building work progressed slowly. The careful selection of timber and the precision in its treatment were indicative of the fact that an architectural masterpiece was in the making rather than an ordinary summer villa. The work was supervised by the only licensed master carpenter-builder from Zakopane, Maciej Gąsienica Józkowy, under the watchful eyes of Gnatowski, Witkiewicz and Władysław Matlakowski (1850–1895). Matlakowski was a doctor, who undertook systematic research and documentation of the ornamentation and construction methods of the Podhale region. His two richly illustrated ethnographic volumes, *Budownictwo ludowe na Podhalu* (*Vernacular Building in Podhale*, 1892) and *Zdobienie i sprzęt ludu polskiego na Podhalu* (*Decorations and Household Objects of Polish Folk in Podhale*, 1901; see fig.2.9), would become a source for artists, including Wyspiański (see Chapter 2). The work on Willa Koliba was carried out by the team of Highlander builders including Jasiek Stachoń, Staszek Bobak and Klimek Bachleda, with Highlander master-craftsmen Józef Kaspruś Stoch (1869–1910) and Wojciech Brzega (1872–1941) undertaking woodcarving work on the principal rafters, doorframes, ceiling beams, etc. In later years Brzega would become a co-founder of the Podhale Arts Society and his furniture workshop in Ulica Kościeliska, one of Zakopane's main thoroughfares, would count Karol Kłosowski as a designer (see Chapter 8).

The architecture of Willa Koliba harmonised with the bespoke interior decoration scheme. The style of most of its

6.3
Dining room in Willa Koliba, with Zygmunt Gnatowski's Podhale Highlander ethnographic collection
Photograph by Antoni Święch, 1894
Tatra Museum, Willa Koliba

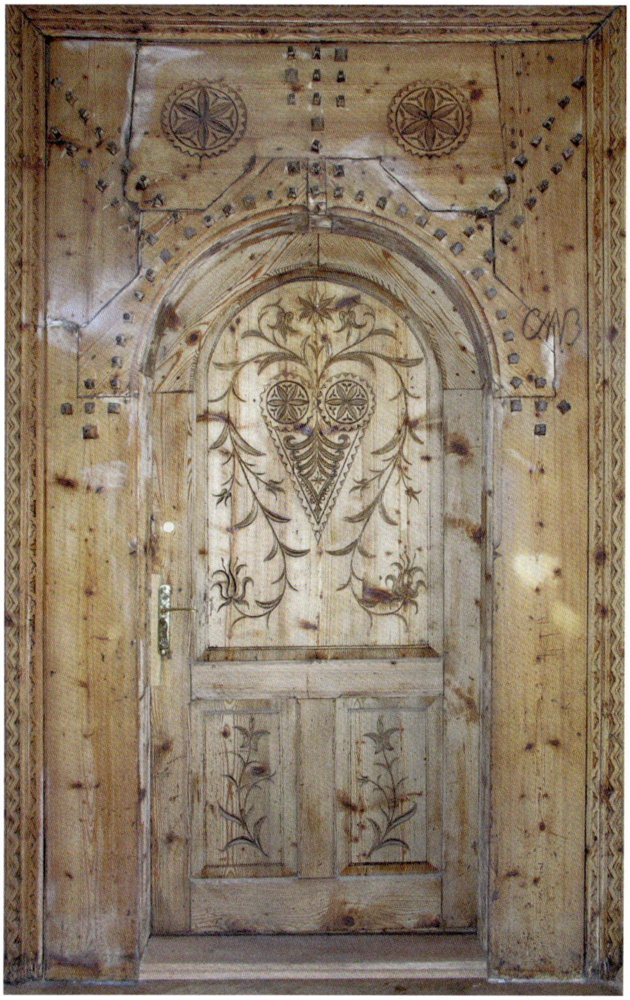

6.4
Door at Willa Oksza, 1896, designed by Stanisław Witkiewicz, displaying staple Zakopane Style ornamentation of *parzenica* and six-petal rosette (derived from Podhale folk culture), as well as a stylised lily motif introduced by Witkiewicz
Tatra Museum, Willa Oksza

contents referenced the furnishings and everyday objects of the Podhale region in terms of their shape, construction and ornamentation; this extended to furniture, tiled and stone stoves, curtain rails, curtains, picture frames, even door handles and escutcheons (figs 6.0 and 6.3). A few years later, in the second volume of his two-part work *Styl Zakopiański* (*The Zakopane Style*, 1904 and 1911), Witkiewicz would discuss the role that Willa Koliba was to play in Polish architecture:

> the chief aim . . . was to build a house which would once and for all dispel any reservations regarding the possibility of reconciling vernacular architecture with the requirements for more complex and refined standards of comfort and beauty, a house which could defy any criticisms and disarm any prejudices, which would prove that it is possible to have a house and a dwelling in the Zakopane Style and to be certain that the house will not collapse, and will provide a shelter from rainy weather, the wind and the cold, and to have all modern comforts, whilst being simultaneously surrounded with an atmosphere of beauty, not inferior to other styles, and in addition being distinctively Polish. The aim was to assimilate all the most distinctive and most crystallised elements of Highlander architecture, and to develop the others, currently in their infancy, to an extent appropriate for higher lifestyle requirements, but without losing their distinctive character.[13]

In keeping with the Podhale tradition, Zakopane Style wooden villas were constructed of spruce, obtained locally, whilst furniture was chiefly made of deciduous wood – oak and ash. The foundations of buildings were constructed primarily from granite boulders, less often from limestone. Podhale ornamentation was generally geometrical, with a limited range of stylised plant motifs (see fig.6.4). These included the hexagonal star (also known as a six-petal rosette), *leluja* (stylised lily), *słoneczko* (semicircular motif of the sun's rays) and *parzenica*, the latter being a heart-shaped motif that adorned Highlanders' embroidered trousers as well as woodcarvings. This folk ornamentation was augmented by motifs of mountain plants, including bracken, carline thistle (fig.6.1), edelweiss and twigs of stone pine.

Willa Koliba had been regarded as the masterpiece of the Zakopane Style until the construction of Witkiewicz's magnum opus, the House Under the Firs (Dom pod Jedlami), in 1897. In the meantime the style had found its first enthusiasts in and

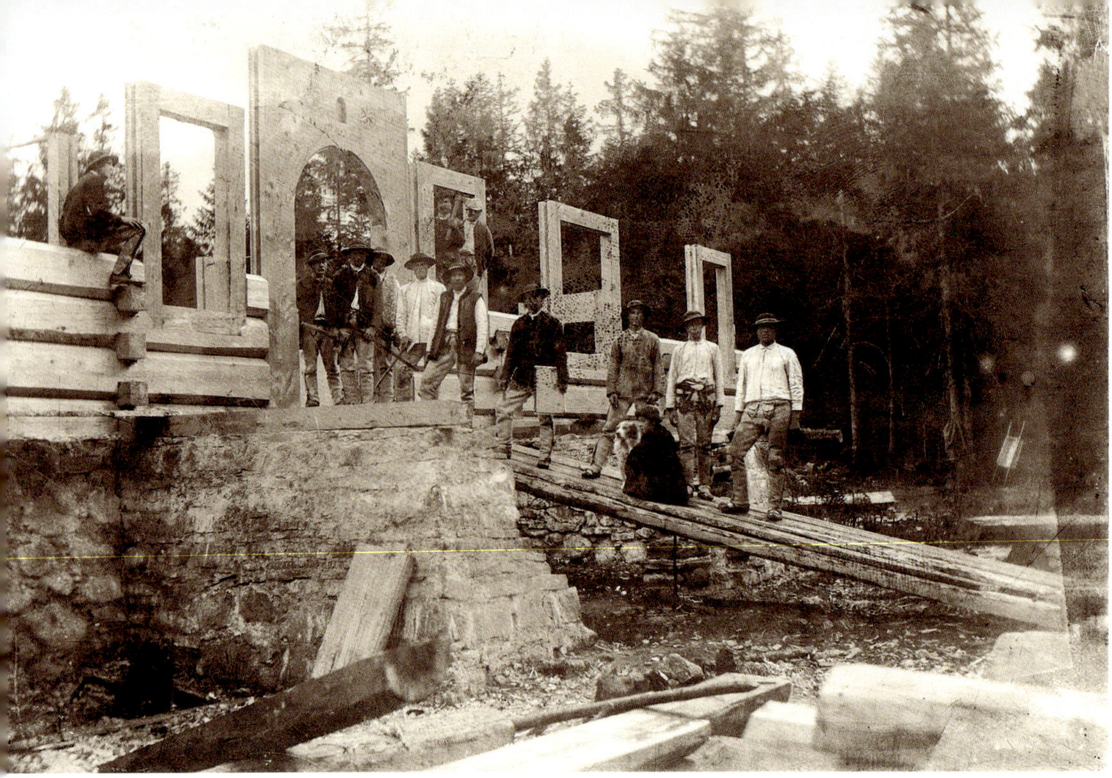

6.5 (LEFT)
Willa Oksza under construction – Highlander carpenter-builders and Stanisław Ignacy Witkiewicz with a dog
Photograph by Stanisław Witkiewicz, 1895
Tatra Museum

6.6 (OPPOSITE)
Chapel of St John the Baptist, in the Church of the Holy Family, Zakopane, designed by Stanisław Witkiewicz, 1895–1901

beyond Zakopane. For example, Witkiewicz designed Willa Pepita in Zakopane for Dr Bronisław Chrostowski (built in 1893), and a manor house for Count Mikołaj Rey, in Przyborów near Dębica (completed in 1894). The latter represented the first attempt at applying the Zakopane Style principles to a brick building. In 1895 Witkiewicz began planning the decorative scheme for the new parish church, the Church of the Holy Family in Ulica Krupówki in Zakopane, designed in a historicist style by Józef Pius Dziekoński. The realisation of his schemes for the Chapels of Our Lady of the Rosary and St John the Baptist in the latter church, the first use of the Zakopane Style in an ecclesiastical building, began a year later (fig.6.6).[14]

The year 1896 also saw the creation of further houses designed by Witkiewicz – Korwinówka (later renamed 'Willa Oksza') at Ulica Zamoyskiego for the Kossakowski family (fig.6.5), and 'Zofiówka' at Ulica Chałubińskiego for the Sas Doliński family. The Zakopane Style was simultaneously becoming of interest to a wider group of professional architects.

Witkiewicz designed what was to become the crowning achievement of the Zakopane Style, the House Under the Firs, for Jan Gwalbert Pawlikowski (1860–1939), an economist, publicist, lover of the Tatras, mountaineer, pioneer conservationist and future Chairman of the Podhale Arts Society (see Chapter 8).[15] His son, Jan Gwalbert Henryk Pawlikowski (1891–1962), writer and poet, was the second husband of the poet, playwright and painter Maria Pawlikowska-Jasnorzewska, and the couple lived in the house (see Chapter 10). The house had become a meeting place for major Polish and international cultural figures. The English painter Lawrence Alma-Tadema visited.

Witkiewicz, who had been actively involved in selecting a suitable plot of land for the villa, particularly favoured the Koziniec Hill, because of the tempting prospect of creating a design on a slope using a high exposed stone foundation creating a basement storey. This would create great impact, whilst offering scope for original design ideas. Construction commenced in the early autumn of 1896. Witkiewicz supervised every detail, working in tandem with the Highlander master carpenter-builder Wojciech Gąsienica Roj (1839–1924), who was also a blacksmith and a distinguished Tatra mountaineering guide. Six Highlander master carpenter-builders were in charge of the work, most notably Zapotoczny (first name unknown) and Jan Obrochta Bartuś (1850–1925).

After the rough stone basement storey was erected, construction of the wooden framework that comprised the main part of the building followed. The rafters were in place by 1 April 1897, and within two weeks, by Easter, the roof

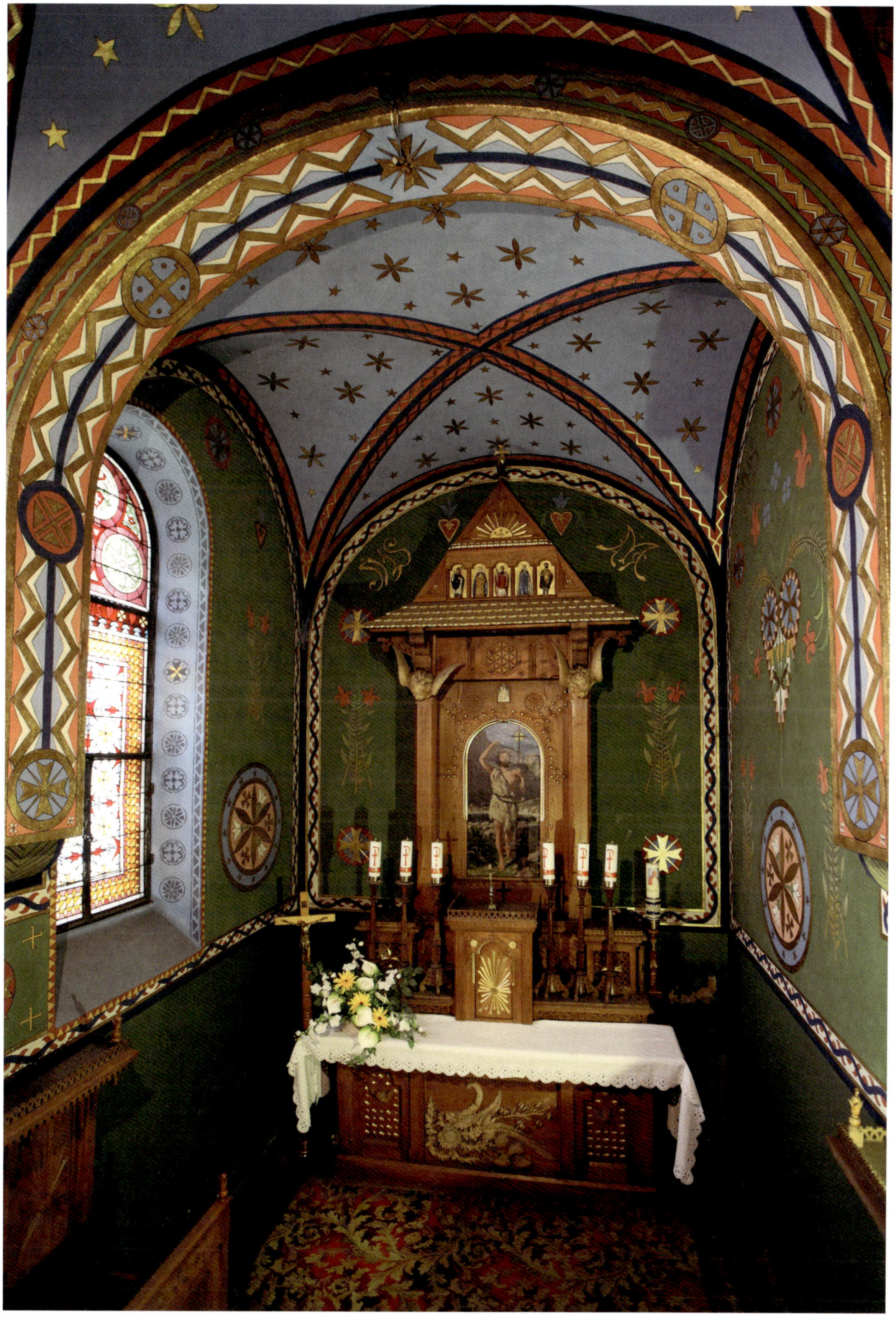

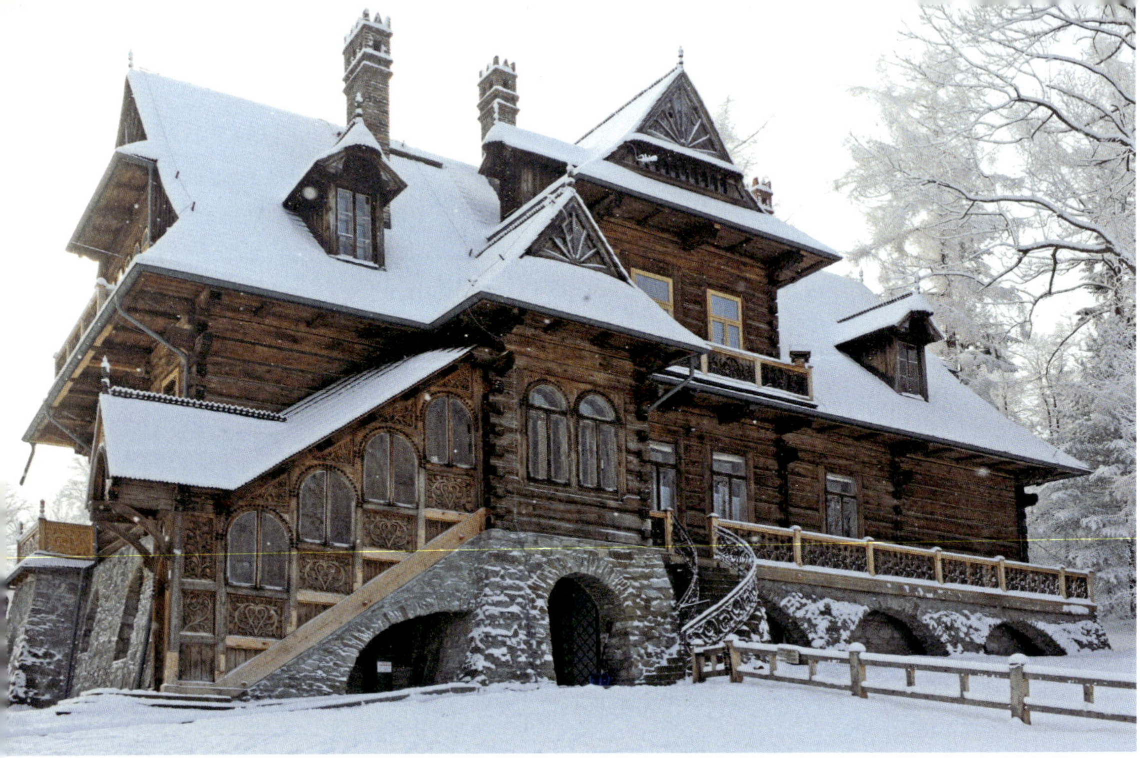

6.7 (TOP)
House Under the Firs, designed by Stanisław Witkiewicz, 1896–7: exterior view in winter
House Under the Firs Trust (Stowarzyszenie Dom pod Jedlami)

6.8 (BOTTOM)
Archive photograph from 1906 of the well at the House Under the Firs, designed by Witkiewicz in that year
Tatra Museum

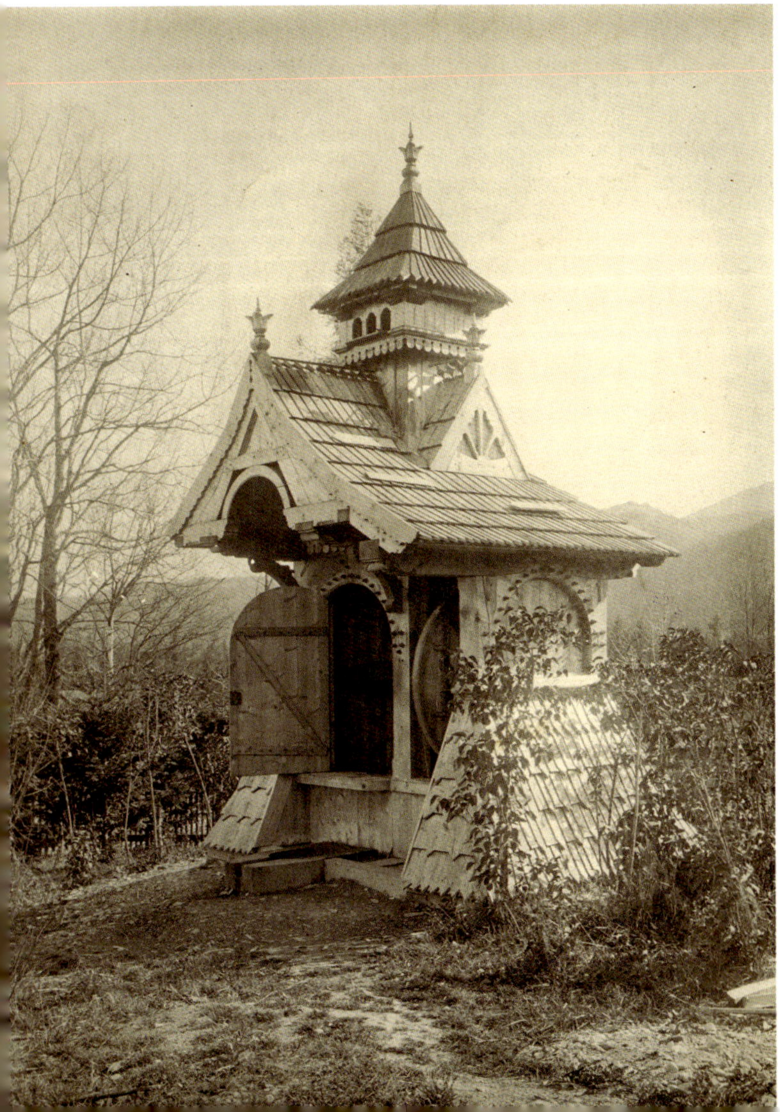

was covered with wooden shingle. The following months saw the finishing of the interiors, the installation of tiled and stone stoves and the laying of wooden floors. At the end of April Pawlikowski was still in need of a stove for the dining room, having contacted the director of the School of Pottery (Szkoła Garncarska) in Kołomyja (now Kolomyia), Aleksander Klimaszewski, regarding this. By the summer a few of the rooms were ready, and the Pawlikowski family spent their first holidays in the House Under the Firs. However, the house was still lacking the hooded stove in the dining room and the fireplace in the sitting room, as well as most of the furniture, which was to be created between 1898 and 1903. By the summer of 1898 a gate and fence were erected, probably together with the caretaker's lodge and a coach house. At the same time Witkiewicz completed his design for a stove-cum-fireplace for the white chamber (sitting room), which would come to fruition in April 1901 (see fig.14.6). The vernacular well in front of the house was constructed in 1906, also according to Witkiewicz's design (fig.6.8).

From the outset Witkiewicz was assisted in furniture design by his closest collaborators: Highlander master-craftsmen including Stoch, Brzega, Kazimierz Sieczka and Andrzej Krzeptowski. In 1898 Witkiewicz's designs for a dresser, a table and a bench were executed for the dining room, probably by

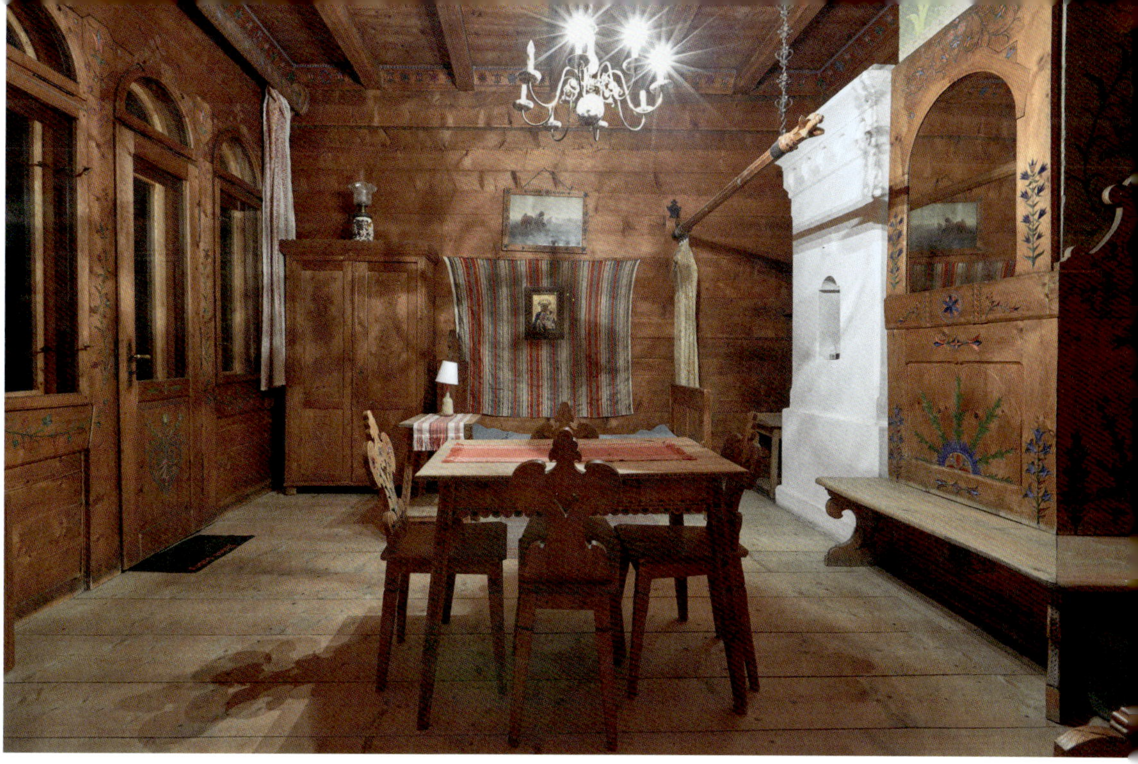

6.9 (TOP)
The Painted Chamber at House Under the Firs
House Under the Firs Trust (Stowarzyszenie Dom pod Jedlami)

6.10 (BOTTOM)
Chair with painted decoration, from the Painted Chamber, House Under the Firs
House Under the Firs Trust (Stowarzyszenie Dom pod Jedlami)

Kazimierz Sieczka. The chairs are also attributed to Witkiewicz. The small table for the samovar was apparently designed by another associate, Wiktor Gosieniecki (1876–1956).

The choice of paintings and kilims to decorate the walls proved challenging. In the spring of 1899 Pawlikowski purchased Witkiewicz's painting *Sheep in the Mist* (1899–1900; see Chapter 17; fig.13.4). A painting by Leon Dembowski, *Tatra Landscape* (1890), also hung in the sitting room. In 1900 four embroidered curtains, worked by Maria Witkiewicz to her husband's design, were hung in the white chamber (sitting room) (see fig.13.4). An interesting attempt at painted decoration of the walls, stove, chimney breast, doors and windows, as well as the furniture in the western room in the attic (now the Painted Chamber; fig.6.9) probably dates from this period. The masterful furniture for the sitting room (figs 6.10, 10.2) and for Wanda Pawlikowska's room was made by Wojciech Brzega in 1902. The armchair and bed were highly regarded by their owners, and most probably by Witkiewicz himself. The House Under the Firs was the fifth building designed by Witkiewicz. Even before it was fully finished and furnished, this architectural masterpiece was due to be presented at the Exposition Universelle in Paris in 1900.

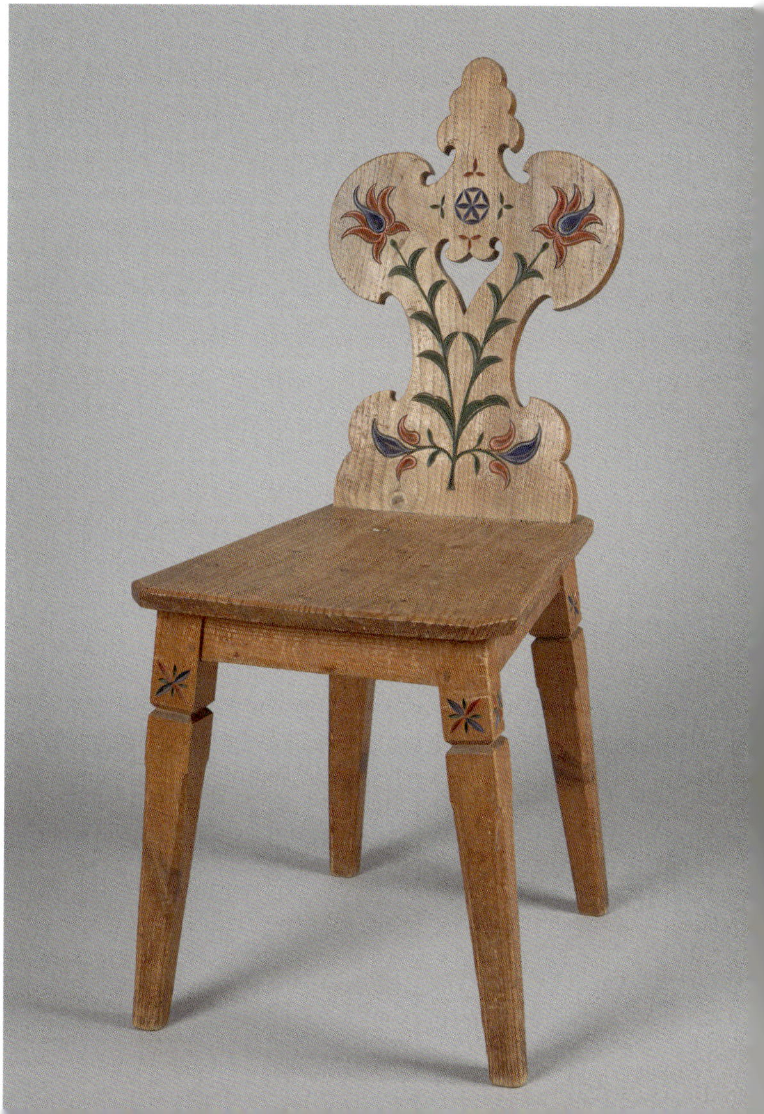

The idea of presenting the Zakopane Style on the international arena emerged towards the end of 1898.

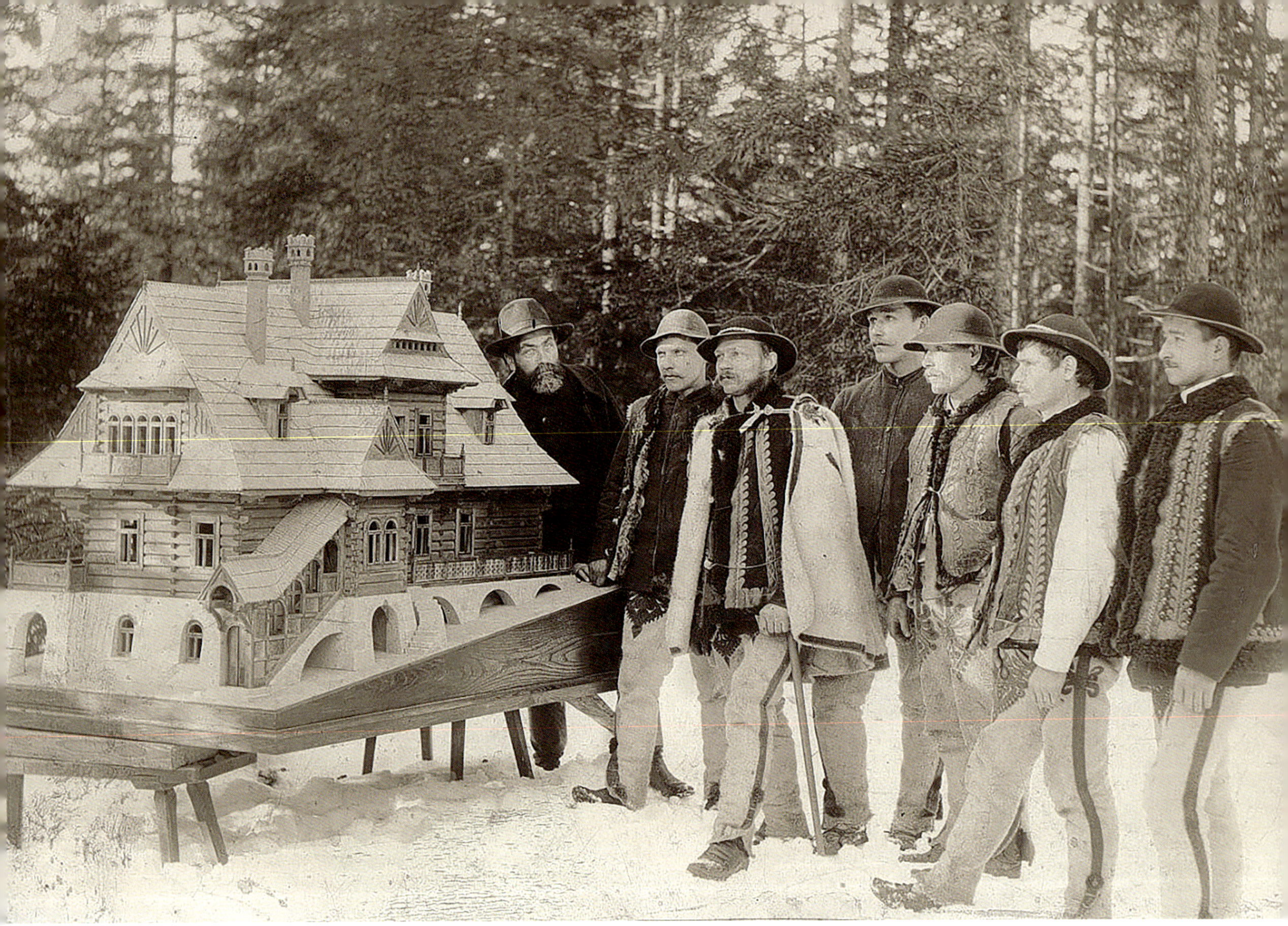

It is intrinsically connected with the story of the making of the remarkable architectural model of the House Under the Firs, which survives to this day in the Tatra Museum collection (figs 6.11 and 6.12). On 29 November 1898 Marian Sokołowski, Professor of Art History at the Jagiellonian University, curator and patriot, wrote to Witkiewicz on behalf of the Galicia Art Department Committee for the Exposition Universelle, 'regarding securing for the exhibition photographs or drawings of facades and architectural designs of all buildings based on your designs in Zakopane, and if possible a model of one of your buildings, e.g. the one at "Kozieniec" [*sic*]'.[16] Sokołowski's personal letter followed a day later in which he stated that he would like 'the architecture of Zakopane to be showcased as well as possible at the Paris Exposition'.[17] Arranging the exhibition was entrusted to the architect and Lviv Polytechnic professor Julian Zachariewicz and after his death to the architect Edgar Kováts, Director of the Wood Industry Vocational School in Zakopane, probably because of the prospect of using the School's resources to help with the preparation of the show. Witkiewicz put forward the whole curatorial concept and layout of the Zakopane Style display.

He also proposed the specifications for the making of the House Under the Firs architectural model in terms of its scale and execution. Thanks to Witkiewicz's article in the local press, we know the names of the Highlander makers of the maquette and the varieties of wood used in its construction. One of the

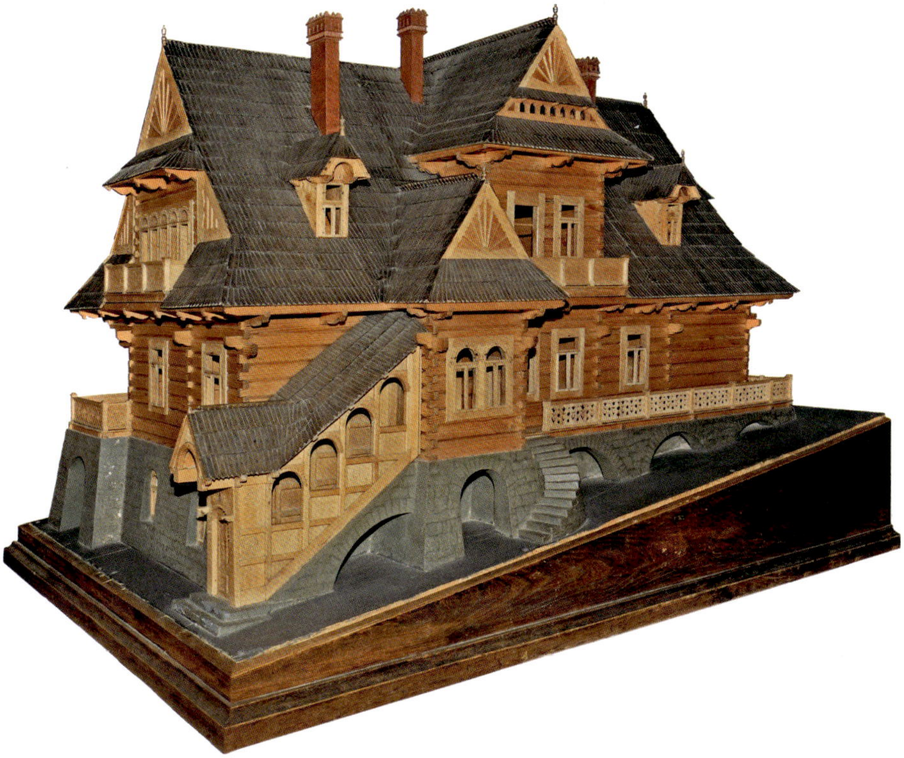

6.11 (OPPOSITE)
Stanisław Witkiewicz (far left) and the makers of the House Under the Firs architectural model, 1899
Tatra Museum

6.12 (LEFT)
Architectural model of the House Under the Firs made for the Exposition Universelle in Paris in 1900
Tatra Museum

master carpenter-builders who supervised the construction of Pawlikowski's villa, Jan Obrochta Bartuś, took part, together with Józek Giewont, Jasisko Dudek, Józef Mikuda, Wojtek Bednarz, Gawlak (first name unknown), Jędruś Walczak, Wojtek Żwijac and Jędruś Gąsienica.[18] Witkiewicz outlined the contribution made by each craftsman, emphasising that 'for a Highlander a couple of lines and a few comments are a sufficient briefing'.[19] He noted that great precision, skill and confidence were required for the execution of carved ornamentation on such tiny elements. It is no wonder that the work was mostly done by Wojciech Gąsienica Roj.

Covering the roof of the model with tiny bits of wooden shingle presented particular difficulties. Witkiewicz believed that the construction methods should closely follow the building of the house itself, with no shortcuts. He noted that 'Wojtek Bednarz exhibited exceptional patience and skill, making 8000 pieces of shingle, while Ignacy Hoły produced turned finials jutting from the gables and decorating the posts of the staircase and balcony balustrades, neatly and carefully'.[20]

The model was first sent to the National Museum in Kraków where it was displayed on a high plinth. On 5 January 1900 Sokołowski enthusiastically reported that the model 'reigns, and is the object of everyone's admiration'.[21] Due to insufficient funds to pay all the makers, Jan Gwalbert Pawlikowski came to Witkiewicz's help, sending '200 fl. for the cost of the model'.[22]

Regrettably, despite all the efforts, the model was not destined to receive the international exposure that it deserved. Wojciech Brzega, at the time a student at the Paris École Normale Supérieure des Beaux-Arts, visited the exhibition on 24 April and first wrote to Witkiewicz about the fate of the model – being left uninstalled on the ground by the wall, so that only two sides were visible, even though the rest of the exhibition had been properly put up.[23] On enquiring about the 'Tatra-style house' at the Austrian pavilion, Kazimierz Skórzewski, owner of the Dębiny estate in the Toruń county, was directed to 'a crate nearby, on the terrace, with the comment that there was no room for it!?!? and that it was being returned to Kraków'.[24] In the August issue of *Przegląd Zakopiański* (*Zakopane Overview*), Witkiewicz wrote:

> The model was thrown out of the exhibition, and the final echo from Paris is an official letter in German from

6.13 (RIGHT)
Chapel of the Sacred Heart of Jesus, Jaszczurówka, designed by Stanisław Witkiewicz, 1904–7

6.14 (OPPOSITE)
The Tatra Manor (1903, designed by Wandalin Beringer) and, behind it, the Tatra Museum (1913–22, designed by Stanisław Witkiewicz and Franciszek Mączyński)
Photograph by Henryk Poddębski, 1936
Tatra Museum

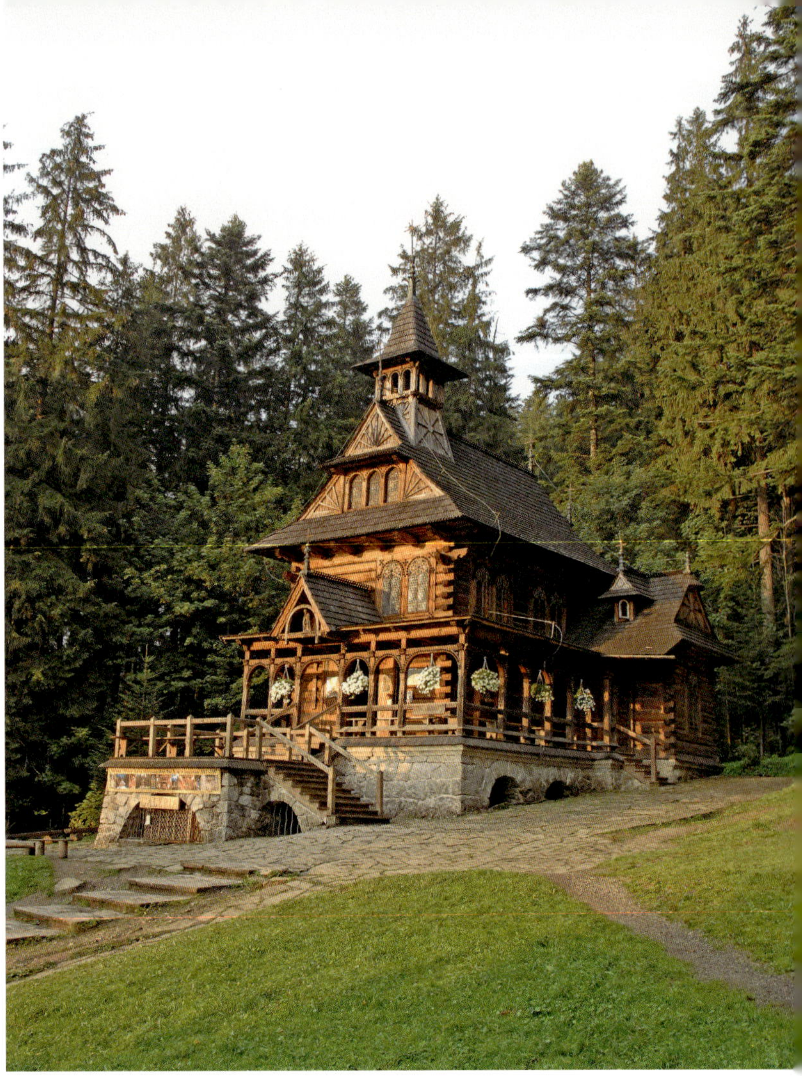

> the Commissariat, stating that the model could not be displayed due to lack of space and hence I am summoned in order to collect the model, without further delay, since *the costs of storing it in Paris are very high!*[25]

Witkiewicz placed all the blame on the Commissioner of the Department of Art, Julian Fałat, whom he accused of lack of diligence, and of 'ignorance, an inability to appreciate the value and significance of an artistic movement like the Polish vernacular revival, lack of understanding of its dignity, seriousness and civilising impact, and a lack of solidarity with the intellectual aspirations of Polish society'. He was writing with regret: 'instead of receiving glory, which was to convert the doubtful, the model will return from Paris damaged and burdened with fines; none of the intended visitors has seen it, nobody has had the opportunity to critique it or to compare with other similar developments elsewhere.'[26] Witkiewicz was, however, able to showcase the model at the Polish Applied Arts Society exhibition in 1902, held at the National Gallery in Kraków and then in Warsaw at the Zachęta, the gallery of the Society for the Encouragement of the Fine Arts (Towarzystwo Zachęty Sztuk Pięknych).

Witkiewicz continued his engagement with the Zakopane Style. The wooden Chapel of the Sacred Heart of Jesus in Jaszczurówka (fig.6.13), constructed in 1904–7, is regarded as his supreme achievement in ecclesiastical architecture. According to Witkiewicz, the challenging application of the Zakopane Style to brick and stone architecture was the key to the style's further development and dissemination. Only a limited number of such buildings came to life – in Zakopane (fig.6.14), Jaworowa, Łańcuchów (Jan Stecki's manor house), Konstancin, Sosnowiec, Warsaw, Nałęczów and Lviv.

Witkiewicz, like other protagonists of the Arts and Crafts movement, attempted to create a style which would embrace not only architecture, interior design, internal fixtures and fittings, and furnishings (stoves, fireplaces, furniture, clocks, tea and coffee services, curtains, lace napkins, even pianos), so-called lesser architecture (caretaker's lodges, wells, gates) and complete decorative schemes, but also fashion for both women (dresses, shoes) and men (sleeveless jackets). As he wrote:

> apart from the four elementary pieces of furniture which constitute the most basic needs of a human dwelling – the bed, table, chairs and wardrobe . . .

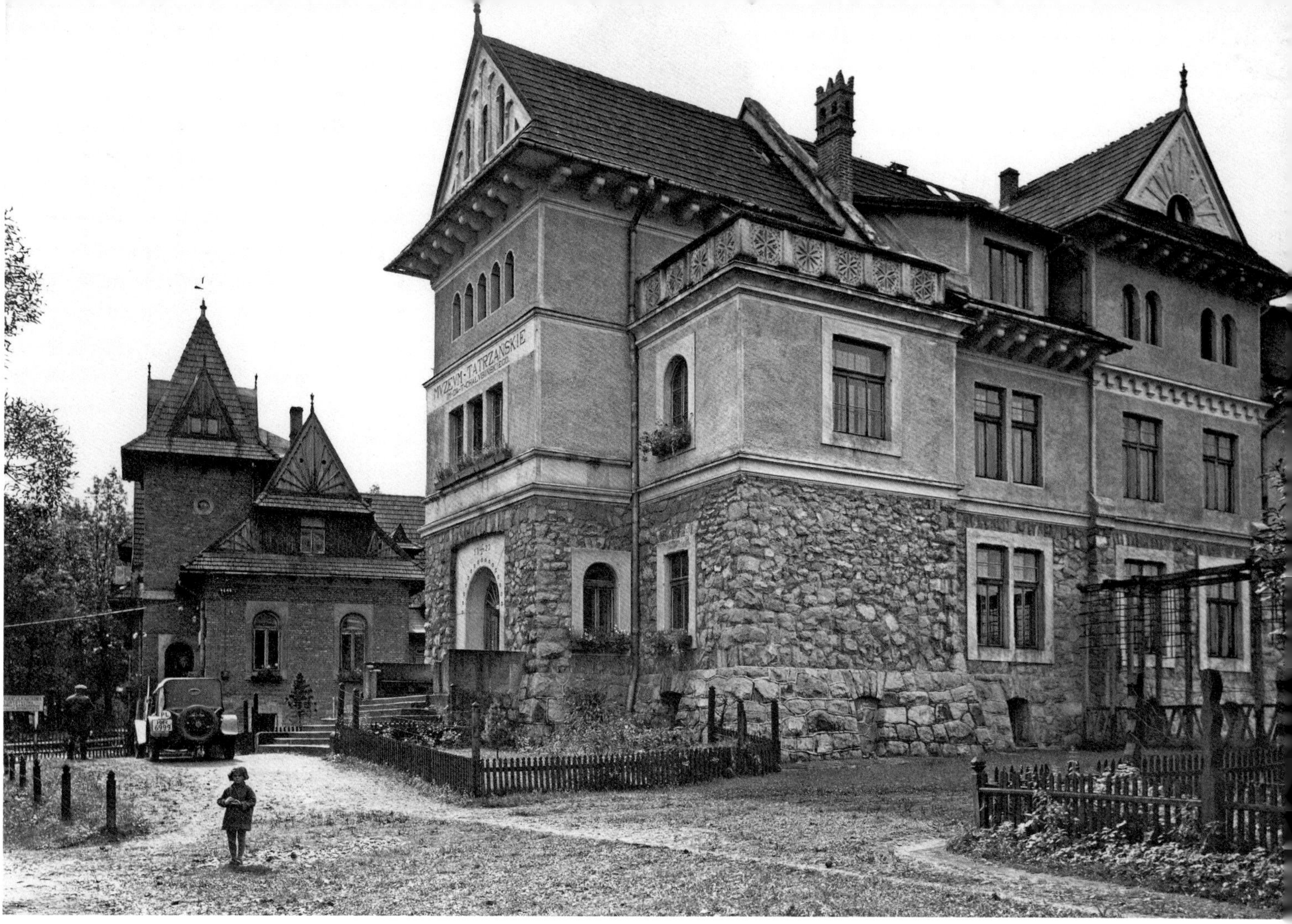

the complex and more refined needs of the lives of the richer classes require many items for which there were no models in the Highlanders' hut, because there was no necessity for them in their lives. Wash-stands and dressing-tables, sofas and armchairs, chaise-longues and poufs, small cupboards, mirrors, large and small desks, a whole range of other pieces which naturally did not exist in a hut, and which had to be created independently, given the new needs. Similarly, hundreds of little things, from inkwells, candlesticks, ashtrays, paper-knives, pen-holders, to tie-pins or needle-cases and lots of other tiny implements, indispensable for contemporary life – all of these things had to be created from such forms as appeared in vernacular architecture and crafts.[27]

Although only 13 buildings were erected after Witkiewicz's designs in Zakopane and elsewhere, there were over a hundred designed by professional architects, including Tadeusz Stryjeński, Zygmunt Dobrowolski, Kazimierz Kreczmer, Eugeniusz Wesołowski and Jan Witkiewicz-Koszczyc, as well as by master carpenter-builders – Witkiewicz's close collaborators, notably Jan Obrochta Bartuś and Wojciech Roj. The Zakopane Style developed in both wooden and brick architecture, embracing secular and ecclesiastical buildings alike. Witkiewicz's collaborators in the design of furniture and other domestic equipment included Józef Kaspruś Stoch, Wojciech Brzega, Stanisław Barabasz (1857–1949), Wiktor Gosieniecki, and many others. Zakopane Style became a national design movement which facilitated the preservation of the Polish cultural identity at the time of the country's political non-existence.

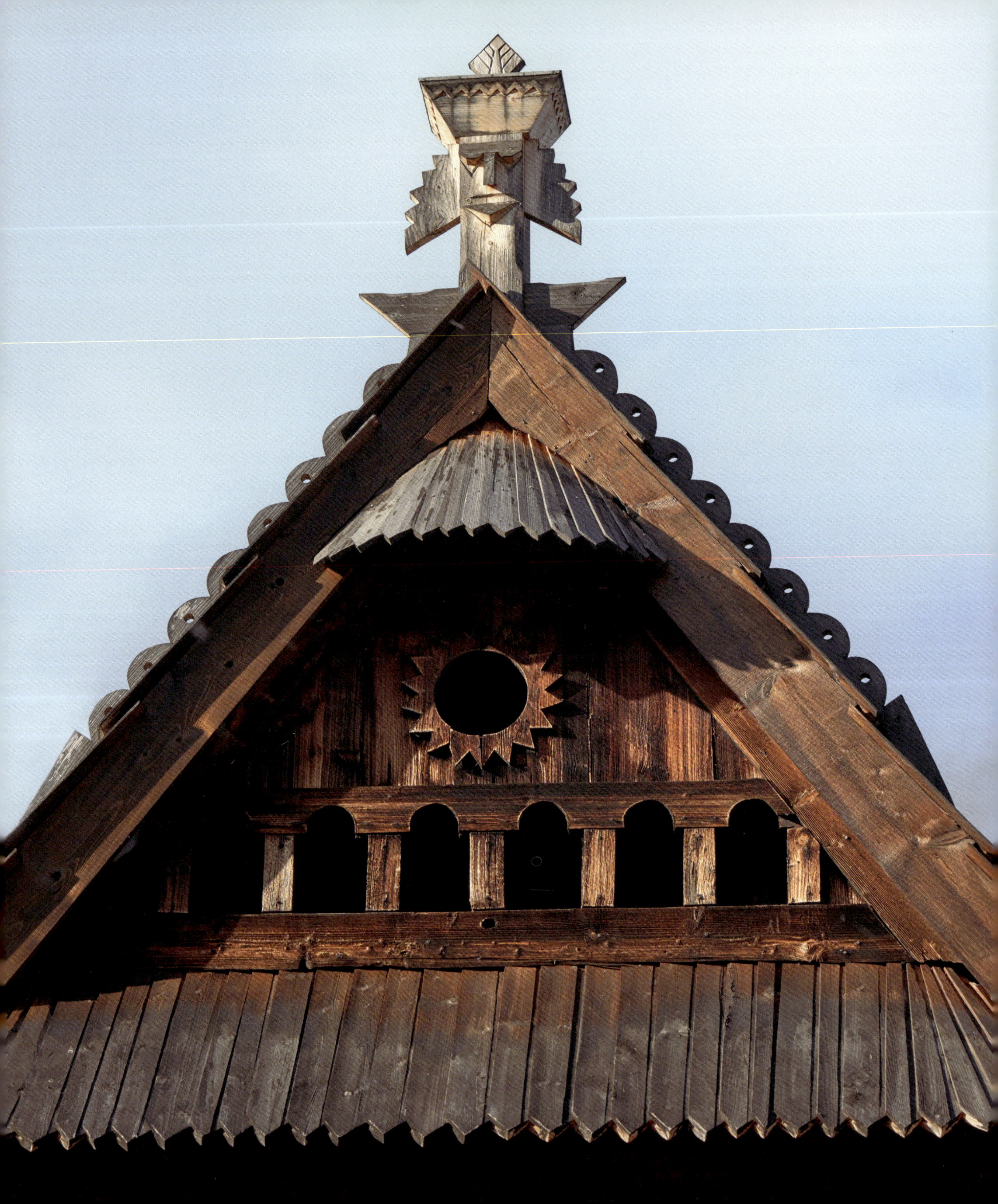

7

Karol Kłosowski and the Silent Villa: Living the Arts and Crafts Life in the Tatras

Edyta Barucka

Karol Kłosowski's life and work in the Silent Villa (Willa Cicha) in Zakopane epitomises the ideal way of living of an artist-craftsman around 1900: rural, domestic, creative and within a larger community of like-minded individuals.[1] Unlike Stanisław Witkiewicz (see Chapter 6), Kłosowski never rose to all-national prominence, but his work as an artist, teacher and designer did not go unacknowledged. In Polish art history he is first and foremost recognised as one of the founding members of the Podhale Arts Society and a designer of lacework, which received international recognition in the International Exposition of Modern Industrial and Decorative Arts in Paris in 1925. Kłosowski's contribution to the Polish Arts and Crafts, though belated, was consistent and individual enough to deserve recognition for its intrinsic value and originality. The Silent Villa, in particular, holds a special position not only in the history of the vernacular revival in the Tatras, but also in that of artists' wooden houses and studios in Northern Europe. This chapter sets out to offer a discussion of the Silent Villa as the artistic house that both lies at the heart of Kłosowski's lifelong creative pursuits and bears compelling testimony to their beauty, quality and vitality.[2] To give a more adequate picture of his progression as an artist, it opens with a brief survey of Kłosowski's education in the then Austria-Hungary.

When Kłosowski first came to Zakopane in 1896 from his native village of Pilatkowice in Podolia (now western Ukraine) he was 14. He had already displayed considerable drawing skills and a deft hand at making paper cuttings and was sent to Zakopane to learn ornamentation and figurative sculpture at the Wood Industry Vocational School. The moment could not have been more opportune for a future artist. As Teresa Jabłońska writes: 'Around 1900, Zakopane "seethed" with art. The village had become, next to Kraków and in artistic relationship with it, the cultural centre of the Young Poland movement . . . It was then that the younger generation of artists, who lived or stayed for longer periods of time in Zakopane, attracted attention.'[3] The village boasted two vocational crafts schools: the Wood Industry Vocational

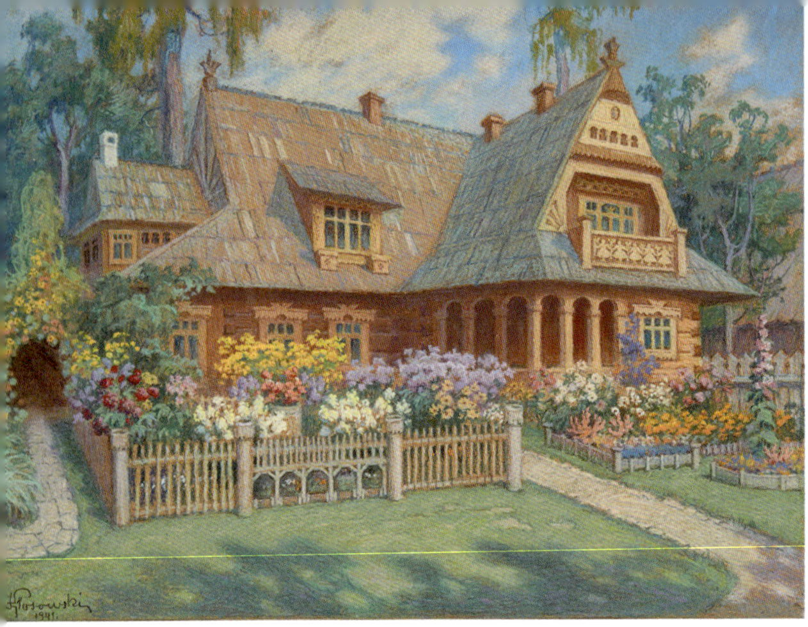

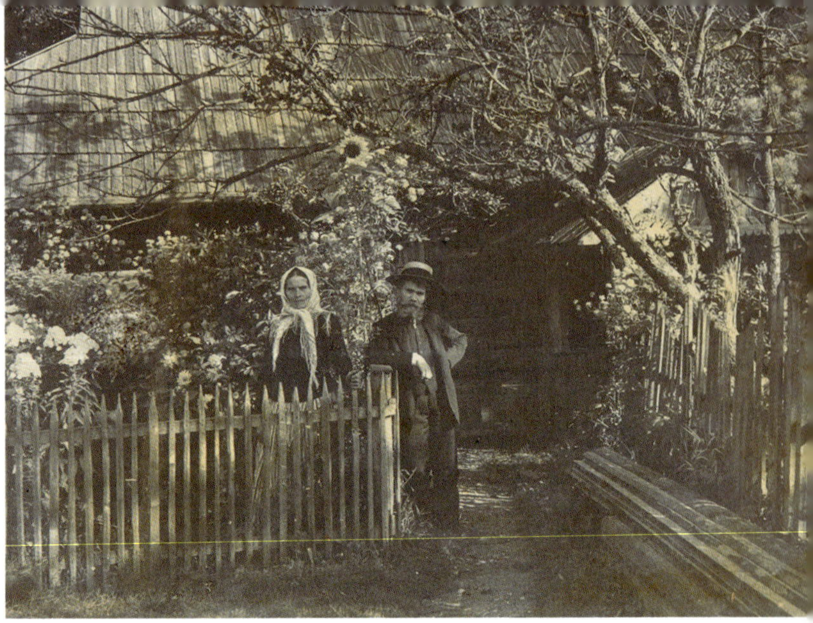

School had opened in 1876, and the School of Lacemaking (Szkoła Koronkarska) in 1883. Both were founded with a view to educating young people from the area in useful skills and with the ultimate goal of providing economic relief to a region of notorious poverty.[4] In 1899 the railway line was opened in Zakopane, making it more accessible to guests coming for holidays and to tuberculosis patients coming for treatment. Kłosowski's own decision to return to Zakopane in 1907, after a hiatus of over five years spent studying art, was partly dictated by his ill health and the onset of tuberculosis.[5]

During his early years at the Wood Industry Vocational School, Kłosowski stayed in a Highlander *chata* (a generic name for a local hut) in Ulica Kościeliska, run as a guest house by the Gąsienica Sobczak sisters and known as Sobczakówka. From Zakopane he went on to study at the School of Decorative Arts in Kraków, modelled on the Viennese Kunstgewerbeschule, and afterwards at the Academy of Fine Arts in Vienna. In 1904 he was back in Kraków, studying at the Academy of Fine Arts under such renowned painters as Stanisław Wyspiański and Leon Wyczółkowski.[6] In 1907, having returned to Zakopane, he married Katarzyna Gąsienica Sobczak (1866–1915) and moved into his wife's house. Sobczakówka thus became Willa Cicha (the Silent Villa), Karol Kłosowski's home until the end of his long life in 1971. His wife, 16 years older than himself, was a Highlander poetess and in an early photograph they are shown together in front of the Silent Villa with Katarzyna wearing a characteristic Highlander headscarf (fig.7.1, right). In 1915 Katarzyna died and Kłosowski later remarried a teacher of lacemaking, Jadwiga Marusińska.

The Silent Villa sits comfortably in Ulica Kościeliska, a historic thoroughfare of Zakopane, lined with vernacular wooden buildings. An old wooden church, which was the hub of community life, and the chapel, founded by Katarzyna's ancestors, are within walking distance, as is Witkiewicz's Willa Koliba (see Chapter 6). It may be safely assumed that for Kłosowski, educated in woodcarving, the presence of Koliba did not go unnoticed during his early years in Zakopane (see fig.6.2). When he returned as an artist himself to live nearby, Koliba was no longer the only house in the village in the Zakopane Style. Kłosowski was well aware of Witkiewicz's stylistic endeavour, and Witkiewicz too was a member of the Podhale Arts Society, instituted in 1909, which subscribed to the ethos of the equal standing of decorative and fine arts. A year later Kłosowski also joined the Kilim Association, founded in Zakopane and responsible for sustaining the tradition of handwoven kilims,[7] and in 1912 he became professionally anchored in the Tatras, when he was offered a teaching position at the Wood Industry Vocational School, followed a year later by a permanent appointment at the School of Lacemaking.

The Silent Villa, Kłosowski's patiently hand-crafted home, was developed piecemeal in the course of over twenty years. Unlike Koliba, designed by Witkiewicz as a flagship project, Kłosowski's work on Willa Cicha was restricted by the existing structure of a Highlander *chata*, and his ideas unfolded slowly.[8]

7.0 (P.104)
Silent Villa, Zakopane, front gable above the balcony, decorated and crowned with a finial sculpted by Kłosowski, after 1915. The sculpture represents the head of Jánošík, a legendary Highlander highwayman

7.1 (OPPOSITE)
LEFT: Karol Kłosowski's drawing of the Silent Villa dated 1941, showing the house and the garden after all extensions and alterations
59 × 72 CM
RIGHT: Photograph of Karol Kłosowski and his wife Katarzyna in front of the Silent Villa, taken presumably between 1907 and 1915
Private Collection. By Descent from the Artist

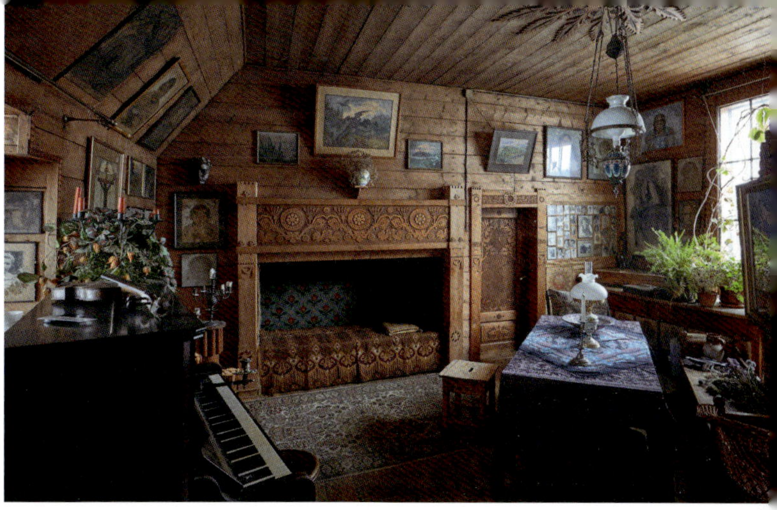

7.2
Silent Villa, interior of Karol Kłosowski's study with a built-in bed, carved and lined with hand-woven kilims, designed by Kłosowski. All wooden features in the studio were designed and hand-crafted by the artist

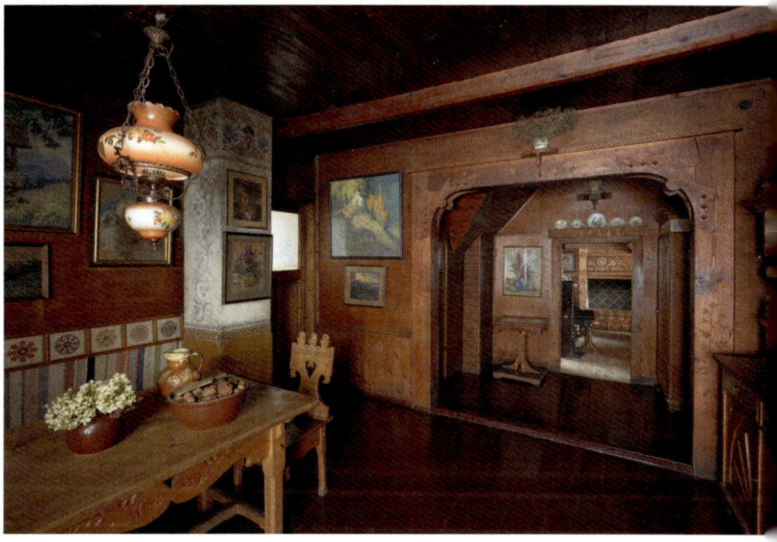

7.3
Silent Villa, interior of the dining room with one of the two stoves added by Kłosowski. The decorative frieze with *gadziki* (little reptiles) running along the stove, as well as other ornamentation, were designed and painted by the artist. On the walls are Kłosowski's pastel drawings and paper cuttings

Witkiewicz sought to adapt vernacular forms in grander houses and as a result his villas were much more sophisticated in their spatial arrangements and ornamentation than traditional Highlander huts (see figs 0.10 and 6.7). Kłosowski likewise transformed the traditional two-chamber *chata* into an artistic house of considerable spatial and functional complexity. He achieved this, however, by retaining the original scale and progressing gradually through a series of sympathetic extensions and alterations. What both houses share is their Arts and Crafts unity of the inside and the outside, dedication to hand-crafted detail in the interiors, drawing inspiration from local sources and nature, and first and foremost, the celebration of beauty in everyday life.[9]

The original wooden house Kłosowski moved into in 1907 is described in the conservation management plan from 2013 as follows:

> It is an exceptional, unique wooden house in the Zakopane Style with ornamental features from Podolia region. The present-day house was developed through enlargements and extensions from a traditional Highlander hut belonging to the Gąsienica Sobczak family, dating back to *ca.* mid-19th century (or perhaps even earlier, as there is a shelf in the vestibule bearing the date 1819) into a commodious family seat of the artistic Kłosowskis.[10]

In the early stages the attic was converted into the artist's studio, lit with two dormer windows facing south and north. In the last stage of the development in the 1920s, a new wing and a deep, open porch, supported by posts with decorative capitals, were added. The porch, with a comfortable built-in bench, extends into the front garden and still today serves as a south-facing 'garden room', giving a strong sense of interconnectedness between the house and the garden.[11]

Kłosowski was a keen horticulturalist and an experienced gardener, and he is credited with the acclimatisation of a number of non-native species of flowers and shrubs into Zakopane. In old drawings and photographs the front garden he established looks uniquely cottagey in the otherwise severe climate of the Tatra mountains and it has survived as such until this day with its roses, hollyhocks, delphiniums and

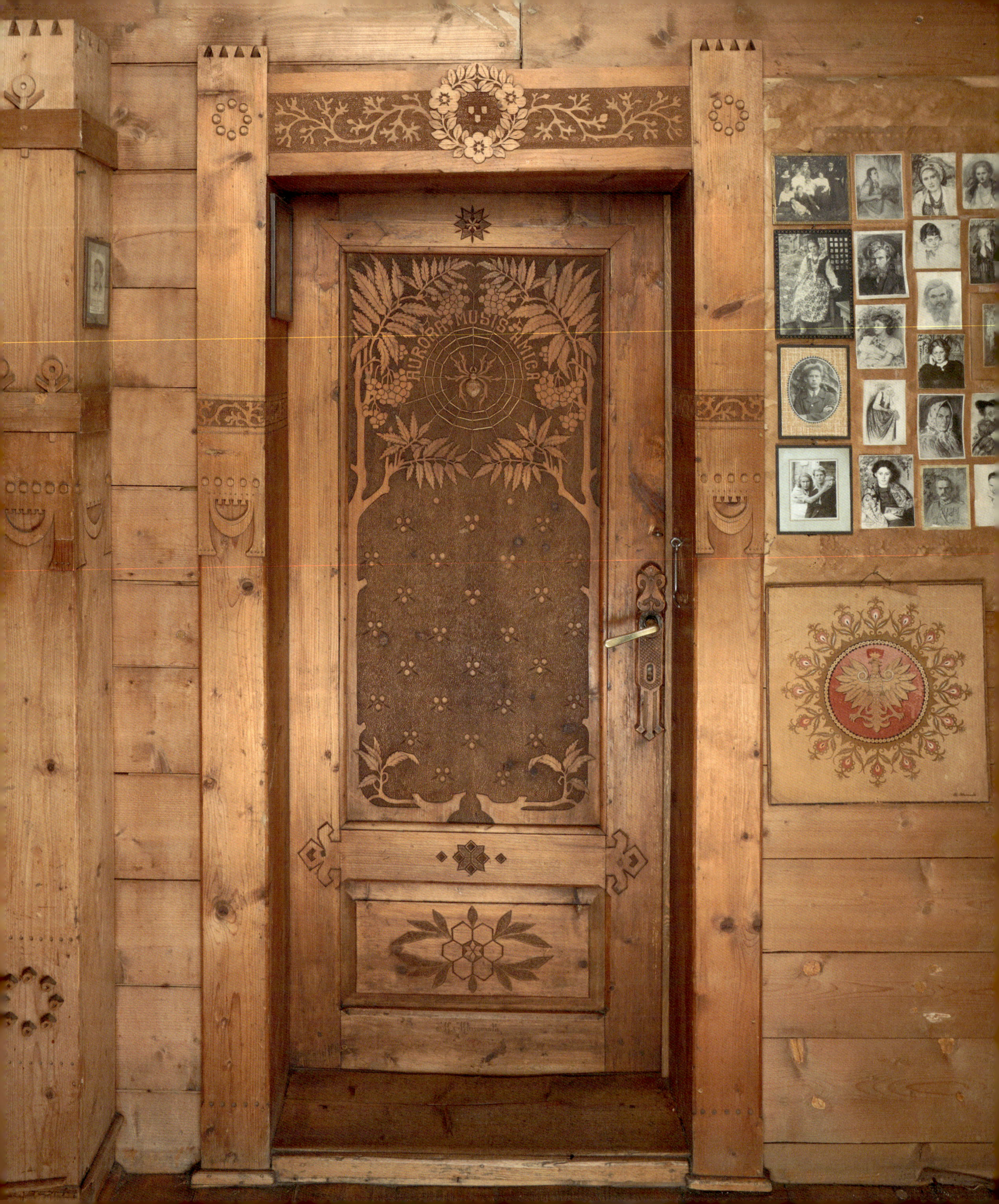
AURORA MUSIS AMICA

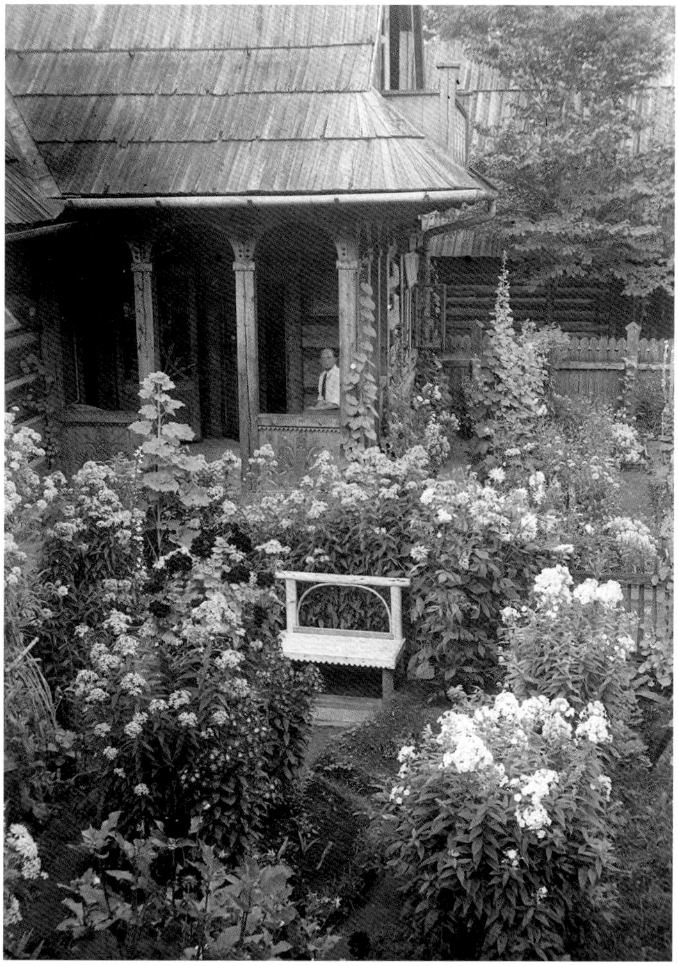

7.4 (OPPOSITE)
Silent Villa, wooden door in the artist's studio with carved decoration featuring a spider's web and the Latin inscription '*Aurora Musis Amica*', designed and carved by Karol Kłosowski, probably after 1915

7.5 (LEFT)
Silent Villa in a period photograph featuring lush vegetation in a garden and an open porch used as a 'garden room'
Private Collection. By Descent from the Artist

verbascums (fig.7.5). Clematis and Virginia creeper climbed the walls and posts, and ferns, meadowsweet, jasmine and quinces grew nearby. In the backyard there was a meadow of wild flowers and knee-high grass. Fruit and berry plants and trees were cultivated too, and maples and sycamore trees, among others, completed the arrangement.[12] Kłosowski's dedication to nature was not confined to gardening, but – in the spirit of the time – extended into his art and interior design. His sketchbook contains watercolour studies of common flowers, such as the one of a sweet pea, highlighting the linear rhythm of its sinuous tendrils and gently purplish hue of its flowers.

The ornamental motifs Kłosowski used in the Silent Villa share the subtle fretwork quality with his lacework and paper cuttings,[13] and they often draw upon the indigenous plants and animals of Podhale, as well as upon Highlander culture. Some of them, such as a spider's web or a pair of crickets, repeated in other designs, are charged with more private and personal meanings. The web carved on the door of the studio, set within a decorative framing of intertwined twigs of rowan-berry, with a Latin inscription '*Aurora Musis Amica*' ('Dawn is a Friend of the Muses') above, while clearly a metaphor for lacemaking, may be also viewed as Kłosowski's artistic statement on his own work as an artist-craftsman. Equally, one may only wonder if a pair of crickets, painted in a symmetrical composition on a stove and repeated on the wooden door, makes a reference to Charles Dickens's Christmas book *The Cricket on the Hearth: A Fairy Tale of Home* (1845), which was published in Polish translation in 1914; or to music which, together with gardening, held a privileged place in Kłosowski's life.

Kłosowski's creative energy was not spent solely on the architectural extensions to the house and its internal and external decorations. It extended to the outbuildings, such as a shed for livestock, and included the entrance gate, a fence to a garden plot and a number of domestic objects and features, such as sledges for children and a mailbox, the making of all of which was treated with equal care and dedication. When Kłosowski was working on the Silent Villa, the Arts and Crafts Movement was in retreat, replaced by the advance of early 20th-century modernism. Artists were experimenting with new forms and ideas, leaving behind vernacular and natural inspirations. Kłosowski, however, consistently pursued his own goals. The Silent Villa was his labour of love and he adhered with remarkable integrity to the ideals that he had embraced early in his life and chose to cultivate until the end.

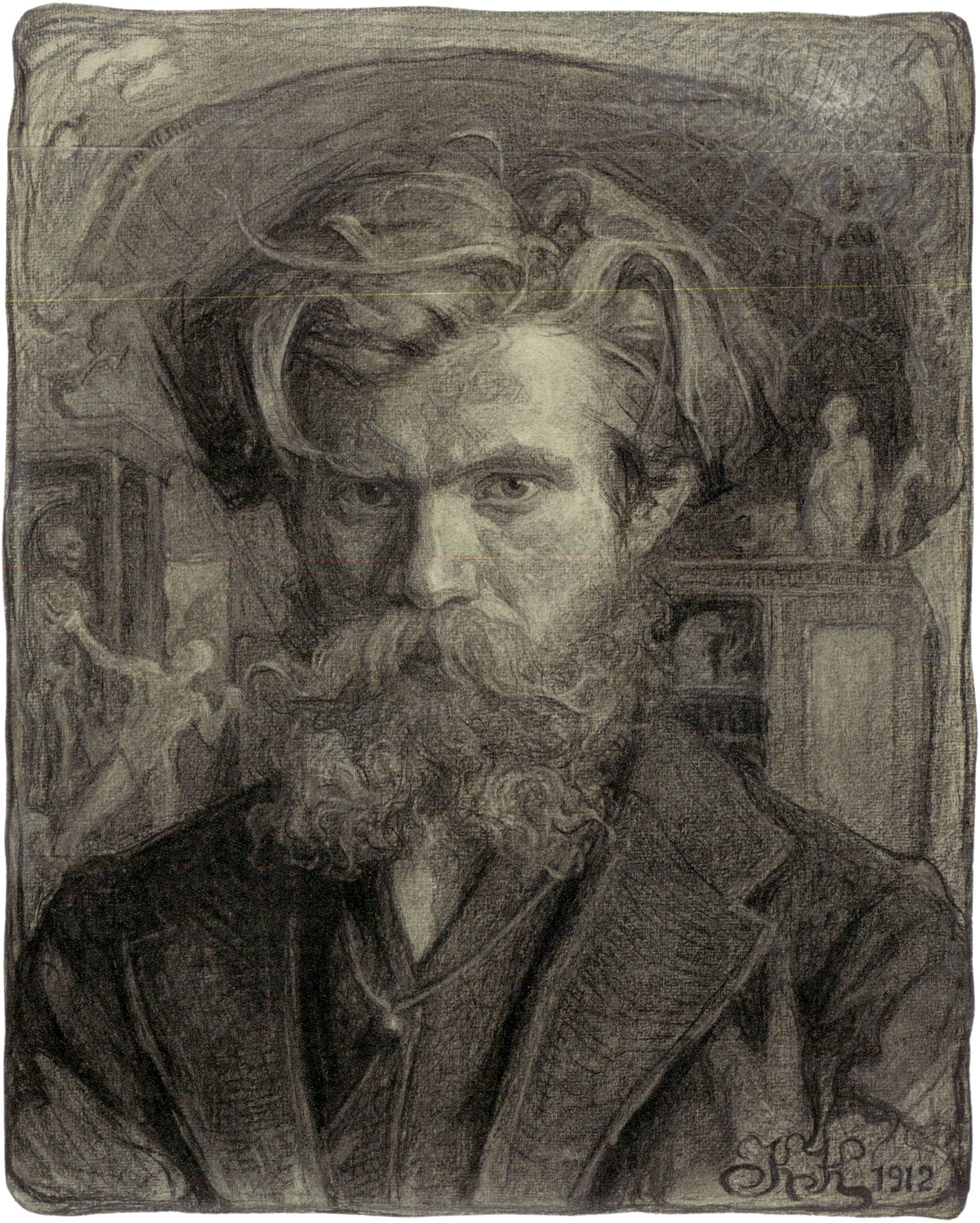
1912

8

Karol Kłosowski (1882–1971): The Last Young Poland Artist and a Genius for Ornament

Julia Griffin

This chapter is dedicated to Ms Ula Bukowska, Mr Jacek Bukowski and Mr Zygmunt Kłosowski, with appreciation for their efforts to preserve their grandfather's legacy.

Karol Kłosowski's masterful creation of the Silent Villa – a *Gesamtkunstwerk* of outstanding originality and quality (see Chapter 7) – in itself deserves a place for him amongst the ranks of foremost international Arts and Crafts designers. What is little known is that Kłosowski left behind an incredibly rich and versatile creative output, going beyond the legacy of the Silent Villa, including a highly accomplished body of paintings as well as a wide range of decorative and applied arts objects.[1] A half-orphan from a poor peasant family with no prospects for a higher education, Kłosowski was a child prodigy, whose artistic talent won him a series of scholarships to study at the best vocational craft schools and art academies in Galicia and abroad. During his passionate lifelong preoccupation with the arts, spanning over eighty years, Kłosowski produced around a thousand pictures, numerous furniture designs, architectural woodcarvings, kilims, around five hundred paper cuttings, several hundred lacework and embroidery designs (including a large number of richly decorated traditional Highlander bodices), posters, book arts and typographical ornaments, designs for domestic and ecclesiastical decorative schemes, as well as a series of wooden roadside shrines.

Despite its remarkable variety, Kłosowski's art and design practice displays a great coherence of vision. It is guided by his belief in cultural democracy – the value of beauty in everyday life and everyone's right to it, as well as the equality of all arts and crafts in fulfilling that purpose. To an equal extent, it is informed by his patriotism and, with it, his quest to cultivate Poland's unique cultural heritage, best preserved in vernacular and folk-art traditions. This artistic philosophy is not only self-evident in the work but is also expressed in Kłosowski's numerous articles and his textbook *Wycinanki: Komponował w mot. lud i naturalist.* (*Paper Cuttings: Designs Based on Folk and Naturalist Motifs*, 1923).[2] He stated: 'pragmatism only serves

8.0 (p.110)
Karol Kłosowski
Self-Portrait, 1912
Charcoal on paper
45 × 36 cm
Tatra Museum

8.1 (OPPOSITE)
Karol Kłosowski
A Wayside Shrine (from Podhale), undated
Pastel on paper
60.5 × 57.5 cm
Private Collection. By Descent from the Artist

the sustainance of a vegetative form of human existence. It is beauty which gives life fullness, dignity and worth.'[3] Kłosowski's resulting oeuvre is characterised by a central integration of fine and decorative arts, combined with an underlying joy of making, frequently in the face of adversity. Each item is of exquisite design and execution, and notable emotive impact. This chapter goes on to show that Kłosowski counts amongst Young Poland's most original painters, designers and master-craftsmen, and that he had a Morrisean genius for ornament.

Anthems in paint and chalk: microcosms of Polishness and the celebration of handiwork

According to Kłosowski's autobiographical account,[4] painting was the first art form he took up, at the age of six. Using a piece of charcoal from the stove, the only material available to him, he would decorate the walls of his humble peasant's cottage with floral ornamentation. For the purpose, he soon developed a range of paints made from natural pigments from plants and minerals he found in the nearby river. In no time his talent was acknowledged by the local peasant community, who paid him to decorate their cottages. Kłosowski recorded his excitement at receiving his first pencil at the age of eight, a milestone in his art. It was thanks to his drawing ability, deemed outstanding by others, that Kłosowski attracted the attention of the chairman of the village school, who financed his art education. This culminated in his graduation from the Kraków Academy of Fine Arts, where Kłosowski distinguished himself by winning five student prizes between 1903 and 1907. It seems that, of all his teachers, Stanisław Wyspiański and Teodor Axentowicz (1859–1938) left the biggest impression on his own distinctive arts practice. During his studies in Vienna and travels in Rome, he came into contact with European Symbolism, including the work of Arnold Böcklin (1827–1901). In his fantastical *Self-Portrait* (1912; fig.8.0), Kłosowski projects his identity as a fully fledged professional artist, posing as an elegantly dressed gentleman against the backdrop of a well-equipped studio, complete with a skeleton, and the suggestion of anatomical casts coming alive. Although he had come a long way since painting the walls in peasant cottages, he still chose to use charcoal, perhaps self-reflecting on the journey.[5]

Kłosowski's prolific painting output was versatile in both media and subject matter, including allegories, landscapes, still lifes and portraiture, worked in oils, pastels, coloured chalks and charcoal. The artist stated that he created the bulk of his paintings for his own gratification. As an accomplished portraitist, he produced striking likenesses of eminent figures, including a number of philanthropists associated with Zakopane, many to commission. The internationally renowned actress Helena Modrzejewska (or Modjeska, 1840–1909), who founded the Zakopane School of Lacemaking, sat for him, as did Count Władysław Zamoyski (1853–1924), early ecologist, who saved the Zakopane forests from eradication by purchasing them. His portrait is now in the Tatra Museum. Kłosowski's likeness of Józef Sieczka (1846–1925), a prominent benefactor of Zakopane and director of the Podhale Bank, presides over the bank's headquarters in Ulica Krupówki to this day.

However, it was local nature and the material culture of the Highlanders that held the greatest fascination for Kłosowski, and, for him, best embodied Young Poland's longing to capture

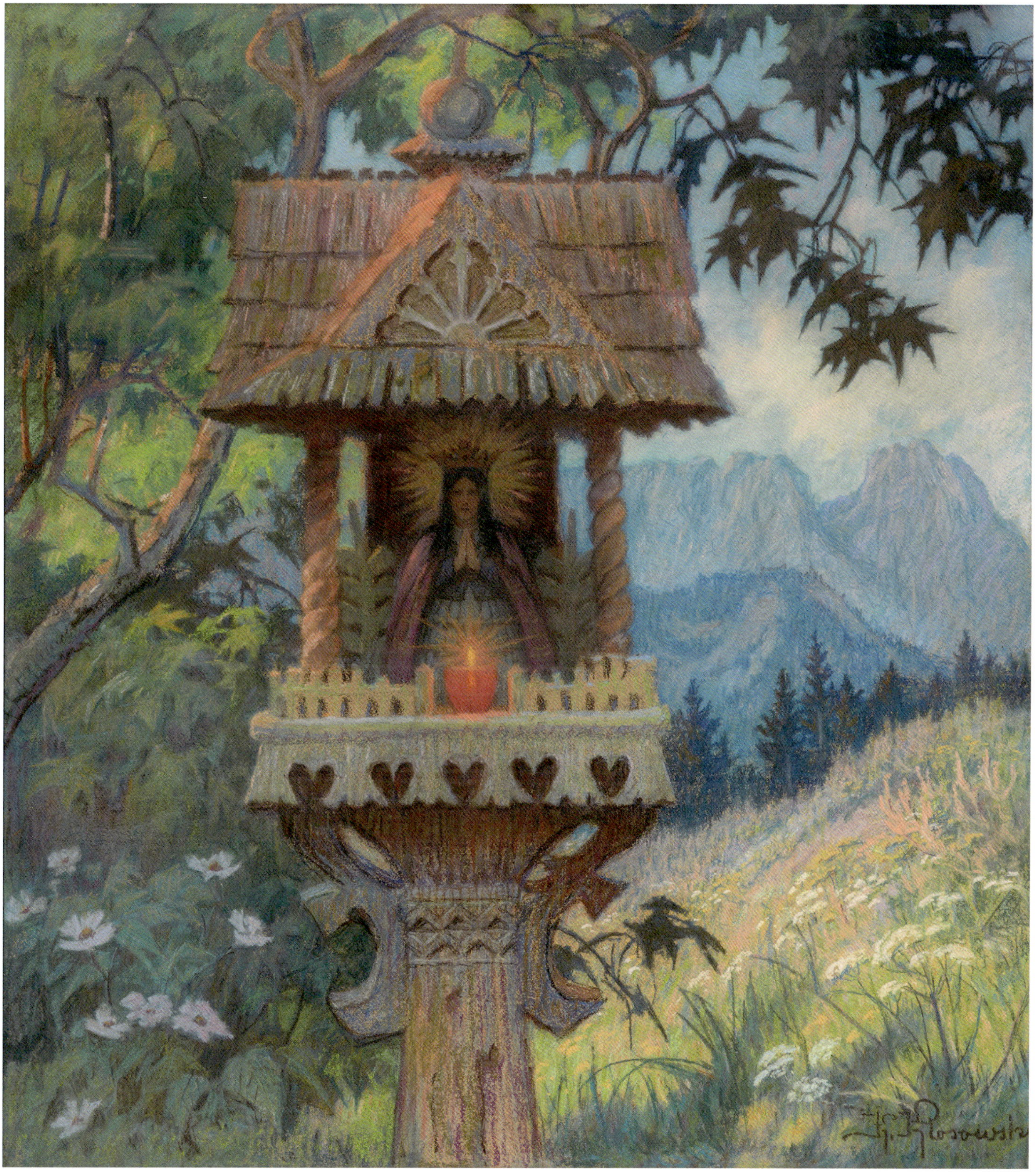

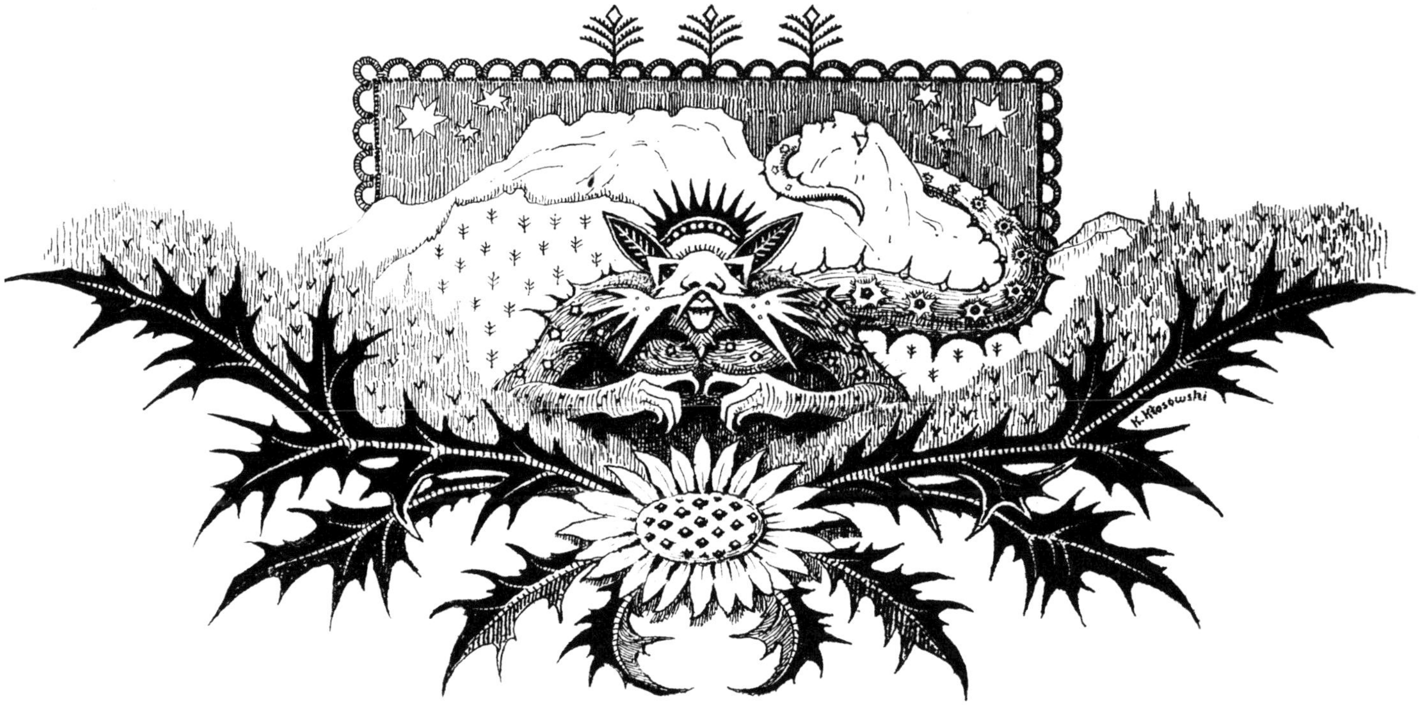

the essence of Polishness. He created a group of evocative representations of Highlander women in traditional costumes, as well as a series of pictures featuring the iconographic motif of the Catholic Virgin Mary shrine in a wild Tatra landscape, in which the Madonna was depicted as the Queen of Poland watching over her country's people. In *A Wayside Shrine (from Podhale)* (fig.8.1), Kłosowski put together several powerful symbolic elements which collectively represent a distilled microcosm of Polishness and a sense of hope for regaining independence. These include the wooden shrine's distinctive vernacular features, the rustic Madonna who seems to have come alive, the lit candle, the beauty and grandeur of the Tatras landscape and, specifically, the silhouette of the mountain known as the Sleeping Knight of Giewont, about to wake up to help the indomitable Polish people. The picture's head-on perspective draws the viewer in, creating the sense of a heartening personal encounter with the shrine.

The Sleeping Knight of Giewont was another recurring motif in Kłosowski's diverse art and craft output, making an appearance in his lace designs (held at the Tatra Museum), on an undated poster advertising Zakopane as a year-round health spa and tourist and sports resort and in his prolific book arts. Kłosowski designed book covers as well as vignettes for magazines – notably *Dziś i Jutro* and *Zawod i Życie*, both aimed at reinforcing values of citizenship among young adults. Both his cover for the book *Uśmiech Tatr* (*The Smile of the Tatras*, 1932)[6] and the related vignette (fig.8.2) featured the Sleeping Knight as well as the Tatra dragon. Much of Kłosowski's creative output evokes the realm of magic and legend.

The celebration of handwork is an ongoing preoccupation in Kłosowski's paintings – a number of which feature women engaged in lacemaking and spinning. *At Bobbin Lacemaking (Legend)* (fig.8.3) features a crowned maiden, modelled from the artist's daughter Helena, absorbed in this craft popularised locally by the School of Lacemaking. The altar-like composition presents bobbin lacemaking as a sacred activity.

Kłosowski's highly original and technically accomplished pictorial work is characterised by an exquisite sense of colour, fairy-tale quality, as well as romanticism, spirituality and emotive intensity, perhaps surpassed only by the Pre-Raphaelites. Moreover, by virtue of its style and subject matter, it has an inherently decorative quality, closely linked to his applied arts.

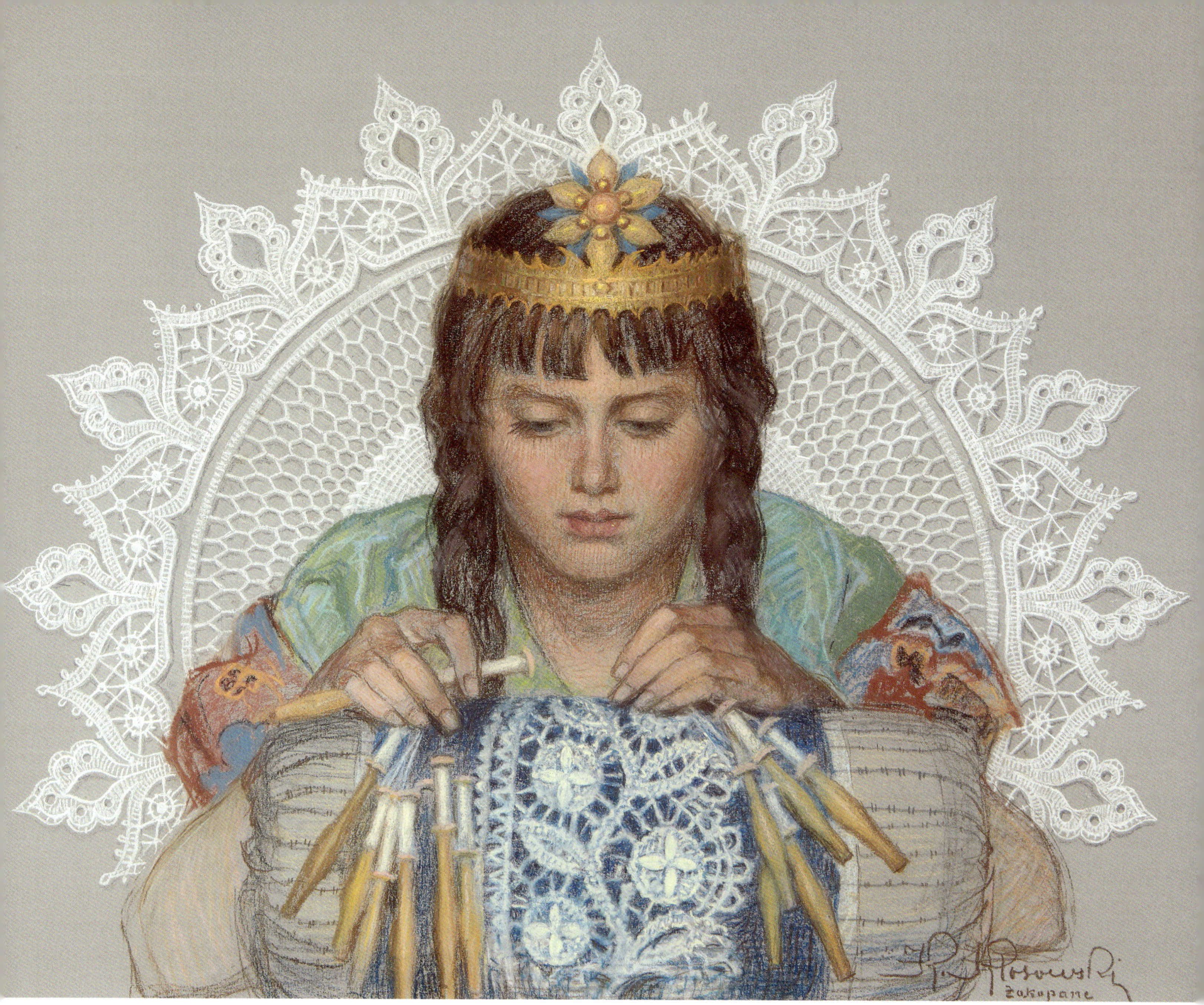

8.2 (OPPOSITE)
Karol Kłosowski
The Tatra Dragon by Giewont Mountain, book ornament
Ink on paper, historical photograph
Private Collection. By Descent from the Artist

8.3 (ABOVE)
Karol Kłosowski
At Bobbin Lacemaking (Legend), undated
Chalk on paper
63 × 75 cm
Private Collection. By Descent from the Artist

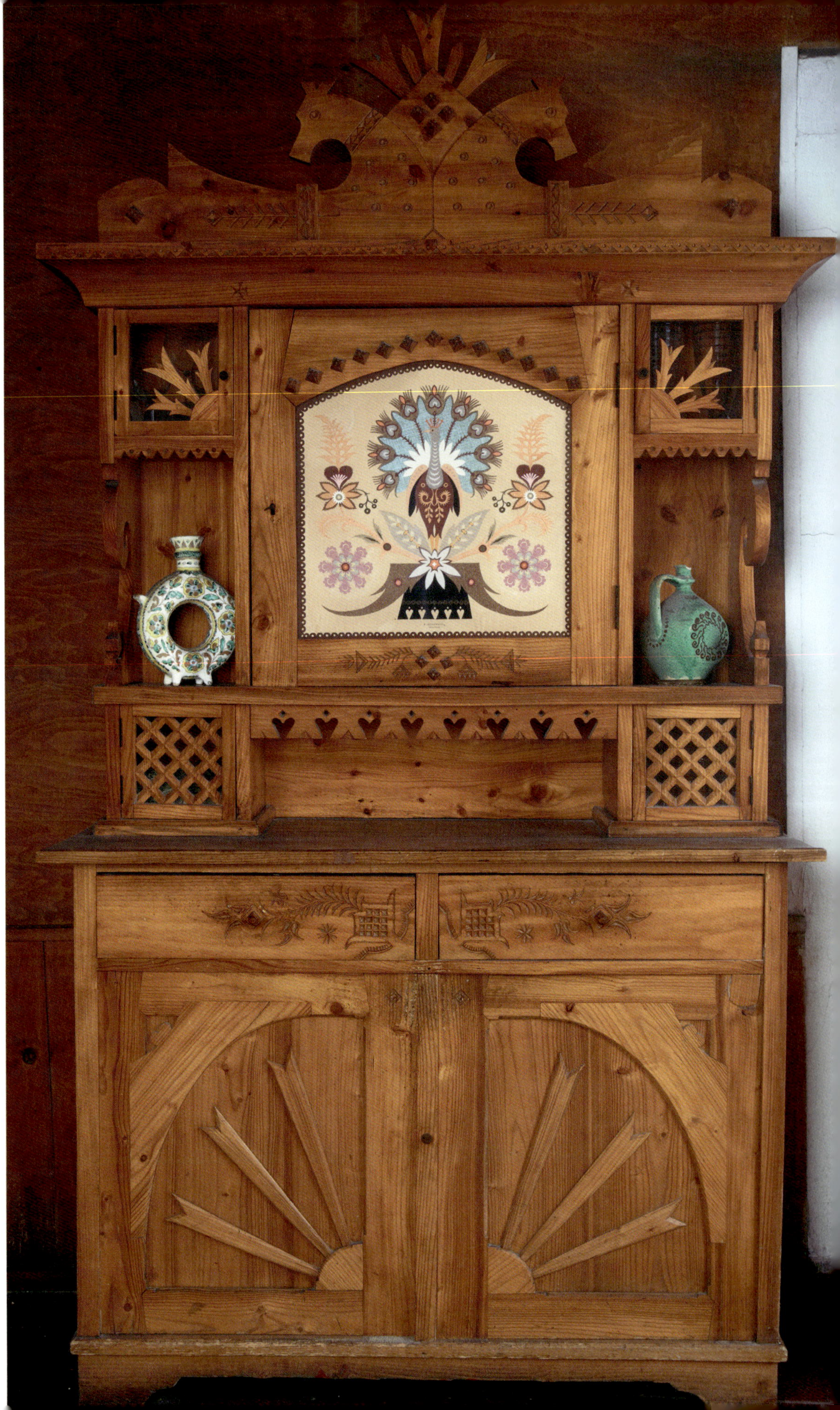

8.4
Dresser, undated, designed by Karol Kłosowski, executed by Wojciech Brzega
Wood customised with paper cutting
214 × 112 × 43 cm
Private Collection. By Descent from the Artist

Kłosowski as an Arts and Crafts designer: cultural politics of ornament

Ever since settling in Zakopane in 1907, Kłosowski became a fixture on the local Arts and Crafts scene and pursued a great number of different crafts, all driven by his urge for beauty, genius for ornament and the aspiration to distil a sense of Polishness.

Between 1907 and 1909 he worked as a designer in the vernacular furniture workshop of Wojciech Brzega (1872–1941) in Ulica Kościeliska, in close proximity to the Silent Villa. Brzega was a foremost master-craftsman and a close collaborator of Witkiewicz, with whom he had co-created numerous decorative schemes, not least the furnishings of Willa Koliba and the House Under the Firs. On this account he is considered a major exponent of the Zakopane Style (see Chapter 6). By the spring of 1909, together with Brzega and a group of local makers, Kłosowski created the Podhale Arts Society, whose dual purpose was to support modern artists and to propagate and raise the standards of folk arts and vernacular craft traditions from the region.[7] Although formally independent from the Zakopane Style, the Society's handcrafted designs reflected similar values. Their exhibition organised in Brzega's house in the summer of 1909 met with critical acclaim and elicited a patriotic response from numerous reviewers. One critic reported:

> everyone who cares about the word and notion of Fatherland should attend this exhibition to realise that our own native culture offers extraordinary riches and beauty . . . this exhibition has once and for all proven that there will never again be the need to populate Polish homes and sitting rooms with German-style 'alt-deutsch' furniture, and for those who will go and see stencilled wall frieze designs, will instantaneously go off their thoughtless, monotonous and lifeless counterparts from Vienna and Berlin. This exhibition brings together so much life, beauty and strength, and everything is so lovely, our own, Polish.[8]

Kłosowski's photographic archive at the National Museum in Warsaw (Muzeum Narodowe w Warszawie) contains examples of his exquisite designs for wall friezes and ornaments, featuring birds and stylised flowers and plants, such as nasturtiums and bracken, as well as carved panelling for domestic and church interiors.[9] Whilst no furniture designs for Brzega's workshop appear to have survived, the furnishings of the Silent Villa offer the best insight into Kłosowski's furniture practice; the great majority of pieces, including tables, stools, benches, shelves, cabinets and the intricate dining-room dresser (fig.8.4), were made by him. The dresser combines traditional Podhale and Zakopane Style elements such as the wooden fretwork, the sunrays on the doors and the heart-shaped decorative edges, together with Kłosowski's own idiosyncratic motifs blended with Podolian influences. The piece has been customised with his multicoloured peacock paper cutting.

As a member of the Zakopane Kilim Association, established in 1910, Kłosowski was a prolific designer of brightly coloured decorative woven textiles, featuring geometric, floral and figurative patterns. One symmetrical design showing two Highlander highwaymen warming themselves up by a campfire reflects Kłosowski's sense of

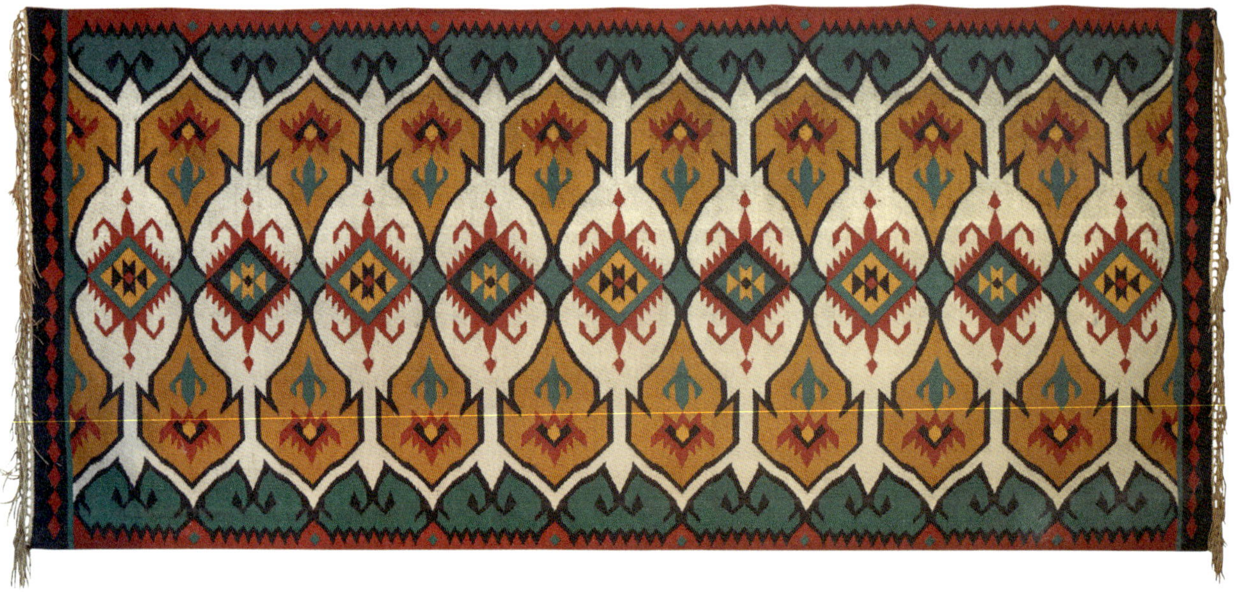

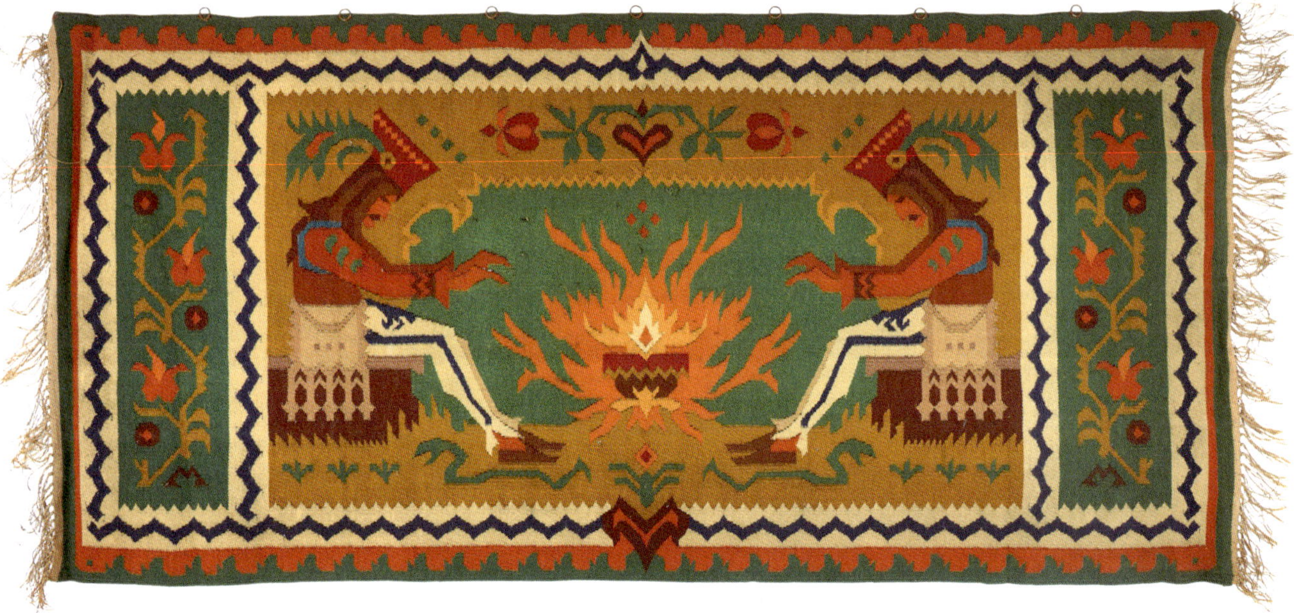

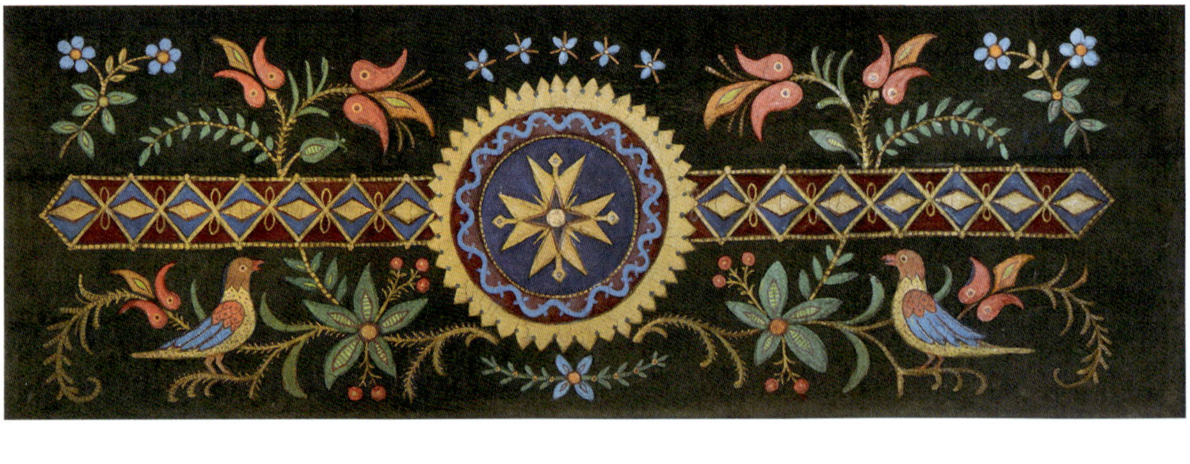

8.5
Karol Kłosowski
Ornamental Textiles
TOP TO BOTTOM:
Kilim with a geometric pattern, undated, after 1910
Kilim with Highlander Highwaymen, undated, after 1910
One of three altar frontals from Madonna of Częstochowa Old Church in Zakopane, after 1945
88 × 195 cm; 90 × 186 cm; 80 × 180 cm
Private Collection. By Descent from the Artist; Madonna of Częstochowa Old Church in Zakopane

humour, and recalls the iconography of another form of Podhale folk art – glass painting. Kłosowski's preoccupation with textiles extended to producing altar frontals with birds and flowers painted on serge (fig.8.5).

Kłosowski had a chance to share his genius for ornament as a crafts teacher at the Wood Industry Vocational School (1912) and as the Creative Director and teacher of composition at the School of Lacemaking (1913–31). As recalled by the artist, the latter appointment had an explicitly stated patriotic mission: 'The Lviv State Department requested that I transform the character of the school from the Austro-German tradition to a distinctively Polish spirit, by getting rid of the excessive Art Nouveau influence and instead basing lace designs on native motifs.'[10]

Kłosowki's lacework legacy at the School won a gold medal at the International Exposition of Modern Industrial and Decorative Arts in Paris in 1925, when the designs and workmanship were compared with the most accomplished pieces from Brussels. Notably, in founding the School of Lacemaking, Modrzejewska transplanted the virtually unknown craft technique of bobbin lacework into Podhale, hitherto mainly associated with embroidery and woodcarving. Kłosowski in turn revolutionalised the Zakopane lacework idiom by introducing native Tatra plants and wildlife drawn directly from nature, alongside adapting Podhale ornamental motifs typically used in other crafts. Kłosowski created lace designs evoking a fairy-tale world of mountain flowers (e.g. edelweiss, carline thistle, mountain lily, dandelion seedheads), trees and leaves (e.g. fir branches, pine cones; vine, oak and chestnut leaves), populated by spiders, butterflies, snakes and owls, as well as occasionally cockerels from the back yard (fig.8.6). Kłosowski extolled the moral advantages of bobbin lacemaking, stating that it not only 'provides the noblest delight through the joy of making' but also 'instills the cult of real beauty and ethics within a nation'.[11] Within this relatively new technique, Kłosowski succeeded at creating a distinctively Polish style of Zakopane lacework and making it famous in the international arena.[12]

However, it was the apparently humble paper cutting that should perhaps be viewed as the single most significant art form within Kłosowski's diverse output due to the ideological implications of this medium. The paper cutting is one of the most traditional manifestations of Polish folk art. It flourished in the 19th century, being commonly used by peasants from diverse regions of the Polish lands under partition to decorate the interior of their cottages – initially in the windows as a substitute for net curtains and subsequently as colourful ornaments used for decorating the walls, usually beneath pictures, particularly popular at Christmas time (see Chapter 15). They were traditionally made with shears by folding coloured paper along multiple axes of symmetry (from one up to about 16). Kłosowski first tried his hand at paper cuttings at the age of eight, making do with newspapers. Nevertheless, by the time he had turned 11, his designs had become sought-after decorations at local peasants' weddings. He continued to perfect the craft to seek solace following a teenage disappointment in love.

Kłosowski had initially left the art of the paper cutting behind when he moved away from his village in Podolia to pursue a comprehensive, decade-long artistic education. It is notable that with all the benefit of exposure to the world of high art in Vienna and Kraków, Kłosowski chose to revive this

8.6
Karol Kłosowski's genius for ornament
TOP ROW, LEFT TO RIGHT: 'Spider' lace (c.1921, c.15 cm in diametre), 'Vine' lace design (1921, 38.5 × 49.3 cm) and 'Cockerel' lace designs (1924, 52 × 45.8 cm)
TWO BOTTOM ROWS CLOCKWISE:
'Squirrels', 'Eagles', 'Crickets', 'Caterpillars', 'Parzenice' and 'Snakes' papercuttings
Various dimensions (20–22 cm in diametre or longest dimension)
lace, pen and ink on tracing paper, coloured papers
Private Collection. By Descent from the Artist; Tatra Museum, S/5563/79/MT, S/5563/26/MT

modest art form 12 years later, not long after settling down into married life in Zakopane. His initial motive to beautify the Silent Villa for his wife's gratification was to turn into a manifesto of cultural democracy. He never lost the joy of making, which helped sustain him through the loss of his wife in 1915 and during a period in the Second World War when both of his children were sent away and conscripted into forced labour.

Kłosowski's paper cuttings show most clearly his Morrisean genius for repeating patterns and an outstanding sense of colour, presenting a joyful, fantastical and virtually multi-sensory world of chirping crickets, hissing snakes, hairy caterpillars and sprightly squirrels, reminiscent of the rhythmic beauty, enchanting charm and humour of Morris's iconic printed cotton designs such as 'Brother Rabbit' (1882) or 'Strawberry Thief' (1883). What is notable is his strikingly contemporary use of colour, with an ability to harmonise bold and subdued tones in a single composition, and his capacity to abstract details without losing the character of the depicted creatures. Some of Kłosowski's designs were more overtly patriotic, including multiple renditions of the crowned eagle, Poland's national emblem (fig.8.6).

In the early 20th century, paper cutting was becoming a disappearing craft, much to Kłosowski's distress, as peasants began to replace it with cheap German oleographs in the hope of appearing more gentrified.[13] It was then that the medium became Kłosowski's staple mode of artistic expression. It is clear that he viewed it as both a manifesto of cultural democracy and a key repository of authentic national heritage, stating:

> The paper cutting has grown out of the basic human desire for beauty, out of the same motive as behind any other art work created by people from more cultured social strata. In quiet, impoverished villages – in the drabness of life – the populace resort to material and making in search for joy and happiness . . . I strongly hope that in the present time of trying to recover our own style on the basis of our own old models: castles, moss-clad manor houses and roadside shrines, we will create our own architecture; similarly, the paper cutting is a treasure trove of characteristically Polish motifs, which will serve as the basis for creating rich local ornamentation already under way.[14]

Despite a first-rate education and access to the Kraków art world, Kłosowski chose to settle down in the village of Zakopane, where he led the sort of quiet rural existence that Morris longed for but could never experience at Kelmscott due to pressing duties in London. In Zakopane, Kłosowski took up many of the media and art forms he grew up with and embraced the local vernacular traditions, celebrating and elevating the status of folk art. He must not, however, be mistaken for a folk artist. The art forms he deliberately engaged with were his form of cultural politics aimed at distilling Polishness and practising cultural democracy.

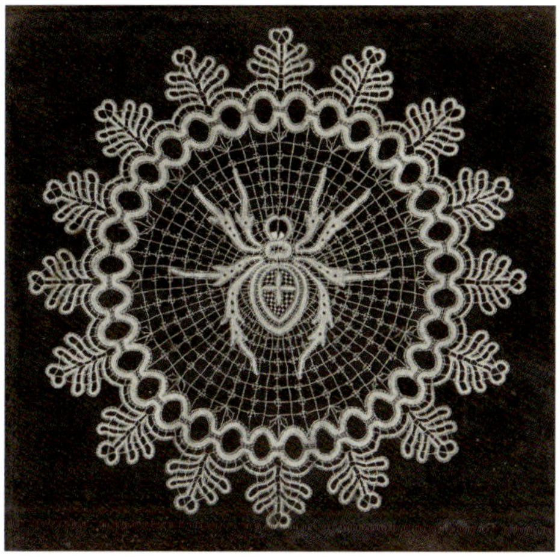
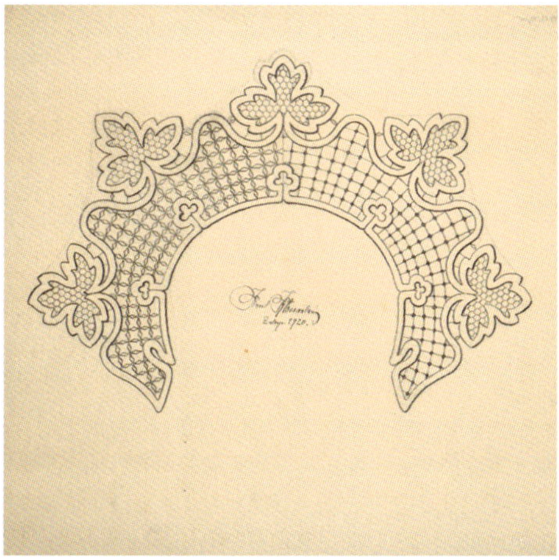
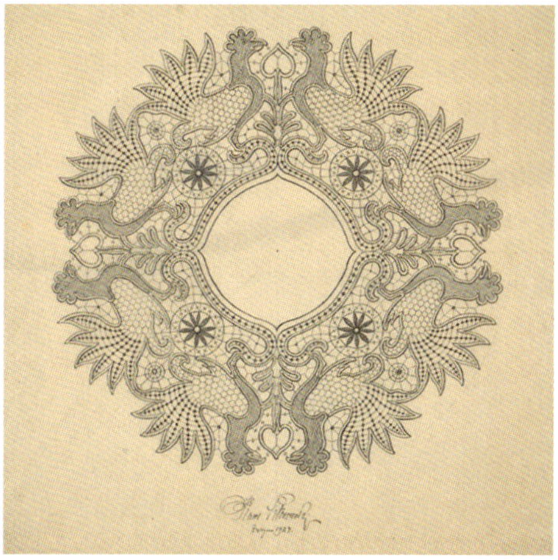
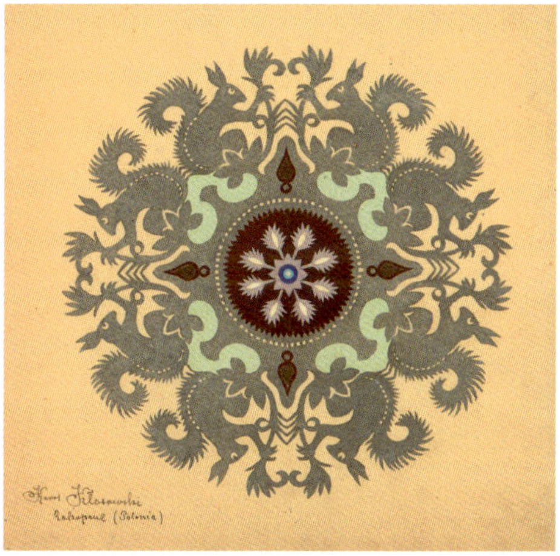
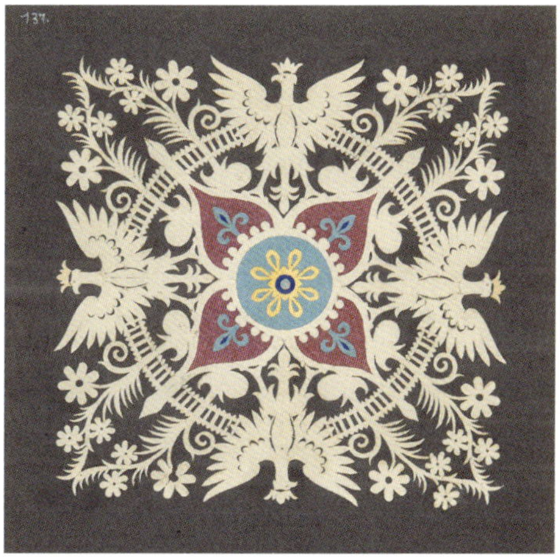
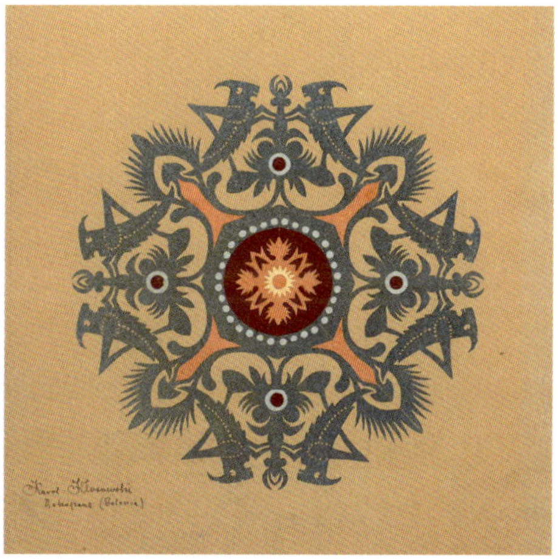
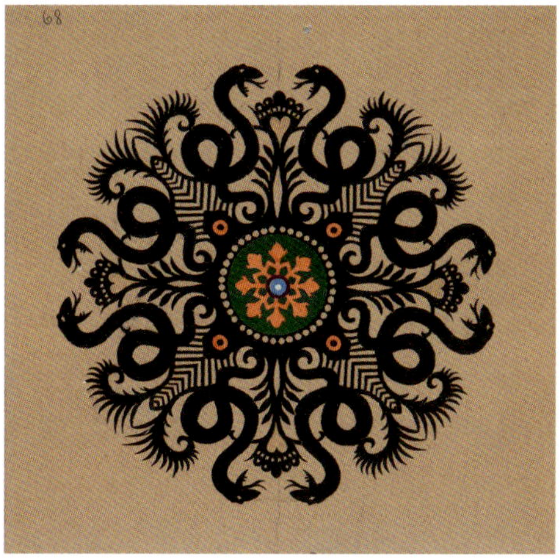
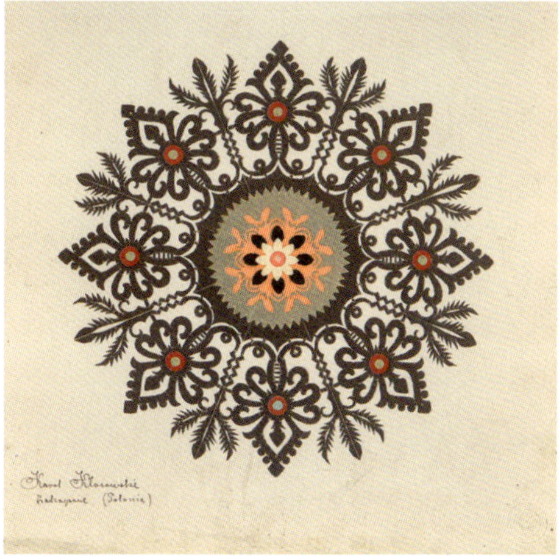
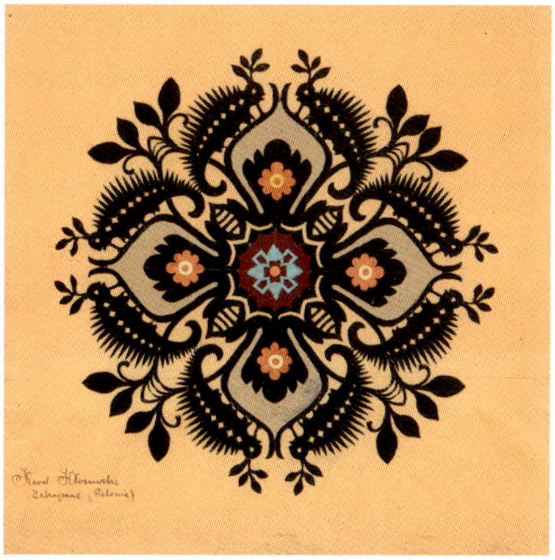

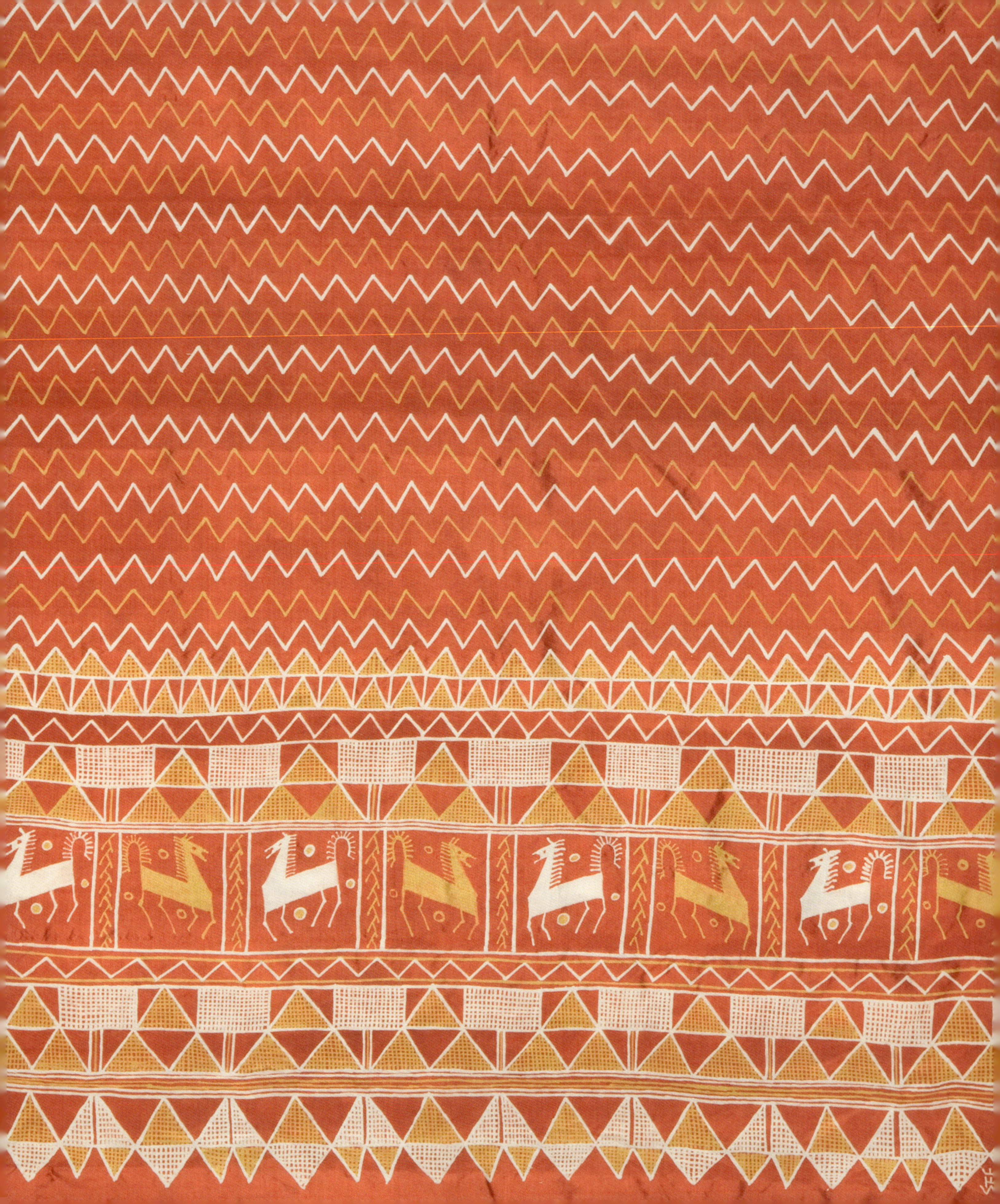

9

'Fine Handwork of Various Professions': The Kraków Workshops

Roisin Inglesby

The Kraków Workshops association was a commercial cooperative of artists, artisans and art professionals founded in Kraków in 1913. In their relatively short existence of only 13 years, they introduced a new kind of design to Poland, synthesising tradition and modernity, expounding new educational techniques, producing notable objects, and launching Polish design on the world stage at the International Exposition of Modern Industrial and Decorative Arts held in Paris in 1925. This chapter aims to introduce the Workshops to an international readership.[1]

From their inception, the Kraków Workshops were intimately associated with the city's Museum of Technology and Industry. It was the Museum's director, Stanisław Till, who instigated the Workshops association's first meeting in January 1913; the other founding members included seven artists, nine artisans, a teacher, and a professor of art history.[2] The Workshops were based in the Museum's building at 9 Ulica Smoleńsk, where they were granted studios in which to run experimental workshops in metalworking, bookbinding and leatherworking, weaving, batik, dyeing, and cabinet-making. This range of artistic pursuits was reflective of the broad-ranging objectives of the association, which aimed to create 'fine handwork of various professions' through the 'joint efforts of artists, people who have the development of the industrial arts at heart, and craftspeople driven to enhance handwork through creating companies whose object is production'.[3]

From the outset, the Workshops shared a fundamental belief that there should be no distinction between the so-called fine and decorative arts. The association was founded on the principle that the material culture of everyday life should be infused with artistic qualities, changing the status of art from something only found in painting and sculpture to an essential element of all creative production. At the centre of this production stood artisanal knowledge and artisanal education, which were seen as the essential source from which to develop a new vocabulary of form, and the means by which this transformation could be accomplished.

The Kraków Workshops differed from its predecessor, the Polish Applied Arts Society, in that the younger members of the Workshops largely rejected the Society's uncritical

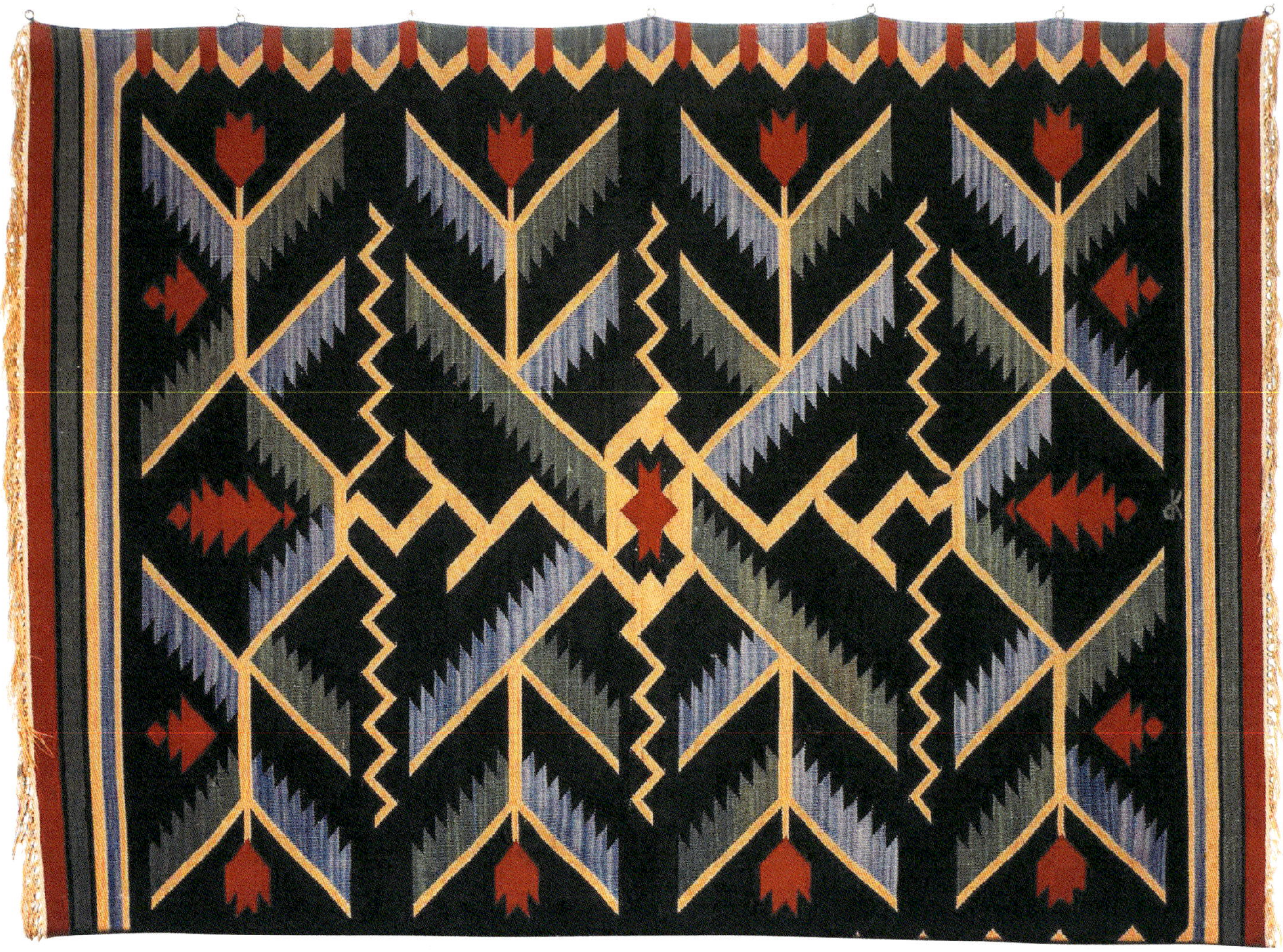

incorporation of folk art, instead seeking a new, functional national style.[4] While the Workshops association embraced traditional craft knowledge, its members were instrumental in forming new theoretical frameworks which blended respect for folk traditions with the drive for original and independent art forms. As Wojciech Jastrzębowski put it, 'we had no time for collecting pieces of folk art, increasing collections, or for propaganda-style publications; we wanted to work as visual artists and make art objects in our own workshops'.[5]

The most important theoretical influence in the early years of the Workshops' existence was Włodzimierz Konieczny. Alongside his work as a sculptor, printmaker and poet, Konieczny developed a theory that argued for the infusion of art into everyday objects and thus everyday life. Drawing on the writings of John Ruskin and Cyprian Kamil Norwid, Konieczny posited that form, material, decoration and function were inextricably linked, and as such there could be no art other than that which was necessary, or useful. Konieczny's ideas echo William Morris's comment that 'nothing can be a work of art which is not useful'.[6] Calling for the eradication of any distinction between the fine and applied arts, he introduced the term 'decorative' to Polish design discourse,[7] arguing that all artists were intrinsically decorators and developing the idea of a 'perfectionist instinct' that drove people to ornament the world around them. While appreciative of folk art and traditional design, Konieczny cautioned against over-reliance

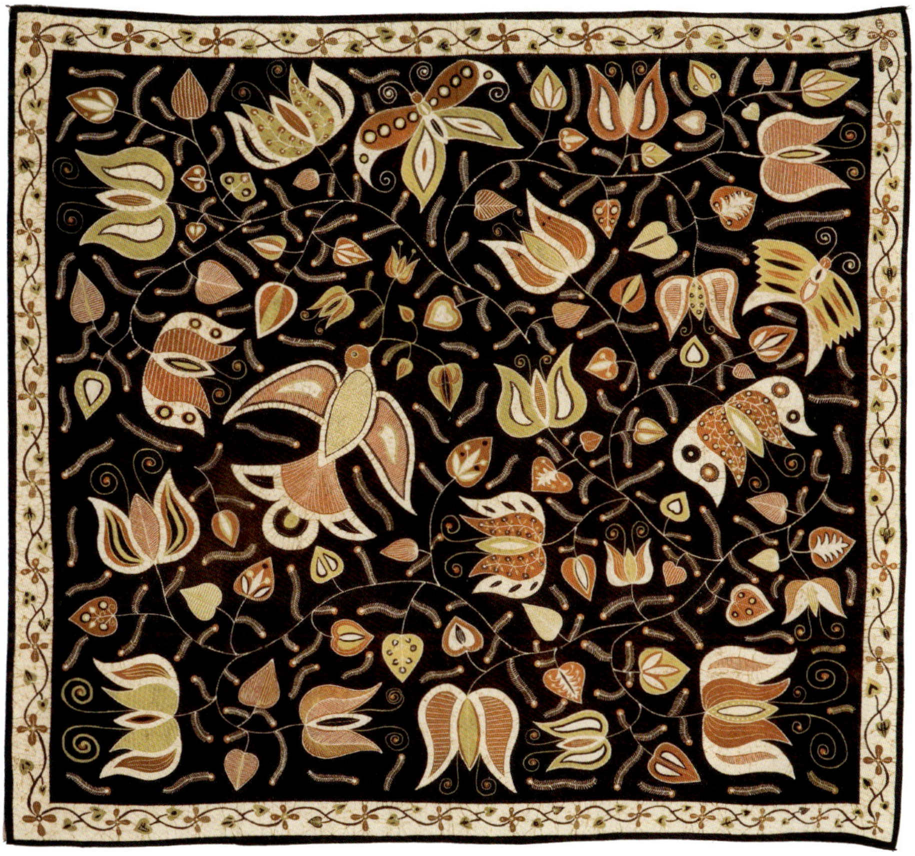

9.0 (p. 122)
Norbert Okołowicz
Batik silk scarf / decorative wall hanging, 1913
Silk with batik decoration
232.5 × 60 cm
National Museum in Kraków, MNK-XIX-3258

9.1 (OPPOSITE)
Wojciech Jastrzębowski
'Saws' kilim, designed *c.*1919, made 1926
Kilim technique, loom with reed
*c.*120 × 150 cm
Maria and Jan Szczepkowski Foundation

9.2 (LEFT)
Zofia Kogut
Scarf, 1921
Silk with batik decoration
117 × 122 cm
National Museum in Kraków, MNK-XIX-3254

on folk motifs, on the basis that, divorced from their original context and media, decorative images lost their intrinsic purpose and thus became inauthentic.[8] Konieczny's theories, published in articles in *Kraków Arts Monthly*, were intrinsic to the Workshops' agenda, cementing the link between the craft-centred ideology of the British Arts and Crafts Movement and the Polish national experience and putting it into workshop practice. In his own words: 'In desiring a Polish art we must desire Polish crafts – without them there can be no Polish art.'[9]

Konieczny was killed in action during the First World War, at the Battle of Kostiuchnówka in 1916. In the following years the intellectual programme of the Workshops was determined by two men with pedagogical interests: Karol Homolacs and Antoni Buszek.

Born near Kraków in 1874, Homolacs was a painter and printmaker who had studied in Vienna, Paris and Munich. He worked as a teacher, and in addition to painting he designed kilims, furniture, metalwork, book covers and illustrations for the Workshops, later becoming a curator at the Museum of Technology and Industry.[10] Homolacs was primarily interested in the role of ornament within design. He argued for a universal understanding of ornament, governed by a set of rules equally applicable to natural history, architecture and art. Rather than being imitative of nature or based in geometry, Homolacs understood true ornament to be the transmission through material of an instinctive artisanal rhythm, derived from 'tribal principles passed down from generation to generation'.[11] Thus the value of folk art lay not simply in imitating its forms, but in intuiting the tribal concepts behind it. Moreover, artisanal technique was the foundation of all art; without it, there could be no beauty.[12]

Homolacs's theories on the 'essential' nature of ornament – that is, ornament derived from an intrinsic rhythmic quality – took form in the objects produced at the Workshops. Arguing that successful ornament depended on the relationship between patterns, Homolacs taught a method by which designs

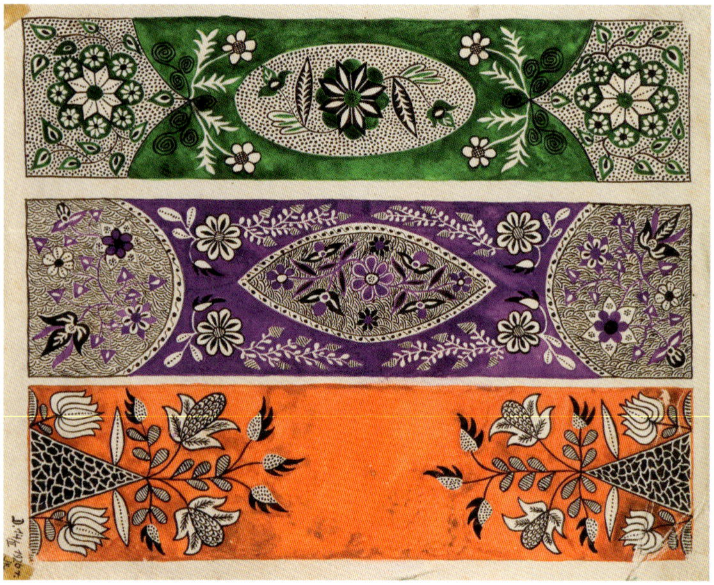
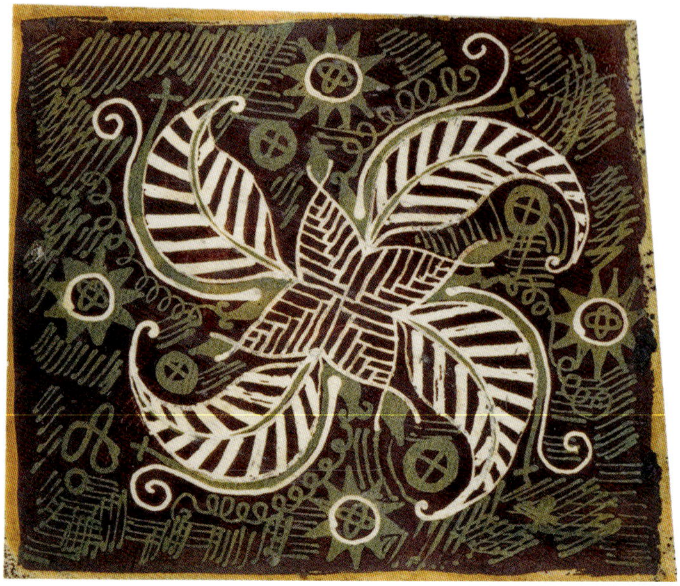

9.3
Pages from batik pattern books developed by peasant women at the Buszek batik workshops at the Kraków Museum of Technology and Industry, undated
24.5 × 30 cm
Seweryn Udziela Ethnographic Museum in Kraków, II/11340/RYS

were built up through small decorative motifs which combined to make an ornamental whole.[13] He lectured on the principles of ornament and produced textbooks on the subject, ensuring that his ideas filtered through to a younger generation of designers. Most significantly, his teachings linked ornament with technique and context, ensuring that practitioners at the Workshops considered the appropriate use of materials and tools in their quest to create new forms.[14]

The Kraków Workshops' particular fusion of creative intuition and technique is best illustrated through the initiatives of Antoni Buszek. A painter, master of painting and dyeing technologies, theoretician and pedagogue, Buszek adopted ideas from the emerging field of developmental psychology to formulate the Buszek Theory, an educational method that encouraged children to use their innate imaginative capacities to create artwork with little or no formal training. Buszek had studied in Paris, where he encountered similar conceptions of intuitive creation at the Atelier Martine, the workshop founded by the fashion designer Paul Poiret (1879–1944) in 1911.[15] At the Martine, young girls from working-class backgrounds were taken to various cultural attractions, such as the Botanic Gardens, and then encouraged to create art based on their experiences, which was subsequently used as the source material for collections of textiles. Buszek employed similar methods in Kraków: uneducated girls were given rudimentary training in the techniques of batik and encouraged to create designs according to their own imagination.[16] Buszek's experiments in the batik workshop were incredibly successful. The workshop was the longest running and most well known of all the studios,[17] and the objects it produced not only made money for the Kraków Workshops but also encapsulate many of the underlying ideas and methodologies behind the Workshops association as a whole.

Batik – a technique of wax-resist dyeing that originated in the Indonesian island of Java – gained international attention after examples were shown at the Exposition Universelle of 1900 in Paris. At the Kraków Workshops, the batik studio combined the Javanese approach with a traditional Polish technique of decorating Easter eggs that also involved wax and dye baths.[18] Buszek and his student Anna Bąkowska, who later ran the batik workshop, studied Javanese working methods and together with colleagues in the dyeing studio developed an innovative process

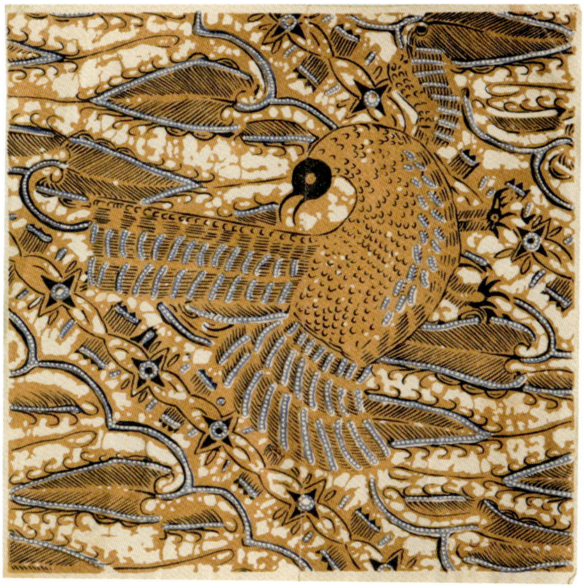

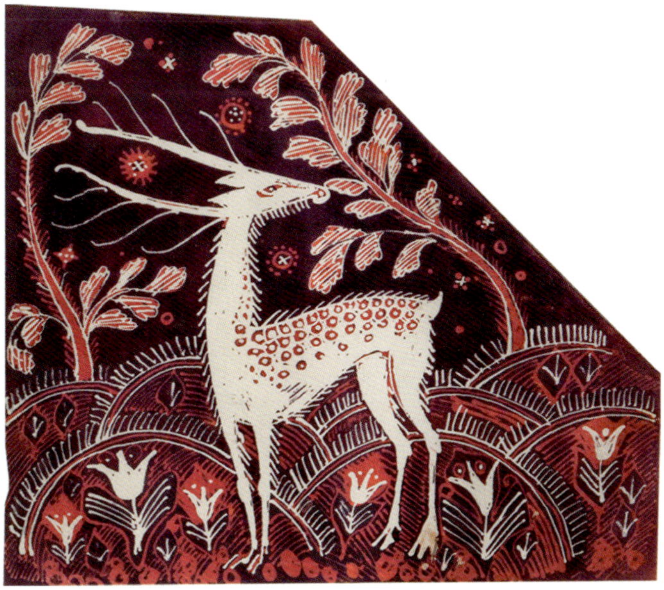

of printing and dyeing that used vegetable dyes from historical recipes in place of modern aniline dyes. An interest in vegetable dyes is found across the design pioneers of the period, with both William Morris in England and students at the Bauhaus weaving workshops in Germany experimenting with natural pigments. The batiks produced at the Kraków Workshops included interior furnishings (wall hangings and tableware such as napkins and coasters), as well as elements of female dress (shawls, headscarves, ribbons, and eventually outfits), and are typically characterised by swirling floral patterns composed of simple shapes. Sometimes symmetry is employed to create an overall sense of harmony; on other occasions the compositional balance is created through the deployment of similar elements arranged according to an internal logic that corresponds to Homolacs's sense of artisanal 'rhythm'.

Among the girls trained by Buszek at the batik workshop were the three Kogut sisters, Maria, Józefa and Zofia, who produced work in accordance with his method, which Józefa described:

> Batik was basically taught without using a pencil [only wax], first on paper, and later on canvas, drawing, using your imagination and whimsy to make various compositions. You had to draw quickly with a marker, filled with a mixture of wax and colophony, heating it over a spirit lamp till it was liquid, since the wax went cold (quickly) and did not make a proper line. Of course, the students initially didn't like the 'daubs' that were produced, but the teachers and various observers . . . expressed their admiration and . . . inspired us all to come up with newer and better patterns.[19]

This intuitive method – bolstered by knowledge of original Javanese examples – was then solidified into coherent designs, as shown in a personal collection of patterns and ornamental motifs devised by Józefa Kogut, which she collated into what appears to be a cross between a diary/scrapbook and a pattern book (fig.9.3), now in the Seweryn Udziela Ethnographic Museum in Kraków.[20]

Alongside the women trained according to the Buszek Theory, many other members of the Kraków Workshops also produced batiks. Norbert Okołowicz, for example, a painter and technologist who ran the dyeing studio in the Workshops' early days, received a silver medal for his batiks at the 1925 Paris Exposition.[21] An early, experimental shawl he produced in 1913 (fig.9.0) reveals the extent to which practitioners at the Workshops used modern, geometric forms in conjunction with the traditional folk motifs incorporated by the peasant women employed by Buszek. Okołowicz's abstracted horses and lace-like triangles and squares are arranged in a repeating composition that vibrates throughout the object; the sense of

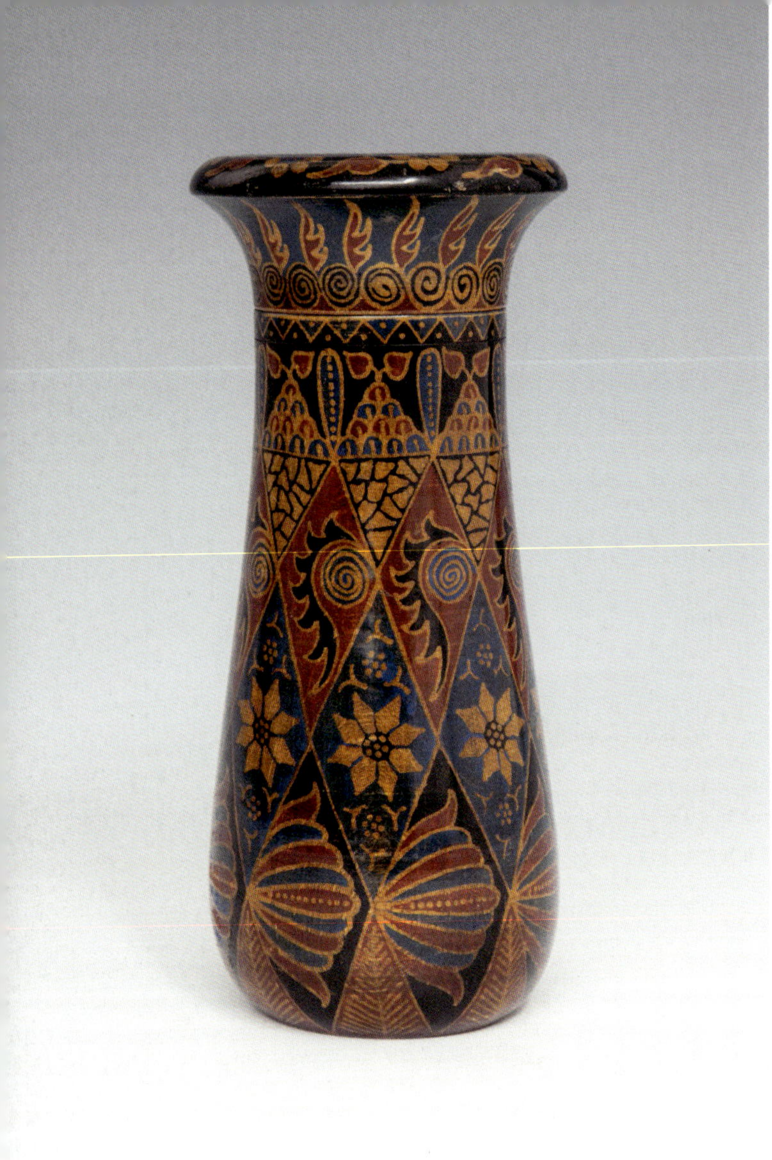

9.4 (LEFT)
Józefa Kogut
Vase with batik decoration, undated
Turned wood with batik decoration
Height 21 cm, rim diameter 9 cm
Seweryn Udziela Ethnographic
Museum in Kraków, MEK 57780

9.5 (OPPOSITE)
Interiors of the batik, cabinetmaking, metalwork and weaving studios at the Kraków Museum of Technology and Industry in 1913–14, including the team of batik artists with studio manager Jerzy Warchałowski
TOP: photograph reproduced from Irena Huml, *Warsztaty Krakowskie*, Wrocław: Zakład Narodowy im. Ossolińskich, 1973; BOTTOM, LEFT TO RIGHT: State Municipal Archive in Kraków, A III/1592; State Municipal Archive in Kraków, A IV/1338; State Municipal Archive in Kraków, A V/1113

rhythm is so strong that the shapes almost appear to march to a beat across the fabric.

The principles of batik production were also applied to other media, including small wooden objects such as boxes, plates and vases (fig.9.4).

As well as being artistically innovative, the batik workshop was commercially successful – the work was extremely popular with foreign visitors and it regularly featured as the first item in the minutes of the Kraków Workshops association's meetings, implying its prominence within the organisation.[22] Indeed, from the outset the Workshops were conceived as a fundamentally practical organisation, enabling artists to make money through the production of saleable products. Alongside the bookbinding studio run by Bonawentura Lenart (see Chapter 16) and a hugely successful toy-making studio (see Chapter 15), the Workshops also produced metalwork and woven kilims.

In addition to the objects produced by the individual workshops, two large-scale collaborative projects stand out, book-ending the Kraków Workshops' existence. The first of these was the interior decoration of the building for the Museum of Technology and Industry, an early commission which gave the Workshops the important opportunity to contribute to an architectural whole.

The commission was undertaken along strictly functional lines and included a grand staircase 'with an exceptionally beautiful decorative balustrade' and sparse, simply ornamented windows and a banister designed by Józef Czajkowski.[23] The building's exterior decoration was undertaken by Jastrzębowski, who, along with Karol Homolacs, Karol Stryjeński (1887–1932) and Karol Maszkowski (1868–1938), was responsible for the furniture, which they designed according to the aesthetic principles of the Workshops: revealed, 'honest' construction; faithful use of materials that showcased the grain of the wood; and simple decorative flourishes. As Till reported: 'The furnishings in the new building are of exclusively Polish production. The simplest materials have been used, generally pine, on occasion larch, and so on. Especial emphasis was placed, however, on very precise workmanship and on strong construction.'[24]

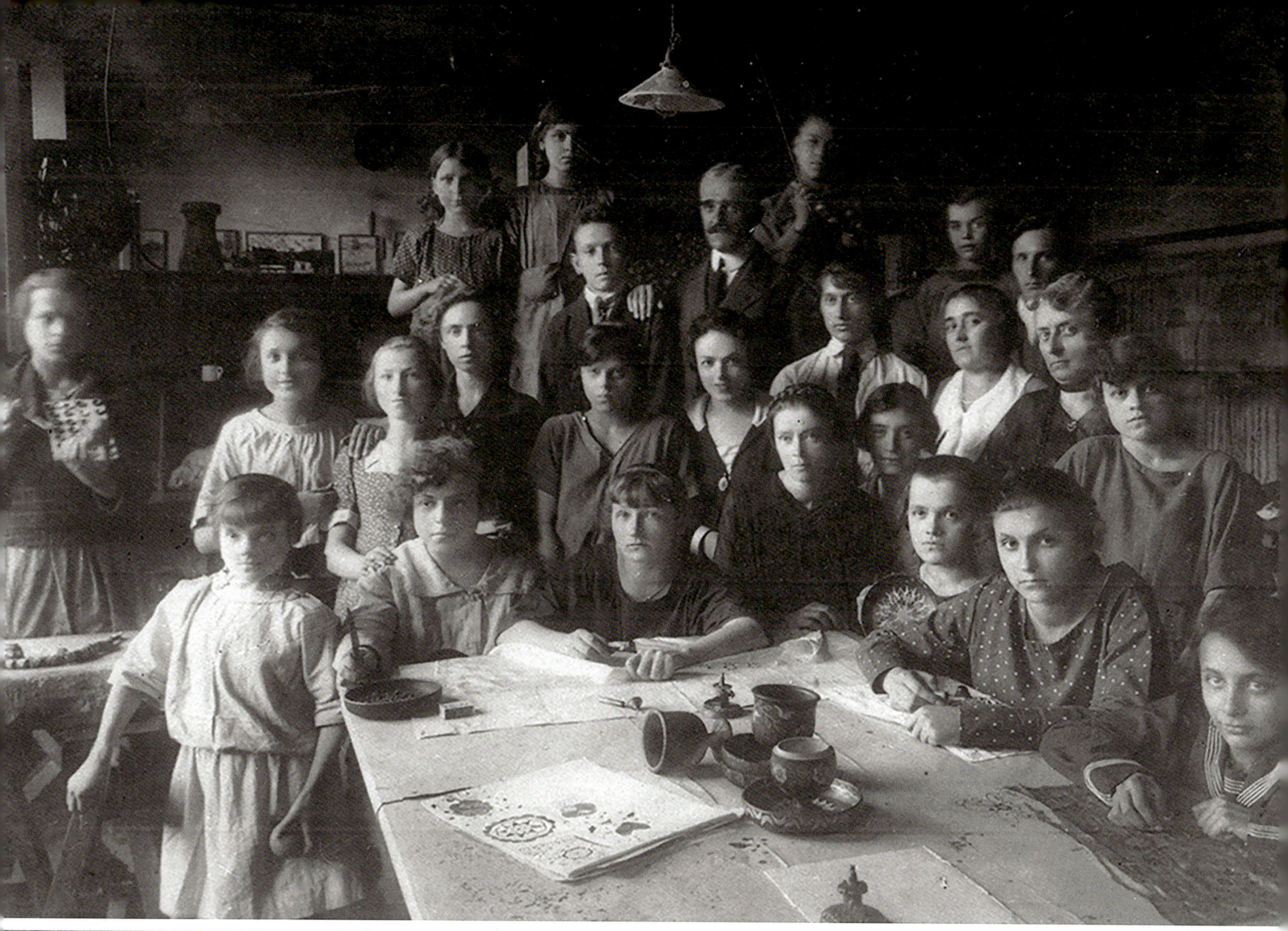

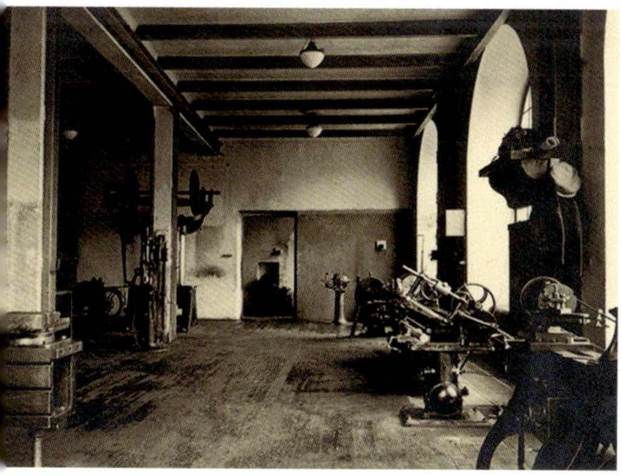

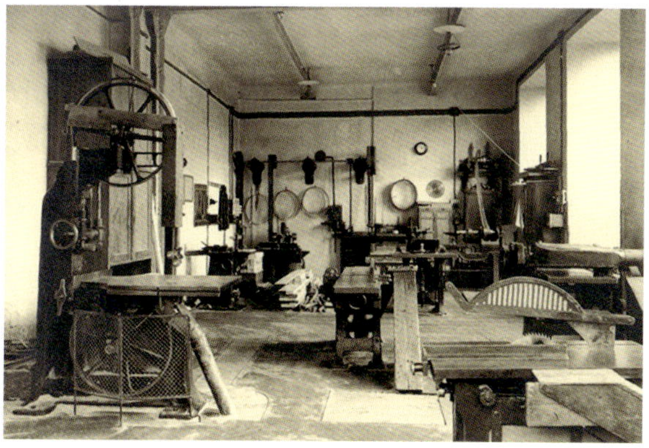

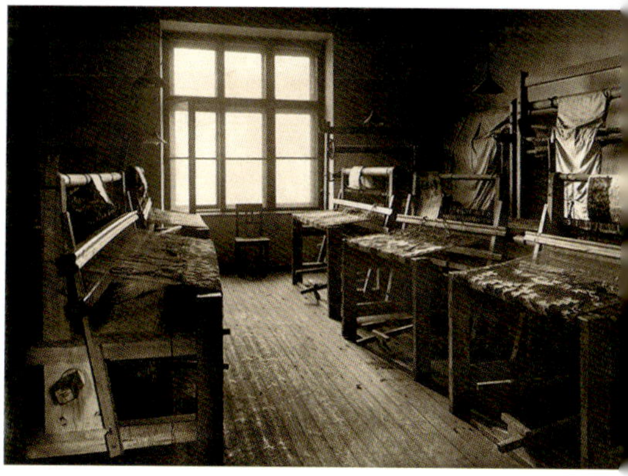

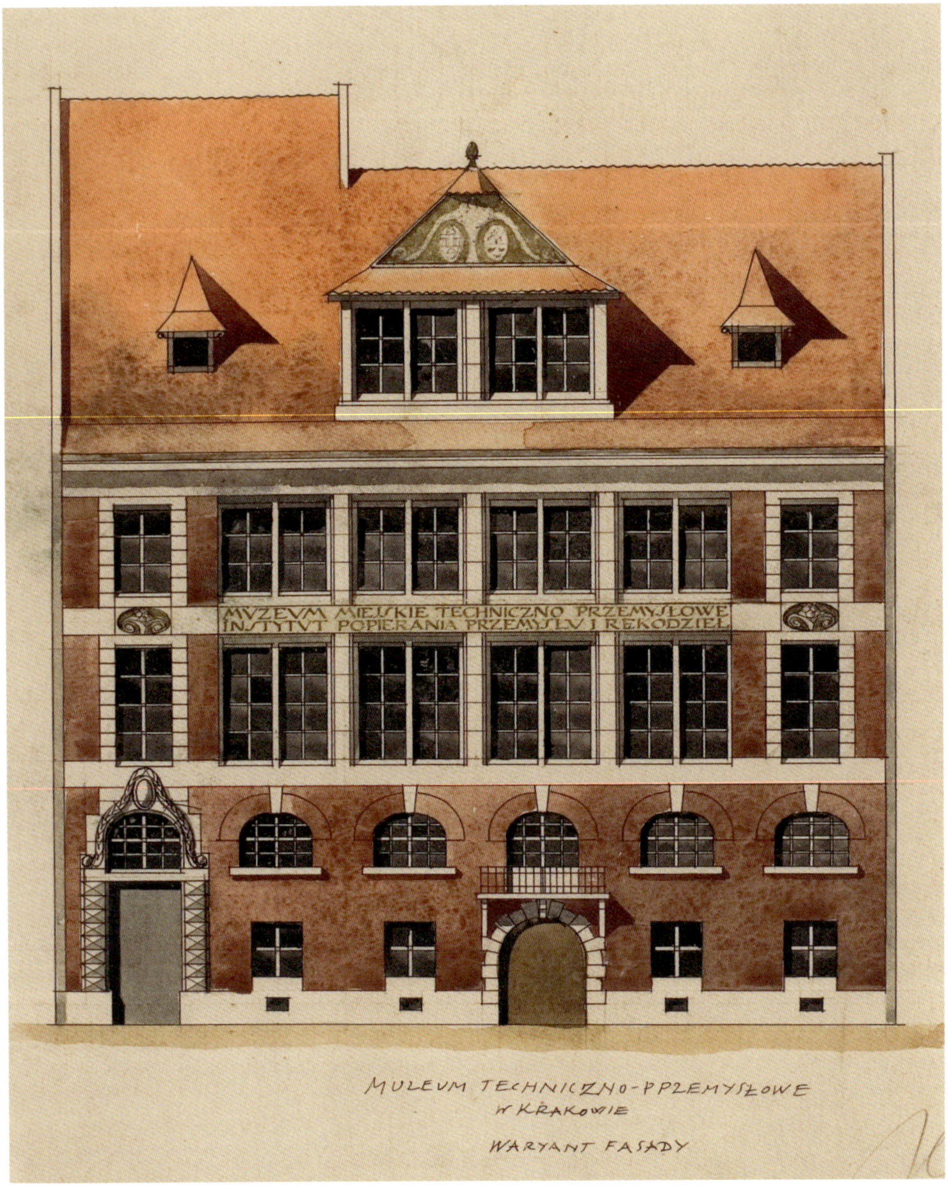

9.6 (LEFT)
Józef Czajkowski
Design of the facade of the Kraków Museum of Technology and Industry, 1909
Watercolour on paper
49 × 38.9 cm
Jan Matejko Academy of Fine Arts in Kraków

9.7 (OPPOSITE)
Wojciech Jastrzębowski
Double seats for the lecture theatre (great hall) in the Museum of Technology and Industry, Kraków, 1913–14
Larch wood
98 × 112.5 × 73.5 cm
Jan Matejko Academy of Fine Arts in Kraków

The second major project undertaken by the Kraków Workshops was their contribution to the International Exposition of Modern Industrial and Decorative Arts held in Paris in 1925. Jerzy Warchałowski was the commissioner of the Polish section of the exhibition; the Kraków Workshops displayed a large array of work, including batik, toys, furniture, weaving and books, garnering 20 of the total 35 Grand Prix awarded to Poland.[25]

However, even the huge success of the Paris Exposition did nothing to alleviate the financial pressures that the Kraków Workshops continually faced throughout the association's existence. In 1923, rising inflation worsened its financial prospects, which were made even more acute by competition from a rival group, the Polish Artistic Industry Society (Towarzystwo Polski Przemysł Artystyczny), which included Karol Homolacs. Despite members such as Warchałowski personally contributing to the association's coffers, the situation proved untenable and the Kraków Workshops went into liquidation in 1926.

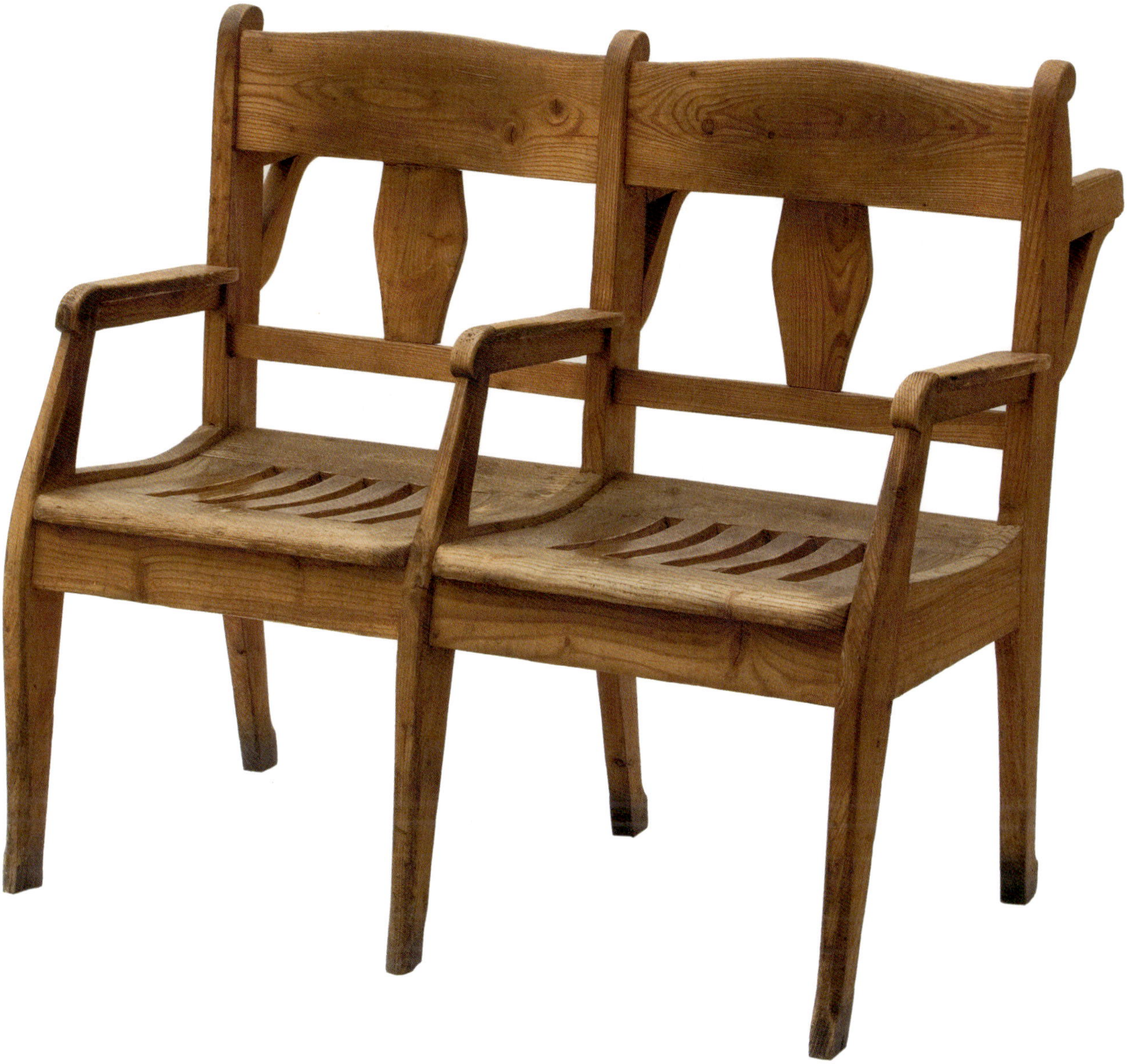

Links with international movements

Wojciech Jastrzębowski held William Morris in high regard, calling him the master of the Kraków Workshops.[26] Nevertheless, while the residual influence of the British Arts and Crafts Movement can be felt through Konieczny's writings and the legacy of the Polish Applied Arts Society, as Szczerski has noted, the Kraków Workshops 'had more in common with artists' and craftsmen's associations formed in Europe at the time, which focused on the development of a modern and synthetic language of form and industrial art rather than on handicrafts revival'.[27] Many members of the Workshops were educated abroad, and the city of Kraków, part of the Austro-Hungarian Empire until 1918, had close ties with Vienna. Some members of the Workshops had in fact trained at the Wiener Werkstätte, an organisation which had been founded in Vienna in 1903 with the intention of raising standards of design through the marriage of art and industry. The Kraków

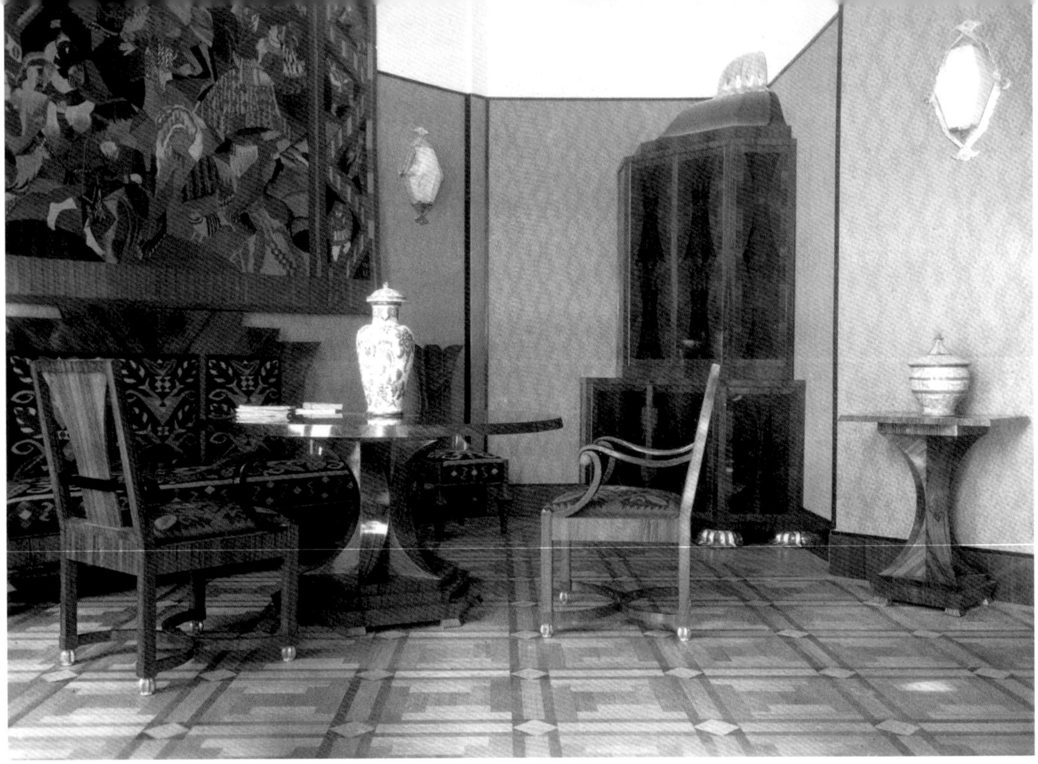

9.8
Lounge area of the exhibition salon in the Polish Pavilion at the International Exposition of Modern Industrial and Decorative Arts, Paris, 1925, designed by Józef Czajkowski and Wojciech Jastrzębowski
Jan Matejko Academy of Fine Arts in Kraków, Main Library Print Room 13 364/125

Workshops, considered by Irena Huml as the 'twin sister' of the Werkstätte,[28] grew partly out of its influence and partly in resistance to competition from Austrian imports.

In Britain, the closest parallel is with the Omega Workshops in London, also established in 1913, by the artist and curator Roger Fry. While there is no evidence of a direct link between the Kraków Workshops and the Omega Workshops, a comparison of the two shows the extent to which the Kraków Workshops were in tune with comparable international initiatives, while simultaneously maintaining a unique national identity.[29]

The Omega Workshops were born out of a sense of horror at the effects of poor commercial taste on the nation's artistic production. Founded along distinctly practical lines – as an arena in which artists could be adequately paid for producing commercially viable designs – the Omega were conceived more as a business model than as a political manifesto, as had been the case with the more traditionally minded Arts and Crafts collectives that had sprung up in England since the death of William Morris in 1896.[30] Like the Kraków Workshops, Fry's mission was aesthetic: the Omega, he declared, would be 'less ambitious than Morris; they do not hope to solve the social problems of production as well as the artistic'.[31]

To these ends, Fry established a system by which artists were essentially kept on a retainer, paid weekly to design for the Omega on a part-time basis and anonymously contributing to a body of work that included painting, interior decoration, furnishing, textiles (including batik) and ceramics. As with the Kraków Workshops, painters formed a substantial element of the Omega Workshops, and while they designed decoration applicable to a range of material culture, these designs were frequently abstracted and applied to a variety of media – a practice that directly contradicted Homolacs's insistence on the integrity of design and purpose.[32] Moreover, while the Kraków Workshops integrated design with manufacture in almost all cases,[33] with the exception of ceramics (which Fry produced himself), the Omega outsourced their designs to specialist workshops.

Fry was familiar with Poland, having travelled there in 1910, in order to purchase Rembrandt's *The Polish Rider* (1650–55) for the American industrialist and collector Henry Clay Frick. Sending a letter to his wife Helen from Vienna in May of that year, Fry recounted his 'very interesting' experience in the country: 'They are a queer, medieval people, but seem to manage their affairs very happily, though the peasants are terribly poor. Kraków is rather an interesting old town, a queer mixture of German, Russian and Turkish. I saw a lot of good pictures there and met a lot of quite interesting people.'[34] Frustratingly, Fry does not mention what he saw or whom he

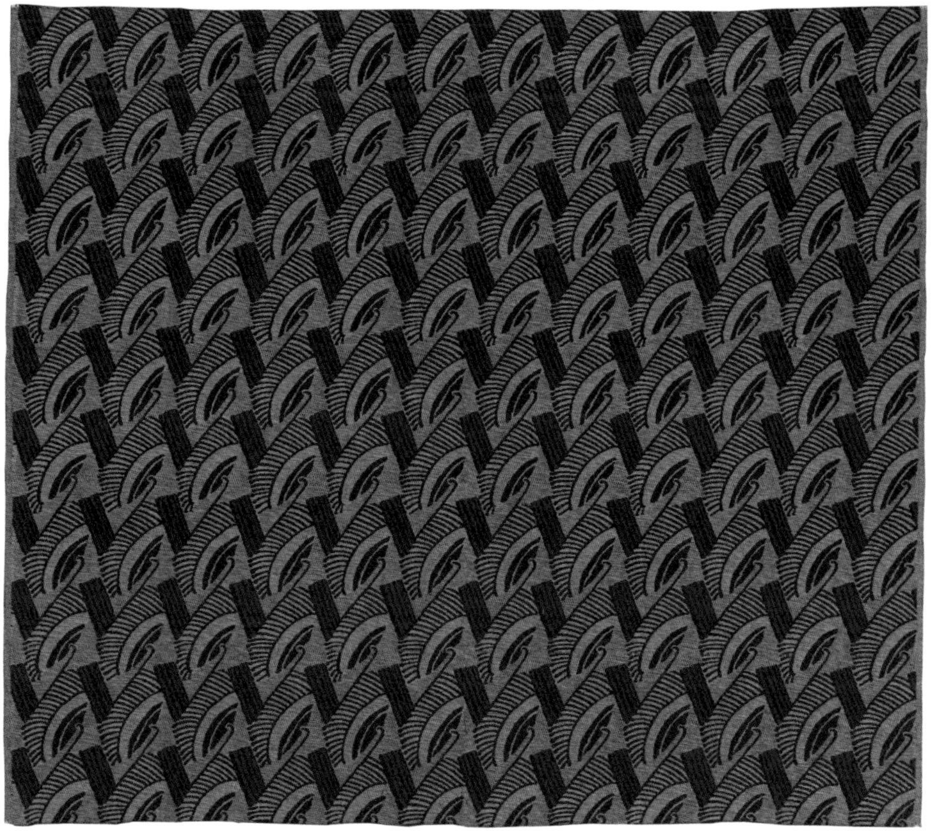

9.9
'Cracow' furnishing fabric, designed by Roger Fry for the Omega Workshops, 1914
Jacquard-woven wool and linen
128.8 × 142.7 cm
Victoria and Albert Museum, London, T.460-1934

met; though he did tell Helen that 'I've seen a lot of pictures and got some new ideas'. While this has been taken to mean inspiration from Polish portraiture,[35] given Fry's interest in the applied arts and the artistic atmosphere of the time in Kraków, a city at the centre of the Polish movement to unify painting and decorative art, it equally does not seem unreasonable to suggest that he was aware of the work of the Polish Applied Arts Society, and that the search for a new formal language in Poland served as one model in the period when he was devising a strategy to renew the decorative arts in Britain. It is also possible that Fry was aware of the Polish context through the French artist Henri Gaudier-Brzeska, who worked with the Omega Workshops prior to his death in 1915, and whose partner, the novelist Sophie Brzeska, was originally from Kraków.

What is certain is that both the Omega Workshops and the Kraków Workshops were influenced by Paul Poiret. Like Buszek, Fry had been hugely impressed by the Atelier Martine, writing that 'My workshop would be carried out on similar lines and might probably work in conjunction with the Ecole Martine, by mutual exchange of ideas and products.'[36] Fry's enthusiasm for the work produced at the Martine stemmed from its spontaneous, intuitive style, a quality that he, like Buszek, also admired in work by children.[37]

Fry showed admiration and sympathy for the Polish people, writing to his wife that 'the Poles are quite simpatico, like Italians or Irish. I suppose all the nice races get sat on.'[38] As such, in addition to his aesthetic appreciation of Eastern European folk art,[39] he may also have had a more personal affinity in mind when, reputedly inspired by newspaper reports of the Battle of Kraków in 1914,[40] he named a fabric design after the city (fig.9.9). The textile – a furnishing fabric made from jacquard-woven wool and linen that was also made into a waistcoat by the Omega Workshops' seamstress Joy Brown – is composed of bold black lines and geometric elements, arranged in a resounding rhythm of repeats that reveals a strong stylistic echo between the Omega and Kraków Workshops.

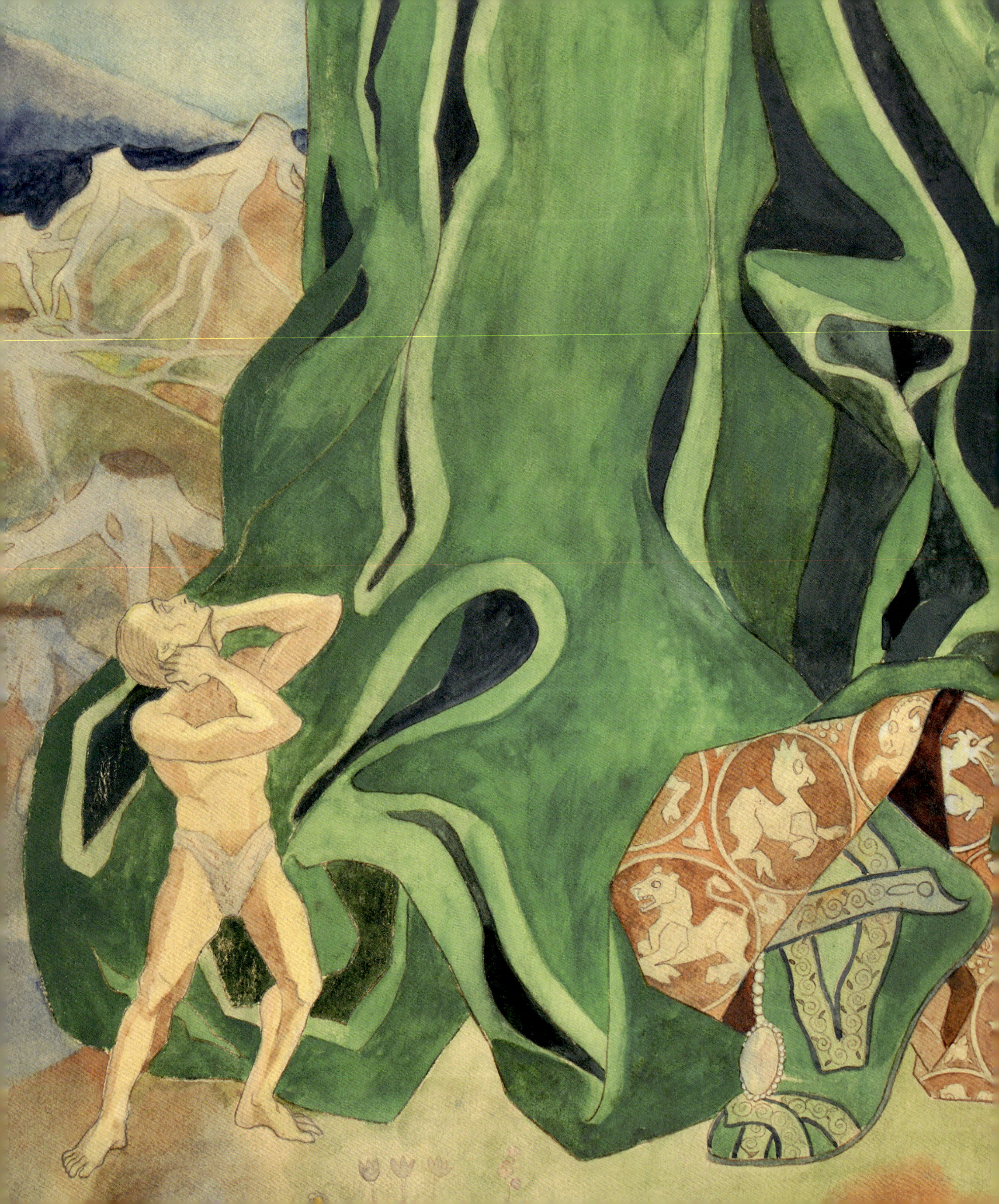

10

Maria Pawlikowska-Jasnorzewska (b. 1891, Kraków, d. 1945, Manchester): The Pictorial Art of Young Poland's Daughter

Barbara Bogoczek and Tony Howard

Maria Pawlikowska-Jasnorzewska, née Kossak, is best known for her epigrammatic lyrical poetry, which has often been set to music – such as her *Ophelia*:

> Oh, I shall have to stay here for a while
> in glassy water, in a seaweed net,
> until this fact and I are reconciled:
> I wasn't loved, it's as simple as that.[1]

She was hailed as 'the Polish Sappho', but like Stanisław Wyspiański she was also a playwright and, crucially, a painter. Looking back to the 1920s, the poet Beata Obertyńska recalled Maria's visual art:

> I saw many of her compositions – small watercolour paintings, routinely preceded by countless preparatory studies from nature, drawings always cast with the same confident, almost masculine flourish, in which she sought to express, honestly and tirelessly, the truth of her vision. They were often weird things, amazing, untainted by any influence and unlike anything else . . . in between a blissful dream and a tormenting nightmare. The meaning? Usually symbolic. Often known only to her. But always testimony to a cool, unfailingly acute observation of life, and with all the panache of a subtle, very contemporary, feminine sensibility. I also remember her psychologically naturalistic portraits of plants! That's the only way to define them. Something *á la* Dürer and Wyspiański, but as though fragmented through the prism of a dewdrop.[2]

Maria's (or Lilka, as she was called at home) earliest watercolours, juvenilia, were infused with the spirit of Art Nouveau – whimsically witty pictures of flowers with the faces of women, sometimes budding together in pools of colour, sometimes swooning alone. As her art developed, it became more intricate, with a precise and skilful attention to detail and increasingly personal layers of meaning. In Obertyńska's words (and to date there have been few considered assessments of

10.0 (p.134)
Maria Pawlikowska-Jasnorzewska
Vision, c.1916
Watercolour and gouache on card
60 × 45 cm
Society of Friends of the Fine Arts, Kraków, cat.65n

10.1
Maria Pawlikowska-Jasnorzewska
Illustration for a Fairy Tale, 1914
Watercolour on paper
23 × 35 cm
Museum of Literature, Warsaw, cat.K.00584

Pawlikowska-Jasnorzewska's painting): 'Herbs, seeds, grasses, leaves and flowers – supernaturally enlarged and incredibly accurate in line and mood, and yet transmuted by her in her own way into enchanted thickets, sea-beds, haze or smoke, often swarming with creatures, half-human, half-insect, fantastically drawn into the tangle of this cabalistic botanical labyrinth.'[3]

I. Roots in Kossakówka

Maria Kossak was born into a family of artists. Both her grandfather Juliusz (1824–1899) and father Wojciech (1856–1942) were celebrated painters, promoting a heroic vision of Polish historical identity, though they were cosmopolitan too. Both married into Polish nobility and settled in Kraków, where Juliusz set up a home soon known as Kossakówka, a vibrant meeting point for artists and intellectuals in which Wojciech and his wife Maria brought up their three children: Jerzy, Magdalena and Maria. Jerzy emulated his father and grandfather while the girls became best known as writers. However, Maria was strikingly multi-talented: by the age of six she had written her first poems, was learning the piano, and had started painting. Obertyńska again:

> Her talent for painting – and the fact that she discarded it completely, prodigally, for the sake of poetry – is hardly ever mentioned. She inherited her ability from her family but her style was totally unlike the Kossak style. One could say she never discarded painting, only changed her technique, trading line and colour for the word. Yet the fact remains that, gifted with two equally powerful talents, she chose one over the other, which she let wither away. Had she chosen otherwise she would surely have made herself a name as the best illustrator of all – unique, capable of creating her own new genre.[4]

Maria's family and home gave her lifelong support and perhaps – until the outbreak of the Second World War – a sense of grounded *joie de vivre* that few artists have enjoyed. Her home education included languages and the study of nature and, well read in Greek myths, the children acted them out in Kossakówka's garden, with friends who included Rafał, the son of the painter Jacek Malczewski. In fact, Maria's artistic biography is part of the story of the children of Young Poland, and of its legacy.

As she stated herself, her education was shaped by her own discoveries in books she avidly borrowed from the library in Ulica Świętego Jana – from Maeterlinck through Nietzsche to Schopenhauer (in that order), whom she considered her teachers.[5] Her Young Poland influences included the naturalist playwright Gabriela Zapolska and the poets Leopold Staff, 'Miriam' (Zenon Przesmycki) and Tadeusz Miciński, as well as writings by Stanisław Przybyszewski. Many of these authors sowed the seeds for her interest in Eastern cultures, spiritualism, the occult and mysticism, as well as a favourite pastime: fortune-telling. She explained: 'All the mystical books are a breath of fresh air for me, they clear my eyes and let me look down from a high mountain on the earth, on life, on humankind, on my life as an individual – and in this condition, losing myself, I find peace.'[6]

But Maria faced the challenging situation of Polish women artists in the first decades of the 20th century, and in particular

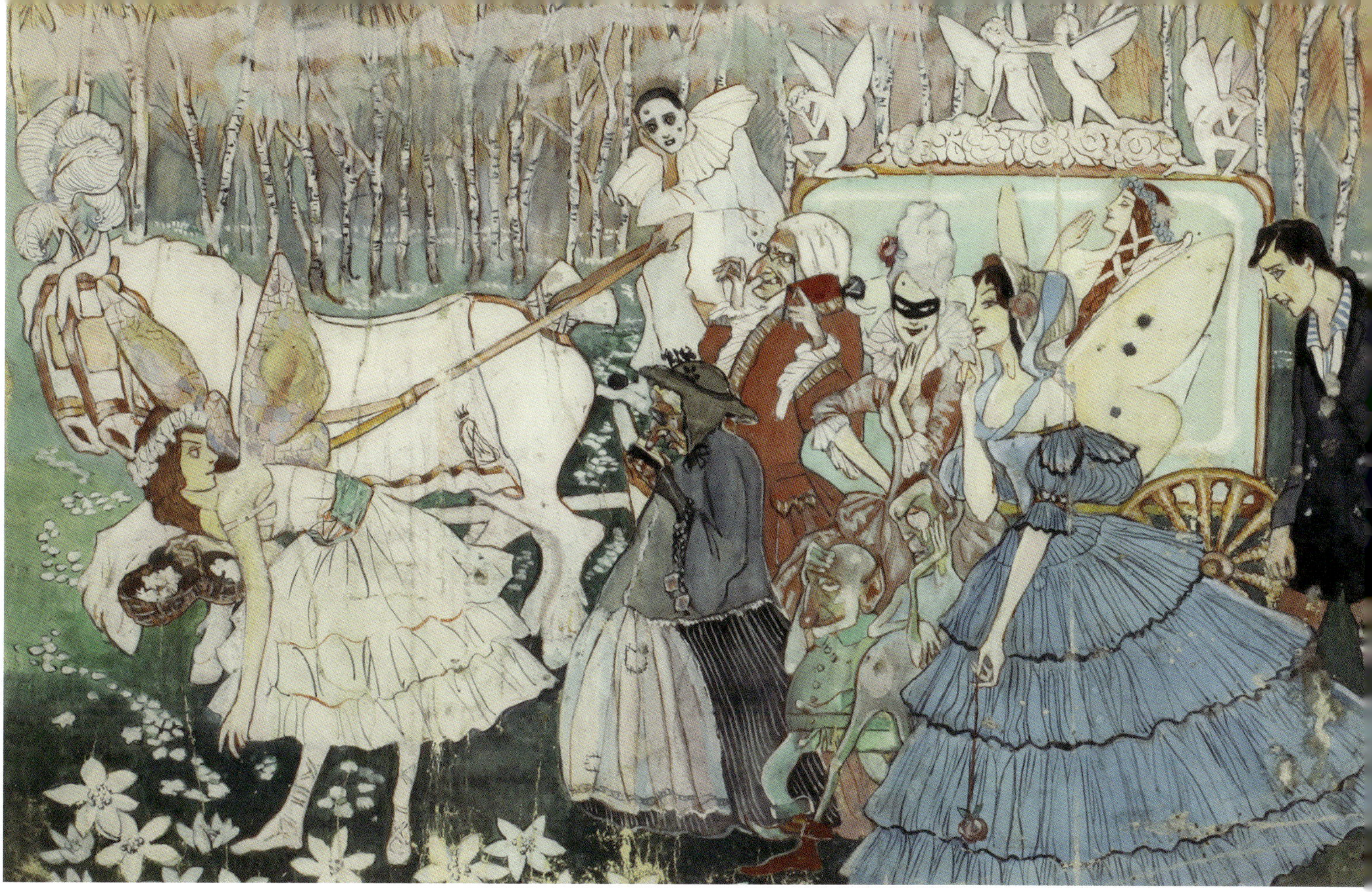

their limited access to the academies. For example, long before the artist and designer Zofia Stryjeńska (1891–1976) became linked to the Kraków Workshops (see Chapter 15), she had shaved her head, dressed as a man, and used her brother's passport to gain entry into the Munich School of Art. Maria, through her father's influence, did attend classes at the Kraków Academy of Fine Arts and received personal tuition, but not until 1917.[7]

On the other hand, the limits to her formal education ensured she would develop her own style. She and her sister had consumed French and German magazines that mingled satire and romance – 'the illustrations fascinated our child minds', Magdalena recalled[8] – and it is possible to see affinities with the graphic styles of Edmund Dulac (1882–1953) or Arthur Rackham (1867–1939). An example of her pre-Academy work is *Illustration for a Fairy Tale* (1914, fig.10.1). Here, against a timeless birchwood background, she depicts what seems to be an 18th-century funeral, where a Pierrot and a ragged young man are weeping but the amused young women decline to join in. The quality of the drawing is striking, as is the flexibility of her technique. Experimenting with watercolour, she reproduces diverse surfaces and textures: tissue-thin translucent wings, the gelatinous flesh of two gnome-like creatures, and the mist. She gives fantasy a satirical sharpness, crowding her intricate images with characters who comment ironically on each other. A winged ballerina gathering star-flowers looks back at a myopic old woman preoccupied by a book. Many of the motifs here appear in her poetry as symbols of spirituality, freedom and self-expression, and as a teenager she had written a poem that expressed both romanticism ('Sadness is the soul of the haze on the pines') and determination: 'I shall go into the horror of experience'.[9] She would always be transmuting experience into art.

Yet to be independent, she believed, as a woman she had to marry. Her intellectual and artistic journey would involve a courageous self-reinvention – a process which was represented very publicly by the successive changes in her surname when she married three times.

10.2
LEFT TO RIGHT:
Wojciech Brzega
Chair for the Sitting Room at the House under the Firs, 1902
House under the Firs Trust (Stowarzyszenie Dom pod Jedlami)

Maria Pawlikowska-Jasnorzewska
Portrait of Seweryna Pawlikowska, c. 1919
Watercolour on paper
c.36 × 26 cm
Inscribed on the reverse: 'Maria Pawlikowska. Portrecik Seweryny Pawl.'
Private Collection. By Descent from the Artist

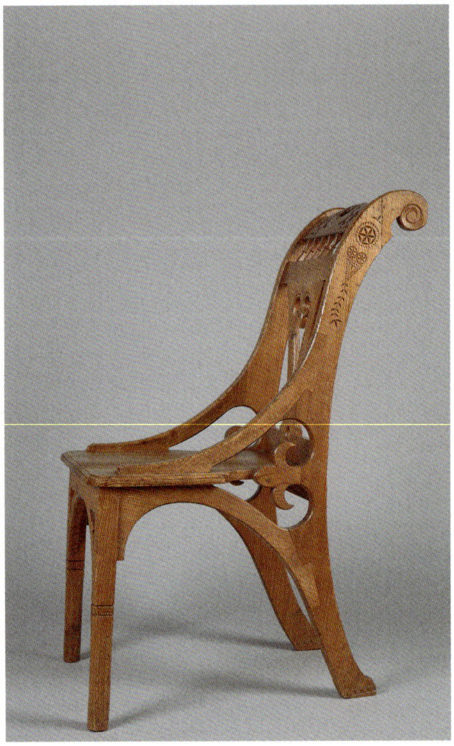

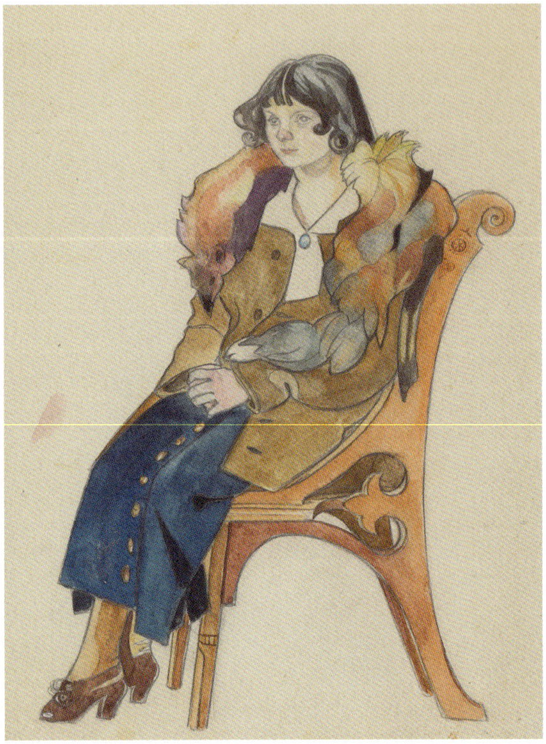

II. Anguish and art

In September 1915 Maria Kossak married Władysław Bzowski, a captain in the Austro-Hungarian cavalry. It was a mismatch; they were incompatible from the start. In 1916 her father wrote to her mother: 'I have no doubt that things will slowly settle between them, but for Lilka art will always be the source of both consolation and success.'[10] And indeed a career in the visual arts seemed probable. She lived with her husband, who was stationed in Mödling near Vienna, and to escape her stifling situation she rented a small studio in the Vienna Kunstverein. There were vivid Art Nouveau elements in her work at that time, which was the period of her most prolific visual output. She exhibited in Kraków at the Numismatic Society (1915) and showed watercolours at the Society of Friends of the Fine Arts (1916). Her sister reported that she also exhibited in the Kraków Academy of Fine Arts, in Zakopane and in Warsaw in the 1920s.[11] The paintings sold well and Maria wrote that Bzowski 'is proud and happy': 'He struts around as if I were a hen who laid a golden egg.'[12] But two allegorical paintings offer radically different perspectives on their marital breakdown – one with a focus on a woman tied to domesticity, one a devastatingly powerful visualisation of the forces underlying their misalliance.

The Poetess and Her Inspiration (1916) is a psychological-symbolic vision of inspiration *confined*. Three figures in three styles – realistic, grotesque and Symbolist – are all aspects of one trapped woman. The central figure looks inseparable from the comfortable world she lives in: the pattern of her clothing connects her to an ormolu table and, squatting on it, a dark oversized teapot. Despite the bourgeois ostentatiousness of the furniture, it is the teapot that most represents her state of confined domesticity. She looks us in the eye, seems unafraid, but is terribly languid. An insect-like creature with an aged human face also appears resigned to disappointment. Behind them, unseen yet dominating the picture, is a glorious butterfly-winged being who combines the colours of nature with the dignity of classical art. But she is in despair, her shoulders taut, her hands covering her eyes. Crucially, the stylistic tensions within this painting make it dynamic. It is an allegory of the inner life of a woman experiencing disillusionment but perhaps on the verge of transformation – a study of potential,

10.3
Maria Pawlikowska-Jasnorzewska
Jan Pawlikowski in Highland Dress, *c.*1918
Watercolour on paper
*c.*36 × 26 cm
Private Collection. By Descent from the Artist

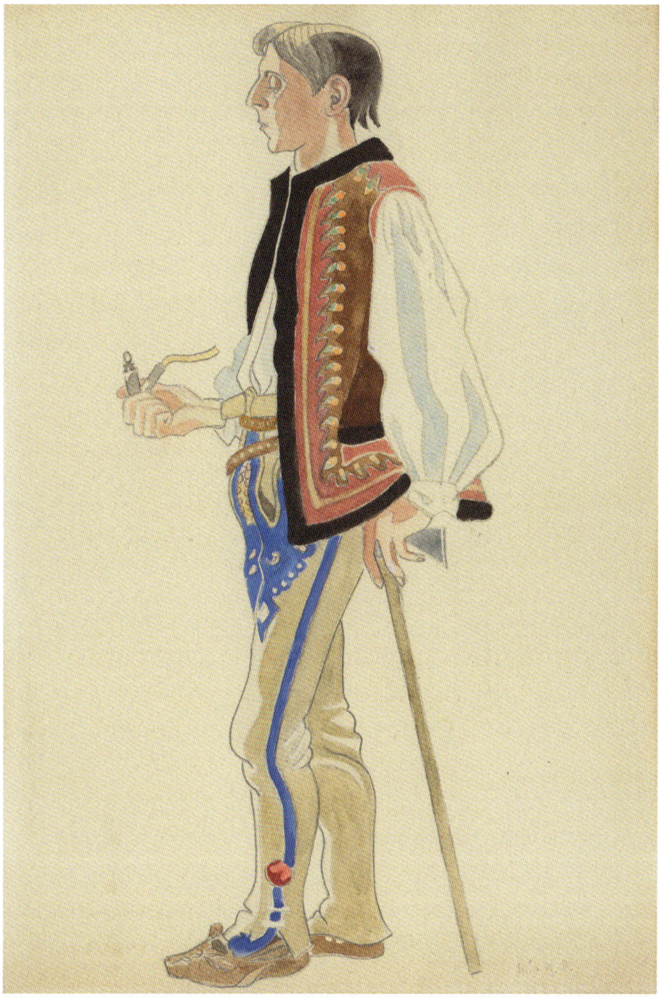

the possibility of flight. Will that winged being ever open her eyes? The painting is similar to another of that painful period, captioned 'Young Women Dreaming and Crying', which suggests the effect of confinement on a whole age group.

But *Vision* (fig.10.0), exhibited in 1916, is very different. It powerfully presents the relationship between the sexes in complex dramatic terms. A male figure stands naked except for a loincloth and with shoulders painfully clenched. He looks up at what could be a steep mountain but which, as the eye adjusts, reveals itself as a long skirt. Into its fabric underlay are woven animalistic images of gender, including an angry lioness and a sort of vulnerable fledgling dragon with wide eyes. A woman's giant bejewelled shoe is emerging, apparently caught in the act of forward movement. And the mountainous landscape beyond them is covered with the vein-like roots and stumps of castrated trees. Freudian . . . ? The man is in fact a portrait of Bzowski, whose sexuality was in question, and the devastated hillside reminds us that this is a work created in wartime. It is Maria's sympathetic but alarming study of masculinity in crisis.

III. Under the Firs, amongst the stars

In October 1916 Maria had met Jan Gwalbert Henryk Pawlikowski in Zakopane. He was a writer, an ecological activist, a pioneer of Tatra tourism and mountain sports – and, like her, a member of one of the key families in the development of turn-of-the-century Polish culture. His uncle Tadeusz Pawlikowski had revolutionised Kraków's Municipal Theatre, while it was his father, the economist, literary scholar and politician Jan Gwalbert Pawlikowski, who commissioned Stanisław Witkiewicz to design the House Under the Firs (see Chapter 6). Maria would live there periodically over the next decade.

There was an immediate attraction, but Maria remained caught in her marriage to Bzowski. This meant an extended period of courtship, secret meetings in romantic locations, and prolific impassioned correspondence, all of which found rich reflection in her art. The process of annulling her first marriage took three years and it was during this period that she professionalised her painting. The wedding finally took place in Wawel in June 1919, a year after Poland's emergence as an independent state *and* the achievement of Polish women's suffrage.

In several works she preserved images of life in the House Under the Firs – some looking back to the Arts and Crafts

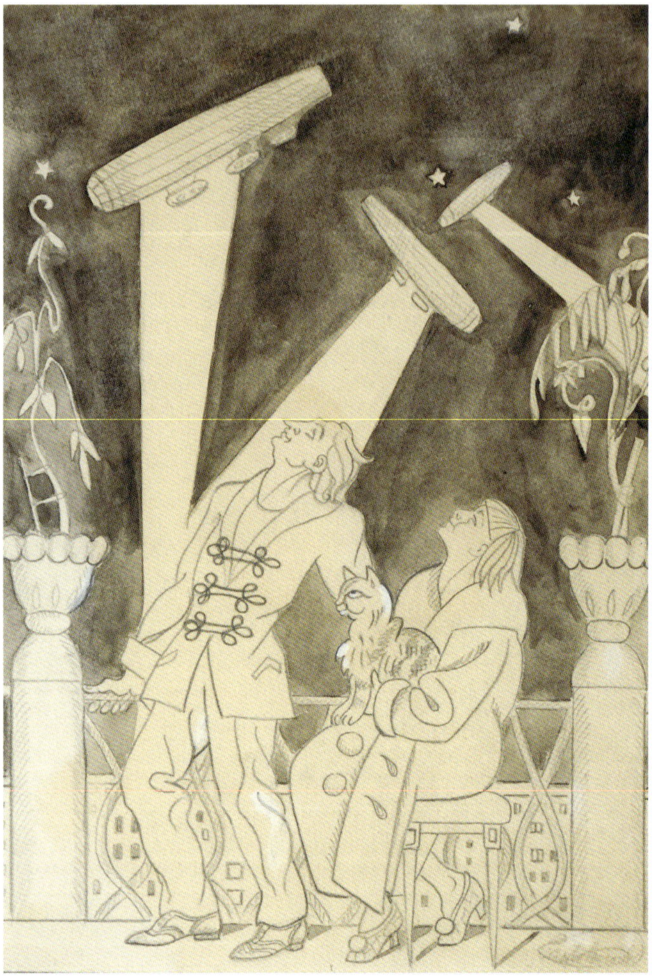

10.4 (LEFT)
Maria Pawlikowska-Jasnorzewska
The Night of the Zeppelins, *c.*1920
Pencil, ink wash and Chinese white on paper
28 × 18.5 cm
Private collection, courtesy of Rempex Auction House

10.5 (OPPOSITE)
Maria Pawlikowska-Jasnorzewska
Jan Pawlikowski in a Cosmic Setting, *c.*1918
Pencil, pastel, watercolour and gouache on paper (unfinished)
*c.*36 × 26 cm
Private Collection. By Descent from the Artist

movement, others gesturing to the future. Pawlikowski, an ethnographer, was collecting folklore and writing a book, *Bajda o niemrawcu* (*Sluggard Tales*), in the Tatra dialect. Maria painted him in a Highlander costume – *strój góralski* – complete with carved pipe and stick. She drew his traditional outfit in careful detail – the russet waistcoat, traditional fastenings, leather *kierpce* shoes – and conveyed even the fabric of the trousers, shadowy folds of 'felted wool' (see fig.10.3). Her sensitive portrait of her sister-in-law Maria Seweryna Pawlikowska, who would die aged 23, shows the sitter posed on a richly carved Wojciech Brzega chair which is still in the House Under the Firs (see fig.10.2). Yet other studies relate to the fact that a circle of *avant-garde* artists soon gathered around the House. They included the anarchic painter-philosopher-playwright Witkacy (or Stanisław Ignacy Witkiewicz, the architect's son), the composer Karol Szymanowski, and the sculptor August Zamoyski with his wife Rita Sacchetto.[14]

Rita Sacchetto was a Zakopane phenomenon. She was a dancer and silent film star who had married Zamoyski in Vienna. Since she had a contract to perform in Poland, they moved to Zakopane in 1918 and lived in another of Witkiewicz's creations, Willa Forma. Many members of this new 'Zakopane set' were part of the Formist group of artists and Sacchetto became central to it, creating dance pieces with a weave of elements - sound, colour and the moving body: Pure Form. She was also an educationalist: she founded a school for girls with a syllabus embracing not only gymnastics, dance and dance history but also drawing, design, languages and scriptwriting. Her dances were often inspired by paintings and she worked with Witkacy on her final Zakopane performance, *Cocaine* (1922). Maria sketched a series of studies of Sacchetto, possibly for a poster, which suggest the Formist influence through blocks of colour and a dynamic, more geometrical, line.[15]

In an astonishing drawing, *The Night of the Zeppelins* (*c.*1920; fig.10.4), Maria blended disparate elements from her vision together, celebrating natural growth, domesticity and respect for tradition, yet revelling in the fantastic possibilities of the future.[16] At this time her style became bold, intimate and challenging and, while probing further the nature of the male–female relationship, touched a spiritual dimension.

A whole series of portraits on paper of Jan Pawlikowski is on a cosmic scale. Here his profile dominates a universe of planets and stars, holding on the palm of his hand variously the globe, a butterfly, or a naked golden couple (recognisably the painter and her husband) entwined in an ecstatic embrace

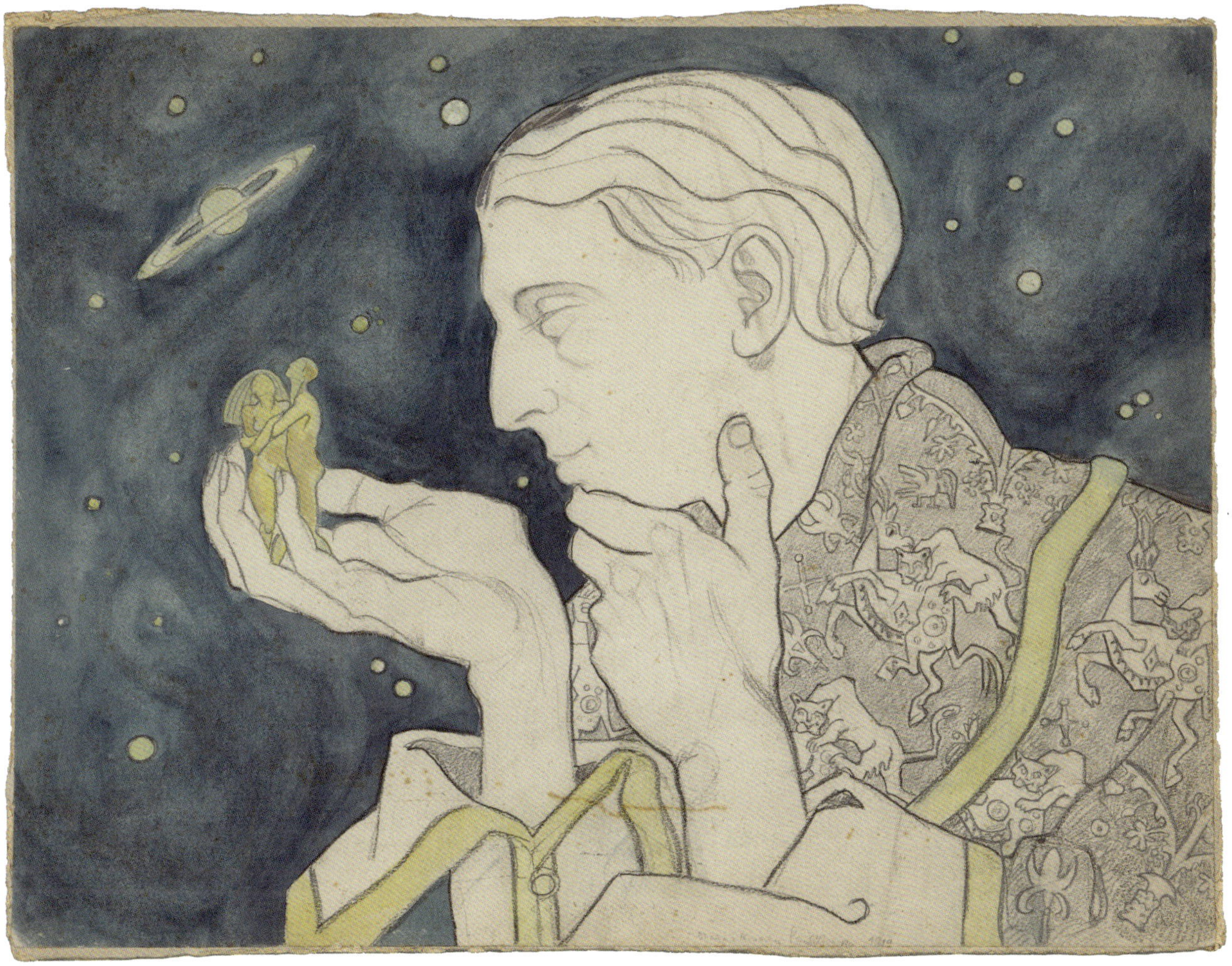

and gazing up into the firmament. He is studying them thoughtfully, eyes narrowed, and in the various versions of this painting he wears rich, heavy robes that again demonstrate Maria's fascination with both textiles and symbolism. In one version (fig.10.5) the robes are decorated with her animal emblems – but now the lioness is feeding contentedly on a compliant deer. The fine lines are meticulous yet firm, the colours are striking, and the central image would recur in one of her most famous poems: 'Whoever wants me to love him . . . must be able to lift me up high in the palm of his hand.'[17]

The series is a shifting conversation. In *Self-Portrait with Elf* (fig.10.6) the relationships are reversed. The tiny suppliant figure with angelic wings is unmistakably Pawlikowski; the artist herself is self-assured, ironic, her long hair elegantly tied with pearls. Now the background is domestic: curtains and a curtain rail instead of stars. The 'elf' kneels on the back of her left hand – while her right hand, resting on her thigh, is faint but disfigured: Maria broke that arm as a child and it never properly healed. In 2020 another version of the composition surfaced at auction (fig.10.7). This time Pawlikowski's giant's robe is decorated with a phoenix, and next to the curtains, where walls should be, we see the stars again.[18] Its signature, 'Maria Kossak-Jasnorzewska', suggests that it dates from the 1930s, after her third marriage (to Stefan Jasnorzewski), and we may wonder why she looked back.
As we shall see, in her highly successful plays she explored elements from her biography, and her poetry often drew inspiration from dreams.

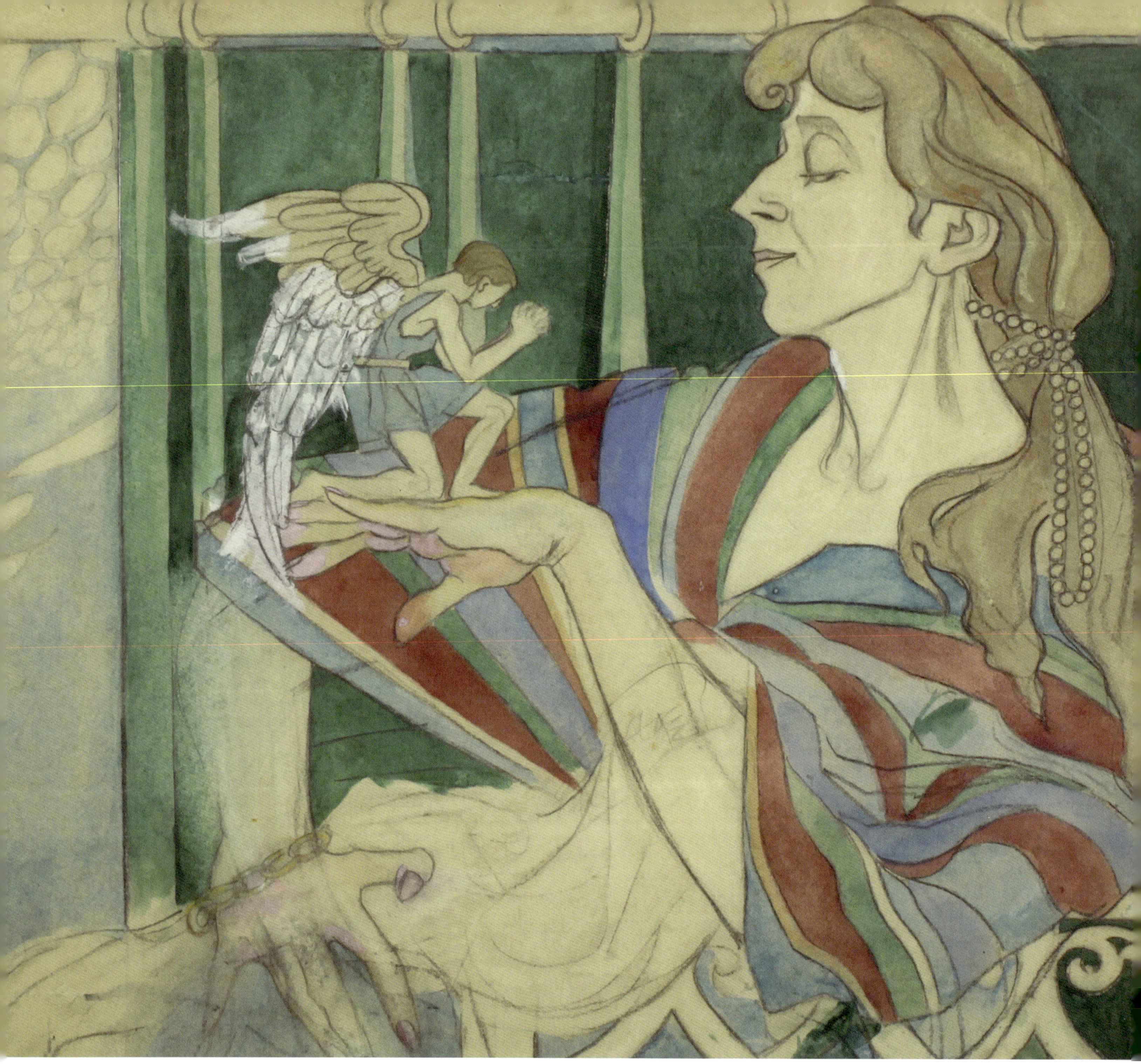

10.6
Maria Pawlikowska-Jasnorzewska
Self-Portrait with Elf, c.1920
Watercolour and pencil on paper
34.5 × 39 cm
Museum of Literature, Warsaw, cat.K.00583

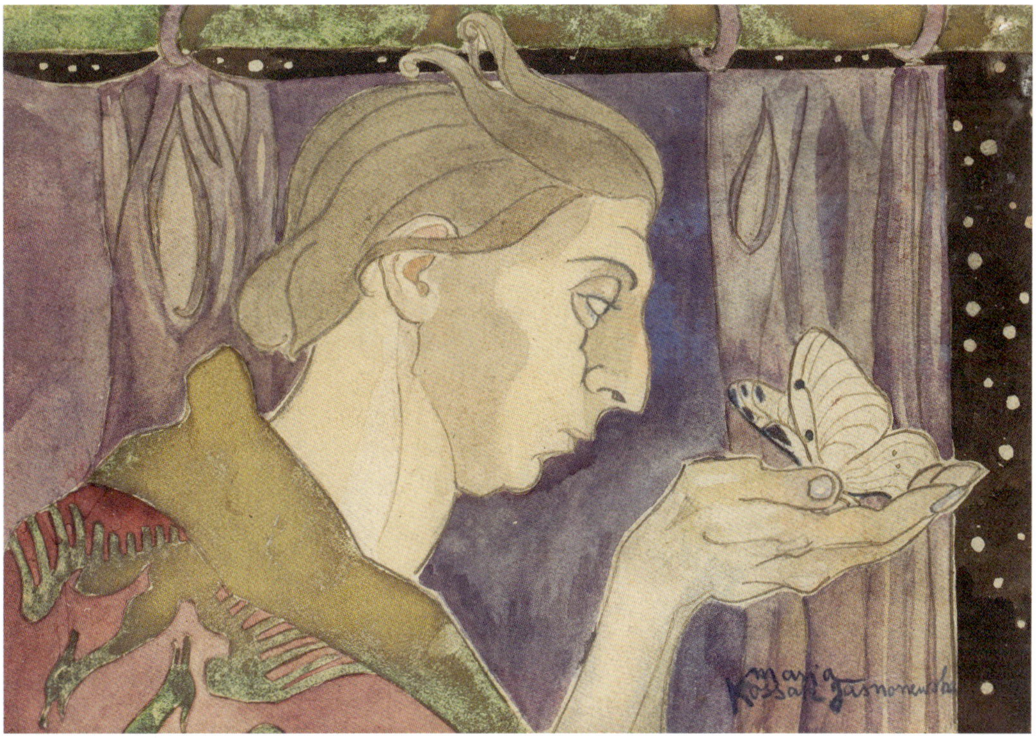

10.7
Maria Pawlikowska-Jasnorzewska
Jan Pawlikowski with Butterfly,
date unknown
Watercolour and pencil on paper
15.5 × 22 cm (dimensions inside mount)
Private collection, courtesy of
Desa Unicum

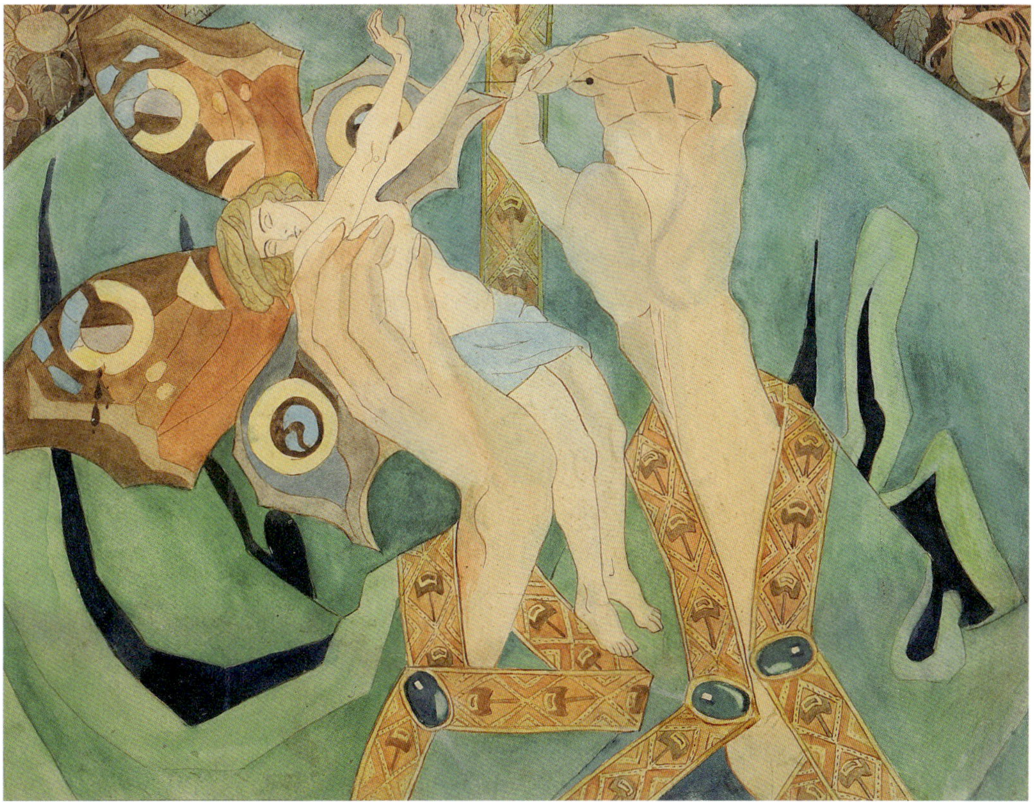

10.8
Maria Pawlikowska-Jasnorzewska
In the Hands of a Sorceress (Woman), undated
Watercolour on paper
34 × 43 cm
Private collection, courtesy of
Okna Sztuki Auction House

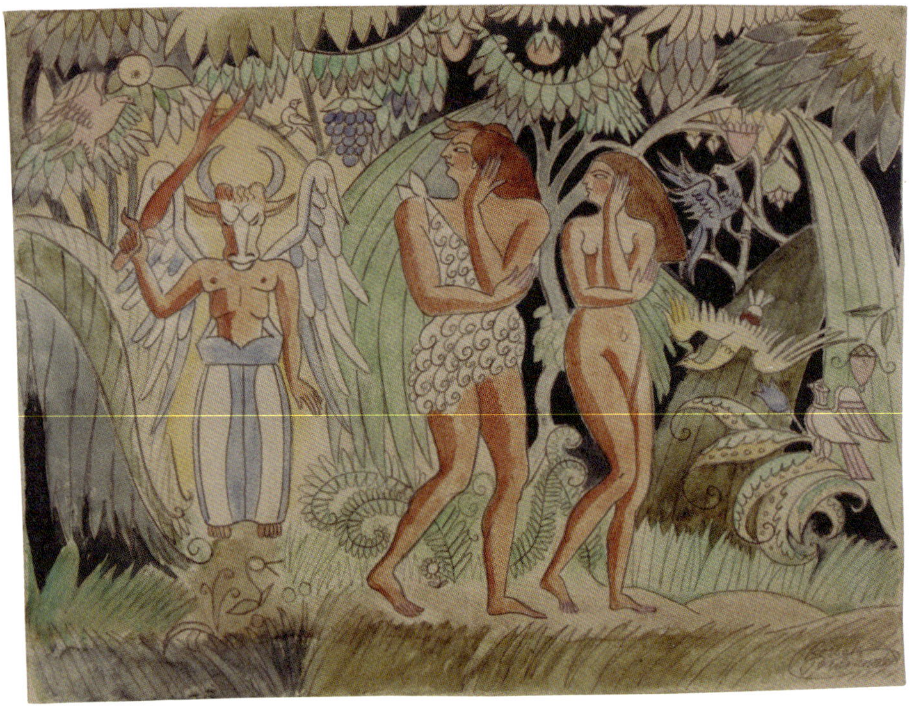

10.9 (LEFT)
Maria Pawlikowska-Jasnorzewska
Adam and Eve – Expulsion from Eden, c.1920
Pencil and watercolour on paper
28 × 30.5 cm
Museum of Literature, Warsaw, K.01267

10.10 (OPPOSITE)
Maria Pawlikowska-Jasnorzewska
Sunset with 'Icaruses' over the City, c.1920
Watercolour and pencil on card
35.5 × 50 cm
Private collection, courtesy of
Rempex Auction House

These celestial paintings together form an interplanetary kaleidoscope or a drama where males and females exchange essential roles. But *In the Hands of a Sorceress* (fig.10.8) confronts us with a radically different perspective. Maria's investigation of strong Formist colours and brutal lines is overwhelming in this cropped close-up. Again, we have one of her inescapable motifs, the hands, but she challenges us to complete the image and understand the nature of the faceless force holding onto the – female? androgynous? crucified? – body. Are we witnessing the plucking of its wings?

IV. Poetry and the city

For many years the Kraków-based Salon of Polish Painters had sold reproductions of such artists as Jan Matejko, Jacek Malczewski and Wojciech Kossak. Their huge range of inexpensive postcards included photographs of classical statuary, Polish landmarks and great Poles (including Wyspiański). Maria designed some new images for them. In England William Morris had popularised delft-style blue-and-white tiles; now she created delft-influenced postcards in a simple lively style, for example featuring a pedlar-entertainer on the road, with balloons or a hurdy-gurdy. She signed them 'Pawik' (little peacock). Pawlikowski disapproved of such a commercial attitude to art. Instead he spurred her on to write poetry. His family helped her to publish her first volumes: *Niebieskie migdały* (*Blue Almonds*) in 1922, followed by *Różowa magia* (*Pink Magic*) in 1924.[19] Yet the pictorial element remained. She adapted her 'delft' style to provide covers and vignettes for both books – a childlike figure with a tambourine for the first, but for the second a conjuror with potions, astrological symbols, and a book which s/he does not seem to need any more, having consumed all the knowledge.[20] Her passionate poetry provoked some misogynistic attacks in Kraków but was received enthusiastically in Warsaw, especially by the Skamander poets, who included Julian Tuwim, Antoni Słonimski and others. *Różowa magia*'s publication was front-page news in the literary magazine *Wiadomości Literackie* (30 March 1924) and given comparable space to the announcement of W.B. Yeats's Nobel Prize.

Maria and Pawlikowski would gradually part. Two powerful but graceful watercolours seem to reflect her change of artistic direction. The first, *Adam and Eve – Expulsion from Eden* (fig.10.9), depicts a strange thick jungle of primordial ferns

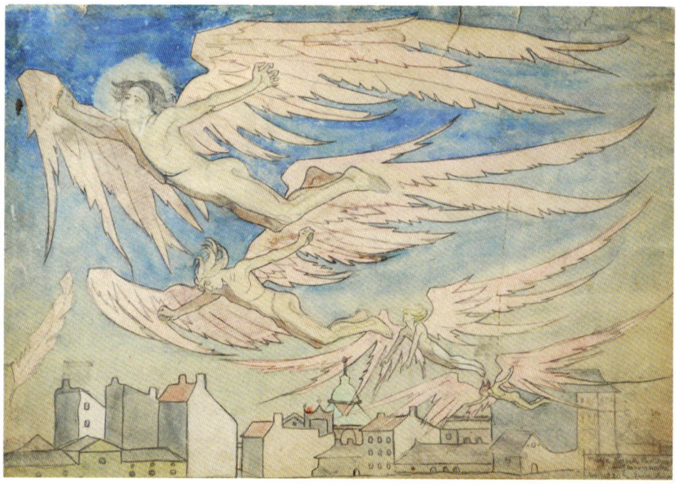

and abundant fruits in which a Minotaur-like creature with angel wings and a forked sword is threatening Eve and Adam. This composition is frieze-like – the eclectic stylisation reflects Maria's interest in Greek and Egyptian art and thought – and the sculpted geometrical shape of their hair mirrors the tail of an inert bird of paradise. In the watercolour known as *Sunset with 'Icaruses' over the City* (fig.10.10) the sense of collective movement and release is completely different. A flock of winged androgynous figures with arms stretched out like swimmers are flying over urban streets. We have seen that the motif of flight is ever-present in her work, and in 1928 she wrote a surreal poem that begins:

> That dream happened again last night. It came to me,
> the dream I love the best, pure ecstasy,
> about swimming in air as if in water . . . .[21]

Ominously, in *Sunset* we can see a feather falling; soon, though, her images of fulfilment embraced modernity, technology . . . and aeroplanes.

V. 'A kind of infernal gravity'

In Paris in 1928, as her second marriage was ending, there was a dreamlike affair with the great Portuguese aviator José Manuel Sarmento de Beires, a theosophist and poet who was later imprisoned and exiled for his involvement in a failed coup against the dictator Salazar. This was also the year when Virginia Woolf gave her lecture *A Room of Her Own*, advocating that for a woman to write she needed experience, a room of her own, and an income. Returning from France, Maria moved out from Kossakówka for good, rented an apartment, and established herself as a playwright. In one radio drama broadcast in 1937, *Złowrogi portret* (*Portrait of Doom*), she talked wittily about the nature of painting, the responsibility of the artist, and the sexual politics of art. Like many of her plays, it explored the social situation of 20th-century women, and was autobiographical. In 1931 she married the Polish pilot Stefan Jasnorzewski. When Germany invaded in September 1939 – on the day of the Warsaw premiere of her play satirising Hitler, *Baba-Dziwo* – they found their way to England, where he took part in the Battle of Britain.

In 1945 Maria Pawlikowska-Jasnorzewska died of cancer in Manchester. She had been reshaping herself as a Polish-English poet, writing of the everyday courage of the survivors of the Manchester Blitz – and the redemptive value of a cup of tea amid devastation. Her fellow exile Antoni Słonimski told her: 'England has given you a kind of infernal Shakespearean gravity.'[22] 'There are still decent writers out there, thank God,' Maria wrote to him. 'For whom, though? Today it would be better to paint, and I keep dreaming about it.'[23] To the last, she kept writing, and she drew. She played with colour, producing blobs of paint and reading her future in them: there would be one more flight. As Beata Obertyńska put it: 'She simply continued her journey through life, leaving behind some shimmering feathers like a peacock.'[24]

2

Objects and Craft Practices in Focus

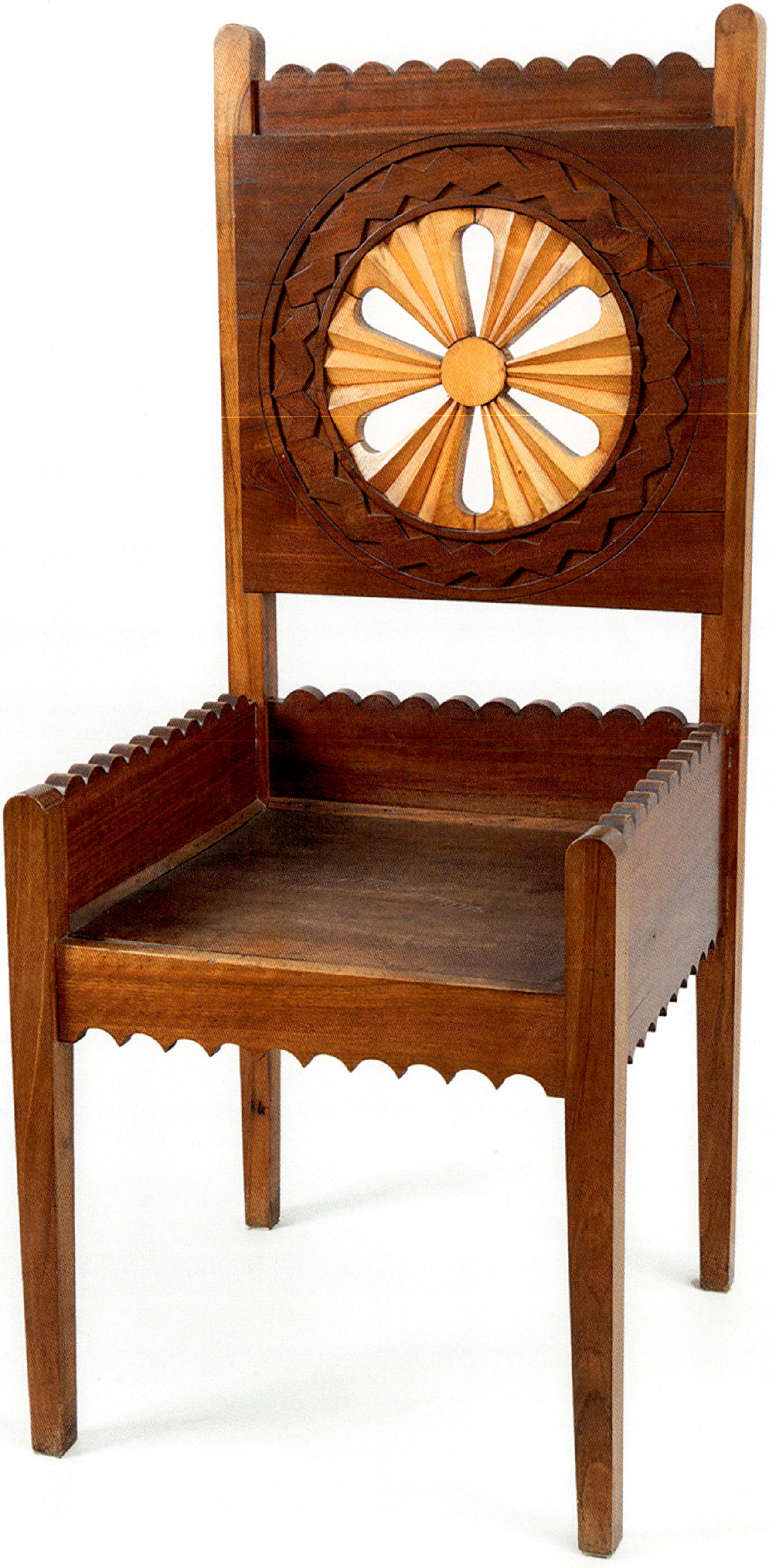

11

Interiors and Furniture

Alicja Kilijańska

John Ruskin's ideas, developed and put into practice by William Morris, found a following among Young Poland artists, architects and social campaigners (see Chapter 1), who strove to participate in the cultural and intellectual life of Europe despite Poland's political non-existence.[1] This found expression in interior decoration schemes and furniture designs.

Ruskin and Morris's ideology was reflected in the activities of the painter and art critic Stanisław Witkiewicz, who settled in Zakopane in 1890. Fascinated by the wooden vernacular architecture of the Podhale region, including the interiors of Highlanders' peasant huts, Witkiewicz recognised its value as exceptional cultural heritage which, if appropriately adapted, would form the basis for a coherent national style. The Zakopane Style was a unique phenomenon in Polish architecture and handicraft (see Chapter 6).[2] Of the villas and ecclesiastical buildings that Witkiewicz designed in Zakopane and its environs from 1892 onwards, the only original decorative scheme preserved in its entirety, including authentic furnishings, can be found in the House Under the Firs (see figs 6.7, 6.8, 6.9 and 6.10).[3] Zakopane Style houses were based on the construction of the Highlander hut, with adaptations and additions made according to need. Witkiewicz was particularly taken by the appealing properties of the room used for festive occasions – the so-called White Chamber. He regarded it as an inspirational model for designing the middle-class dining room. Interiors, including items of furniture – tables, stools, armchairs, wardrobes and dressers – designed by Witkiewicz and his collaborators, including sculptors Wojciech Brzega (fig.11.1) and Stanisław Barabasz, fulfilled their respective functions, while also being endowed with a set of distinctive ornamental features derived from architectural woodcarving and Podhale crafts (such as embroidery). As such, they created a unified style in an interior. Zakopane Style furniture designs were lighter and more sophisticated than their peasant 'prototypes'. Apart from staple furnishings found in a Highlander's hut, amalgam designs of new furniture types were developed to meet the needs of the exacting, contemporary customer. These included desks, dressing tables and armchairs (fig.11.2). The arrival of the 20th century saw a debate about the concept of the Zakopane Style and its validity as a national

11.6a (p.148)
Chair from a set of dining-room furniture from the Żeleński apartment, Kraków, designed by Stanisław Wyspiański, executed by Andrzej Sydor, after 30 October 1904
Walnut and sycamore, carved and polished
120 × 51 × 51 cm
National Museum in Kraków, MNK-IV-Sp-281 (donated by the 'Sztuka' ['Art'] Society of Polish Artists, 1935)

style. Critics claimed it was derivative in nature, based on imitation and compilation, and after all of local character.[4] However, the Zakopane Style has retained its status as an exceptional phenomenon in the history of Polish art – a project which had wider sociopolitical aspirations.[5]

Stanisław Wyspiański was another polymath designer who embarked on shaping the Polish applied arts and a quest for a Polish national style inspired by Polish vernacular crafts and folk art, whilst simultaneously responding to current developments in European art (see Chapters 2, 3 and 4). In 1897 he was one of the co-founders of the 'Sztuka' ['Art'] Society of Polish Artists, and his involvement in the following years extended to curating its shows.[6] Of particular significance was the display of works by 'Sztuka' members, at the Society of Friends of the Fine Arts anniversary exhibition, shown at the Palace of Art in Kraków in the autumn of 1904. Wyspiański created an arrangement of painting and sculpture within an original decorative scheme he developed in the gallery interior, thus pioneering a new approach to the curation of Polish exhibitions.[7] He called the gallery a 'Świetlica' (Great Hall), an Old Polish word for a communal space in a manor house used for festive occasions. The overall scheme was an expression of Wyspiański's fascination with the Polish vernacular crafts. The predominantly grey interior featured accents of colour in the form of the painted wall frieze and embroideries on the grey portières, both adorned with motifs of geranium flowers and leaves. Decorative metalwork (zinc) rosettes protruding from the door frames were based on giant snowflakes, whilst at the same time referencing the jewellery worn by peasants from the Kraków region.[8] The exhibition catalogue written by Wyspiański lists all craftsmen engaged in the work, including Andrzej Sydor with his team of cabinetmakers.[9]

Securing the commission to devise a decorative scheme for the newly built premises of the Medical Society in Kraków was Wyspiański's other prestigious project of 1904. Work commenced concurrently with the development of the 'Świetlica' display, and the design drawings for both schemes indicate overlapping ideas.[10] It was Professor Julian Nowak who came up with the idea of engaging Wyspiański's services. Following the opening of the newly decorated building in 1905, Nowak recalled: 'We had discussed our needs and our means with Mr Wyspiański . . . we had given him free rein and I maintain this is the only way to achieve a beautiful and coherent outcome.'[11]

Wyspiański's interior design encompassed the staircase, the entrance hall, the meeting hall and the reading room. Each space had its distinctive colour scheme, joinery, furniture, textiles and other furnishings. The stained-glass window *Apollo: Copernicus's Solar System* took centre stage within the entrance hall and the staircase (see fig.1.4). The yellow colour of the walls, the metalwork chandeliers made up of giant snowflakes, and a sculptural metal balustrade featuring chestnut flowers and leaves (see fig.2.6), all create an atmosphere of uniqueness and distinction. The ceremonial yet tranquil and measured meeting hall, with walls painted Pompeiian pink, was furnished with modest modernist furniture. Its dark mahogany tones harmonised with the joinery of the doors and the gallery at the back. Wyspiański's introduction of a set of kilims with floral decoration repeating the geranium motif from the painted wall frieze above (and offering insulation from the walls for members seated on the benches) was an innovation (see fig.2.7).[12] The chairs aroused controversy since their simplicity and lightness did not conform to expectations and differed from furniture hitherto used in such interiors. However, they were among the key elements which contributed to the making of a contemporary, modernist interior (fig.11.4).

From the autumn of 1904 Wyspiański was also devising the decorative scheme for Zofia and Tadeusz 'Boy' Żeleński's apartment in Kraków. The bespoke furniture Wyspiański designed for the sitting room, bedroom and dining room was characterised by raw, geometric forms which departed from the received aesthetic of domestic interiors at the turn of the century. As had been the case with the decorative schemes at the 'Świetlica' and the Medical Society, Wyspiański once again treated the items of furniture as a key element within the architectural and artistic composition of the interior. The overall look was complemented by the colour scheme and textiles selected for each interior, in keeping with their characters and functions.[13] As with previous commissions, Wyspiański entrusted the workmanship to Andrzej Sydor's workshop. The Żeleński apartment exemplified a pioneering decorative scheme and custom-made sets of furniture commissioned by a private client. The sitting-room furniture, an armchair and a chair from the bedroom, and a dining-room chair have been preserved (figs 11.5, 11.6a and 11.6.b).[14]

The ethos of the Arts and Crafts Movement found numerous supporters in Kraków at the turn of the century. In 1901 the Polish Applied Arts Society was established; Wyspiański was a co-founder, and other members included architects and artists such as Józef Czajkowski, Karol Tichy and Edward Trojanowski, as well as the art historian and director of the National Museum in Kraków Feliks Kopera, and the lawyer and critic Jerzy Warchałowski, an outstanding leader-organiser and the future director of the Society.[15] The Society's mission was based on the theories of the continuators of Ruskin and Morris ideas, namely Gottfried Semper (1803–1879) and Hermann Muthesius (1861–1927). It called for the revival of native applied arts and supporting such domestic production by various means, namely organising decorative arts competitions and exhibitions, as well as offering versatile learning opportunities for makers, not least through amassing and disseminating a collection of vernacular crafts and folk art.

By virtue of its venue, the Society's first exhibition, in 1902, held at the National Museum in Kraków (before a second showing at the Society for the Encouragement of the Fine Arts in Warsaw), succeeded in introducing applied arts and vernacular crafts to the most significant Polish museum. The three thematic sections of the exhibition – ethnographic, 'contemporary endeavours' and 'historical material' – clearly conveyed the Society's inspirations, intentions and the direction of its future activities.[16]

In 1903 the Polish Applied Arts Society joined forces with the 'Sztuka' society to co-organise a joint exhibition at the headquarters of the Society of Friends of the Fine Arts in Kraków. Many artists were involved with both societies. The applied arts on display comprised furniture and a large number of kilims, embroideries, ceramics, metalwork and prints. Two sets of furniture – for the study by Jan Bukowski, and for the dining room by Ludwik Puget (1877–1942) – deserve special mention, as do individual works by Karol Tichy (a bed) and by Edward Trojanowski (a bookcase (fig.11.8) and a chair). All furniture presented in the exhibition was made by Kraków-based cabinetmakers, among them the Ligęza Brothers and Jan Józef Zabża workshops.[17] Puget's design of dining-room furniture (see fig.11.9) exemplifies the search for a national style based on vernacular crafts/folk art inspirations, and informed by the scholarly study of Polish vernacular wooden architecture. Puget put forward designs which differed from the aesthetic of the then-prevalent Zakopane Style. The dresser and an icebox deserve to be considered as self-contained architectural masterpieces. Their ornamentation is limited to a modest carved fretwork frieze as well as iron hinges and escutcheons symmetrically located on top of the smooth surface of the wood.[18]

Designing the decorative scheme of the Old Theatre in Kraków became another communal artistic project undertaken by the Society's members (1905–6). The larger of two restaurants on the ground floor was designed by Edward Trojanowski, and the smaller by the architect Ludwik Wojtyczko. Józef Czajkowski designed the buffet and a private restaurant room on the second floor. Other smaller private restaurant rooms were designed by Eugeniusz Dąbrowa-Dąbrowski (1870–1941). Each of the above interiors had its own bespoke sets of furniture, comprising tables of varying dimensions, chairs and armchairs, as well as other pieces determined by the function of the space or architectural considerations, such as dressers and glazed cupboards at the buffet. Wojtyczko went to considerable lengths to conceal a heater. He designed a cover in the form of a dresser (fig.11.10), while sofas and mirrors were provided for the private restaurant rooms. Each space featured distinctive painted wall friezes, as well as kilims, lamps and sconces, in keeping with the wood variety and colour of the furniture. Furniture, wall paintings and textiles in the ground-floor restaurants featured ornamentation based on the folk paper cutting as well as decorative motifs drawn from folk chests, such as the heart and the rosette. The majority of furniture was produced in Andrzej Sydor's workshop, and the kilims in Antonina Sikorska's workshop. Similarly, other items were made by Kraków-based firms or craftspeople.[19]

The 1908 Polish Applied Arts Society's exhibition at the Society for the Encouragement of the Fine Arts in Warsaw offered a summary of its members' work over the previous few years. It was dominated by interior decoration schemes, especially furniture for private homes. Wyspiański's furniture for the Żelenski apartment was on show, although the artist had died the previous year. New projects included commissions for Warsaw homes: a bedroom for Leonowa Papieska by Trojanowski, as well as dining-room furniture for the Dziewulski and Reymont households by Wojtyczko and Czajkowski respectively.[20]

As a dynamically developing city with rich middle classes and intelligentsia, Warsaw had become the locus of an important client base who were more eager to invest in modern furnishings than Kraków dwellers.[21] In 1909 the National Museum in Kraków received a gift from the Warsaw doctor Teodor Dunin, including the turn-of-the-century furnishings from his house. The chattels from the Dunin house were the first examples of Art Nouveau and modernist furniture to enter the Museum's collection. The set of furniture designed by the painter Bronisława Poświkowa (1855–1902) (fig.11.11) is noteworthy. The artist ran a school of painting and sculpture for women in Warsaw, and her wide-ranging teaching and creative pursuits included designing textiles, lace and embroideries, as well as ornamentation of ceramics and furniture, the latter two made to commission in the school workshop.[22]

Between 1908 and 1910 the Polish Applied Arts Society undertook more work commissioned by the Dłuski family, the owners of a sanatorium in Zakopane. The sanatorium's interiors were to facilitate rest in an exceptional atmosphere, characterised by simplicity, elegance and spaciousness, being far removed from the usual hospital aesthetic. The long-lost interiors dating to 1909–10 were designed by the Society's members Karol Frycz and Henryk Uziembło, as well as a non-member Jan Rembowski (1879–1923). The latter designed the hallway, corridor and a large sitting room, which he adorned with painted decoration, and stained-glass windows referencing Tatra legends. The furniture characterised by plain, geometrical forms, including small tables, sofas, armchairs and chairs, was made of oak and decorated only with small stars (see also Chapter 17). Uziembło's design for the Music Room was inspired by the Biedermeier and other styles from the first half of the 19th century.[23] In 1909 the painter and stage designer Karol Frycz was entrusted with the decorative schemes for the Reading Room and the Library. Wooden panelling, bookshelves and matching carved joinery were an important element of his arrangement. Comfortable club armchairs loosely referenced English 18th-century chairs. Frycz's scheme, complete with painted mural decoration and suitable lighting, yielded an intimate and mysterious atmosphere.[24]

Karol Frycz achieved a similar effect a year later in the interior of the famous Kraków cafe Jama Michalika (Michalik's Den). The new hall and small annexe upstairs were endowed with carefully laid-out bespoke sets of furniture as well as wooden panelling and matching joinery, stained glass, mirrors and lamps all creating the atmosphere. Upholstered settees, corner armchairs, chairs and stools of every kind as well as tables with marble tops, all placed within the modestly sized space, created a cosy and intimate feel for the visitor (fig.11.12).[25] Frycz, who had studied in Munich and Vienna and came into contact with Morris's ideas during his stay in England in 1904, drew on these influences in his designs, also aided by his great talent for stage design.[26] He was among the artists who reinterpreted older styles in furniture design, while departing from the blind imitation of vernacular/folk art motifs.[27]

The *Architecture and Interiors in a Garden Setting* exhibition in Kraków (1912) was the last major communal undertaking of the Polish Applied Arts Society's members. The show was an attempt to reflect on the best way forward regarding Kraków's development, following the city's recent expansion by the incorporation in 1910 of a few surrounding areas. The inspiration came from Ebenezer Howard's concept of the Garden City. The notion of presenting housing options for all social classes was a novelty in the Polish context. The exhibition had great educational value, and the organisers set out to convince the general public to look for inspiration in Polish provincial vernacular architecture, including the manor houses of the gentry.[28] The Manor House, designed for the exhibition by Józef Czajkowski, drew on English models, in terms of the concept of unity between the interior, the terrace and the surrounding garden. In turn various artists undertook the decoration of specific rooms, including the furniture design: Karol Tichy's Sitting Room, Henryk Uziembło's Dining Room, Edward Trojanowski's Bedroom, Karol Frycz's Maiden's Room, and a Nursery by Edmund Bartłomiejczyk

(1885–1950) (see Chapter 12). The Craftsman's House and the Worker's House, both complete with furnishings designed by Franciszek Mączyński and Karol Maszkowski (fig.11.13), received the greatest amount of attention. The furniture was praised as simple, robust, and simultaneously elegant. The 1912 Kraków exhibition was a unique undertaking and a great success. The architecture, interiors and furniture displayed European design tendencies from around 1910, which had by this time departed from Art Nouveau, in favour of the creative adaptation of historical styles, including Biedermeier combined with elements of native Polish arts. The marked inspiration drawn from British ideas, as well as German art movements such as the Deutscher Werkbund and the Wiener Werkstätte, became an important milestone in the development of modern architecture and interior design in Poland after 1918.[29]

The vital role played by the Kraków Museum of Technology and Industry founded by Adrian Baraniecki in 1868 has already been discussed in Chapter 1.[30] The founder's stay in England and Scotland had a decisive influence on his future decisions – Baraniecki was fascinated by the level of civilisation of British society.[31] Following his death, and in the face of a crisis in 1904–6, discussions took place regarding the future role and operations of the Museum. Jerzy Warchałowski's 1904 text 'O sztuce stosowanej' ('On Applied Art') became a key voice, proposing that the Museum needed to support the development of local craftsmanship on the basis of native models, frequently inspired by the Polish vernacular/folk art tradition.[32] A 1906 article written by the architect Tadeusz Stryjeński contained a concise programme for the Museum, proving convincing to the city's authorities. He became the institution's new director, and was also entrusted with the design and supervision of the construction of its new premises.[33] Building work was completed in 1913, and the same year saw the beginning of collaboration between the Museum of Technology and Industry and the newly formed Kraków Workshops association (1913–26; see Chapter 9), whose members, artists and architects, regarded the artistic elevation of the standard of craft production as the fundamental aim of their activities. Their objective was to be realised on the basis of models drawn from vernacular/folk art, aided by an understanding of traditional craft skills, use of authentic materials and the techniques of making.

Members of the Kraków Workshops were involved in the design and supervision of the production of the furnishings for the interiors of the Museum of Technology and Industry. Sets of furniture for the Reading Room (fig.11.14) and Library, dating from 1913–14, were made according to the designs of the painter and pedagogue Karol Homolacs, and remain *in situ* to the present day.[34] The activities of the Kraków Workshops, which developed in opposition to the Polish Applied Arts Society, concluded a very significant and creative period in the history of Polish applied arts of the 20th century.

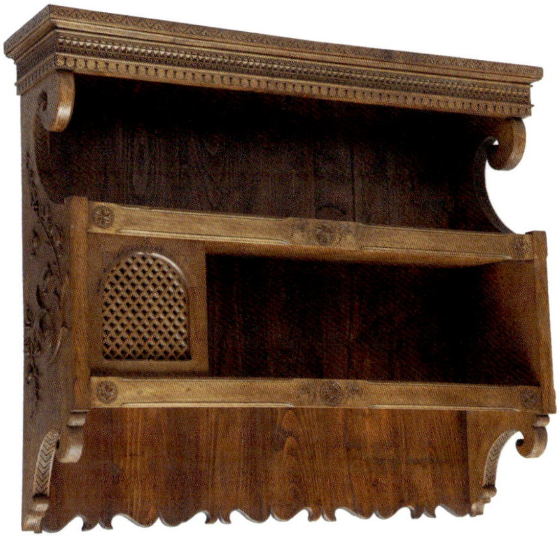

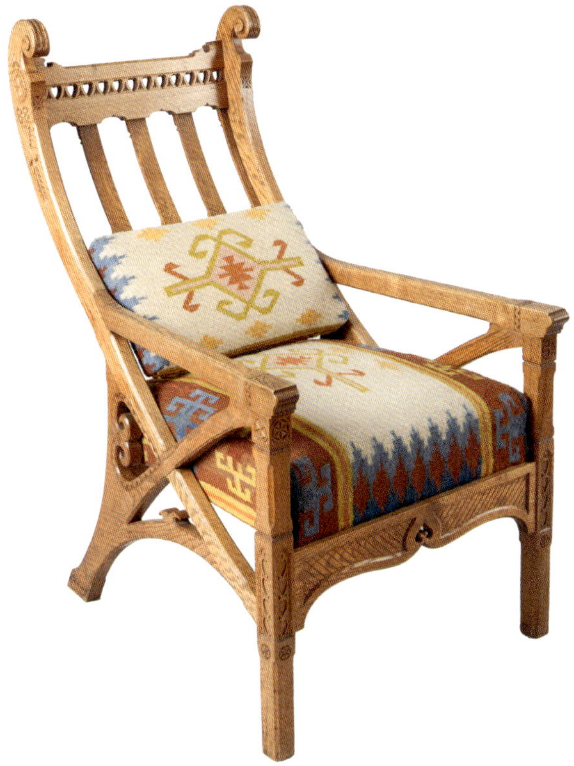

11.1 ↑

Bookcase, Zakopane, designed by Wojciech Brzega, executed by Andrzej Krzeptowski, 1893

Coniferous wood, carved
91 × 110 × 28 cm
National Museum in Kraków, MNK-IV-Sp-931
(Teodor Dunin bequest, 1909)

This is a very early example of the original work of the Zakopane sculptor Wojciech Brzega, a graduate of the Wood Industry Vocational School in Zakopane and the School of Fine Arts in Kraków. Brzega undertook his first Zakopane Style woodcarving in 1892 during the building of Willa Koliba (see Chapter 6), which is how he met Stanisław Witkiewicz, with whom he subsequently collaborated on the furnishings for the House Under the Firs, among other projects.

This hanging three-level bookcase bears the signature 'ZAKOPANE 3/5 1893 / W. BRZEGA KRZEPTOWSKI' inscribed alongside the lower edge, revealing its co-creator, the cabinetmaker Andrzej Krzeptowski, also known as the maker of a chest shown at the first exhibition of the Polish Applied Arts Society in the headquarters of the National Museum in Kraków at Sukiennice in 1902.

The bookcase was presented to the Museum by the Warsaw physician Teodor Dunin, who had purchased Willa Schodnica (1894–7) in Zakopane from the architect Tadeusz Stryjeński in 1905.

11.2 ↑

Armchair, designed by Stanisław Witkiewicz, 1902; executed by Jan Józef Zabża, 1920s

Deciduous wood (Scotch elm, oak), carved, kilim upholstery and cushion
108 × 62 × 54 cm
National Museum in Kraków, MNK IV-Sp-1143 (donated by Janina Glazur, the cabinetmaker's granddaughter, 1998)

This Zakopane Style armchair was created in Kraków in the 1920s in Jan Józef Zabża's workshop. It is a variation of Stanisław Witkiewicz's design dating from 1902, made a year later by Wojciech Brzega in Zakopane. Several similar armchairs were commissioned for Willa Sośnina in Lubień in 1912, and Willa Harenda in Zakopane, belonging to the Kasprowicz family, after 1923. Witkiewicz designed a number of variations of furniture, including those not found in Highlanders' huts, to cater to the needs of interiors occupied by exacting customers. The inspiration for this armchair design came from a Highlander sledge typically with a curved back and armrests.

Zakopane Style furniture retained popularity in the first quarter of the 20th century and was found not only in Zakopane Style houses.

11.3 ↓

(LEFT) **Throne and two seats, Kraków, designed by Stanisław Wyspiański, executed by Andrzej Sydor, 1904**

Solid oak, partly covered with oak veneer, top frieze partially painted in red
Throne: 137 × 72.5 × 69.5 cm; seats: 115 × 72.5 × 69.5 cm
National Museum in Kraków, MNK-IV-Sp-626/1–3
(donated by the Academy of Fine Arts in Kraków, 1973)

(RIGHT) **The throne and two seats featured in the 'Świetlica' (Great Hall) display of the 'Sztuka' Society of Polish Artists, designed by Stanisław Wyspiański, as part of the anniversary exhibition of the Society of Friends of the Fine Arts in Kraków, 1904**

Archival photograph
Museum of Kraków, MHK-FS3995-IX

Furniture and joinery for the 'Świetlica' (Great Hall) installation of the 'Sztuka' ['Art'] Society of Polish Artists, at the anniversary exhibition of the Society of Friends of the Fine Arts, in Kraków, was especially designed by Stanisław Wyspiański as an integral and key part of the scheme. Known from archival photographs and descriptions, the contents comprised joinery (wooden panelling and decorative door frames) as well as bespoke furniture: a bench, a throne and two seats. All of the above components were produced within a month in 1904 by Andrzej Sydor's workshop, with contributions from Julian Praszkiewicz and Stefan Zieliński. Only the oak throne and seats survive. Wyspiański's designs comprised simple, almost cubic forms, far removed from the comfort of functional designs. As intended by Wyspiański, the pieces of furniture were effectively sculptural artistic creations, brought to life by means of shaping raw masses of solid wood while retaining its natural, smooth surfaces. The decoration was restricted to crenellated edges reminiscent of architectural detailing, with the upward-facing inner surfaces of the crenellations painted red.

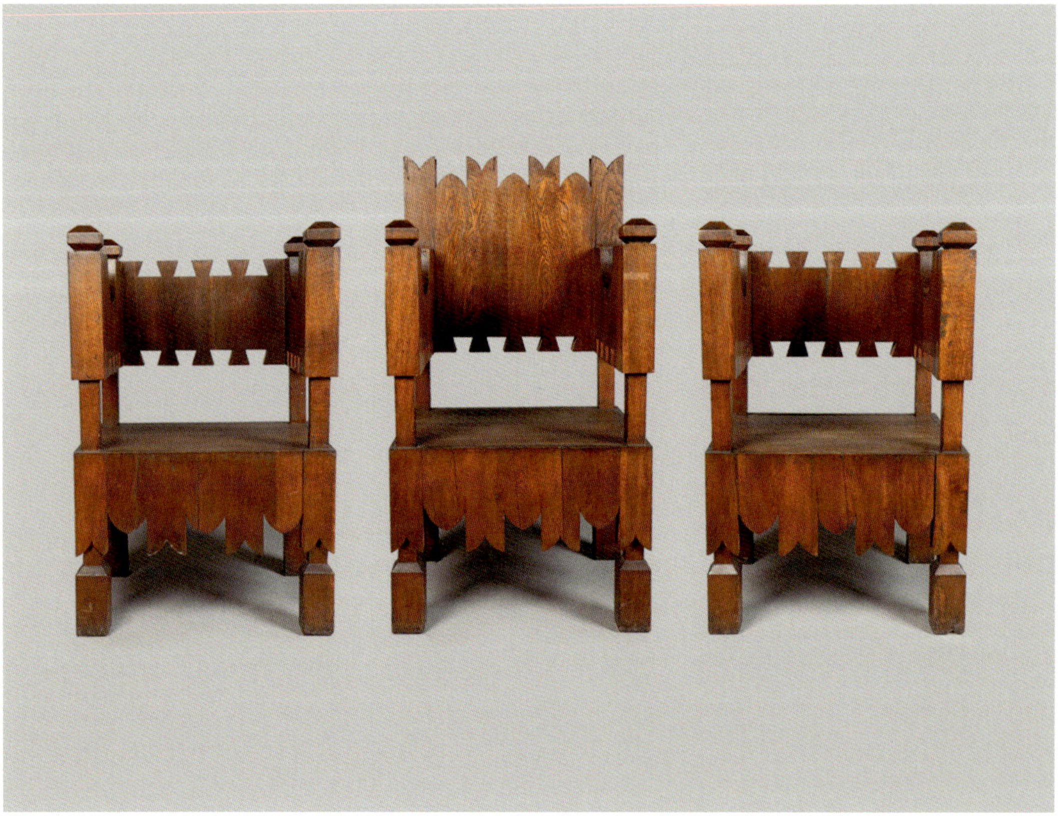

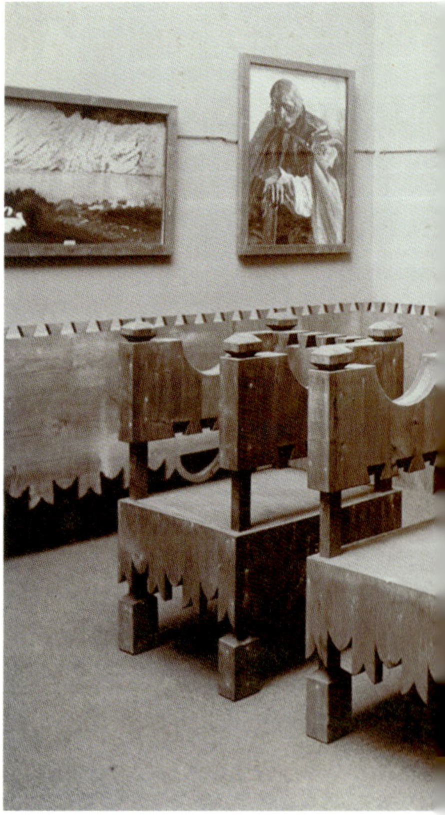

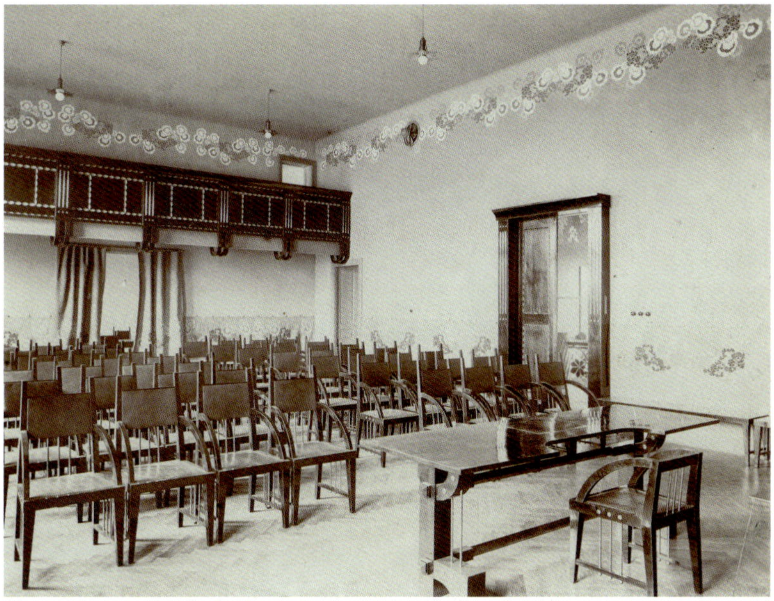

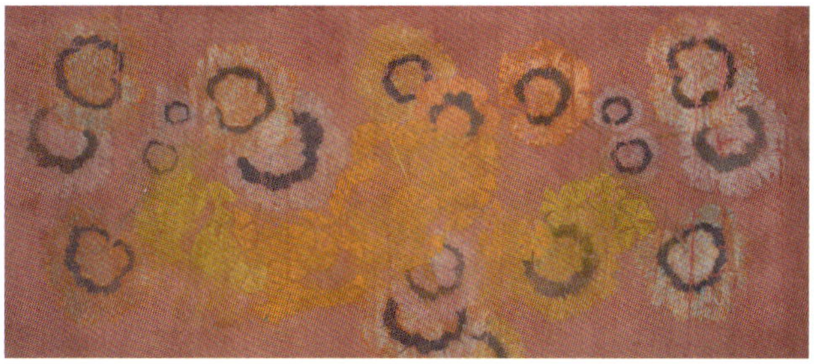

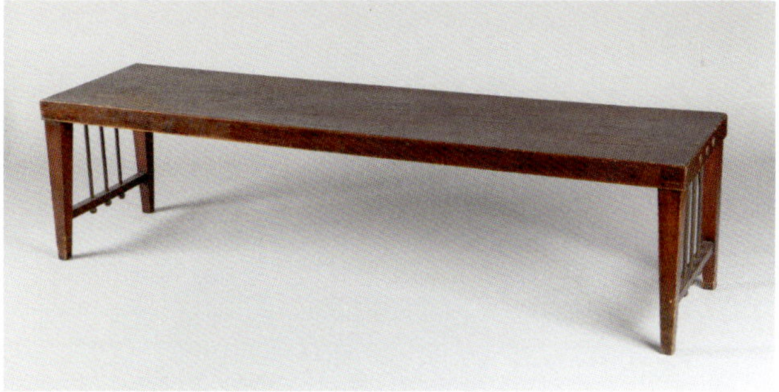

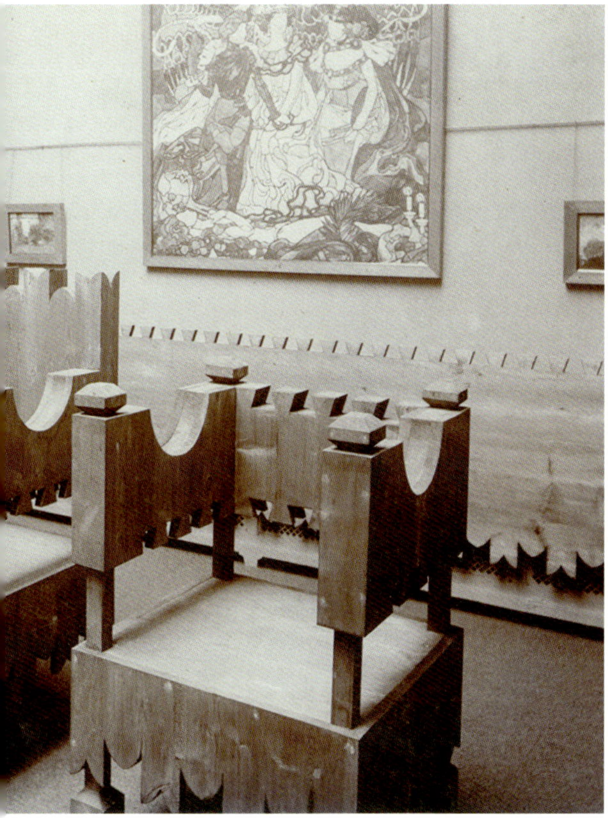

11.4 ↑

(CLOCKWISE FROM LEFT) **The decorative scheme at the meeting hall of the Medical Society headquarters in Kraków, designed by Stanisław Wyspiański, 1904–5; his design for the geranium motif for its wall frieze; and one of its surviving benches (executed by Andrzej Sydor)**

Archival photograph; design: pastel on paper laid on canvas;
bench: solid pine covered with beech veneer, brass
Museum of Kraków, MHMK FS 11971X; National Museum in Kraków, MNK-IV-r.a-13318, MNK-IV-SP-1233

The decorative scheme for the meeting hall in the Medical Society premises was Wyspiański's first complex interior design in a secular public building. As part of the coherent arrangement, the artist designed architectural fixtures and fittings (the joinery of the doors and gallery) as well as the furniture – a set of chairs (known as 'stools'), tables, the President's table, a lectern for the speaker, benches placed along the walls – all made from pine stained a mahogany hue. Decoration of the furniture was restricted to modest gilded brass elements and red leather upholstery of the chairs. The choice of a Pompeiian pink colour for the walls, adorned with a frieze of geranium flowers and leaves, was an important part of the scheme. An analogous motif was repeated in the kilims placed on the walls, as backrests for eight benches for the audience.

11.5 ↓

(LEFT) **Set of furniture from the sitting room at the Żeleński apartment, Kraków: sofa, four 'chairs' (armchairs), three 'stools', designed by Stanisław Wyspiański, executed by Andrzej Sydor, 1905**

Pine wood, double-sided sycamore veneer, polished, fabric
Sofa: 80 × 137.5 × 54 cm; 'chairs': 80 × 70 × 55 cm; 'stools': 63 × 71 × 48 cm
National Museum in Kraków, MNK-IV-Sp-627 1–8 (donated by the Dr Tytus Chałubiński Anti-Tubercular Home Sanatorium (formerly Dr Chramiec's Sanatorium), 1967–8; a gift of the 'Sztuka' ['Art'] Society of Polish Artists, 1935)

(RIGHT) **The decorative scheme at the sitting room at the Żeleński apartment, Kraków, designed by Stanisław Wyspiański**

Photograph reproduced from *Sztuka Stosowana* (1907)

Entries in Wyspiański's diary concerning furniture for Zofia and Tadeusz Żeleński's sitting room date from 18 October 1904 to June 1905. They record the chronology of the creation of specific pieces of furniture, and also confirm the active involvement of Zofia Żeleńska's mother, Eliza Pareńska, in the successive stages of creating the furnishings for the newlyweds' rented apartment in Ulica Karmelicka in Kraków. Surviving pieces include the sofa, four armchairs and three chairs. The original set had also originally included two sofas, a table and a shelf-cum-jardinière, and presumably another chair. The furniture was made from pine with a sycamore veneer. In keeping with the wall colour of the sitting room, the upholstery was executed in dark purplish-red. In 1913 Dr Andrzej Chramiec purchased the furniture for his newly rebuilt tuberculosis sanatorium in Zakopane.

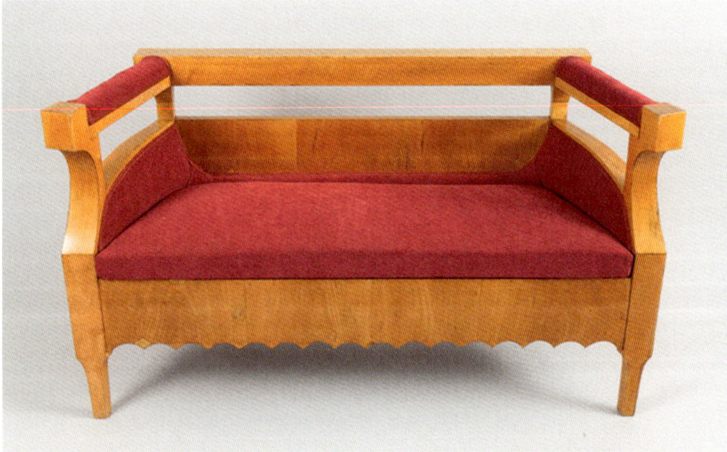

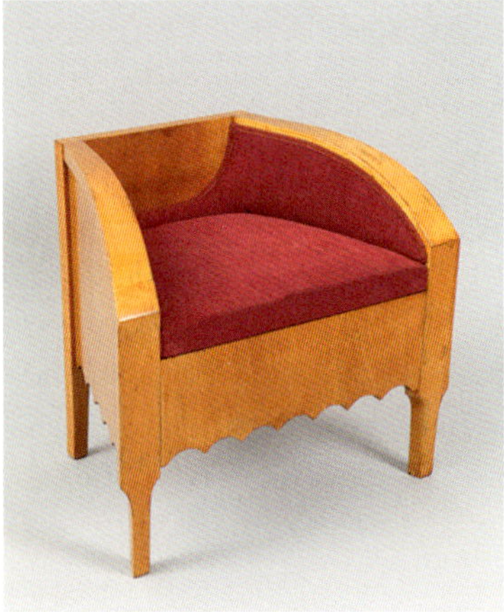

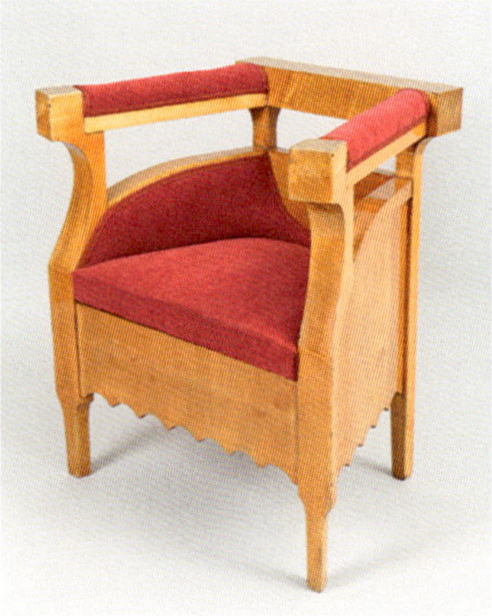

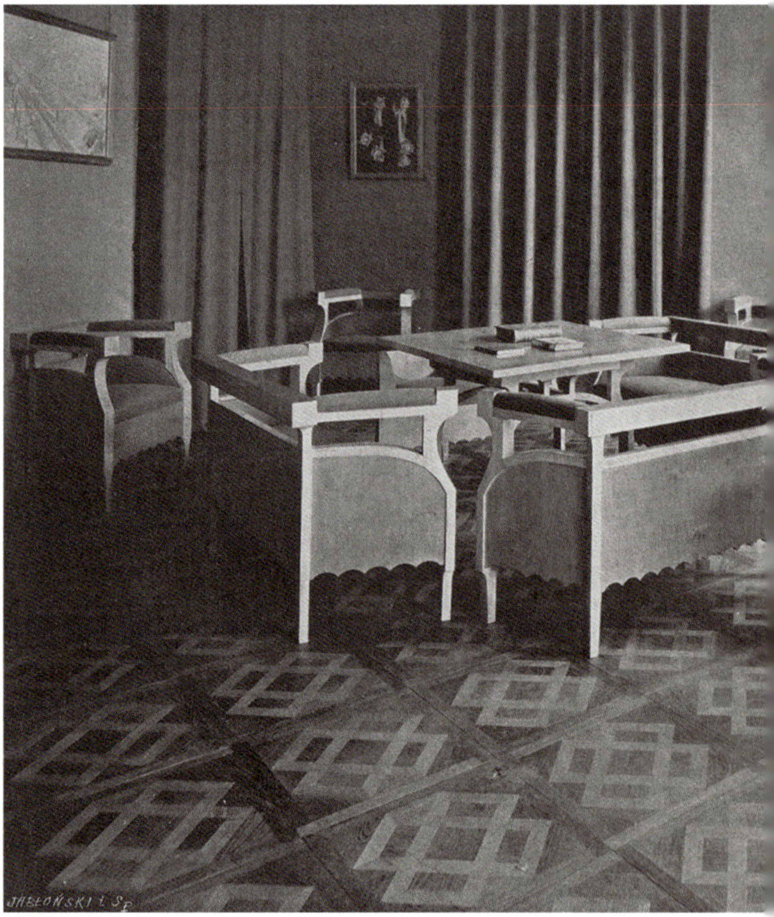

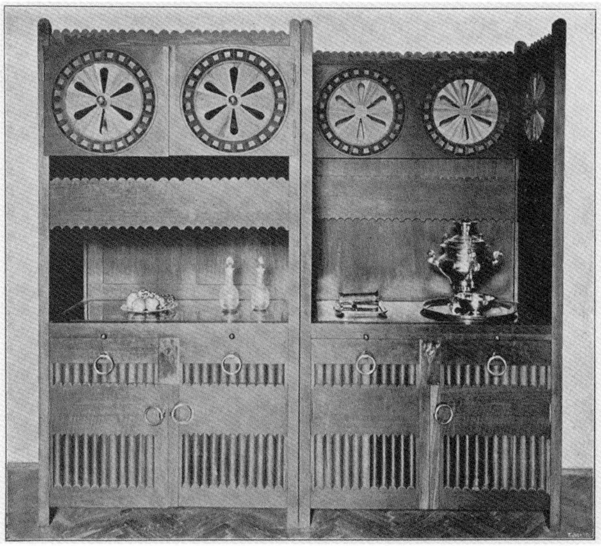

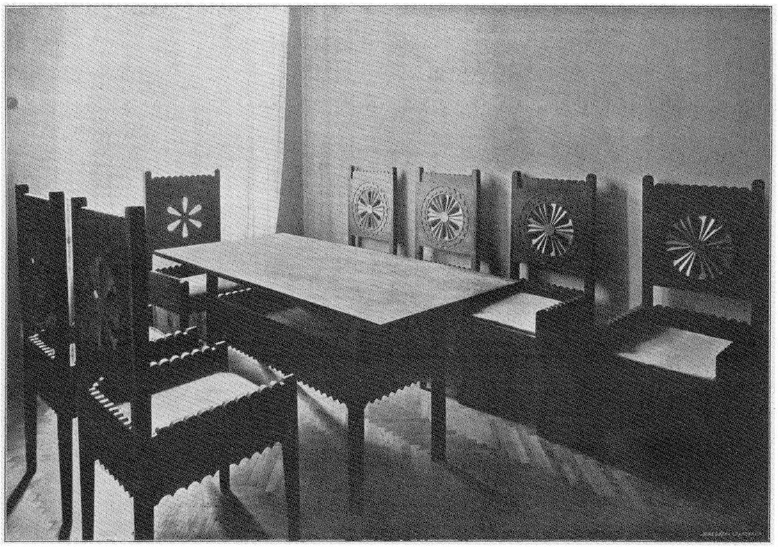

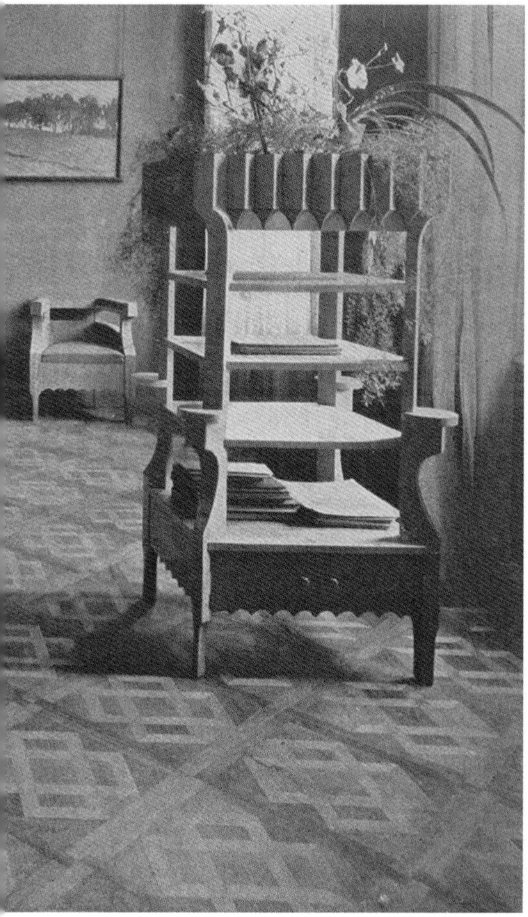

11.6b (see also 11.6a on p.148) ↑

Suite of dining-room furniture from the Żeleński apartment, Kraków, designed by Stanisław Wyspiański, executed by Andrzej Sydor, after 30 October 1904

Photographs reproduced from *Sztuka Stosowana*, (1907)

The set of dining-room furniture that Wyspiański designed for Zofia and Tadeusz Żeleński originally comprised chairs (fig.11.6a), a table and a sideboard. On 30 October 1904, Wyspiański wrote in his diary, 'I am drawing a chair with a star.'[35] The result was a set of monumental, raw furniture, with ornamentation inspired by vernacular woodcarving, and limited to carved friezes and prominent six-petal rosettes of contrasting lighter sycamore wood on the backrests of the chairs and the doors of the two-piece sideboard. These items showed artistry but failed to take into account the everyday needs of their users and the principles of ergonomics.

Details of the decorative scheme of the Żeleński apartment are known from a description contained in Tadeusz 'Boy' Żeleński's essay 'Historia pewnych mebli' ('History of a certain set of furniture'), in which he recalls in an anecdotal manner his collaboration with Wyspiański, as well as events associated with having to live amongst not very comfortable furniture.[36]

11.7 →

(TOP) **Shelves, Kraków, designed by Karol Tichy, made at the State School of Carpentry, Kalwaria Zebrzydowska – Władysław Jarosiński (cabinetmaking), Karol Kudelski (woodcarving), before 1906**

Carved oak
139 × 107 × 39.5 cm
National Museum in Kraków, MNK-IV-Sp-203
(Feliks Jasieński bequest, 1929)

(BOTTOM) **Interior of Feliks Jasieński's apartment in Kraków showing the Tichy shelf, c.1901–1906**

Archival photograph
National Museum in Kraków, MNK XX-f-35401

Karol Tichy designed sets as well as individual pieces of furniture. For example, he designed a bed for the second exhibition of the Polish Applied Arts Society in 1903, and in 1909 he won the competition for a set of bedroom furniture. As early as 1901 the Polish Applied Arts Society organised a competition for a set of shelves displaying a distinctively Polish character. Tichy was announced as the winner the following year. Either of two pieces of surviving furniture may have been the winning design: the one shown here, from the collection of Feliks 'Manggha' Jasieński, or a similar model, reproduced in one of the Society's *Sztuka Stosowana* journals. The latter was made by a team from the State School of Carpentry (Krajowa Szkoła Stolarska) at Kalwaria Zebrzydowska – the cabinetmaker Władysław Jarosiński and the woodcarver Karol Kudelski – with fixtures by the Kraków-based firm of Marcin Jarra.

Both sets of shelves have similar ornamentation and form, which reference the vernacular carpentry traditions. They differ only in the location of their woodcarvings: the first one has a carved door with three relief panels as the sole decoration, whilst the intricate carving of the second is limited to its sides.

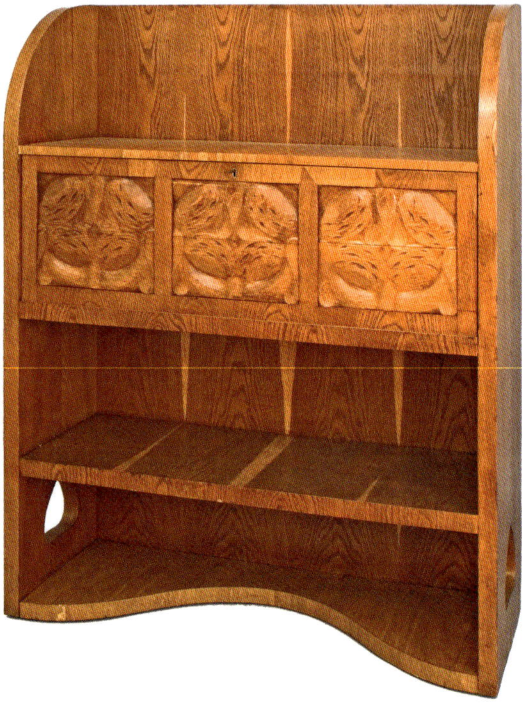

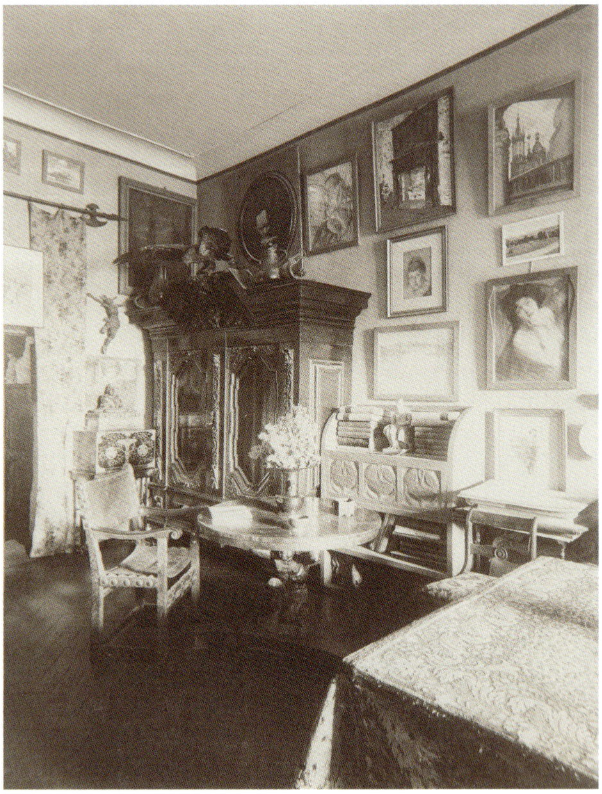

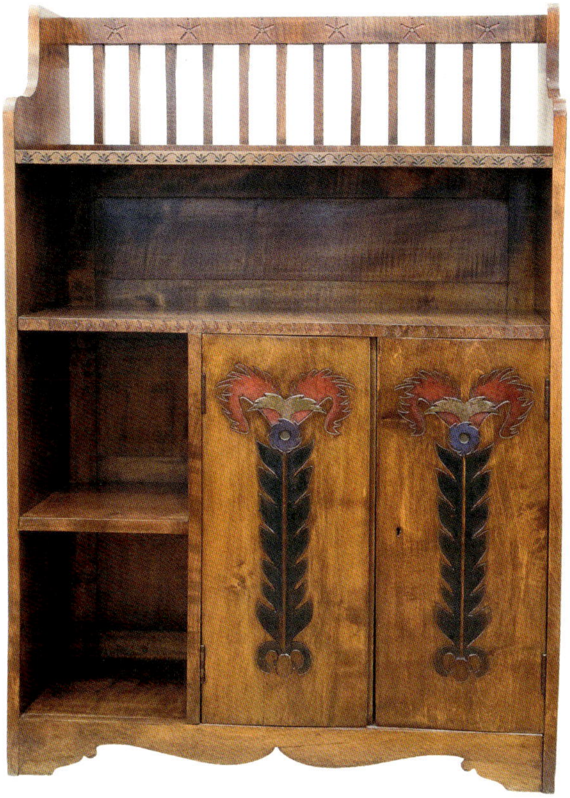

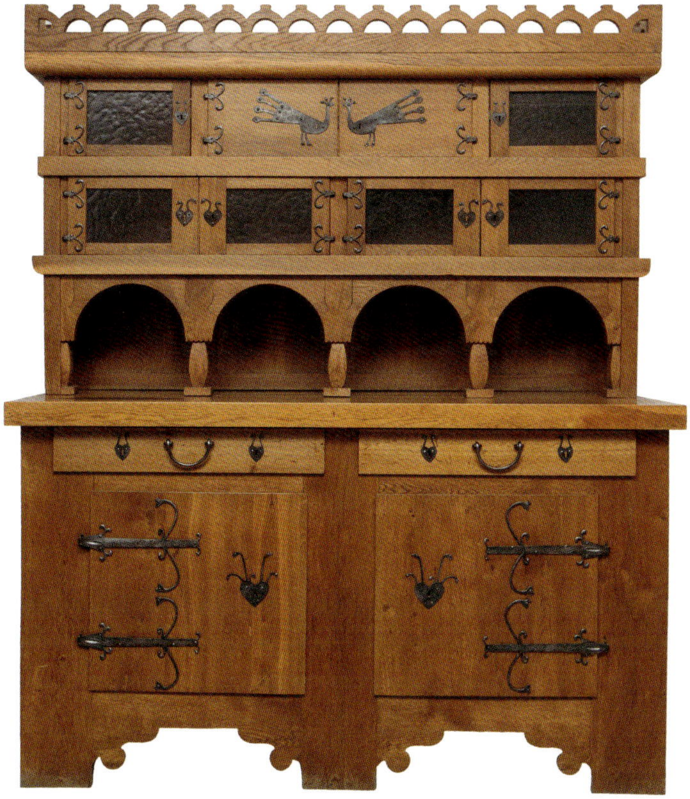

11.8 ↑

Shelves, Kraków, designed by Edward Trojanowski, before 1906

Oak, stained, carved, painted
146 × 100 × 35 cm
National Museum in Kraków, MNK-IV-Sp-204 (Feliks Jasieński bequest, 1929)

Designed by Edward Trojanowski, painter, designer, teacher and co-founder of the Polish Applied Arts Society, this set of shelves is one of several similar recorded designs from the artist's workshop.

Trojanowski's designs showcased at the second exhibition of the Polish Applied Arts Society in 1903 included a shelf and chair made by Jan Józef Zabża. In 1905 he showed another set of shelves, made by the Ligęza Brothers, at the *Modern Textiles and Ceramics* exhibition. The sizeable dresser designed for the larger restaurant at the Old Theatre features analogous compositional solutions and decorative motifs.

This piece, incorporating a two-door cupboard, comes from the collection of the art connoisseur Feliks 'Manggha' Jasieński. The door panels are decorated with carved and painted ornament which evokes a floral paper cutting. The influence of simple, vernacular woodcarving is also discernable in the carved ornamental frieze on the little gallery at the top of the piece.

11.9 ↑

Dresser from a dining-room set, Kraków, designed by Ludwik Puget, executed by Jan Józef Zabża (cabinetmaking) and Stanisław Fijałkowski (metalwork), 1903

Solid oak, forged iron
220 × 184 × 70.3 cm
National Museum in Kraków, MNK-IV-Sp-1235/1
(purchased from Grzegorz Puget under the MKiDN scheme, 2016)

This dresser is part of a set comprising an icebox, two tables and five chairs, which are the only known furniture designs by the sculptor Ludwik Puget. The design dates from an early stage of the artist's career, and evidences his familiarisation with Central European folk art, wooden vernacular architecture and woodcarving. The pierced cornice at the top of the dresser is inspired by wooden arcades, characteristic of the architecture of small towns in 19th-century Galicia. Puget was also an art historian and his interest in Polish wooden sculptures and Gothic architecture is notable. The inspiration for the decorative metalwork was undoubtedly blacksmiths' hinges found on the wooden doors of medieval churches. The dining-room furniture set had remained in Kraków in the possession of the artist and his descendants prior to being acquired by the National Museum there.

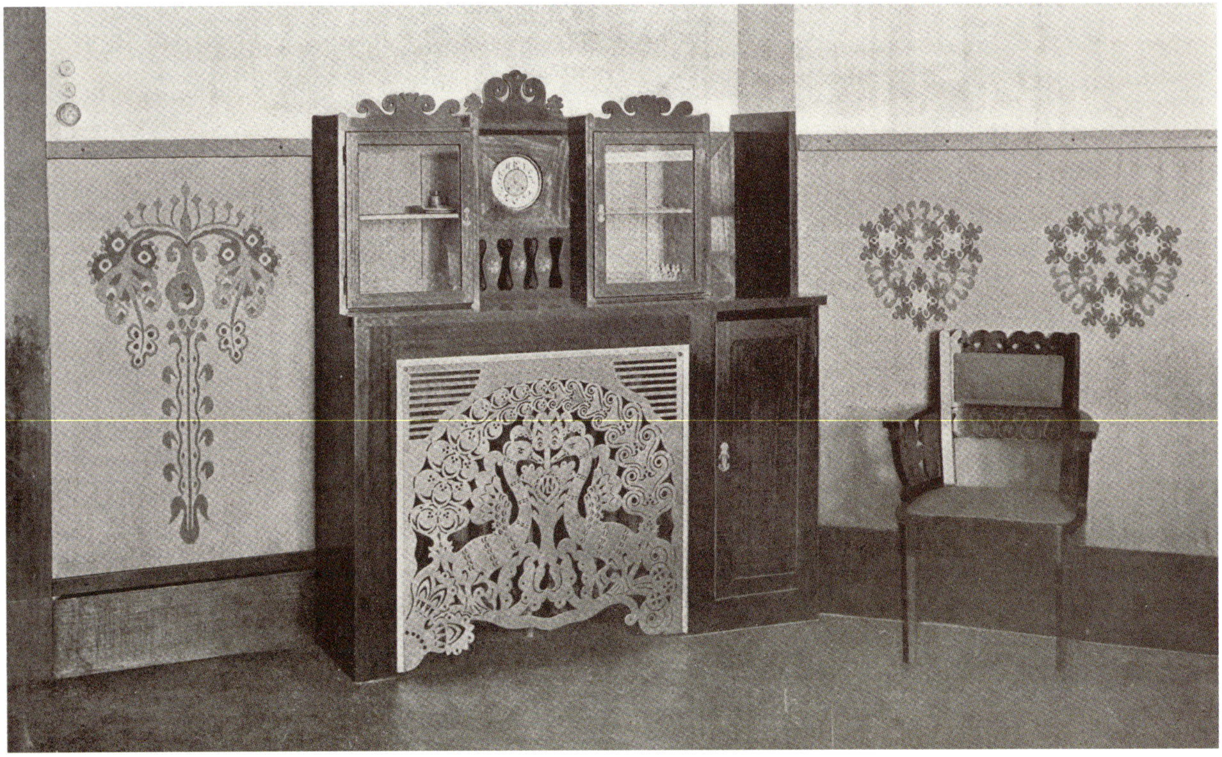

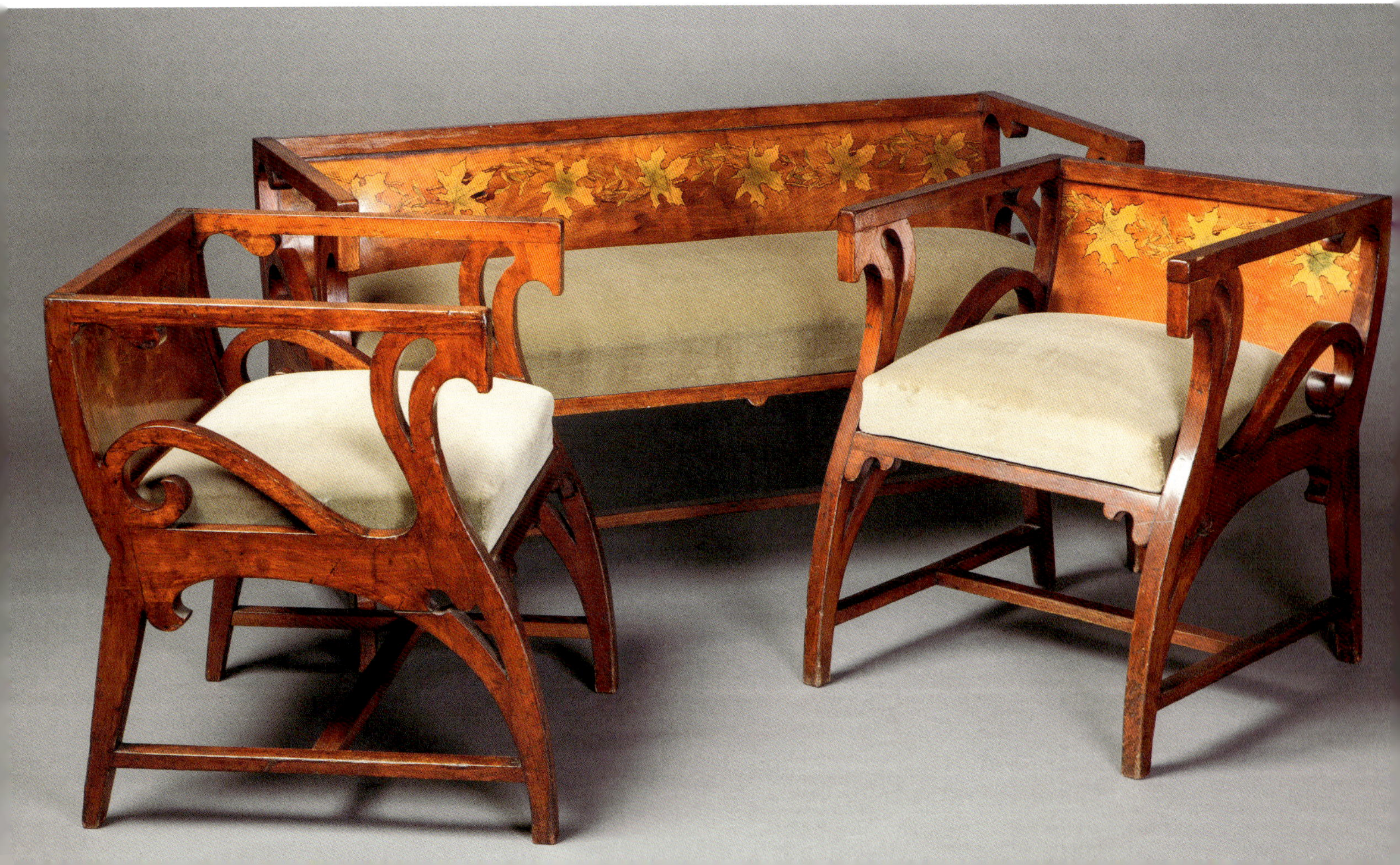

11.10 ←

Heater cover from the smaller restaurant hall in the Old Theatre in Kraków, designed by Ludwik Wojtyczko, 1905–6

Photograph reproduced from *Sztuka Stosowana*, Kraków, no.8–9 (1906), unpaginated

In 1905, as part of the communal design project to decorate the Old Theatre in Kraków, undertaken by the members of the Polish Applied Arts Society, the architect Ludwik Wojtyczko devised the design for the smaller restaurant hall. Due to limited space, the furnishings included only mahogany furniture made in Michał Piela's workshop: tables, a corner settee and two types of chairs. Kilims from Antonina Sikorska's workshop complemented the scheme. The heater posed a considerable challenge to the architect. In order to conceal it, he designed a metal fretwork screen featuring two fantastical birds with stylised peacock tails. He also designed a dresser-like structure to go on top of the screen, comprising a clock and two glazed cases. Folk paper cuttings, collected and reproduced in the periodical *Sztuka Stosowana*, were the inspiration for the intricate fretwork of the screen. The design was skilfully executed by Wojciech Róg, from Karol Uznański's metalwork workshop in Kraków.

11.11 ←

Set of furniture: settee and two armchairs, Warsaw, designed by Bronisława Poświkowa (signed), before 1902

Alder wood polished to imitate mahogany,
batik decoration on wood, reproduction upholstery
Settee: 69 × 136 × 54 cm; armchairs: 69 × 56 × 54 cm
National Museum in Kraków, MNK-IV-Sp-68/1-3
(Teodor Dunin bequest, 1909)

Designing furniture was only a peripheral artistic pursuit for the painter Bronisława Poświkowa. In 1897 a set of her furniture decorated with pokerwork, inspired by Podhale vernacular crafts, was recorded, and two years later a furniture set with colourful floral Art Nouveau style decoration. In 1902 the artist exhibited an Art Nouveau set of furniture for the study at Aleksander Krywult's Salon in Warsaw. In the same year a selection of her applied arts and furniture was on display at her posthumous memorial exhibition at the Society of Friends of the Fine Arts in Lviv, alongside her paintings. Her style was characterised by her predilection for floral and plant forms, which is also evident in the set of furniture from the Dunin household. The backs of two armchairs and the settee are decorated with a broad frieze of maple leaves and flowers in the batik technique on wood. The slender framework of the furniture is characterised by a modernist minimalist form and lightness, emphasised by the straight lines of the low backs and armrests.

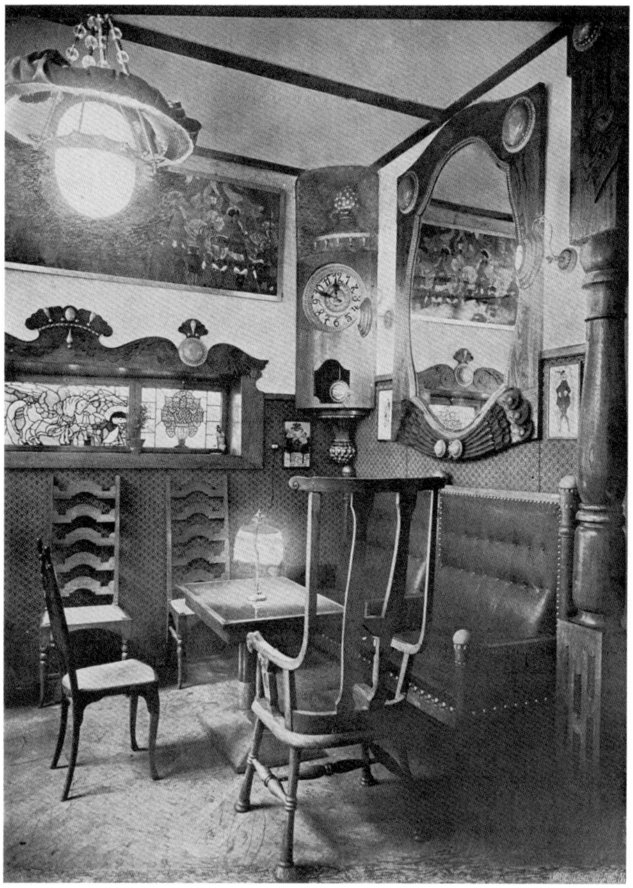

11.12 ↑

Jama Michalika (Michalik's Den) cafe in Kraków, designed by Karol Frycz, 1910

Photograph reproduced from *Sztuka Stosowana*, no.15 (1911), p.3

Jama Michalika cafe in Kraków was the popular meeting place of Young Poland bohemia. Its extraordinary decorative scheme was the work of Karol Frycz, who designed the larger hall and the annexe, the so-called *górka* (upstairs). The small space of the raised annexe was conceived as a uniform whole, in which all branches of the visual arts came together to create a coherent scheme. Elements of joinery and the wooden panelling contain small stained-glass panels and a clock, and a large mirror in a carved frame featuring peacocks presides over the arrangement. In front of the leather-upholstered settees, which line the walls, there are small modernist tables with functional finishes: marble tops and feet covered with metal. Lamps and sconces complete the scheme. Two types of wooden chairs with oversized backrests, whose forms are inspired by German and English furniture from the 18th century, are noteworthy. Craftsmen from Józef Sperling's workshop in Kraków were largely responsible for making the joinery and furniture.

11.13 ↓

(LEFT) **Chair from a craftsman's bedroom, Kraków, designed by Karol Maszkowski, executed by Ambroży Chrobak, 1912**

Solid oak
91 × 43 × 42 cm
National Museum in Kraków, MNK-IV-Sp-448/1
(from the Museum of Technology and Industry)

(TOP AND BOTTOM RIGHT) **Bedroom and sitting-room-cum-dining-room at the Craftsman's House, designed by Karol Maszkowski for the *Architecture and Interiors in a Garden Setting* exhibition in Kraków in 1912**

Photograph reproduced from *Wzory mebli zabytkowych i nowoczesnych*, Kraków: Miejskie Muzeum Przemysłowe im. dra Adrjana Baranieckiego, vol.9-10 (1929)

The painter and interior designer Karol Maszkowski was invited by the Museum of Technology and Industry to design furniture for the Craftsman's House as part of the *Architecture and Interiors in a Garden Setting* exhibition in Kraków in 1912. The model home for a craftsman, designed by Adolf Szyszko-Bohusz (1883–1948), consisted of a carpentry workshop on the ground floor, and on the upper floor a bathroom, kitchen, a room for journeymen and a sitting room with a bedroom alcove. The rooms were endowed with simple furniture made of solid oak, functional and fulfilling the basic needs of residents with limited means. The furniture was made to Maszkowski's designs by Kraków cabinetmakers Ambroży Chrobak (the bed, cupboard, bedside cabinet and chairs for the bedroom) and Michał Marchewczyk (the table, chairs, corner bench and sideboard for the sitting-room-cum-dining-room). Maszkowski proposed two types of chairs. Those for the dining room feature heart-shaped motifs on the backs, referencing folk paper cuttings, and those for the bedroom (which survive in the Museum collections) have simple openwork chair backs composed of vertical slats.

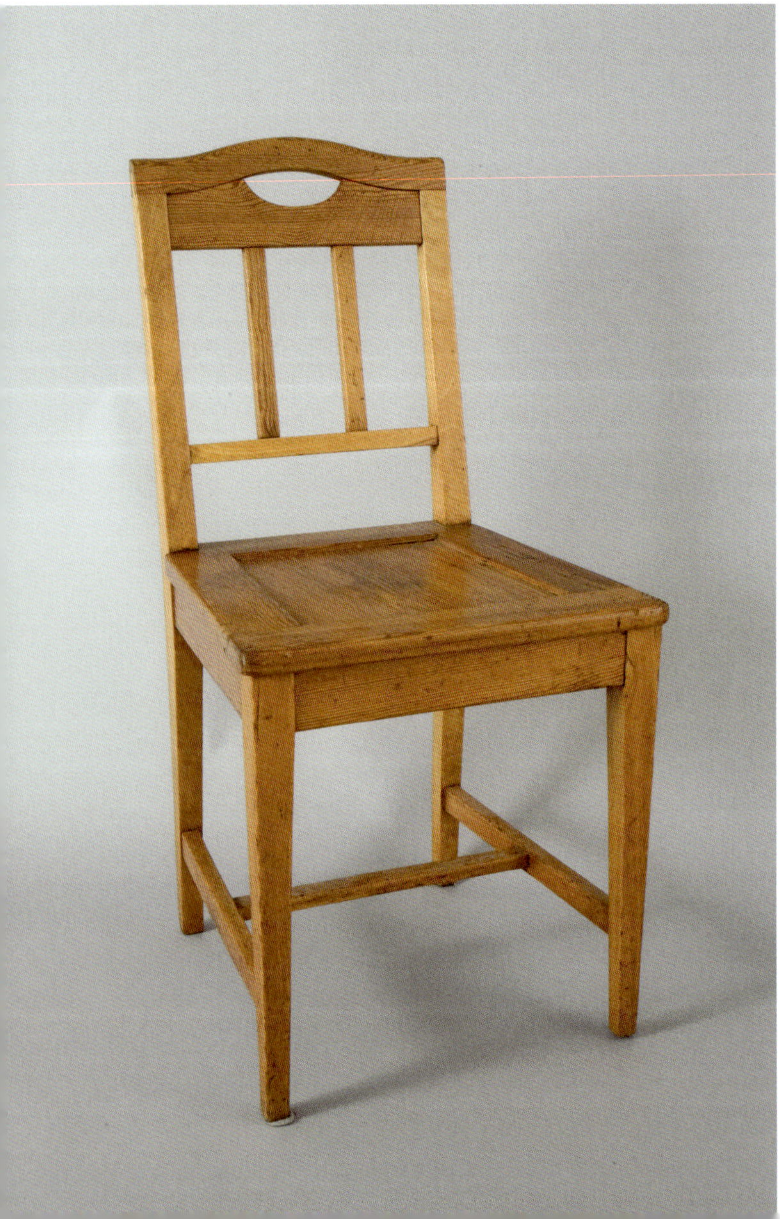

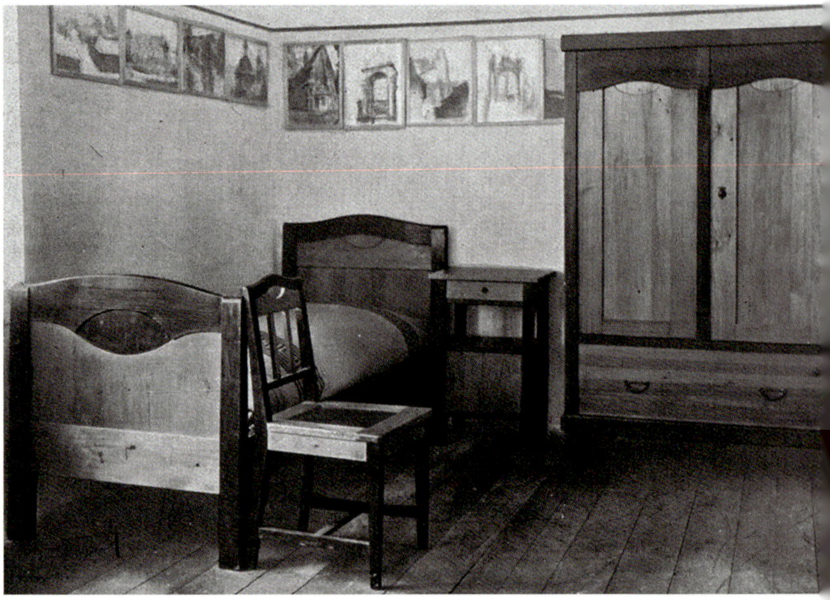

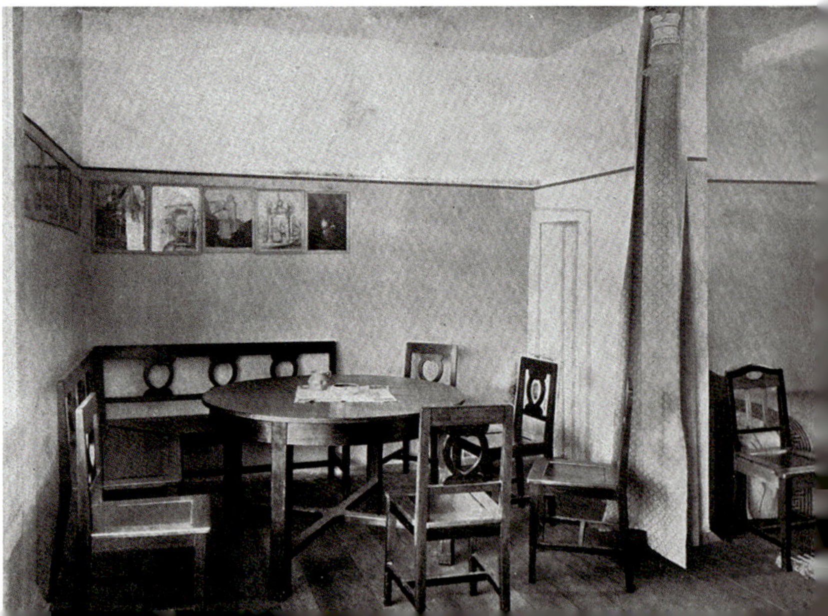

11.14 ↓

Reading Room in the Library of the Museum of Technology and Industry, Kraków, designed by Karol Homolacs, executed by the Kraków Workshops, 1913–14

Museum of Kraków, MHK 3143-N

The decorative scheme of the newly completed Museum of Technology and Industry was the first communal design project undertaken by the members of the newly formed Kraków Workshops (see Chapter 9), and today the building houses the only (partially) surviving examples of the decorative schemes designed by the members of the association. Józef Czajkowski's design of the grand staircase and Karol Stryjeński's design of the modern library spaces and the Librarian's Office are noteworthy, as would have been the lost furnishings of the assembly hall designed by Wojciech Jastrzębowski. The Reading Room scheme including the furniture was single-handedly designed by Karol Homolacs, a founding member of the Kraków Workshops, a versatile artist, teacher and theoretician of art. In accordance with the Workshops' ideological principles, local material (pine, ash and oak) was used for the long tables, sturdily constructed chairs and cupboards, bringing out the properties and structure of the wood. Three table types of varying functions were produced, with surfaces for various library users, i.e. for readers, for visitors consulting the catalogue, and a table fitted with an inbuilt shelf.

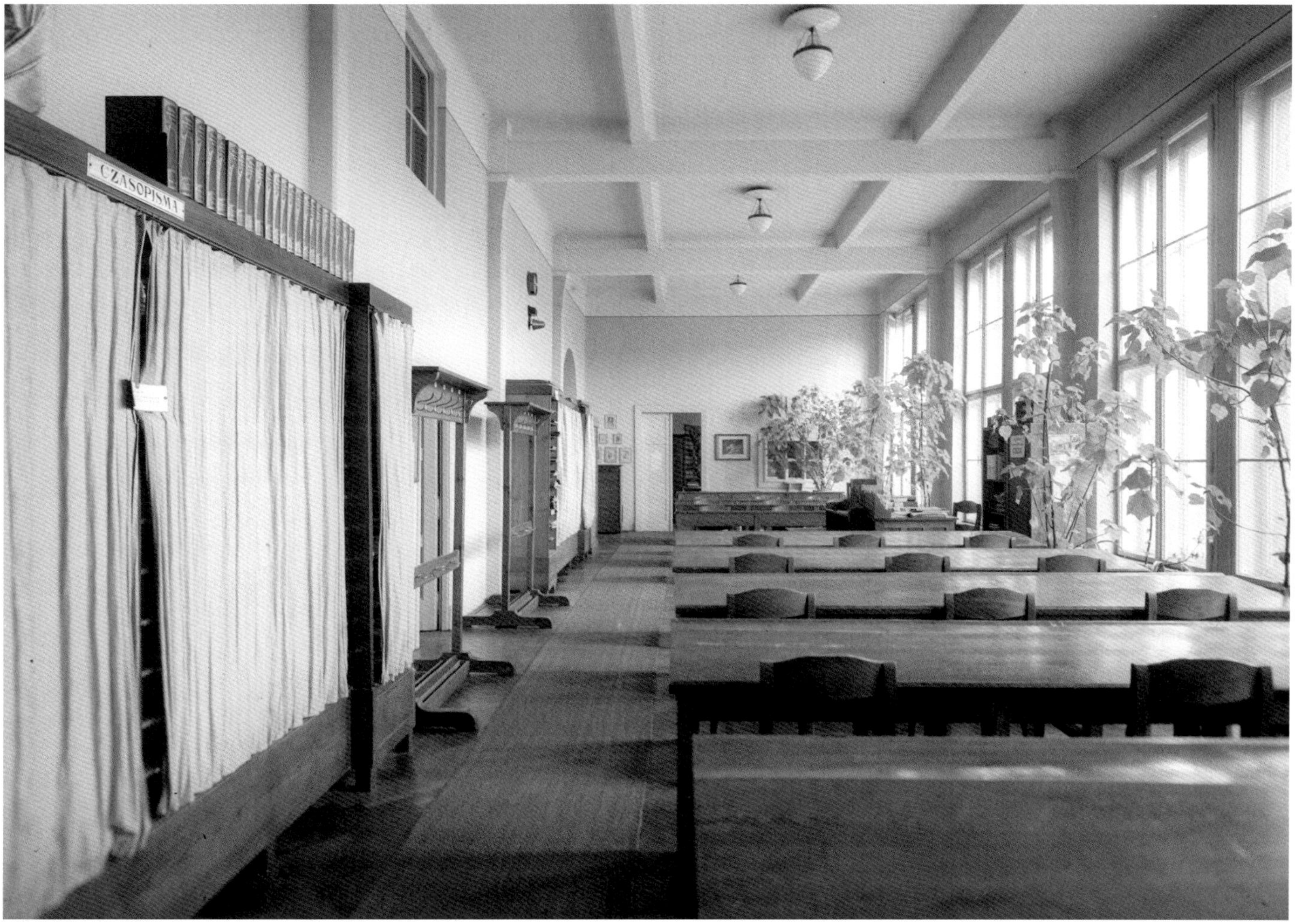

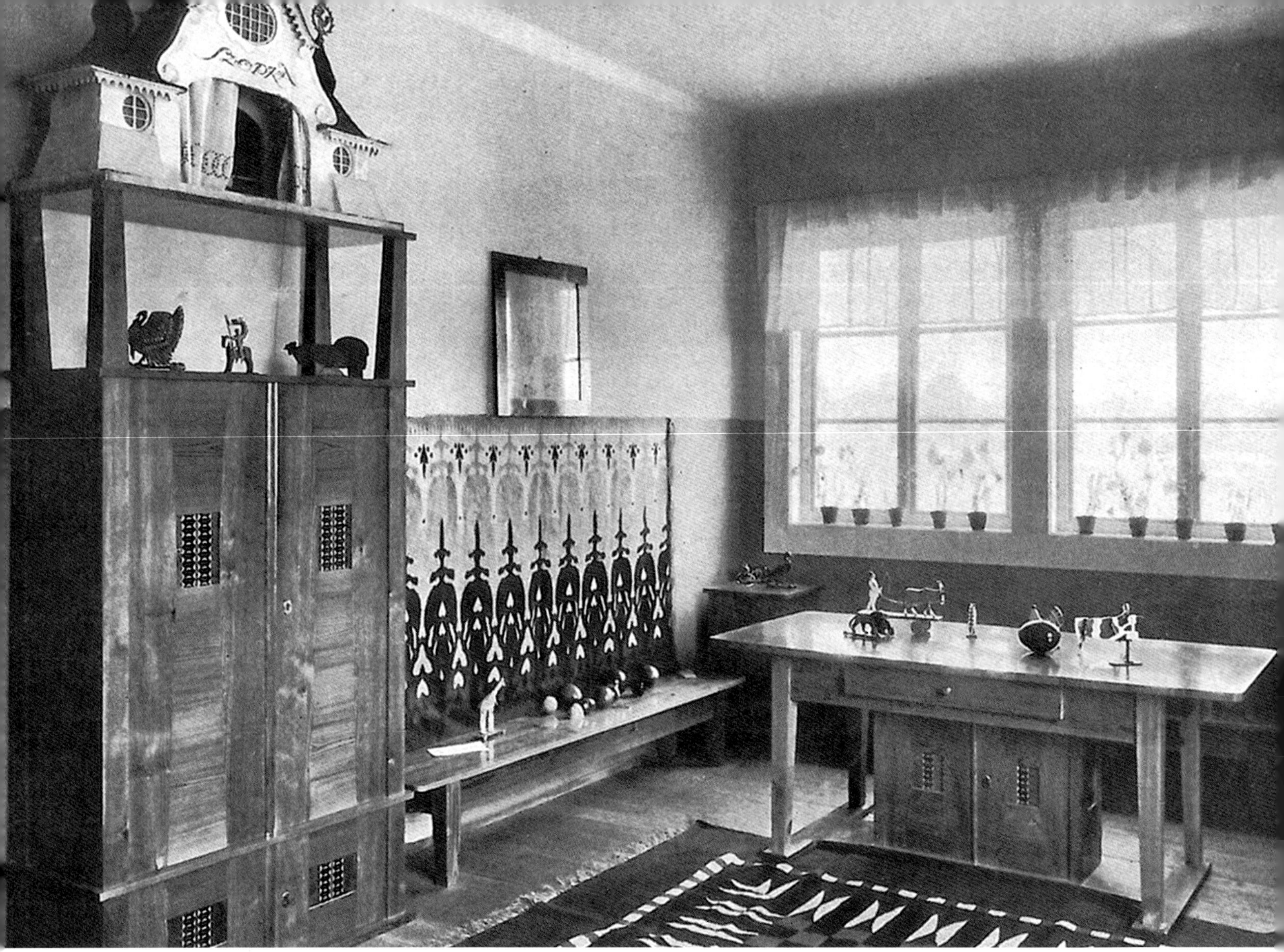
SZOPKA

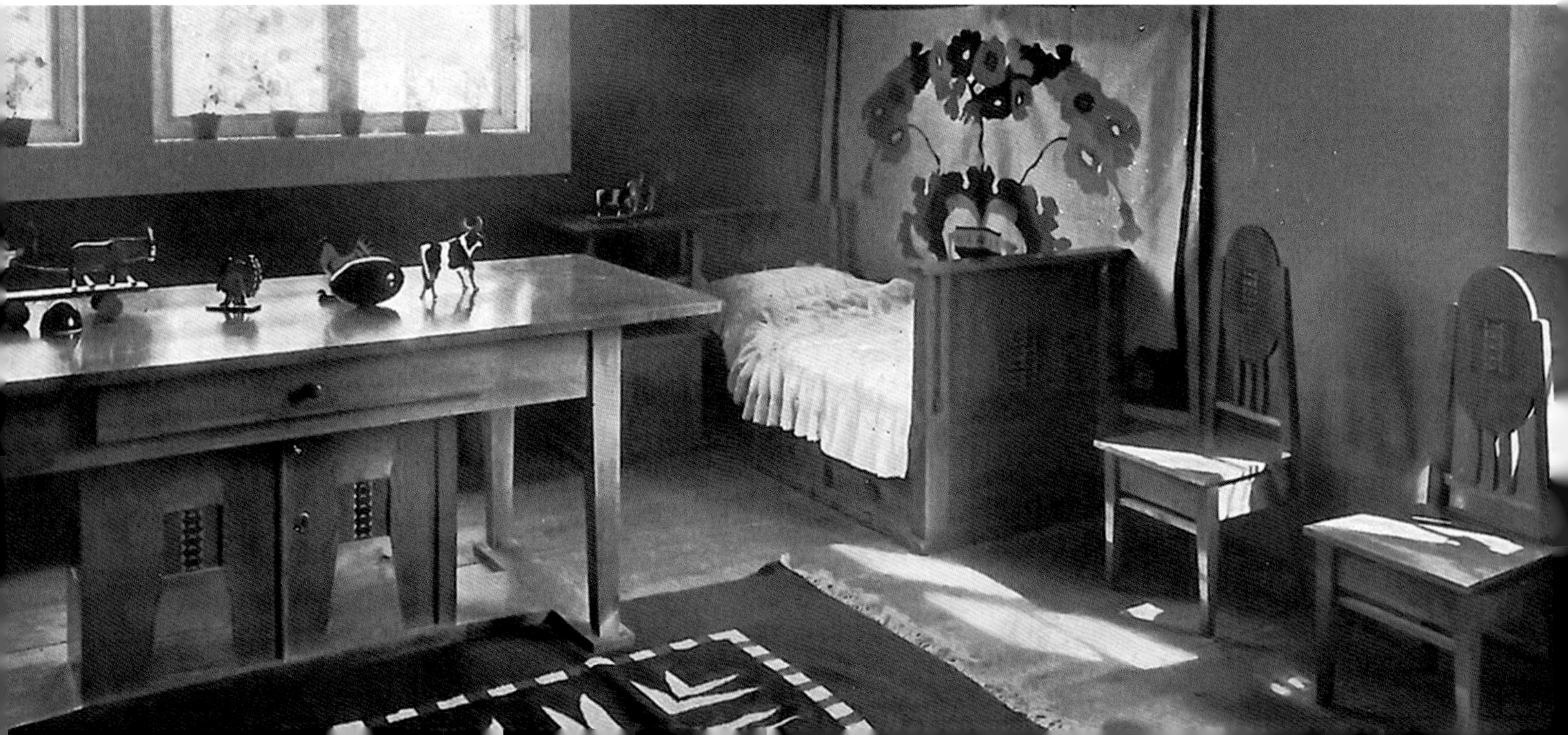

12

Edmund Bartłomiejczyk's Design for a Nursery

Zofia Weiss

A rare set of furniture designed by Edmund Bartłomiejczyk for the *Architecture and Interiors in a Garden Setting* exhibition held in Kraków in 1912 has been preserved at the Wojciech Weiss Museum Foundation (figs 12.0 and 12.1). The foundation looks after the legacy of the great Polish Symbolist and Expressionist painter Wojciech Weiss (1875–1950), a member of numerous turn-of-the-century European arts societies, particularly the Vienna Secession, and an outstanding pedagogue, who inspired many modernist artists.

The *Architecture and Interiors in a Garden Setting* exhibition was both a reflection of strong ties with the Viennese artistic milieu, and testimony to a considerable awareness of novel artistic, architectural and urban planning ideas which originated in England. William Morris's and Ebenezer Howard's writings had become known through Polish translations, and Howard – the founder of the Garden City Movement – honoured the Kraków exhibition with his presence.

The main ideological basis for the exhibition had been formulated a year earlier, in 1911, in the periodical *Architekt*. Its fundamental objective was to present the egalitarian notion of 'one's own home in a garden' to a socially diverse audience, in keeping with 'a powerful . . . movement in this direction in Western societies, particularly in England and Germany'.[1] The projected new symbolism of the manor house was to be freed from its traditional association with the landed gentry and nobility. The manor house was to become the archetypal home – the suburban villa – whilst continuing to signify tradition, national character and closeness to nature.

The surviving suite of furniture from this exhibition, preserved in Weiss's house for over a century, was intended for the 'children's room' of the 'suburban manor-house'. The building itself was designed by the painter and architect Józef Czajkowski. The design of the nursery suite set out to fulfil the exhibition organisers' objectives, namely drawing on the visual language of national art forms, and rediscovering age-old design models and forms left unspoiled by civilisation in the suburbs and countryside. Furthermore, in keeping with the idea of creating 'art for all', accessible to the whole of society, the exhibited furniture designs were to be comfortable, relatively inexpensive, and to comply with the basic principles

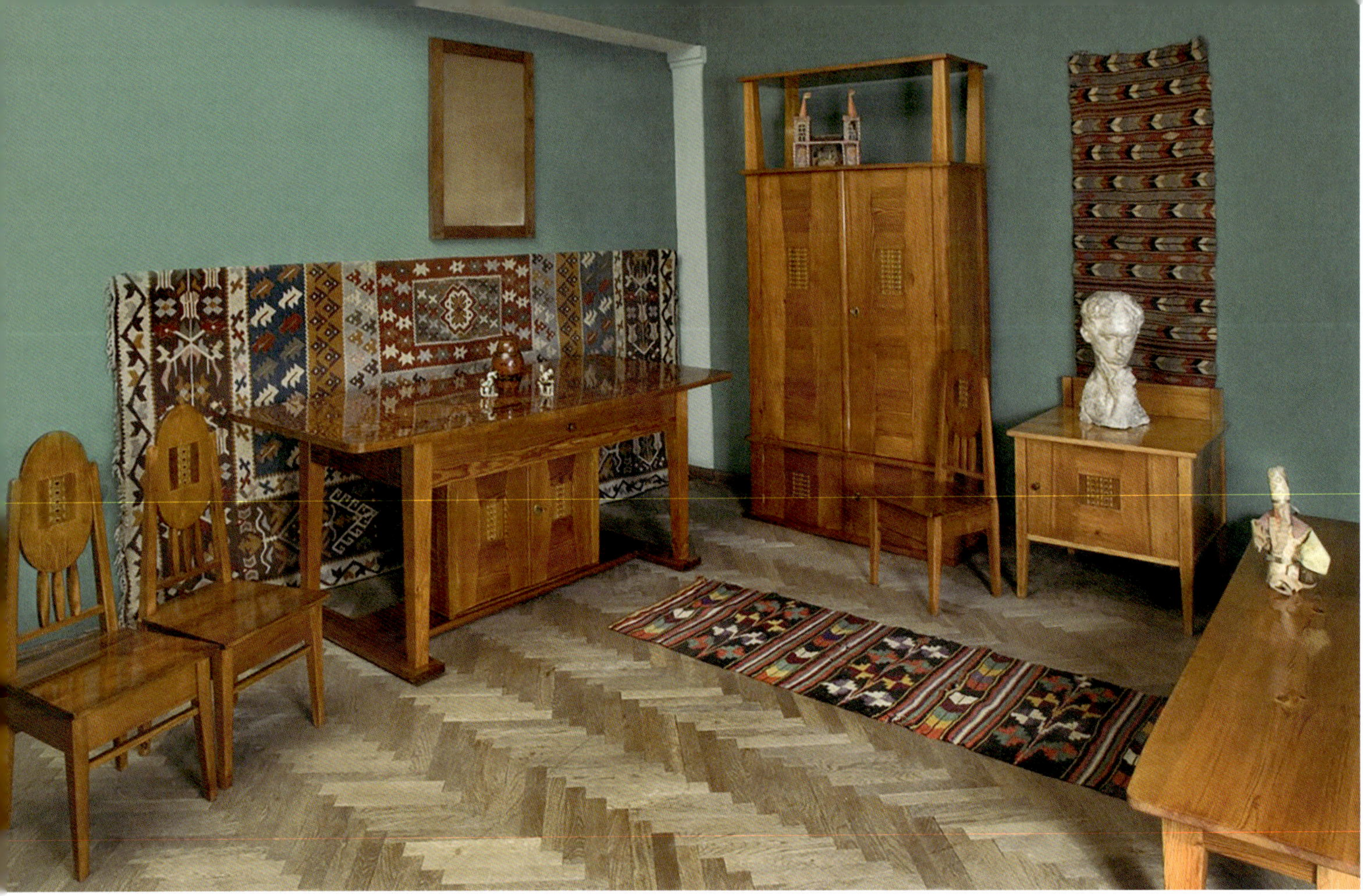

of hygiene. Embracing all of these demands, Bartłomiejczyk's furniture suite is a prime example of a design in keeping with international trends of that period. It enters into a dialogue with the ideas of the Arts and Crafts Movement, very well-known in Poland at this time (see Chapter 1), as well as the principles of the Wiener Werkstätte, widely discussed within the Austro-Hungarian Empire.

The designer, Bartłomiejczyk, known above all as a printmaker and illustrator, studied at the Academy of Fine Arts in Kraków between 1906 and 1909, in the painting studios of Jan Stanisławski (1860–1907) and Wojciech Weiss. He undertook the design of the furniture for the Kraków exhibition while already a student of architecture at the School of Fine Arts in Warsaw. Bartłomiejczyk's outstanding debut in the field of design was to be crowned with international success only years later. At the International Exposition of Modern Industrial and Decorative Arts in Paris in 1925 he was honoured with a gold medal in the field of book arts and posters, while at the International Exposition of Art and Technology in Modern Life in Paris in 1937 he received the Grand Prix in the field of independent print-making.[2]

The furniture suite designed by him for the *Architecture and Interiors in a Garden Setting* was executed in the workshops of Józef Sperling, a Kraków entrepreneur, and subsequently Wojciech Weiss's brother-in-law. Sperling realised the ideal of the integration of fine art and craft within the field of interior design, collaborating with leading architects and painters. Apart from his handicraft workshops, he also ran an 'Atelier for complete furnishings and decorations' in Kraków, which developed into a department store situated in the heart of the town centre.[3]

Most of the pieces of furniture that comprise the remarkable 'children's room' decorative scheme of 1912 have survived to the present, namely a wardrobe, a low square cabinet, a table with an integrated two-door cupboard located beneath the tabletop, two low benches and a chair with dimensions appropriate for a child. Untraced pieces regarded

12.0 (p.166)
Bespoke set of nursery furniture at the *Architecture and Interiors in a Garden Setting* exhibition of 1912 in Kraków, designed by Edmund Bartłomiejczyk
Photographs reproduced from *Sztuka Stosowana*, vol.16 (1912)

12.1
Bespoke set of nursery furniture, 1912, designed by Edmund Bartłomiejczyk, now at the Wojciech Weiss Museum Foundation

as lost include the remaining chairs,[4] a small bed with three drawers, and two accompanying bedside tables. The decorative scheme of the nursery shown in the exhibition itself was complemented by a Christmas crib (on top of the wardrobe) – notably modelled on the suburban manor house – and some wooden toys. Important elements of the overall design included a kilim rug, likewise designed by Bartłomiejczyk, and two more kilim wall hangings on either side of the room – one over the bench designed by the painter Stanisław Gałek, and one over the bed by Kazimierz Brzozowski, a painter and co-founder of the Kilim Association in Zakopane.

Bartłomiejczyk's furniture was made of solid pine. Veneer, made from rotary-cut pine, was used only for the tabletop. This is a technique employed to the present day that involves cutting from the circumference of the trunk, to produce a long, broad sheet of veneer. The resulting, particularly beautiful effect, with a pronounced and irregular grain, is heightened by using a glossy shellac varnish. The other pieces of furniture were also varnished, which brought out their natural ornamentation, composed of nothing other than the structure of the tree from which they were made. This flawless, virginal, natural quality gave rise to furniture characterised by great simplicity of form on the one hand, and great elegance and monumentality on the other. The only added decorative features were small rectangular marquetry elements. These were made of ebony, almost black in tone, together with walnut and sycamore, the latter being the lightest in colour. Small component pieces arranged within these rectangular features form highly stylised folk motifs of peacocks' eyes or fish scales, hugely popular at this time (see also figs 3.6 and 13.1). Bartłomiejczyk's set of furniture clearly references designs by Charles Rennie Mackintosh (1868–1928), particularly the bedroom furniture suite of 1904 at the Hunterian Art Gallery of the University of Glasgow, as well as his furnishings for Hill House, Helensburgh, from 1903. Aside from of its ornamental elements, Mackintosh's inspirational furniture was characterised by the distinctive simplicity of its forms, producing an effect of exceptional elegance.

Despite the fact that the Polish nation had been deprived of its country for over a hundred years and that the partitioning powers' policies had condemned Polish culture to a provincial and peripheral role within the European arts scene, there was a wonderful flourishing of this culture at the turn of the century, against the odds. Polish artists, being fully open to inspiration from Western cultural centres, particularly Paris, London and Vienna, were able to maintain an appropriate balance between external trends and their own national tradition, and in particular certain inherent sensibilities that were characteristic of the Polish nation.

Designs presented at the *Architecture and Interiors in a Garden Setting* exhibition embodied the Young Poland era. They endeavoured to reconstruct the Polish national identity on the basis of the age-old authenticity of the folk culture, including its spirituality, unspoiled by civilisation, combined with the national and patriotic insurrectionist tradition associated with the phenomenon of the landed gentry's manor houses. This is precisely why one reviewer thus summarised the exhibition: 'dreaming of a new Poland, a Poland which has left behind kitsch apartment blocks and pseudo-palaces and has moved into houses . . . conceived out of harmony between form and content . . . close to nature, breathing deeply, houses modelled on the old Polish manor house.'[5]

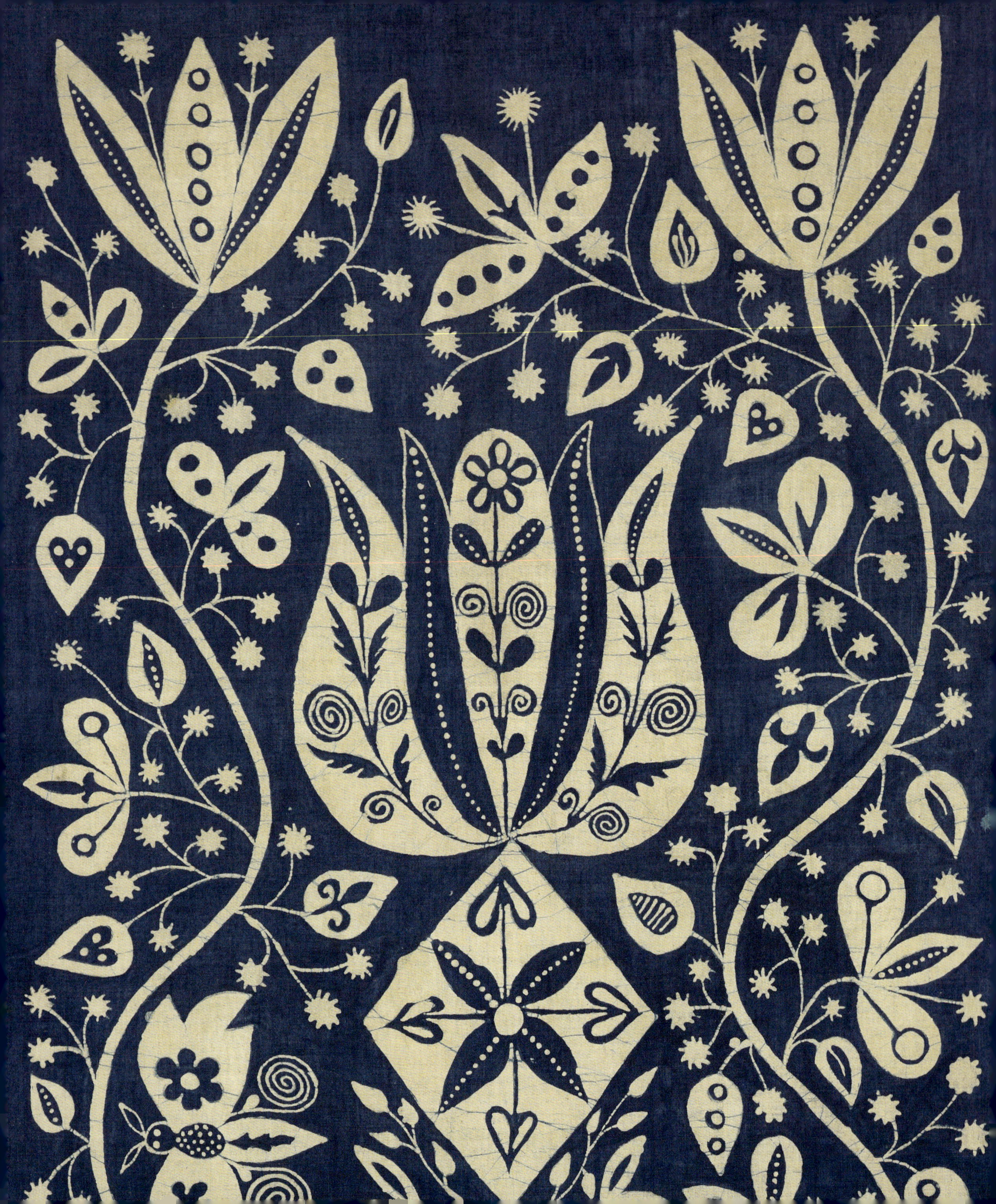

13

Textiles

Joanna Regina Kowalska

Just as had been the case in Britain under the influence of the Arts and Crafts Movement, the Young Poland era witnessed a revival in the design of decorative textiles. Kilims and embroideries were most deeply rooted in the Polish tradition, but unexpected innovations such as painted and stencilled linen friezes (fig.13.2) were also occasionally designed for interiors.

Polish kilims

Although of similar woven technique, a kilim differs significantly from a tapestry. It is double-sided, and small gaps are left at the edges of its patterns during the weaving process. The properties of this technique mean that it is impossible to attain a completely flowing line in a design. Due to the ease of execution, kilim-making had long remained the sole domain of the peasantry. While tapestry-weaving was developing in Western Europe, kilim workshops were being established on aristocratic estates in Polish lands under the partitions. Manor-house kilims modelled on tapestries had enjoyed great popularity in the 18th century, featuring mainly floral motifs. The south-eastern territories of Galicia were renowned for folk kilims decorated with geometrical designs. The last third of the 19th century saw renewed interest in the beauty of such hand-woven textiles in comparison with factory products, and efforts to preserve the tradition of kilim-making. The most famous centres of production were in Gliniany (now Hlyniany), Okno (now Wikno) and Kosów (now Kosiv).

Kilims were the favourite decorative textile of Young Poland artists. They were an indispensable part of the Polish Applied Arts Society exhibitions. In the modern interior kilims were used to adorn walls, tables, floors and sofas. Even the most famous artists produced kilim designs. The spirit of the folk kilim was best evoked in compositions featuring rhythmically

13.0 (p.170)
Wojciech Jastrzębowski (concept originator and co-designer)
Co-designed and executed by Józefa Kogut in collaboration with Franciszka Delkowska (Kraków Workshops)
Batik wall covering, 1924
Part of a dining-room interior decoration scheme presented at the International Exposition of Modern Industrial and Decorative Arts in Paris in 1925
Monochrome wax batik on canvas
283 × 63 cm
National Museum in Kraków, MNK-XIX-3274

arranged motifs, such as 'Peacock's Eyes', designed by Józef Czajkowski (fig.13.1).

Later on the Zakopane-based Kilim Association, founded in 1910, attached great importance to traditional materials and dyeing techniques. The State Exhibition of Ancient and Modern Kilims, in Lviv in 1913, had a wide-ranging influence. The kilim remained one of the chief means of artistic expression for the next generations of artists who grew out of the Polish Arts and Crafts movement.

Embroideries and appliqué in interior decoration

Embroidery was, relatively speaking, the cheapest and most accessible decorative technique. It was part of the standard education for women, which is why both female artists and housewives alike practised it with great proficiency and sensitivity. Embroidered napkins, tablecloths and wall hangings could transform an interior, giving it a modern feel, as long as the maker was able to choose a design embracing the latest trends within the decorative arts of the period.

Artists associated with the Kraków milieu began designing embroideries around 1900. Men commissioned female embroiderers to carry out their designs, precisely reflecting the artist's concept (figs 13.3 and 13.4). Women artists, on the other hand, realised their own designs, working on the piece from the original concept to execution. Their textiles were therefore more coherent in terms of subject matter, style and technique (figs 13.5, 13.6 and 13.7).

Fashion and the national style

At the dawn of the 20th century, fashion in Polish lands under the partitions followed Western trends. Style-conscious men and women looked particularly to Paris. Their outfits emulated Parisian or Viennese fashions in terms of shapes, quality of fabrics and workmanship. As had been the case in Western Europe, fashion was increasingly valued, assuming the distinctive features of the style prevalent in high art. Fashion quietly entered the world of the decorative arts.

At the same time the aspiration to create an all-encompassing national style, extending to dress, was increasingly coming to prominence. In a country now dismembered by three partitioning powers, a distinctively 'Polish' national costume would be vital in cultivating the national identity, occasioning patriotic feelings and strengthening a sense of self-worth. The Zakopane Style (see Chapter 6), inspired by the Highlanders from the Podhale region, became one of the most vibrant influences on Young Poland fashion. The year 1902 was the turning point in the popularisation of Zakopane Style fashion: it saw the publication of Feliks 'Manggha' Jasieński's article, calling for the design of a 'Polish dress' (fig.13.10).[1] The gown's originality was to be determined by accessories rather than by a fashionable cut in keeping with international trends. Jasieński's designs featured Zakopane lace, a Highlander shepherd's belt, and embroideries with traditional Highlander motifs. The first dress in the Zakopane Style was made and exhibited in the same year, at the first Polish Applied Arts Society exhibition. Whilst the frock had a fashionable silhouette, it was the polychrome folk embroideries which proclaimed its 'Zakopane' pedigree. A dress collection inspired by Highlander culture went on sale at the Warsaw-based Bogusław Herse fashion house in 1902, which was testimony to the success of the Zakopane Style in fashion. Artists such as the sisters Leona and Karolina Bierkowska (1855–1925 and 1855–1931) and Bronisława Rychter-Janowska (1872–1953) also designed 'Polish' dresses inspired by folklore. Folk elements appeared in clothes and accessories made in both private homes and artisan workshops alike (figs 13.8 and 13.9). The zenith of the aspirations to create a national style in fashion came in 1908, when the Circle of Polish Women Artists organised the exhibition *Fashion Applied to Products of State Industry* in Kraków. It presented exceptional products of craftsmanship, including a collection of designs for 'Polish' clothes by Czesław Jankowski, combining inspiration from Highlander, Kraków and aristocratic dress.

Students at craft schools also designed items of fashion. The best-known schools were the School of Lacemaking in Zakopane (fig.13.10) and the State School of Embroidery (Krajowa Szkoła Hafciarska) in Maków Podhalański (fig.13.11). The idea of establishing these schools emerged in 1867, when Galicia was granted autonomy. It conformed to the Positivist programme of 'grassroots work' and also enjoyed the support of the imperial authorities. Interestingly, the girls at both schools were taught techniques not traditionally practised in their native villages: lacemaking had been unknown in Zakopane, and Maków Podhalański had been famed for its monochrome embroidery (i.e. whitework) and not the polychrome variety taught at the school. Despite imposing alien techniques, the artistic directors of both craft schools drew on a wealth of local folk art motifs. The resulting objects were very modern in their expression, whilst rooted in tradition in iconographic terms.[2] Batik scarves in 'Javanese-Kraków' style also became particularly fashionable in Kraków. Made by girls from local villages in the Kraków Workshops (see Chapter 9), they occasioned demand from fashionable ladies (figs 13.12 and 13.13).

The ideals of the revival of handicrafts and the creation of a national style found a highly original expression in fashion during the Young Poland era.

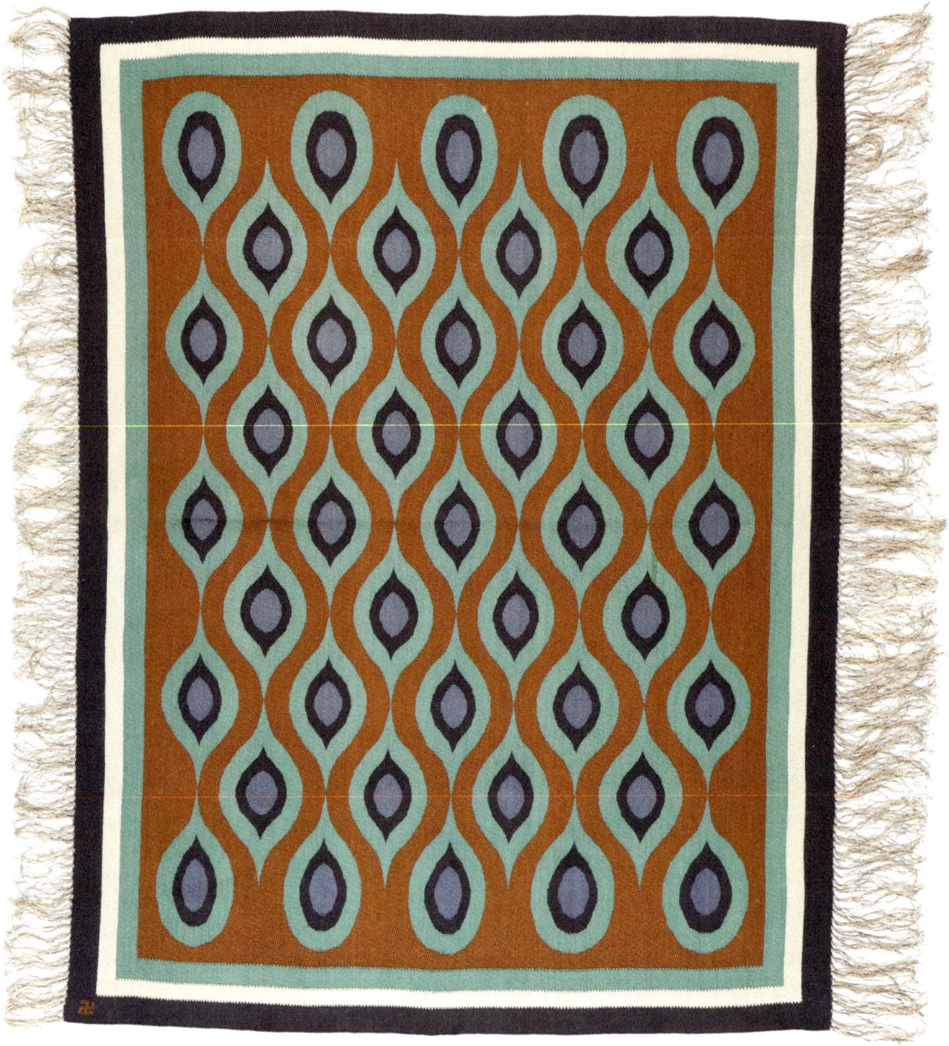

13.1 ↑

'Peacock's Eyes' kilim, early 20th century, designed by Józef Czajkowski, executed by the workshop of Antonina Sikorska in Czernichów; in the left corner the woven signature of the workshop in the form of a swastika

Linen and wool, loom-woven in kilim technique
194 × 148 cm
National Museum in Kraków, MNK XIX-5124
(Feliks Jasieński bequest, 1929)

The work of Józef Czajkowski, one of the founders of the Polish Applied Arts Society, is characterised by an exceptional sensitivity to the calls for the revival of handicrafts. Interiors designed by him combined folk art inspirations with the influence of high art. He excelled at utilising the properties of the kilim technique for creating highly decorative textiles.

The peacock's-eye motif had a special significance in Kraków, since it had long been present in folk embroidery, and peacocks' feathers adorned Krakowiak peasants' caps. Czajkowski used this typical Kraków motif as the chief ornament in his decorative scheme for the city of Kraków president's apartments (1907).

In keeping with the style of decorative art prevalent around 1900, the striking composition of the 'Peacock's Eyes' kilim endows it with local colour. Czajkowski created a similar kilim as a table-covering for the dining room of the Polish Nobel Prize winner Władysław Reymont, author of the four-volume novel *Chłopi* (*The Peasants*, 1904–9), depicting Polish rural life with ethnographic precision.

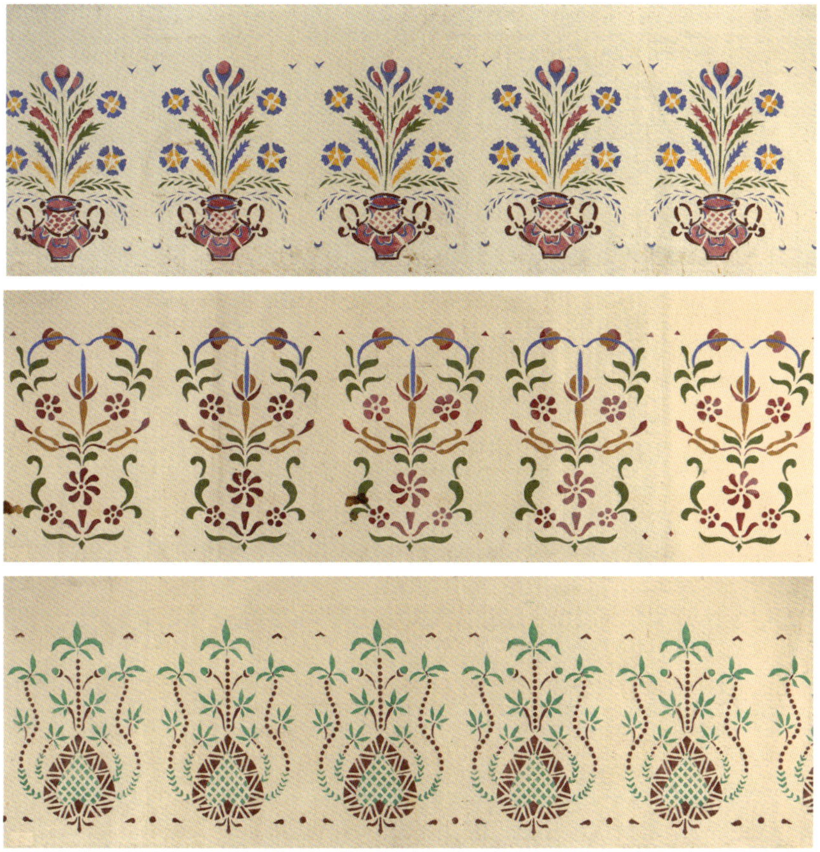

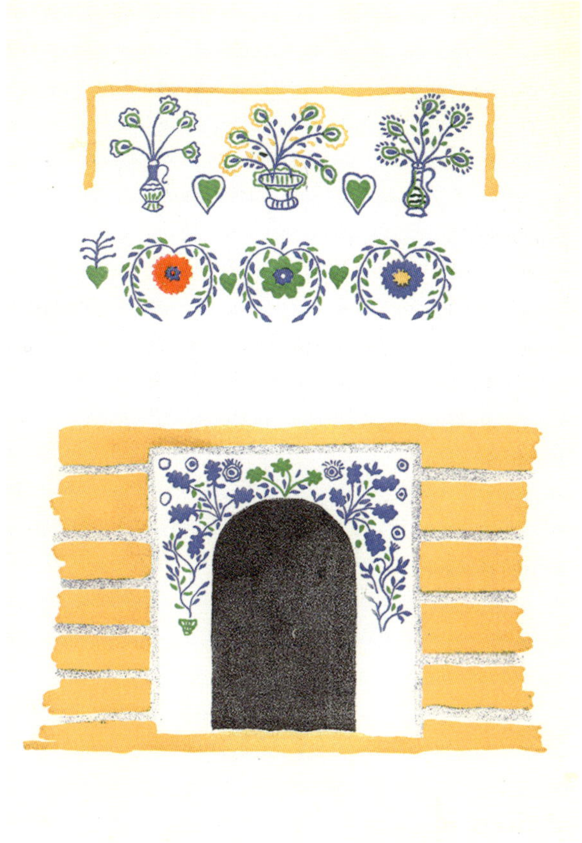

13.2 ↑

(LEFT) **Decorative friezes, Kraków, early 20th century, designed by Stanisław Wyspiański**

Natural linen, stencil-printed by hand
76 × 400 cm
National Museum in Kraków, MNK XIX-9388, MNK XIX-9389, MNK XIX-9390
(Feliks Jasieński bequest, 1929)

(RIGHT) **Lithograph showing Hanka Czepcówna's wall paintings in a peasant cottage in the village of Bronowice Wielkie (internal wall and external wall above the doorway, respectively), 1901, based on a drawing by Józef Czajkowski, reproduced in *Wydawnictwo Towarzystwa Polska Sztuka Stosowana: materiały*, vol.4, (1904)**

Three long linen friezes designed by Stanisław Wyspiański had been preserved in the collection of Feliks 'Manggha' Jasieński, one of the leading patrons of Young Poland art. They are decorated with repeating motifs clearly derived from folk ornamentation. Flowers in a vase, arranged as a symmetrical bouquet, were a common motif in the art of local villages. Hanka Czepcówna, daughter of Błażej Czepiec from Bronowice Wielkie, decorated the whitewashed wall of their peasant cottage with a frieze located between the window and the ceiling, featuring a motif of bouquets in jugs, simplified in form and restricted in colour (blue, green and yellow). A print based on Józef Czajkowski's copy of this decoration was published in 1904 in the journal of the Polish Applied Arts Society.[3] Textiles designed by Wyspiański greatly resemble Czepcówna's work (see also fig.2.9). These linen cloth friezes must have been in perfect harmony with the austere interiors which he designed, given their minimalist colour schemes and raw visual impact.

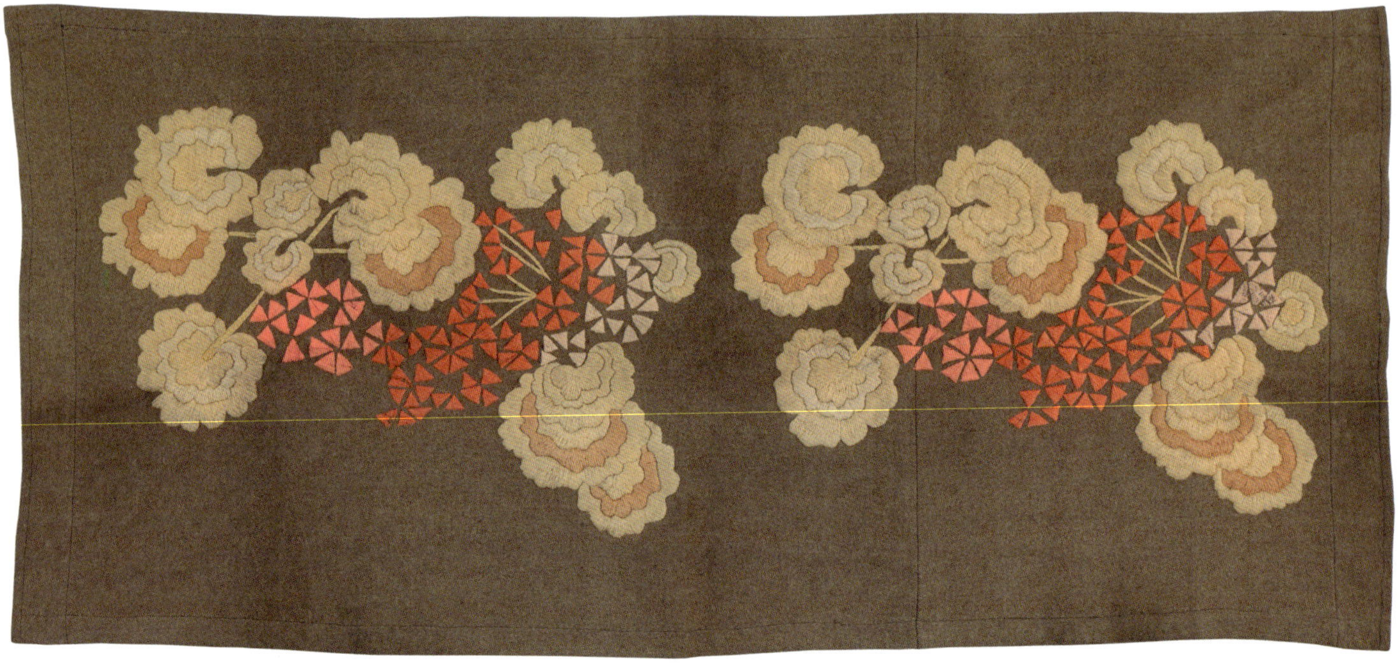

13.3 ↑

'Geraniums' embroidered pelmet, c.1904, designed by Stanisław Wyspiański; woollen cloth by Zajączek & Lankosz partnership, Kęty; embroidery by Helena Czeremuga

Woollen cloth, flat embroidery in woollen yarn
104 × 224 cm
National Museum in Kraków, MNK XIX-9413 (purchased 1980)

The style of the 'Świetlica' (Great Hall) presented at the exhibition of the 'Sztuka' ['Art'] Society of Polish Artists in 1904 (see Chapter 11) recalls the atmosphere of the Polish Middle Ages. Stanisław Wyspiański chose geraniums as the primary ornamental motif for the decorative scheme of the interior. The flowers were so popular in Kraków that they were nicknamed *krakowiaki*. The monumental asceticism of the 'Świetlica' is brought into relief by the choice of materials. Broad-hewn planks were used for the furniture, harmonising with the portières and pelmets made of thick grey woollen cloth. The austerity of the textiles was softened by the light colours of the wool used in the embroideries, departing significantly from the tonality of actual plants.

13.4 →

Curtains in the Zakopane Style, Zakopane, 1900, designed by Stanisław Witkiewicz, worked by Maria Witkiewiczowa

Woollen cloth, hand-embroidered in chain, stem and buttonhole stitch
480 × 114 cm
House Under the Firs Trust

The most familiar Zakopane motif was the embroidered *parzenica* adorning men's trousers. Its evolution indicates that it was not only artists who took inspiration from folk ornamentation, but also that Highlanders came under the influence of artists and attempted to respond to 'urban' expectations. In so far as it had appeared on men's trousers, during the second half of the 19th century the *parzenica* had a very simple form executed in black cord. In time this motif was filled out with polychrome embroidery and its shape became more complex. This process coincided with the arrival of Young Poland artists in Zakopane.

These curtains made by the Witkiewiczes are decorated with *parzenice*, rosettes and lilies. They harmonise perfectly with the Turkish carpets and cushions decorating the sitting room of the House Under the Firs.

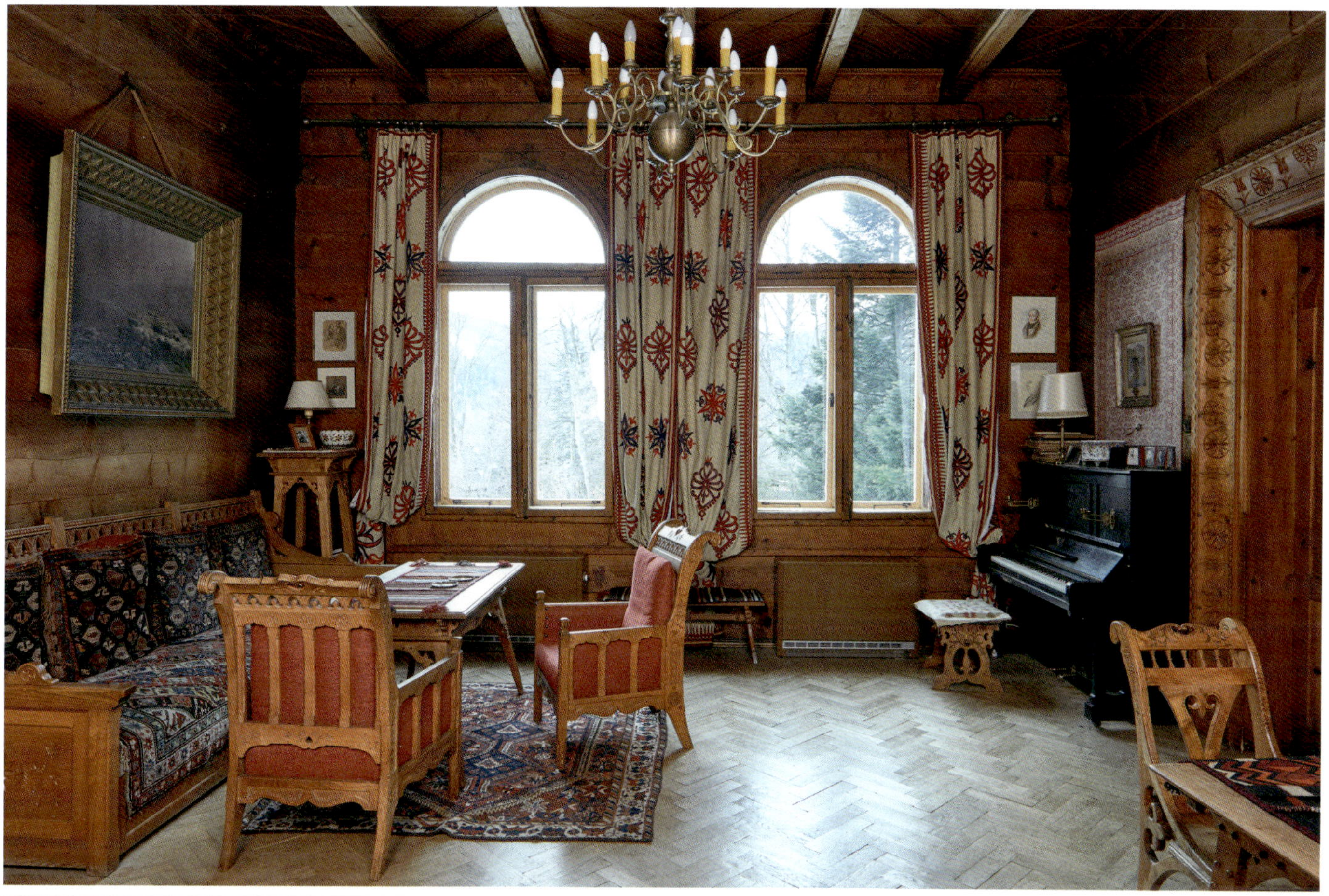

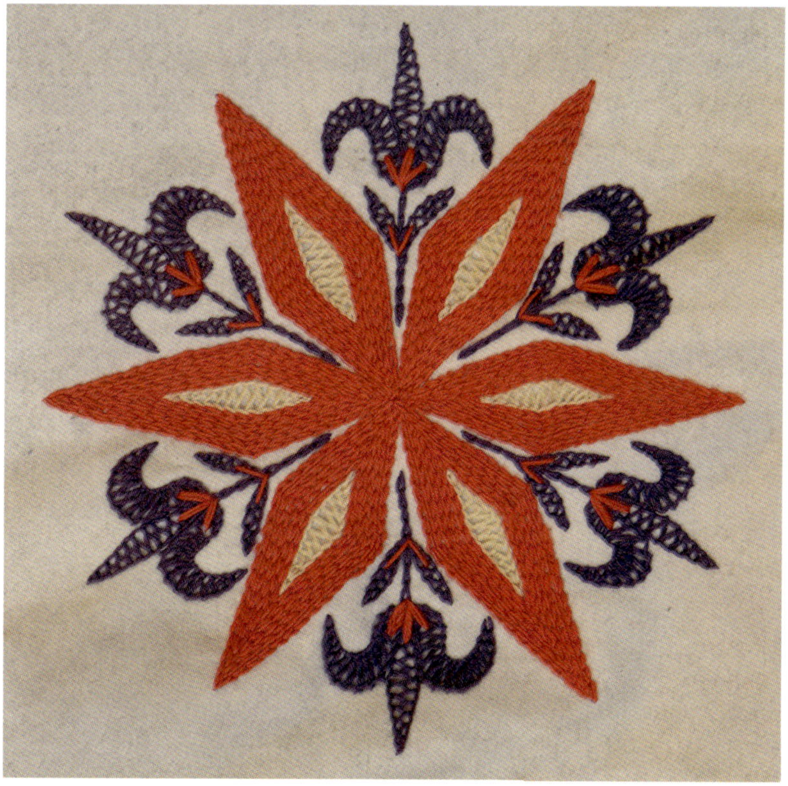

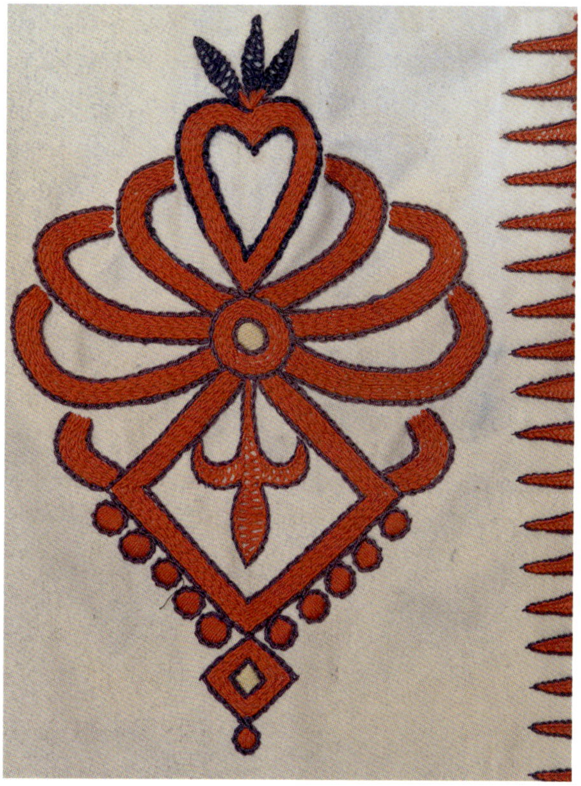

13.5 →

'Dandelion' embroidered blind, Kraków, after 1901, by Maria Giżbert-Studnicka; embroidered signature on the lower right: 'Giżbert'

Silk fabric, shaded embroidery with twist threads
250 × 121 cm
National Museum in Kraków, MNK XIX-10348 (transferred from the Department for the Protection of Monuments of the Administration of the City of Kraków, 1986)

Following her studies in Paris, Maria Giżbert-Studnicka (1868–1955) settled in Kraków and joined the Young Poland artistic circle. Sensitive to indigenous nature, she made beautiful representations of wild flowers. The composition adorning this embroidered blind, a clump of wilting dandelions, combines a luminosity characteristic of Impressionist painting with a decorative linearity. The artist has managed to achieve the effect of overlapping textures, greatly popular in the decorative arts, in the areas depicting seedheads. In Symbolist terms, the artist employs contrasts: the opportunistic vitality of wild flowers is juxtaposed with the sadness of dead, abandoned snail-shells.

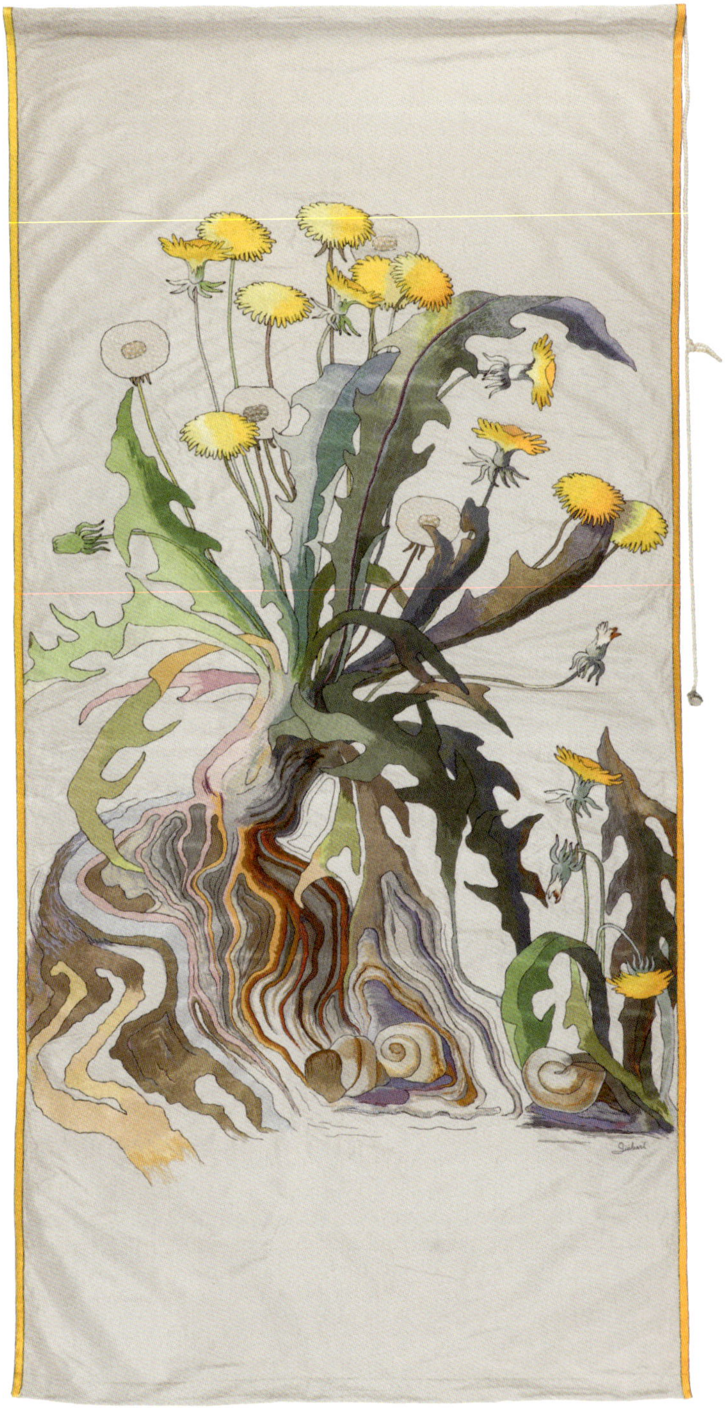

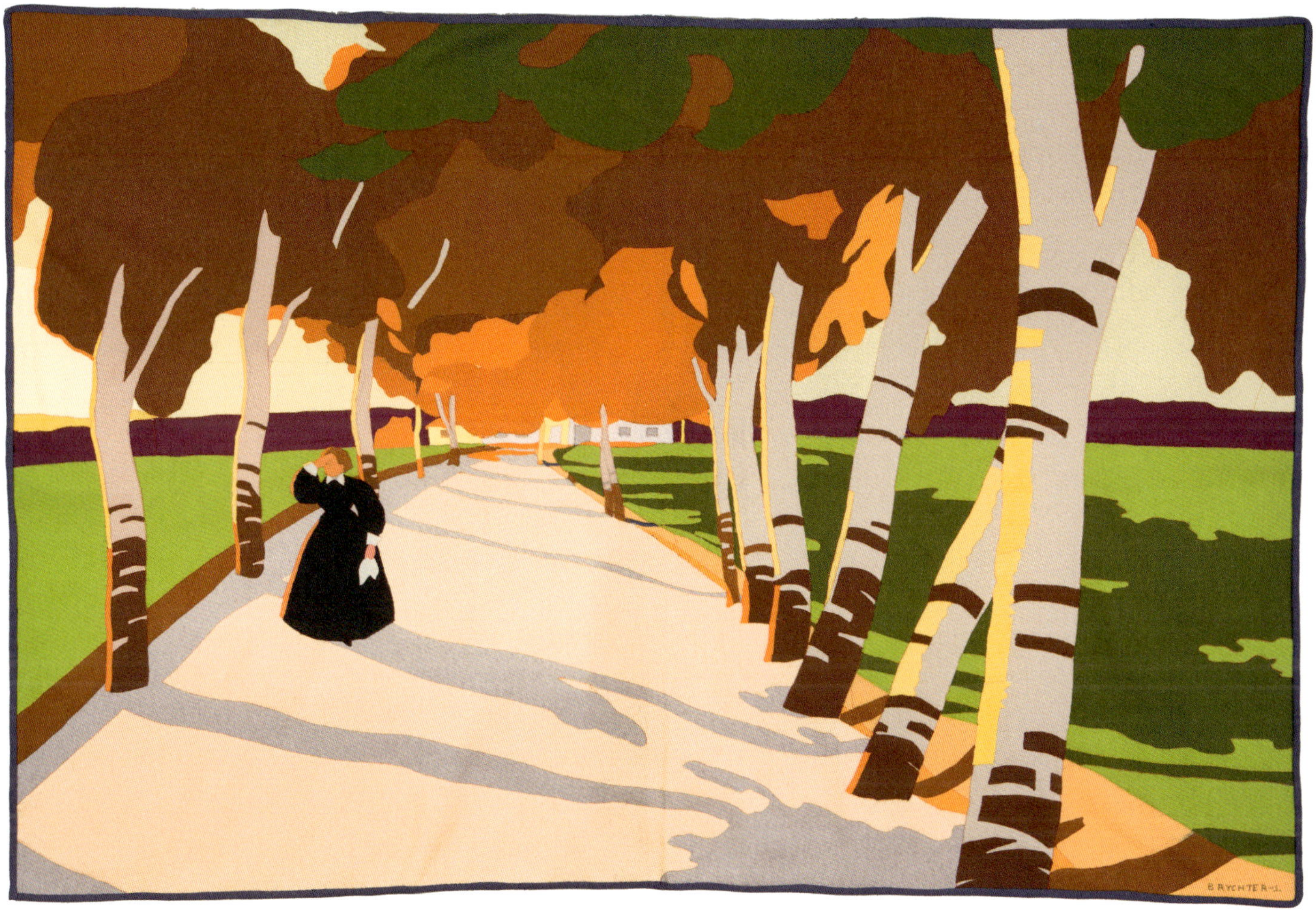

13.6 ↑

'Avenue of Birches' wall hanging, 1910, by Bronisława Rychter-Janowska; embroidered signature in lower right corner: 'B. Rychter-J'

Woollen cloth, pieced work and appliqué
97 × 145.5 cm
National Museum in Kraków, MNK XIX-6075
(from the Museum of Technology and Industry, 1952, purchased from the artist 1911)

Bronisława Rychter-Janowska is regarded above all as a eulogist of Polish manor houses. She is best known for her paintings, but she also experimented successfully with other techniques. 'Pictures painted with cloth' constitute the most original part of her oeuvre. The appliqué and pieced work techniques predetermine the minimalist character of the works made up of flat areas of colour. 'Avenue of Birches' maintains a strong tonal composition with a fiery orange tone as a central point. The artist has succeeded in conveying the atmosphere of a hot afternoon.

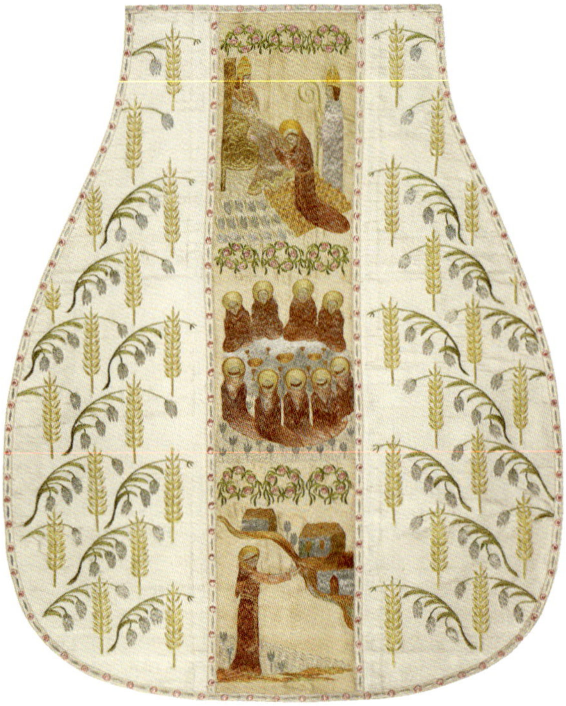

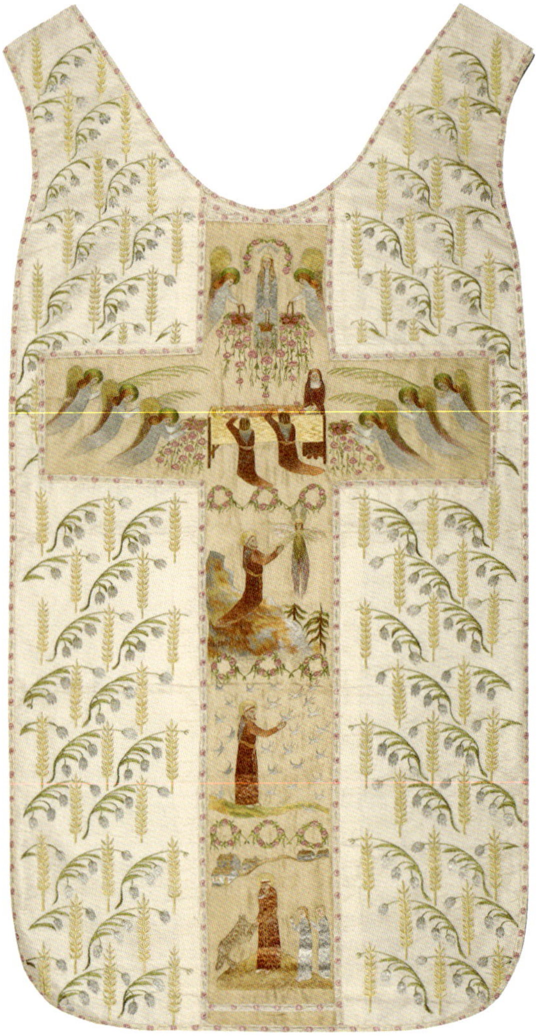

13.7 ↑

Embroidered chasuble, Lviv, 1911–12, by Maria Szymonowiczowa (née Młodzianowska)

Ribbed silk ground, silk hand-embroidery, worked in running, satin and stem stitch
Back 107 × 67.5 cm, front 78 × 62 cm
National Museum in Kraków, MNK XIX-10272/1-2 (from the Museum of Technology and Industry, 1952, presented by Stefan Stasiak)

This chasuble was never used in the liturgy. It was produced especially for the exhibition *Embroidery and its Applications* organised by the Musée Industriel in Paris in 1912. The back and front were exhibited separately and are not sewn together.

The lives of Saints Francis and Clare are a pretext for the depiction of the beauty of nature, greatly lauded by them. Sheaves of corn symbolically refer to the Eucharist, and sprigs of lily-of-the-valley express a fascination with the beauty of the humblest of flowers. The simplified form of the depictions corresponds to the austerity of the Franciscan saints' lives. The artist perfectly adapted the composition of the embroidery to the ideological content of the chasuble.

Maria Szymonowiczowa (*c.*1880–?) was the sister of Kazimierz Młodzianowski, an artist associated with the Polish Applied Arts Society, and the first director of the Kraków Workshops. She was undoubtedly very familiar with ideas regarding the decorative arts revival. Stefan Stasiak, Orientalist, Professor at the Jan Kazimierz University in Lviv, who presented the chasuble to the National Museum in Kraków, was for some years her life partner.

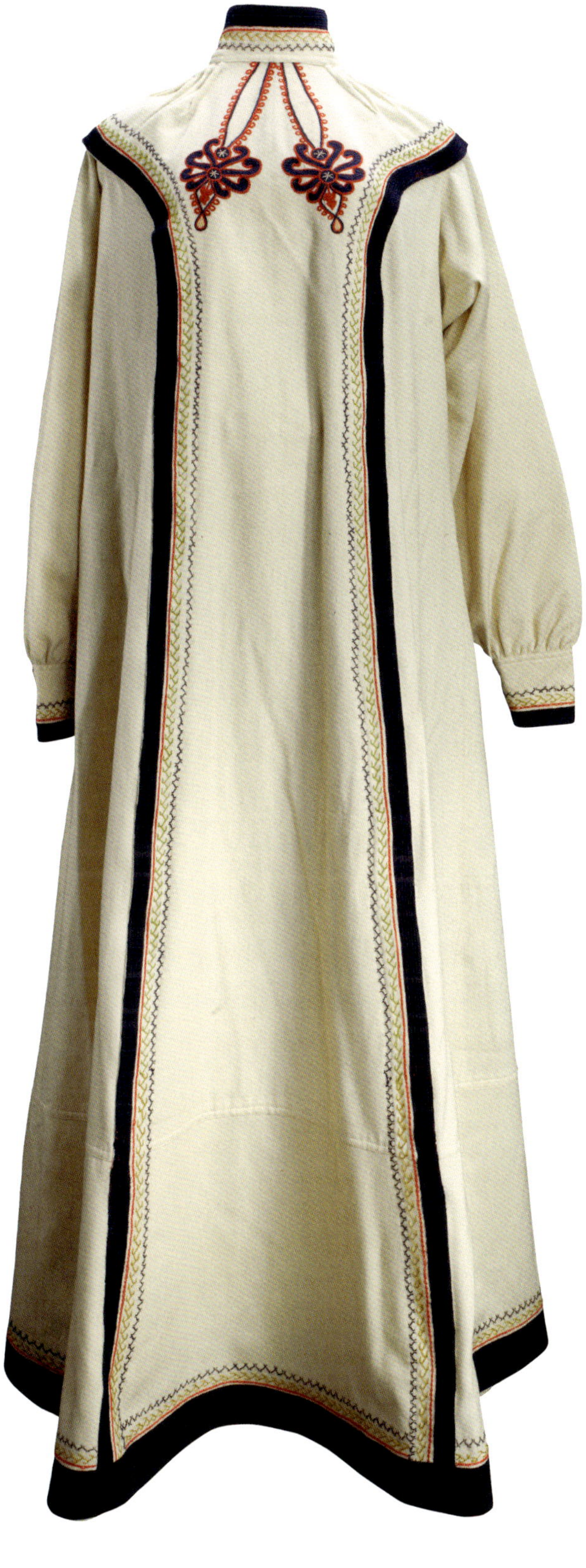

13.8 →

Dress in the Zakopane Style, Kraków, beginning of the 20th century, by Maria Łabęcka

Woollen cloth, machine and hand-sewn construction, decorated with hand-embroidered woollen yarn in chain, 'Zakopane', fern and back stitch with some appliqué
Length of front 157 cm, length of back 162 cm, perimeter at base 367 cm
National Museum in Kraków, MNK XIX-4606 (purchased from Henryk Jasieński, 1964)

According to family tradition, this dress was made by Maria Łabęcka (1869–1933), sister-in-law of Feliks 'Manggha' Jasieński, the leading collector and patron of Young Poland artists. It was made in a milieu in which the ideas of the Zakopane Style and the question of the national character of attire were ardently discussed. The colouring of the dress and the style of ornamentation are an example of the application of the Zakopane Style to women's fashion. Many of the embroidered motifs seem directly transferred from traditional Highlander trousers. The embroidery techniques used have been chosen with exceptional care – all the stitches are characteristic of the Podhale region. This is a typical 'reformed' dress: ungathered at the waist, flowing down in loose folds, worn without a corset. Such dresses were generally worn at home. In one's own domestic setting, among friends, one could appear in avant-garde 'Zakopane' dress without encountering criticism from less progressive acquaintances.

13.9 →

Woman's shoe in the Zakopane Style, Zakopane, 1904, by Antoni Wojciechowski

Leather with contrasting suède and varnished areas, hand-sewn with appliqué decoration
Height to shoe top 14–18 cm, length of sole 27 cm
National Museum in Kraków, MNK XIX-3483 (from the Museum of Technology and Industry, 1952, donated by Antoni Wojciechowski, 1904)

Antoni Wojciechowski, a Zakopane shoemaker based at 71 Ulica Krupówki, succeeded in making women's shoes to a fashionable design in the Zakopane Style. The uppers are decorated with appliquéd ornaments following a soft, undulating line, modelled on folk ornamentation of the Podhale region. Wojciechowski saw lilies, six-petal rosettes and *parzenice* daily in his immediate surroundings – on furniture, utensils and dress.

The craftsman offered two shoes to the Museum of Technology and Industry, one black-and-white, the other gold-and-black, together with the information that they had won a gold medal at an exhibition in Paris in 1904. The exhibition was probably the first Paris Fair. He made only one shoe from each pair, and must have been particularly proud of them, since he donated them almost immediately after his return from Paris.

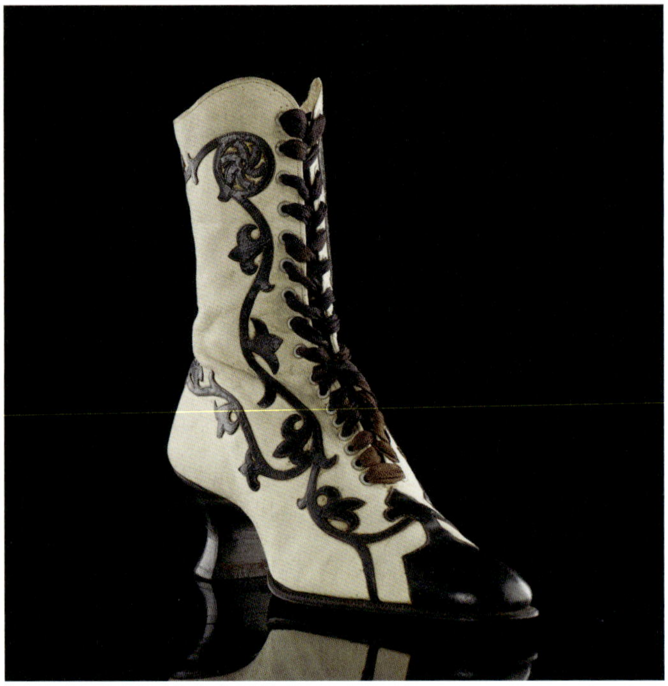

13.10 ↱

(LEFT) 'At home' dress of brown woollen cloth, designed by Feliks Jasieński, drawn by Henryk Uziembło, reproduced in Feliks Jasieński's article 'O sukni polskiej', *Ilustracja polska*, vol.2, no.7 (1902), p.146

(RIGHT) Collar in the Zakopane Style, c.1900, made at the School of Lacemaking, Zakopane

Linen, bobbin lace
Width 12.5 cm, perimeter at neck 50 cm
National Museum in Kraków, MNK XIX-3123
(Feliks Jasieński bequest, 1929)

Established in 1883 at the initiative of the great actress Helena Modrzejewska, the School of Lacemaking in Zakopane aimed to provide local girls with the opportunity to learn a craft and thus gain a livelihood. Its artistic aim was also very important – the Zakopane Highlanders had previously not made lace, so local motifs drawn from embroideries, wooden carvings and metalwork had to be adapted to the requirements of a new technique. One of the most recognisable motifs of Zakopane bobbin lace became the edelweiss flower.

'Edelweiss collars' are recorded in the School's chronicle in 1895. Feliks 'Manggha' Jasieński, the first owner of the collar shown here, valued the significance of Zakopane lace. A lace collar designed by Stanisław Witkiewicz was to serve as an accessory for one of Jasieński's designs for a 'Polish dress' dating from 1902, also shown here.

13.11 ↳

Handbag, 1900, made at the State School of Embroidery, Maków Podhalański

Linen cloth, hand-embroidered in silk and crewel wools in satin, fern and knotted stitches with a raffia handle and woollen pom-poms
33 × 26.2 cm
National Museum in Kraków, MNK XIX-5984 (from the Museum of Technology and Industry, 1952, presented by the Municipal Industrial Museum in Lviv)

The State School of Embroidery was founded in 1896. Its artistic director was Leona Bierkowska, a painter fascinated with folklore, who designed dresses in Polish style. Monochrome embroideries (i.e. whitework) adorning peasant shirts were most characteristic of the Maków Podhalański district, but the school chiefly taught polychrome embroidery. Its products very quickly gained renown both in Poland and abroad. Sleeveless jackets from Maków were very popular in Vienna, and women's blouses adorned with coloured embroidery, made from homespun linen, an ideal summer material, were especially popular in Sweden, Britain and America, as the Polish press emphasised. The Maków School was particularly keen to ensure that the embroidered motifs derived from the vernacular traditions of the Podhale people. This handbag was shown in the Galician pavilion at the Exposition Universelle in Paris in 1900.

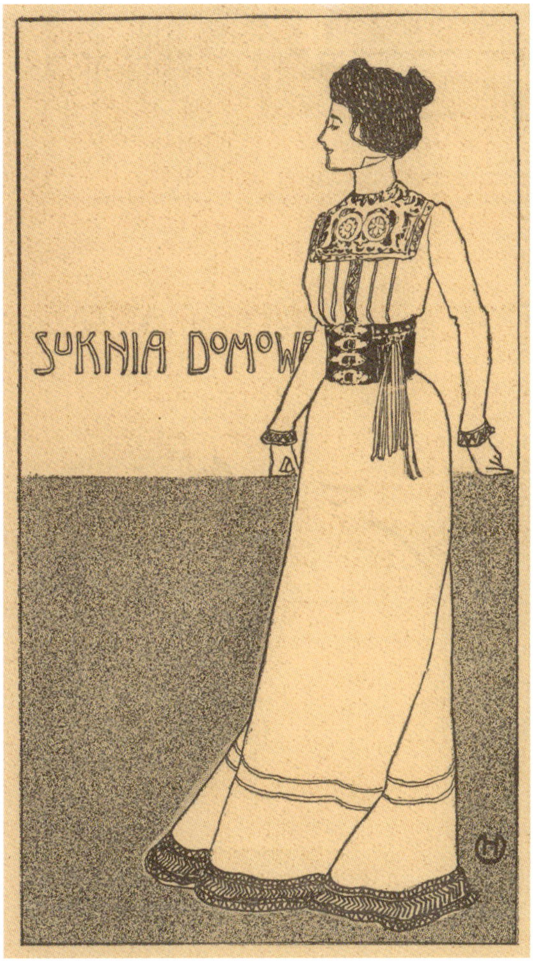
SUKNIA DOMOW

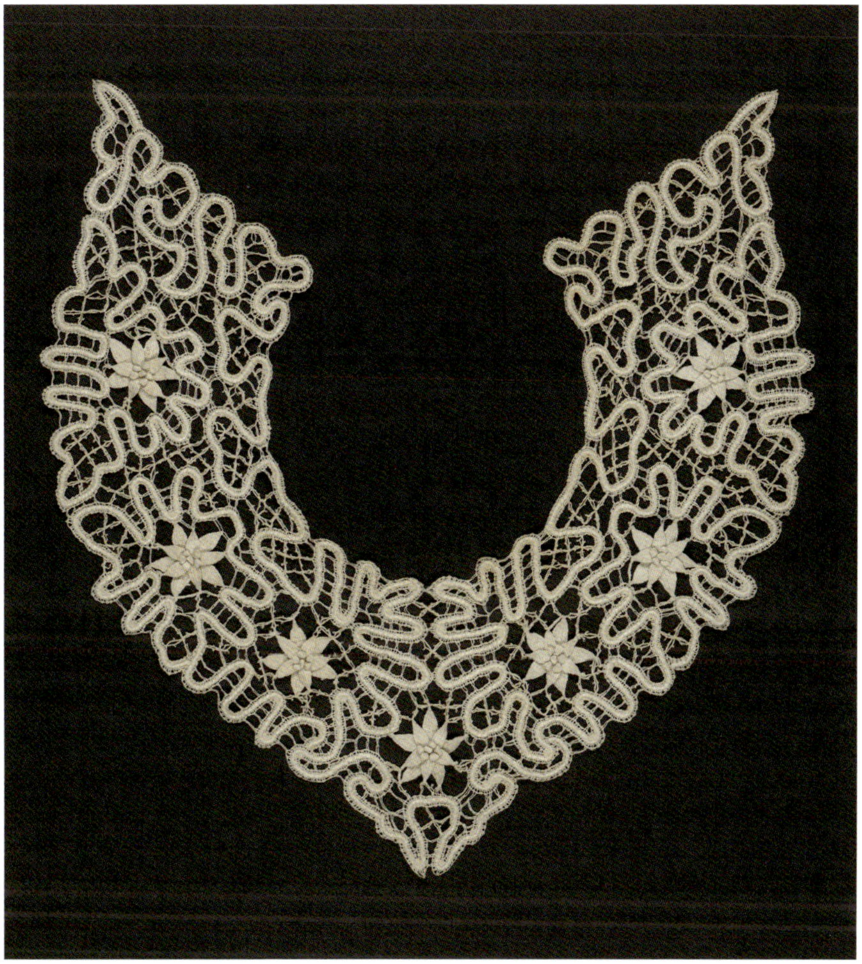

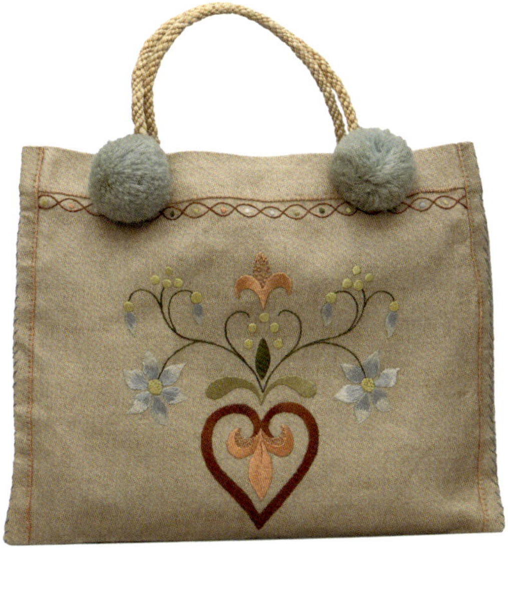

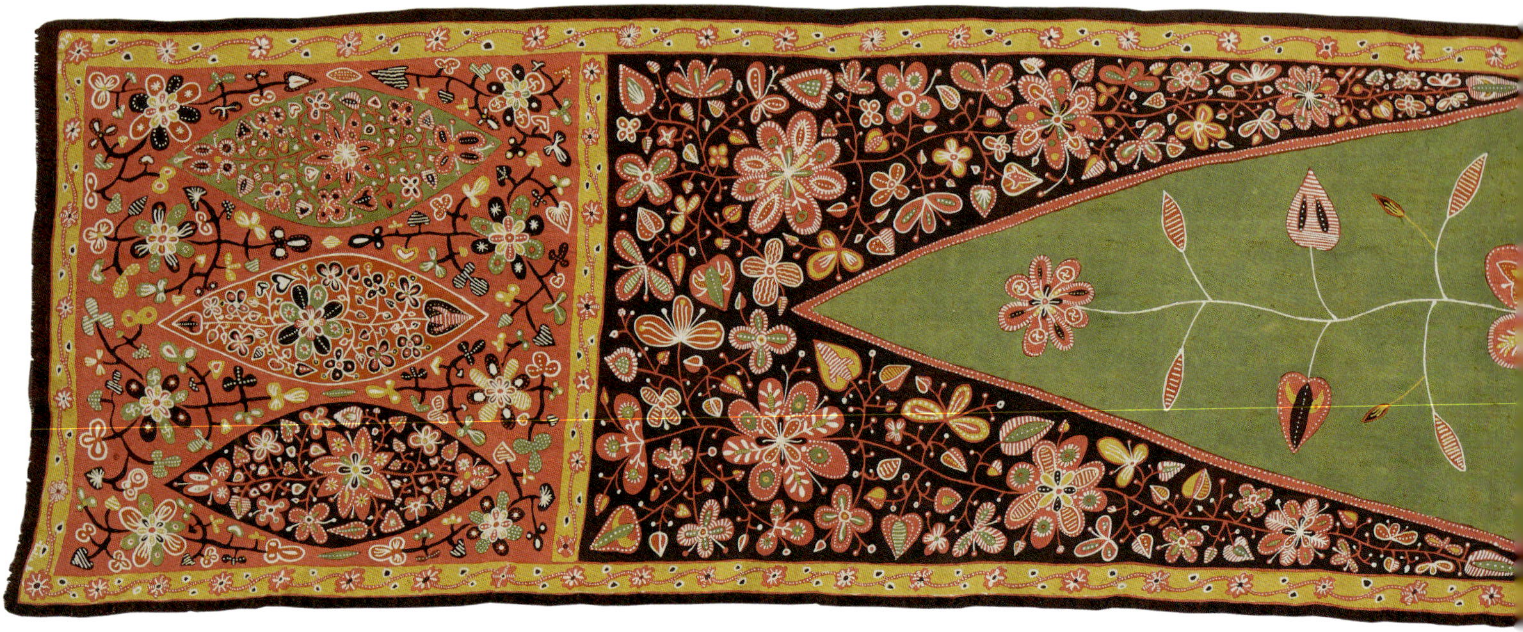

13.12 ↑

Batik shawl, 1921, by Zofia Kogut, Kraków Workshops; signature in batik in one corner 'Zofia K', in another the inscription 'KW 672'

Silk fabric of plain weave decorated with multicoloured wax batik
47.5 × 248 cm
National Museum in Kraków, MNK XIX-3255 (Feliks Jasieński bequest, 1929)

Antoni Buszek can be credited with introducing the batik technique to Polish lands under the partitions. In 1913 Buszek opened a batik workshop within the Kraków Workshops, chiefly employing young women from villages near Kraków (see Chapter 9). One of the first was Maria Kogut, who also brought along her two younger sisters, Józefa and Zofia. In their work the girls would embody their teacher's conviction that the ability to decorate was innate in everyone. This shawl by Zofia Kogut indicates the extent to which her work was, however, exposed to and informed by external influences. The overall composition of the scarf evokes *kontusz* sashes, an element of the Polish nobleman's costume. Individual motifs can nevertheless be traced back to local folk art, while the principle of their arrangement in a masterly network filling the entire surface of the textile recalls the aesthetic of Javanese batiks in the Museum of Technology and Industry's collection at this time.

13.13 →

Batik coasters, 1920s, made by the Kraków Workshops

Silk fabric of plain weave, multicoloured wax batik, hem-stitch edging
13 × 13 cm
National Museum in Kraków, MNK XIX-11816/1-12
(donated by Anna Pawłowska, 2013)

The batik workshop of Antoni Buszek led to the popularisation of the technique of batik in Kraków. Ladies from the Kraków intelligentsia also wanted to learn its secrets. One of them was the writer Magdalena Samozwaniec, younger sister of the poet Maria Pawlikowska-Jasnorzewska (see Chapter 10). After completing a course in 'painting in wax on silk', she set up her own workshop. Wall hangings, scarves and napkins produced by her apparently enjoyed great success. She coined the description 'batik in Javanese-Kraków style'.

This set of coasters belonged to Janina Pawłowska (1894–1988), from the Bardel family of Kraków intelligentsia. Janina pursued handicrafts all her life – she sewed and embroidered, even hand-wove kilims herself. The technique of batik also undoubtedly attracted her attention. She purchased these coasters probably because she was fascinated by their simplicity and the inventiveness of their designer; 12 different varieties of floral motifs appear.

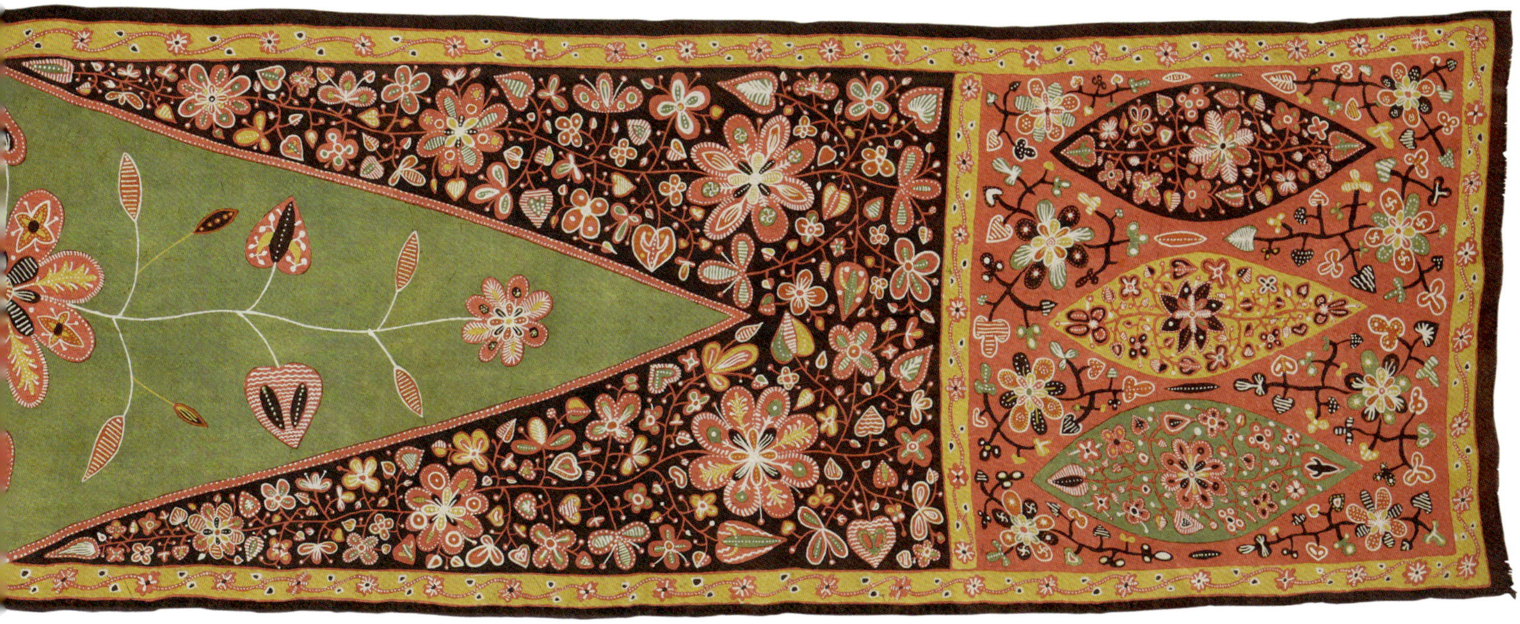

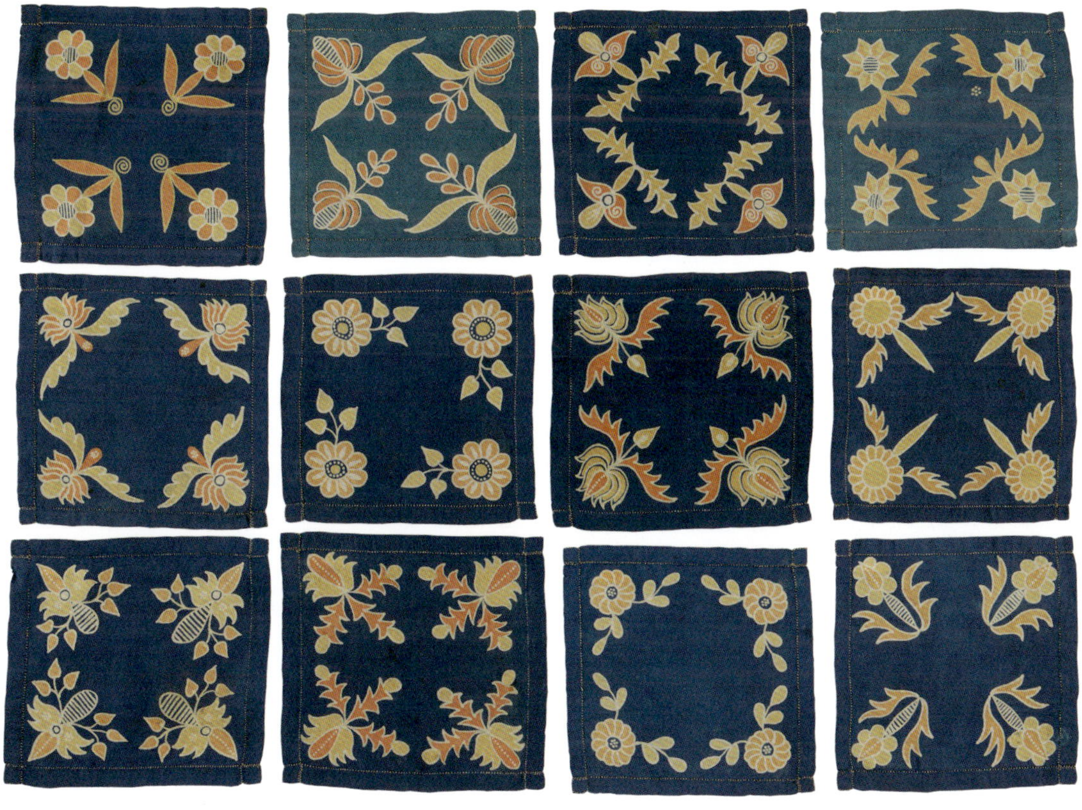

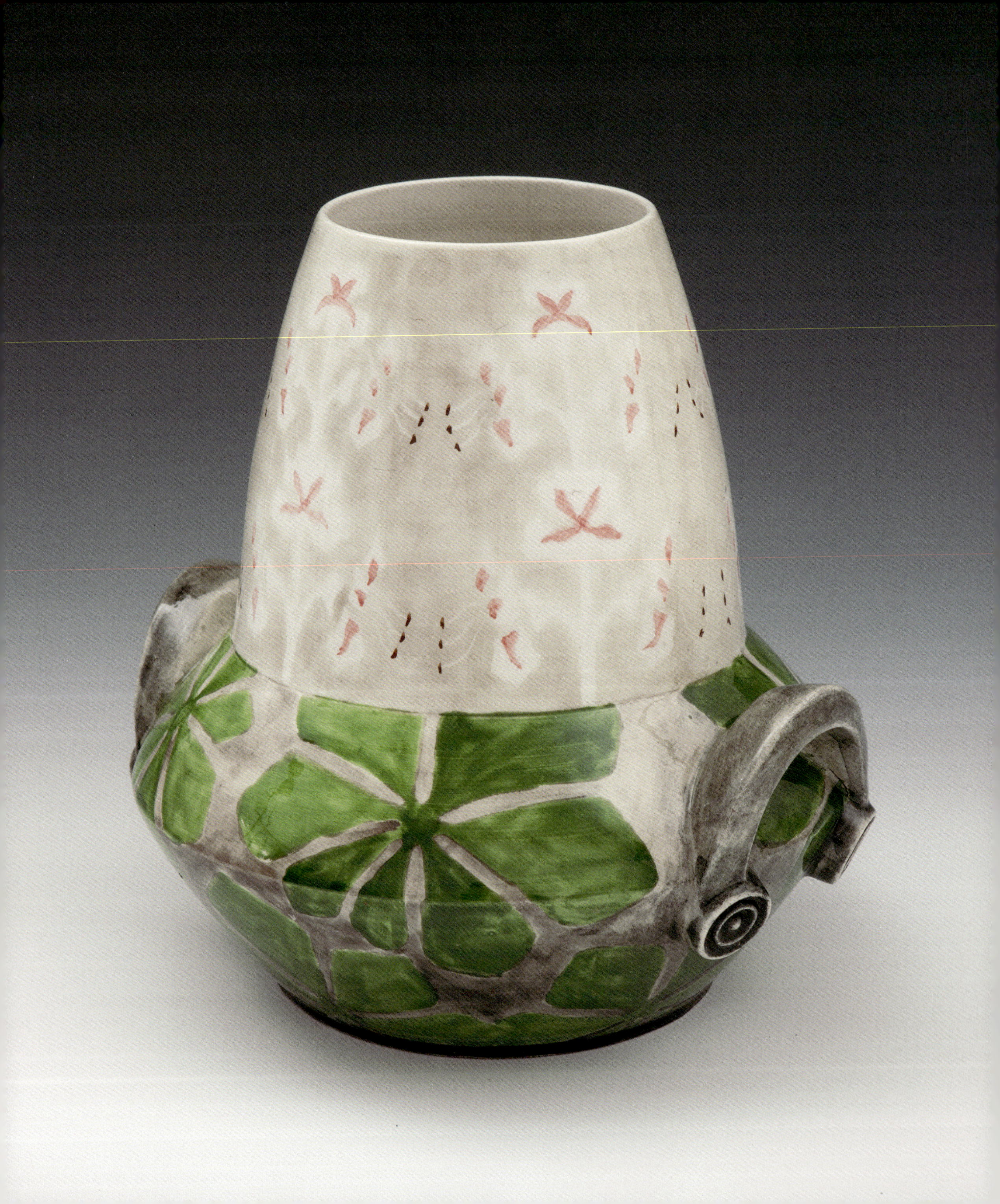

14

Ceramics

Bożena Kostuch

For Polish ceramicists the era of Young Poland was one of searching and of experimentation. A surfeit of historical styles, as well as awareness of the poor quality of industrial production and its negligible aesthetic value, resulted in a search for inspiration from a range of sources. Thus ceramics reflected Art Nouveau, an interest in the art of the Far East, elements of Symbolism and Naturalism deriving from trends in sculpture, and a reaching down into the nation's roots, in the form of both folk art and archaeological ceramics.

Folk art, with its decorativeness, modesty, utilitarian aspect, and the honesty of its execution, became an inexhaustible source of inspiration. It was folk art, in fact, that was to be the basis for the quest to create a national style embracing all aspects of life, and pottery was one of the fields that was to supplement it with object types not used by the peasantry (fig.14.1).[1] Theoreticians and artists also perceived a need to eliminate the division between fine art and applied art, and to restore crafts to their rightful status. These tendencies coincided with ideas expressed by the British creators of the Arts and Crafts Movement, for whom a reliance upon the past and on local traditions had a fundamental significance, as did an emphasis on the role of craftsmanship and the ethos of handiwork, the importance of materials, techniques and construction, and the resulting methods of creation. Changes also took place in the selection of subjects for ceramic works and in their decoration in the context of the Young Poland movement – these were drawn from folk tales, instead of history and mythology, and folk types and scenes observed in everyday life took the place of allegories. Wild flowers were preferred to cultivated roses, and alongside chestnut leaves there appeared sprigs of raspberry or fern leaves, while pseudo-stylised ornamentation was superseded by motifs drawn from folk paper cuttings.

In Polish lands, divided between three partitioning powers, individual regions developed according to differing legal and economic systems. This influenced the development of local ceramic manufacturing as well as artistic and technical education. In the Prussian partition-zone before 1919, there were only German ceramics factories; those wanting to work in ceramics in the Austrian partition-zone had to take into account the remarkably developed Czech industry; on the other hand, in the Russian zone several factories producing faience were active, as well as a porcelain factory in Ćmielów, whose roots went back to the years around 1800. But, for obvious

14.0 (p.186)
Jan Szczepkowski
Vase with Chestnut Flowers and Leaves motif, 1905
Made by J. Niedźwiecki i Ska in Kraków
Faience with underglaze painting
24 cm
National Museum in Kraków, MNK-IV-C-1342
(from the Museum of Technology and Industry,
donated by Adam Kirchmayer, 1919)

reasons, it could not be the ceramics industry itself, geared as it was to the market, that would initiate the revival of ceramics, even though attempts were made at improving the quality of production, and new decorations and 'national' forms were timidly introduced. Neither could craft and technical schools be a source of renewal, since they concentrated on practical and economic aims, and their influence was slight.[2] The School (later Academy) of Fine Arts in Kraków was only concerned with the fine arts; the applied arts and artistic crafts were firmly excluded. And yet the new tendencies which appeared in Polish ceramics in the years around 1900 can in fact be traced back to a considerable extent to the milieu of the Kraków Academy. Their chief advocate was Konstanty Laszczka (1865–1956), a sculptor educated in Paris, who in 1899 had been summoned to Kraków, and as a pedagogue reformed the teaching of sculpture. He repudiated the division between fine and applied arts, and saw beauty in a 'delicate artistic decoration' as much as in a 'majestic statue' or a 'figurative painting'.[3] For Laszczka all sculptural materials had equal worth, and 'the vitality [of his] talent' expressed itself in his desire to 'master the mysteries of technique, by using ever-new materials: bronze, terracotta, maiolica, plaster'.[4] He inculcated such an approach in his students, and several of them became interested in ceramics.

Laszczka, who came from a lowly rural family, saw the enormous potential of folk culture and willingly drew upon it. He made numerous images of peasants from the Kraków region (fig.14.2). Some of his works were reproduced in faience at the J. Niedźwiecki i Ska factory in the Dębniki district of Kraków, where the artist fired his ceramics.[5] One of his pupils, Jan Szczepkowski, was the artistic director of this factory during the period 1902–7. It was celebrated for the high quality of its products – delicate artistic faience with original painted

14.1 →

Service in the Zakopane Style, designed by Stanisław Witkiewicz, 1898, executed by the Manufacture Nationale de Sèvres in France, 1900–1901

Relief-decorated porcelain, gilded
Coffee pot: height 21 cm; milk jug: height 12 cm; larger cup: height 8 cm, diameter 10 cm; saucer: diameter 15.3 cm; smaller cup: height 6.8 cm, diameter 13.2 cm; coffee cup: height 7.2 cm, diameter 5.1 cm; saucer: diameter 9.4 cm.
National Museum in Kraków, MNK-IV-C-3618/1-8 (donated by Stanisław Witkiewicz, 1902)

Stanisław Witkiewicz was inspired by the forms of utensils and decorative motifs encountered in the Podhale region. The intention was for city-dwellers to make use of these products, so among them there were also types of objects never used by the Highlanders themselves, such as porcelain services for coffee and tea. Manufactured in France, the set described as 'in the Polish style', was exhibited in 1901 at a Parisian ceramics store, and in consequence peasant vessels 'received their official baptism as "works of art" in the form of services of Sèvres porcelain'.[9] Only two services were made – for Witkiewicz, and for Dr Karol Benni, the intermediary in his contacts with Sèvres. A few cups remained in Sèvres.

decoration frequently of a domestic character, or else with folk inspirations (fig.14.3). Products also included items aimed at unrefined customers. These were both 'objects for ordinary use' and 'purely artistic objects'. In an interview given to the Kraków newspaper *Czas*, Szczepkowski recalled medallions depicting Polish monarchs and heroes, as well as devotional figures, such as *Christ Falling Beneath the Cross*. The factory relied on 'a market for such figures among the masses, in Kalwaria'. It was hoped that they would replace 'cheap German and Tyrolean' products, which dominated devotional items at this time.[6] A desire to replace foreign manufactures, as well as a sense of responsibility to the less privileged sectors of society, were significant elements in Szczepkowski's earlier creative work.

Wacław Bębnowski (1865–1945) and Stanisław Jagmin (1879–1961) also emerged from the Kraków School of Fine Arts (later Academy). Works by Bębnowski belong to the aesthetic of Art Nouveau, but the artist took interest in pottery found during archaeological excavations, and introduced pre-Slavic forms into his works. Inspiration of the same kind also appeared in the work of Jagmin, who at the start of his ceramic career made 'smoked' vessels, thus imitating folk ceramics,

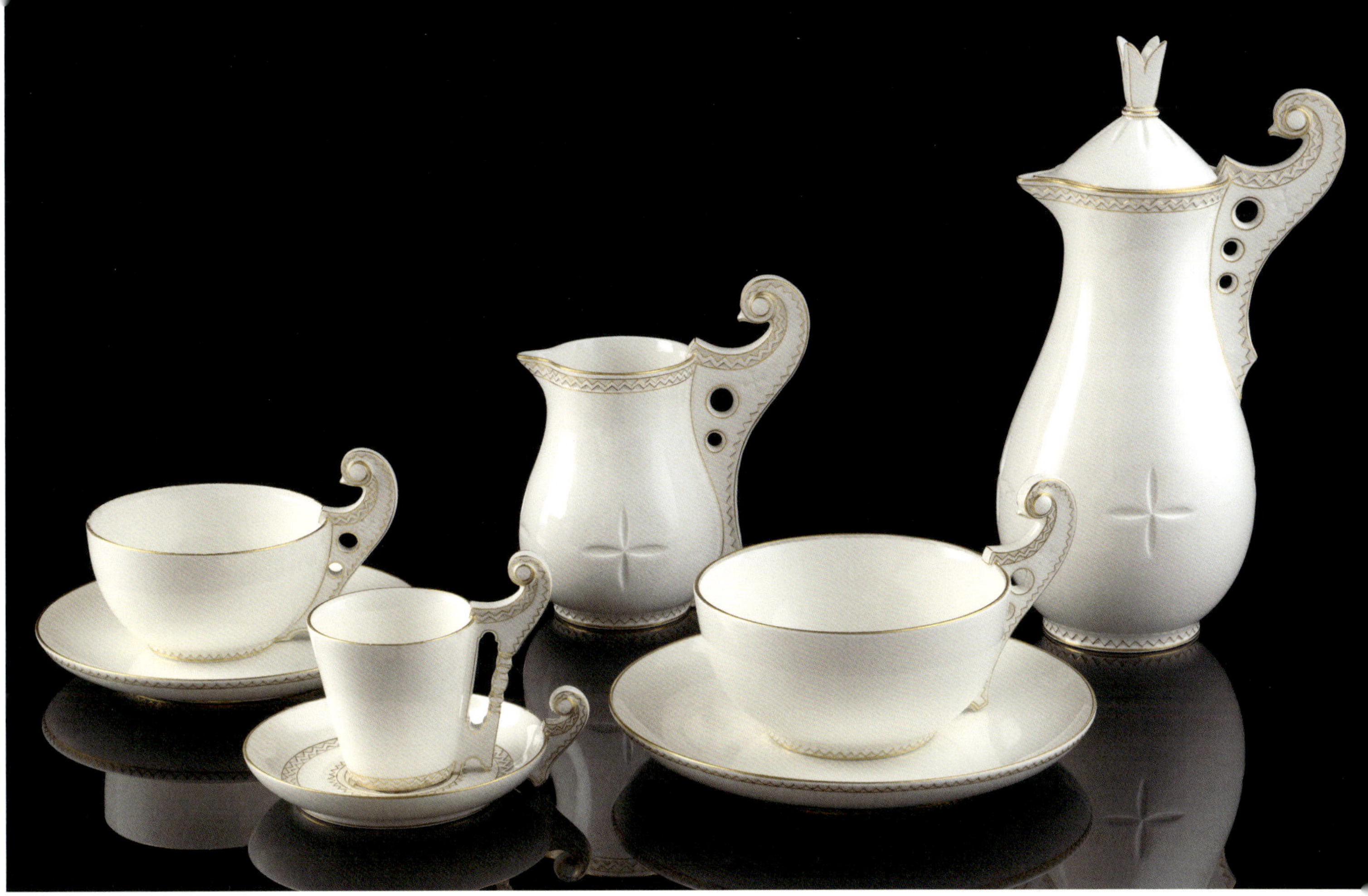

so-called *siwaki*.[7] Jagmin is, however, acknowledged universally as the first 'modern' Polish artist-potter. Under the influence of French ceramicists he concentrated on the glazes with which he covered simple vessels, effectively introducing abstract forms of expression into ceramics (fig.14.4). He was also a pioneer of the application of artistic ceramics to architecture. Jagmin was the first artist to exhibit his ceramics at 'the shrine of fine art', the Society for the Encouragement of the Fine Arts in Warsaw (1906),[8] thereby equating 'pots' with paintings and sculptures.

Two women potters working in Kraków also deserve to be mentioned. Maria Ludwika Męcina-Krzesz (1863–1949) had a studio in the Dębniki district, so may have collaborated with the Niedźwiecki factory, located nearby. Zofia Szydłowska (1887–1944), in turn, worked in very difficult circumstances, in an ordinary apartment, yet despite this her works were rated highly and in popular demand (fig.14.5). After Poland regained its independence, neither artist returned to making ceramics, but both had prepared the way for other women potters.

The Niedźwiecki factory, in which artistic faience was produced, manufactured tiled stoves, which were of great importance in the Polish climate. Numerous firms and workshops were engaged in the production of tiles. These generally had historicising decoration in dark colours, although at the beginning of the 20th century new designs were introduced – tiles adorned with flowing plant ornamentation and lighter tonality. Few Polish stoves have survived *in situ*, however, and collectors generally own only individual tiles (fig.14.7).

These individual creative artists, together with the Niedźwiecki factory, mark the beginnings of modern Polish ceramics, although new approaches and new subjects also gradually spread to industry, as can be seen in examples from the work of both the porcelain factory in Ćmielów (fig.14.8) and the manufactory producing delicate decorative faience in Pacyków (fig.14.9). The transformations initiated during the era of Young Poland brought remarkable results during the interwar period.

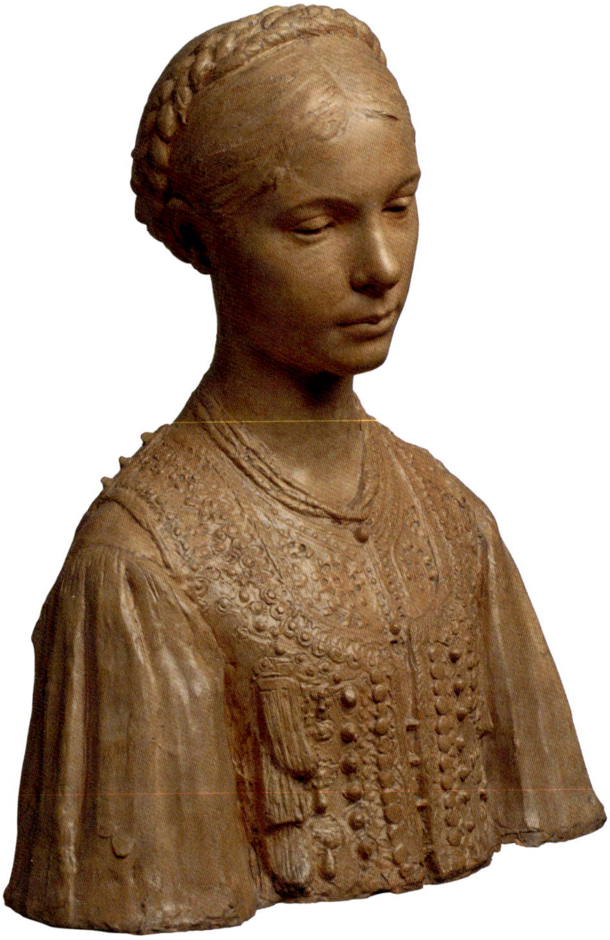

14.2 ↑

Konstanty Laszczka, *Portrait of a Peasant Girl in a Kraków Costume*, 1905

Terracotta
Height 50 cm
National Museum in Kraków, MNK-II-rz-718
(donated by Feliks Jasieński, 1920)

The outstanding sculptor and ceramicist Konstanty Laszczka was one of the makers fascinated with the peasantry. His diverse output included heads and half-length figures of elderly women, overworked men, and young girls lost in thought, their necks encircled with ropes of beads, dressed in decorative Kraków bodices. This terracotta bust is representative of the artist's early works in terms of both subject and material. At the beginning of the 20th century Laszczka collaborated with the J. Niedźwiecki i Ska factory in Kraków, producing his own works in faience – vases with sculptural elements, medallions for architectural settings, and figures.

14.3 →

Vase with a raspberry motif, bowl with branches of acacia, plate with lily-of-the-valley sprigs, c.1905, designed by Jan Szczepkowski, executed by the J. Niedźwiecki i Ska factory in Dębniki, Kraków, decorated by Stefan Witold Matejko

Faience with underglaze painting
Vase: height 40 cm; bowl: height 8.5 cm, diameter 21.5 cm;
plate: diameter 25.5 cm
National Museum in Kraków, MNK-IV-C-1355, IV-C-1352, IV-C-1348
(from the Museum of Technology and Industry, donated by Adam Kirchmayer, 1919)

The biggest vase was designed by Jan Szczepkowski, Artistic Director of the J. Niedźwiecki i Ska factory, who gave his ceramics slightly geometrical forms. He also designed two services for coffee and tea inspired by folk productions, simplified undecorated figures representing a nightwatchman and a dancing Kraków couple, and various decorative vessels. The decoration of the objects presented here was by Stefan Witold Matejko (1871–1933), an artist and a master-craftsman in mosaic, stained glass and mural painting, and they were aimed at higher social groups.

14.4 →

Vases, 1905–19, by Stanisław Jagmin

Clay, poured glazes
Heights 18.5 cm, 11.5 cm, 16 cm, 3 cm, 8.4 cm
National Museum in Kraków, MNK-IV-C-5438, IV-C-5419, IV-C-5439, IV-C-5442, IV-C-5430 (donated by Feliks Jasieński, 1920, and Stanisław Ursyn-Rusiecki, 1937)

Stanisław Jagmin was the first artist to make ceramic sculptures and bibelots on a large scale, and also the first to experiment with ceramic glazes. Following his return from Paris in 1905, he began making ceramics without any traditional painted decoration. Their beauty depended on the glaze, its colour and texture, and the moment when it cooled on the surface of the vessel. In 1906 he presented his works at the Society for the Encouragement of the Fine Arts in Warsaw, which was a turning point in awarding artistic status to ceramics in the partitioned lands of Poland.

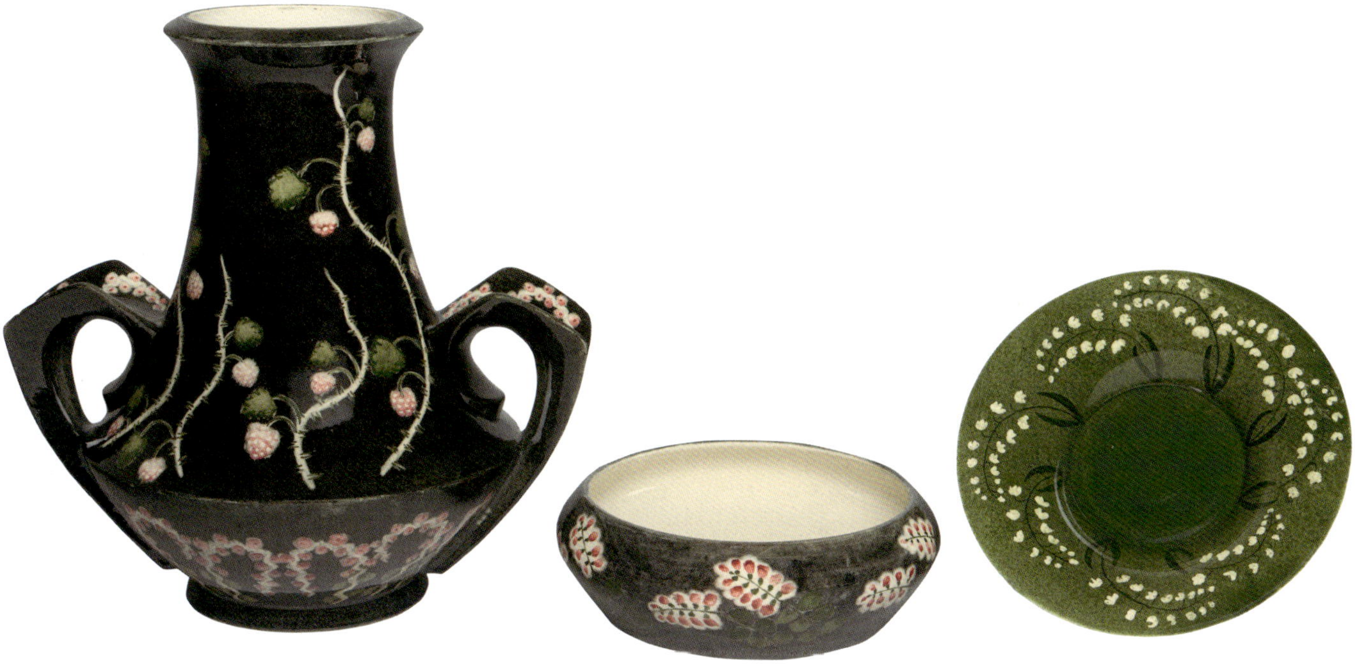

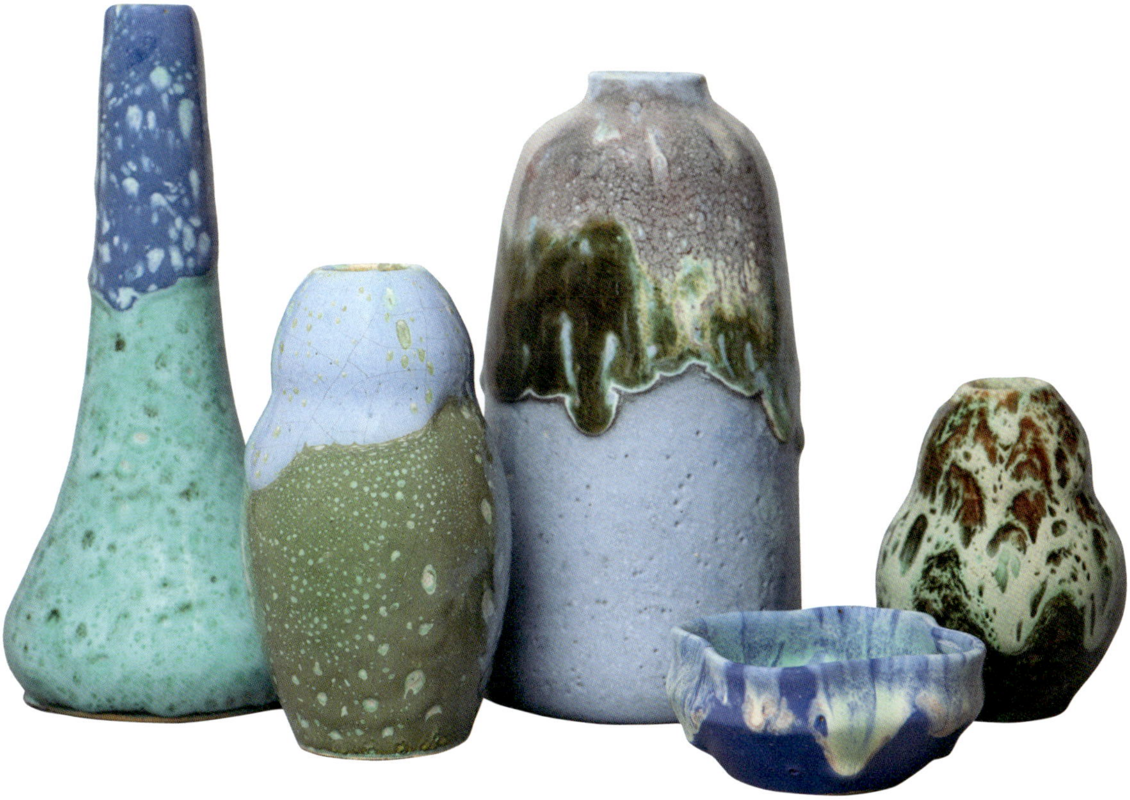

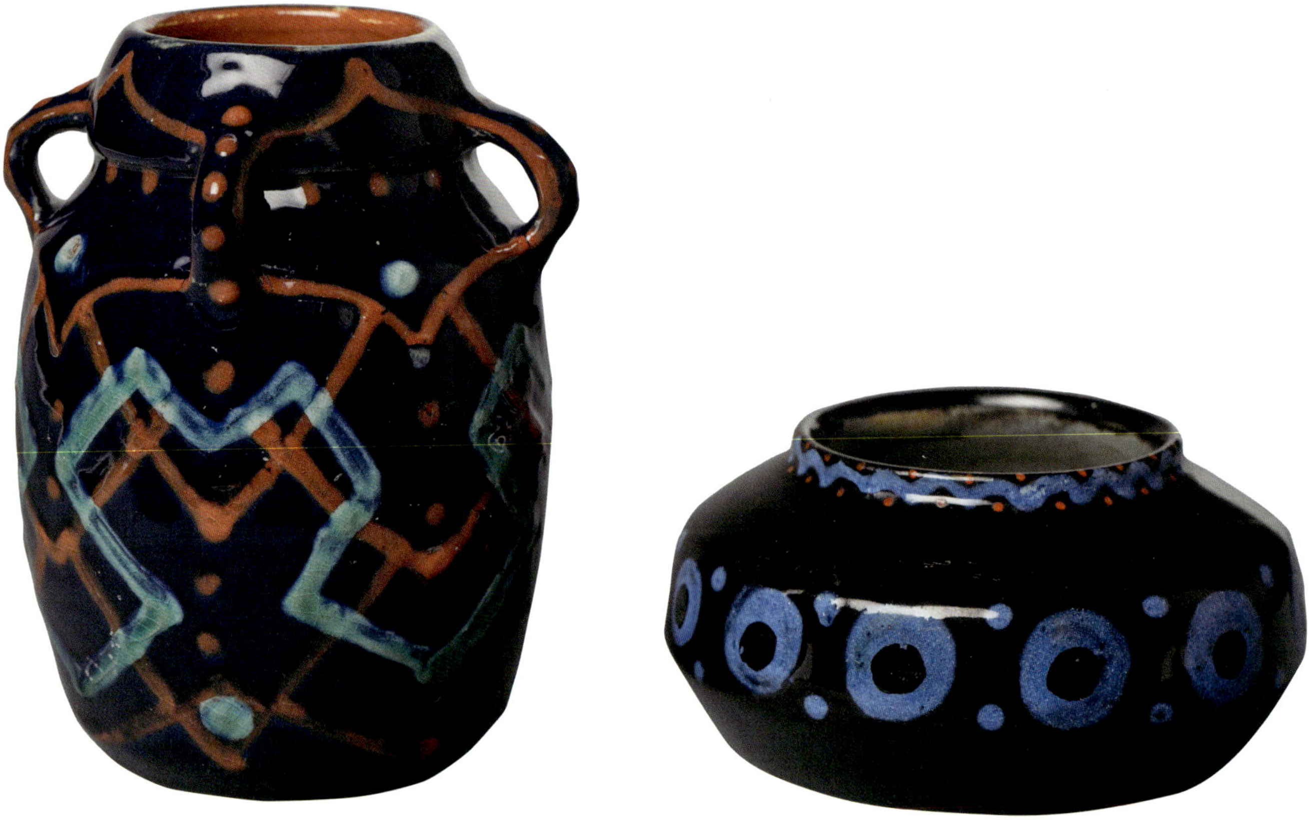

14.5 ↑

Vases, c.1910, by Zofia Szydłowska

Painted clay, glazed
Heights 13.5 cm, 6.1 cm
National Museum in Kraków, MNK-IV-C-5365, IV-C-5366 (donated by Feliks Jasieński, 1920)

At the beginning of the 20th century, women were generally only involved in painting designs on finished pieces of ceramics. Educated in Munich, Zofia Szydłowska, who made modestly decorated vessels, some of which drew on pre-Slavonic pottery urns, was one of only two women who in 1913 joined the Kraków Workshops. Szydłowska's work was praised by the press, and described as 'maiolica changing colour with the hues of the rainbow'.[10] Little of her work has survived.

14.6 →

Stove for the House Under the Firs, designed by Stanisław Witkiewicz, 1898, executed by the factory of Jan Lewiński in Lviv, 1900–1901

Clay decorated artistically, painted, glazed, sculpted
Height *c.*400 cm
House Under the Firs Trust

Designed by Stanisław Witkiewicz for the Pawlikowski family, the House Under the Firs in Zakopane is the quintessential example of the Zakopane Style in terms of both architecture and interior decoration (see Chapter 6). The design for the sitting-room stove dates from 1898. It was executed at Jan Lewiński's manufactory in Lviv,[11] and put in place in 1901, but failed to conform to its owners' taste.[12] Cream-coloured tiles are adorned with typical Zakopane ornaments, although the chief decorative element is a large figure of a bear holding the clock face, and it is this that occasioned the most controversy. Today, however, the stove is regarded as an interesting example of tiling from the turn of the century.

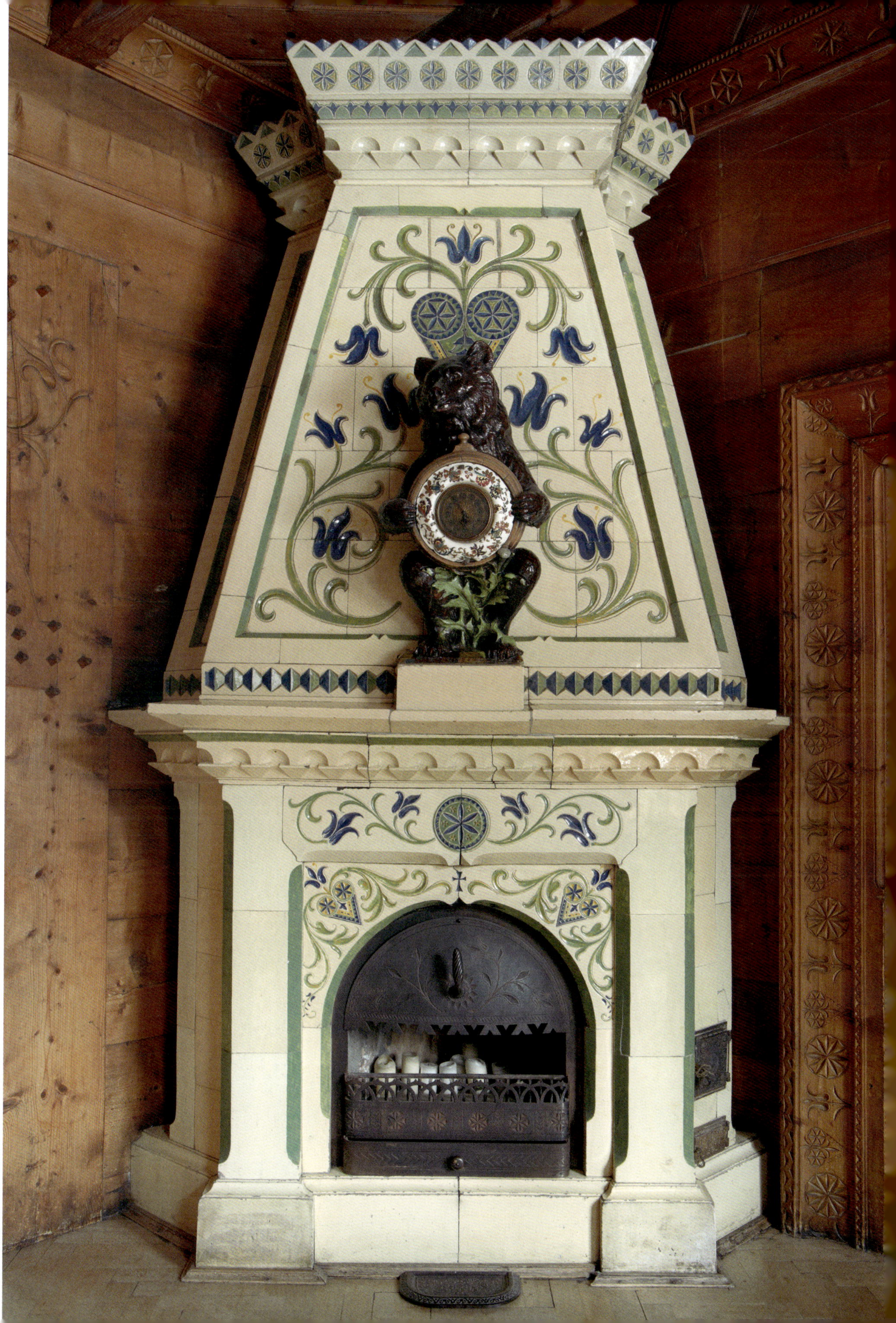

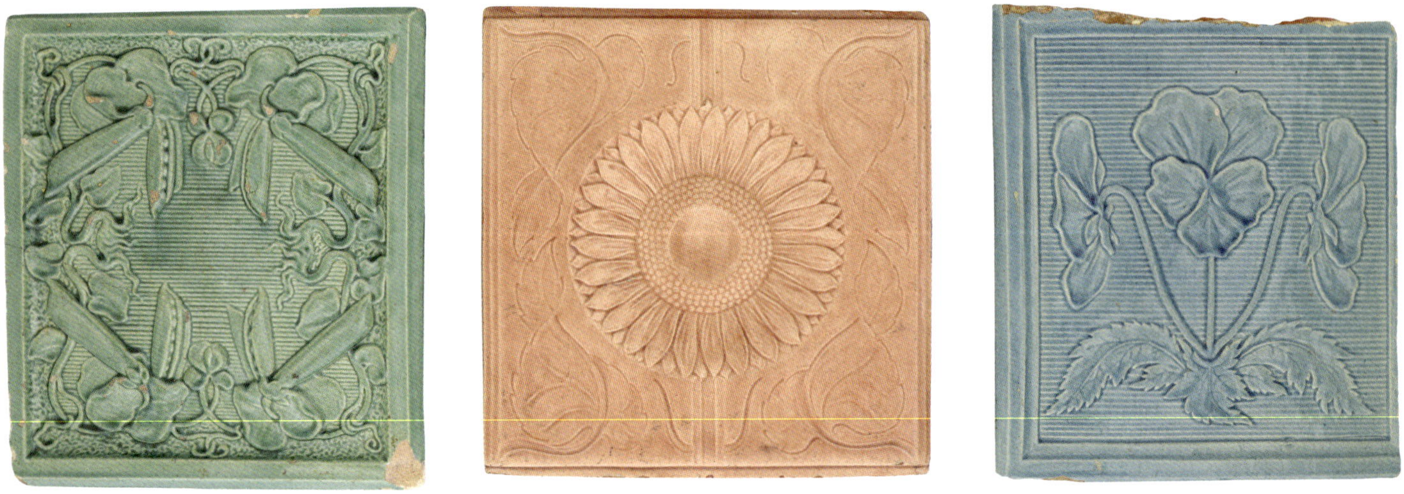

14.7 ↑

Collection of stove tiles with motifs of peas, a sunflower and pansies, made by the J. Niedźwiecki i Ska factory in Dębniki, Kraków, beginning of the 20th century; the State School of Pottery, Kołomyja (now Kolomyia), before 1912; and the tileworks of Jakub Horowitz in Kraków, beginning of the 20th century

Clay decorated artistically, glazed
25.5 × 19.5 cm; 21.0 × 21.0 cm; 22.0 × 18.5 cm
National Museum in Kraków, MNK-IV-C-6632 (donated by Adam Dubin, 2003); MNK-IV-C-1782 (from the Museum of Technology and Industry); MNK-IV-C-7247 (donated by Andrzej Karbowski, 2015)

Stoves with enclosed hearths, covered in ceramic tiles with modelled decoration, were incomparably more popular than open stoves in Polish lands. They often had decorative superstructures, with sections separated by profiled cornices. The tiles themselves had historicising motifs, plant motifs and Art Nouveau designs, and the Niedźwiecki firm also produced tiles with Highlander motifs. The tiles here derive from three different manufactories.

14.8 →

Cup and saucer, 1900–1914, made by the Porcelain and Ceramic Products Factory in Ćmielów

Painted porcelain, gilded
Cup: height 6.7 cm, diameter 6.8 cm; saucer: diameter 14.7 cm
National Museum in Kielce, MNKi/R/3241/1-2
(donated by Grażyna and Wiesław Stachurski, 2006)

At the beginning of the 20th century the factory in Ćmielów, in Poland under the Russian partition, was the only manufactory of porcelain in Polish lands. Popular, traditional, historicising forms and decorations executed using transfer techniques predominated. New fashions were gradually introduced, and painting was occasionally executed by hand. The example here combines characteristic gilded decoration with hand-painted thistles, and provides evidence of the timid introduction of innovation into industrial production.

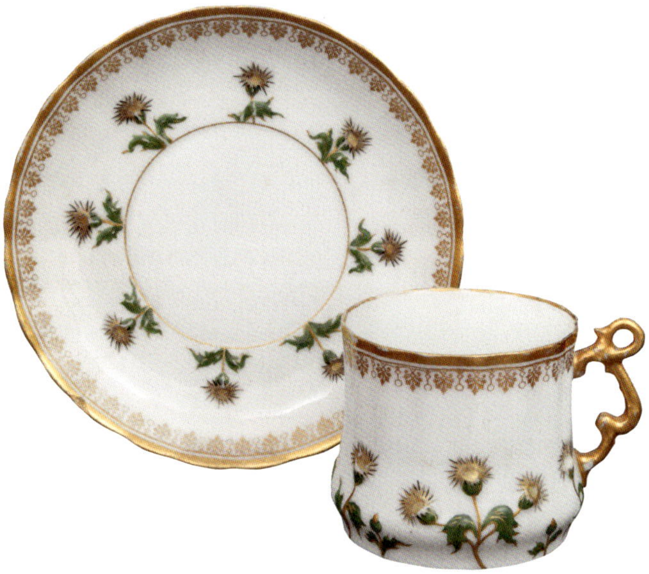

14.9 →

A Pair of Women in Peasant Costumes, 1912–14, designed by Władysław Gąbkowski, made by the First Galician Factory for Artistic Faience and Terracotta in Pacyków

Faience with underglaze painting
Height 24.5 cm
National Museum in Kraków, MNK-IV-C-1391 (from the Museum of Technology and Industry, donated by Stanisław Ursyn-Rusiecki, 1937)

The faience manufactory in Pacyków, in Eastern Galicia, founded in 1912, was appreciated for its high-quality figures and figurines. It produced pieces representing genre scenes; portraits of well-known individuals; animals; and figures made after sculptures by famous foreign artists, as well as by contemporary Polish artists from the Lviv milieu. Folk subjects also featured. The piece here belongs to the group of regional, local representations, and is signed, although nothing is known about its author.

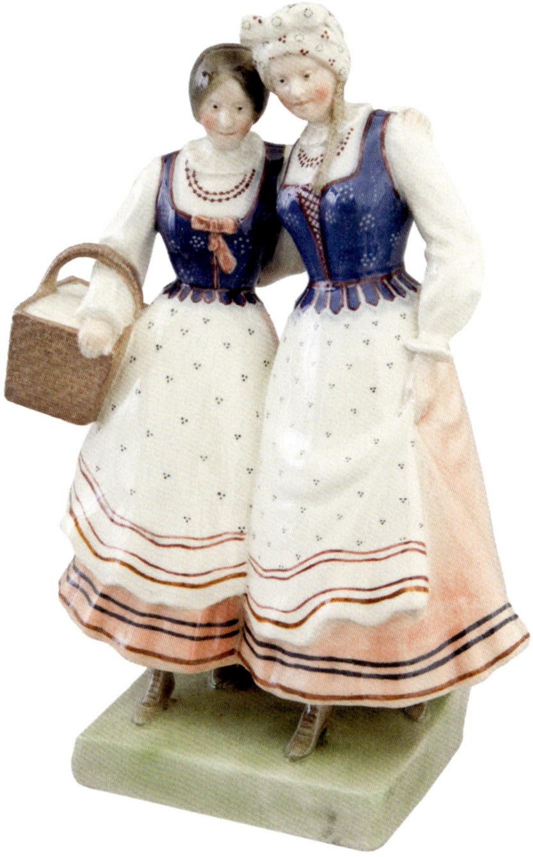

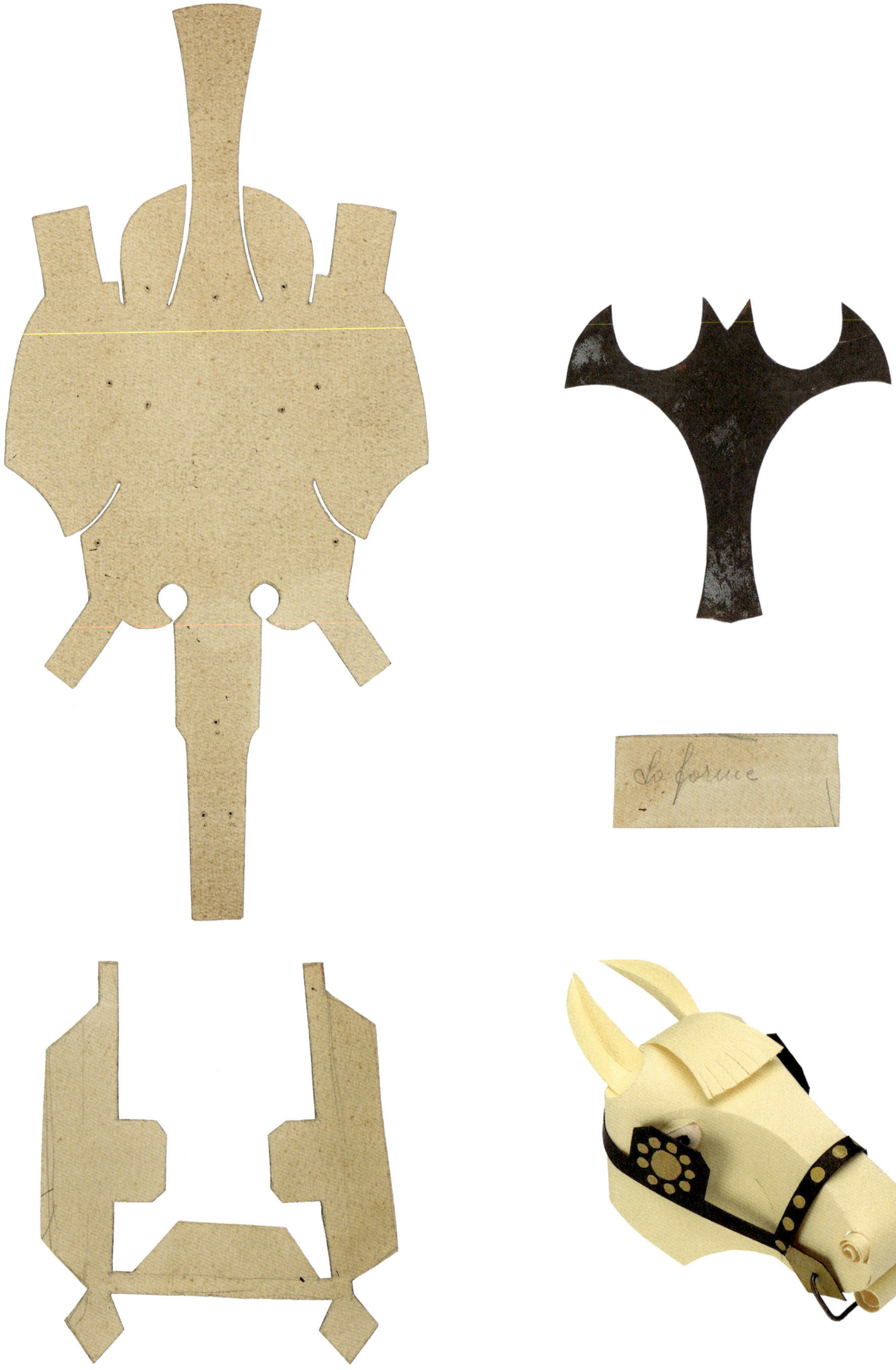
La forme

15

Children's Toys and Christmas-Tree Decorations from the Kraków Workshops

Anna Myczkowska-Szczerska

The legacy of the Kraków Workshops association, active in the years 1913–26 (see Chapter 9), deserves special attention among designers, mainly as the Polish version of the Arts and Crafts Movement, in the Art Deco idiom, but also as a laboratory for the Polish applied arts.[1] The call for the integration of the fine and applied arts coincided with the quest for a national mode of expression in art and design produced in a country that was coming around to the prospect of independence, and liberated at the end of the First World War. The group brought together remarkable representatives of the applied arts – artists, architects and craftsmen – whose works enjoyed success at the International Exposition of Modern Industrial and Decorative Arts in Paris in 1925.

The Kraków Workshops headquarters – at the Museum of Technology and Industry, the 'living museum' opened in 1868 and founded by Adrian Baraniecki on the model of English institutions created in the spirit of the Arts and Crafts Movement (see Chapter 1) – provided the context for the association's wide-ranging activities.[2] The Museum's studios and workshops were the site of the design and production as well as the educational activities of the Workshops. The latter played a key role in the interwar period, when the poor standards of creativity in the lands destroyed by the First World War became widely discussed amongst artistic circles. The training of craftsmen, as well as the art education of children carried out by professional artists and teachers educated by them, were seen as the solution. It is in this context that the Kraków Workshops association and the Museum developed their ideological-patriotic and social-pedagogic programme.

Members of the Workshops delivered museum training courses and lectures for craftspeople. Children and teenagers working and studying under the auspices of the Workshops were able to attend classes in the batik and toy-making studios directed by Jerzy Warchałowski, former chairman of the Polish Applied Arts Society and briefly by Antoni Buszek. The curriculum comprised batik, decoration of wooden objects, toys made of turned wood and ornamentation. Painted decorations were chiefly derived from the children's imagination.

The painter and printmaker Zofia Stryjeńska designed the wooden toys, whose forms drew on both folk art and manor-

15.0 (p.196)
Original templates for the 'Horse' Christmas-tree decoration (see also fig.15.10) together with a metal plate facilitating the modelling of the figure, *c.*1913–21, designed by Zdzisław Gedliczka, and a modern artist's reconstruction of the decoration, 2020, by Anna Myczkowska-Szczerska
Cardboard, tin plate, haricot beans (eyes), wire
Height of template: 19 cm
Template (currently lost): private collection of the artist's son, Adam Gedliczka

house culture.[3] Stryjeńska was one of Poland's most popular interwar artists. Although she was an heir to Young Poland's legacy, she developed an individual style, employing decorative forms (close to Art Deco) and rich colouring, frequently inspired by folk art. The same qualities also characterised her outstanding work as an illustrator, stage designer and toy-maker. Her toys were honoured with the *Diplôme d'honneur* at the Paris Exposition in 1925.[4] Stryjeńska's toys created under the auspices of the Kraków Workshops represented legendary figures associated with Kraków (Pan Twardowski, fig.15.1; Lajkonik (a bearded character in oriental costume riding a hobby horse); a dragon, fig.15.4), representatives of social groups (nobleman, street vendor, Orthodox Jew), indigenous folk types (Highlander, fig.15.2, Krakowiak, fig.15.3), harlequins, Saint Nicholas, as well as a remarkable series of birds: a goose, turkey, swallow, woodpecker, peacock and heron (figs 15.5 and 15.6). These were simple in form, both in visual and technical terms. They comprised elements of varying sizes turned in wood, sometimes modified with additional cuts, and interconnected by means of metal wires and springs. What is particularly noteworthy is the logic and brilliance of the toys' construction, resulting from an understanding of the properties of the material and how to work it; their refined and beautifully proportioned forms; and their appealing 'decorative' potential, virtually begging to be covered in colourful paint and surface ornamentation. Stryjeńska occasionally painted her toys herself, whilst the children embellished them with the batik technique, in watercolour and oil paints under the supervision of Antoni Buszek and Jerzy Warchałowski. Surviving examples evince thoroughness and precision, care taken to achieve a harmony of colours, as well as conscious application of ornament – a subject explored in depth by Karol Homolacs, another member of the Workshops (see Chapter 9).

Christmas-tree decorations also lent themselves to finding a national mode of artistic expression, in opposition to the hitherto dominant German models.[5] Polish artists rose to the challenge, elevating Christmas decorations to the status of stylistically distinctive decorative arts. There were calls for introducing courses for teachers and instructors, and publishing Christmas decoration textbooks containing designs. In 1919 a toy-making school opened at the Museum of Crafts and Applied Art (Muzeum Rzemiosł i Sztuki Stosowanej) in Warsaw, an initiative supported by the Ministry of Industry and Trade. Its activities were inaugurated with a paper department (making Christmas-tree decorations).[6] Folk art provided a key source of inspiration, although it was not assimilated uncritically.

Besides Stryjeńska, others at the Kraków Workshops who designed Christmas-tree decorations included Wojciech Jastrzębowski (fig.15.7), Zygmunt Lorec (1891–1963)[7] and Zdzisław Gedliczka (1888–1957). Gedliczka's designs stand out:[8] their visual and constructive coherence and contemporary appearance make it possible to view them as an open-ended system which would lend itself to continuation by means of developing new models today. His set of decorations includes heads of an ox, a horse, Saint Nicholas and the Devil, as well as an insect, a crayfish, a fish, a piece of fruit and a 'horse' (possibly originally 'a rocking horse') (figs 15.8, 15.9 and 15.10).[9] Thus the chief characters associated with the celebration of Christmas are represented: stable animals, Saint Nicholas celebrated during Advent, the fish as both a symbol of Christianity and a Christmas Eve dish. The Devil (fig.15.8) is a notable exception, as in the Polish lands he tends to appear in Nativity plays and carol-singing groups instead.[10] The decorations are intended for serial production – they were made from cardboard templates. Enclosed metal plates (as shown in fig.15.0) aided the precise scoring to guide the bending, which in turn generated the three-dimensional form. Gedliczka introduced ingenious methods for turning two-dimensional forms into three-dimensional ones, namely the technique of ribbing – opening out a series of parallel strategic cuts that transform a flat piece of card into a solid (see 'Fish' in fig.15.9), frequently in combination with bending into an arch (see the abdomen of the 'Insect' and the horns of the 'Ox' and 'Devil' – figs 15.8, 15.9 and 15.10). Gedliczka employed construction methods that stabilised the form of the Christmas decorations, which were appropriate for the material (pulp-coloured card) and techniques of production (cutting, bending into an arch, glueing and curling, e.g. of the tongue of the 'Devil', or of the antennae of the 'Insect' – figs 15.8 and 15.10). His designs clearly combine coloured cardboard, haricot beans (used for eyes) and areas of colour applied using gold or copper paint and black Indian ink (e.g. spots on the 'Devil' and 'Crayfish', copper-coloured antennae, wings and abdomen of the 'Insect', etc.). His colours are distinctive and lively; each figure is on the whole monochromatic with shimmering accents, contrasting with the dark green backdrop of the Christmas tree. According to family accounts, Zdzisław Gedliczka received an order from France for a train wagon-load full of these ornaments.

Kraków Workshops Christmas-tree decorations were displayed at the Museum of Technology and Industry and popularised as designs. These were disseminated under the auspices of the League for Assistance to Industry (Liga Pomocy Przemysłowej), an organisation founded in Lviv in 1903, with a branch in Kraków, which brought together auxiliary associations and supported the development of home industry. For example, it supported the State Institute for the Promotion of Handicrafts and Industry (Krajowy Instytut Popierania Rękodzieł i Przemysłu), founded in 1907, which worked in tandem with the Museum of Technology and Industry.[11]

Apart from their evident commercial dimension, the main significance of the Kraków Workshops' craft practices – even on such a small scale as the making of Christmas-tree decorations and toys – was pedagogical. The Workshops educated craftsmen, but also future consumers, thereby realising the principle of the dissemination of the ideal of beauty as expressed by one of the foremost national poets, Cyprian Kamil Norwid,[12] whose work was rediscovered and appreciated in the Young Poland era. It was no coincidence that toys became the object of educators; the appealing and gratifying task of producing them highlighted the celebration of the process of making, and hence the design process itself, so significant for the development of modern industrial design.[13]

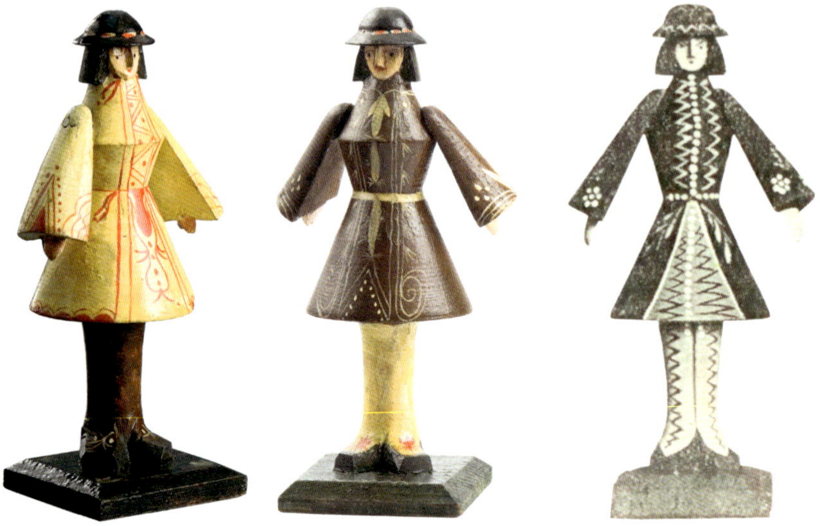

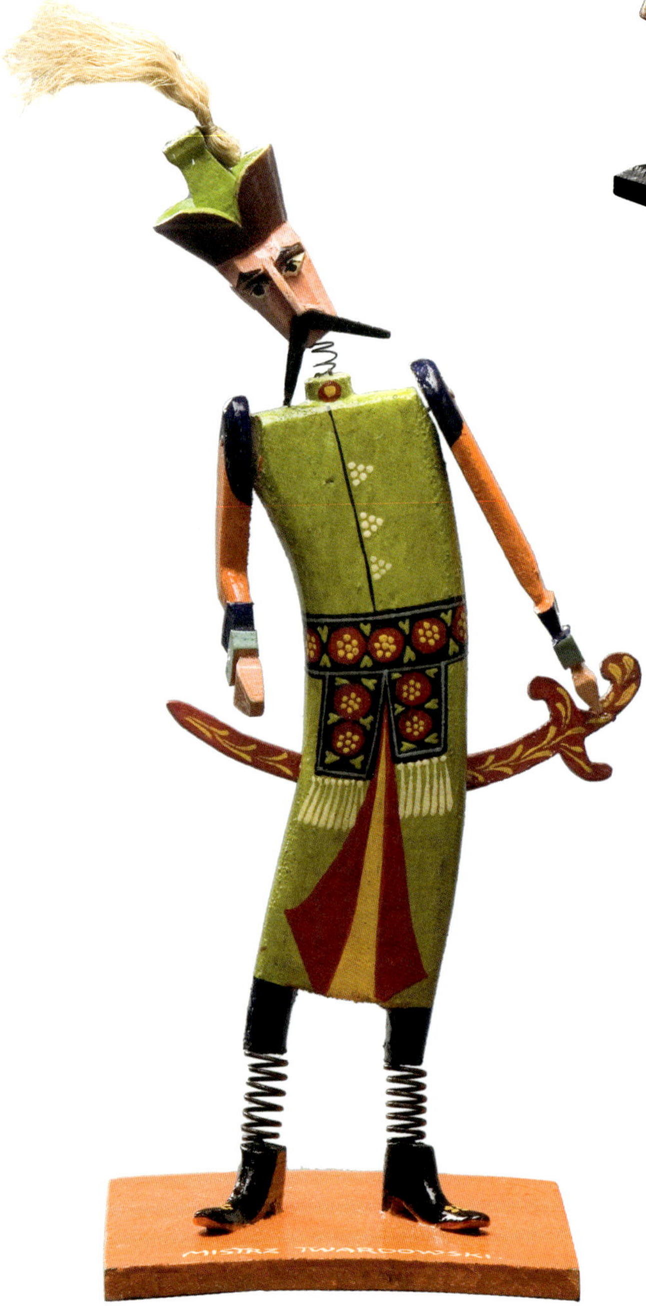

15.1 ←

'Master Twardowski' toy, 1918, designed and with painted decoration by Zofia Stryjeńska, made by the Kraków Workshops

Carved wood, painted, lacquered, metal springs
Height 36 cm, dimensions of base 12 × 13 cm
Seweryn Udziela Ethnographic Museum in Kraków, MEK 27745

'Master Twardowski', one of the most familiar of the series of toys designed by Zofia Stryjeńska, depicts a Polish nobleman with a Sarmatian moustache, and in traditional dress comprising a caftan and split-sleeved coat tied with a Słuck sash, a feathered hat and a sabre. A version with an even more dynamic pose was reproduced in the general report of the 1925 Paris Exposition. Figures of noblemen appear in the catalogue of Stryjeńska's solo exhibition at the Zachęta, the Society for the Encouragement of the Fine Arts in Warsaw in 1919. Twardowski is one of the characters from Kraków legends that inspired Stryjeńska – she also designed a Lajkonik and a dragon (fig.15.4). Fixed to its base, as is typical of toys from the Kraków Workshops, it is nevertheless flexibile – the head and feet are attached to the torso with springs, and the arms, nailed to the torso, are also mobile.

15.2 ←

(LEFT AND CENTRE) **Two versions of the 'Góral Sabała' toy, 1919, designed by Zofia Stryjeńska, made by the Kraków Workshops – painted by children under the direction of Jerzy Warchałowski**

Turned wood, painted and lacquered
Height 14.5 cm
Seweryn Udziela Ethnographic Museum in Kraków, MEK 27721, 27719

(RIGHT) **Photograph reproduced from *Płomyk: Tygodnik illustrowany dla dzieci i młodzież y*, vol.16, no.18, 1931, p.413**

Folk figures were an important category of toys from the Kraków Workshops, among them Highlanders in Podhale costume, with hats, trousers and *gunia* (also known as *cuha*) or possibly a sheepskin coat. This one bears the name of Sabała (correctly Jan Krzeptowski from Kościelisko, 1809–1894), a storyteller and musician, symbol of the Highlander material culture admired by the Young Poland movement, the godfather of Stanisław Ignacy Witkiewicz (son of Stanisław, founder of the Zakopane Style – see Chapter 6). The selection here indicates the wide variety of possibilities in adding painted decoration to a relatively simple turned form. The form necessitated proper application of fields of colour and ornament, adhering to sections and elaborating the detail in specific directions. This may have been a significant element in developing aesthetic sensitivity in young artists, learning how ornament highlights form. A virtually identical figure, labelled 'Kraków Toy', was reproduced in 1931 in issue 18 of *Płomyk*, an illustrated weekly for children and teenagers, urging them to make one, and showing a figure possibly made at the Kraków Folk Industry Workshop (Krakowska Wytwórnia Przemysłu Ludowego).

15.3 →

'Krakowianka' and 'Krakowiak' toys, 1916–17, designed and with painted decoration of 'Krakowiak' by Zofia Stryjeńska, made by the Kraków Workshops – 'Krakowianka' painted by children under the direction of Jerzy Warchałowski

Turned wood, painted and lacquered
Heights 13 cm, 14 cm
Seweryn Udziela Ethnographic Museum in Kraków,
MEK 27716, 27715

Figures depicting townspeople constituted a separate group of toys produced by the Kraków Workshops. They included Krakowiaks, Orthodox Jews and street vendors. The use of pieces of turned wood did not stand in the way of conveying the distinctive appearance of the figures represented. Toys painted by children depict the overall character of the Krakowiak costume, which had different local variations. The male figure here is dressed in a blue caftan with red lining and tassels, with trousers tucked into tall black boots and a cap in the form of a four-cornered red hat; while the female figure wears a close-fitting embroidered jacket, or *katana*, a long, flowery skirt and red boots. The Kraków costume played an important role as a type of Polish national costume, and provided inspiration for Young Poland artists.

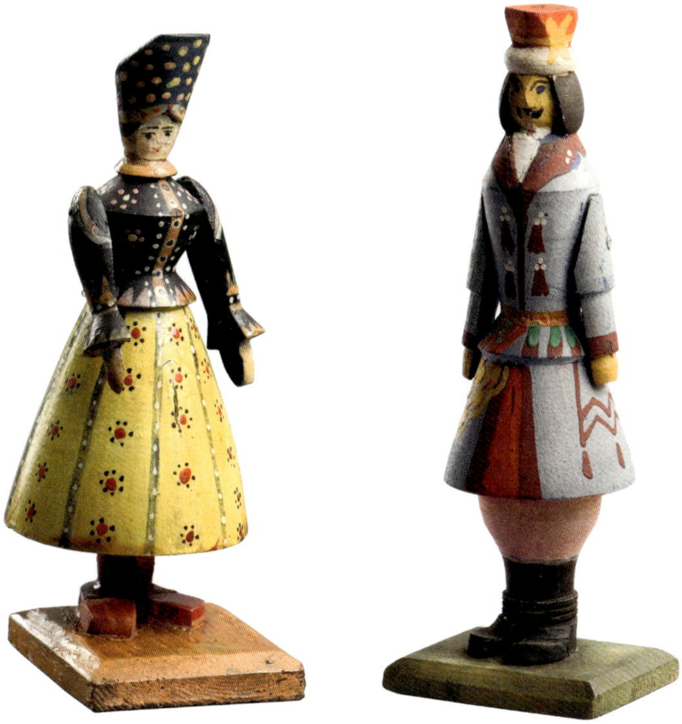

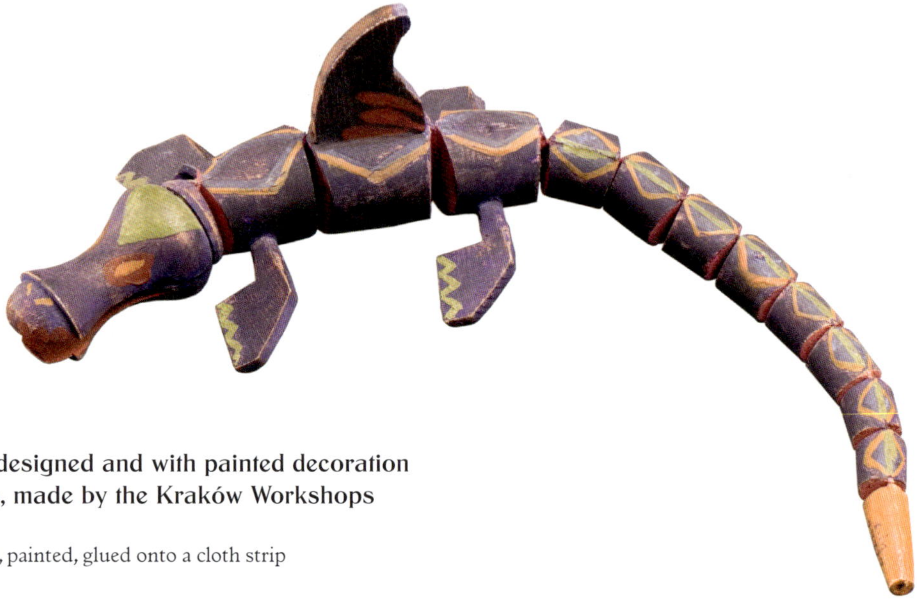

15.4 →

'Dragon' toy, 1918, designed and with painted decoration by Zofia Stryjeńska, made by the Kraków Workshops

Turned and carved wood, painted, glued onto a cloth strip
Length 37 cm
Seweryn Udziela Ethnographic Museum in Kraków, MEK 27727

The dragon is associated with the popular Kraków legend of the Wawel Dragon – a fearsome giant reptile said to reside within Wawel Hill. It was designed by Zofia Stryjeńska, taking an Indonesian toy as a model. The dragon is made up of a 12-part body with a tail comprising sections cut in half and glued to a cloth strip. When sawn, these sections have been appropriately profiled to leave a wedge-shaped space between them. Such a construction means that, when held in the hand, the dragon writhes like a snake. Four legs and a fin as well as a geomentric pattern give the toy a fantastical legendary feel.

15.5 →

'Woodpecker' toy, 1918, designed and with painted decoration by Zofia Stryjeńska, made by the Kraków Workshops

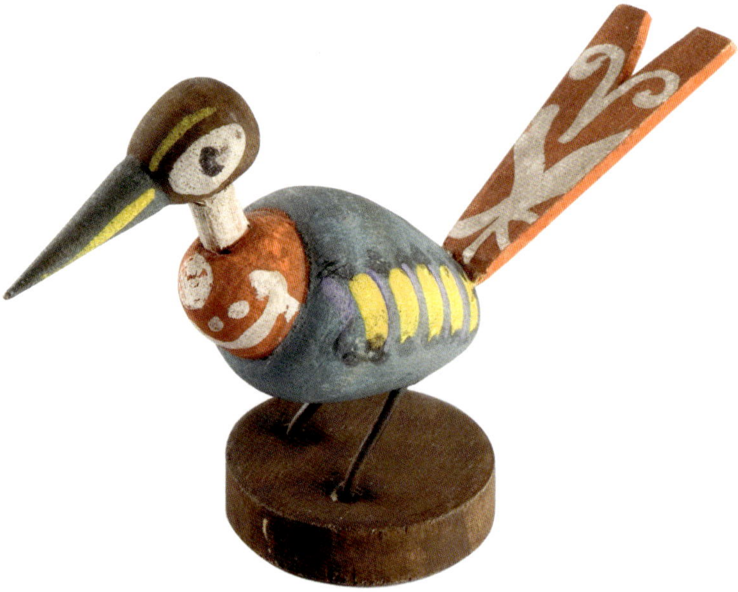

Turned and carved wood, painted with water-based paints
Length 12 cm, diameter of base 4 cm
Seweryn Udziela Ethnographic Museum in Kraków, MEK 27743

Just like other toys by the Kraków Workshops representing birds and animals, the 'Woodpecker' displays a high level of stylisation, inevitable given the serial manufacture of the toys. Turning simple solid figures resulted in minimalist forms, leaving room for the surface decorators to show off – both professional artists and children working under their direction, in whom was instilled a love of high-quality handicraft combined with native models and a quest for beauty and compositional harmony. The painted decoration of the woodpecker, achieved with great panache, is an excellent example of a departure from naturalism in favour of the decorative rhythm of shapes and colours.

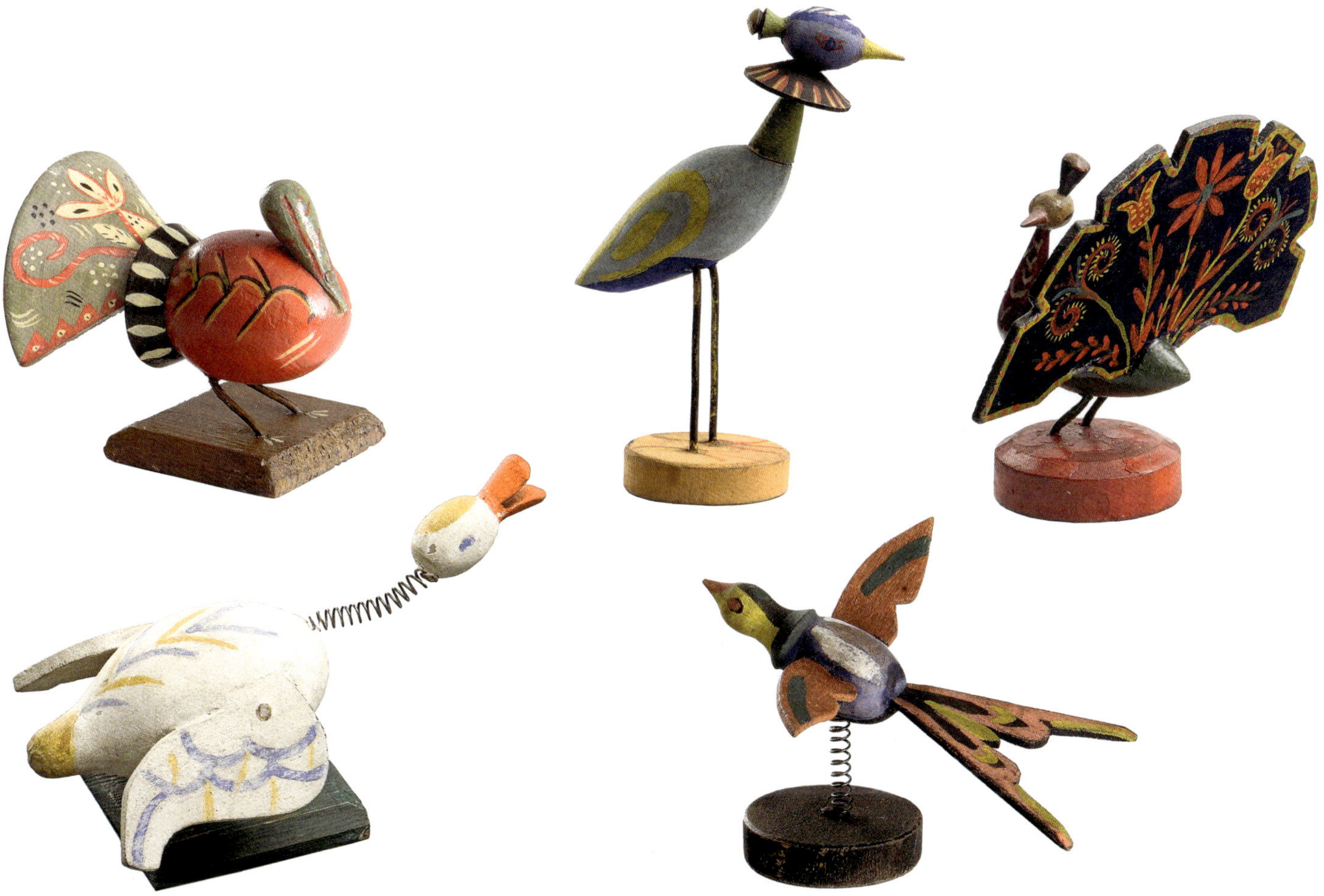

15.6 ↑

Series of bird toys: 'Turkey', 'Heron', 'Peacock', 'Goose', 'Swallow', 1918–19, by Zofia Stryjeńska (design and painted decoration of 'Heron', 'Goose' and 'Swallow', and design of 'Peacock') and the Kraków Workshops (design of 'Turkey', and production of all) – 'Turkey' and 'Peacock' painted by children under the direction of Jerzy Warchałowski

Turned wood, painted (including lacquered), metal elements (wire, spring)
Various dimensions (widths of bases 4–5 cm)
Seweryn Udziela Ethnographic Museum in Kraków, MEK 27733, 27737, 27741, 27742, 27734

The series of birds produced at the Kraków Workshops include domesticated, decorative and wild birds. In spite of this diversity the series retains a formal and constructional homogeneity. It recalls folk images of birds produced from the end of the 19th century in Stryszawa. The birds are made of wooden turned elements (heads, bodies), together with parts cut from wooden boards (wings and tails). Relatively large smooth surfaces lend themselves to rich painted decoration, some inspired by nature, some by folk ornament. The result is the interplay of two- and three-dimensional elements – visible, for example, in the construction of the birds' legs, which are made of thick wire with the claws painted flat on the bases.

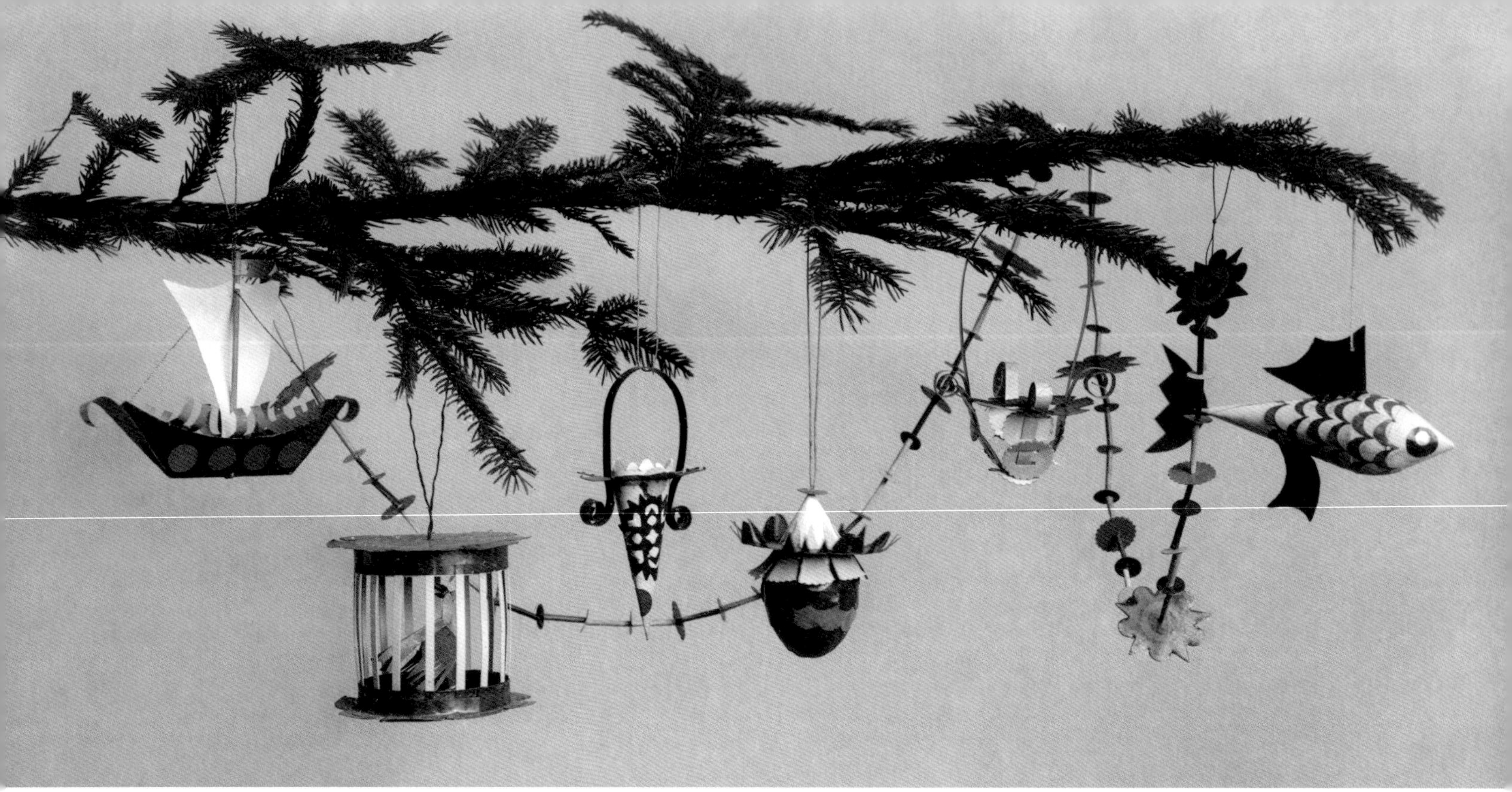

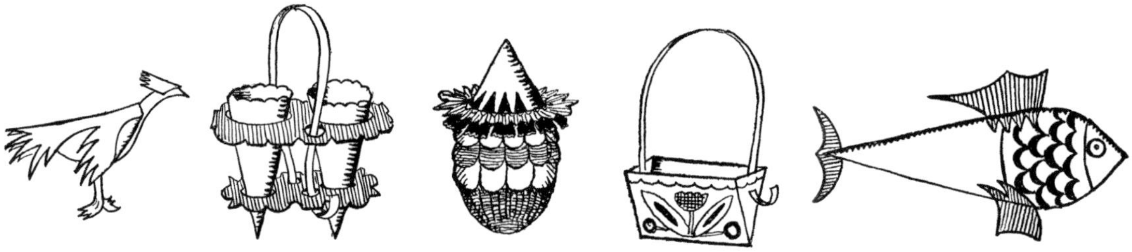

15.7 ↑

(TOP) **Toys for the Christmas tree from the Kraków Workshops, 1913–26, designed and produced by the Kraków Workshops, including most probably Wojciech Jastrzębowski ('Bird in a Cage')**

Paper, straw, blown eggshells
Various dimensions
Museum of Kraków, MHK 644-N

(BOTTOM) **Drawings by Maria Werten to accompany her publication *Ozdoby choinkowe*, offprint originally printed in the quarterly *Praca Ręczna w szkole* (*Handiwork at School*), no.3, Warsaw, 1928**

Apart from three reproductions included in *Rzeczy Piękne* (the magazine of the Museum of Technology and Industry, whose title translates as *Beautiful Things*) – 'Ox', 'Fish' (fig.15.9) and 'Devil' – the photograph above is the only known photographic source documenting finished Christmas-tree decorations from the Kraków Workshops. Some of the objects shown can be identified with the help of a 1928 article by Maria Werten, titled *Ozdoby choinkowe* (*Christmas Decorations*), and its accompanying illustration.[14] The author draws attention to Kraków Workshops designs, among them a bird with flapping wings, part of the Christmas-tree decoration 'Bird in a Cage' designed by Wojciech Jastrzębowski. In addition to the single hanging ornaments visible in the photograph, there is also a chain made up of pieces of straw strung onto a thread and alternating with paper circles. The forms of the pine cone (fourth from the left in the photograph) and fish are constructed out of blown eggshells. In the case of the pine cone, its paper scales are made with the assistance of a punch to facilitate serial production of the decoration.

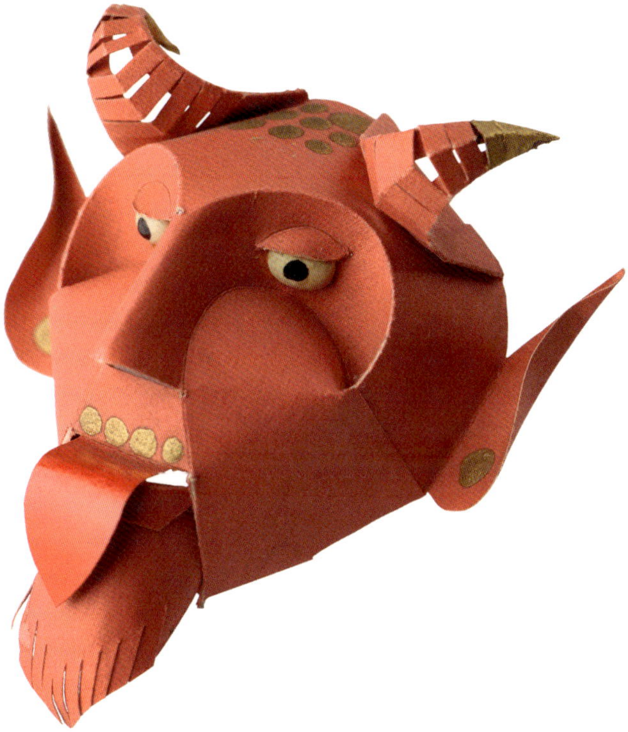

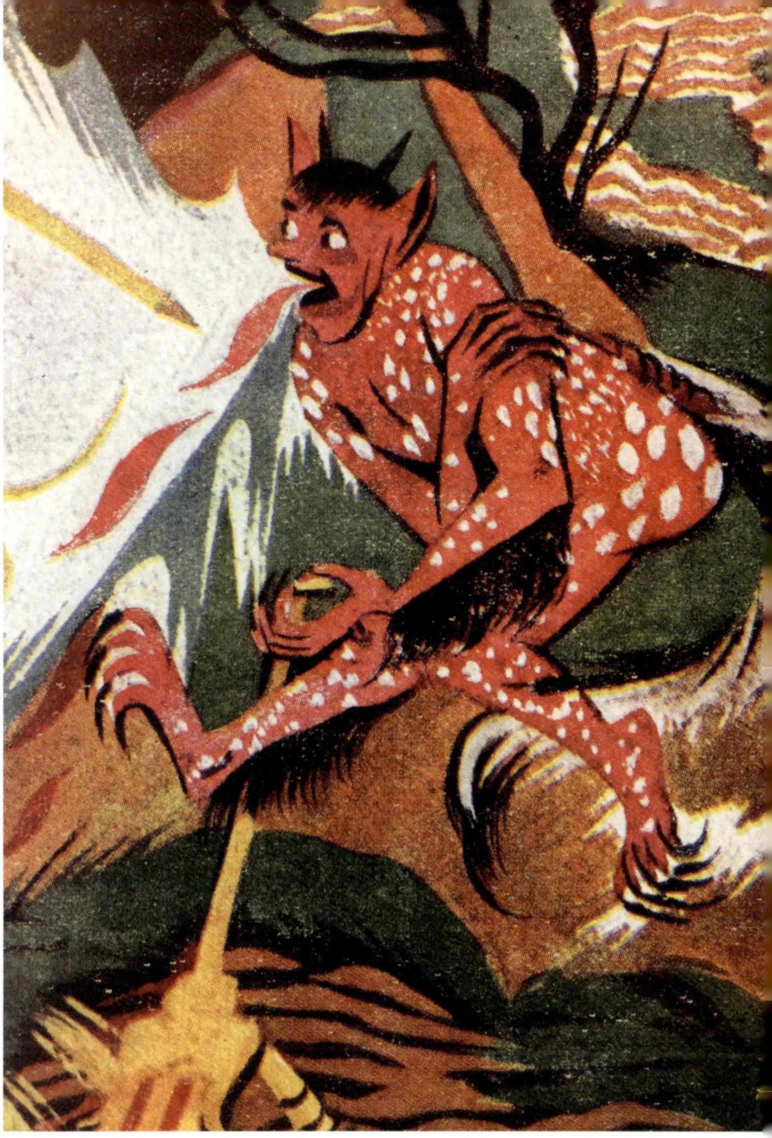

15.8 ↑

(LEFT) **'Devil' Christmas-tree decoration, 1921, designed by Zdzisław Gedliczka, with a League for Assistance to Industry label**

Cardboard, paper, haricot beans (eyes), black Indian ink, golden pigment
Height 11 cm
National Museum in Kraków, MNK IV-V-108

(RIGHT) **Detail of an illustration by Zofia Stryjeńska in *Rzeczy Piękne*, 1927, no.4**

According to Professor Adam Gedliczka, the artist's son, the Devil enjoyed particular popularity as part of the dressing of the Christmas tree at home. There was probably also the angel (whole figure with wings) to balance the Devil. The Devil does not normally appear among popular Christmas-tree ornaments, in which small birds, fish, clowns, baskets, pendants, peacock's eyes and decorative geometrical forms predominated. Yet it is the most striking of the figures in Gedliczka's selection, not only in terms of incorporating this unexpected character into the Christmas tree but also in purely visual terms: a flaming red head with dripped gold spots, curved horns, enormous ears, contrasting white eyeballs and a protruding tongue. Zofia Stryjeńska produced a similar depiction of the Devil as an illustration for a story by Kazimierz Przerwa-Tetmajer, Young Poland's foremost exponent – 'Jak baba diabła wyonacyła' ('How woman cheated the Devil'), from the short-story collection *Na Skalnym Podhalu* (*In the Rocky Podhale*, 1901–12).[15] In her own distinctive style she emphasised the dynamism of the figure by means of flat fields of colour in contrast with expressive details and a strong outline.

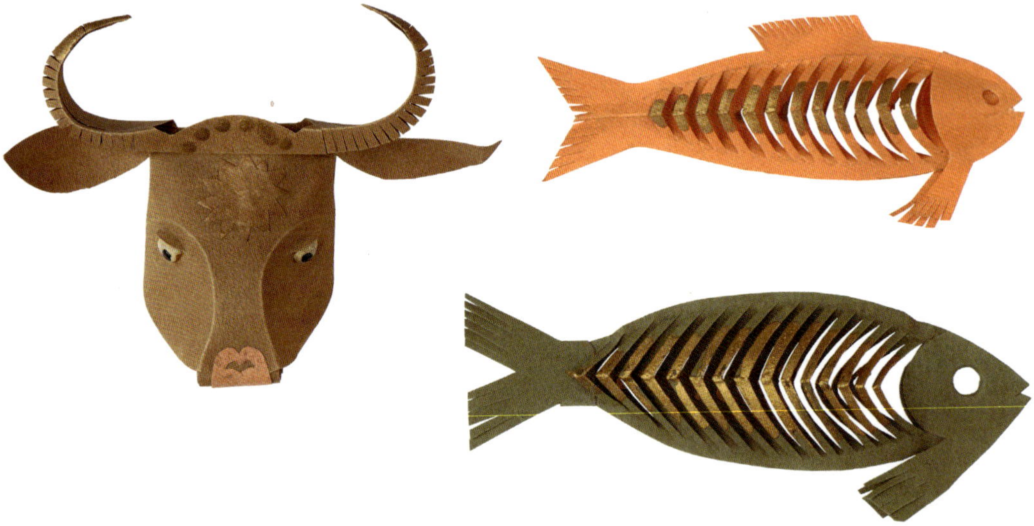

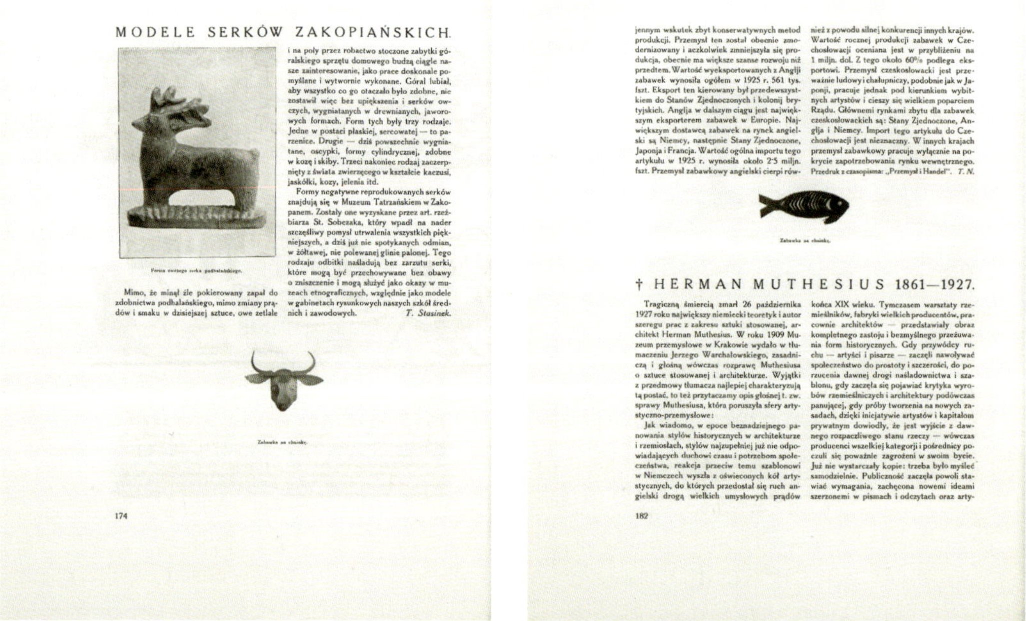

MODELE SERKÓW ZAKOPIAŃSKICH.

Mimo, że minął źle pokierowany zapał do zdobnictwa podhalańskiego, mimo zmiany prądów i smaku w dzisiejszej sztuce, owe zetlałe i na poły przez robactwo stoczone zabytki góralskiego sprzętu domowego budzą ciągle nasze zainteresowanie, jako prace doskonale pomyślane i wytwornie wykonane. Góral lubiał, aby wszystko co go otaczało było zdobne, nie zostawił więc bez upiększenia i serków owczych, wygniatanych w drewnianych, jaworowych formach. Form tych były trzy rodzaje. Jedne w postaci płaskiej, sercowatej — to parzenice. Drugie — dziś powszechnie wygniatane, oscypki, formy cylindrycznej, zdobne w kozę i skiby. Trzeci nakoniec rodzaj zaczerpnięty z świata zwierzęcego w kształcie kaczusi, jaskółki, kozy, jelenia itd.

Formy negatywne reprodukowanych serków znajdują się w Muzeum Tatrzańskiem w Zakopanem. Zostały one wyzyskane przez art. rzeźbiarza St. Sobczaka, który wpadł na nader szczęśliwy pomysł utrwalenia wszystkich piękniejszych, a dziś już nie spotykanych odmian, w żółtawej, nie polewanej glinie palonej. Tego rodzaju odbitki naśladują bez zarzutu serki, które mogą być przechowywane bez obawy o zniszczenie i mogą służyć jako okazy w muzeach etnograficznych, względnie jako modele w gabinetach rysunkowych naszych szkół średnich i zawodowych. *T. Stasinek.*

174

jennym wskutek zbyt konserwatywnych metod produkcji. Przemysł ten został obecnie zmodernizowany i aczkolwiek zmniejszyła się produkcja, obecnie ma większe szanse rozwoju niż przedtem. Wartość wyeksportowanych z Anglji zabawek wynosiła ogółem w 1925 r. 561 tys. fszt. Eksport ten kierowany był przedewszystkiem do Stanów Zjednoczonych i kolonij brytyjskich. Anglja w dalszym ciągu jest największym eksporterem zabawek w Europie. Największym dostawcą zabawek na rynek angielski są Niemcy, następnie Stany Zjednoczone, Japonja i Francja. Wartość ogólna importu tego artykułu w 1925 r. wynosiła około 2·5 miljn. fszt. Przemysł zabawkowy angielski cierpi również z powodu silnej konkurencji innych krajów. Wartość rocznej produkcji zabawek w Czechosłowacji oceniana jest w przybliżeniu na 1 miljn. dol. Z tego około 60% podlega eksportowi. Przemysł czeskosłowacki jest przeważnie ludowy i chałupniczy, podobnie jak w Japonji, pracuje jednak pod kierunkiem wybitnych artystów i cieszy się wielkiem poparciem Rządu. Głównemi rynkami zbytu dla zabawek czeskosłowackich są: Stany Zjednoczone, Anglja i Niemcy. Import tego artykułu do Czechosłowacji jest nieznaczny. W innych krajach przemysł zabawkowy pracuje wyłącznie na pokrycie zapotrzebowania rynku wewnętrznego.
Przedruk z czasopisma: „Przemysł i Handel". *T. N.*

† HERMAN MUTHESIUS 1861—1927.

Tragiczną śmiercią zmarł 26 października 1927 roku największy niemiecki teoretyk i autor szeregu prac z zakresu sztuki stosowanej, architekt Herman Muthesius. W roku 1909 Muzeum przemysłowe w Krakowie wydało w tłumaczeniu Jerzego Warchałowskiego, zasadniczą i głośną wówczas rozprawę Muthesiusa o sztuce stosowanej i architekturze. Wyjątki z przedmowy tłumacza najlepiej charakteryzują tą postać, to też przytaczamy opis głośnej t. zw. sprawy Muthesiusa, która poruszyła sfery artystyczno-przemysłowe:

Jak wiadomo, w epoce beznadziejnego panowania stylów historycznych w architekturze i rzemiosłach, stylów najzupełniej już nie odpowiadających duchowi czasu i potrzebom społeczeństwa, reakcja przeciw temu szablonowi w Niemczech wyszła z oświeconych kół artystycznych, do których przedostał się ruch angielski drogą wielkich umysłowych prądów końca XIX wieku. Tymczasem warsztaty rzemieślników, fabryki wielkich producentów, pracownie architektów — przedstawiały obraz kompletnego zastoju i bezmyślnego przeżuwania form historycznych. Gdy przywódcy ruchu — artyści i pisarze — zaczęli nawoływać społeczeństwo do prostoty i szczerości, do porzucenia dawnej drogi naśladownictwa i szablonu, gdy zaczęła się pojawiać krytyka wyrobów rzemieślniczych i architektury podówczas panującej, gdy próby tworzenia na nowych zasadach, dzięki inicjatywie artystów i kapitałom prywatnym dowiodły, że jest wyjście z dawnego rozpaczliwego stanu rzeczy — wówczas producenci wszelkiej kategorji i pośrednicy poczuli się poważnie zagrożeni w swoim bycie. Już nie wystarczały kopie: trzeba było myśleć samodzielnie. Publiczność zaczęła powoli stawiać wymagania, zachęcona nowemi ideami szerzonemi w pismach i odczytach oraz arty-

182

15.9 →

(TOP) **'Ox' and 'Fish' Christmas-tree decorations, 1921, designed by Zdzisław Gedliczka, with a League for Assistance to Industry label**

Cardboard, paper, haricot beans (eyes), black Indian ink, golden pigment
Height of 'Ox': 11 cm; length of 'Fish': 12 cm
National Museum in Kraków, MNK IV-V-107, MNK IV-V-106/1-2

(BOTTOM) **Pages from *Rzeczy Piękne*, 1927, nos 10–11**

Apart from the 'Devil', 'Horse', 'Insect' and 'Crayfish', the 'Ox' and 'Fish' are the only decorations which survive to date. They appeared under the auspices of the League for Assistance to Industry, and came to the National Museum in Kraków as part of the legacy of the Museum of Technology and Industry, the headquarters of the Kraków Workshops. 'Fish', 'Ox' and 'Devil' have an exceptionally expressive synthetic form, transforming them into sign-pictograms. Notably, it is in this capacity that their silhouettes were used as typographical ornaments by *Rzeczy Piękne*, the Museum of Technology and Industry's magazine.

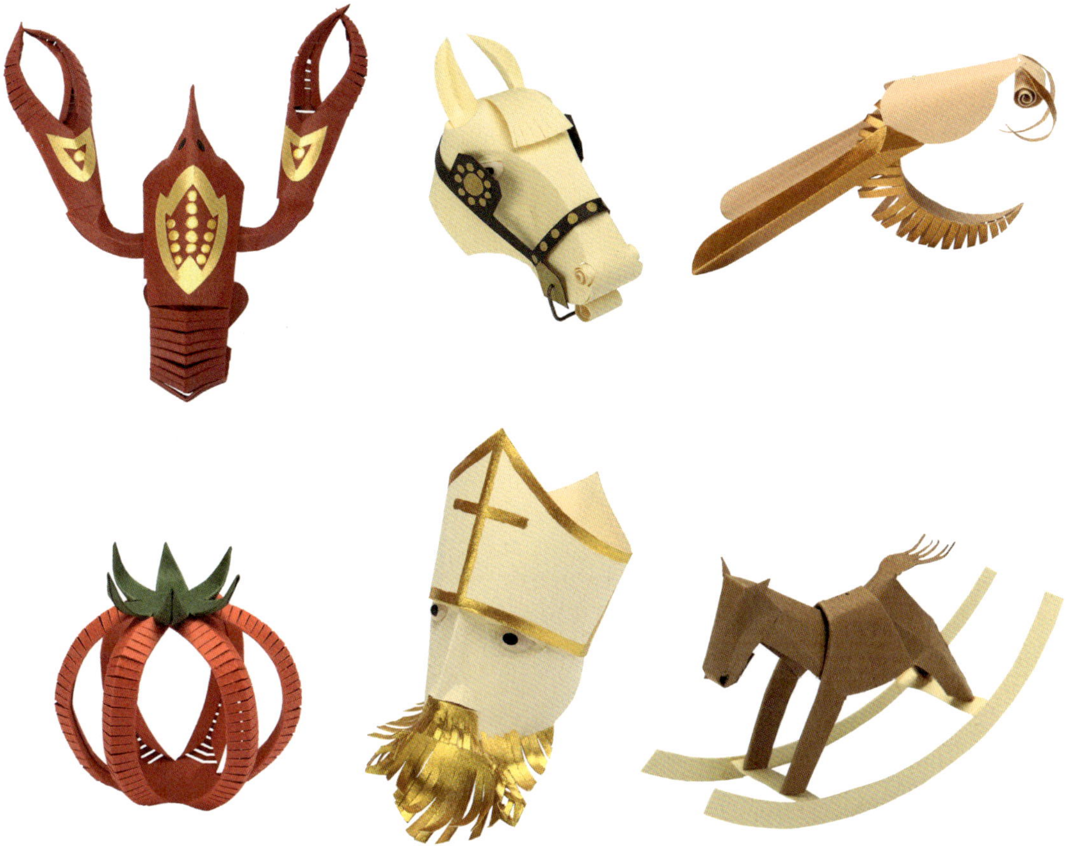

15.10 →

Selection of artist's reconstructions by Anna Myczkowska-Szczerska, 2020 (on the basis of a combination of original templates, archival research and several surviving originals) of Christmas-tree decorations originally designed by Zdzisław Gedliczka between 1913 and 1926, together with the constructional principle for curved elements: 'Crayfish', 'Horse', 'Insect' (Grasshopper – attributed to Gedliczka), 'Fruit', 'Saint Nicholas', 'Rocking Horse'

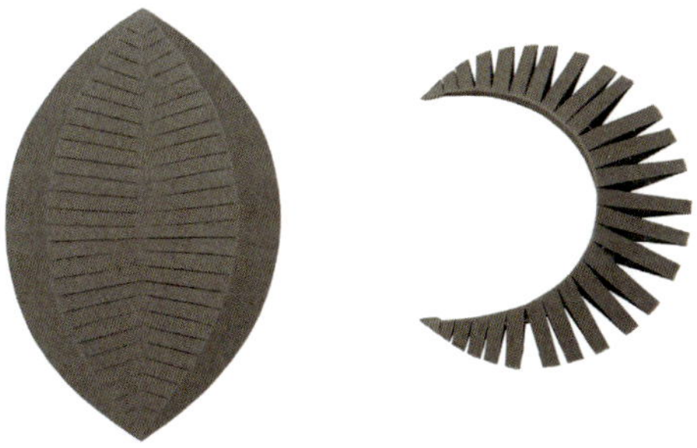

Cardboard and paper, haricot beans (eyes), bookbinder's glue,
black Indian ink, water-based pigment
Heights respectively 11 cm, 8 cm, 5.5 cm, 6 cm, 11.5 cm, 6 cm

The set presented here, together with the ornaments 'Devil' (fig.15.8), 'Ox' and 'Fish' (fig.15.9), represents the full range of Christmas decorations designed by Zdzisław Gedliczka known to us today. Their coherence and unity with respect to style and materials used is striking, and extends to the colour scheme, finishing, scale, and the construction of all elements. Despite obvious differences in form, their overall level of complexity, accessories and ornamental details are comparable across the whole series. Characteristic features include the precisely executed curved scoring which is the basis for shaping the three-dimensional forms. Together with a series of parallel cuts, they allow the creation of dynamically rounded forms; this is particularly evident in the curved horns of the 'Ox' and 'Devil', the pincers of the 'Crayfish' and the abdomen of the 'Insect'. Such a manner of construction eliminates the need for glue, or reduces it to a minimum. Rolled strips of cardboard imitate eyes ('Insect') and nostrils ('Ox', 'Horse'). The figures of the 'Crayfish' and 'Insect' (Grasshopper) in the collections of the National Museum in Kraków display rich ornamental gilding, while the surviving specimen of the 'Horse' has enabled the reconstruction of the bridle (fig.15.0). 'Fruit', 'Saint Nicholas' and 'Rocking Horse' are artist's re-creations based on the original templates, since the original made-up decorations remain untraced.

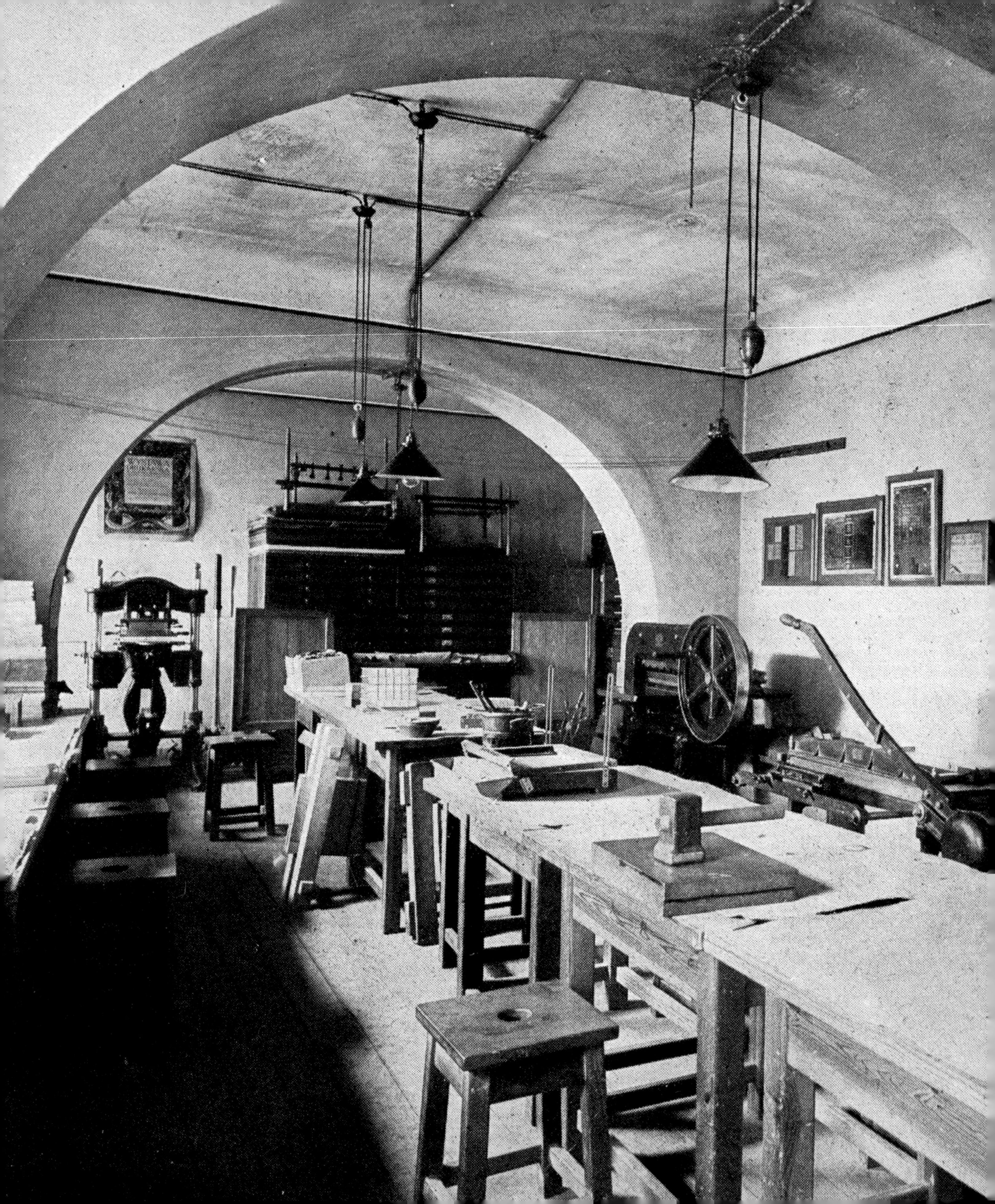

16

The Book Beautiful

Monika Paś

Attempts to raise the aesthetic status of the book, begun in England by William Morris (see Chapter 2), spread at the turn of the 20th century to many European countries. Poland was no exception, even though its lands were occupied by three partitioning powers. These ideas were integral to the art of Young Poland, which had inherent patriotic undertones and a wide reach. Book arts encompass several disciplines, including illustration, typography, graphic design and bookbinding. This chapter focuses on the achievements of Kraków-based bookbinders, since their activities played a significant role in inculcating the ideal of the 'book beautiful' in Poland. Innovative works were also produced in other locations, such as Warsaw, Lviv and Poznań.

During this period Kraków belonged to the Austro-Hungarian Empire, where an Industrial Law had been promulgated in 1850. This restricted the role of craft guilds, which had hitherto been solely responsible for controlling economic life in terms of accepting trainees and journeymen, granting master-craftsmen trade certificates, determining the price of products, and regulating the number of workshops in individual towns. Increasing mechanisation of the bookbinding trade had facilitated production, whilst causing a decline in fine handicraft. This resulted in a low aesthetic and technical standard in an unexacting and undiscerning local market. The revival in bookbinding in Kraków at the turn of the century was associated with the activities of the Museum of Technology and Industry, established by Adrian Baraniecki in 1868 (see Chapter 1). The Museum promoted the notion of fine handicraft in accordance with the aesthetic principles of John Ruskin, whom Baraniecki had met in London.[1] Amongst its aims, it endeavoured to raise the standard of home craftsmanship, by means of creating an accessible study collection and organising popular lectures, competitions and professional training courses for craftspeople, as well as exhibitions of their work.

16.0 (p. 208)
The bookbinding studio at the first premises of the Museum of Technology and Industry in Kraków at the Franciscan monastery, 1908–13
Archival photograph, reproduced from: Kazimierz Witkiewicz, *Kunszt introligatorski Bonawentury Lenarta* (*The Bookbinding Craft of Bonawentura Lenart*), Kraków: Muzeum Techniczno-Przemysłowe, 1932

Competitions announced by the Museum in 1894 ('for works of jewellery and bookbinding') and 1908 ('for an exemplary book cover') called for completed bookbindings based on bespoke designs and made to set specifications.[2] They did not, however, produce satisfactory results. Experts from the judging panels drew attention to the entries' numerous technical shortcomings, as well as unimaginative use of ornamentation, and the latter's unfitness for purpose with respect to the book's construction or subject matter.[3]

A turning point and a key initiative was the establishment at the Museum of Technology and Industry in 1909 of a professional bookbinding studio with state-of-the art equipment and tools, supplied also with Morris's Golden Type font.[4] Bonawentura Lenart (1881–1973), an expert bookbinding tutor from the Industrial School (Szkoła Przemysłowa) in Kraków, was appointed as its director.[5] His influence cannot be overstated. The curriculum included practical bookbinding techniques and the technology of materials, composition, drawing and typography, as well as basic book-keeping, law and Health and Safety, all of which were useful for running a workshop. Bookbinding courses for journeymen and masters aimed at raising their professional qualifications, familiarising them with best practice, and promoting the ideal of the 'book beautiful'. Seen as a uniform whole, it was characterised by close correlation between the book's physical artistry and the contents.

In November 1909 the State Department (the administrative and executive organ of the Galicia Diet in the years 1856–1914) organised a course for bookbinders at the Museum of Technology and Industry, engaging Paul Adam, from Düsseldorf, as tutor. Bindings produced on this course were exhibited alongside several former submissions to the 1908 competition, together with works made by Lenart's students at the Museum workshop, several of Lenart's own bindings, and examples of antique works loaned by the National Museum and State Archive in Kraków.[6] Reviewing the exhibition, Jerzy Warchałowski, co-founder of the Polish Applied Arts Society, praised the work of Lenart and his students, commending their good taste and masterly execution.[7]

Lenart was an artisan whose professional training followed ancient guild tradition. After completing an apprenticeship in Galicia in 1899, he went on to gain bookbinding experience in various European cities. Thanks to his international education, he was familiar with the ideas of John Ruskin, William Morris and the artist and bookbinder Thomas James Cobden-Sanderson (1840–1922). In a 1908 article on 19th-century bookbinding he wrote about Cobden-Sanderson with great admiration.[8] Lenart received a scholarship from the State Department and the State Institute for the Promotion of Handicrafts and Industry in Kraków, which enabled him to visit vocational schools in Germany, Holland and England in 1910–11. He visited London, where George Sutcliffe was teaching at the Camberwell School of Arts and Crafts.[9] As such Lenart came into contact with the direct lineage of Morris's disciples: Sutcliffe was a former student of Douglas Bennett Cockerell (1870–1945), who was part of Morris's circle as the brother of Sydney, the secretary of the Kelmscott Press. Cockerell had been apprenticed to T.J. Cobden-Sanderson at the Doves Bindery in Hammersmith, before setting up his own art press, Douglas Cockerell & Son. There Lenart perfected his skills, attending classes in bookbinding and book-cover ornamentation, and familiarising himself with Cockerell's theories of modern binding-decoration, limiting this to straight lines, small flowers, leaves and dots. He also worked in the bookbinding workshop of Edgar Green. He grafted his experiences onto Polish soil, completely breaking away from the imitation of historicist styles, and promoting the individual treatment of each book. As director of the Museum's bookbinding studio, he created bindings unique in artistic terms, whose decoration harmonised with the subject matter of the book. In technical terms they were faultlessly executed, and made using the finest materials.

In 1911 the Museum organised two further courses for bookbinders, both led by Lenart – the first in hand-gilding, the second in both manual and machine-gilding of book-edges, the embossing of inscriptions, composition using the simplest tools, and the technology of bookbinding materials. Graduates had the opportunity to apply their skills to binding ecclesiastical books and conserving old missals.[10] The output of each course and competition was showcased in an exhibition of the graduates' works.[11] The prayer books were exhibited at the *Piotr Skarga First Exhibition of Contemporary Ecclesiastical Art*, which opened in Kraków on 7 December 1911.[12] The choice of prayer books as the object of the course was undoubtedly dictated by the forthcoming exhibition, coupled with the fact that they are typically small, making them particularly suitable for practising newly acquired skills. The Museum workshops aimed at equipping master bookbinders with the necessary skills to be able to closely collaborate with the artist responsible for conceiving the design. Bindings created under Lenart's guidance are characterised by practical construction and sensitivity to the properties of the materials used, painstaking execution and simple ornamentation, always in keeping with the nature of the book. This is exemplified by the prayer books, where, alongside meticulous use of hand tools for stamping, details such as the design and colour of the endpapers correspond with the turn-ins of the cover material. They are undoubtedly influenced by Lenart's exposure to British bookbinding during his stay in London. Accordingly, course attendees were entrusted with decorating bookbindings with very simple stamps, creating a decorative motif relating to the content of the book by means of juxtaposing them in a particular manner on the surface of the cover. The Latin and the Greek cross were amongst the most common designs, created by means of the rhythmic juxtaposition of two or three stamps using the techniques of blind- and gold-stamping. The covers preserved in the National Museum in Kraków demonstrate the diversity of visual effects achieved with the same stamps arranged in different configurations, in such a way that the composition is never repeated.[13]

Established in 1887, the workshop of another Kraków-based master bookbinder, Robert Jahoda (1862–1947), operated in parallel with Lenart's state-of-the-art studio at the Museum.[14] Like Lenart, Jahoda was a craftsman partially educated abroad. Apart from publishers' bindings produced by around thirty qualified workmen, Jahoda also undertook one-off commissions for bibliophiles and special occasions, made to designs by famous artists. Thanks to his collaboration with architects and painters, Jahoda's workshop became a laboratory where new styles were tested and innovative works realised. It broke away from hackneyed ornamentation, and, in his own designs, Jahoda was able to draw on historical motifs as a springboard for creating fresh and original works. For example, he developed the use of leather intarsia, achieving unusually painterly effects upon the book cover. Jahoda's workshop also experimented

16.1 →

Rozmowy ktore myal Krol Salomon mądry z Marchołtem grubym a sprosnym . . . (The Conversations which Wise King Solomon had with Fat and Ribald Marchołt . . .)

Publication address: Harlem: published by Ludwik Bernacki;
printer: Harlem Joh. Enschedé en Zonen, 1913
Binding: Bonawentura Lenart, Kraków, 1914
Cardboard, pig's leather, blind-stamped
26.5 × 19 cm
National Museum in Kraków, MNK IV-MO-302
(from the Museum of Technology and Industry, 1950)

This is the first volume of the publication *Inkunabuły Polskie* (*Polish Incunabula*), a series established by Ludwik Bernacki, historian of Polish literature, editor and librarian. The copy is from a limited and numbered edition. The binding designed and executed by Lenart is a characteristic example of his work, displaying a precisely composed and carefully made 'expressive binding', by virtue of the decorative elements being closely associated with the subject matter of the book. The rhythmically repeated initials of the protagonists appear within a clear, geometrical arrangement based on the module of the square. The characters' initials are juxtaposed with motifs symbolic of them, namely the crown of King Solomon and the caduceus of Marchołt. These form a decorative border surrounding the central section of the front cover, featuring the title. This publication was intended for wealthy bibliophiles.

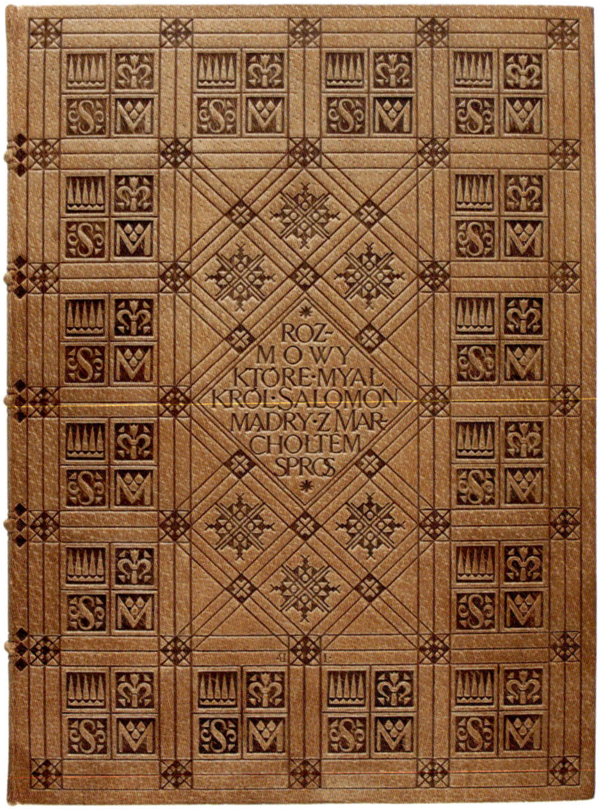

with batik technique around the year 1921. This was used to decorate paper or fabric endpapers, as well as whole bindings, particularly for small books of poetry. The technique yielded excellent results as batik enabled precise harmonisation of the endpapers' design with the whole binding. Throughout its existence, Jahoda's workshop produced exquisitely executed bindings made from prime-quality materials with no technical imperfections. Presented at exhibitions both at home and abroad, they were highly rated and won top awards (including a Diploma at the Exposition Universelle in Paris in 1900, the Great Gold Medal at the *Frühlings Ausstellung* in Vienna in 1907, and the Gold Medal at the *Internationale Ausstellung für Buchgewerbe und Graphik* in Leipzig in 1914).[15]

This overview has sought to outline the achievements of Polish material culture in the field of fine bookbinding and bibliophilism in the years around 1900, which in artistic terms emulated production in other European centres. It would be difficult to overstate the activities of Lenart and Jahoda, both of whom exerted enormous influence on bookbinding in Poland after it regained independence in 1918. Both of them trained many skilful craftsmen and left behind numerous remarkable works. Lenart's legacy also includes theoretical works on the 'book beautiful' – particularly *Konserwacja książki zabytkowej i jej oprawy* (*Conservation of Historic Books and their Bindings*, 1926) and *Piękna książka jako zespół czynników materialnych* (*The Book Beautiful as a Set of Physical Constituents*, 1928).

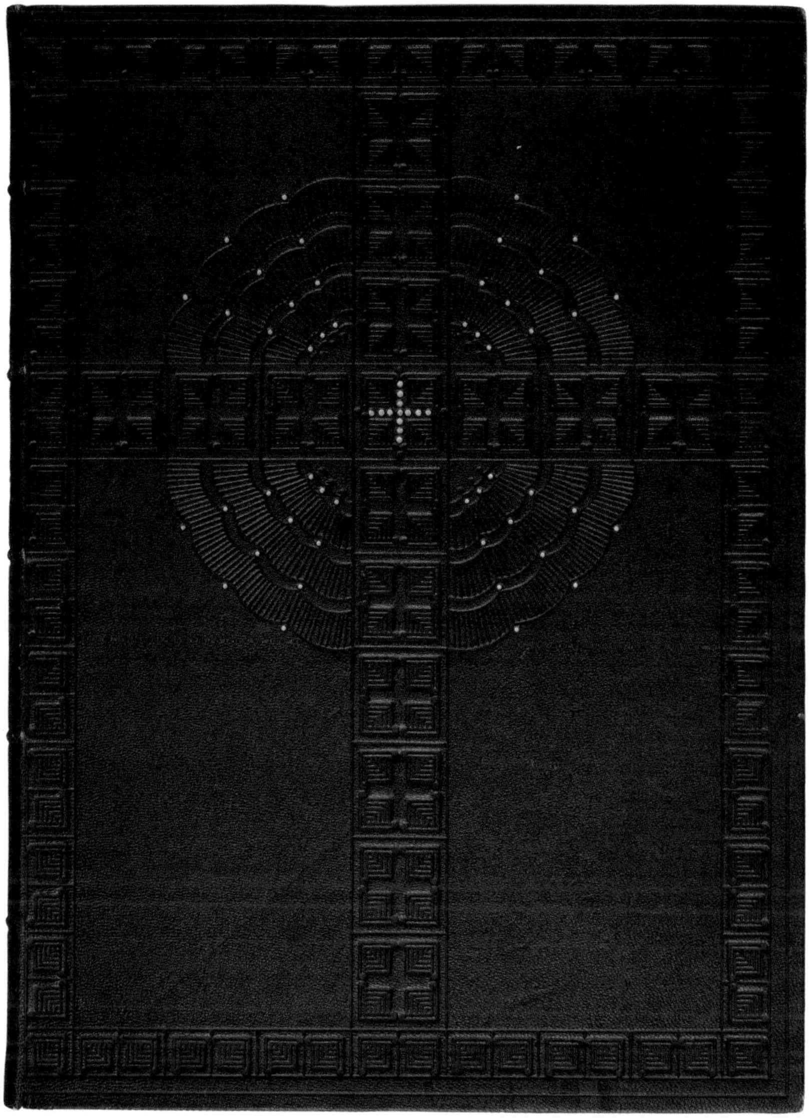

16.2 ↑

Missae pro defunctis ad commodiorem ecclesiarum usum ex Missali romano desumptae . . .

Publication address: Ratyzbona, Rzym, Neo Eboraci & Cincinnati, 1911; printer: Friderici Pustet
Binding: the journeyman Józef Lachowski, a participant in the bookbinding course at the Museum of Technology and Industry in Kraków under the supervision of Bonawentura Lenart, Kraków, 1911
Cardboard, goat's leather, blind- and silver-stamped
36 × 26 cm
National Museum in Kraków, MNK IV-MO-252
(from the Museum of Technology and Industry, 1950)

The decoration of the cover, executed by means of rhythmically applied hand tools, in the form of a short line, curve and dot, is an excellent example of the principles promulgated by Lenart. The basic element, from which the composition is composed, consists of lines arranged in the form of a square. The border is made up of individual squares, while four squares placed together comprise the motif which, repeated 16 times, forms the basic decoration in the shape of a Latin cross filling the entire surface of the cover. Its rays are composed of straight lines, curves and dots. A few silver-punched points combining into a Greek cross are situated within the crossing of the arms of the Latin cross, together with undulating lines of rays. A very refined effect of light and shade has been achieved by the use of extremely simple means, undoubtedly inspired by the bindings of Douglas Cockerell.

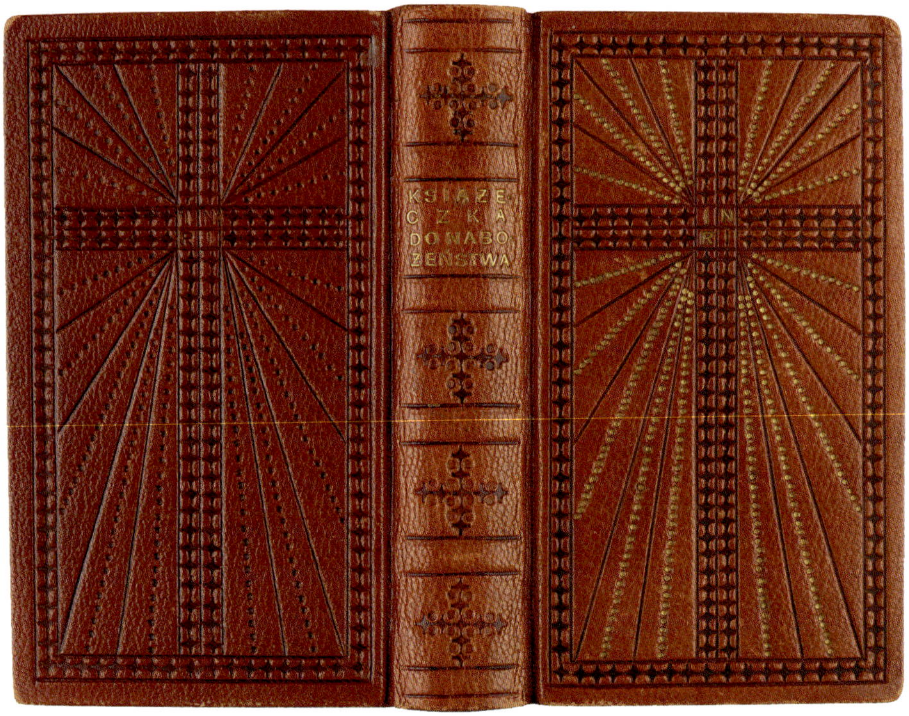

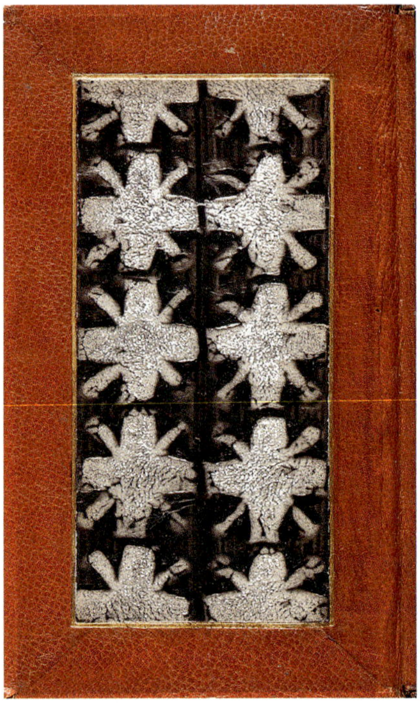

16.3 ↑

Adam Morawski, *Książeczka kieszonkowa do nabożeństwa dla wszystkich stanów oraz rady i rozmyślania ułożył* Adam Morawski, *'Ora et Labora' (A Pocket Missal for All Conditions, Together With Advice and Reflections, Arranged by Adam Morawski, 'Ora et Labora')*

Publication address: Geberthner i Wolff; printer: Druk W.L. Anczyca i Spółki, Kraków
Binding: bookbinding course at the Museum of Technology and Industry in Kraków under the supervision of Bonawentura Lenart, 1911
Cardboard, Morocco leather, blind- and gold-stamped, endpapers in stamped paper 11.3 × 7.2 cm
National Museum in Kraków, MNK IV-MO-267
(from the Museum of Technology and Industry, 1950)

The front cover of the prayer book is decorated with a border of blind-stamped stripes in the shape of an arch, enclosing a Latin cross formed from doubled stripes. The gold-stamped acronym 'INRI' is placed at the intersection of the arms of the cross, the background filled with a sunburst composed of blind-stamped straight lines, alternating with lines formed from gold-stamped points. The decoration of this binding shares the same compositional scheme applied to the binding of the *Missale Romanum* (fig.16.5), but with punches of a different cut, and within a smaller format, achieving a different visual effect.

The endpapers of the book were made from patterned paper, of which the half that is stuck to the inner side of the cover is surrounded by a leather frame. The paper was probably made during the endpapers-making course organised by the Museum. Its participants learned how to make marbled papers using starch paste and carrageenan, the latter enabling the effect of various colours spreading across the surface of the paper without mixing with one another. Here a simple, geometrical design has been achieved on natural-coloured paper covered with black starch-paste paint by means of displacing the paint with a stamp or roller using a hand-cut ornament. Lenart paid great attention to endpapers, which he regarded as an integral part of the complete binding. Papers produced by him personally, usually composed within a geometrical, chessboard arrangement, are characterised by much more complex lettering and figurative motifs, making a direct reference to the content of the bound book.

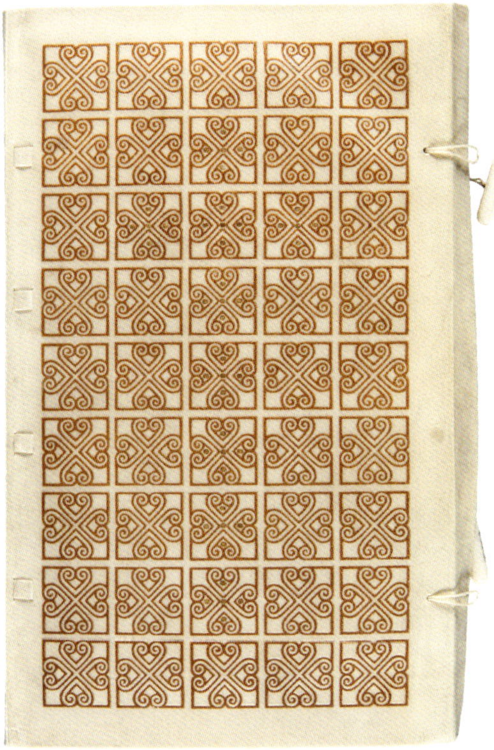

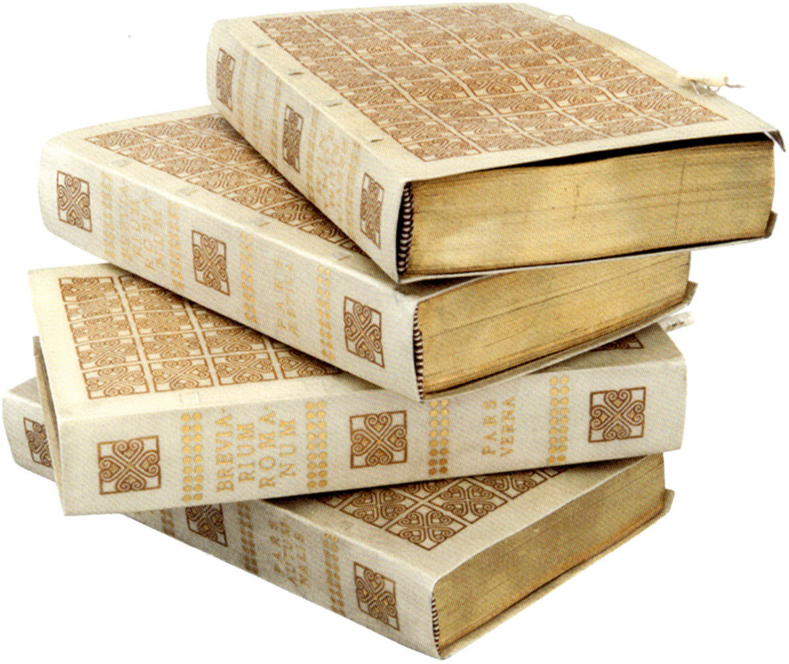

16.4 ↑

Breviarum Romanum ex decreto SS. Concilii Tridentini restitutum . . ., vol.1

Publication address: Ratyzbona, Rzym, Neo Eboraci & Cincinnati, 1911;
printer: Friderici Pustet
Binding: bookbinding course at the Museum of Technology and Industry in Kraków under the supervision of Bonawentura Lenart, 1911
Parchment, machine-stamped, gold-stamped, ivory
18.6 × 10.8 cm
National Museum in Kraków, MNK IV-MO-250/1
(from the Museum of Technology and Industry, 1950)

This was the first of four volumes of the *Breviarum Romanum*, all in identical parchment bindings. The covers are decorated with a dense chessboard arrangement featuring concentrically arranged machine-stamped heart motifs placed within a square. It was therefore possible to recreate the same decoration on successive volumes. This very elegant and aesthetically tasteful binding has been achieved by means of the contrast between the white parchment and a simple geometrical brown ornament, and glittering gold-stamped dots arranged in the form of a cross, together with the gilding of the page-edges and the introduction of clasps upon ivory pegs.

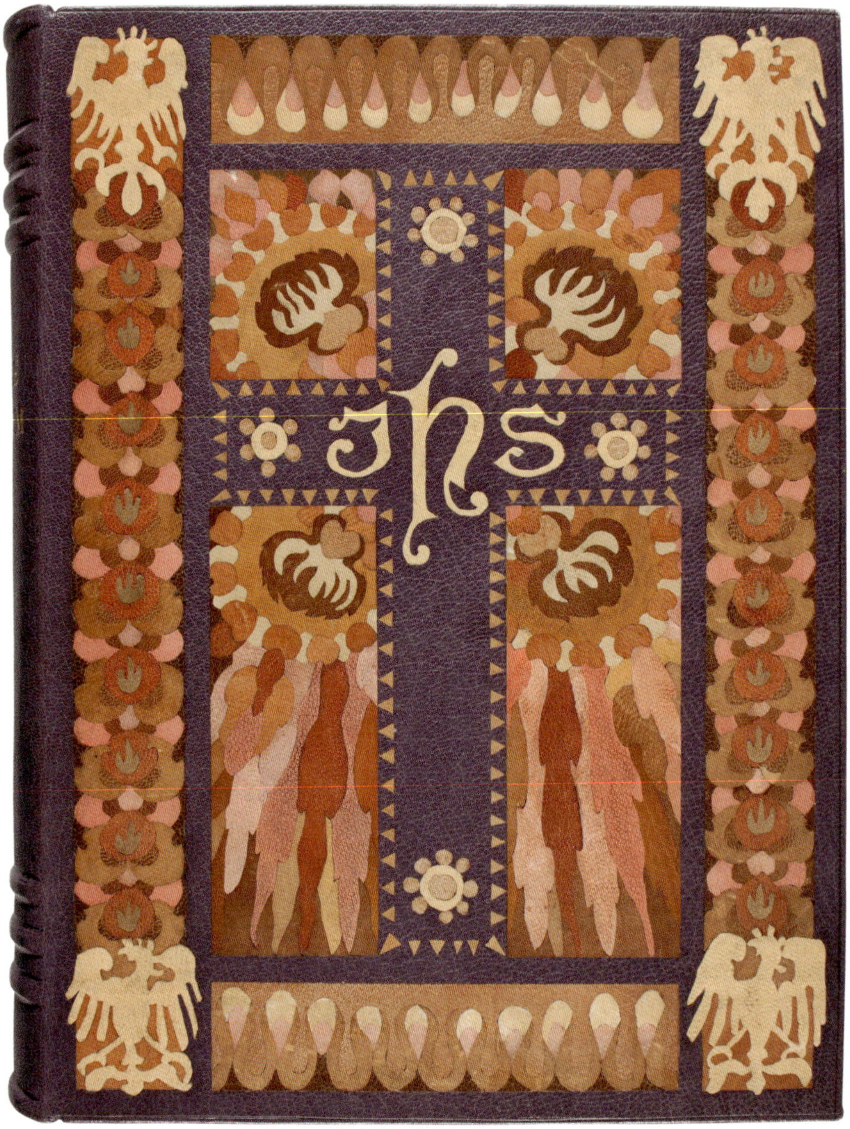

16.5 ↑

Missale Romanum ex decreto SS. Concilii Tridentini restitutum . . .

Publication address: Romae; Tornari; Sumptibus et Typis Societ. S. Joannis Evang. – Desclée et Soc., S. Sedis Apostolicae et S. Rituum Congr. Typograph, 1911
Binding: designed by Henryk Uziembło, executed by Gustaw Baer in the Bookbinding Workshop of Robert Jahoda, Kraków, 1912
Cardboard, goat's skin, dyed, leather intarsia
34 × 25 cm
National Museum in Kraków, MNK IV-MO-308
(from the Museum of Technology and Industry, 1950)

The painterly effect of the binding has been achieved by cutting out ornamental motifs from polychrome-dyed leathers and inserting them into openings in the leather background. The sole figurative elements are images of the White Eagle (the Polish national emblem), conveying a patriotic undertone. The bookbinding was produced especially for an exhibition of ecclesiastical art in Vienna in 1912. Thanks to an original design and flawless technical execution, this binding attracted widespread attention amongst visitors. As an unfortunate consequence, this work (along with other works produced by Jahoda's workshop) has at times been erroneously used by scholars as an illustration of the achievements of Austrian bookbinding.[15]

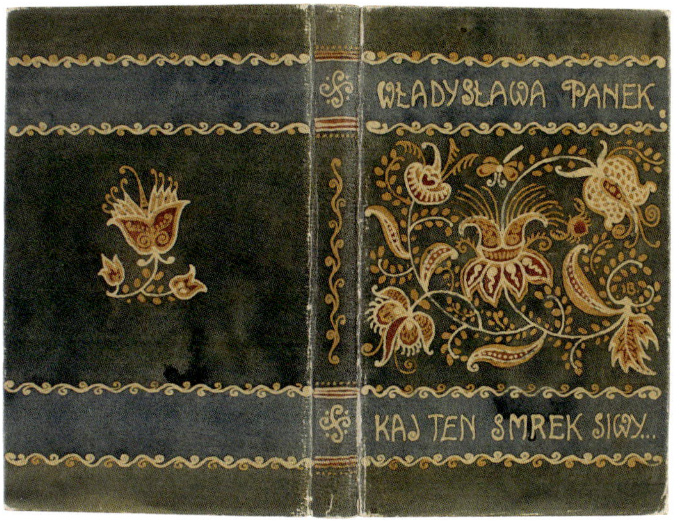

16.7 ←

Design for a binding for an edition of the story by Władysława Panek, 'Kaj ten smrek siwy . . .' ('When this grey spruce . . .')

Irena Bojarska, Kraków, 1921
Cardboad, bookbinding cloth, paper, batik
20.7 × 12.7 (27) cm
National Museum in Kraków, MNK IV-MO-335
(from the Museum of Technology and Industry, 1950)

The cardboard binding was first covered in fabric, onto which paper was pasted, creating the effect of a lightly tooled surface. The decoration is executed in the batik technique, featuring a composition with stripes. The upper and lower stripes contain the name of the author and the title of the work, while the broader central stripe is filled with stylised floral motifs showing the influence of folk art, displaying parallels with the batik designs executed on wood and fabric at the Antoni Buszek batik workshops at the Museum of Technology and Industry (see Chapter 9). The colour scheme of the binding, featuring brown, green and blue, with slight accents of red, has faded. Batik was first used in the binding of books by the Dutch binder Johannes Aarnout Loebèr, and in Poland by Robert Jahoda, who commissioned the present work.

16.6 →

Visitors' Book of the Museum of Technology and Industry, 1914

Workshops of the Museum of Technology and Industry, Kraków
Cardboard, ribbed silk, flat and satin embroidery using cotton thread, endpapers of printed patterned paper
20 × 18 cm
National Museum in Kraków, MNK IV-V-501 (from the Museum of Technology and Industry, 1950)

The historic visitors' book presented here is an unlined notebook, partially filled with memorial inscriptions by guests visiting the Museum. The front cover of the binding is adorned with an embroidered floral ornament depicting a stylised branch of a flower, displaying folk art influence. It echoes the aesthetic of batik works produced at the Buszek workshops. It can be assumed that the volume was produced at the Museum. As the first inscription in the volume dates from 1921, and the date '1914' appears at the bottom of the composition, it appears that the volume had originally had a different purpose. Many more examples of bindings using this type of stylised embroidered decoration must have been made during the Young Poland era and the interwar period, but this subject requires further research.

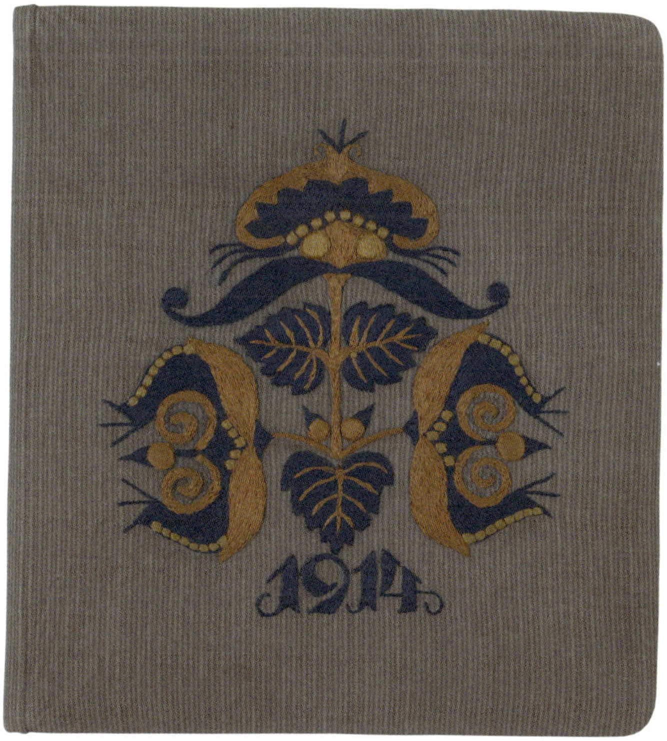

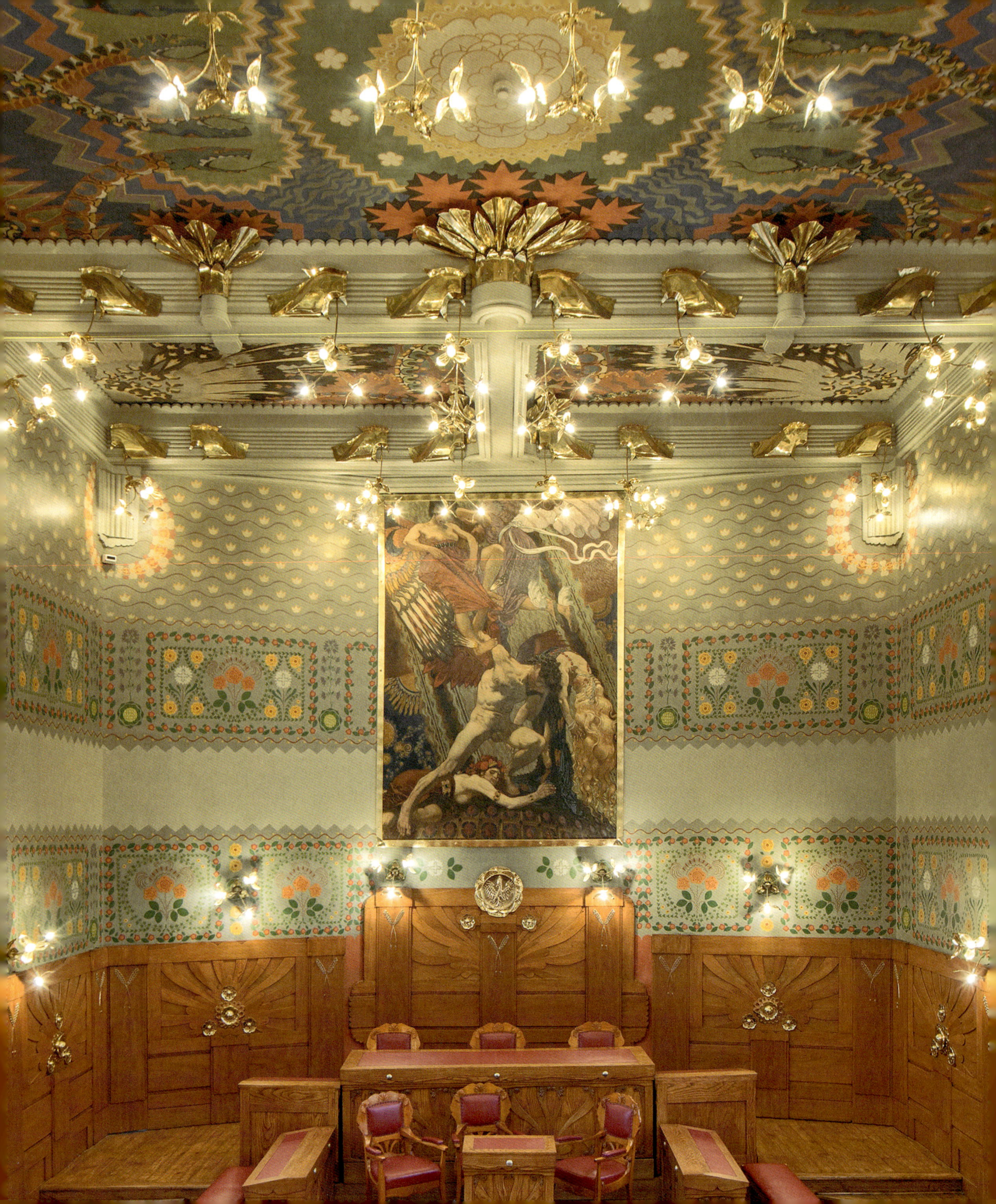

17

Painting

Piotr Kopszak

Ever since the beginning of the partitions of Poland there has been the need to use the visual arts as carriers of patriotic values. It was the success of Jan Matejko's historical paintings that confirmed the key importance of Polish art as a vehicle for affirming and cultivating the Polish national identity. Allegories of suffering Polonia that had become prevalent in popular imagery immediately after the loss of independence in 1795 reappeared a century later in works by Young Poland painters such as Jacek Malczewski (figs 17.1 and 17.7) and Stanisław Wyspiański (fig.0.3). Artists continued to draw on national history as important subject matter, although overt references to Polish history were minimised in favour of myth and allegory, which was the case in Leon Wyczółkowski's pictures such as the *Druid Stones* (1894).[1] His *Giewont* (1898, fig.17.4) refers to the legend of the Sleeping Knights, who will one day wake up to liberate Poland.

Young Poland painting provides a useful lens through which to view the key preoccupations of the movement. Subject matter revolved around metaphors of the dormant nation, spirituality and religion, history and the celebration of nature. The art of the psychological portrait was at its height then. French Symbolism influenced intimist images of people in interiors. Folk subjects, present in Polish art since the end of 18th century, found their avid interpreters in artists often working in artistic colonies, such as Bronowice near Kraków.

Young Poland visual arts were characterised by immense variety in stylistic terms. The 'Sztuka' ['Art'] Society of Polish Artists (see Editors' Introduction), which advocated the individuality of the artist rather than any artistic claims, brought together exponents of different art tendencies, including Impressionism, Symbolism and Expressionism. As Jan Cavanaugh argues, one of the defining qualities (and paradoxes) of Young Poland art was that it was both culturally autonomous from the rest of Europe and simultaneously cosmopolitan.[2]

Artists in Poland were becoming familiar with the Pre-Raphaelites and the British Arts and Crafts Movement (see Chapter 1), disseminated in art journals and books by Polish authors, as well as translations of John Ruskin, William Morris and Walter Pater (1839–1894). Perhaps the earliest mention of

17.0 (p.218)
Józef Mehoffer
Conference Room in the Chamber of Commerce and Industry in Kraków, 1906
Interior decoration scheme featuring the painting *Taming of Elements* mirrors the spatial arrangement of vernacular wooden churches. The ornamentation of murals derives from peasants' wooden chests.

the Pre-Raphaelites appeared in 1877 in the Warsaw magazine *Echo literackie i artystyczne*.[3] Its author paid special attention to the recently opened Grosvenor Gallery in London and paintings by Edward Burne-Jones.[4]

By the end of the 19th century, academic ideals were giving way to modern sentiments, among them the growing appreciation of the applied arts. Józef Mehoffer wrote about the role of painting in interior decoration in his essay 'Uwagi o sztuce i jej stosunku do natury' ('Remarks on art and its relationship to nature'):[5]

> A picture is a gem, priceless and modest at the same time, the artist is an artisan in the most noble sense of the word, because he creates a thing, an object of high value. The picture, even though it represents some content and artistic value, does not cease to be a thing having its own physicality made up of canvas, paints and the frame. . . . The most beautiful impact a painting can have would be its close link with a person, who understands it, feels its beauty, having bought it at the price of sacrifice and venerating it. Such a painting, placed in the best, most advantageous place in the drawing room filled with expensive furniture will dominate as a richest jewel, adorned as it deserves.[6]

The subject of recent history predominated in Malczewski's proto-surrealist paintings, often full of allusions to poetry of the Polish Romantic bard Juliusz Słowacki. They adorned the homes of the Kraków intelligentsia. Malczewski was influenced by Pre-Raphaelite painting, especially by Burne-Jones, as was his younger follower, the Czech artist Vlastimil Hofmann (1881–1970) (fig.17.9). Hofmann's eerie realism was combined with a veneration for Renaissance painting. Teodor Axentowicz, famous for the distinctive style of his female portraits, also settled in Kraków in 1897. He was one of the first artists to depict the Hutsuls in their colourful folk costumes.

Landscape was considered one of the most modern genres around 1900. Jan Stanisławski was another hugely popular Kraków-based artist (fig.17.3). His tiny paintings reducing landscape to a few brushstrokes are important evidence of proto-abstract tendencies and the influence of Symbolist ideas of the correspondence between music and painting. In accordance with the ideas of Ruskin and Morris, Stanisławski devoted much effort to documenting places threatened by destruction – such as village huts with straw roofs and monuments of historical importance. Another landscape painter, Ferdynand Ruszczyc (1870–1936), a close friend of Stanisławski, was educated at the St Peterburg Academy of Fine Arts. In his diary he quotes William Morris.[7] The School of Fine Arts in Warsaw, founded in 1905, where Ruszczyc taught landscape painting, was heavily influenced by the Arts and Crafts Movement.[8] Ruszczyc was also very successful as a book designer, and on this account he was compared to Morris.[9] He was also an active member of the 'Sztuka' society. One of his most successful paintings was *Nec Mergitur* (1904–5, fig.17.6). The writer and socialist Bolesław Limanowski compared it to stained glass made by Wyspiański (see Chapters 2, 3 and 4). The idea that Ruszczyc tried to obtain the effect of stained glass in painting is further supported by the popularity of stained glass as an iconographic motif in Young Poland painting.[10]

Among the most popular paintings decorating Kraków homes were portraits of children by Wyspiański. The artist did not consider them to be an important part of his output; he did them quickly, sometimes making replicas, but this does not change the fact that they rate among the best of his portraits.[11] Although portraits of children had been a popular genre since the 18th century,[12] unlike Axentowicz's female portraits or Stanisławski's landscapes, Wyspiański's depictions of children can hardly be considered as purely decorative objects. Wyspiański imbued his children with an aura of sadness and melancholy (see fig.2.5), also found in children's portraits by Olga Boznańska (1865–1940), whose talent he publicly praised.

The art critic and artist Stanisław Witkiewicz never abandoned his realist style, but his own paintings were the best complement to his Zakopane Style interiors (see Chapter 6). Their distinctive decorative frames, featuring mountain flora and Zakopane Style ornamentation, were an integral part of the paintings. The white chamber in the House Under the Firs, built for Jan Gwalbert Pawlikowski and his family, can be considered as one of the best-preserved and most coherent Polish Arts and Crafts interiors. The drawing room is furnished with chairs and table designed by Witkiewicz and Wojciech Brzega. The centrepiece is however the painting *Sheep in the Mist* (1899–1900) by Witkiewicz, displayed prominently above the sofa. It fits the interior so well, one could think that it had been painted for that purpose, but in fact it was chosen by Pawlikowski.[13] Its frame is decorated with folk ornament. Another painting, *Winter Landscape from Tatra Mountains* (after 1890),[14] features a similar, meticulously carved frame with a motif of bracken.

Paintings played a significant role in one of the best-known interiors designed by Stanisław Wyspiański – the apartment of Zofia and Tadeusz 'Boy' Żeleński (1904–5; see Chapter 11). Preserved photographs of the apartment show paintings in an evenly spaced-out grouping at eye level, almost as if they were hanging on display at one of the 'Sztuka' society exhibitions, which Wyspiański arranged. It seems Wyspiański did not go as far as Witkiewicz, designing special frames for the paintings destined for the apartment. Żeleński wrote that 'the furnishings did not include any paintings other than Wyspiański's own creations'.[15] However, there is no evidence that paintings were chosen by Wyspiański or painted especially for the purpose.

There is more than a hint of medievalism in the otherwise very modern arrangement of the Chamber of Commerce and Industry in Kraków by Mehoffer (1906; see fig.17.0). There is only one painting in the room – *Taming of Elements* – otherwise covered by intricate ornamental wall painting. A heroic male nude is depicted in a struggle against the personifications of the elements, Earth, Water, Air and Fire. Almost like an altarpiece, the painting takes centre stage, displayed above the table where the head of the assembly sat. It plays an important role in the decorative scheme of the building, its ornamental style perfectly fits the colourful wall paintings loosely inspired by folk motifs.

This kind of integration of painting with architecture was developed further in the Dłuski Sanatorium in Zakopane and the interior of the famous Kraków cafe Jama Michalika (1910; see Chapter 11; see fig.11.12), designed by Karol Frycz with important contributions by Henryk Uziembło (a stained-glass panel depicting Irena Solska as a female centaur), both of whom studied art in London. The Dłuski Sanatorium was set up by Kazimierz Dłuski and his wife Bronisława, sister of the physicist Marie Skłodowska-Curie (better known simply as Marie Curie), who financed the project by donating part of her Nobel Prize money. Dłuski Sanatorium attracted both the exponents and followers of the Zakopane Style as well as members of the Polish Applied Arts Society.[16] Among

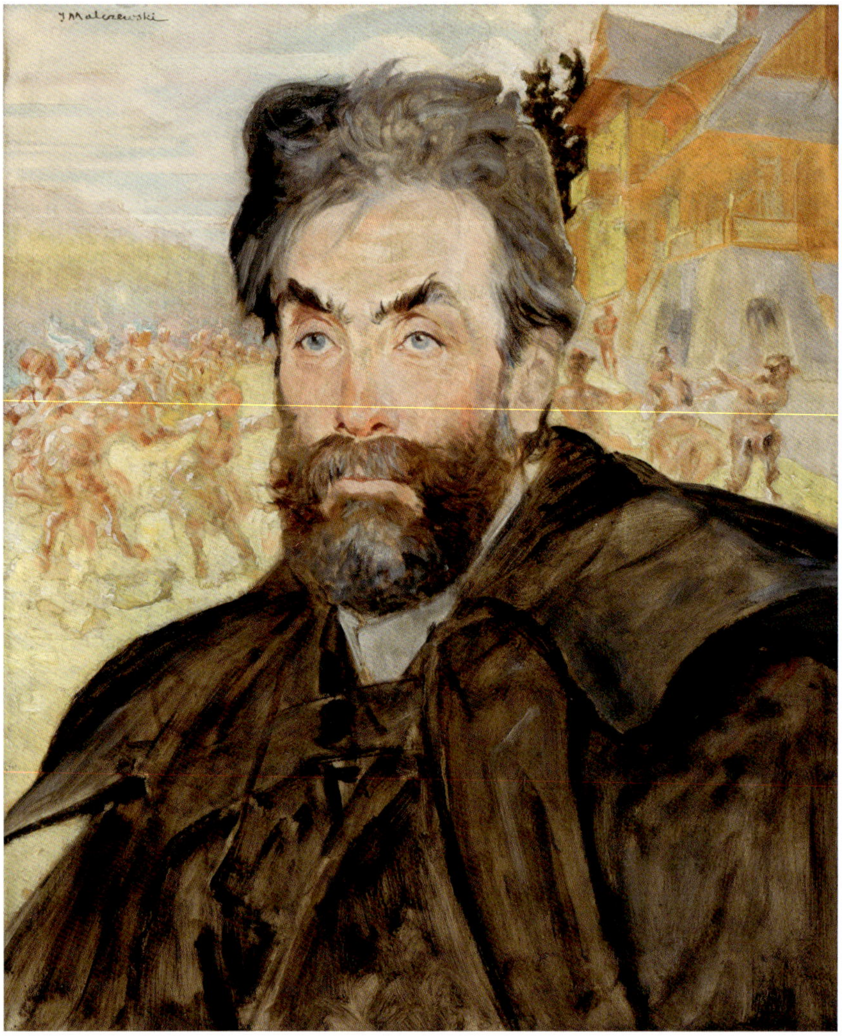

the most impressive elements of the decorative scheme were figurative wall friezes by one of the patients of the sanatorium, Jan Rembowski (in or before 1910).[17] Rembowski's paintings of Highlanders marching form an integral part of the salon (fig.17.5). They covered entire walls, forming a continuum with the painted wainscoting. An interesting effect was achieved by juxtaposing them with stained glass, showing the Spirit of the Faery of the Tatra Mountains and the motif of ducks in flight.[18] The iconography of the cycle could have been inspired by the play *Queen of the Tatra Mountains* (*Królowa Tatr*, 1904) by Adolf Walewski, as well as by one of the most popular works of Young Poland – the mystical novel *Nietota: Księga tajemna Tatr* (*Nietota: The Secret Book of the Tatra Mountains*, serialised in 1908–9 and published in full in 1910) by Tadeusz Miciński.[19] The cycle was open to patriotic interpretations, whilst also referencing regaining good health – an appropriate subject for a sanatorium. This *Gesamtkunstwerk* incorporated the view from the windows. Behind the Spirit of the Tatras one could see the mountains, including Giewont with its sleeping knight silhouette.[20]

By 1910 the ideas of the Arts and Crafts Movement had already become well adopted, so it was only natural to have a portrait painted by another advocate of the Pre-Raphaelites, Edward Okuń. The wife of the owner of Warsaw's most popular clothing store sat for one, posing against the backdrop of a medieval-style tapestry that could have been bought in London.[21]

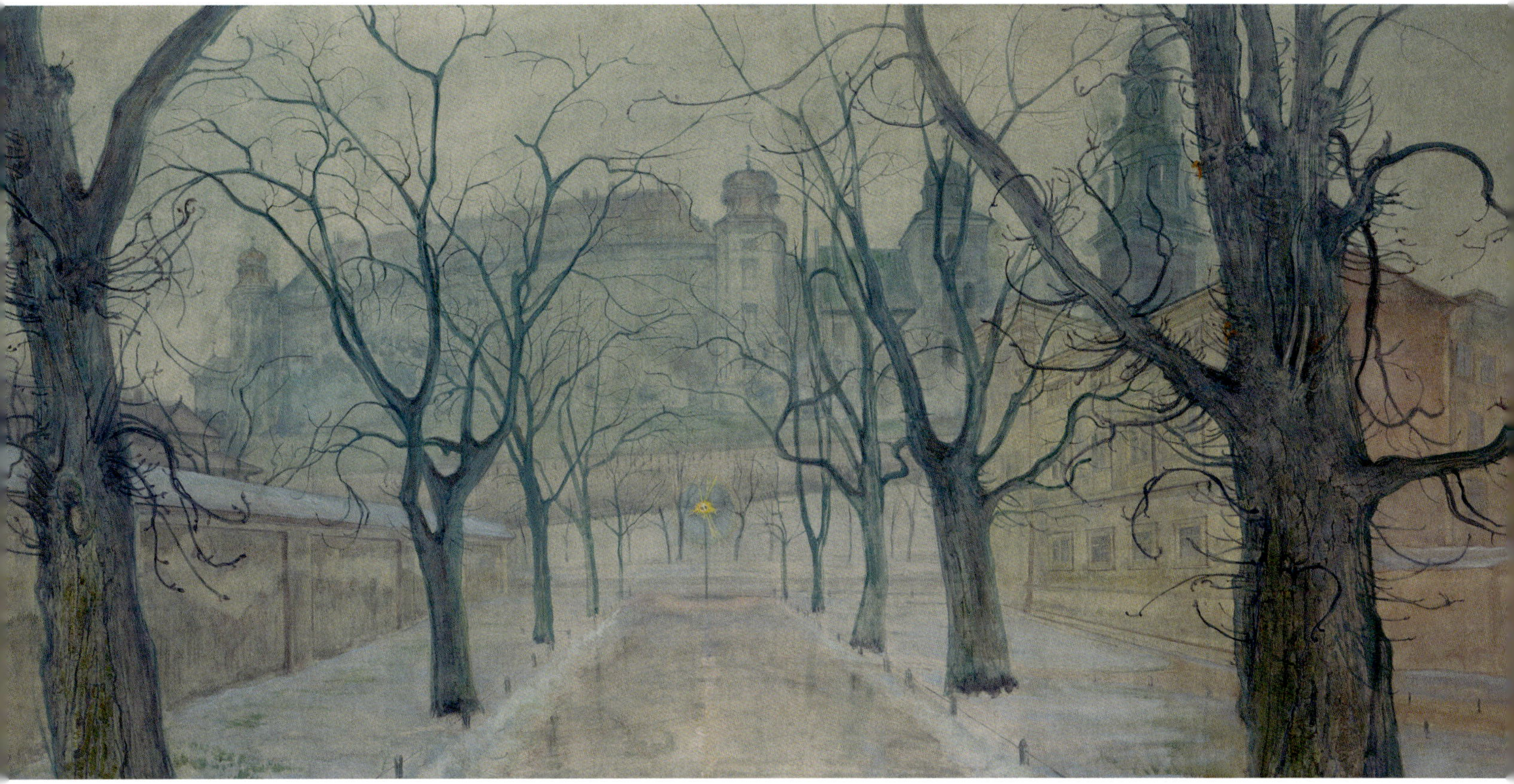

17.1 ←

Jacek Malczewski, *Portrait of Stanisław Witkiewicz*, c.1897

Oil on board
61 × 49 cm
National Museum in Kraków, MNK II-b-108

This is a portrait of Witkiewicz depicted in front of his masterpiece House Under the Firs in Zakopane (see Chapter 6). In the background, fauns and Highlanders can be seen dancing in a circle. In Malczewski's paintings, fauns often represented artists and members of the intelligentsia. Showing them dancing together with the Highlanders could be Malczewski's ironical interpretation of the idea of incorporating folk motifs into high art, proposed by Witkiewicz. Malczewski frequented the House Under the Firs. Another member of the circle recalled that the Pre-Raphaelites were often the subject of conversations. Educated in Munich, Witkiewicz belonged to a group of Polish artists who introduced Realism and early Symbolism (inspired by German *Stimmungsmalerei*, meaning 'mood painting') into Polish art, under the guidance of Adam Chmielowski (Saint Brother Albert).

17.2 ↑

Stanisław Wyspiański, *Morning at the Foot of Wawel Hill*, 1894

Oil on canvas
100 × 201 cm
National Museum in Kraków, MNK ND-7791

Wawel Hill, with Wawel Castle, which was the seat of Polish kings, and Wawel Cathedral, where they were crowned and buried, became a Pantheon for Poles (see Chapter 4). Once Austrian Army barracks, it became a (never-used) residence of the Emperor Franz Joseph. The Austrian Army left Wawel in 1904–11. The project for the reconstruction of Wawel Hill proposed by Stanisław Wyspiański incorporated a monumental sculpture by Wacław Szymanowski (1859–1930) consisting of 52 figures representing Polish kings, queens and important personages led by the personification of Fate. Wawel was often depicted by Polish artists. Wyspiański's unusual interpretation incorporates elements of Impressionism while giving the view strong symbolic meaning enhanced by the presence of a lonely lantern in the foreground, either coming on or still alight at the crack of dawn.

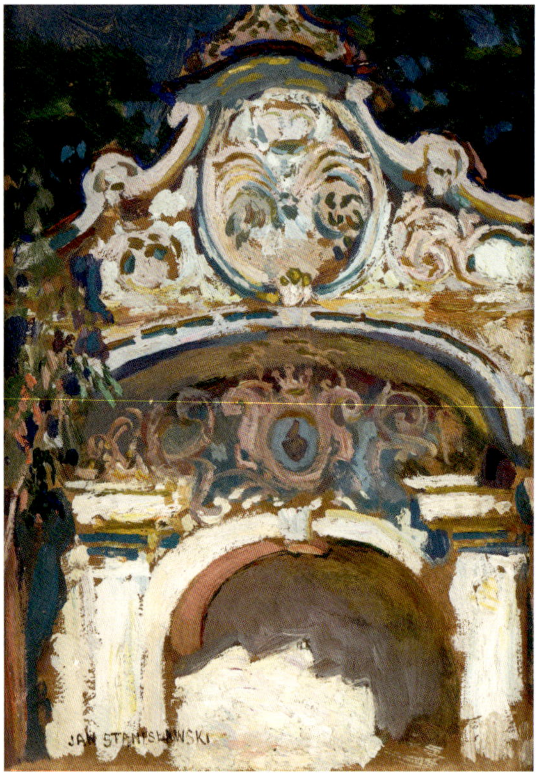

17.3 ←

Jan Stanisławski, *Vasa Gate in Kyiv*, 1903

Oil on cardboard
22 × 16 cm
National Museum in Kraków, MNK II-b-586

Stanisławski managed to create his own school of landscape painting. He was conscious of the changes to landscape and monuments brought about by modern civilisation and, in accordance with Ruskin's ideas, tried to preserve for posterity the memories of villages and cities bound to be destroyed. The gate depicted by Stanisławski fortunately survived. It was built in the 1740s when Kyiv (Kiev) was no longer part of the Polish-Lithuanian Commonwealth; it is now called the Zaborovsky Gate and is part of the walls surrounding the St Sophia Cathedral.[22]

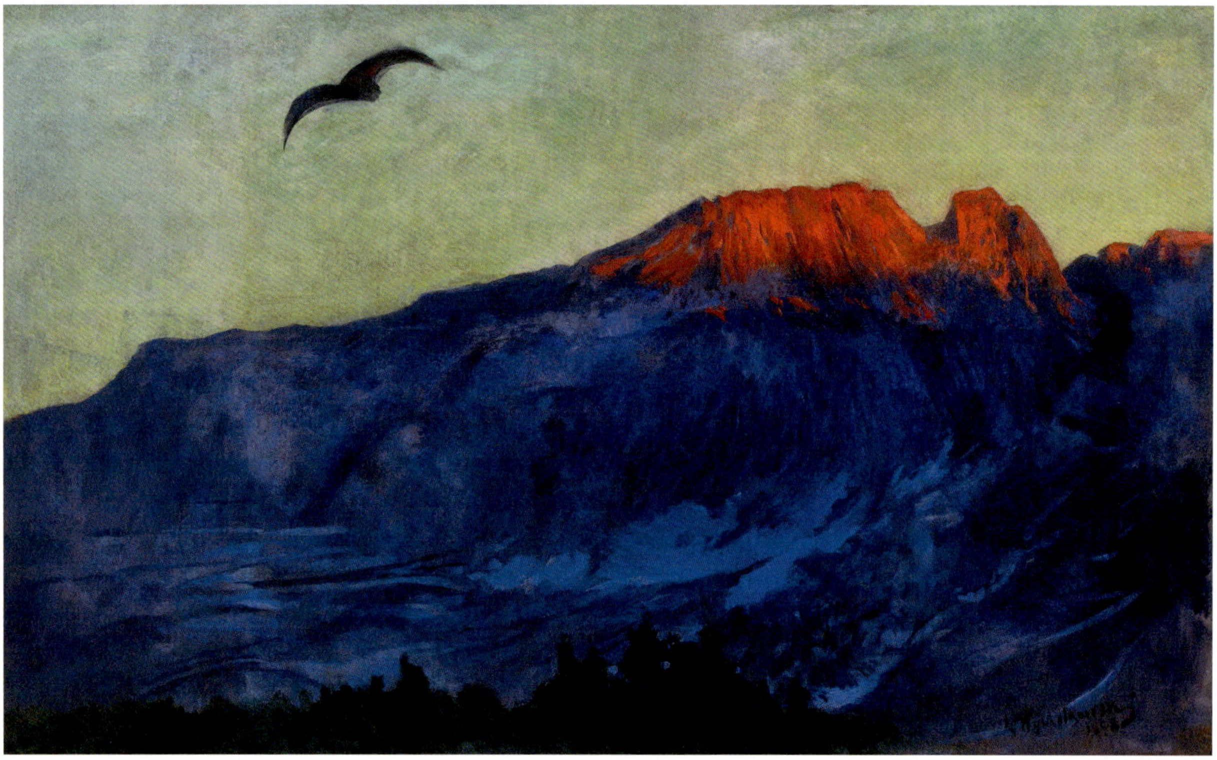

17.4 ↵

Leon Wyczółkowski, *Giewont*, 1898

Oil on canvas
101 × 159 cm
Private collection

Tadeusz Miciński wrote that Ararat and Fujiyama are symbols of national existence for the Armenians and Japanese.[23] Giewont played a similar role in Poland. Its silhouette, which looks like a sleeping man, gave rise to the legend of the sleeping knight, who would wake up one day to liberate Poland. Wyczółkowski often depicted Giewont in various techniques in his series *Tatra Legends*. The motif of a man turned into a mountain appeared four years earlier in his *Druid Stones*, based on James Macpherson's *Poems of Ossian*, a cycle of epic poems published from 1760 as translations of ancient Scottish folk tales.

17.5 ↓

Jan Rembowski, *Highlanders Marching* painting cycle for Dłuski Sanatorium, 1909–10

Oil on canvas
Central panel: 202 × 262 cm
National Museum in Kraków, MNK II-b-122

This is the central panel from a series of wall paintings which decorated the Theatre Room at the Dłuski Sanatorium. They collectively represented a group of Highlander men, women and children in traditional costumes marching at dawn with a characteristic expression of looking ahead – interpreted as a metaphor for Poland's march towards independence. As part of a frieze for a decorative scheme, the picture is a prime example of Young Poland's central integration of the fine and decorative arts. It is also a celebration of the Highlanders' strength of character and lifestyle, offering an insight into Rembowski's originality as a painter.

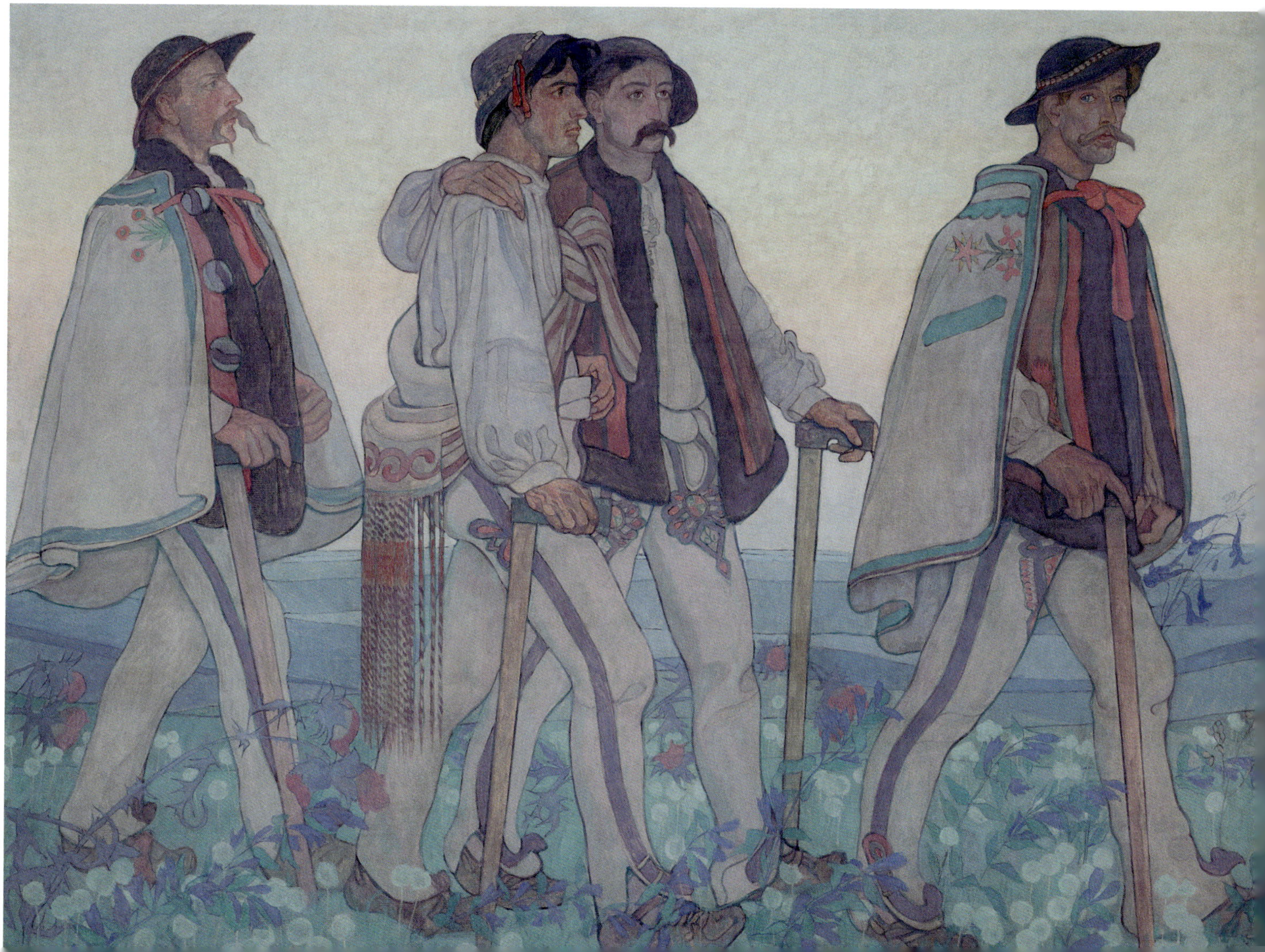

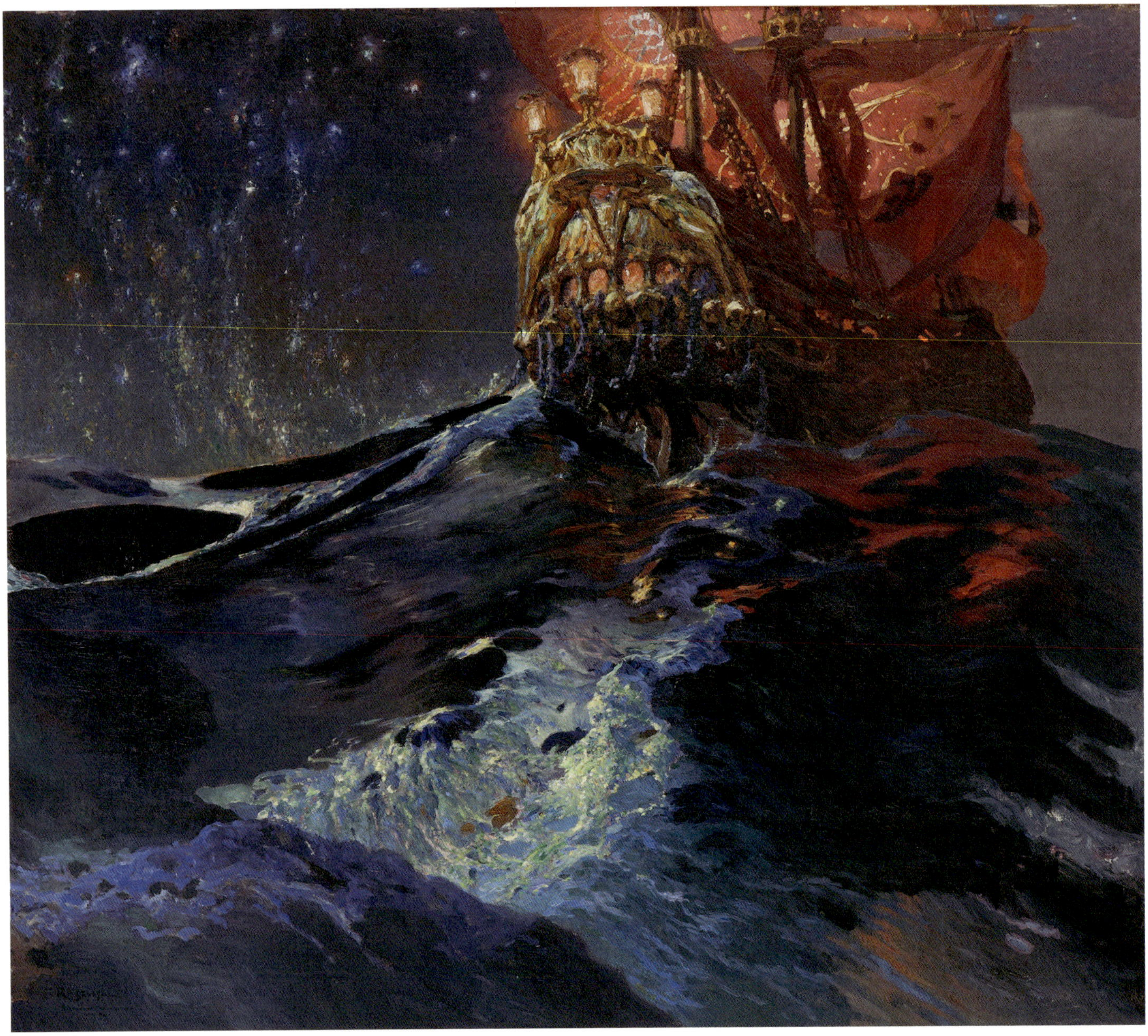

17.6 ↑

Ferdynand Ruszczyc, *Nec Mergitur*, 1904–5

Oil on canvas
203 × 219 cm
Lithuanian National Museum of Art, Vilnius, LDM T 2691

Originally the title was *Legenda żeglarska* (*Sailing Legend*). The ancient ship navigating turbulent waters was considered an apt representation of Poland withstanding the blows of fate, which led to its change in title to *Nec Mergitur*, a Latin expression meaning 'yet it does not sink'. Ruszczyc was acquainted with Morris's and Ruskin's ideas. He also worked as a designer. In 1911 he presented tableaux vivants based on Pre-Raphaelite paintings, which he titled *Sny o pięknie* (*Dreams about Beauty*).[24] Arts and Crafts ideas also inspired a series of paintings of an old manor house in Bohdanów, where respect for history was combined with a love of beautiful objects.

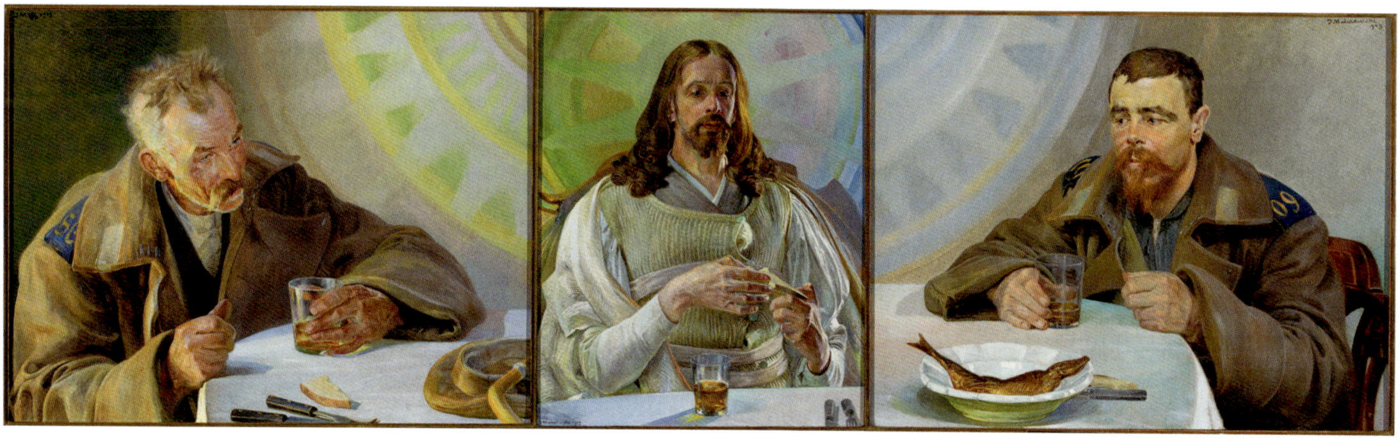

17.7 ↑

Jacek Malczewski, *Christ in Emmaus* (triptych), 1909

Oil on cardboard
Left part: 73 × 92 cm; middle part: 93 × 73 cm; right part: 73 × 92 cm
National Museum in Warsaw, MP 1909/1–3 MNW

Jadwiga Puciata-Pawłowska noted an affinity with the art of Edward Burne-Jones in Malczewski's *Poisoned Wells* cycle (begun in 1900, with five parts completed in 1905–6).[25] Malczewski probably knew the works by Burne-Jones in the collection of his patron, the art historian Karol Lanckoroński. Like Burne-Jones, Malczewski sought inspiration in the art of the Renaissance, and like Renaissance artists he depicted biblical personages in modern dress. Two disciples are dressed in heavy coats similar to those worn by exiles in Siberia. Glasses of tea and a herring also suggest this is where the meeting with Christ takes place. Malczewski was strongly influenced by the work of Juliusz Słowacki, especially *Anhelli*, a visionary quasi-biblical tale of exiles sent to Siberia after the uprising of 1830–31.

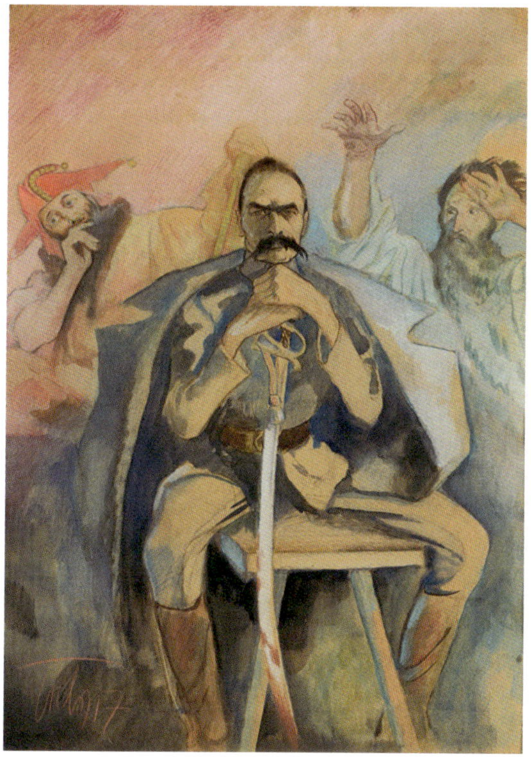

17.8 ←

Kazimierz Sichulski
Portrait of Józef Piłsudski with Wernyhora and Stańczyk, 1917

Watercolour, gouache, crayon, ink, pencil and pastel on cardboard
89 × 63 cm
Polish Army Museum

Just like Teodor Axentowicz and Fryderyk Pautsch, Kazimierz Sichulski was fascinated by the folk art of the Hutsul region. He studied at the Academy of Fine Arts in Kraków and became a follower of his teacher Stanisław Wyspiański. Sichulski created designs for stained-glass windows and monumental paintings and caricatures. He was invited to make caricatures of British Members of Parliament. When staying in Zakopane for medical examination, Sichulski drew Piłsudski between Stańczyk, the jester of King Sigismund I Jagiellon, shown as in the painting *The Prussian Homage* (1879–82) by Jan Matejko, and Wernyhora – the mythical Ukrainian prophet known from works of Juliusz Słowacki, shown in a pose taken from an 1862 painting by Matejko of the same character.

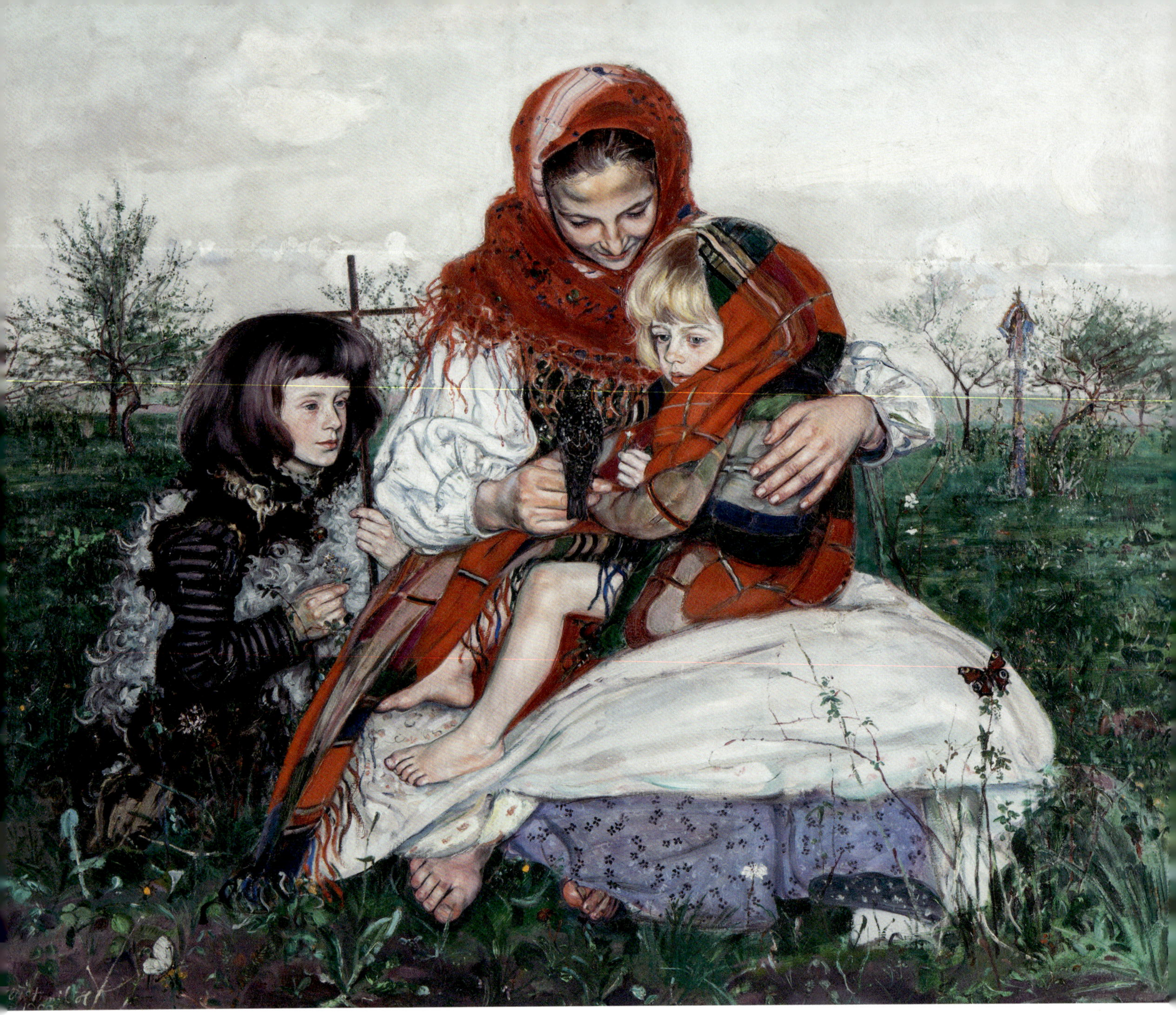

17.9 ↑

Vlastimil Hofmann
Madonna with a Starling, 1909

Oil on canvas
109 × 129 cm
Raczyński Foundation, at the National Museum in Poznań, MNP FR 25

Vlastimil Hofmann – like Jacek Malczewski, his teacher at the School of Fine Arts in Kraków – often used compositional and iconographical devices found in Renaissance paintings. He frequently included children and old people in his modern versions of the *sacra conversazione*. It is possible that Hofmann was not aware of the symbolism of the goldfinch in Renaissance paintings, which was a reference to Christ's Passion, and instead painted a starling, much more common in Poland. The Madonna is dressed in a folk costume, further underlining the artist's desire to make the meaning of the biblical scene more relatable to his contemporaries.

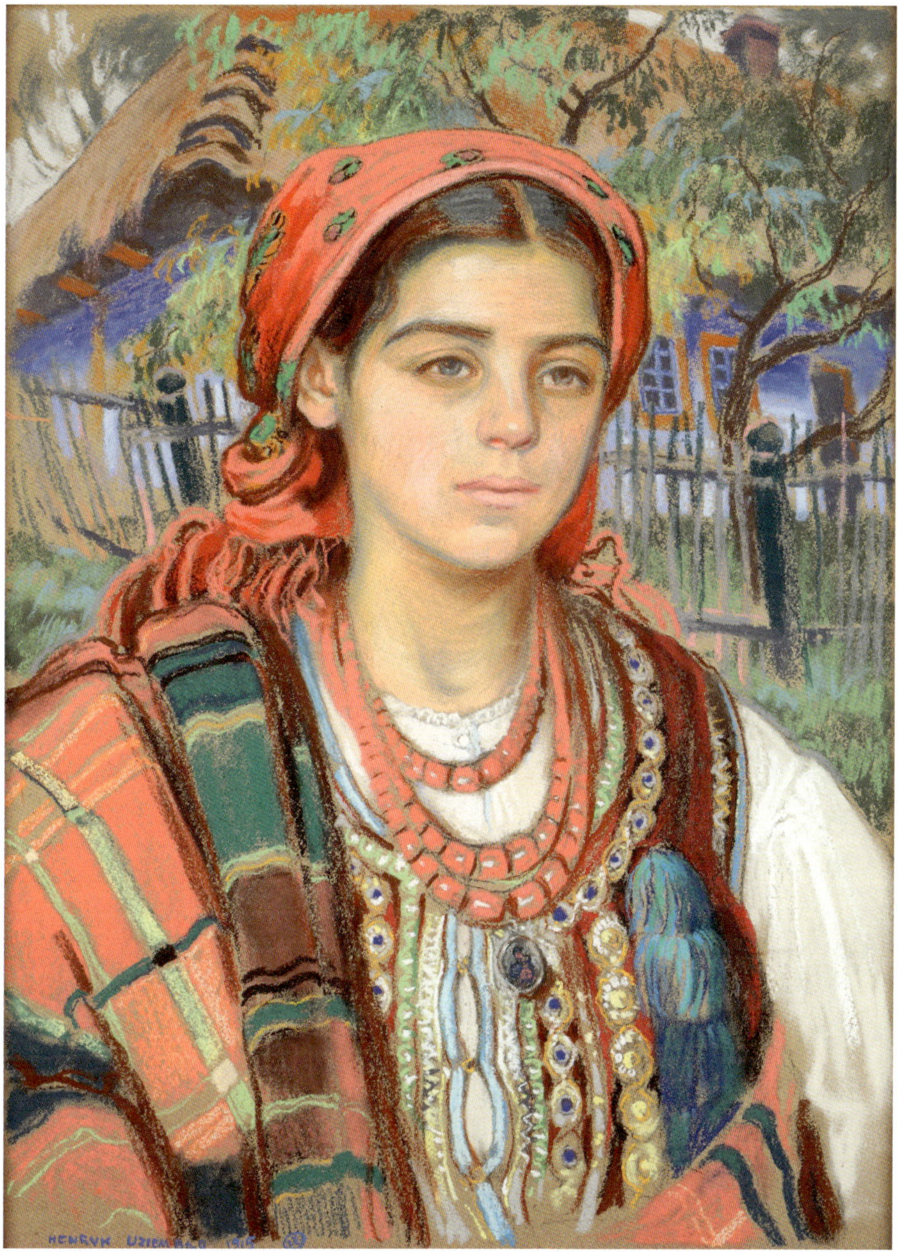

17.10 ↑
Henryk Uziembło
***A Peasant Girl in Traditional Krakovian Folk Costume from the Village of Bronowice near Kraków*, 1915**

Pastel on cardboard
70.5 × 51 cm
Museum of Kraków, Rydlówka Manor House Branch, MHK 2860/III

This image conveys the importance of the village of Bronowice as a physical hub as well as an emblem of idyllic country life and the unification of the divided nation by means of intermarriages between peasant girls and the middle classes and/or gentry. This was immortalised by Wyspiański in his most popular play, *The Wedding* (1901), bringing renown to the village. The picture is also an accomplished celebration of the peasant girl's beauty, and in that sense Uziembło invites comparisons with some of Dante Gabriel Rossetti's works such as *The Beloved* (1865–6).

Notes

Items listed in the Select Bibliography are referred to throughout these notes in the form 'Author/Editor Year' only, while items not listed there are given in full at first mention, then 'Author/Editor Year, op.cit.' thereafter.

Preface

1. This may have been at the suggestion of the brothers D.G and W.M Rossetti whose father had been forced into political exile in Britain for supporting Italian revolutionary nationalism. Kościuszko was the Polish army officer and statesman who gained fame for his leadership of the first national insurrection during the partitions.
2. Cavanaugh previously suggested that Wyspiański's Polonia is fainting whilst also hinting at the message of death and resurrection (Cavanaugh 2000, pp.188–9). A close study by Magdalena Laskowska suggests Polonia is shown dying, based on the verse from Wyspiański's dramatic narrative, *Królowa Polskiej Korony* (*Queen of the Polish Crown*): 'widzę jej twarz . . . zda się, że kona' ('I can see her face . . . it seems she is dying'), created as a literary commentary on the pictorial version of the subject (12 November 1893). Stanisław Wyspiański, *Pisma Pośmiertne, II: Wiersze – Fragmenty Dramatyczne – Uwagi*, Kraków: Wilhelm Feldman, 1910, p.83.
3. Tadeusz 'Boy' Żeleński, 'Historia pewnych mebli', *Kurier Poranny, niedzielny dodatek ilustrowany*, no.322 (20 November 1927), p.4, quoted in Cavanaugh 2000, p.184.

Editors' Introduction

1. Livingstone and Parry (eds) 2005, p.10.
2. ibid.
3. ibid., p.12.
4. ibid., p.12.
5. Stanisław Wyspiański, in *Czas*, 3 March 1905 (evening edition), p.2. Wyspiański's manuscript of this poem was dated 2 March 1905 and was originally owned by Tadeusz 'Boy' Żeleński. The Editors extend special thanks to Barbara Bogoczek and Tony Howard for their translation.
6. Cavanaugh 2000, pp.1–2.
7. See Cavanaugh 2000.
8. A similar point about the coexistence of national and international tendencies in European Art Nouveau was made in Howard 1996.
9. Crowley 1992.
10. Andrzej Szczerski, *Wzorce tożsamości: recepcja sztuki brytyjskiej w Europie Środkowej około roku 1900*, Kraków: Towarzystwo Autorów i Wydawców Prac Naukowych Universitas, 2002.
11. Szczerski 2015.
12. Barucka 2010; Barucka 2020; Supińska-Polit 2004.
13. Szczerski 2005.
14. Blakesley 2006, pp.137–58. Other significant publications in Polish are the pioneering study by Irena Huml – Huml 1978 – and Krzysztofowicz-Kozakowska 2003. See also: Purchla (ed.) 2001; Brockington 2009; Clegg 2006.
15. Artur Górski, 'Młoda Polska', *Życie: Tygodnik Ilustrowany Literacki, Artystyczny, Naukowy i Społeczny*, 1898, no.15 (9 April), p.170; no.16 (16 April), pp.181–2; no.18 (30 April), p.206; no.19 (7 May), pp.217–18; no.24 (18 June), pp.278–9; no.25 (25 June), p.299.

Chapter 1

1. This chapter contains excerpts from my monograph, *Views of Albion: The Reception of British Art and Design in Central Europe, 1890–1918*, Oxford: Peter Lang, 2015 (Szczerski 2015) and includes results of new research after the book's publication.
2. Wyspiański 1998, p.59.
3. Quoted in Krajewska 1972, p.85.
4. Ignacy Matuszewski, *Słowacki i nowa sztuka (modernizm)*, Kraków: Gebethner i Wolff, 1902, p.86.
5. Helena d'Abancourt, 'Od tłomacza', preface to Robert de La Sizeranne, *Malarstwo współczesne Anglii*, Kraków: Spółka Wydawnicza Polska, 1901, pp.3–4. Subsequent quotations ibid.
6. Zenon Przesmycki, *Pisma zebrane*, vol.A, part II, Warsaw: Nakład Jakóba Mortkowicza, 1911, pp.821–2.
7. Beiersdorf 1991.
8. Adrian Baraniecki, 'Muzeum Techniczno-Przemysłowe w Krakowie', memorandum, *c.*1864, unpaginated, quoted in Piotr Hapanowicz, 'Adrian Baraniecki: prekursor polskiego muzealnictwa przemysłowego', *Muzealnictwo*, vol.57 (2016), p.98.
9. See Tondos 2004.
10. Stanisław Witkiewicz, *Dziwny człowiek*, Lviv: Towarzystwo Wydawnicze, 1903, p.95.
11. Antoni Chołoniewski, 'Panna Sienkiewiczówna i Ruskin', *Biesiada Literacka*, vol.52, no.29 (1901), p.57.
12. Stanisław Eljasz-Radzikowski, *Styl zakopiański*, Kraków and Lviv: Towarzystwo Wydawnicze w Lwowie, 1901, p.29.
13. Stanisław Witkiewicz, *Na przełęczy*, Lviv: Towarzystwo Wydawnicze, 1906, p.87.
14. Biriulow 1996, p.49.
15. Kazimierz Mokłowski, *Sztuka ludowa w Polsce*, Lviv: H. Altenberg, 1903, p.324.
16. Jerzy Warchałowski, untitled (editorial), *Wydawnictwo Towarzystwa Polskiej Sztuki Stosowanej: materiały*, no.1 (1902), pp.2–3.
17. Tadeusz Dobrowolski, *Sztuka Młodej Polski*, Warsaw: Państwowe Wydawnictwo Naukowe, 1963, p.379.
18. Crowley 1992, p.31.
19. Wojciech Jastrzębowski, 'Geneza, program i wyniki działalności "Warsztatów Krakowskich" i "Ładu"', *Polska Sztuka Ludowa*, vol.VI, no.1 (1952), pp.13–22.
20. ibid.
21. ibid., p.17.

Chapter 2

1. I would like to thank Linda Parry and Magdalena Laskowska for their ongoing mentorship and help with this chapter, including generously sharing information and archival materials. Many thanks also to Anna Wende-Surmiak, Alison Smith, Anna Kozak, Zbigniew Moździerz, Helena Pitoń, Anna Rudzińska, Rowan Bain, Roisin Inglesby, Tony Howard, and Anna and Piotr Dudkiewicz.
2. J.W. Mackail, *The Life of William Morris*, vol.1, London, New York and Bombay: Longmans, Green & Co., 1901, p.224.
3. For more information on the Probus Barczewski Endowment Prize see Jan Hulewicz, *Akademia Umiejętności w Krakowie 1873–1918: zarys dziejów*, Wrocław and Warsaw: Zakład Narodowy im. Ossolińskich, Wydawnictwo PAN, 1958.
4. Wilfrid Blunt, *Sydney Carlyle Cockerell*, London: Hamish Hamilton, 1964, p.59.
5. Zenon Parvi, 'Ze Wspomnień o Wyspiańskim', in Leon Płoszewski (ed.), *Wyspiański w oczach współczesnych*, Kraków: Wydawnictwo Literackie, 1971, vol.1, pp.38–9.
6. Morris's engraving of *Primavera* by Feliks Jasiński (1892) was photographed in his study by Emery Walker around 1896. For more on *Primavera* in Wyspiański's Paris studio see letter from Stanisław Wyspiański to Karol Maszkowski, 25 October 1891, in Rydlowa (ed.) 1997, p.133, quoted in Magdalena Laskowska, '"Cudze zbiory": Zespół luźnych reprodukcji, kart książkowych, wycinków oraz fotografii ze spuścizny po Stanisławie Wyspiańskim w kolekcji Muzeum Narodowego w Krakowie', forthcoming article in conference proceedings *Sztuka książki ok. 1900. W 150. rocznicę urodzin Stanisława Wyspiańskiego*, Kraków: National Museum in Kraków, 2021. The collected letters of Stanisław Wyspiański have been published in four volumes: Vol.I – correspondence with Józef Mehoffer, Henryk Opieński and Tadeusz Stryjeński (Rydlowa (ed.) 1994); Vol.II (published first) – correspondence with Lucjan Rydel (Rydlowa and Płoszewski (eds) 1979); Vol.III – correspondence with Karol Maszkowski (Rydlowa (ed.) 1997); Vol.IV – miscellaneous correspondence (Rydlowa (ed.) 1998).
7. The drawing appeared in *Teka Grona Konserwatorów Galicyi Zachodniej*, Kraków: Grono Konserwatorów Galicyi Zachodniej, vol.I, 1900, p.296.
8. Architect Tadeusz Stryjeński's description in Marian Gorzkowski (ed.), *Jan Matejko: epoka lat dalszych, do końca życia artysty, z dziennika prowadzonego w ciągu lat siedemnastu*, Kraków: Drukarnia Związkowa, 1898, p.414.
9. Rydlowa and Płoszewski (eds) 1979, part 1, p.390.
10. William Morris, 'The Lesser Arts', in *Hopes and Fears for Art*, New York, London and Bombay: Longmans, Green & Co., 1905, pp.1–37.
11. Letter from Wyspiański to Stanisław Eljasz Radzikowski, 26 August 1904, in Rydlowa (ed.) 1998, p.278.
12. See also argument made in Szczerski 2015, pp.270–71.
13. Henryk Uziembło, 'Jego korekta', *Czas*, 27 November 1932, cited in Gaweł and Laskowska 2019, p.36.
14. Gaweł and Laskowska 2019, p.31.
15. Elżbieta Skierkowska, *Wyspiański artysta książki*, Wrocław: Zakład Narodowy im. Ossolińskich, 1960, p.192.
16. Antoni Gawiński, 'O książkach Wyspiańskiego', *Przegląd Biblioteczny*, 1908, no.2, pp.86–7.
17. For an English translation of this study, see: *The Hamlet Study and The Death of Ophelia*, translated by Barbara Bogoczek and Tony Howard, London: Shakespeare's Globe, 2019.
18. National Museum in Kraków, MNK III-SW-MP-4 and MNK III-SW-19-20; Laskowska 2021, op.cit.
19. Szczerski 2015, p.283.
20. Letter from Wyspiański to Rydel, Rydlowa and Płoszewski (eds) 1979, part 1, p.316, quoted in Charazińska, Rudzińska and Milicer 2007, p.96.
21. Rydlowa and Płoszewski (eds) 1979, part 1, p.282.
22. Financial records at the National Archive in Kraków, APKr, 'Akta związane ze Stanisławem Wyspiańskim', StW 7. I am grateful to Magdalena Laskowska for this information.
23. Szczerski 2015, pp.139–40.
24. I am grateful to Linda Parry for pointing out the similarity of Wyspiański's decorative scheme at the Medical Society to the 'Horse-chestnut Leaves' plate from the *Grammar of Ornament*. Gaweł and Laskowska 2019,

p.25; Bałus 2007, p.93. Morris frequently used illustrations in his lectures of the types also used by Owen Jones.
25. Letter from Wyspiański to Antonina Sikorska, 18 December 1904, cited in Alina Doboszewska (ed.), *Kalendarz życia i twórczości 26 marca 1898-grudzień 1907 Stanisława Wyspiańskiego*, Kraków: Wydawnictwo Literackie, 1995, pp.327–8. *Kalodont* was a toothpaste brand produced by F.A. Sarg's Sohn & Co. from Vienna, first sold in Austria-Hungary in 1887.
26. Godyń and Laskowska 2017, pp.381–3.
27. Tanya Harrod, '"For Love and Not for Money": reviving "peasant art" in Britain 1880–1930,' in *The Lost Arts of Europe. The Haslemere Museum collection of European Peasant Art*, edited by David Crowley and Lou Taylor, Haslemere: Haslemere Educational Museum, 2000, pp.13–4, 18.
28. Janet Pennington, 'Sussex Chairs', *Regional Furniture*, vol.9 (1995), pp.81–7.
29. Małgorzata Palka and Agnieszka Kowalska, *Teatralia Stanisława Wyspiańskiego. Katalog Zbiorów MHK*, Kraków: Muzeum Historyczne Miasta Krakowa, 2011, pp.173, 181–5.
30. Letter from Stanisław Wyspiański to Adam Chmiel, 25 July 1904, in Rydlowa (ed.) 1998, p.207.
31. The textile artist Bronisława Rychter-Janowska made the costumes and props.
32. Godyń and Laskowska 2017, pp.371–2, 390. Even though Wyspiański referred to the motif on the dining-room chair as the 'Lithuanian Sun' it closely reflects the ornamentation of the Podhale six-petal rosette.
33. All his plays were banned under the Russian and Prussian partition, apart from *The Wedding*.
34. Doboszewska (ed.) 1995, op.cit., pp.357–9.
35. Adolf Nowaczynski, 'On i Ja', *Wiadomosci Literackie*, 3 June 1928, p.2.

Chapter 3

1. Marjan Dienstl, *Znaczenie Wyspiańskiego dla polskiego zdobnictwa*, Lviv: Towarzystwo Wydawnicze we Lwowie, 1908, p.6.
2. I am grateful to Julia Griffin for her comments on this chapter. For a history of the Franciscan Church, see Zdzisław Gogola, 'Rys historyczny bazyliki Franciszkanów w Krakowie', in *Studia z dziejów kościoła Franciszkanów w Krakowie*, edited by Zdzisław Kliś, Kraków: Wydawnictwo Unum, 2006, pp.25–43.
3. For a monographic study of the decorative scheme at the Franciscan Church, see Bałus 2007, pp.71–110.
4. Morawińska 2000, p.16.
5. Szczerski 2015, p.137.
6. Letter from Stanisław Wyspiański to Lucjan Rydel, 16 November 1894, in Rydlowa and Płoszewski (eds) 1979, part 1, pp.263–4.
7. In the Jagiellonian Museum, private collections, and National Museum in Kraków, respectively.
8. Quoted in: Kazimierz Lewandowski, 'Przedwiośnie "Młodej Polski"', *Kurier Literacko Naukowy (IKC)*, vol.33 (1935), p.111.
9. Letter from Wyspiański to Lucjan Rydel, 3 July 1897, in Rydlowa and Płoszewski (eds) 1979, part 1, p.479.
10. Jadwiga Puciata-Pawłowska (ed.), *Józef Mehoffer: Dziennik*, Kraków: Wydawnictwo Literackie, 1975, p.269.
11. ibid., p.275.
12. Bałus 2007, p.75.
13. ibid., p.77.
14. Letter from Wyspiański to Rydel, 15 December 1894, in Rydlowa and Płoszewski (eds) 1979, part 1, p.266.
15. ibid.
16. Charazińska, Rudzińska and Milicer 2007, p.166, cat.no.II/13; Leon Płoszewski et al. (eds), *Stanisław Wyspiański: Pisma prozą. Juvenilia*, Kraków: Wydawnictwo Literackie, 1966, p.286.
17. Bałus 2007, p.82.
18. Godyń and Laskowska 2017, p.68.
19. Rydlowa and Płoszewski (eds) 1979, part 1, p.282.
20. ibid., p.71, footnote 27.
21. Bałus 2007, p.95.
22. Maria Stokowa (ed.), 'Kalendarz życia i twórczości 1 marca 1890-ostatnie dni marca 1898 Stanisława Wyspiańskiego', in *Stanisław Wyspiański: Dzieła zebrane*, vol.16/ II, Kraków: Wydawnictwo Literackie, 1982, p.292.
23. Godyń and Laskowska 2017, p.72.
24. Letter from Wyspiański to Rydel, 9–10 May 1896, in Rydlowa and Płoszewski (eds) 1979, part 1, p.323.
25. In Wyspiański's letter to Rydel dated 8 September 1897 he wrote: 'I will give for free, and will do for free (so long as they give me the nave) two frescoes beneath the vaulting, where the milky way is' – ibid., pp.493–4. I am most grateful to Professor Wojciech Bałus for drawing my attention to this quotation.
26. Danuta Czapczyńska-Kleszczyńska and Tomasz Szybisty, *Korpus witraży z lat 1800–1945 w kościołach rzymskokatolickich metropolii krakowskiej i przemyskiej, vol. 1, Archidiecezja krakowska. Dekanaty krakowskie*, edited by Wojciech Bałus and Tomasz Szybisty, Kraków: Corpus Vitrearum Polska: Imedius Agencja Reklamowa, 2014, pp.169–87.
27. Letter from Wyspiański to Rydel, 8 September 1897, in Rydlowa and Płoszewski (eds) 1979, part 1, pp.493–4.
28. Anon., *Sprawozdanie Dyrekcyi Towarzystwa Przyjaciół Sztuk Pięknych w Krakowie z czynności za rok 1897*, Kraków: Towarzystwo Przyjaciół Sztuk Pięknych, 1898, p.16.
29. Józef Ryszkiewicz, 'Z konkursu Tow. Zachęty Sztuk Pięknych w Królestwie Polskiem', *Tygodnik Illustrowany*, 12 February 1898, p.128.
30. Danuta Czapczyńska-Kleszczyńska, 'Dzieje witraży Stanisława Wyspiańskiego w kościele OO. Franciszkanów w Krakowie', *Rocznik Krakowski*, vol.70 (2004), pp.61–88.
31. Władysław Ekielski, 'Wspomnienia o Wyspiańskim', in *Wyspiański w oczach współczesnych*, edited by Leon Płoszewski, vol.1, Kraków: Wydawnictwo Literackie, 1971, pp.352–64 (p.360).
32. Wojciech Bałus, 'Stanisław Wyspiański i krakowski kościół Franciszkanów', in *Studia z dziejów kościoła Franciszkanów w Krakowie*, edited by Zdzisław Kliś, Kraków: Wydawnictwo Unum, 2006, p.219.
33. Adam Bochnak, 'Kilka anegdotycznych wiadomości o Stanisławie Wyspiańskim (Ze wspomnień Juliana Pagaczewskiego)', in Płoszewski (ed.) 1971, op.cit., vol.2, p.409.
34. Lewandowski 1935, op.cit.
35. Bałus 2006, pp.222–3.
36. ibid., p.223.
37. Stanisław Przybyszewski, 'Exegi monumentum . . .', s. 394–401, in Płoszewski (ed.) 1971, op.cit., vol.1, p.40.
38. National Museum in Kraków, MNK III-r.a-2675/1-39.
39. Władysław Łuszczkiewicz, *Poradnik dla zajmujących się utrzymywaniem i restauracją kościołów i kościelnych sprzętów*, offprint from *Przegląd Katolicki*, Warsaw: Drukarnia F. Czerwińskiego, 1887, vol.1, p.26.
40. ibid., p.31.
41. Wacław Husarski, 'Matejkowska spuścizna', *Tygodnik Illustrowany*, 10 December 1932, p.810.
42. Letters from Wyspiański to Lucjan Rydel, 22 May and 18 and 27 June 1890, in Rydlowa and Płoszewski (eds) 1979, part 1, pp.38, 40, 105 and 125.
43. Letter from Wyspiański to Lucjan Rydel, 22 May 1890, in ibid. p.38.
44. Płoszewski et al. (eds) 1996, p.12.
45. Wiesław Juszczak (ed.), *Teksty o malarzach: antologia polskiej krytyki artystycznej 1890–1918*, Wrocław: Zakład Narodowy im. Ossolińskich, 1976, p.392.
46. Alicja Okońska, *Stanisław Wyspiański*, Warsaw: Wiedza Powszechna, 1971, p.101.
47. Stokowa (ed.) 1982, op.cit., p.259.
48. Rydlowa and Płoszewski (eds), part 2, p.185, footnote 3.
49. Leonard Lepszy, 'Wyspiański i Malczewski', *Głos Literacki i Społeczny (Głos Narodu)*, no.10 (10 March 1901), p.6.
50. Dienstl 1908, op.cit., p.16.
51. Juszczak (ed.) 1976, op.cit., p.392.
52. ibid., p.389.
53. Anon., 'Dookoła twórczości Wyspiańskiego: z przemówień i głosów prasy', *Tygodnik Illustrowany*, 10 December 1932, p.809.
54. Szczerski 2015, p.137.
55. Antoni Buszek, 'Ze wspomnień szkolnych o Stanisławie Wyspiańskim', in Płoszewski (ed.) 1971, op.cit., vol.2, pp.412–15.

Chapter 4

1. See: Gaweł 2017, pp.181–2; Purchla 1979.
2. Metropolitan Basilica of St Stanisław and St Wacław.
3. Wojciech Bałus, 'Wawel: mowa przeszłości', in *Figury losu*, Kraków: Universitas, 2002, pp.50–61.
4. Rydlowa and Płoszewski (eds) 1979, part 1, p.298.
5. Drawings in the collections of the National Museum in Kraków – see Godyń and Laskowska 2017, pp.253–8, cat.nos V.10–V.17; as well as in the collection of the National Museum in Warsaw – see Charazińska, Rudzińska and Milicer 2007, pp.127–9, cat.nos I/96/1–8.
6. For a perceptive interpretation of the project for the stained-glass windows, see Bałus 2007, pp.173–225.
7. 'Kazimierz Wielki' was serialised in *Czas* in 1900 (nos 149–152) and privately published by Wyspiański in the same year as a *Czas* offprint. The following year he privately published the second edition, typeset at Księgarnia Gebethnera (Gebethner's Bookshop): Stanisław Wyspiański, *Kazimierz Wielki*, Kraków: Drukarnia Uniwersytetu Jagiellońskiego, 1901.
8. Rydlowa and Płoszewski (eds) 1979, part 1, p.378.
9. Mossakowski 2012.
10. Wyspiański 1910, pp.17–19. The Editors extend special thanks to Barbara Bogoczek and Tony Howard for their translation of this poem.
11. Godyń and Laskowska 2017, pp.240–43.
12. Stanisław Wyspiański and Władysław Ekielski, 'Akropolis: Projekt zabudowania Wawelu obmyślany przez . . .', *Architekt*, vol.9, nos 5–6 (1908), pp.49–57 (online: http://bcpw.bg.pw.edu.pl/dlibra/publication?id=1169&tab=3).
13. ibid., p.57.

Chapter 5

1. This chapter is a version of the following text: Anna Rudzińska, *Chochoły*, in Iwona Danielewicz and Agnieszka Rosales Rodriguez (eds.), *Polska. Siła obrazu*, exhibition catalogue [catalogue entry no.76], National Museum in Warsaw, 2020, forthcoming.
2. For the most comprehensive bibliography on Wyspiański's *Chochoły*, see the catalogue entry on the picture in Charazińska, Rudzińska and Milicer 2007, pp.124–5, cat.no.I/93; see also Łukasz Kossowski, *Wielka fala: Inspiracje sztuką Japonii w polskim malarstwie i grafice*, Warsaw and Toruń: Tako, 2016,

p.301, cat.no.460. The pastel as well as the eponymous *Chochoły* first came into the public domain in 1925 thanks to the publication of Stanisław Przybyszewski and Tadeusz Żuk-Skarszewski's book *Stanisław Wyspiański: Dzieła malarskie*, Bydgoszcz: Instytut Wydawniczy 'Biblioteka Polska', 1925 (the index was compiled by Stanisław Świerz). The picture did not become iconic in the sense of being widely known until 1925 and mostly after 1945.
3. Wyspiański 1901, op.cit., verses XLVI–XLVIII.

Chapter 6

1. This chapter presents our original research, and builds on some of our books published by the Tatra Museum, including Zbigniew Moździerz, *The Zakopane Style Trail*, Zakopane: Muzeum Tatrzańskie, 2014.
2. Some of Witkiewicz's other architectural designs also remained unrealised.
3. Stanisław Witkiewicz, 'Styl zakopiański', *Kurier Warszawski*, no.279 (1891), p.3.
4. See: Jabłońska 2019; Moździerz 2001; Crowley 1992.
5. For wider context about the Arts and Crafts movement in the Tatras, see Barucka 2010 and Barucka 2020.
6. Tomsk province received only administrative exiles, while the Eastern Siberian provinces received criminal exiles and hard-labour convicts.
7. Szczerski 2015, p.276.
8. See Jabłońska and Moździerz 1994.
9. Stanisław Witkiewicz, 'Tatry w śniegu', *Wędrowiec* 1886, nos 46–48, 52; Witkiewicz's drawings also appeared in the English press: Adam Gielgud, 'In the Polish Carpathians', *The English Illustrated Magazine*, no.60 (September 1888) – see fig.0.10 in the present volume.
10. In *Kurier Warszawski*, no.279 (1891), unpaginated.
11. Serialised in *Tygodnik Illustrowany*, 1889–90.
12. See Moździerz 2005, pp.125–32.
13. Witkiewicz 1911, p.3.
14. See Moździerz (ed.) 2007, pp.12–31.
15. For a monograph with bibliography, see Moździerz 2003.
16. Jagiełło (ed.) 1979, no.276, p.540.
17. ibid., no.277, p.541.
18. See Eljasz-Radzikowski 1901, op.cit., photo.5 (after p.24). For more on the creators of the model, see Moździerz 2003, pp.179–92.
19. Stanisław Witkiewicz, 'Na wystawę paryską', *Przegląd Zakopiański*, no.5 (1 February 1900), p.35.
20. ibid., p.36.
21. Jagiełło (ed.) 1979, no.285, p.555.
22. ibid., no.77, pp.247–8 and no.78, p.248.
23. Stanisław Witkiewicz, 'Sprawy stylu zakopiańskiego', *Przegląd Zakopiański*, vol.2, no.33 (1900), p.293.
24. ibid.
25. ibid.
26. ibid., p.294.
27. Witkiewicz 1904, p.5.

Chapter 7

1. The core of the argument on the Silent Villa elaborated in this chapter was published in Barucka 2020, pp.109–34. It is republished here with the kind permission of the Finnish National Gallery.
2. Kłosowski's work as a decorative artist is discussed in Chapter 8.
3. Jabłońska 2015, p.209.
4. The economic and political aspects of the developments in Zakopane are discussed at greater length and set into a broader context of Polish crafts revival in the 19th century in Barucka 2010, pp.71–99.
5. His other reason, later acknowledged in Karol Kłosowski's reminiscences, was being in love with his future wife, Katarzyna: Lisek 2007, p.16.
6. Kłosowski's studies are discussed in greater detail in Chapter 8.
7. Huml 2009, pp.20–135 (p.42).
8. In the course of time Koliba was also remodelled and extended.
9. The ideas on the house of the British Arts and Crafts architects and designers are discussed in Supińska-Polit 2004, chapter 2.
10. Barucka 2020, p.127. The quote and a discussion of the extensions and alterations to the house are drawn from the first well-informed architectural survey on the Silent Villa in the unpublished Conservation Management Plan by Agata Nowakowska-Wolak from 2013.
11. M.H. Baillie Scott envisaged a 'garden room' as adjoining the house and facing south; the place that 'may be formed by an extension of the roof supported by posts': Mackay Hugh Baillie Scott, *Houses and Gardens: Arts and Crafts Interiors*, Woodbridge: Antique Collectors' Club, 1995 (first published in 1906), pp.68–9.
12. A more complete survey of plants, based on recollections of Urszula Bukowska, Karol Kłosowski's granddaughter is in Barucka 2020, pp.128–9.
13. Kłosowski's dedication to paper cuttings coincided with the growing appreciation of the technique among art lovers and critics, as evidenced, for example, in the early issues of the Polish Applied Arts Society's journal *Wydawnictwo Towarzystwa Polskiej Sztuki Stosowanej: materiały*.

Chapter 8

1. For more on Kłosowski's creative output, see Lisek 2007. Dating of the artist's works is problematic as he did not inscribe a date on them.
2. Karol Kłosowski, *Wycinanki: Komponował w mot. lud i naturalist.*, part 1, Zakopane: [publisher unknown], 1923.
3. Karol Kłosowski, 'Z trosk o estetykę uzdrowiska, ochronę przejawów naszej sztuki i inne dolegliwości', unidentified press cutting, Private Collection. By Descent from the Artist.
4. Karol Kłosowski, *Przebieg Życia i Pracy* (*My Life and Work*), 1961, pp.1–7, manuscript, Private Collection. By Descent from the Artist. The bulk of biographical information in this chapter is based on this source, unless otherwise stated.
5. This self-portrait may have been painted at the time when the artist was covering for Władysław Skoczylas as the tutor of ornamental and anatomical drawing at the Wood Industry Vocational School.
6. Marza Ostrawicka, *Uśmiech Tatr*, Warsaw: Gebethner i Wolff, 1932.
7. Lisek 2007, p.19.
8. Andrzej Schroder, 'Wystawa przemysłu artystycznego w stylu zakopiańskim', *Słowo Polskie*, no.351 (1909), p.12.
9. Karol Kłosowski Photographic Archive, no. 1271/28-33/85, Iconography and Photography Department, National Museum in Warsaw.
10. Kłosowski 1961, op.cit., p.6.
11. Karol Kłosowski, 'Koronki Klockowe', *Zawód i Życie* (1941), p.26, loose press cutting, Private Collection. By Descent from the Artist.
12. Kowalska 2013.
13. Kłosowski 1923, op.cit., pp.1–3.
14. ibid.

Chapter 9

1. The chapter draws largely on the pioneering scholarship of Irena Huml, Maria Dziedzic, David Crowley and Andrzej Szczerski. Irena Huml's seminal monograph *Warsztaty Krakowskie*. Wrocław: Zakład Narodowy im. Ossolińskich, 1973, served as a basis for the first half of Dziedzic (ed.) 2009, published in English- and Polish-language versions and distributed in Poland. The only two English-language sources on the Workshops published in the UK are Szczerski 2015, pp.238–94, and Crowley 1992, pp.44–72. I am very grateful to Anna Myczkowska-Szczerska for her help in accessing the relevant sources.
2. For information on the organisational structure of the Kraków Workshops, see Huml 2009, pp.57–60.
3. Quoted in ibid., p.58.
4. For more information on the Polish Applied Arts Society, see Editors' Introduction and Chapter 1.
5. Quoted in Huml 2009, p.63.
6. William Morris, *Hopes and Fears for Art*, London: Ellis & White, 1882, p.31.
7. Huml 2009, p.54.
8. ibid., p.57.
9. Włodzimierz Konieczny, 'Sztuka i rzemiosła', *Krakowski Miesiecznik Artystyczny*, Yr 1 (1911), no.7, pp.75–7, quoted in Huml 2009, p.55.
10. For further biographical details, see Dziedzic (ed.) 2009, p.429.
11. ibid., p.94.
12. ibid., p.95.
13. ibid., p.94.
14. ibid., p.96.
15. ibid., p.85.
16. ibid., p.87.
17. ibid., p.108.
18. In fact, the word 'batik' was not commonly used in Poland until 1913, when the term was popularised thanks to a book on Javanese nature and art by a botanist, Michał Siedlecki. Until then the technique was known as the 'Easter egg technique': ibid., p.277.
19. From Józefa Kogut's letter to Irena Huml, *c.*1970, quoted in Dziedzic (ed.) 2009, p.275.
20. I am grateful to Professor Maria Dziedzic for kindly providing this information.
21. For further biographical details see Dziedzic (ed.) 2009, p.433.
22. I am grateful to Professor Maria Dziedzic for kindly providing this information.
23. Huml 2009, p.100.
24. ibid., p.103.
25. ibid., p.80.
26. Szczerski 2015, p.272.
27. ibid., p.271.
28. ibid., p.21.
29. I am grateful to Andrzej Szczerski for initially drawing my attention to the parallels between the two movements. See ibid., pp.414–15. For further information on the connections between Polish artists and the Bloomsbury Group, see ibid., p.413.
30. Although Fry was an old friend of C.R. Ashbee and A.H. Mackmurdo, he was dismissive of the second generation of Arts and Crafts enterprises, such as Ashbee's Guild of Handicraft.
31. Collins 1984, p.30.
32. Morris was also vehemently against this practice and with a few notable exceptions produced designs specifically for a designated medium.
33. A notable exception is the stained glass at the Museum of Technology and Industry, made by the firm of S.G. Żeleński.
34. Sutton (ed.) 1972, vol.1, pp.331–2.
35. Spalding 1977, unpaginated.
36. Quoted in Collins 1984, p.9.
37. Fry organised the first exhibition of children's art in England, in 1917. An *Art of the Child* exhibition was organised in Poland by the Ministry of Art and Culture in 1919 which included batiks made by members of Buszek's workshop.
38. Sutton (ed.) 1972, vol.1, p.332.

39. Szczerski 2015, p.402.
40. This observation came from Fry's daughter, Pamela; Fry himself is not known to have ever explained the reason behind the name.

Chapter 10

1. Pawlikowska-Jasnorzewska 2000, p.79.
2. Beata Obertyńska, 'Lilka', *Wiadomości*, London 1969, no.47, quoted in Pryzwan 2015, pp.55–6.
3. ibid., p.56.
4. ibid., p.55.
5. In a 1926 questionnaire quoted in Elżbieta Hurnikowa, *Maria Pawlikowska-Jasnorzewska: zarys monograficzny*, Katowice: Wydawnictwo Naukowe Śląsk, 1999, p.25.
6. Letter to Jan Gwalbert Henryk Pawlikowski, quoted in Magdalena Samozwaniec, *Zalotnica niebieska*, Warsaw: Świat Książki, 2012, p.129.
7. She may have taken classes there with the Symbolist and Expressionist painter Wojciech Weiss. His granddaughter Zofia Weiss's private collection includes his hand-written list of all of his students, to which the name 'Pawlikowska' was added later. Equally, however, this might relate to the successful painter Aniela Pawlikowska, née Aniela Wolska (1901–1980).
8. Samozwaniec 2012, op.cit., p.10.
9. ibid., p.9.
10. Quoted in Anna Nasiłowska, *Maria Pawlikowska-Jasnorzewska czyli Lilka Kossak*, Toruń: Algo, 2010, p.44.
11. Website devoted to the Kossak family: http://www.bg.agh.edu.pl/KOSSAK/maria.html. More recently her work was included in the exhibition *Polish Women Artists* at the National Museum in Warsaw (1991), and in 2006 there was an exhibition dedicated to her in Warsaw's Adam Mickiewicz Museum of Literature: *Portrait of a Poetess in the Context of the Kossaks*.
12. Nasiłowska 2010, op.cit., p.44.
13. Several versions exist, with varied poses: in the villa he was her model.
14. Others included Zofia and Karol Stryjeński and the leading Formist artists Leon Chwistek and Zbigniew Pronaszko who promoted Maria's paintings.
15. She collaborated with Witkacy on plays which are now lost.
16. In 1920 the new Polish state purchased a zeppelin from France and called it 'Lech'.
17. He left her for Waleria Kończyńska, with whom he had a child. She was a member of Sacchetto's dance company.
18. The auction catalogue mistakenly listed it as 'Woman with a Butterfly'. There is indeed an androgynous quality to this image of Pawlikowski.
19. In Polish *Niebieskie migdały* has idiomatic suggestions of 'daydreaming'.
20. She was fascinated by the Tarot and designed her own deck.
21. Pawlikowska-Jasnorzewska 2000, p.37.
22. Letter from Antoni Słonimski to Maria Pawlikowska-Jasnorzewska, 2 February 1941, Adam Mickiewicz Museum of Literature, Warsaw, ref.no.874000071.
23. Letter from Maria Pawlikowska-Jasnorzewska in Blackpool to Antoni Słonimski, 25 March 1941. Quoted in Pryzwan 2015, p.139.
24. Beata Obertyńska quoted in Pryzwan 2015, p.56.

At the time of writing, MPJ's known paintings and drawings are very widely dispersed, and their dating is often provisional. For example, the gigantic figure in the work known as *In the Hands of a Sorceress* (dated after 1920 when it was sold at auction) apparently revisits the imagery of *Vision* (fig.10.0), which was exhibited during World War I. Further research may reveal a closer connection between the two works.

Chapter 11

1. Huml 1978, pp.9–11; Szczerski 2015, p.20.
2. Huml 1978, pp.11; Zbigniew Moździerz, 'Koncepcja stylu narodowego Stanisława Witkiewicza i jego realizacja', in *Stanisław Witkiewicz: Człowiek, artysta, myśliciel: materiały z sesji zorganizowanej w osiemdziesiątą rocznicę śmierci artysty, Zakopane, 20–22 października 1995*, edited by Zbigniew Moździerz, Zakopane: Towarzystwo Muzeum Tatrzańskiego, Muzeum Tatrzańskie im. T. Chałubińskiego, 1997, pp.293–328 (p.276).
3. Jabłońska and Moździerz 1994, pp.109–11.
4. ibid., p.58.
5. Szczerski 2015, p.19.
6. Godyń and Laskowska 2017, pp.365–6.
7. Huml 1978, p.16.
8. ibid., p.18.
9. Stanisław Wyspiański, 'Spis dzieł pomieszczonych w budynku Towarzystwa Przyjaciół Sztuk Pięknych w Świetlicy 2-ej, Towarzystwo Artystów Polskich 'Sztuka' z siedzibą w Krakowie, spisał Stanisław Wyspiański', unpublished list, 1904, unpaginated [p.4], National Museum in Kraków. Wyspiański was known for his attitude to craftsmen, carpenters, embroiderers and master metalworkers, and was the first exhibition-organiser to include their names in catalogues, with the same status as those of artists.
10. Godyń and Laskowska 2017, p.317.
11. Julian Nowak, 'Dom Towarzystwa Lekarskiego w Krakowie', *Architekt*, vol.6, no.4 (1905), pp.50–55.
12. Beiersdorf 2006, pp.74–81.
13. Huml 1978, p.21; Sieradzka 1996, p.135.
14. Godyń and Laskowska 2017, pp.387–93.
15. Huml 1978, pp.23–4.
16. *Katalog I: Wystawy Towarzystwa Polska Sztuka Stosowana*, Kraków: Museum Narodowe, 1902, pp.3–19 and 23–9; the exhibition, augmented in autumn 1902 with work by Warsaw craftspeople, was shown at the Society for the Encouragement of the Fine Arts.
17. *Katalog VII: Wystawa Towarzystwa Artystów Polskich 'Sztuka' i II. Wystawa Towarzystwa 'Polska Sztuka Stosowana'*, 11 November to 31 December 1903; the spelling of the name of the carpenter Jan Józef Zabża follows that provided by his granddaughter Janina Glazur.
18. Kilijańska 2005.
19. Agata Wójcik, '"Myśl artystyczna", która przeniknęła do "knajp": wnętrza restauracyjne w Starym Teatrze w Krakowie projektu artystów związanych z towarzystwem Polska Sztuka Stosowana', *Modus* (Kraków), vol.18 (2018), pp.123–49 (pp.125–7, 130).
20. *Wystawa Krakowskiego Towarzystwa 'Polska Sztuka Stosowana' w gmachu Towarzystwa Zachęty Sztuk Pięknych w Warszawie, luty 1908 r*, exh.cat., Kraków: Drukarnia Uniwersytetu Jagiellońskiego, 1908, pp.8–9.
21. Huml 1978, p.33.
22. Lidia Kuchtówna, 'Bronisława Poświkowa', in *Polski Słownik Biograficzny*, vol.27/4, no.115, Wrocław: Zakład Narodowy im. Ossolińskich, 1983, pp.710–11.
23. Agata Wójcik, 'Mikrokosmos polskiej sztuki przełomu XIX i XX wieku: wystrój wnętrz sanatorium i willi doktorstwa Bronisławy i Kazimierza Dłuskich w Zakopanem', *Quart: kwartalnik Instytutu Historii Sztuki Uniwersytetu Wrocławskiego*, vol.3 (2018), pp.33–65 (pp.40–53).
24. ibid., p.56.
25. Matyaszewska 2015, pp.386–7.
26. Hanna Bartnicka-Górska, 'Karol Józef Frycz', in *Słownik artystów polskich i obcych w Polsce działających*, edited by Jolanta Maurin-Białostocka, Wrocław: Zakład Narodowy im. Ossolińskich, 1975, vol.2, p.252 – she mentions Hubert von Herkomer.
27. Wójcik 2018 ('Mikrokosmos polskiej . . .'), op.cit., p.59.
28. Agata Wójcik, 'Projekty wnętrz i mebli zaprezentowane na "Wystawie architektury i wnętrz w otoczeniu ogrodowem", w Krakowie w 1912 roku', *Roczniki Humanistyczne*, vol.67, no.4 (2019), pp.109–40 (pp.111–12).
29. ibid., p.132.
30. Beiersdorf 1991, p.132.
31. Józef Rostafiński, 'Adrjan Baraniecki, twórca Muzeum Przem. 1828–1891', *Przemysł i Rzemiosło*, vol.1 (1921), p.3.
32. Jerzy Warchałowski, 'O sztuce stosowanej', *Czas*, 10 and 11 June 1904, pp.1–2.
33. Bolesława Kołodziejowa, 'Miejskie Muzeum Przemysłowe im. dra. Adriana Baranieckiego w Krakowie', *Rozprawy i Sprawozdania Muzeum Narodowego w Krakowie*, vol.11 (1976), pp.186–230 (p.200).
34. Dziedzic (ed.) 2009, pp.168–72.
35. Rydlowa (ed.) 1998, part 1, p.378.
36. Tadeusz 'Boy' Żeleński, 'Historia pewnych mebli', in *O Wyspiańskim*, Kraków: Wydawnictwo Literackie, 1973, pp.69–76 (p.71, fig.34).

Chapter 12

1. Jerzy Warchałowski, 'Wystawa architektury i wnętrz w otoczeniu ogrodowem w Krakowie w r. 1912', *Architekt*, vol.12, no.8 (August 1911), pp.114–18.
2. Tadeusz Leszner, *Edmund Bartłomiejczyk: grafika, rysunki, akwarele*, exh.cat., Warsaw: CBWA, 1956.
3. Łomnicka and Weiss 2020.
4. Three additional chairs have been produced as faithful replicas of the sole surviving example of this piece.
5. Anon., 'Krakowska wystawa architektury', *Świat*, no.44 (1912), p.3 (from a collection of press cuttings at the State Municipal Archive in Kraków, no.29/576/38, K.81); quoted after: Agata Wójcik, 'Projekty wnętrz i mebli zaprezentowane na "Wystawie architektury i wnętrz w otoczeniu ogrodowem", w Krakowie w 1912 roku', *Roczniki Humanistyczne*, vol.67, no.4 (2019), pp.112–13.

Chapter 13

1. Feliks Jasieński, 'O sukni polskiej', *Ilustracja polska*, vol.2, no.7 (1902), p.146.
2. See: Sieradzka 1991; Anna Sieradzka, *Nie tylko peleryna: Moda okresu Młodej Polski w życiu i sztuce*, Warsaw: DiG, 2003, pp.73–4; Kowalska 2013; Elżbieta Piskorz Branekowa, *Polskie hafty i koronki: zdobienia stroju ludowego*, Warsaw: Muza, 2005, pp.278–89; Beata Biedrońska-Słotowa and Joanna Regina Kowalska, *Za modą przez wieki: Ubiory z kolekcji Muzeum Narodowego w Krakowie / Following fashion through the ages: garments from the collections of the National Museum of Cracow*, translated by Jessica Taylor-Kucia, Kraków: Muzeum Narodowe w Krakowie, 2003, pp.95–6.
3. *Wydawnictwo Towarzystwa Polska Sztuka Stosowana: materiały*, vol.4 (1904), plate 4.

Chapter 14

1. The most complete realisation of the attempt to create a national style took the form of the 'Zakopane Style': see Chapter 6. For porcelain in the Zakopane Style, see Kostuch 2005.
2. Towards the end of the 19th century there were three schools of pottery in the Austrian partition-sector, of which the best-known was that in Kołomyja (now Kolomyia), in Eastern Galicia.
3. Konstanty Laszczka, *Keramos*, Warsaw: 'Książka', 1948, p.7.

4. 'Stosław', 'W pracowni artystów naszych: Konstanty Laszczka', *Świat*, 4 May 1907, p.13.
5. The J. Niedźwiecki i Ska factory began as a manufactory of tile stoves, and produced artistic products in 1900–1910, when it belonged to Adam Kirchmayer and Beata (née Matejko) Kirchmayer.
6. *Czas*, 29 July 1904, p.3. Kalwaria Zebrzydowska is a place of pilgrimage to the south of Kraków.
7. A *siwak* is an unglazed clay vessel whose steel-grey colour is obtained by cutting off air flow during final phase of firing.
8. 'Ceramika St. Jagmina w "Zachęcie"', *Tygodnik Illustrowany*, 23 June 1906, p.487.
9. Andrzej Potocki, 'Sztuka na wystawie paryskiej: VI', *Tygodnik Illustrowany*, 15 September 1900, p.729.
10. Ewa Łuskina, 'Wnętrze', *Zdrój*, 2 June 1918, p.187.
11. As well as being an architect, Jan (Iwan) Lewiński was the owner of a construction firm and a factory producing building materials, tiled stoves and ceramic products.
12. Magdalena Michalczuk-Gędziorowska, 'Opis Domu pod Jedlami', in *Dom pod Jedlami i jego twórca: Studia i wspomnienia*, edited by Wiesław A. Wójcik, Kraków: Wydawnictwo Znak Kraków, 1997, p.185.

Chapter 15

1. For their contributions and assistance that made this chapter possible, I would greatly like to thank: Julia Griffin for sharing materials from her search in the National Museum in Kraków, which allowed me to verify my own 2009 reconstructions of Christmas-tree decorations by Zdzisław Gedliczka; Monika Paś, Curator in the Decorative Arts Department of the Museum, and Józefa Krysińska, manager of the Stores in the same Department, for helpfully giving me access to the collections in the Stores; Professor Maria Dziedzic and Professor Adam Gedliczka for consultations; and Agata Pleciak and Anna Szwaja for taking photographs and for making them available to me.
2. The activities of the Kraków Workshops are most thoroughly presented in the researches of Irena Huml: see Huml 2009.
3. Toys appeared in the catalogue of the solo exhibition of the artist's work at the Society for the Encouragement of the Fine Arts in Warsaw in 1919, as well as in the general report of the 1925 Paris Exposition. See Lenartowicz 2008.
4. ibid.
5. See, among others, M.W., 'O ozdobach choinkowych', *Kurjer Warszawski*, 26 November 1927, p.7.
6. See 'Kronika: Szkoła zabawkarstwa', *Rzeczy Piękne*, vol.2, no.4 (1919), p.23; important publications from the 1920s include books by Maria Gerson-Dąbrowska, Felicja Gosieniecka, Barbara Strasburger, Bluszcz Publishing Society and Maria Werten. Maria Werten, *Ozdoby choinkowe*, offprint originally printed in the quarterly *Praca Ręczna w szkole* (*Handiwork at School*), Organ Towarzystwa Miłośników Robót Ręcznych (Publication of the Handiwork Lovers Society), no.3, Warsaw, 1928 (in the quarterly, pp.37–61), referred to the Workshops' decorative designs; creators of Polish Christmas-tree decorations also include Jacek Mierzejewski (1883–1925) and Jan Kurzątkowski (1899–1964).
7. Designs reproduced in *Płomyk: Tygodnik ilustrowany dla dzieci i młodzieży*, e.g.: 1926, nos.15, 16 and 17; 1927, no.10.
8. See Gedliczka 2012.
9. A fruit, St. Nicholas's head, and a horse are only known from versions reconstructed from the original templates in the family archive of the designer's son, Adam Gedliczka (reconstructed in 2009 for the publication Dziedzic (ed.) 2009).
10. See Ginalska 1961.
11. The League embraced Galicia and Kraków, together with the city of Gdańsk. Its branch in Kraków was the Association for Industrial Assistance (Towarzystwo Pomocy Przemysłowej, founded in 1909; earlier the 'With Your Own Strength' Association (Towarzystwo 'O własnych siłach'), founded in 1902), which collaborated with the Museum of Technology and Industry. The programme of the League included educational and exhibition activities, including, in the field of toy-making, the introduction of its own brand for national products, and the export of native products. See Dariusz Piotr Kruk, 'Instytucjonalne formy wspierania rozwoju przemysłu Galicji w dobie autonomii', *Zeszyty Naukowe*, vol.6, no.942 (Kraków: Uniwersytet Ekonomiczny w Krakowie, 2015), pp.93–105.
12. Norwid 1851.
13. See Kinchin and O'Connor 2012.
14. Maria Werten, *Ozdoby choinkowe*, op. cit.
15. Reproduced in *Rzeczy Piękne*, vol.VI, no.4, April 1927.

Chapter 16

1. Kazimierz Witkiewicz, *Kunszt introligatorski Bonawentury Lenarta*, Kraków: Muzeum Techniczno-Przemysłowe, 1932, p.10. Witkiewicz reported the meeting. He worked at the Library of the Museum of Technology and Industry from 1912 onwards. For further information about Baraniecki's apparent meeting with Ruskin, see Szczerski 2015, p.259. Baraniecki lived in Great Britain in the second half of the 1860s (see Chapter 1). Other early 20th-century authors also mentioned Baraniecki's alleged meeting with Ruskin, but this fact remains unsubstantiated by archival evidence. See: Alicja Kilijańska, 'The Technical-Industrial Museum in Kraków (1868-1950): The Director, Dr Adrian Baraniecki and the Beginnings of the Institution 1868-1891', unpublished paper given at the workshop: 'From London to Vienna and Central Europe: Museums of Art & Design in the Habsburg Empire', V&A Research Department, 8 and 9 December 2017, organised by the University of Birmingham and the V&A.
2. *Czas* (Kraków), 8 June 1894, p.2; *Czas*, 29 September 1908, evening edition, p.2. In the case of the 1894 competition, the task was to prepare a folder for letters, and an anniversary book (necessarily in a Renaissance style). The 1908 competition stipulated a book cover, but did not impose any style guidelines, thus marking a notable departure from historicism.
3. *Czas*, 8 June 1894, pp.3–4; *Architekt* (Kraków), vol.9, no.12 (1908), pp.155–6.
4. Magdalena Koziak-Podsiadło, 'Kształcenie introligatorów przy Muzeum Techniczno-Przemysłowym w Krakowie w latach 1908–1913', *Annales Universitatis Paedagogicae Cracoviensis. Studia ad Bibliothecarum Scientiam Pertinentia*, vol.15 (2017), p.247.
5. Bolesława Kołodziejowa, 'Miejskie Muzeum Przemysłowe im. dra Adriana Baranieckiego w Krakowie', *Rozprawy i Sprawozdania Muzeum Narodowego w Krakowie*, vol.11 (1976), p.216.
6. *Czas*, 1 December 1909, evening edition, p.2; Jerzy Warchałowski, 'Książka (dokończenie) II', *Czas*, 15 December 1909, evening edition, p.2.
7. Jerzy Warchałowski, 'Książka I', *Czas*, 14 December 1909, evening edition, pp.1–2; Jerzy Warchałowski, 'Książka (dokończenie) II', *Czas*, 15 December 1909, evening edition, pp.1–2.
8. Bonawentura Lenart, 'Sztuka introligatorska w XIX stuleciu', *Polski Poradnik Graficzny*, vol.3 (1908), p.42.
9. *Miejskie Muzeum Techniczno-Przemysłowe, Krajowy Instytut Popierania Rękodzieł i Przemysłu w Krakowie: Sprawozdanie Dyrekcyi za R. 1910*, Kraków: Miejskie Muzeum Techniczno-Przemysłowe, 1910, p.18; *Sprawozdanie Dyrekcyi Miejskiego Muzeum Techniczno-Przemysłowego, Krajowego Instytutu Popierania Rękodzieł i Przemysłu w Krakowie za rok 1911*, Kraków: Muzeum Techniczno-Przemysłowe, Krajowy Instytut Popierania Rękodzieł i Przemysłu, 1912, p.28.
10. *Sprawozdanie* . . . 1912, ibid., p.57.
11. *Katalog wystawy introligatorskiej w Miejskiem Muzeum Techniczno-Przemysłowem w Krakowie*, exh.cat., Kraków: Miejskie Muzeum Techniczno-Przemysłowe, [1910].
12. *Pierwsza wystawa współczesnej sztuki kościelnej im. Piotra Skargi w Krakowie MDCCCCXI*, exh.cat., Kraków: Towarzystwo Przyjaciół Sztuk Pięknych, 1911, pp.56–8.
13. Monika Paś, 'Zespół opraw modlitewników prezentowanych na Pierwszej Wystawie Sztuki Kościelnej im. Piotra Skargi w 1911 roku w Krakowie' / 'The set of prayer book covers presented at the First Piotr Skarga Exhibition of Contemporary Church Art in Kraków in 1911' [in:] *Sacrum et Decorum. Materiały i studia z historii sztuki sakralnej / Materials and Studies on the History of Sacred Art*, R. XI 2018, Rzeszów: Uniwersytet Rzeszowski, Wydział Sztuki Uniwersytetu Rzeszowskiego, Centrum Dokumentacji Współczesnej Sztuki Sakralnej, 2019, pp.81–97. (bilingual edition).
14. *Encyklopedia wiedzy o książce*, Wrocław: Zakład Narodowy im. Ossolińskich, 1971, p.1043; *Słownik pracowników książki polskiej*, Warsaw and Łódź: Państwowe Wydawnictwo Naukowe and Stowarzyszenie Bibliotekarzy Polskich, 1972, p.355.
15. Leszek J. Sibila, 'Wybrane oprawy książkowe, projekty opraw książkowych, dyplomów i tek adresowych krakowskiego mistrza introligatorskiego Roberta Jahody z lat 1892–1912: Ze zbiorów Muzeum Historycznego Miasta Krakowa', in *Rocznik Muzeum Papiernictwa*, Duszniki-Zdrój: Muzeum Papiernictwa, 2012, vol.6, p.35.
16. S.A. Levetus, 'The art of the book in Austria', in *The Art of the Book: A Review of Some Recent European and American Work in Typography, Page Decoration and Binding*, edited by Charles Holme, London, Paris and New York: The Studio, 1914, pp.202–30 (p.214).

Chapter 17

1. Jerzy Malinowski sees here the influence of the *Poems of Ossian*: Jerzy Malinowski, *Malarstwo polskie XIX wieku*, Warsaw: DiG, 2003, p.283.
2. See Cavanaugh 2000.
3. *Echo literackie i artystyczne* (Warsaw), 3 September 1877, p.6.
4. Notably, until the end of the 20th century connections between 19th-century Polish and British art had only been noticed in passing. I dealt with this problem in my paper 'Burne-Jones Seen from Poland before 1914', delivered at the conference *Reassessing Burne-Jones* at the Ashmolean Museum in Oxford (February 2019).
5. Józef Mehoffer, 'Uwagi o sztuce i jej stosunku do natury', *Przegląd Polski*, vol.124 (1897), pp.1–30.
6. ibid., p.20.
7. Ferdynand Ruszczyc, *Dziennik: Część pierwsza: Ku Wilnu 1894–1919*, Warsaw:

Artystyczna Oficyna Wydawnicza 'Secesja', 1994, p.151 (entry for 14 February 1904).

8. Ksawery Piwocki, *Historia Akademii Sztuk Pięknych w Warszawie 1904–1964*, Wrocław, Warsaw and Kraków: Zakład Narodowy im. Ossolińskich, 1965, pp.23–9.
9. ibid., p.237.
10. For instance in *Against the Background of a Stained Glass Window: Peacock* (1908) by Kazimierz Stabrowski, *Sarcophagi* (1895–1900) by Leon Wyczółkowski, a view of the interior of Chartres Cathedral, France (1903) by Józef Pankiewicz, or views of Notre-Dame Cathedral in Paris (1912) by Konrad Krzyżanowski.
11. Michał Haake, 'Portret – portret dziecka', in *Przemyśleć wszystko . . . : Stanisława Wyspiańskiego modernizacja wyobraźni zbiorowej*, edited by Małgorzata Okulicz-Kozaryn, Mateusz Bourkane, Michał Haake, Poznań: Wydawnictwo Poznańskiego Towarzystwa Przyjaciół Nauk, 2009, p.121.
12. ibid.
13. Moździerz 2003, pp.167–8.
14. National Museum in Warsaw, inv.MP 720 MNW.
15. 'Boy' (Tadeusz Żeleński), 'Historia pewnych mebli', in *Reflektorem w mrok*, Warsaw: Państwowy Instytut Wydawniczy, 1981, pp.145–53 (p.152).
16. See also Łomnicka and Weiss 2020.
17. They are in the collection of the National Museum in Kraków.
18. For photographs of the interior, see Wójcik 2018 ("'Myśl artystyczna" . . .'), op.cit., pp.42–3.
19. *Nietota: Księga tajemna Tatr* was initially serialised in the magazine *Sfinks* between April 1908 and May/June 1909.
20. Reinhard-Chlanda 2011.
21. Edward Okuń, *Portrait of Mrs. Herse*, 1908, National Museum in Warsaw, MP 191 MNW.
22. I am grateful to Alina Kondratiuk and Professor Waldemar Deluga for help in identifying the subject of this painting.
23. Tadeusz Miciński, *Do źródeł duszy polskiej*, quoted in: *Młoda Polska: Słowa, obrazy, przestrzenie – W hołdzie Stanisławowi Wyspiańskiemu*, exh.cat., Warsaw: Muzeum Literatury im. Adama Mickiewicza, 2007, p.216.
24. Aleksandra Majerska, 'Ferdynand Ruszczyc (1870–1936) Psychologiczna charakterystyka stylu', *Nike*, 1939, no.1, p.26.
25. Jadwiga Puciata-Pawłowska, *Jacek Malczewski*, Wrocław, Warsaw and Kraków: Zakład Narodowy im. Ossolińskich, 1968, pp.146–7.

Select Bibliography

Titles listed here are those which would be useful specifically to English-speaking readers (by virtue of either being in English or, for example, being richly illustrated monographs on particular artists or phenomena), as well as standard, seminal books in Polish which tend to be cited widely. Articles are included only if absolutely key.

Antos, Janusz, 'Karol Stryjeński. Narodowe art déco', in *Rzeczy niepospolite: Polscy projektanci XX wieku*, edited by Czesława Frejlich, Kraków: 2+3D Fundacja Rzecz Piękna, 2013, pp.68–77.

Bajda, Justyna, *Młoda Polska*, Wrocław: Wydawnictwo Dolnośląskie (series: 'A to Polska właśnie'), 2003.

Bałus, Wojciech, 'Stanisław Wyspiański i krakowski kościół Franciszkanów', in *Studia z dziejów kościoła Franciszkanów w Krakowie*, edited by Zdzisław Kliś, Kraków: Wydawnictwo Unum, 2006, pp.217–33.

Bałus, Wojciech, *Sztuka sakralna Krakowa w wieku XIX, część 2: Matejko i Wyspiański*, Kraków: Universitas, 2007.

Barucka, Edyta, 'Redefining Polishness: the revival of crafts in Galicia around 1900', *Acta Slavica Iaponica*, vol.28 (2010), pp.71–99.

Barucka, Edyta, 'The Vernacular Revival in the Polish Tatras *c.*1900: arts, patronage, collecting and documentation', in *European Revivals: From Dreams of a Nation to Places of Transnational Exchange*, edited by Anna-Maria von Bonsdorff, Riitta Ojanperä and Hanna-Leena Paloposki, Helsinki: Finnish National Gallery (FNG Research 1), 2020, pp.109–34.

Beiersdorf, Zbigniew, 'Miejskie Muzeum Przemysłowe im. dr Adriana Baranieckiego', *Rocznik Krakowski*, vol.57 (1991), pp.129–64.

Beiersdorf, Zbigniew, 'Dom Lekarski: siedziba Towarzystwa Lekarskiego krakowskiego jako dzieło sztuki', in *Księga jubileuszowa Towarzystwa Lekarskiego w Krakowie*, edited by Igor Gościński and Aleksander B. Skotnicki, Kraków: Krakowskie Towarzystwo Edukacyjne – Oficyna Wydawnicza AFM, 2006, pp.55–133.

Beiersdorf, Zbigniew, and Jacek Purchla, *Dom pod Globusem, dawna siedziba krakowskiej Izby Handlowej i Przemysłowej*, Kraków: Wydawnictwo Literackie, 1988.

Biriulow, Jurij, *Secesja we Lwowie*, translated by Janusz Derwojed, Warsaw: Wydawnictwo Krupski i S-ka, 1996.

Blakesley, Rosalind Polly, *The Arts and Crafts Movement*, London: Phaidon Press, 2006.

Brockington, Grace (ed.), *Internationalism and the Arts in Britain and Europe at the Fin de Siècle*, Oxford, Bern, Berlin, Brussels, Frankfurt am Main, New York, Vienna: Peter Lang, 2009.

Cavanaugh, Jan, *Out Looking In: Early Modern Polish Art, 1890–1918*, Berkeley, CA: University of California Press, 2000.

Charazińska, Elżbieta, Anna Rudzińska and Ewa Milicer, *Jak meteor . . . Stanisław Wyspiański (1869–1907): Artyście w setną rocznicę śmierci*, exh.cat., Warsaw: Muzeum Narodowe w Warszawie, 2007.

Clegg, Elizabeth, *Art, Design and Architecture in Central Europe, 1890–1920*, New Haven, CT: Yale University Press, 2006.

Collins, Judith, *The Omega Workshops*, London: Secker & Warburg, 1984.

Crowley, David, *National Style and the Nation-State: Design in Poland from the Vernacular Revival to the International Style*, Manchester and New York: Manchester University Press, 1992.

Crowley, David and Lou Taylor (eds.), *The Lost Arts of Europe. The Haslemere Museum. A Collection of European Peasant Art*, Haslemere: Haslemere Educational Museum, 2000.

Czubińska, Magdalena (ed.), *Fin de siècle w Krakowie: Grafika użytkowa, tkaniny, rzemiosło artystyczne / Fin de Siècle in Cracow: Applied Graphics, Textiles, Decorative Art*, translated by Monika Myszkiewicz and Jessica Taylor-Kucia, Kraków: Muzeum Narodowe w Krakowie, 2006.

Dobrowolski, Władysław Józef, and Maria Fredro-Boniecka, *Konstanty Laszczka*, Warsaw: Arkady, 1959.

Dziedzic, Maria (ed.), *The Kraków Workshops 1913–26*, translated by Søren Gauger and Robin Gill, Kraków: Wydawnictwo Akademii Sztuk Pięknych w Krakowie, Jan Matejko Academy of Fine Arts Publishing House, 2009.

Gaweł, Łukasz, *Stanisław Wyspiański: Na chęciach mi nie braknie . . .*, Kraków: Muzeum Narodowe w Krakowie, 2017.

Gaweł, Łukasz, and Magdalena Laskowska, *Wyspiański Nieznany / Unknown Wyspiański*, exh.cat., Kraków: Muzeum Narodowe w Krakowie, 2019.

Gedliczka, Adam (ed.), *Zdzisław Gedliczka 1888–1957*, Kraków: Wydawnictwo Akademii Sztuk Pięknych w Krakowie, Jan Matejko Academy of Fine Arts Publishing House, 2012.

Ginalska, Maria, *Polskie Boże Narodzenie*, London: B. Świderski, 1961.

Godyń, Danuta, and Magdalena Laskowska, *Wyspiański*, translated by Marta Herudzińska-Oświecimska et al., exh. cat., Kraków: Muzeum Narodowe w Krakowie, 2017 (reprinted 2018 and 2019).

Griffin, Julia, 'Kelmscott Manor. Mr. Morris's Country Place', in *Routledge Companion to William Morris*, edited by Florence Boos, London: Routledge, 2020, pp.87–144.

Howard, Jeremy, *Art Nouveau: International and National Styles in Europe*, Manchester: Manchester University Press, 1996.

Huml, Irena, *Polska sztuka stosowana XX wieku*, Warsaw: Wydawnictwo Artystyczne i Filmowe, 1978

Huml, Irena, 'The Kraków Workshops', in *The Kraków Workshops 1913–26*, edited by Maria Dziedzic, translated by Søren Gauger and Robin Gill, Kraków: Jan Matejko Academy of Fine Arts Publishing House, 2009, pp.20–135.

Jabłońska, Teresa, *Sztuki Piękne pod Tatrami / Fine Arts at the Foot of the Polish Tatra Mountains*, translated by Adrian Smith, Zakopane: Tatrzański Park Narodowy and Muzeum Tatrzańskie, 2015.

Jabłońska, Teresa, *Stanisław Witkiewicz's Zakopane Style*, translated by Adrian Smith and Anna Wende-Surmiak, Olszanica: Bosz, 2019.

Jabłońska, Teresa, and Zbigniew Moździerz, *'Koliba' – pierwszy dom w stylu zakopiańskim*, Zakopane: Muzeum Tatrzańskie im. dra Tytusa Chałubińskiego, 1994.

Jagiełło, Michał (ed.), *Listy o stylu zakopiańskim (1892–1912): Wokół Stanisława Witkiewicza*, Kraków: Wydawnictwo Literackie, 1979.

Kilijańska, Alicja, 'Rzemiosło artystyczne', in *Fin de siècle w Krakowie: Grafika użytkowa, tkaniny, rzemiosło artystyczne / Fin de Siecle in Cracow: Applied Graphics, Textiles, Decorative Art*, translated by Monika Myszkiewicz and Jessica Taylor-Kucia, Kraków: Muzeum Narodowe w Krakowie, 2005, pp.80–110.

Kinchin, Juliet, and Aidan O'Connor, *Century of the Child: Growing by Design, 1900–2000*, New York: The Museum of Modern Art, 2012.

Kostuch, Bożena, 'Service à thé et café en porcelaine produit à la manufacture de Sèvres, exemple de la recherche d'un style national dans la céramique polonaise', *Sèvres: revue de la Société des Amis du Musée National de Céramique*, vol.14 (2005), pp.93–7.

Kowalska, Joanna Regina, 'Lace inspired by the folk art of Podhale: The National

School of Lace-Making in Zakopane and its influence on fashion in the first fifty years of its existence', in *Lace, Fashion and Transparency: ICOM's Costume Committee Proceedings from the Annual Conference, 21–27 October 2012, Brussels, Belgium*, edited by Corinne ter Assatouroff, Brussels: Bruxelles ICOM, 2013, pp.107–13.

Kowalska, Joanna Regina, 'Secesyjne hafty, aplikacje i inkrustacje w kolekcji Muzeum Narodowego w Krakowie', *Pamiętnik Sztuk Pięknych: Fin de siècle odnaleziony: Mozaika przełomu wieków*, vol.10 (2015), pp.119–28.

Kozakevych, Olena, 'Działalność Ligii Pomocy Przemysłowej na terenach Galicji Wschodniej w pierwszym trzydziestoleciu XX stulecia', in *Stan badań nad wielokulturowym dziedzictwem dawnej Rzeczypospolitej*, vol.6, edited by Wojciech Walczak and Karol Łopatecki, Białystok: Instytut Badań nad Dziedzictwem Kulturowym Europy, 2013, pp.55–78.

Krajewska, Wanda, *Recepcja literatury angielskiej w Polsce w okresie modernizmu (1887–1918): informacje, sądy, przekłady*, Wrocław: Zakład Narodowy im. Ossolińskich, Wydawnictwo PAN, 1972.

Krzysztofowicz-Kozakowska, Stefania, *Art déco en Pologne*, Brussels: Galerie KBC, 2001.

Krzysztofowicz-Kozakowska, Stefania, *Sztuka Młodej Polski*, Kraków: Wydawnictwo Kluszczyński, 2003.

Kulig-Janarek, Krystyna, Zofia Gołubiew, *Zawsze Młoda!: Polska sztuka około 1900 / Forever Young! Poland and its Art around 1900*, exh.cat., Kraków: Muzeum Narodowe w Krakowie, 2017

Laskowski, Andrzej, 'The Stained Glass Revival in Galicia in the Second Half of the Nineteenth Century', *The Journal of Stained Glass*, vol.xxv (2001), pp.10–26.

Lenartowicz, Światosław (ed.), *Zofia Stryjeńska 1891–1976: Wystawa w Muzeum Narodowym w Krakowie, październik 2008–styczeń 2009*, Kraków: Muzeum Narodowe w Krakowie, 2008.

Lisek, Teresa Maria, 'Karol Kłosowski (1882–1971): Życie i twórczość, Life and work', *Rocznik Podhalański* (Zakopane), vol.10 (2007), pp.7–54.

Livingstone, Karen, and Linda Parry (eds), *International Arts and Crafts*, London: V&A Publications, 2005.

Łomnicka, Katarzyna, and Zofia Weiss, *Józef Sperling – kreator i przedsiębiorca*, Kraków: Inter Line SC, 2020.

Matyaszewska, Elżbieta, 'Przestrzeń kawiarni i przestrzeń sztuki: Jama Michalika w Krakowie, fin de siècle i Młoda Polska', *Pamiętnik Sztuk Pięknych*, vol.10 (2015), pp.383–93.

Morawińska, Agnieszka, 'Wyspiański . . . "Nieśmiertelność strasznie samotna"', in *Stanisław Wyspiański: Opus magnum*, Kraków: Muzeum Narodowe w Krakowie, 2000, pp.15–30.

Mossakowski, Stanisław, *King Sigismund Chapel at Cracow Cathedral (1515–1533)*, Kraków: IRSA and Zamek Królewski na Wawelu, 2012.

Moździerz, Zbigniew, 'The Zakopane Style and the Vernacular Movement in European architecture in the second half of the 19th century', in *Vernacular Art in Central Europe*, edited by Jacek Purchla, Kraków: International Cultural Centre, 2001, pp.307–22.

Moździerz, Zbigniew, *Dom 'Pod Jedlami' Pawlikowskich*, Zakopane: Muzeum Tatrzańskie, 2003.

Moździerz, Zbigniew, *Gmach Muzeum Tatrzańskiego*, Zakopane: Muzeum Tatrzańskie, 2005.

Moździerz, Zbigniew (ed.), *Kaplica Najświętszego Serca Jezusowego w Jaszczurówce (1907–2007)*, Zakopane: Towarzystwo Muzeum Tatrzańskiego, 2007.

Norwid, Cyprian Kamil, *Promethidion*, Paris: L. Martinet, 1851.

Okońska, Alicja, *Stanisław Wyspiański*, Warsaw: Wiedza Powszechna, 1971.

Oleszkiewicz, Małgorzata, 'O zabawkach z Warsztatów Krakowskich', in Światosław Lenartowicz, *Zofia Stryjeńska, 1891–1976: Wystawa w Muzeum Narodowym w Krakowie, październik 2008–styczeń 2009*, Kraków: Muzeum Narodowe w Krakowie, 2008, pp.278–9.

Omilanowska, Małgorzata, 'Styl zakopiański i jego konotacje europejskie', *Rocznik Podhalański*, vol.13 (2018), pp.14–16.

Parry, Linda (ed.), *William Morris*, London: Philip Wilson Publishers in association with V&A Publishing, 1996.

Pawlikowska-Jasnorzewska, Maria, *Motyle: poesje wybrane / Butterflies: Selected Poems*, translated by Barbara Bogoczek and Tony Howard, Kraków: Wydawnictwo Literackie, 2000.

Pleciak, Agata, *Ozdoby choinkowe Warsztatów Krakowskich sto lat później*, M.A. thesis under the supervision of Maria Dziedzic and Stanisław Półtorak, Kraków: Archiwum Wydziału Form Przemysłowych Akademii Sztuk Pięknych w Krakowie, 2015.

Pryzwan, Mariola, *Lilka: Maria Pawlikowska-Jasnorzewska we wspomnieniach i listach*, Kraków: MG, 2015.

Purchla, Jacek, *Jak powstał nowoczesny Kraków: studia nad rozwojem budowlanym miasta w okresie autonomii galicyjskiej*, Kraków: Wydawnictwo Literackie, 1979.

Purchla, Jacek (ed.), *Vernacular Art in Central Europe*, Kraków: International Cultural Centre, 2001.

Reinhard-Chlanda, Małgorzata, 'Witraże w sanatorium dra Dłuskiego w Zakopanem', in *Witraże secesyjne: tendencje i motywy*, Kraków: Legnica, 2011, pp.68–70.

Romanowska, Marta, *Stanisław Wyspiański*, Kraków: Kluszczyński, 2000.

Rydlowa, Maria (ed.), *Listy Stanisława Wyspiańskiego do Józefa Mehoffera, Henryka Opieńskiego i Tadeusza Stryjeńskiego* (Stanisław Wyspiański, *Listy zebrane*, vol.I), Kraków: Wydawnictwo Literackie, 1994.

Rydlowa, Maria (ed.), *Listy Stanisława Wyspiańskiego do Karola Maszkowskiego* (Stanisław Wyspiański, *Listy zebrane*, vol.III), Kraków: Wydawnictwo Literackie, 1997.

Rydlowa, Maria (ed.), *Listy Stanisława Wyspiańskiego różne – do wielu adresatów* (Stanisław Wyspiański, *Listy zebrane*, vol.IV), Kraków: Wydawnictwo Literackie, 1998.

Rydlowa, Maria, and Leon Płoszewski (eds), *Listy Stanisława Wyspiańskiego do Lucjana Rydla* (Stanisław Wyspiański, *Listy zebrane*, vol.II), Kraków: Wydawnictwo Literackie, 1979.

Sieradzka, Anna, *Peleryna, tren i konfederatka: O modzie i sztuce polskiego modernizmu*, Wrocław, Warsaw and Kraków: Zakład Narodowy im. Ossolińskich, 1991.

Sieradzka, Anna, 'Stanisław Wyspiański jako prekursor stylu Art Déco w polskim rzemiośle artystycznym', in *Rzemiosło artystyczne: materiały sesji Oddziału Warszawskiego Stowarzyszenia Historyków Sztuki*, edited by Ryszard Bobrow, Warsaw: Stowarzyszenie Historyków Sztuki – Fundacja ATK Akademii Teologii Katolickiej, 1996.

Smith, Alison (ed.), *Symbolist Art in Poland: Poland and Britain c. 1900*, exh.cat., London: Tate Publishing, 2009.

Spalding, Frances, 'The paintings of Roger Fry', unpublished PhD thesis, Sheffield Hallam University, 1977.

Supińska-Polit (now Barucka), Edyta, *Dom Arts & Crafts: geneza i idea*, Warsaw: Neriton, 2004.

Supińska-Polit (now Barucka), Edyta, '"The world is different here": Arts and Crafts in the Polish Tatras', *Journal of the Scottish Society for Art History*, vol.9 (2004), pp.41–6.

Sutton, Denys (ed.), *Letters of Roger Fry*, London: Chatto & Windus, 1972.

Szczerski, Andrzej, *Views of Albion: The Reception of British Art and Design in Central Europe, 1890–1918)*, translated by Ewa Kanigowska-Gedroyć, Marcin Łakomski and Aleksandra Sobczak, Oxford: Peter Lang, 2015 (originally published in Polish in 2002).

Szczerski, Andrzej, 'Central Europe', in *International Arts and Crafts*, edited by Karen Livingstone and Linda Parry, London: V&A Publications, 2005, pp.238–51.

Szczerski, Andrzej, 'Sources of modernity: the interpretations of vernacular crafts in Polish design around 1900', *The Journal of Modern Craft*, vol.1, no.1 (March 2008), pp.55–76.

Szczerski, Andrzej, *Cztery nowoczesności: teksty o sztuce i architekturze polskiej XX wieku*, Kraków: Studio Wydawnicze DodoEditor, 2015.

Szczerski, Andrzej, and Piotr Kopszak, *Śladami Prerafaelitów: artyści polscy i sztuka brytyjska na przełomie XIX i XX wieku / In the Footsteps of the Pre-Raphaelites: Polish Artists and British Art Around 1900*, Wilanów: Muzeum Pałac w Wilanowie, 2006.

Szybisty, Tomasz (ed.), *Witraże secesyjne: tendencje i motywy*, Kraków and Legnica: Stowarzyszenie Miłośników Witraży 'Ars Vitrea Polona' and Wydawnictwo Edytor, 2011.

Tondos, Barbara, *Styl zakopiański i zakopiańszczyzna*, Wrocław: Zakład Narodowy im. Ossolińskich, 2004.

Weiss, Zofia, *1900, Weiss at the crossroads: with selected critical texts*, Kraków: Fundacja Muzeum Wojciecha Weissa, Wojciech Weiss Museum Foundation, 2014.

Weiss, Zofia, with Katarzyna Łomnicka, *Władysław Jarocki*, translated by Władysław Chłopicki, Katarzyna Dziemian and Marta Kapera, exh.cat., Zakopane: Miejska Galeria Sztuki im. Wł. hr. Zamoyskiego, Count Zamoyski Municipal Art Gallery, and Kraków: Wydawnictwo Akademii Sztuk Pięknych im. Jana Matejki w Krakowie, Jan Matejko Academy of Fine Arts Publishing House, 2015

Weiss, Zofia, and Katarzyna Łomnicka, *Konstanty Laszczka*. Kraków: Wydawnictwo Akademii Sztuk Pięknych im. Jana Matejki w Krakowie, Jan Matejko Academy of Fine Arts Publishing House, 2017.

Wiszniewska, Anna, *Stanisław Jagmin, 1875–1961: rzeźbiarz i ceramik-eksperymentator.* Warsaw: Instytut Sztuki PAN, 2012.

Witkiewicz, Stanisław, *Styl zakopiański, zeszyt 1: Pokój jadalny*, Lviv: Wydawnictwo H. Altenberga, 1904.

Witkiewicz, Stanisław, *Styl zakopiański, część 2: Ciesielstwo*, Lviv: Wydawnictwo H. Altenberga, 1911.

Wyspiański, Stanisław, *Acropolis: The Wawel Plays*, translated and introduced by Charles S. Kraszewski, London: Glagoslav Publications, 2017.

Wyspiański, Stanisław, *The Hamlet Study and The Death of Ophelia* (1904), translated by Barbara Bogoczek and Tony Howard, London: Shakespeare's Globe, 2019.

Wyspiański, Stanisław, *The Wedding* (1901), translated by Noel Clark, London: Oberon Books, 1998.

About the Academic Editors

JULIA GRIFFIN (née Dudkiewicz) is a Courtauld-trained art historian and curator specialising in the Arts and Crafts Movement and Victorian art. Her PhD explores William Morris and D.G. Rossetti's occupancy of Kelmscott Manor (Central Saint Martins, University of the Arts London). She is a Young Poland Project Curator. Julia has been responsible for a number of exhibitions and rehangs, including the City's Collection Displays (2015) at the Guildhall Art Gallery, for which she was awarded the Freedom of the City of London. She is a contributor to *The Routledge Companion to William Morris* (London: Routledge, 2020).

PROFESSOR DR HAB. ANDRZEJ SZCZERSKI is Director of the National Museum in Kraków and Professor in the Institute of Art History at the Jagiellonian University. He is a Young Poland Project Curator. He has published extensively on 20th-century art, design and architecture, including a pioneering study *Views of Albion: The Reception of British Art and Design in Central Europe, 1890–1918* (Oxford: Peter Lang, 2015). He has curated exhibitions on 19th- and 20th-century art and architecture. In 2009 he co-curated *Symbolism in Poland and Britain* at Tate Britain in London.

About the Copy-Editor

ABIGAIL GRATER is a freelance editor and French-to-English translator who works for publishers, major museums, cultural organisations and individual authors around the world, specialising in art and architectural subjects. She studied Art History at the University of St Andrews and has a lifelong passion for the Arts and Crafts Movement.

About the Contributors

DR EDYTA BARUCKA is an independent art and architectural historian who has published books on the idea and genesis of the British Arts and Crafts house and the European Garden City Movement, as well as a series of articles on the Polish crafts revival in the 19th century.

BARBARA BOGOCZEK is a translator and interpreter based in London. Her literary translations, with Tony Howard, include Wyspiański's *The Hamlet Study and the Death of Ophelia* (London: Shakespeare's Globe, 2019) and the works of Tadeusz Różewicz and Maria Pawlikowska-Jasnorzewska.

PROF. TONY HOWARD is Professor of English and Comparative Literature at the University of Warwick. His publications include *Women as Hamlet: Performance and Interpretation in Theatre, Film and Fiction* (Cambridge: Cambridge University Press, 2007).

ROISIN INGLESBY is Curator at the William Morris Gallery and a Young Poland Project Curator. She was previously Assistant Curator of Designs at the Victoria and Albert Museum, Curator of Architectural Drawings for Historic Royal Palaces and Curatorial Assistant at Tokyo Teien Metropolitan Art Museum. Her work focuses on Morris's international connections, with exhibitions including *Pioneers: William Morris and the Bauhaus* (2019). She is currently working on a project examining the relationship between Morris and the Japanese Mingei movement.

ALICJA KILIJAŃSKA is Head of the Decorative Arts and Material Culture Department at the National Museum in Kraków with responsibility for glass, goldwork, furniture, clocks, intaglios and cameos, as well as overall management of the Decorative Arts displays. She studied Art History at the Jagiellonian University and is a member of the International Council of Museums (ICOM). She is also a Lecturer in the History of the Decorative Arts at the Faculty of Scenography, Jan Matejko Academy of Fine Arts in Kraków.

DR PIOTR KOPSZAK is an art historian, publisher, and Curator at the National Museum in Warsaw, specialising in 19th-century Polish art and art criticism. He co-curated *Symbolism in Poland and Britain* at Tate Britain in 2009, among other exhibitions; has published several popular books on Polish artists; translated Walter Pater's *The Renaissance* (Warsaw: Fundacja Aletheia, 1998); and is involved in numerous projects in the field of digital humanities.

DR BOŻENA KOSTUCH is an art historian, museologist, and Ceramics Curator at the National Museum in Kraków, specialising in Polish ceramics from the 19th and 20th centuries.

JOANNA REGINA KOWALSKA is Textiles Curator at the National Museum in Kraków. She holds two Master's degrees, in History and Art History, as well as a diploma in Museology from the Jagiellonian University. She completed technical courses at the Centre International d'Étude des Textiles, Lyon, in 2013–14. She is the Vice Chair of the ICOM Costume Committee, and has authored many publications and curated numerous exhibitions on the history of fashion.

MAGDALENA LASKOWSKA is an art historian and Curator of Drawings and Watercolours at the National Museum in Kraków with responsibility for Stanisław Wyspiański's works. She was a co-curator of the recent exhibitions *Stanisław Wyspiański* (2017–18) and *Unknown Wyspiański* (2019) and has published extensively on the artist's life and work.

DR HAB. ZBIGNIEW MOŹDZIERZ is a historic buildings conservation advisor and architectural historian. Specialising in 19th- and 20th-century architecture, especially the Zakopane Style, he is the author of numerous publications in this field. He is a long-time Research Fellow at the Tatra Museum, and currently lectures at the Faculty of Architecture at the Podhale State Higher Education School in Nowy Targ.

DR HAB. ANNA MYCZKOWSKA-SZCZERSKA is Assistant Professor at the Faculty of Industrial Design, Jan Matejko Academy of Fine Arts in Kraków. A graphic designer with a passion for paper art, she has published books on information design.

MONIKA PAŚ is an art historian, Books, Metalwork, Plastics, Organic Media, Iconography and Academic Aids Curator at the National Museum in Kraków, author of articles and catalogues, and curator of exhibitions and displays in the field of artistic handicrafts and material culture.

ANNA RUDZIŃSKA is Curator at the Department of Prints and Drawings at the National Museum in Warsaw, with responsibility for drawings, watercolours and pastels produced by 19th and early 20th-century Polish artists.

DR ALISON SMITH is Chief Curator at the National Portrait Gallery, London. In 2009 she co-curated *Symbolism in Poland and Britain* at Tate Britain, London.

ZOFIA WEISS is an art historian, art critic and curator focusing on Polish and European art of the years around 1900 and their lasting impact on contemporary art. Currently President of the Wojciech Weiss Museum Foundation, she previously worked at the Art History Institute of the Jagiellonian University and in the National Museum in Kraków.

ANNA WENDE-SURMIAK is Director of the Tatra Museum in Zakopane and a President of the International Mountain Museums Alliance, which she co-founded in 2015. She studied French and languages and is a trained museologist, French translator and teacher. She is currently leading a £6.6 million capital project to restore the Tatra Museum's nine historic buildings including the main headquarters.

*For clarity, Polish academic titles have been used, where applicable. 'Hab.' stands for a post-doctoral qualification

Index

Page numbers in italics refer to illustrations.

Image credits

Image photography credits are as follows:

Note: all photos of objects belonging to the National Museum in Kraków (NMK), Bank PKO S.A., privately owned works by Karol Kłosowski, views of the Silent Villa and the Franciscan Church, as well as figs 6.9, 6.10, 10.2, 10.3, 10.5, 13.4, 14.6, were kindly taken by the NMK Photographic Department.

© A. & E. Ciołek: fig.10.8
© Tomasz Kalarus: figs 9.3, 9.6; (with pre-press by Piotr Hrehorowicz): 9.7, 15.1, 15.2, 15.3, 15.4, 15.5, 15.6; (digital image by Tomasz Kalarus): 9.8
© Wiktoria Kaławak: fig.1.5
© Stanisław Kolowca (archive photo)/ Museum of Kraków: fig.15.7 (top)
© Marcin Koniak: fig.10.7
© Paweł Mazur: figs 4.5, 17.0
© Dawid Moździerz: figs 6.2, 6.4, 6.6, 6.7, 6.13
© Paweł Murzyn: fig.6.12
© Agata Pleciak/Anna Szwaja: fig.15.0
© Anna Szwaja: fig.15.10
© Robert Wancerz: figs 10.4, 10.10
© Marcin Wąsik: fig.9.4
© Joanna Wolańska: fig.1.0
© Michał Zieliński: fig.6.0